THE SEASONS

The earth revolves around the sun once a year in an anti-clockwise direction. The earth is tilted at an angle of $66\frac{1}{2}$ degrees to the plane of its orbit and always points into space in the same direction. In June the northern hemisphere is tilted towards the sun – days are longer and it is generally warmer. The southern hemisphere is pointing away from the sun. It is cooler and the days are shorter – the southern winter. In December the reverse is the case.

Equinox – One of the two times in the year when day and night are of equal length, owing to the Sun being overhead at the Equator.

Solstice – One of the two times in the year, midway between the two equinoxes, when the Sun is overhead at one of the Tropics (Cancer or Capricorn) and is at its highest latitude from the Equator ($23\frac{1}{2}°$ North or South).

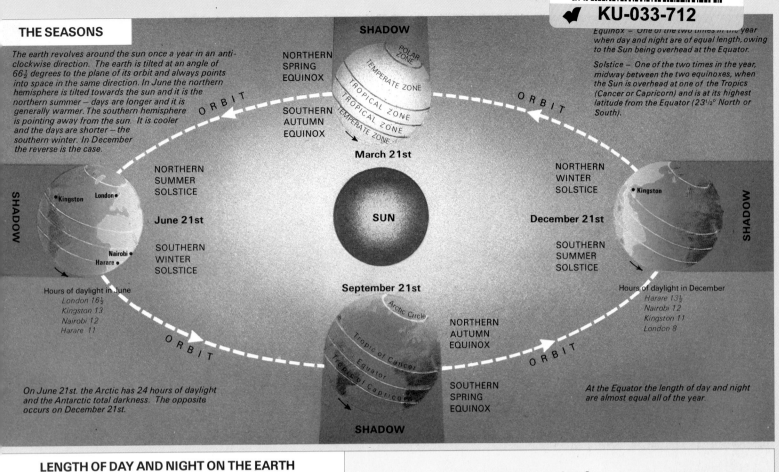

SHADOW

NORTHERN SPRING EQUINOX

SOUTHERN AUTUMN EQUINOX

POLAR ZONE
TEMPERATE ZONE
TROPICAL ZONE
TROPICAL ZONE
TEMPERATE ZONE

March 21st

NORTHERN SUMMER SOLSTICE

June 21st

SOUTHERN WINTER SOLSTICE

SUN

NORTHERN WINTER SOLSTICE

December 21st

SOUTHERN SUMMER SOLSTICE

SHADOW

SHADOW

Kingston · London ·

Nairobi ·
Harare ·

· Kingston

Hours of daylight in June
London 16½
Kingston 13
Nairobi 12
Harare 11

Hours of daylight in December
Harare 13½
Nairobi 12
Kingston 11
London 8

September 21st

Arctic Circle
Tropic of Cancer
Equator
Tropic of Capricorn

NORTHERN AUTUMN EQUINOX

SOUTHERN SPRING EQUINOX

SHADOW

On June 21st. the Arctic has 24 hours of daylight and the Antarctic total darkness. The opposite occurs on December 21st.

At the Equator the length of day and night are almost equal all of the year.

LENGTH OF DAY AND NIGHT ON THE EARTH

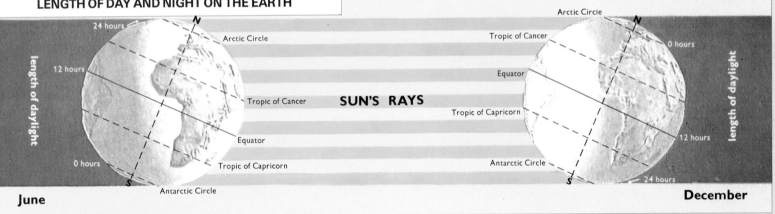

24 hours
12 hours
length of daylight
0 hours

N
Arctic Circle
Tropic of Cancer
Equator
Tropic of Capricorn
S
Antarctic Circle

SUN'S RAYS

Arctic Circle
Tropic of Cancer
Equator
Tropic of Capricorn
Antarctic Circle

N
0 hours
length of daylight
12 hours
S
24 hours

June

December

TIME

The Year – the time taken by the Earth to revolve around the Sun, or 365¼ days.

The Month – the approximate time taken by the Moon to revolve around the Earth. The twelve months of the year in fact vary from 28 (29 in a Leap Year) to 31 days.

The Week – an artificial period of 7 days, not based on astronomical time.

The Day – the time taken by the Earth to complete one rotation on its axis.

The Hour – 24 hours make one day. Usually the day is divided into hours A.M. (ante meridiem or before noon) and P.M. (post meridiem or after noon), although most timetables now use the 24-hour system, from midnight to midnight, for example, 1p.m. = 13.00 hours.

SUNRISE AND SUNSET

From the diagrams below it is possible to find out the time of sunrise or sunset on a given date and for latitudes between 60°N and 60°S.

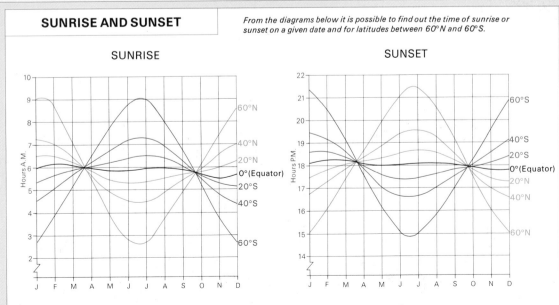

SUNRISE

Hours A.M.

60°N
40°N
20°N
0°(Equator)
20°S
40°S
60°S

J F M A M J J A S O N D

SUNSET

Hours P.M.

60°S
40°S
20°S
0°(Equator)
20°N
40°N
60°N

J F M A M J J A S O N D

PHILIPS' MODERN SCHOOL ATLAS

Contents

Front Endpaper: Astronomical Geography

British Isles

4 Physical ~ 1:4M
Geology ~ 1:16M
5 Administrative ~ 1:4M
6 Climate
7 Transport
8 Population
9 Agriculture
10 Energy and Industry
11 Employment, Leisure and Trade
12-13 Climate Graphs
14-15 South and South-East England ~ 1:1M
16 South-West England ~ 1:1M
17 Wales ~ 1:1M
18-19 Northern England ~ 1:1M
20-21 Scotland: South ~ 1:1M
22-23 Scotland: North ~ 1:1M
24-25 Ireland ~ 1:1,25M

Europe

26 Physical ~ 1:20M
27 Political ~ 1:20M
28 Climate and Natural Vegetation ~ 1:40M
29 Economic ~ 1:20M
30-31 Themes
32-33 Statistics
34-35 France and Western Europe ~ 1:4M
36 Low Countries and Lower Rhine ~ 1:2M
37 Spain and Portugal ~ 1:5M
38-39 Mediterranean Lands ~ 1:10M
40-41 Italy and the Balkan States ~ 1:5M
42-43 Central Europe ~ 1:5M
44-45 Scandinavia and the Baltic Lands ~ 1:6M
46-47 European Russia and Turkey ~ 1:10M
48-49 Union of Soviet Socialist Republics ~ 1:20M

Asia

50 Physical ~ 1:50M
51 Political ~ 1:50M
52 Climate and Natural Vegetation ~ 1:100M
53 Economic ~ 1:50M
54-55 Statistics (including Oceania)
56-57 South-West Asia ~ 1:15M
The Holy Land ~ 1:1,5M
58-59 South Asia ~ 1:10M
60-61 China and Korea ~ 1:15M
62 Japan ~ 1:7,5M
63 South-East Asia ~ 1:15M
64-65 Pacific Ocean ~ 1:54M

Australia and New Zealand

66-67 Australia ~ 1:12M
Political ~ 1:80M
68 Climate and Natural Vegetation ~ 1:60M
69 Economic ~ 1:20M
70 South-East Australia ~ 1:4,5M
71 New Zealand ~ 1:6M
Samoa, Fiji and Tonga Islands ~ 1:12M

Africa

72 Physical ~ 1:40M
73 Political ~ 1:40M
74 Climate and Natural Vegetation ~ 1:80M
75 Economic ~ 1:40M
76-77 Statistics
78-79 Northern Africa ~ 1:15M
80-81 Central and Southern Africa ~ 1:15M

Edited By

B.M. Willett, *Cartographic Editor*

D. Gaylard, *Assistant Cartographic Editor*

and L. Prince-Smith, J. Russell, R. Smith and A. Wells
George Philip Ltd., London

Maps prepared by

George Philip Cartographic Services Ltd., London under
the direction of A.G. Poynter, *Director of Cartography*.

© 1989   George Philip Ltd., London

Eighty-fifth Edition

ISBN 0 540 05557 3 (Paperback Edition)
0 540 05554 9 (Hardback Edition)

Printed in Great Britain by Redwood Offset, Trowbridge

Contents

North America

82	Physical ~ 1:35M
83	Political ~ 1:35M
84	Climate and Natural Vegetation ~ 1:70M
85	Economic ~ 1:32M
86-87	Statistics (including South America)
88-89	Canada ~ 1:15M
	Alaska ~ 1:30M
90-91	United States ~ 1:12M
	Hawaiian Islands ~ 1:10M
92-93	Basin of the St Lawrence and North-East United States ~ 1:6M
94-95	Mexico, Central America and the West Indies ~ 1:15M
	Panama Canal ~ 1:1M
	Jamaica, Trinidad and Tobago, Leeward and Windward Islands ~ 1:5M

South America

96	Physical ~ 1:30M
97	Political ~ 1:30M
98	Climate and Natural Vegetation ~ 1:70M
99	Economic ~ 1:30M
100-101	South America: North ~ 1:16M
102	South America: South ~ 1:16M

The World

103	Polar Regions ~ 1:50M
104-105	Physical ~ 1:80M
106-107	Structure, Volcanoes and Earthquakes
108-109	Climatic Regions, Soils and Vegetation
110-113	Climate Statistics
114	Temperature and Ocean Currents
115	Pressure, Winds and Annual Precipitation
116-117	Density of Population
118-119	Population of Cities
120	Languages and Religions
121	International Organisations
122-123	Population Trends
124-125	Quality of Life
126-127	Economic Facts of Life
128-129	Political ~ 1:80M
130-131	Time and Distance

Index

Back Endpaper: Map Projections

General Reference

SETTLEMENTS

Settlement symbols in order of size

⌂ LONDON   ■ Osaka   ◉ Venice   ◎ Andropov   ○ Toledo   ○ Cromer   ∘ Interlaken

Settlement symbols and type styles vary according to the scale of each map and indicate the importance of towns on the map rather than specific population figures.

ADMINISTRATION

——— International Boundaries

— — — International Boundaries
(Undemarcated or undefined)

•••••••• Internal Boundaries

International boundaries show the 'de facto' situation where there are rival claims to territory.

COMMUNICATIONS

═══ Motorways in UK

⌒ Principal Roads

⌐---⌐ Tracks and Seasonal Roads

⌐---⌐ Road Tunnels

⌒ Principal Railways

----- Railways under construction

⌐---⌐ Railway Tunnels

≍ Passes

••••••• Principal Canals

⌐—⌐ Principal Oil Pipelines

✿ Principal Airports

PHYSICAL FEATURES

⌒ Perennial Streams

------- Seasonal Streams

⌒ Seasonal Lakes and Salt Flats

 Swamps and Marshes

▦ Permanent Ice and Glaciers

Wells in Desert

▲ 8848 Elevations in metres

▼ 8050 Sea Depths in metres

1134 Height of Lakes

1 : 4 000 000

50   0   50   100   150 km

GEOLOGY
1 : 16 000 000

SOUTHERN LIMIT OF GLACIATION

Tertiary — sand, clays	Lavas
Mesozoic — chalk, clays, limestone, sandstone	Granites
Upper Palaeozoic — coal, limestone, sandstone	Major Faults
Lower Palaeozoic — sandstone, shales, slates	
Pre-Cambrian — gneiss, quartzite, schists	

See pp. 106-107 for Geological Time Scale

m
1000
400
200
100
0
50
100
200

Shetland Is.

Unst
Yell
Fetlar
St. Magnus B.
Out Skerries
Whalsay
Mainland
Foula
Bressay

Orkney Is.
Mainland
Hoy
Westray
Rousay
Sanday
Stronsay
N. Ronaldsay
Start Point
Pentland Firth
Dunnet Hd.
John o' Groats
Duncansby Hd.

ATLANTIC OCEAN

Outer Hebrides

Inner Hebrides

NORTH WEST HIGHLANDS

Grampian Mountains

Southern Uplands

Cheviot Hills

Pennine

NORTH SEA

Dogger Bank

IRISH SEA

Central Plain

Wicklow Mountains

Mts. of Kerry

CELTIC SEA

Cambrian Mountains

Cotswolds

The Fens

The Wash

Chiltern Hills

North Downs

The Weald

South Downs

Dartmoor

Bodmin Moor

Exmoor

ST. GEORGE'S CHANNEL

ENGLISH CHANNEL

Strait of Dover

Land's End

Isles of Scilly

Lizard Point

1:4 000 000

50 0 50 100 150 km

The DISTRICTS of Northern Ireland have been numbered
and can be identified by reference to this table.

1	Londonderry	14	Craigavon
2	Limavady	15	Armagh
3	Coleraine	16	Newry & Mourne
4	Ballymoney	17	Banbridge
5	Moyle	18	Down
6	Larne	19	Lisburn
7	Ballymena	20	Antrim
8	Magherafelt	21	Newtownabbey
9	Cookstown	22	Carrickfergus
10	Strabane	23	North Down
11	Omagh	24	Ards
12	Fermanagh	25	Castlereagh
13	Dungannon	26	Belfast

ORKNEY

Kirkwall

HIGHLAND

SHETLAND

Lerwick

WESTERN
ISLES
Stornoway

ATLANTIC

OCEAN

HIGHLAND
Inverness
GRAMPIAN
SCOTLAND
Aberdeen

TAYSIDE
Dundee

FIFE
CENTRAL Glenrothes
Stirling
Edinburgh
Glasgow LOTHIAN

STRATHCLYDE
Newtown
St. Boswells
BORDERS
NORTHUMBERLAND
DUMFRIES Morpeth
AND Dumfries Newcastle
GALLOWAY TYNE AND
Carlisle WEAR
Durham
DURHAM
CUMBRIA CLEVELAND
Middlesbrough
Northallerton
NORTH
YORKSHIRE

NORTH
SEA

DONEGAL
Lifford
NORTHERN
IRELAND
Fermanagh

Sligo
SLIGO
MAYO
Castlebar

ROSCOMMON
Roscommon

GALWAY
Galway

IRELAND

CLARE
Ennis
Limerick
LIMERICK

KERRY
Tralee

ISLE OF
MAN
Douglas

IRISH SEA

Carrick-on-
Shannon
LEITRIM
Monaghan
MONAGHAN
Cavan
CAVAN
LOUTH
Dundalk
Longford
LONGFORD
Mullingar An Uaimh
WESTMEATH (Navan)
MEATH
Tullamore Dublin
OFFALY KILDARE Dublin
Port Laoise Naas
LAOIS Wicklow
WICKLOW
Kilkenny Carlow Wicklow
TIPPERARY CARLOW
KILKENNY WEXFORD
Clonmel Wexford
WATERFORD Waterford

CORK
Cork

LANCASHIRE
Preston WEST
YORKSHIRE
Wakefield
GREATER Barnsley
MANCHESTER SOUTH
MERSEYSIDE Manchester YORKSHIRE
Liverpool
ENGLAND
Chester DERBYSHIRE Lincoln
Mold CHESHIRE NOTT- LINCOLNSHIRE
Caernarfon INGHAM-
GWYNEDD CLWYD Matlock SHIRE
Nottingham
Stafford
STAFFORD- Leicester NORFOLK
SHIRE LEICESTERSHIRE Norwich
Shrewsbury
SHROPSHIRE WEST
WALES MIDLANDS NORTH- CAMBRIDGE-
Birmingham AMPTON- SHIRE
WARWICK- SHIRE SUFFOLK
POWYS Warwick Northampton
HEREFORD SHIRE Bedford Cambridge
Llandrindod AND Worcester BEDFORD- Ipswich
Wells WORCESTER SHIRE
Gloucester BUCK-
DYFED INGHAM- Hertford
GLOUCESTER- Aylesbury SHIRE ESSEX
Carmarthen SHIRE Oxford HERTFORD- Chelmsford
GWENT OXFORDSHIRE SHIRE
WEST Cwmbran GREATER
GLAMORGAN MID Reading LONDON
Swansea GLAMORGAN Cardiff Bristol BERKSHIRE Kingston
SOUTH AVON WILTSHIRE Maidstone
GLAMORGAN Trowbridge SURREY KENT
HAMPSHIRE
SOMERSET Winchester WEST
Taunton SUSSEX EAST
SUSSEX
DEVON DORSET Chichester Lewes
Exeter Dorchester Newport
ISLE OF
WIGHT

NORTH
CHANNEL

St. George's Channel

CELTIC

SEA

CORNWALL
Truro

ENGLISH CHANNEL

FRANCE

ST. GEORGE'S CHANNEL

○ Norwich   Administrative headquarters
MERSEYSIDE   Metropolitan counties
Antrim   Former Northern Ireland
counties

Projection: *Conical with two standard parallels*

West from Greenwich   0   East from Greenwich
COPYRIGHT, GEORGE PHILIP & SON. LTD.

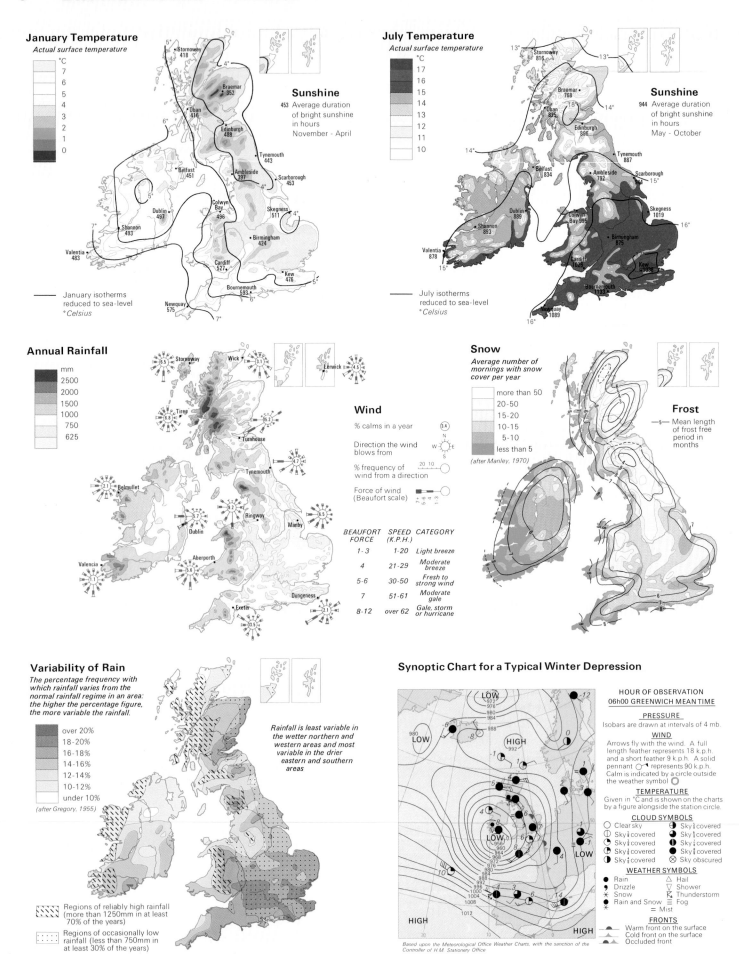

January Temperature

Actual surface temperature

°C
7
6
5
4
3
2
1
0

Sunshine

453 Average duration of bright sunshine in hours November - April

—— January isotherms reduced to sea-level °Celsius

July Temperature

Actual surface temperature

°C
17
16
15
14
13
12
11
10

Sunshine

944 Average duration of bright sunshine in hours May - October

—— July isotherms reduced to sea-level °Celsius

Annual Rainfall

mm
2500
2000
1500
1000
750
625

Wind

% calms in a year

Direction the wind blows from

% frequency of wind from a direction

Force of wind (Beaufort scale)

BEAUFORT FORCE	SPEED (K.P.H.)	CATEGORY
1-3	1-20	Light breeze
4	21-29	Moderate breeze
5-6	30-50	Fresh to strong wind
7	51-61	Moderate gale
8-12	over 62	Gale, storm or hurricane

Snow

Average number of mornings with snow cover per year

more than 50
20-50
15-20
10-15
5-10
less than 5

(after Manley, 1970)

Frost

—5— Mean length of frost free period in months

Variability of Rain

The percentage frequency with which rainfall varies from the normal rainfall regime in an area: the higher the percentage figure, the more variable the rainfall.

over 20%
18-20%
16-18%
14-16%
12-14%
10-12%
under 10%

(after Gregory, 1955)

Rainfall is least variable in the wetter northern and western areas and most variable in the drier eastern and southern areas

Regions of reliably high rainfall (more than 1250mm in at least 70% of the years)

Regions of occasionally low rainfall (less than 750mm in at least 30% of the years)

Synoptic Chart for a Typical Winter Depression

HOUR OF OBSERVATION
06h00 GREENWICH MEAN TIME

PRESSURE
Isobars are drawn at intervals of 4 mb.

WIND
Arrows fly with the wind. A full length feather represents 18 k.p.h. and a short feather 9 k.p.h. A solid pennant represents 90 k.p.h. Calm is indicated by a circle outside the weather symbol

TEMPERATURE
Given in °C and is shown on the charts by a figure alongside the station circle.

CLOUD SYMBOLS

○ Clear sky		◐ Sky ¾ covered	
◔ Sky ⅒ covered		◕ Sky ⅞ covered	
◑ Sky ¼ covered		● Sky ¹⁰⁄₁₀ covered	
◑ Sky ⅜ covered		◒ Sky obscured	
◑ Sky ½ covered			

WEATHER SYMBOLS

● Rain		△ Hail	
, Drizzle		▽ Shower	
* Snow		↯ Thunderstorm	
* Rain and Snow		≡ Fog	
		≡ Mist	

FRONTS
Warm front on the surface
Cold front on the surface
Occluded front

Based upon the Meteorological Office Weather Charts, with the sanction of the Controller of H.M. Stationery Office

COPYRIGHT. GEORGE PHILIP & SON LTD.

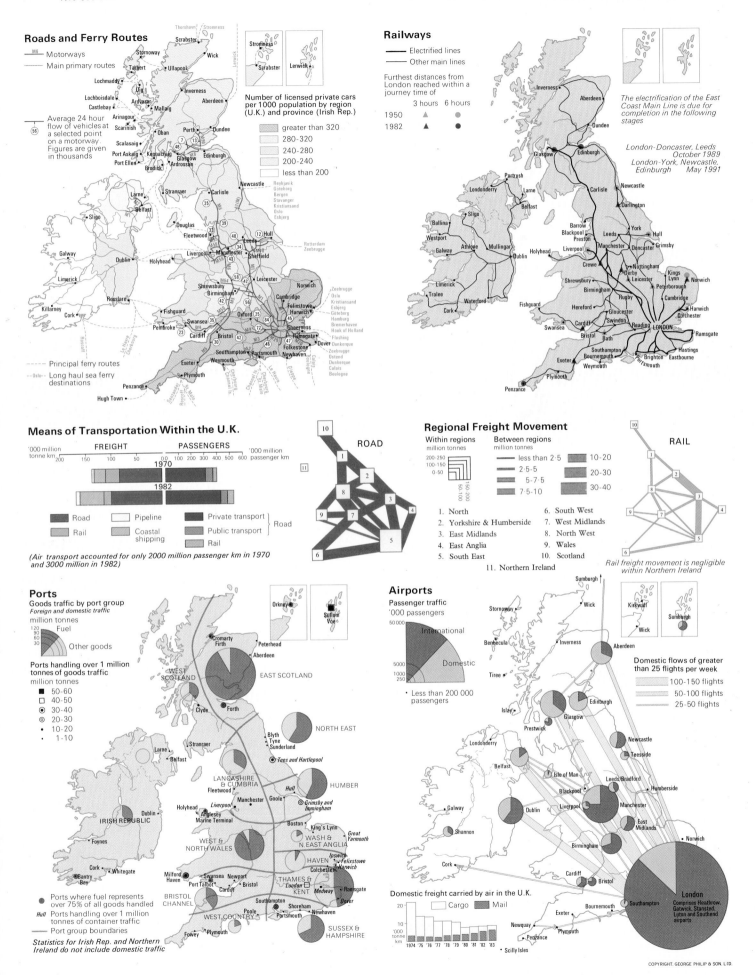

Roads and Ferry Routes

— M6 — Motorways
----- Main primary routes

(56) Average 24 hour flow of vehicles at a selected point on a motorway. Figures are given in thousands

Number of licensed private cars per 1000 population by region (U.K.) and province (Irish Rep.)

greater than 320
280-320
240-280
200-240
less than 200

----- Principal ferry routes
--Oslo-- Long haul sea ferry destinations

Railways

—— Electrified lines
—— Other main lines

Furthest distances from London reached within a journey time of
3 hours   6 hours
1950
1982

The electrification of the East Coast Main Line is due for completion in the following stages

London-Doncaster, Leeds October 1989
London-York, Newcastle, Edinburgh May 1991

Means of Transportation Within the U.K.

'000 million tonne km   FREIGHT   PASSENGERS   '000 million passenger km
200 150 100 50 0.0 100 200 300 400 500 600

1970
1982

Road
Rail
Pipeline
Coastal shipping
Private transport
Public transport } Road
Rail

(Air transport accounted for only 2000 million passenger km in 1970 and 3000 million in 1982)

ROAD

Regional Freight Movement

Within regions million tonnes
200-250
100-150
0-50
50-100
150-200

Between regions million tonnes
less than 2.5
2.5-5
5-7.5
7.5-10
10-20
20-30
30-40

1. North
2. Yorkshire & Humberside
3. East Midlands
4. East Anglia
5. South East
6. South West
7. West Midlands
8. North West
9. Wales
10. Scotland
11. Northern Ireland

RAIL

Rail freight movement is negligible within Northern Ireland

Ports

Goods traffic by port group
Foreign and domestic traffic
million tonnes
120
90
60
30
Fuel
Other goods

Ports handling over 1 million tonnes of goods traffic
million tonnes
■ 50-60
□ 40-50
◉ 30-40
◎ 20-30
• 10-20
· 1-10

● Ports where fuel represents over 75% of all goods handled
Hull Ports handling over 1 million tonnes of container traffic
—— Port group boundaries

Statistics for Irish Rep. and Northern Ireland do not include domestic traffic

Airports

Passenger traffic
'000 passengers
50 000
International
5000
Domestic
1000
250

• Less than 200 000 passengers

Domestic flows of greater than 25 flights per week
100-150 flights
50-100 flights
25-50 flights

Domestic freight carried by air in the U.K.
Cargo   Mail
20
10
'000 tonne km
1974 '75 '76 '77 '78 '79 '80 '81 '82 '83

London Comprises Heathrow, Gatwick, Stansted, Luton and Southend airports

COPYRIGHT. GEORGE PHILIP & SON. LTD.

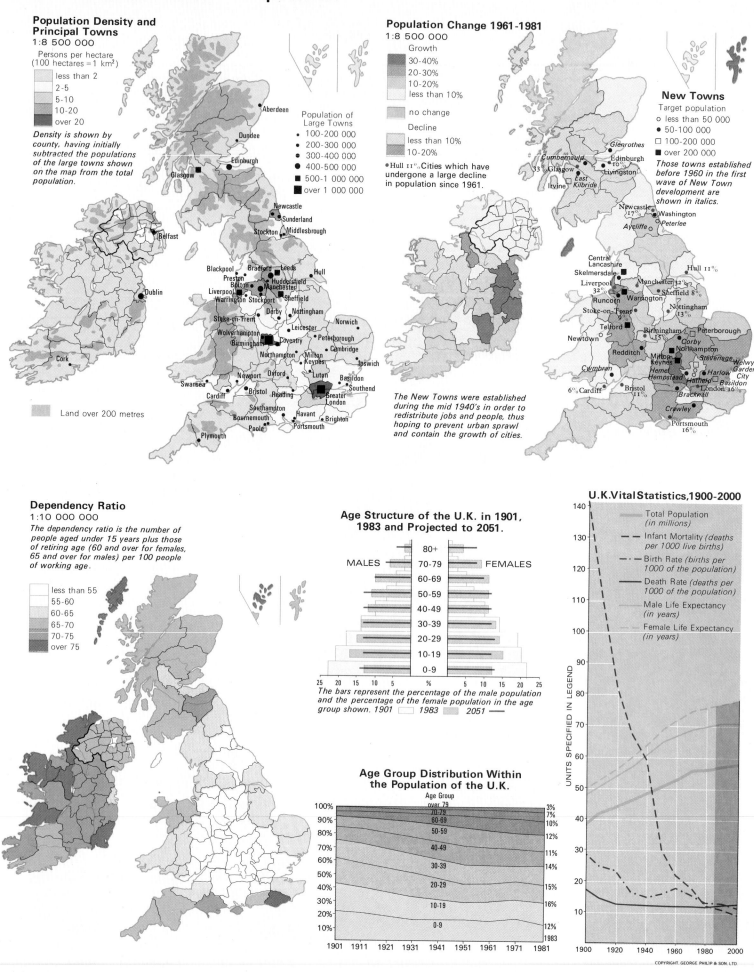

Population Density and Principal Towns

1:8 500 000

Persons per hectare
(100 hectares = 1 km²)

- less than 2
- 2-5
- 5-10
- 10-20
- over 20

Density is shown by county, having initially subtracted the populations of the large towns shown on the map from the total population.

Population of Large Towns
- • 100-200 000
- • 200-300 000
- • 300-400 000
- ● 400-500 000
- ■ 500-1 000 000
- ■ over 1 000 000

Land over 200 metres

Population Change 1961-1981

1:8 500 000

Growth
- 30-40%
- 20-30%
- 10-20%
- less than 10%

no change

Decline
- less than 10%
- 10-20%

● Hull 11% Cities which have undergone a large decline in population since 1961.

The New Towns were established during the mid 1940's in order to redistribute jobs and people, thus hoping to prevent urban sprawl and contain the growth of cities.

New Towns

Target population
- ○ less than 50 000
- ● 50-100 000
- □ 100-200 000
- ■ over 200 000

Those towns established before 1960 in the first wave of New Town development are shown in italics.

Dependency Ratio

1:10 000 000

The dependency ratio is the number of people aged under 15 years plus those of retiring age (60 and over for females, 65 and over for males) per 100 people of working age.

- less than 55
- 55-60
- 60-65
- 65-70
- 70-75
- over 75

Age Structure of the U.K. in 1901, 1983 and Projected to 2051.

MALES   FEMALES

80+
70-79
60-69
50-59
40-49
30-39
20-29
10-19
0-9

25 20 15 10 5 % 5 10 15 20 25

The bars represent the percentage of the male population and the percentage of the female population in the age group shown. 1901 ☐ 1983 ☐ 2051 ▬

Age Group Distribution Within the Population of the U.K.

Age Group
over 79 — 3%
70-79 — 7%
60-69 — 10%
50-59 — 12%
40-49 — 11%
30-39 — 14%
20-29 — 15%
10-19 — 16%
0-9 — 12%

1901 1911 1921 1931 1941 1951 1961 1971 1981

U.K. Vital Statistics, 1900-2000

— Total Population *(in millions)*

- - - Infant Mortality *(deaths per 1000 live births)*

-·-·- Birth Rate *(births per 1000 of the population)*

── Death Rate *(deaths per 1000 of the population)*

── Male Life Expectancy *(in years)*

- - - Female Life Expectancy *(in years)*

UNITS SPECIFIED IN LEGEND

1900 1920 1940 1960 1980 2000

COPYRIGHT. GEORGE PHILIP & SON. LTD

Agricultural Land Use Capability
1:10 000 000

NORTHERN IRELAND AND THE IRISH REPUBLIC
(Land Use Range)
- Wide
- Somewhat Limited
- Limited
- Very Limited
- Extremely Limited

GREAT BRITAIN
(Land Quality)
- First Class
- Good
- Good and Medium
- Medium
- Medium and Poor
- Poor
- Urban Areas

The land use capability classification assesses the value of land for agricultural purposes according to physical conditions and type of management.

Leading Agricultural Enterprises
1:10 000 000
- Crops
- Dairy
- Beef
- Sheep
- Pigs
- Horticulture
- Crofting

The leading enterprises shown on this map are those which use the most man-days in each district.

Principal Crops
Production ('000 tonnes)

	Production
Wheat	10 801
Barley	7517
Oats	343
Potatoes	5493
Sugar Beet	7494
Fruit	3559
Hops	9

Yield of Selected Crops in the U.K.
tonnes/ha.
1939 / 1983
WHEAT, BARLEY, OATS, SUGAR BEET, POTATOES

Number and Size of Agricultural Holdings in the U.K.

Average Size of Holding (hectares)

	1940	1980
England and Wales	33.8	60.2
Scotland	81.8	96.2
Northern Ireland	13.7	24.2

- over 100 ha.
- 50-100 ha.
- 40-50 ha.
- 20-40 ha.
- 5-20 ha.
- 2-5 ha.
- under 2 ha.

1940 1950 1960 1970 1980

Self-Sufficiency of the U.K. in Agricultural Production
(home production given as a percentage of total consumption)

PRODUCT	1969	1977	1982
Wheat	42%	61%	96%
Barley	90%	121%	130%
Potatoes	91%	95%	96%
Sugar	33%	40%	49%
Cheese	45%	67%	71%
Butter	12%	40%	49%
Beef	77%	72%	83%
Pork	101%	62%	67%
Poultry	100%	100%	99%

Fishing
1:10 000 000
Quantity of fish landed by domestic vessels at major ports, (port districts in Scotland.)

- less than 10 000 tonnes
- 10-50 000 tonnes
- 50-100 000 tonnes
- over 100 000 tonnes

Ullapool, Fraserburgh, Peterhead, Aberdeen, SCOTLAND, Ayr
Burtonport, Killybegs, Howth, Galway, Dunmore East, Castletownbere, Newlyn, Falmouth, Plymouth, Brixham, Milford Haven, Fleetwood, WALES, ENGLAND, North Shields, Whitby, Scarborough, Bridlington, Hull, Grimsby, Lowestoft

- Predominantly deep sea fish (demersal)
- Predominantly shallow water fish (pelagic)
- Predominantly shellfish

Forestry
- Forested Areas
- Newly planted areas
- Restocking of existing areas

The graphs show the area of forest planted annually by the Forestry Commission.

ha. SCOTLAND 2000 1000 1975 1980 1984
ha. WALES 2000 1000 1975 1980 1984
ha. ENGLAND 3000 2000 1000 1975 1980 1984

Area of Agricultural Land Under Selected Enterprises

TOTAL AREA
- Others 4%
- Rough Grazing 32%
- Arable 37%
- Permanent Pasture 27%

18 734 728 hectares

CEREALS
- Oats 3%
- Maize and Rye 1%
- Barley 54%
- Wheat 42%

3 960 569 hectares

HORTICULTURE
- Soft Fruit 8%
- Greenhouse Crops 6%
- Orchard Fruit 18%
- Vegetables 68%

222 024 hectares

OTHER CROPS
- Others 2%
- Turnips, Kale, Peas, Beans and other stock feeding crops 26%
- Rape 26%
- Sugar Beet 23%
- Potatoes 23%

842 339 hectares

Quantity of Fish Landed by British Vessels in all Fishing Areas
'000 tonnes
- Demersal Fish
- Pelagic Fish
- Shellfish

1950 1960 1970 1980 1983

Number and Size of Livestock Holdings in the U.K.
'000 holdings
- over 1000 head
- 500-1000 head
- 200-500 head
- 100-200 head
- 50-100 head
- 10-50 head
- under 10 head

DAIRY CATTLE, BEEF CATTLE, PIGS, SHEEP

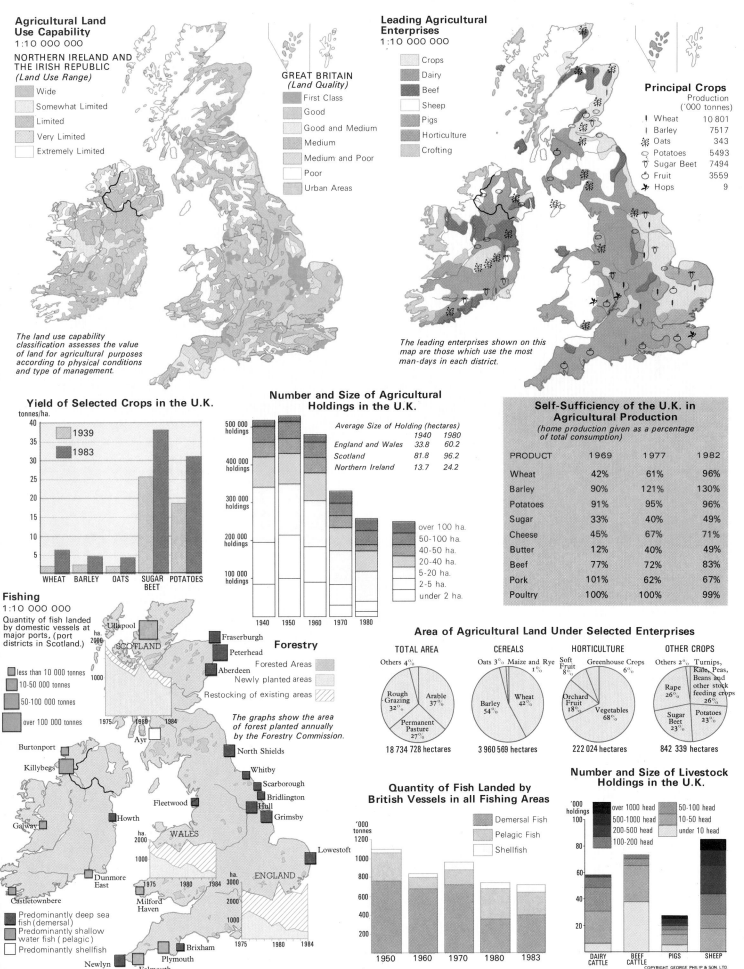

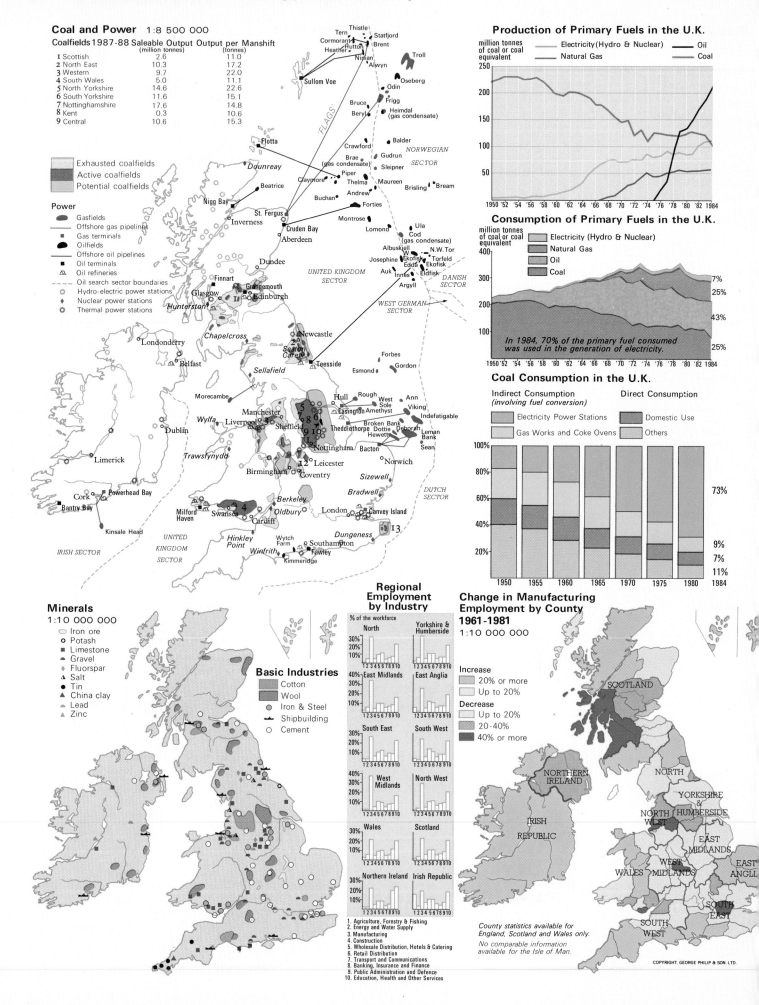

Coal and Power 1:8 500 000

Coalfields 1987-88

		Saleable Output (million tonnes)	Output per Manshift (tonnes)
I	Scottish	2.6	11.0
2	North East	10.3	17.2
3	Western	9.7	22.0
4	South Wales	5.0	11.1
5	North Yorkshire	14.6	22.6
6	South Yorkshire	11.6	15.1
7	Nottinghamshire	17.6	14.8
8	Kent	0.3	10.6
9	Central	10.6	15.3

Exhausted coalfields
Active coalfields
Potential coalfields

Power

- Gasfields
- Offshore gas pipelines
- Gas terminals
- Oilfields
- Offshore oil pipelines
- Oil terminals
- Oil refineries
- Oil search sector boundaries
- Hydro-electric power stations
- Nuclear power stations
- Thermal power stations

Production of Primary Fuels in the U.K.

million tonnes of coal or coal equivalent

Electricity (Hydro & Nuclear) — Oil
Natural Gas — Coal

Consumption of Primary Fuels in the U.K.

million tonnes of coal or coal equivalent

Electricity (Hydro & Nuclear)
Natural Gas
Oil
Coal

7%
25%
43%
25%

In 1984, 70% of the primary fuel consumed was used in the generation of electricity.

Coal Consumption in the U.K.

Indirect Consumption (involving fuel conversion)

Electricity Power Stations
Gas Works and Coke Ovens

Direct Consumption

Domestic Use
Others

73%
9%
7%
11%

1950 1955 1960 1965 1970 1975 1980 1984

Minerals

1:10 000 000

- Iron ore
- Potash
- Limestone
- Gravel
- Fluorspar
- Salt
- Tin
- China clay
- Lead
- Zinc

Basic Industries

- Cotton
- Wool
- Iron & Steel
- Shipbuilding
- Cement

Regional Employment by Industry

% of the workforce

North
Yorkshire & Humberside
East Midlands
East Anglia
South East
South West
West Midlands
North West
Wales
Scotland
Northern Ireland
Irish Republic

1. Agriculture, Forestry & Fishing
2. Energy and Water Supply
3. Manufacturing
4. Construction
5. Wholesale Distribution, Hotels & Catering
6. Retail Distribution
7. Transport and Communications
8. Banking, Insurance and Finance
9. Public Administration and Defence
10. Education, Health and Other Services

Change in Manufacturing Employment by County 1961-1981

1:10 000 000

Increase

20% or more
Up to 20%

Decrease

Up to 20%
20-40%
40% or more

County statistics available for England, Scotland and Wales only.

No comparable information available for the Isle of Man.

SCOTLAND
NORTHERN IRELAND
IRISH REPUBLIC
NORTH
YORKSHIRE & HUMBERSIDE
NORTH WEST
WALES
WEST MIDLANDS
EAST MIDLANDS
EAST ANGLIA
SOUTH EAST
SOUTH WEST

COPYRIGHT. GEORGE PHILIP & SON, LTD.

EMPLOYMENT

Employment in the U.K. by Industry

Numbers employed '000
25000
20000
15000
10000
5000

1931 1941 1951 1961 1971 1981 1984

- 62% Services
- 7% Transport
- 26% Manufacturing
- 3% Mining & Energy Supply
- 2% Agriculture, Forestry & Fishing

Employment by County

£ Over 75% employed in Services

Over 30% employed in Manufacturing

Over 5% employed in Agriculture

County statistics available for England, Scotland and Wales only.

UNEMPLOYMENT
1:10 000 000

Unemployment Rate by County, 1985

- over 20%
- 16-20%
- 12-16%
- 8-12%
- less than 8%

The unemployment rate is the number of unemployed expressed as a percentage of the working population (employed labour force plus the unemployed)

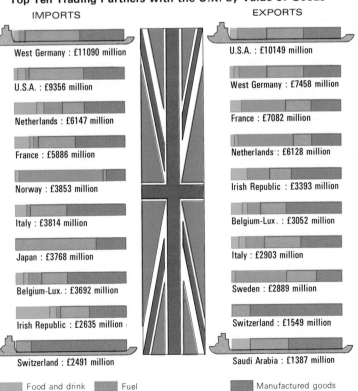

Leisure
1:8 500 000

- National Parks National Park Direction Areas (Scotland)
- National Forest Parks
- Areas of Outstanding Natural Beauty (England & Wales) National Scenic Areas (Scotland)

Coastal Conservation Zones (Scotland) Heritage Coasts (England & Wales)
Long Distance Footpaths
Navigable Waterways
Canals

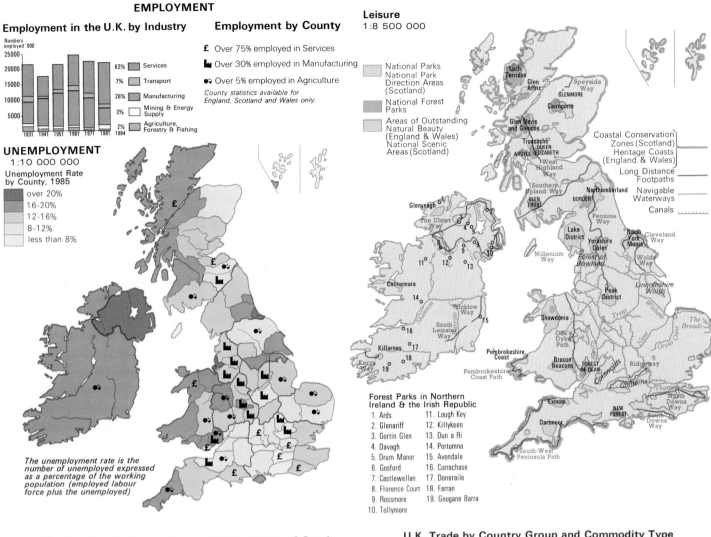

Forest Parks in Northern Ireland & the Irish Republic

1. Ards
2. Glenariff
3. Gortin Glen
4. Davagh
5. Drum Manor
6. Gosford
7. Castlewellan
8. Florence Court
9. Rossmore
10. Tollymore
11. Lough Key
12. Killykeen
13. Dun a Ri
14. Portumna
15. Avondale
16. Currachase
17. Doneraile
18. Farran
19. Gougane Barra

Top Ten Trading Partners with the U.K. by Value of Goods

IMPORTS

West Germany : £11090 million
U.S.A. : £9356 million
Netherlands : £6147 million
France : £5886 million
Norway : £3853 million
Italy : £3814 million
Japan : £3768 million
Belgium-Lux. : £3692 million
Irish Republic : £2635 million
Switzerland : £2491 million

EXPORTS

U.S.A. : £10149 million
West Germany : £7458 million
France : £7082 million
Netherlands : £6128 million
Irish Republic : £3393 million
Belgium-Lux. : £3052 million
Italy : £2903 million
Sweden : £2889 million
Switzerland : £1549 million
Saudi Arabia : £1387 million

- Food and drink
- Raw materials
- Fuel
- Machinery and equipment
- Manufactured goods

U.K. Trade by Country Group and Commodity Type
(percentages are given by value of trade)

IMPORTS 1973 / 1983
33% 46% 17% 16% 15% 14% 9% 8% 10% 10% 13% 2% 8% 4%

EXPORTS 1973 / 1983
33% 45% 16% 12% 16% 15% 10% 5% 7% 10% 15% 11% 3% 2%

Country Groups
- E.E.C.
- Other European
- North America
- Other Developed
- Oil Exporters
- Other Developing
- Centrally Planned Economies

IMPORTS 1973 / 1983
20% 12% 7% 13% 11% 11% 31% 21% 35% 39%
£59841 million / £65993 million

EXPORTS 1973 / 1983
3% 7% 7% 3% 3% 40% 22% 38% 47% 30%
£46002 million / £60533 million

Commodity
- Food and Drink
- Raw materials
- Fuel
- Machinery and equipment
- Manufactured goods

Total Value of Trade *(at current prices)*

Balance of Payments (£ million)

		1967	1977	1987
CREDITS	Visibles *(Exports)*	5241	31682	79422
	Invisibles	3310	21351	80010
	Total	8551	53033	159432
DEBITS	Visibles *(Imports)*	5840	34006	89584
	Invisibles	2992	19177	72352
	Total	8832	53183	161936
BALANCE		−281	−150	−2504

Visible trade involves transactions of goods while invisible trade involves transactions of money and services.

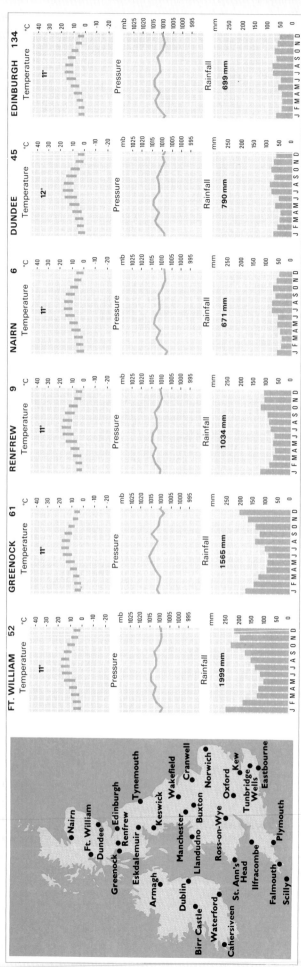

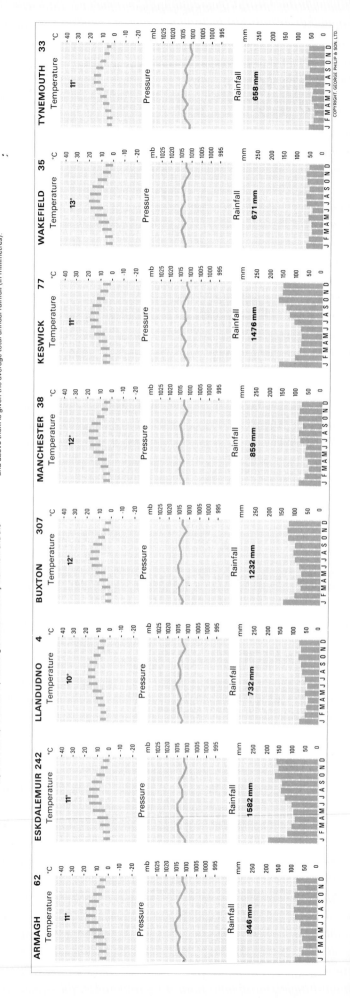

The climate graphs should be used in conjunction with the maps illustrating the climate of the British Isles on page 6. The stations have been selected to show climatic variations throughout the British Isles. On each graph the name of the station is followed by its height in metres above sea level, so that comparisons between stations can be made allowing for elevation. Temperature is shown by a bar, the top of the bar representing the mean monthly maximum and the bottom of the bar the mean monthly minimum temperature. A mid point between these is the mean monthly temperature; the mean annual range of temperature (in degrees Celsius) is given above the graph. The line on the pressure graphs shows the mean monthly pressure (in millibars and reduced to sea level). The rainfall graphs show the average monthly rainfall and above them is given the average total annual rainfall (in millimetres).

NORWICH 34 — Temperature 13° · Pressure · Rainfall 650 mm

CRANWELL 62 — Temperature 13° · Pressure · Rainfall 597 mm

OXFORD 63 — Temperature 13° · Pressure · Rainfall 653 mm

ILFRACOMBE 8 — Temperature 10° · Pressure · Rainfall 973 mm

ROSS-ON-WYE 68 — Temperature 12° · Pressure · Rainfall 709 mm

ST. ANN'S HEAD 43 — Temperature 9° · Pressure · Rainfall 945 mm

DUBLIN 16 — Temperature 10° · Pressure · Rainfall 696 mm

BIRR CASTLE 53 — Temperature 10° · Pressure · Rainfall 828 mm

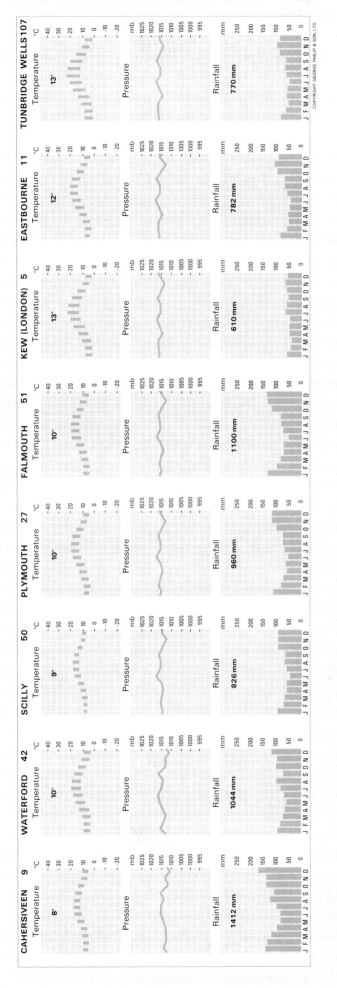

TUNBRIDGE WELLS 107 — Temperature 13° · Pressure · Rainfall 770 mm

EASTBOURNE 11 — Temperature 12° · Pressure · Rainfall 782 mm

KEW (LONDON) 5 — Temperature 13° · Pressure · Rainfall 610 mm

FALMOUTH 51 — Temperature 10° · Pressure · Rainfall 1100 mm

PLYMOUTH 27 — Temperature 10° · Pressure · Rainfall 960 mm

SCILLY 50 — Temperature 9° · Pressure · Rainfall 826 mm

WATERFORD 42 — Temperature 10° · Pressure · Rainfall 1044 mm

CAHERSIVEEN 9 — Temperature 8° · Pressure · Rainfall 1412 mm

1:1 000 000

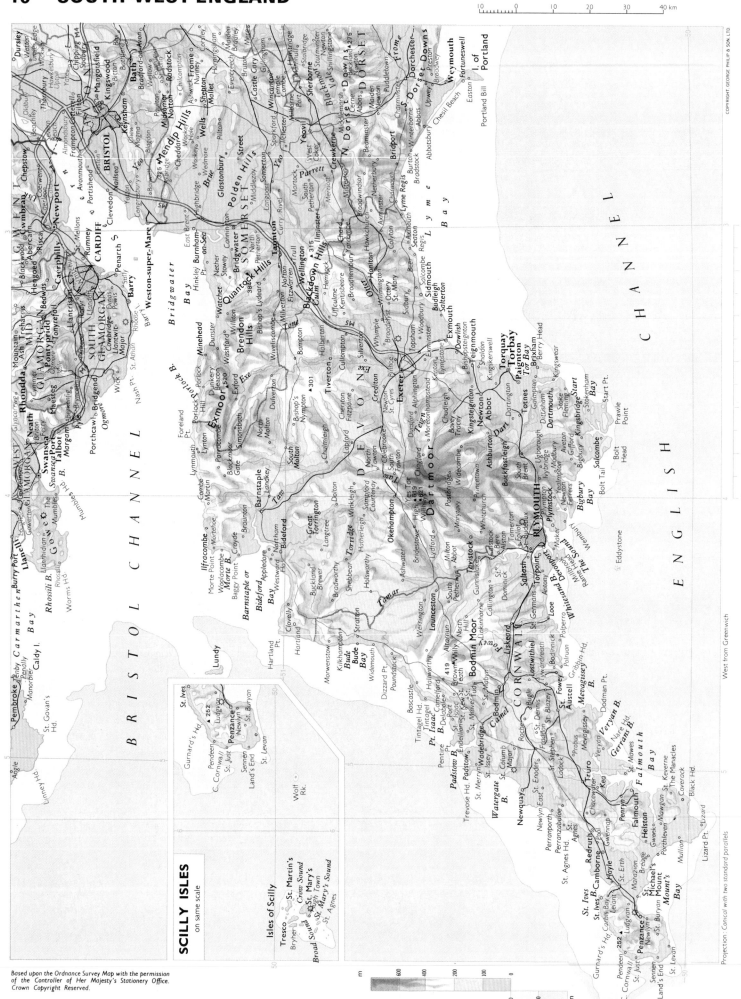

SCILLY ISLES
on same scale

West from Greenwich

Projection : Conical with two standard parallels

1:1 000 000

10 0 10 20 30 40 km

Map labels (Wales and surrounding regions):

The Skerries, Carmel Head, Wylfa Head, Cemaes Bay, Amlwch, Llanfechell, Parys Mt. 128, Moelfre, Dulas B., Red Wharf B., Puffin I., Gt. Ormes Hd., Llandudno, Lt. Ormes Hd., Rhos-on-Sea, Colwyn Bay, Kinmel Bay, Rhyl, Prestatyn

LIVERPOOL, Bootle, St. Helens, Prescot, Newton le Willows, Warrington, Wallasey, Hoylake, West Kirby, MERSEYSIDE, Huyton, Garston, Widnes, Runcorn, Birkenhead, Bebington, Bromborough, Speke, Frodsham, Helsby, Weaverham, M56, Ellesmere Port, Neston, Connah's Quay, Flint, Northop, Mynydd Isa, Mold, Buckley, Hope, Treuddyn, Caergwrle, Brymbo, Minera, CHESHIRE, Chester, Winsford, Tarvin, Kelsall, Tarporley, Wardle, Nantwich

Holyhead, Holyhead B., Holy I., Holy Hd., Valley, Bodedern, Llanerchymedd, Benllech, Pentraeth, Beaumaris, Menai Bridge, Bangor, Anglesey, Penmaenmawr, Conwy, Deganwy, Old Colwyn, Abergele, St. Asaph, Rhuddlan, Mostyn, Holywell, Gwalchmai, Llangefni, Gaerwen, Caerhun, Llanfairfechan, Dolgarrog, Llanfair Talhaiarn, Henllan, Denbigh, Llandyrnog, Bylchau, Ruthin, Llanarmon, Llansannan, Llangernyw

Aberffraw, Newborough, Malltraeth B., Menai Str., Caernarfon, Waunfawr, Carnedd Llewelyn 1062, Trefriw, Betws-y-Coed, Capel Curig, Pentrefoelas, Cerrigydrudion, Gwyddelwern, CLWYD, Corwen, Llangollen

Caernarfon Bay, Penygroes, Snowdon 1085, Llanberis, Dolwyddelan, Penmachno, Blaenau Ffestiniog, GWYNEDD, Ffestiniog, Arenig Fawr 853, Bala, L. Tegid (Bala L.), Glyn Ceiriog, Llanarmon Dyffryn Ceiriog, Berwyn Mts., Cefn-mawr, Ruabon, Wrexham, Overton, Whitchurch

Clynnog-fawr, Llanaelhaiarn 564, Nefyn, Tudweiliog, Lleyn Peninsula, Llanystumdwy, Llannor, Pwllheli, Porthmadog, Tremadog, Maentwrog, Trawsfynydd 853, Llanuwchllyn, Aran Fawddwy 905, Llanfihangel, Llandrillo, Llanfyllin, Oswestry, Chirk, Whittington, Wem, Ellesmere, Prees, Market Drayton

Aberdaron, Rhiw, Llanbedrog, Abersoch, Criccieth, Harlech, Talsarnau, Dina Mawddwy, Mallwyd, Llanfair Caereinion, Welshpool, Guilsfield, Shrewsbury, Shawbury, Myddle

Braich-y-pwll, Bardsey Sd., Bardsey I., Porth Neigwl, Trwyn Cilan, St. Tudwal's Is., Tremadog Bay, Llanbedr, Llanaber, Llanelltyd, Dolgellau, Dinas Mawddwy, Corris, Cemmaes Road, Wynnstay, Tregynon, Berriew, Long Mt., Westbury, Bayston Hill, Condover, Minsterley, Bicton, Wellington, The Wrekin 407, Coalbrookdale, Ironbridge, Broseley

Barmouth, Fairbourne, Llwyngwril, Llangelynin, Cader Idris 892, Tal-y-llyn, Abergynolwyn, Cwrt, Tywyn, Machynlleth, Carno, Caersws, Trefeglwys, Newtown, Kerry, Clun, Church Stretton, Stiperstones 528, Lydham, Montgomery, Chirbury, SHROPSHIRE, Craven Arms, Clee Hills 541, Clun Forest, Clun Castle, Clunbury

Cardigan Bay, Borth, Talybont, Plynlimon (Pumlumon) 752, Llangurig, Llanidloes, Severn, Rhayader, Beguildy, Knighton, Clee Hills

Aberystwyth, Rheidol, Devil's Bridge, Ystwyth, Ysbyty Ystwyth, Llanilar, Llanrhystyd, Pontrhydfendigaid, Llanon, Llanddewi-Brefi, Elan, Elan Village, Reservoirs, Drygarn Fawr 645, Newbridge on Wye, Llandrindod Wells, Penybont, Radnor Forest, New Radnor, Presteigne, Kingsland, Leominster, Wigmore, Brimfield, Mortimer's Cross, Tenbury, HEREFORD AND WORCESTER

Aberaeron, Mynydd Bach 361, Tregaron, POWYS, Rhayader, Radnor, Hundred House, Newchurch, Eardisley, Pembridge, Weobley, Bodenham

New Quay, Llanarth, Llangranog, Cemaes Hd., Aberporth, St. Dogmaels, Cardigan, Llandygwydd, Cenarth, Newcastle Emlyn, Llandysul, DYFED, Llanybyther, Lampeter, Pumsaint, Llanwrtyd Wells, Builth Wells, Llanafan-fawr, Llanganten, Painscastle, Clifford, Hay-on-Wye, Dorstone, Credenhill, Hereford, Madley, Lugwardine

Nevern, Cilgerran, Boncath, Llechryd, Bettws Bledrws, Llanwenog, Llandysilio, Llandovery, Mynydd Eppynt, Upper Chapel, Llyswen, Talgarth 811, Longtown, Ewyas Harold, Peterchurch, Pontrilas

Fishguard B., Strumble Hd., Fishguard, Goodwick, Newport, Dinas Hd., Mynydd Prescelly 536, Greenway, Crymych, Trelech, Llanpumsaint, Llandovery, Myddfai, Senny Bridge, Brecon, Black Mountains, Ross-on-Wye, Llanvihangel Crucorney, Pandy, Much Dewchurch

St. David's Hd., St. David's, Ramsey I., Solva, St. Brides Bay, Haverfordwest, Camrose, Wolf's Castle, Letterston, Mathry, Llandissilio, Whitland, St. Clears, Carmarthen, Llanarthney, Llandeilo, Mynydd Du, Black Mt., Forest Fawr, Brecon Beacons 886, Crickhowell, Abergavenny, Monmouth, Mitchel Troy, Coleford, Forest of Dean, Lydney

Skomer I., Skokholm I., St. Ann's Head, Dale, Milford Haven, Neyland, Pembroke Dock, Pembroke, Angle, Johnston, Templeton, Narberth, Laugharne, Llanstephan, Kidwelly, Pontardulais, Llanelli, Pontarddawe, Resolven, Glyn Neath, Hirwaun, Aberdare, Mountain Ash, Merthyr Tydfil, New Tredegar, Bargoed, Blackwood, Abercarn, Pontypool, Abersychan, Abertillery, Ebbw Vale, Blaenavon, Brynmawr, Tredegar, Rhymney, GWENT, Usk, Raglan, Chepstow

Linney Hd., Milford Haven, Pembroke, Manorbier, Caldy I., Tenby, Saundersfoot, Begelly, Pendine, Carmarthen Bay, Burry Port, Loughor, Gorseinon, Gowerton, WEST GLAMORGAN, Neath, Briton Ferry, Glyncorrwg, Treorchy, Rhondda, MID GLAMORGAN, Treharris, Caerphilly, Bedwas, Risca, Cwmbran, Caerleon M4, Newport, Caerwent

St. Govan's Hd., Rhossili B., Rhossili, Worms Hd., Gower, The Mumbles, Swansea, Port Talbot, Margam, Porthcawl, Bridgend, Maesteg, Llantrisant, Pontypridd, Pontyclun, SOUTH GLAMORGAN, Cowbridge, Llantwit Major, Penarth, CARDIFF, St. Mellons, Rumney, Marshfield, Caldicot, Severn Beach, Oldbury

Mumbles Hd., Ogmore, Wick, Llanharan, St. Athan, Barry, Nash Pt., Sully, Dinas Powys, Barry I., Weston-super-Mare, BRISTOL, AVON, Avonmouth, Portishead, Clevedon, Nailsea, Filton

BRISTOL CHANNEL

Bridgwater Bay, Mendip Hills 325, Congresbury, East Brent, Banwell, Cheddar, Axbridge, Blagdon, Chew Magna

Projection: Conical with two standard parallels

West from Greenwich

m
1000
800
600
400
200
100
0
50
100
m

1 : 1 000 000

10   0   10   20   30   40 km

Continuation
Northwards
on same scale

NORTH SEA

TYNE AND WEAR

Hartley
Earsdon
Whitley Bay
Tynemouth
Wallsend
South Shields
Jarrow
Gateshead
Sunderland
Washington
Houghton-le-Spring
Ryhope
Seaham
Murton
Easington Colliery
Horden

Seaton Delaval
wcastle-
upon-
Tyne
Hebburn
Birtley
Chester-le-
Street
Hetton-le-Hole
Sacriston
Durham
Brandon
Wheatley
Hill
Castle Eden
Willington
Trimdon
Hartlepool

Peterlee

nnymoor
Sedgefield
Ferryhill
Shildon
Wolviston
Billingham
Stockton-on-Tees
Teesside
Middlesbrough
Thornaby
on Tees
Eston

Greatham
Redcar
Marske by the Sea
Saltburn by the Sea
Staithes
Kettle Ness

Newton Aycliffe

Gainford
Darlington
Eaglescliffe
Yarm
CLEVELAND
Guisborough
Loftus
Hinderwell
Lythe

BORDERS

Preston
Duns
Chirnside
Westruther
Greenlaw
Berwick-upon-Tweed
Tweedmouth
Scremerston

Merse
Swinton
Norham
Holy I.
Budle Bay
Farne Is.
Bamburgh

Earlston
Gordon
Coldstream
Leitholm
Barmoor
Castle
Lowick
Beal
N. Sunderland
Seahouses
Beadnell

Kelso
Maxwellheugh
Flodden
Till
Belford
Mindrum
Deddington

Newtown
St. Boswells
Roxburgh
Town
Yetholm
Wooler
Chatton
Embleton

Ancrum
Jedburgh
Morebattle
The Cheviot
816
Breamish
Glanton
Aln
Alnwick
Longhoughton
Lesbury
Alnmouth

Bonchester
Bridge
Alwinton
Corner
Rothbury
Shilbottle
Warkworth
Coquet I.
Amble
Felton
Hauxley
Broomhill

Catcleugh
Rochester
Simonside
441
Rothbury
Longhorsley
Thirston
Druridge B.

Peel Fell
602
Kielder
Res.
Elishaw
Otterburn
Rede
Widdrington
Ellington

Kielder
Falstone
NORTHUMBERLAND
Pegswood
Ashington
Newbiggin-
by-the-sea

Sighty
Crag
519
Bellingham
Kirkwhelpington
Cambo
Whalton
Morpeth
Wansbeck
Bedlington

Redesmouth
Ridsdale
Stannington
Cowpen
Cramlington
Blyth

Wark
N. Tyne
Birtley
Belsay
Ponteland
Seaton Delaval
Hartley

HADRIAN'S WALL

Humshaugh
Chollerton
Stamfordham
Brunton
Gosforth
Longbenton
Whitley B.
Tynemouth

Gilsland
Greenhead
Haydon
Bridge
Corbridge
Newcastle-upon-Tyne
Wallsend
South Shields
Jarrow

Cold Fell
622
Haltwhistle
Lambley
Allen
Catton
Painshawfield
Slaley
Prudhoe
Ryton
Newburn
Whickham
Blaydon
Gateshead
TYNE AND
WEAR

Alston
Allendale
Town
Allenheads
Derwent
Edmondbyers
Leadgate
Castleside
Lanchester
Stanley
Consett
Birtley
Sunderland
Washington
Houghton-
le-Spring

Hexham
Haydon
Bridge
Leadgate
Annfield Plain
Chester-le-
Street
Hetton-le-Hole
Easington

Collier Law
516
Sacriston
Durham
A1(M)

NORTH YORK MOORS

Wiske
Hutton
Rudby
Stokesley
Great
Ayton
Egton
Castleton
Whitby
Hawsker
Robin Hood's Bay

Rudby
Broughton
Esk
Goathland
Fylingdales
Moor
Sleights
Hayburn Wyke

Northallerton
Osmotherley
Laskill
Rosedale
Abbey
Saltergate
Scalby
Scalby Ness

Cleveland Hills
454
Hodge
Dove
Cloughton

Brompton
Helmsley
Kirkbymoorside
Ebberston
Scarborough

Hambleton
Hills
Rievaulx
Pickering
Thornton
Dale
Snainton
Seamer
Cayton

Thirsk
Sowerby
Carlton
Miniott
Ampleforth
Hovingham
Vale of Pickering
Rye
Sherburn
Ayton
Eastfield
Filey

YORKSHIRE
Helperby
Easingwold
Stillington
Malton
Rillington
Burton
Fleming
Hunmanby
Filey Bay

Ripon
Fountains
Abbey
Boroughbridge
Aldborough
Sheriff Hutton
Strensall
Norton
Settrington
Rudston
Flamborough

Pateley
Bridge
Ripley
Killinghall
Whixley
Green
Hammerton
Haxby
Sledmere
Wetwang
Great
Driffield
Burton
Agnes
Nafferton
Flamborough
Head

Harrogate
Knaresborough
Marston
Moor
Fulford
Fridaythorpe
246
Stamford Bridge
Bridlington
Bridlington
Bay

YORKSHIRE WOLDS

Spofforth
Nidd
Wetherby
Pocklington
Skipsea

Otley
Guiseley
Yeadon
Baildon
Harewood
Collingham
Tadcaster
Escrick
Barmby
Moor
Middleton on the
Wolds
Beeford
Hornsea

Wharfe
Cawood
Sherburn
Riccall
Barlby
Holme
Leven
Aldbrough

LEEDS
Garforth
Rothwell
Selby
Market Weighton
Cottingham
Beverley
Sproatley

WEST
YORKSHIRE
Morley
Castleford
Knottingley
Howden
Ouse
Brough
South Cave
Hessle
KINGSTON-UPON-HULL
Marfleet
Hedon
Burstwick
Withernsea

Batley
Normanton
Pontefract
Snaith
Goole
Whitton
Winterton
Barton upon
Humber
New
Holland
Paull
Keyingham
Patrington
Sunk
Island
Easington

and Dewsbury
Mirfield
Ossett
Wakefield
Hemsworth
South
Kirkby
Royston
Stainforth
Adwick le
Street
Thorne
Crowle
Belton
Barrow upon
Humber
Burton upon Stather
Roxby
Immingham
Keelby
Stallingborough
Grimsby
Spurn Hd.

Kirkburton
Denby
Dale
Darton
Wombwell
Doncaster
Hatfield
Isle
of
Axholme
Scawby
Scunthorpe
Barnetby
Laceby
Waltham
Cleethorpes

Penistone
Barnsley
Worsbrough
Mexbrough
New
Rossington
Epworth
Kirton in
Lindsey
Broughton
Brigg
Caistor
Humberston
Mouth of the Humber

SOUTH YORKSHIRE
Hoyland Nether
Wath
Swinton
Conisbrough
Bawtry
Misterton
Owston
Ferry
Waddingham
Usselby
North
Thoresby
Grainthorpe
Donna Nook
North Somercoates

Rawmarsh
Rotherham
Maltby
Tickhill
Blyton
Caenby
Corner
West Rasen
Tetney
Saltfleet

SHEFFIELD
Thurcroft
Dinnington
Beckingham
Gainsborough
Faldingworth
Market Rasen
South
Elkington
Saltfleetby
Louth
Manby

Dronfield
Eckington
Worksop
Carlton
Lindrick
Lea
Kexby
Welton
Stainton
Wragby
Hainton
Scamblesby
Withern
Mablethorpe
Sutton-on-Sea

Chesterfield
Bolsover
Mansfield Woodhouse
East
Retford
East
Markham
Saxilby
LINCOLNSHIRE
Wragby
Ulceby
Cross
Alford
Willoughby
Chapel St. Leonards

Clay Cross
Staveley
Whitwell
Tuxford
North
Hykeham
Lincoln
Washingborough
Bardney
Horncastle
Partney
Burgh le
Marsh
Ingoldmells Pt.

Matlock
Sutton
in Ashfield
Kirkby-in-
Ashfield
Ollerton
North
Collingham
Branston
Bracebridge
Heath
Metheringham
Woodhall
Spa
Mareham
le Fen
Spilsby
Skegness

Alfreton
Ravenshead
Blidworth
Southwell
Eakring
Waddington
Scopwick
Coningsby
East-Fen
Wainfleet
All Saints
Gibraltar
Pt.

Ripley
Heanor
Eastwood
Hucknall
Arnold
Navenby
Billinghay
West
Fen
Sibsey
Wrangle

Belper
Ilkeston
Stapleford
NOTTINGHAM
Carlton
Radcliffe-on-Trent
Leadenham
Ruskington
Sleaford
Brothertoft
Holland Fen
Heckington
Old Leake
Benington
Boston
Fishtoft

DERBY
Mickleover
Beeston
West
Bridgford
Bingham
Long
Eaton
Balderton
Newark-on-Trent
Cranwell
Grantham
Honington
Swineshead
Kirton
Sutterton

The Wash

NORFOLK

Thornham
Brancaster
Holkham
Blakeney
Cley
Weybourne
Holt

Hunstanton
Heacham
Burnham
Market
Wells
next-the-Sea
Little
Walsingham
Melton
Constable

Snettisham
Docking
Fakenham
Dersingham

West from Greenwich

East from Greenwich

COPYRIGHT. GEORGE PHILIP & SON, LTD.

Based upon the Ordnance Survey Map with the permission
of the Controller of Her Majesty's Stationery Office.
Crown Copyright Reserved.

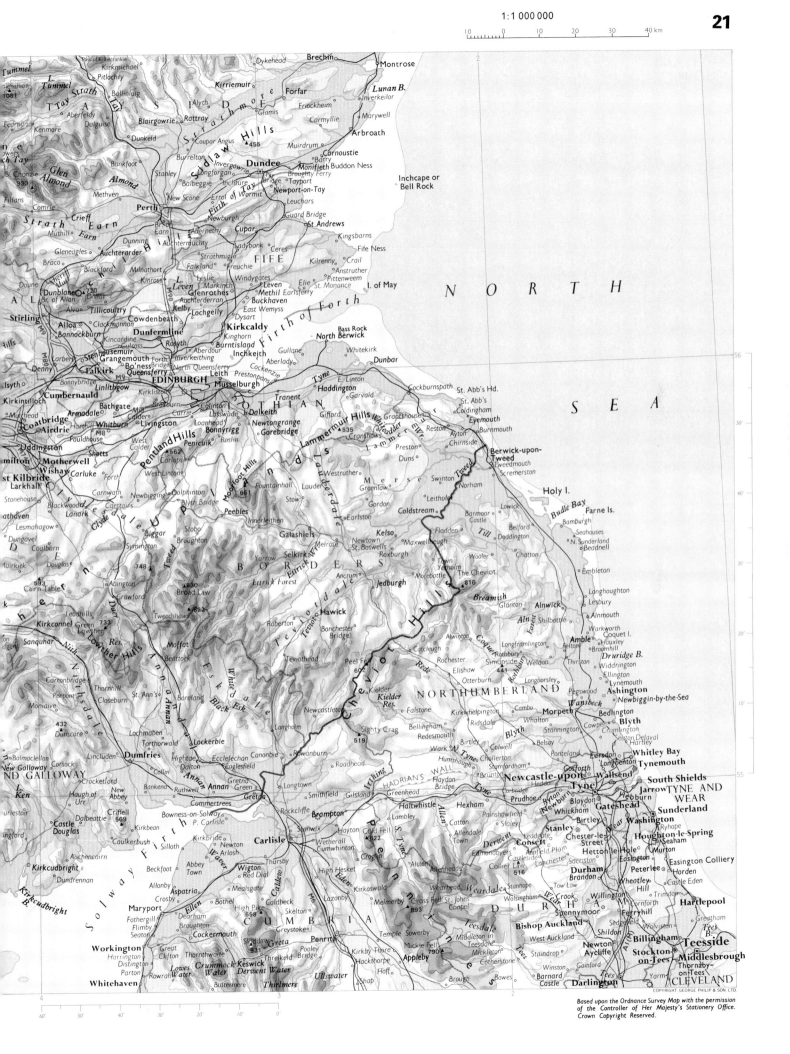

SHETLAND ISLANDS
on same scale

Projection: Conical with two standard parallels

SHETLAND

Herma Ness
Haroldswick
Bluemull Sd.
Baltasound
Balta
Unst
Cullivoe
Uyeasound
Mu Ness
Ramna Stacks
Whale Firth
Fetlar
Point of Fethaland
Colfgrave Sd.
The Snap
The Faither
North Roe
Ronas Hill 450
Mid Yell
Yell
Burravoe
Esha Ness
Hillswick
Lunna Ness
St. Magnus Bay
Brae
Skaw Taing
Out Skerries
Muckle Roe
Voe
Whalsay
Papa Stour
Sd. of Papa
Sandness
The Haa
S Nesting Bay
Walls
Score Hd.
Vaila
Easter Skeld
Lerwick
I. of Noss
Gruting Voe
Scalloway
Bressay
Bard Hd.
Hamnavoe
West Burra
293
Bressay Sd.
Helli Ness
Kettla Ness
Hoswick
Mousa
St. Ninian's I.
Scousburgh
Boddam
Fitful Hd.
B. of Quendale
Sumburgh Hd.

Outer Hebrides / Western Isles

Butt of Lewis
South Dell
Port of Ness
Ness
Borve
Cellar Hd.
Barvas
North Tolsta
Tolsta Hd.
Carloway
Shawbost
Back
Tiumpan Hd.
Gallan Hd.
Great Bernera
291
Newmarket
Broad Bay
Portaguiran
Uig
Callanish
Stornoway
Melbost
Eye Peninsula
L. Roag
Bayble
575
Gisla
Lewis
Chicken Hd.
Aird Brenish
Loch Langavat
Balallan
Crossbost
Lochs
L. Erisort
Scarp
Kintaravay
Park
Cromore
Gravir
Husinish
N. Harris
571
Kebock Hd.
Husinish Pt.
Ardourlie Castle
799
Beinn Mhor
L. Shell
W. L. Tarbert
Ardhasig
L. Seaforth
Sd. of Shiant
Shiant Is.
Taransay
Tarbert
WESTERN
Toe Hd.
Sd. of Taransay
Scalpay
Harris
E. L. Tarbert
Pabbay
Scarastavore
S. Harris
Sd. of Pabbay
Leverburgh
Berneray
Rodel
Haskeir Is.
Renish Pt.
Rubha Hunish
Griminish Pt.
ISLES
Sollas
North Uist
Lochmaddy
Paible
L. Maddy
Vaternish Pt.
Clachan
Carinish
L. Eport
Monach Is.
Baleshare
347 Eaval
Grimsay
Ronay
Gramisdale
Benbecula
Ardivachar Pt.
Wiay
L. Bee
Bagh nam Faoileann
Howmore
South Uist
605 Hecla
Rubha Ardvule
620 B. Mhor
L. Eynort
Daliburgh
Lochboisdale
L. Boisdale
Sound of Barra
Sd. of Eriskay
Greian Hd.
Eriskay
Barra
384
Castlebay
Bruernish Pt.
Vatersay
Sandray
Pabbay
Mingulay
Berneray
Barra Head
241

Skye and mainland

C. Wrath
Kyle
L. Inchard
Kinlochbervie
L. Laxford
Handa I.
Scourie
B. S.
Eddrachillis Bay
Pt. of Stoer
Drumbeg
Quinag
Stoer
809
Assynt
L. Assy
Rhu Coigach
Lochinver
Canisp 847
Enard Bay
Elphin
Ledm
Summer Isles
L. Lurgainn
Croma Hill
Greenstone Pt.
L. Broom
Coigach
Strathka
Mellon Charles
Ullapool
Ardchar
L. Ewe
Aultbea
An Teallach 1062
Melvaig
Poolewe
Fionn Loch
Braemore
Longa I.
Henderson
L. Gairloch
Gairloch
L. na Sealga
Kerrysdale
L. Maree
Talladale 981
Slioch
W
Fannich
Kilmaluag
L. Sgur
1053
Kinlochewe
Achnasheen
Vaternish Pt.
Rona
L. Torridon
Fasag
Torridon
Loch Snizort
Uig
Trotternish
Sound of Raasay
Shieldaig
Achnashellach
Stein
The Storr 719
Applecross Forest
Coulags
Carron
Monar Forest
Milovaig
Lephin
Applecross
1052 L. Monar
Dunvegan Head
Roskhill
Portree
L. Kishorn
Lochcarron
Dunvegan
488
Raasay
Stromemore
Sgurr na Lapa
Bracadale
Toscaig
Kishorn
Plockton
1150
Fernilea
Coillore
Crowlin Is.
Mullardoch
L. Bracadale
L. Harport
Carron
Stromeferry
Minginish
Carbost
Drynoch
Scalpay
Kyle of Lochalsh
Auchtertyre
Carn Eige
Glenbrittle
Sligachan
Kyleakin
Darnie
1821
Glen Affr
Cuillin Hills 1009
Bla Bheinn 928
Broadford
L. Alsh
L. Affr
Rubh' an Dunain
Glenelg
Invershiel
A Chralaig
Glen M
Soay Sd.
Soay
L. Scavaig
Elgol
L. Eishort
Eilean Iarmain
The Saddle 1010
A Chralaig 1120
Glen She
Canna
Teangue
L. Hourn
Glen Shiel
L. Cluanie
Sanday
Canna
Kinloch
Armadale
Ardvasar
Sound of Sleat
Ladhar B. 1019
L. Quoich
Sd. of Canna
Rhum 810
Pt. of Sleat
Mallaig
Knoydart
Tomdoun
Cuillin Sound
Morar
L. Nevis
1040
Glen Garry
Eigg
Arisaig
Loch Morar
Sgurr na Ciche
L. Arkaig
983
Sd. of Eigg
394
Lechailort
Culvain
Caledonian Canal
Muck
Sd. of Arisaig
Glenfinnan
Kinlocheil
Shona
882
Moidart
L. Eil
Fort William
L. Moidart
Kinlochmoidart
Loch Shiel
S
Ben Nevis
Pt. of Ardnamurchan
Ardnamurchan
Salen
Ardgour
1347
Coll
Kilchoan
527
Mingary
Sunart
888
North Ballachulish
L. Sunart
Strontian
Corran
Sorisdale
L. Leven
Clabhach
Caliach Pt.
Kingairloch
Arinagour
Calgary
Tobermory
Drimnin
South Ballachulish
Morvern
1148
Tiree
Dervaig
L. Frisa
Sd. of Mull
STRATH
Scarinish
L. Tuath
Lochaline
Loch Linnhe
L. Etive
Treshnish Isles
Salen
Lismore I.
Hynish B.
Tiree Passage of
Hynish

m scale
1000
800
600
400
200
100
0
m
50
100

DISTRICTS IN
NORTHERN IRELAND

1 Londonderry
2 Limavady
3 Coleraine
4 Ballymoney
5 Moyle
6 Larne
7 Ballymena
8 Magherafelt
9 Cookstown
10 Strabane
11 Omagh
12 Fermanagh
13 Dungannon
14 Craigavon
15 Armagh
16 Newry and Mourne
17 Banbridge
18 Down
19 Lisburn
20 Antrim
21 Newtownabbey
22 Carrickfergus
23 North Down
24 Ards
25 Castlereagh
26 Belfast

1:1 250 000

10 0 10 20 30 40 50 km

COPYRIGHT GEORGE PHILIP & SON LTD

Projection: Conical with two standard parallels

West from Greenwich

ATLANTIC OCEAN

LEINSTER

MUNSTER

Provinces & Counties: WICKLOW, KILDARE, OFFALY, LAOIS, CARLOW, WEXFORD, KILKENNY, WATERFORD, TIPPERARY, LIMERICK, CLARE, CORK, KERRY

Selected places:

Dún Laoghaire (Dunleary), Bray, Bray Head, Greystones, Newtownmountkennedy, Newcastle, Wicklow, Wicklow Hd., Kilbride, Rathnew, Avoca, Arklow, Courtown, Riverchapel, Ballycanew, Gorey, Cahore Pt.

Wicklow Mountains, Poulaphouca Res., Lugnaquilla 926, Vartry Res., Blackwater, Castlebridge, Wexford, Wexford Harbour, Rosslare Harbour, Rosslare, Greenore Pt., Tuskar Rock, Carnsore Pt., Broadway, Churchtown, Saltee Is.

Enniscorthy, Bunclody, New Ross, Vinegar Hill, Oilgate, Clonroche, Killurin, Foulksmills, Bannow Bay, Bagenbun Hd., Fethard, Baginbun Hd., Hook Hd., Duncannon, Arthurstown, Ballyhack, Passage East, Cheekpoint, Tramore, Tramore Bay, Dunmore East, Brownstown Hd.

Waterford, Carrick on Suir, Clonmel, Comeragh Mts. 792, Monavullagh Mts. 726, Dungarvan, Dungarvan Harbour, Helvick Hd., Ringville, Mine Hd.

Lismore, Cappoquin, Tallowbridge, Tallow, Ardmore, Ardmore Head, Youghal, Youghal Bay, Ballymacoda, Knockadoon Hd.

Kilkenny, Thomastown, Inistioge, Graiguenamanagh, Mullinavat, Callan, Kells, Windgap, Carrick-on-Suir

Cahir, Cashel, Tipperary, Golden Vale, Galty Mts. 920, Galtymore, Aherlow, Mitchelstown, Fermoy, Kilworth Mts., Araglin

Thurles, Templemore, Roscrea, Nenagh, Silvermine Mts., Arra Mts., Slieve Felim Mts., Newport 694

Limerick, Shannon, Bruff, Bruree, Kilmallock, Charleville, Buttevant, Doneraile, Mallow, Kanturk, Newmarket, Millstreet, Macroom, Blarney

Cork, Cork Harbour, Cobh, Passage West, Crosshaven, Carrigaline, Kinsale, Kinsale Harbour, Old Head of Kinsale, Courtmacsherry, Courtmacsherry Bay, Clonakilty, Clonakilty Bay, Rosscarbery, Rosscarbery Bay, Galley Hd., Toe Hd., Castletownshend, Glandore Harbour, Baltimore, Sherkin I., C. Clear, Clear I., Cape Clear, Fastnet Rock

Bandon, Dunmanway, Skibbereen, Ballydehob, Shehy Mts. 537, Boggeragh Mts., Nagles Mts., Knocknaskagh, Mushera 648, The Paps

Bantry, Bantry Bay, Whiddy I., Glengarriff, Castletown Bearhaven, Bere Haven, Bear I., Dursey Hd., Dursey I., Crow Hd., Sheeps Hd., Mizen Hd., Three Castle Hd., Goleen, Toormore, Durrus, Kilcrohane

Caha Mts., Slieve Miskish Mts., Hungry Hill 686, Allihies, Ballydonegan, Ballydonegan B.

Killarney, Killorglin, Caragh L., Macgillycuddy's Reeks, Carrauntoohil 1041, Mangerton Mt. 840, Kenmare, Kenmare R., Sneem, Derrynane, Waterville, Caherdaniel, Caherciveen, Valentia I., Valentia Har., Portmagee, Bolus Hd., St. Finian's Bay, Cahersiveen

Tralee, Tralee B., Castlemaine, Castlemaine Harbour, Dingle, Dingle Bay, Slea Hd., Dunmore Hd., Mt. Eagle, Brandon 953, Brandon Hd., Brandon Pt., Smerwick Har., Sybil Pt., Ballydavid Hd., Ballyferriter

Stack's Mts. 357, Castleisland, Abbeyfeale, Listowel, Tarbert, Ballylongford, Glin, Foynes, Shannon, Mouth of the Shannon, Loop Hd., Kilrush, Kilkee, Carrigaholt, Doonbeg, Quilty, Miltown Malbay, Spanish Pt., Lahinch, Liscannor Bay, Cliffs of Moher, Hags Hd., Ennistymon, Ennis, Shannon Airport, Newmarket on Fergus, Sixmilebridge, Killaloe, Scariff, L. Derg, Tulla, Corofin, Gort

CLARE

Galway, Galway Bay, Black Hd., Burren, Kinvara, Ballyvaghan, Kilcolgan, Clarinbridge, Oranmore, Athenry, Loughrea, Portumna, Ballinasloe, Banagher, Birr, Roscrea

Inishmore, Inishmaan, Inisheer, Aran Is. (Galway), North Sound, South Sound, Gregory Sound

m 1000 800 600 400 200 100 0

m 50 100

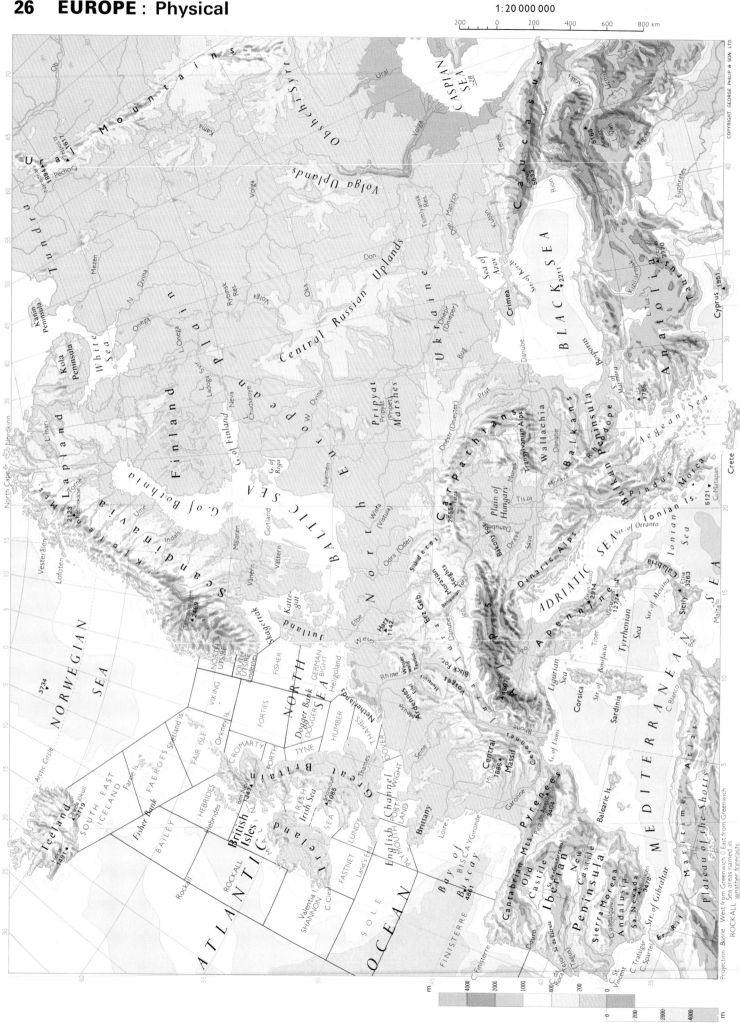

1:20 000 000

Projection : Bonne. West from Greenwich 0 East from Greenwich
Sea areas named in
ROCKALL weather forecasts

1:20 000 000

200 0 200 400 600 800 km

UNION OF SOVIET SOCIALIST REPUBLICS

Nizhny Tagil · Sverdlovsk · Chelyabinsk · Magnitogorsk · Orenburg · Perm · Izhevsk · Ufa · Kuybyshev · Kazan · Kirov · Gorki · Saratov · Penza · Tambov · Voronezh · Tula · Orel · Kursk · Kharkov · MOSCOW · Yaroslavl · Ivanovo · Kostroma · Rybinsk · Vologda · Smolensk · Vitebsk · Mogilev · Gomel · Kaluga · Bryansk

Ob · Irtysh · Tobol · Ural · KAZAKHSTAN · Guryev · CASPIAN SEA · Baku · AZERBAIJAN · Tbilisi · ARMENIA · Yerevan · GEORGIA · Erzurum

N. Dvina · Kotlas · Arkhangelsk · Onega · White Sea · Murmansk

Leningrad · Chudskoye · RUSSIA · W. Dvina · WHITE RUSSIA · Minsk · Pripyat (Pripet) · Zhitomir · Kiev · Dnepr (Dnieper) · Dnepropetrovsk · Krivoy Rog · Nikolayev · Odessa · Kherson · MOLDAVIA · Kishinev · U. Dnestr (Dniester) · Lvov · Zaporozhye · Donets · Rostov · Taganrog · S. of Azov · Krasnodar · Stavropol · Volga · Volgograd · Astrakhan · Don

FINLAND · Helsinki · Tampere · Tallinn · ESTONIA · Riga · LATVIA · LITHUANIA · Kaunas · Vilnius · Kaliningrad · Białystok · Brest · Bug · Lublin · Debrecen

L. Ladoga · Vyborg · Kronstadt · G. of Bothnia · Luleå · Vaasa · Oulu · Kemi

Tornio · Luleå · Piteå · Umeå · Stockholm · Uppsala · SWEDEN · Gävle · Örebro · Göteborg · Jönköping · Vänern · Vättern · Malmö · Öland · Gotland

NORWAY · Oslo · Bergen · Stavanger · Trondheim · Trondheim · Tromsø · Narvik · Sogne Fd. · Hardanger Fd.

ICELAND · Reykjavik

ATLANTIC OCEAN · Faroe Is. (Don.) · Shetland Is. · Orkney Is. · Hebrides

UNITED KINGDOM · SCOTLAND · Aberdeen · Dundee · Glasgow · Edinburgh · Newcastle · N.I. · Belfast · IRELAND · Dublin · Cork · C. Clear · Isle of Man · ENGLAND · Liverpool · Manchester · Leeds · Sheffield · Hull · Birmingham · Leicester · WALES · Cardiff · Swansea · Bristol · Southampton · Plymouth · Portsmouth · LONDON · English Channel · Is. of Scilly

NORTH SEA · DENMARK · COPENHAGEN · Aarhus · Aalborg · Kiel · Skagerrak · Kattegat

GERMANY · Hamburg · Bremen · Hanover · Magdeburg · BERLIN · Leipzig · Dresden · Halle · EAST · WEST · Essen · Dortmund · Cologne · Düsseldorf · Frankfurt · Bonn · Karl-Marx-Stadt (Chemnitz) · Elbe · Nuremberg · Stuttgart · Munich · Mannheim · Wiesbaden

NETHERLANDS · Amsterdam · The Hague · Rotterdam · Groningen · BELGIUM · Brussels · Antwerp · LUX. · LIECH. · Strasbourg · Rouen · Le Havre · Seine · PARIS

FRANCE · Nantes · Loire · Limoges · St. Etienne · Lyons · Dijon · Bordeaux · Garonne · Toulouse · Marseilles · Toulon · Nice · Monaco · Rhône · Ushant · Brest · BAY OF BISCAY

SWITZERLAND · Basle · Zürich · Bern · Geneva · AUSTRIA · VIENNA · Salzburg · Graz · Innsbruck

POLAND · WARSAW · Łódź · Wrocław (Breslau) · Poznań · Szczecin · Bydgoszcz · Gdańsk · Kraków · Katowice · Odra · Vistula (Wisła)

CZECHOSLOVAKIA · PRAGUE · Brno · Bratislava

HUNGARY · BUDAPEST · Miskolc

ROMANIA · BUCHAREST · Cluj · Timişoara · Braşov · Ploieşti · Constanţa · Danube · Galaţi

YUGOSLAVIA · Belgrade · Zagreb · Ljubljana · Sarajevo · Split · Niš · Skopje

BULGARIA · Sofia · Plovdiv · Varna

ALBANIA · Tiranë

GREECE · ATHENS · Thessaloníki · Piraeus · Pátrai · Crete

ADRIATIC SEA · ITALY · Venice · Milan · Turin · Genoa · Bologna · Florence · ROME · Naples · Bari · Taranto · Palermo · Messina · Catania · Sicily · Sardinia · Corsica · Cagliari · Ajaccio · Ionian Sea · Tyrrhenian Sea · Pantelleria (Ital.) · Trieste · Tiber

SPAIN · MADRID · Barcelona · Valencia · Zaragoza · Bilbao · Valladolid · Murcia · Alicante · Córdoba · Sevilla · Málaga · Granada · Cádiz · Gibraltar (Br.) · Balearic Is. · Mallorca (Majorca) · Menorca · Ibiza · Palma · Ebro · Duero · Guadiana · Guadalquivir · La Coruña · Oporto · Vigo

PORTUGAL · Lisbon · Douro

MEDITERRANEAN SEA · BALTIC SEA · BLACK SEA · White Sea

TURKEY · Ankara · Istanbul · İzmir · Bursa · Adana · Konya · Antalya · Kayseri · Diyarbakır · ANATOLIA · CYPRUS · Nicosia · Limassol

SYRIA · Aleppo (Halab) · Homs · IRAQ · Baghdad · Mosul · Euphrates · Tigris

IRAN (PERSIA) · Tabriz · Araks

MOROCCO · Rabat · Fès · Meknès · Tangier · Str. of Gibraltar · Oran · ALGERIA · Algiers · Constantine · Annaba · TUNISIA · Tunis · Sousse · MALTA · Valletta · Oued

LONDON Capital Cities

Projection: Bonne · West from Greenwich 0 East from Greenwich

1:20 000 000

200 0 200 400 600 800 km

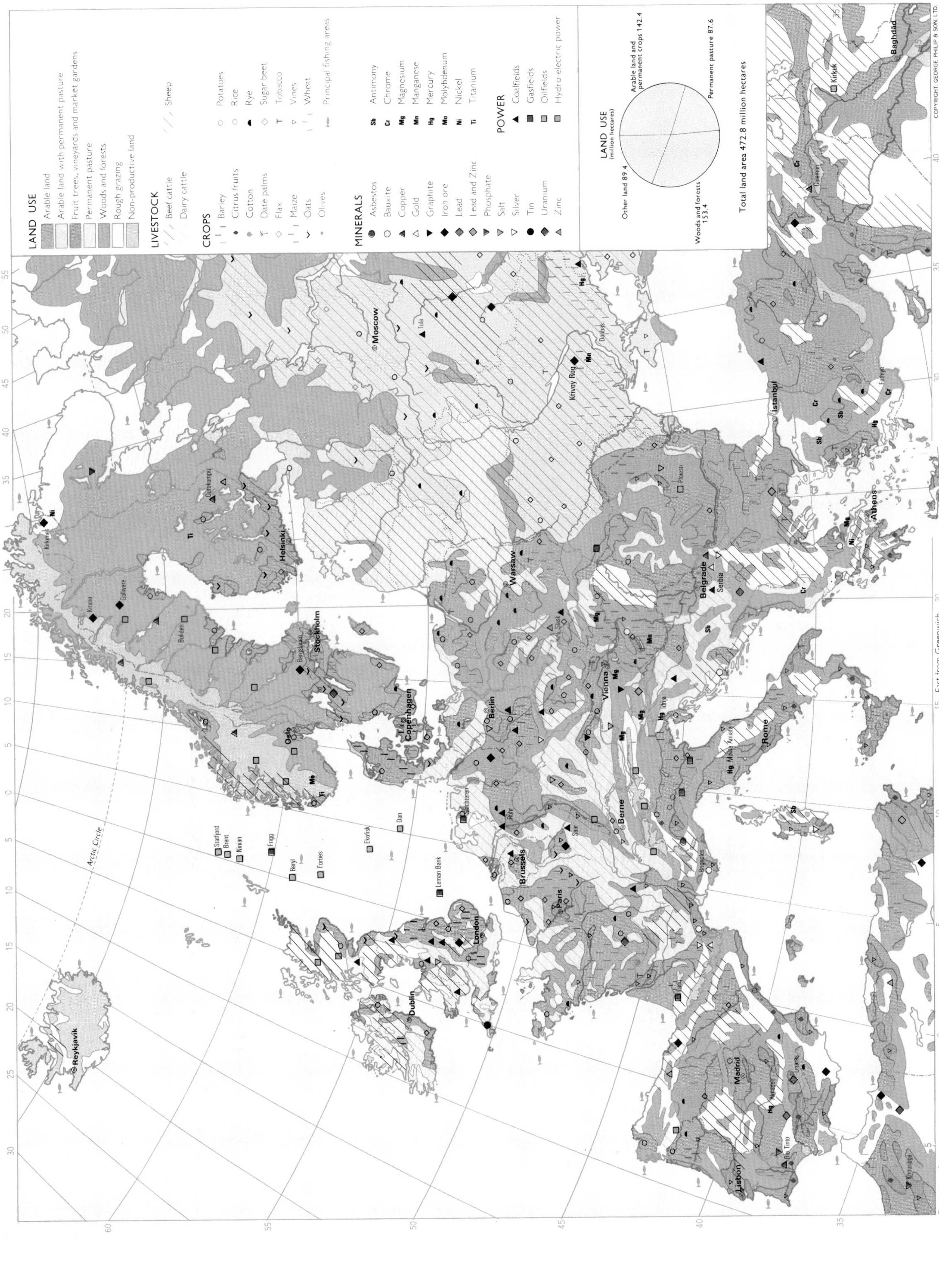

LAND USE
- Arable land
- Arable land with permanent pasture
- Fruit trees, vineyards and market gardens
- Permanent pasture
- Woods and forests
- Rough grazing
- Non-productive land

LIVESTOCK
- Beet cattle
- Dairy cattle
- Sheep

CROPS
- Barley
- Citrus fruits
- Cotton
- Date palms
- Flax
- Maize
- Oats
- Olives
- Potatoes
- Rice
- Rye
- Sugar beet
- Tobacco
- Vines
- Wheat
- Principal fishing areas

MINERALS
- Asbestos
- Bauxite
- Copper
- Gold
- Graphite
- Iron ore
- Lead
- Lead and Zinc
- Phosphate
- Salt
- Silver
- Tin
- Uranium
- Zinc

- **Sb** Antimony
- **Cr** Chrome
- **Mg** Magnesium
- **Mn** Manganese
- **Hg** Mercury
- **Mo** Molybdenum
- **Ni** Nickel
- **Ti** Titanium

POWER
- Coalfields
- Gasfields
- Oilfields
- Hydro electric power

LAND USE
(million hectares)

Arable land and permanent crops 142.4

Permanent pasture 87.6

Other land 89.4

Woods and forests 153.4

Total land area 472.8 million hectares

Projection: Bonne

Reykjavik

Arctic Circle

Kokemäki · Ni
Koskenniska
Ti
Oulunkumpu
Kiruna
Tallivaara
Boliden
Bergslagen
Stockholm
Helsinki

Moscow
Tula
Krivoy Rog · Mn
Donbas

Oslo
Mo
Ti
Copenhagen
Stavanger
Brent
Ninian
Frigg
Beryl
Forties
Ekofisk
Dan
Leman Bank
Slochteren
Ruhr
Saar

London
Dublin

Brussels
Paris
Berne

Berlin
Warsaw
Sisak
Mg

Vienna
Mg
Mg
Mg
Belgrade
Serbia
Sb
Mn
Ljung
Hg
Idrija
Almadén
Rome

Madrid
Lisbon
Hg
Almadén
Rio Tinto
Tharsis

Istanbul
Cr
Sb
Hg
Cr
Cr
Athens
Ni · Mg
Sb

Kirkuk
Baghdad
Cr

East from Greenwich

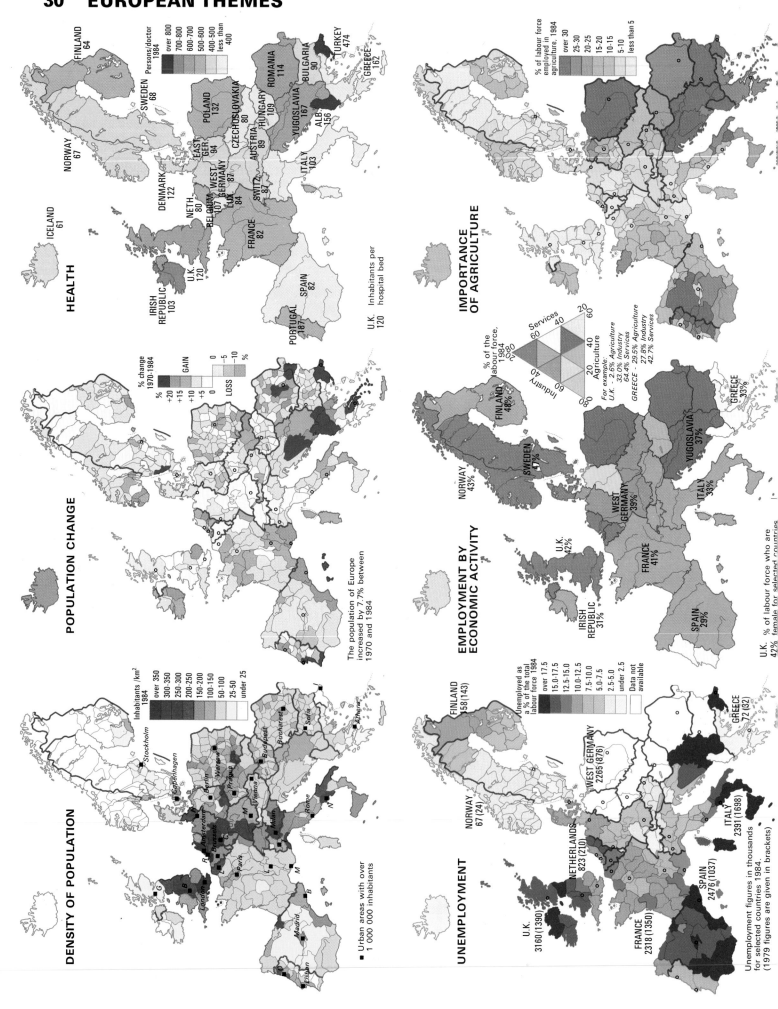

HEALTH

Persons/doctor 1984

over 800	
700-800	
600-700	
500-600	
400-500	
less than 400	

FINLAND 64
SWEDEN 68
NORWAY 67
ICELAND 61
IRISH REPUBLIC 103
DENMARK 122
NETH. 80
BELGIUM 107
WEST GERMANY 87
LUX. 84
EAST GER. 94
POLAND 132
CZECHOSLOVAKIA 80
HUNGARY 109
AUSTRIA 89
SWITZ. 87
U.K. 120
FRANCE 82
SPAIN 82
PORTUGAL 187
ITALY 103
YUGOSLAVIA 167
ALB. 156
ROMANIA 114
BULGARIA 90
GREECE 162
TURKEY 474

Inhabitants per hospital bed
U.K.   120

POPULATION CHANGE

% change 1970-1984

GAIN
+20	
+15	
+10	
+5	
0	
-5	
-10	

LOSS
%

The population of Europe increased by 7.7% between 1970 and 1984

DENSITY OF POPULATION

Inhabitants /km² 1984

over 350	
300-350	
250-300	
200-250	
150-200	
100-150	
50-100	
25-50	
under 25	

Stockholm
Copenhagen
Berlin
Warsaw
Prague
Vienna
Budapest
Bucharest
Sofia
Athens
Amsterdam
Brussels
Paris
Milan
Rome
London
Madrid
Lisbon

■ Urban areas with over 1 000 000 inhabitants

IMPORTANCE OF AGRICULTURE

% of labour force employed in agriculture, 1984

over 30	
25-30	
20-25	
15-20	
10-15	
5-10	
less than 5	

EMPLOYMENT BY ECONOMIC ACTIVITY

% of the labour force, 1984

Services
Agriculture
Industry

For example:
U.K. - 2.6% Agriculture
33.0% Industry
64.4% Services
GREECE - 29.5% Agriculture
27.8% Industry
42.7% Services

NORWAY 43%
SWEDEN 47%
FINLAND 48%
U.K. 42%
IRISH REPUBLIC 31%
WEST GERMANY 39%
FRANCE 41%
SPAIN 29%
ITALY 33%
YUGOSLAVIA 37%
GREECE 33%

U.K.   % of labour force who are 42% female for selected countries

UNEMPLOYMENT

Unemployed as a % of the total labour force 1984

over 17.5	
15.0-17.5	
12.5-15.0	
10.0-12.5	
7.5-10.0	
5.0-7.5	
2.5-5.0	
under 2.5	
Data not available	

NORWAY 67 (24)
FINLAND 158 (143)
U.K. 3160 (1390)
NETHERLANDS 823 (210)
WEST GERMANY 2265 (876)
FRANCE 2318 (1350)
SPAIN 2476 (1037)
ITALY 2391 (1698)
GREECE 72 (32)

Unemployment figures in thousands for selected countries 1984.
(1979 figures are given in brackets)

STANDARDS OF LIVING

Gross Domestic Product (GDP) is a measure of a country's total production of goods and services.

NORWAY £37.9 bn. (3.7%)

FINLAND £34.0 bn. (2.7%)

SWEDEN £63.3 bn. (3%)

DENMARK £38.8 bn. (1.8%)

NETH. £94.1 bn. (1.5%)

WEST GERMANY £449.9 bn. (2.1%)

AUSTRIA £44.4 bn. (2.8%)

SWITZERLAND £66.9 bn. (0.7%)

U.K. £313.6 bn. (1.1%)

IRISH REP. £12.4 bn. (3.2%)

BELGIUM £55.2 bn. (1.8%)

FRANCE £357.7 bn. (2.5%)

YUGOSLAVIA £32.3 bn. (5.3%)

ITALY £243.1 bn. (2.2%)

GREECE £21.2 bn. (3.0%)

SPAIN £94.1 bn. (1.8%)

PORTUGAL £14.0 bn. (4.0%)

Gross Domestic Product per person in 1981
- £7-8000
- £6-7000
- £5-6000
- £4-5000
- £3-4000
- £2-3000
- £1-2000

Gross Domestic Product in 1983 in £ billions
(% annual average growth 1973-83 is given in brackets)

INFLATION

The rate of inflation shows the increase in the price of a broad selection of household goods and services in each country.

ICELAND

NORWAY, FINLAND, SWEDEN, DENMARK, NETH., U.K., IRISH REP., BELG., WEST GERMANY, SWITZ., FRANCE, EAST GER., POLAND, CZECH., AUSTRIA, HUNGARY, ROMANIA, BULGARIA, YUGOSLAVIA, ITALY, SPAIN, PORT., GREECE, TURKEY

Average annual rate of inflation 1973-83
- over 20%
- 15-20%
- 10-15%
- 5-10%
- 0-5%

ENERGY CONSUMPTION

NORWAY +2.6%

FINLAND +2.1%

SWEDEN +0.4%

DENMARK -1.2%

NETH. +0.6%

BELG. -0.7%

E. GER. -2.0%

WEST GERMANY -0.4%

SWITZ. +0.5%

POLAND +2.5%

CZECH. -1.8%

HUNGARY +0.5%

ROMANIA +3.8%

BULGARIA +4.3%

YUGOSLAVIA +3.1%

ALB. +6.5%

GREECE +3.8%

U.K. -1.4%

IRISH REP. +2.7%

FRANCE +0.5%

ITALY +0.1%

SPAIN +2.3%

PORTUGAL +3.7%

Energy consumption per person in kilograms of oil equivalent in 1983
- over 6000
- 5-6000
- 4-5000
- 3-4000
- 2-3000
- 1-2000
- under 1000

+0.4% % average annual change in consumption 1973-83

TRADE ORGANISATIONS

ICELAND, NORWAY, FINLAND, SWEDEN, DENMARK, NETH., U.K., IRISH REP., BELG., Brussels, Geneva, FRANCE, SWITZ., WEST GERMANY, EAST GER., POLAND, CZECH., AUSTRIA, HUNGARY, ROMANIA, BULGARIA, YUGOSLAVIA, ALB., ITALY, SPAIN, PORT., GREECE

E.F.T.A. (European Free Trade Association) H.Q. Geneva

COMECON (Council for Mutual Economic Assistance) H.Q. Moscow

E.E.C. (The European Economic Community) H.Q. Brussels
- The Six in 1957 (Pop. 170 000 000)
- The Nine in 1973 (Pop. 256 000 000)
- The Ten in 1981 (Pop. 270 000 000)
- The Twelve in 1986 (Pop. 321 000 000)

DEFENCE ORGANISATIONS

ICELAND, NORWAY, FINLAND, SWEDEN, DENMARK, NETH., U.K., IRISH REP., BELG., WEST GERMANY, EAST GER., POLAND, CZECH., 'The Iron Curtain', FRANCE, SWITZ., AUSTRIA, HUNGARY, ROMANIA, BULGARIA, YUGOSLAVIA, ALB., ITALY, SPAIN, PORT., GREECE, TURKEY

- N.A.T.O. Countries (North Atlantic Treaty Organisation)
- Warsaw Pact Countries
- Non-aligned or neutral

Major Military Bases
- U.S. Forces
- Other N.A.T.O. Forces (U.K., France, Canada, Neth. and Belg.)
- U.S.S.R. Forces

* France is a member of N.A.T.O. but its armed forces are not formally committed.

TRANSPORT

FINLAND, NORWAY, SWEDEN, DENMARK, WEST GERMANY, NETH., BELG., SWITZ., U.K., FRANCE, ITALY, GREECE, SPAIN, PORT.

CARS
Number of cars per 1000 persons
- 350-400
- 300-350
- 250-300
- 200-250
- 150-200
- 100-150
- under 100

MOTORWAYS
Length of motorway in kilometres per thousand km² of land area for selected countries

10   5   0

COPYRIGHT GEORGE PHILIP & SON LTD

	Population								Land			Agriculture		
	Total	Density	Birth Rate	Death Rate	Life Expectancy	Growth 1965-80	Growth 1980-86	Urban	Area	Arable	Forest	Agricultural Population	Index of Production	Food Intake
	th.	persons per km²	per th. popn.	per th. popn.	yrs.	av. % per annum	av. % per annum	%	th. km²	th. km²	th. km²	% of total popn.	1979-81 = 100	calories per day
Albania	3022	112	26	6	71	2.5	2.1	39	27	7.1	10	52	108	2726
Austria	7565	91	11	11	74	0.3	0	56	83	15	32	6.8	105	3514
Belgium *	9913	330	12	11	75	0.3	0	89	30	8	7	2.2	104	3679
Bulgaria	8959	81	13	11	72	0.5	0.2	69	111	41	39	14	106	3663
Czechoslovakia	15534	124	14	12	70	0.5	0.3	66	125	52	46	11	119	3465
Denmark	5121	122	11	11	75	0.5	0	86	42	26	4.9	5.6	126	3547
Finland	4918	16	12	10	75	0.3	0.5	67	305	24	232	9.5	112	3026
France	55392	101	14	10	77	0.7	0.5	77	546	189	146	6.4	108	3359
Germany, East	16624	157	13	13	72	-0.2	-0.1	78	106	47	30	9	109	3791
Germany, West	61048	250	10	12	75	0.3	-0.2	86	244	75	73	4.3	115	3474
Greece	9966	76	11	9	76	0.7	0.5	66	131	40	26	27	99	3721
Hungary	10627	116	12	14	71	0.4	-0.1	57	92	53	16	14	109	3482
Iceland	243	2.4	16	7	77	0.8	1.1	90	100	0.1	1.2	8	97	3142
Ireland	3537	51	17	10	74	1.2	0.8	57	69	8	3.3	15	106	3831
Italy	57221	195	10	10	77	0.6	0.3	72	294	122	64	8.8	101	3538
Luxembourg *	363	140	12	11	73	0.9	0.1	82	2.6					
Malta	385	1283	14	7	73	0.2	1	85	0.3	0.1	0	4.3	119	2682
Netherlands	14563	428	13	9	77	0.9	0.5	93	34	8.9	3	4.3	111	3343
Norway	4169	14	13	10	77	0.6	0.3	71	308	8.6	83	6.4	105	3239
Poland	37456	123	17	10	72	0.8	0.9	60	305	148	87	24	116	3280
Portugal	10291	112	13	10	73	0.6	0.5	30	92	28	36	19	105	3161
Romania	23174	101	16	11	71	1.1	0.5	55	230	106	63	24	125	3385
Spain	38668	77	12	8	76	1	0.6	77	499	204	156	13	105	3358
Sweden	8370	20	12	11	77	0.5	0.1	86	412	30	264	4.5	103	3097
Switzerland	6504	163	12	9	77	0.5	0.3	60	40	4.1	11	4.8	108	3432
United Kingdom	56963	235	13	12	75	0.2	0.1	92	242	71	23	2.2	112	3131
Yugoslavia	23271	91	15	9	71	0.9	0.7	46	255	78	94	26	102	3602
U.S.S.R.	280144	13	16	11	70	0.9	1	66	22272	2322	9350	16	117	3440

* Many figures for Luxembourg included in Belgium.

Population. This is the United Nations' estimate for the mid-year 1986 (thousands)

Population Density. This is the quoted population total divided by the quoted land area (persons per square kilometre).

Birth Rates and Death Rates. These are the registered or United Nations' estimated rates per thousand population.

Life Expectancy. This figure indicates the number of years that a child born today can expect to live if the levels of death of today last throughout its life. The figure is the average of that for men and women. The figure for women is usually higher than that for men (U.K. Male 72, female 78 years).

Population Growth. This shows the average annual percentage change in population for two periods, 1965–1980 and 1980–1986.

Urbanization. This is the percentage of the total population living in urban areas. The definition of urban is that of the individual nation and usually includes quite small towns.

Land Area. This is the total area of the country minus the area covered by major lakes and rivers (thousand square kilometres).

Arable Land and Permanent Crops. This excludes fallow land but includes temporary pasture (thousand square kilometres).

Forest and Woodland. This includes natural and planted woodland and land recently cleared of timber which will be replanted (thousand square kilometres).

Agricultural Population. This is the percentage of the economically active population working in agriculture. It also includes those people working also in forestry, hunting and fishing.

Index of Agricultural Population. The base period for this index is 1979–1981 and it shows the level of production in each country in 1986 in comparison with that of the earlier period. Only edible crops and meat are included.

Food Supply. The figures are the average intake per person in calories per day for the year 1985.

Trade		Education		Health	Energy	Consumer Price Index	G.N.P.		G.D.P.		Loans & Debt		
Imports	Exports	Primary	Secondary					Growth per capita	Part formed by Agric.	Part formed by Indust.			
US$ per capita	US$ per capita	% of age group	% of age group	Popn. per doctor	Consumption in kg of oil equiv. per capita	1980 = 100	US$ per capita	% per year 1965-86	%	%	end 1986 US$ millions	as % of G.N.P.	
		97	69		1664								Albania
2990	3451	99	79	400	3400	131	9990	3.3	3	38	202	0.3	Austria
6681	6704	95	96	400	4809	145	9230	2.7	2	33	516	0.6	* Belgium
1524	1490	100	100	410	4590		3800		18	57			Bulgaria
1355	1317	97	39	360	4845	111	5000		7	59			Czechoslovakia
4467	4160	98	100	480	3821	158	12600	1.9	6	28	842	1.3	Denmark
3119	3326	100	100	530	5475	162	12160	3.2	8	37	350	0.6	Finland
2336	2256	100	96	580	3640	167	10720	2.8	4	34	4876	0.8	France
1649	1668	100	79	520	5915		6800		9	74			Germany, East
3130	3986	96	74	450	4464	121	12080	2.5	2	40	3651	0.5	Germany, West
1139	567	100	86	430	1932	366	3680	3.3	17	29	15015	38	Greece
903	862	98	72	400	2985	159	2020	3.9	17	41	13567	60	Hungary
3417	3033	100		488		1034	10710	2.4	10	20			Iceland
3285	3578	100	96	780	2436	191	5070	1.7	14	45	58	0.3	Ireland
1738	1709	98	75	340	2539	211	8550	2.6	5	39	2424	0.5	Italy
		100		495	9000	141	14260	4	2	33			* Luxembourg
1887	1037	100		383	1180	101	3310	8.1	3	37			Malta
5170	5455	95	100	540	5201	122	10020	1.9	4	34	1747	1.2	Netherlands
4880	4382	97	97	520	8803	180	15400	3.4	4	41	921	1.4	Norway
308	322	100	78	570	3369	586	2070		17	50	35200	49	Poland
938	704	100	47	540	1284	347	2250	3.2	10	40	13929	50	Portugal
494	541	98	75	680	3405		2500		16	57	5309		Romania
907	703	100	91	450	1928	204	4860	2.9	6	37			Spain
3906	4452	98	83	490	6374	167	13160	1.8	3	35	1167	1.1	Sweden
6310	5761	100		410	4052	126	17680	1.4	2	21	424	0.3	Switzerland
2218	1877	100	89	650	3802	152	8870	1.7	2	43	1667	0.3	United Kingdom
505	445	96	82	550	2041	1312	2300	3.9	12	42	13174	20	Yugoslavia
317	347	100	99	270	4949	104	104		15	51			U.S.S.R.

Andorra, Land 0.5/Popn. 47; Faeroe Is. 1.4/46; Gibraltar 0.01/29; Liechtenstein 0.2/27; Monaco 0.0015/27; San Marino 0.06/22; Svalbard 62/3.

Trade. The trade figures are for the year 1986. The total trade figures have been divided by the population and are a measure of the country's external trade (U.S. $ per capita).

Education. The ages of primary school are taken to be 6–11 years and secondary school 12–17 years. The percentage of total school age group in this type of education is shown.

Energy. All forms of energy have been converted to their equivalent in oil. Firewood and other traditional forms used in developing countries are not included and so the energy consumption in those countries is understated (kilograms of oil equivalent per capita).

Consumer Price Index. The base year is 1980 which is 100 and the level of consumer prices in 1986 or 1987 are shown in relation to the base year. It is a measure of inflation.

G.N.P. (Gross National Product) This figure is an estimate of the average production per person measured in U.S. dollars and for 1986. The G.N.P. measures the value of goods and services produced in a country, plus the balance, positive or negative, of income from abroad, for example investments, interest on capital, money returned from foreign labour, etc. The rate of change is the average annual percentage change during the period 1965–1986 in the G.N.P. The G.D.P. (Gross Domestic Product) is the G.N.P. minus the foreign balances. The adjoining two columns show the percentage contribution to the G.D.P. made by the agricultural and mining and manufacturing sectors.

Loans and Debts. This figure in millions of U.S. dollars shows the external public debt at the end of 1986. This is then shown as a percentage of the annual G.N.P. The figures in red show official development assistance made by the developed countries and also as a percentage of the donor country's G.N.P.

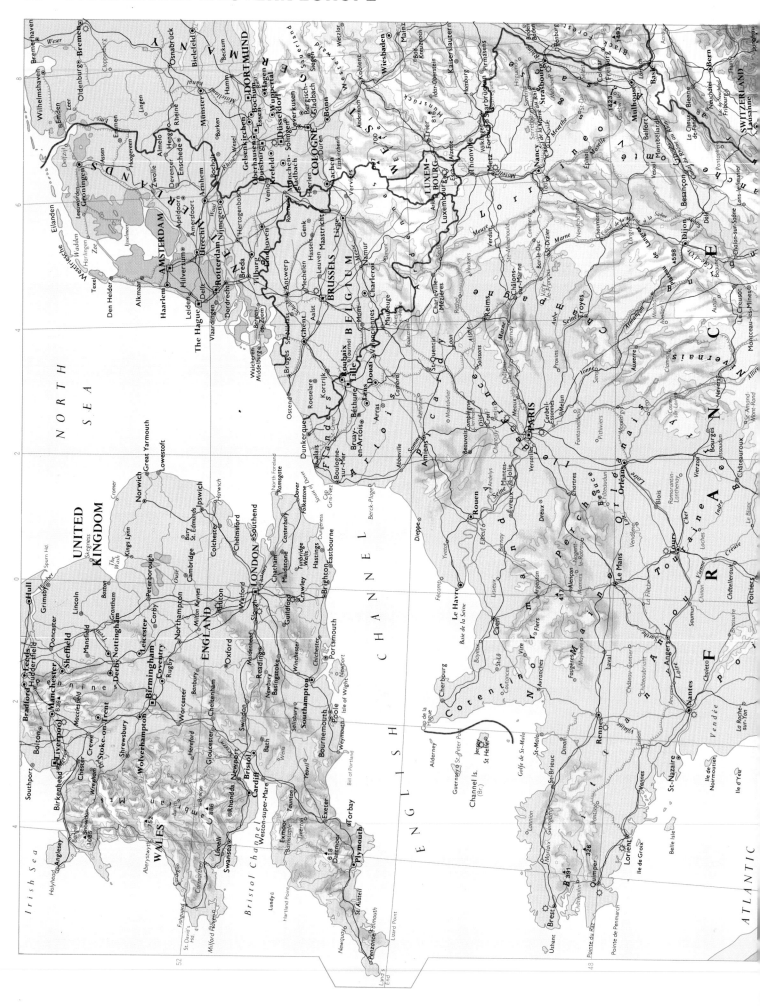

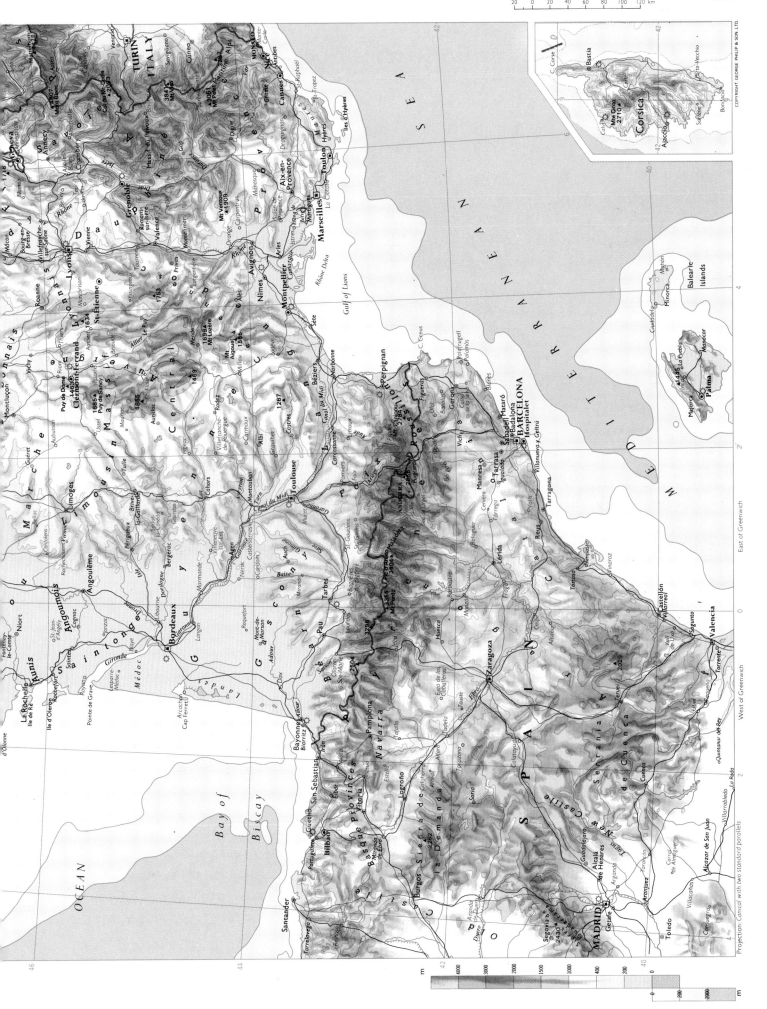

1:2 000 000

10 0 10 20 30 40 50 60 70 80 km

NORTH SEA

NETHERLANDS

BELGIUM

GERMANY

FRANCE

LUXEMBOURG

FRISIAN ISLANDS

Projection: Conical with two standard parallels

East from Greenwich

COPYRIGHT GEORGE PHILIP & SON, LTD

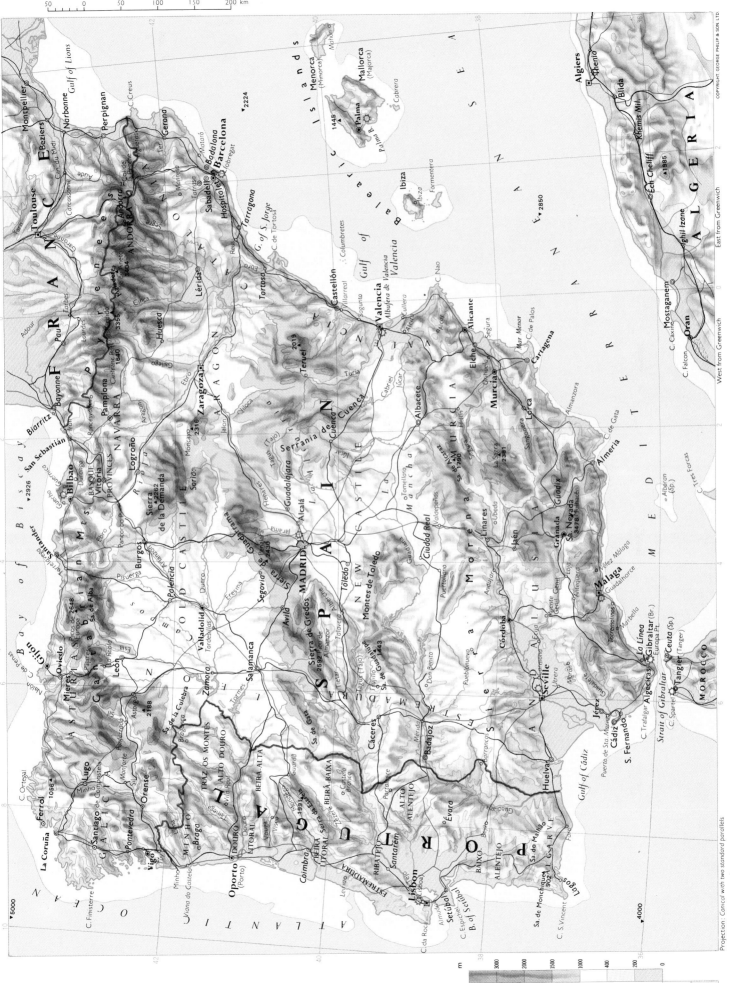

1:5 000 000

50   0   50   100   150   200 km

Projection: Conical with two standard parallels

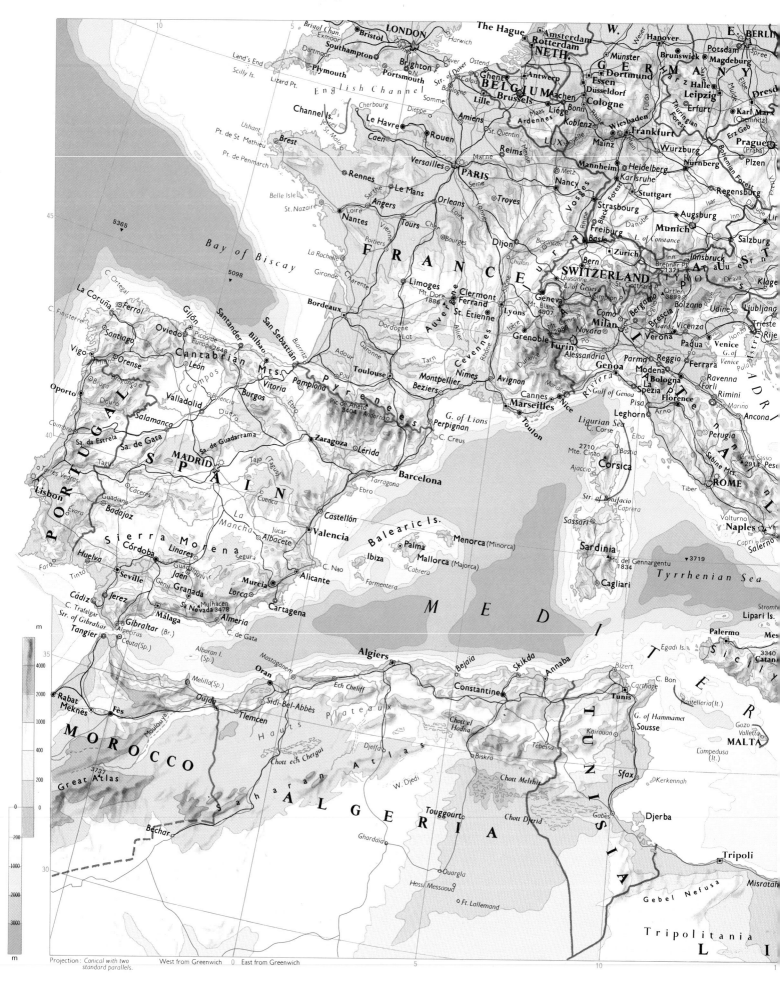

1:10 000 000

100   0   100   200   300   400 km

P O L A N D

Poznan
Łódź
Wrocław
Warsaw (Warszawa)
Brest
Pripyat Marshes
Chernigov
Sumy
Kharkov
Volgograd

Radom
Lublin
Zhitomir
Kiev
Poltava
Desna
Voroshilovgrad
Donets
Tsimlyansk Reservoir

Chorzów
Kraków
Przemyśl
Lvov
Vinnitsa
U. S. S. R.
Kremenchug
Dnepr (Dnieper)
Gorlovka
Makeyevka
Shakhty

Ostrava
Jablunka P.
2550
2655
RUTHENIA
Cherkassy
Dneprodzerzhinsk
Kirovograd
Dnepropetrovsk
Donetsk
Novocherkassk
L. Manych Gudilo

CHOSLOVAKIA
Košice
Chernovtsy
Iași
U K R A I N E
Zaporozhye
Zhdanov
Taganrog
Rostov

Bratislava
Miskolc
Debrecen
Pietrosul 2305
MOLDAVIA
Kishinev
Odessa
Nikolayev
Melitopol
Sea of Azov
Krasnodar
Stavropol
Armavir

Budapest
HUNGARY
Oradea
Pietrosul 2102
Siret
Kherson
Kerch Str.
Kuban

Szeged
Arad
ROMANIA
Cluj
Brașov
Galați
G. of Karkinitk
Crimea
Novorossiysk

Subotica
Timișoara
Sibiu
Negoiu 2535
Transylvanian Alps
Brăila
Simferopol 1545
Barumi

Novi Sad
Belgrade
Craiova
Pitești
Ploești
Bucharest (București)
Constanța
Sevastopol

BOSNIA
Sarajevo
SERBIA
Niš
Sofia
BULGARIA
Ruse
Danube
Varna
B L A C K   S E A
Trabzon

MONTENEGRO
Skopje
Stara Zagora
Plovdiv
Rhodope
Edirne
Istanbul
Canik (Pontine) Mts.

ALBANIA
Tirane
GREECE
Thessaloniki
Limnos
Sea of Marmara
Bursa
Ankara
T U R K E Y
Sivas
Kayseri

Athens
Piraievs
Izmir
Eskişehir
Afyon
Konya
Adana
Aleppo
SYRIA

CYPRUS
Nicosia
Famagusta
Larnaca
Limassol
Beirut
LEBANON
Damascus

Crete
Iráklion
Rhodes
Antalya

M E D I T E R R A N E A N   S E A

Alexandria
Cairo
Port Said
Ismailia
Suez
ISRAEL
JORDAN
Amman
Jerusalem

E G Y P T
Sinai Pen.

B Y A
Cyrenaica
Benghazi
Tobruk
Gulf of Sidra

COPYRIGHT. GEORGE PHILIP & SON. LTD.

- - - - - Division between Greeks and Turks
in Cyprus; Turks to the North.

MALTA
1:1 000 000
0   10 km

S.E. EUROPE
POLITICAL
1:25 000 000

Projection: Conical with two standard parallels

1:5 000 000

50   0   50   100   150   200 km

East from Greenwich

1:5 000 000

50   0   50   100   150   200 km

CENTRAL EUROPE POLITICAL
1:25 000 000

DENMARK
Copenhagen
Amsterdam
Hamburg
Berlin
WEST GERMANY
Bonn
BELGIUM
LUX.
FRANCE
Brussels
POLAND
Warsaw
U.S.S.R.
Kiev
EAST
Prague
CZECHOSLOVAKIA
Lvov
Bern
SWITZ.
Liechtenstein
Vienna
AUSTRIA
Budapest
HUNGARY
ROMANIA
Trieste
ITALY
Bucharest
Monaco
San Marino
Belgrade
YUGOSLAVIA
Rome
BULGARIA
Sofia

COPYRIGHT GEORGE PHILIP & SON LTD

ICELAND

At the same scale as main map

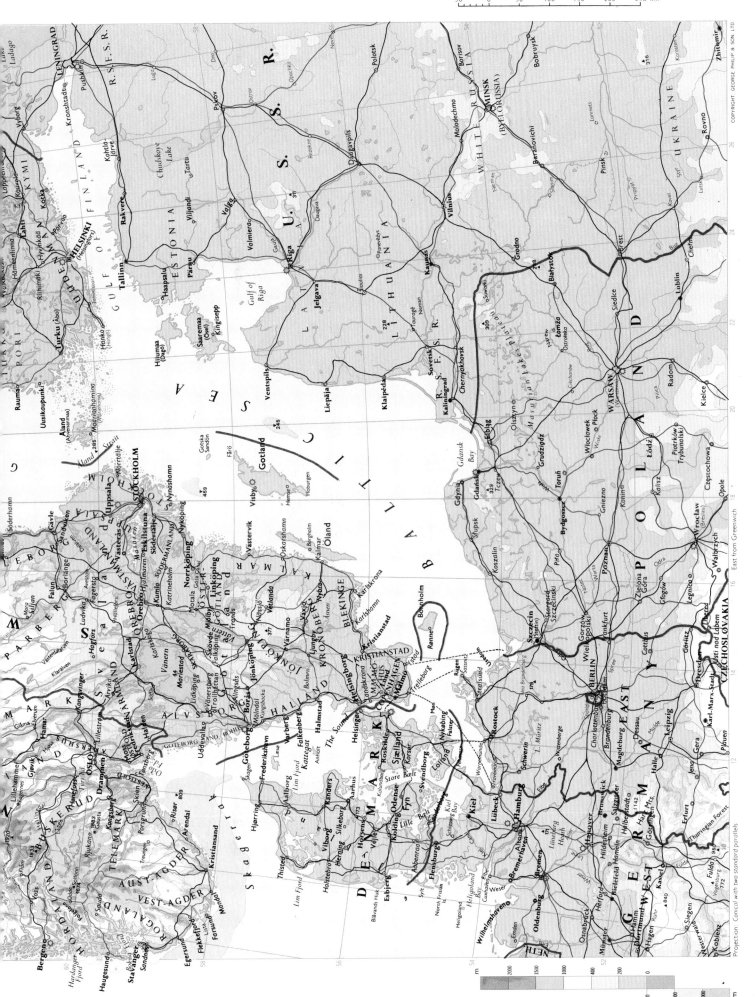

1 : 6 000 000

50   0   50   100   150   200   250 km

COPYRIGHT GEORGE PHILIP & SON LTD

Projection: Conical with two standard parallels

East from Greenwich

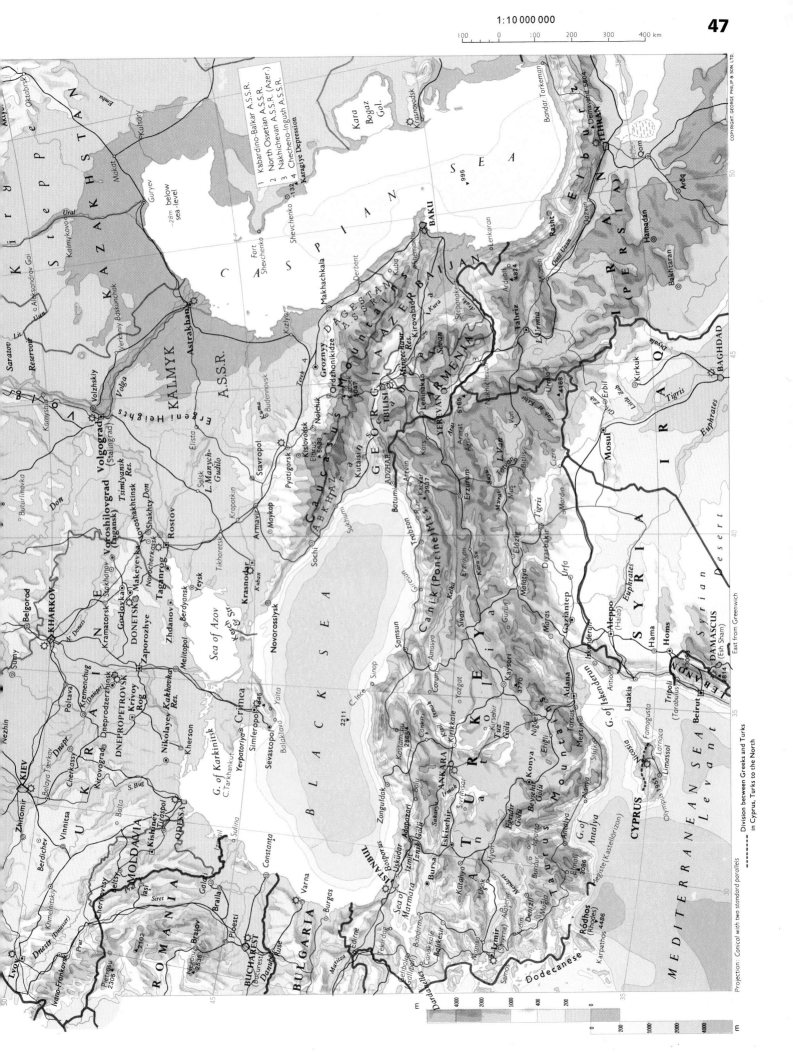

1:10 000 000

100   0   100   200   300   400 km

1 Kabardino-Balkar A.S.S.R.
2 North Ossetian A.S.S.R.
2a Nakhichevan A.S.S.R. (Azer.)
3 Checheno-Ingush A.S.S.R.
4 Karagiye Depression

Projection: Conical with two standard parallels

East from Greenwich

----------- Division between Greeks and Turks
           in Cyprus, Turks to the North

m   4000 2000 1000 400 200 0

m   0 200 1000 2000 4000

R.S.F.S.R.
1. Daghestan A.S.S.R.
2. Kabardino–Balkar A.S.S.R.
3. Mari A.S.S.R.
4. Mordovian A.S.S.R.
5. North Ossetian A.S.S.R.
6. Tatar A.S.S.R.
7. Udmurt A.S.S.R.
8. Chuvash A.S.S.R.
9. Checheno–Ingush A.S.S.R.
     AZERBAIJAN
10. Nakhichevan A.S.S.R.
     GEORGIA
11. Abkhaz A.S.S.R.
12. Adzhar A.S.S.R.

Projection: Conical Orthomorphic with two standard parallels

East from Greenwich

1:50 000 000

500   0   500   1000   1500   2000 km

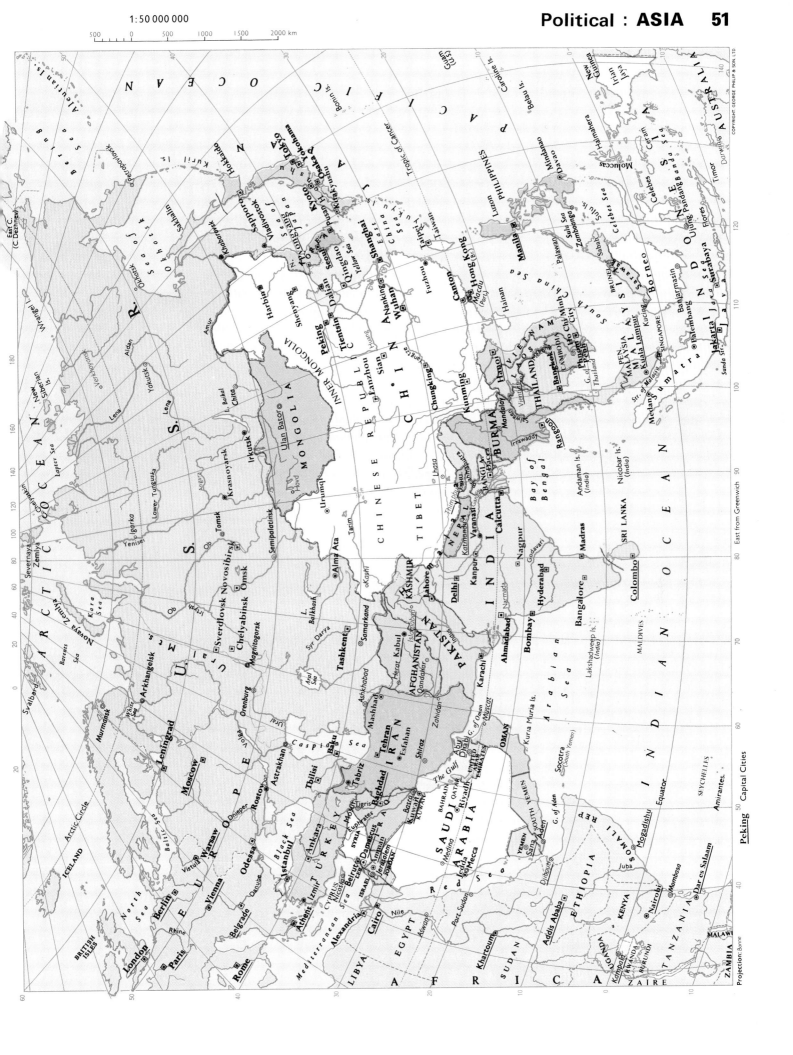

1:50 000 000

500   0   500   1000   1500   2000 km

COPYRIGHT GEORGE PHILIP & SON, LTD.

Projection: Bonne

Peking   Capital Cities

East from Greenwich

PACIFIC OCEAN

ARCTIC OCEAN

INDIAN OCEAN

U. S. S. R.

MONGOLIA

CHINESE REPUBLIC OF CHINA

TIBET

INDIA

IRAN

SAUDI ARABIA

PAKISTAN

AFGHANISTAN

TURKEY

IRAQ

AUSTRALIA

PHILIPPINES

INDONESIA

MALAYSIA

BURMA

THAILAND

VIETNAM

LAOS

CAMBODIA

NEPAL

BANGLADESH

SRI LANKA

EUROPE

AFRICA

Tokyo · Osaka · Kyoto · Nagoya · Yokohama
Sapporo · Hakodate
Seoul · Pusan
Peking · Tientsin · Shanghai · Nanking · Wuhan
Canton · Hong Kong · Macau
Manila
Ulan Bator
Moscow · Leningrad
Tehran · Esfahan · Shiraz
Baghdad · Kuwait · Riyadh
Delhi · Calcutta · Bombay · Madras · Bangalore · Hyderabad
Karachi · Lahore
Kabul · Herat · Qandahar
Ankara · Istanbul · Izmir
Cairo · Alexandria
Jakarta · Surabaya
Kuala Lumpur · Singapore
Bangkok
Hanoi · Ho Chi Minh · Phnom Penh
Rangoon · Mandalay
Kathmandu
Colombo

London · Paris · Rome · Berlin · Vienna · Warsaw · Belgrade · Athens

Addis Ababa · Nairobi · Dar es Salaam · Mogadishu · Khartoum

ETHIOPIA · **SOMALI REP** · **KENYA** · **TANZANIA** · **SUDAN** · **EGYPT** · **LIBYA**

ICELAND · **BRITISH ISLES**

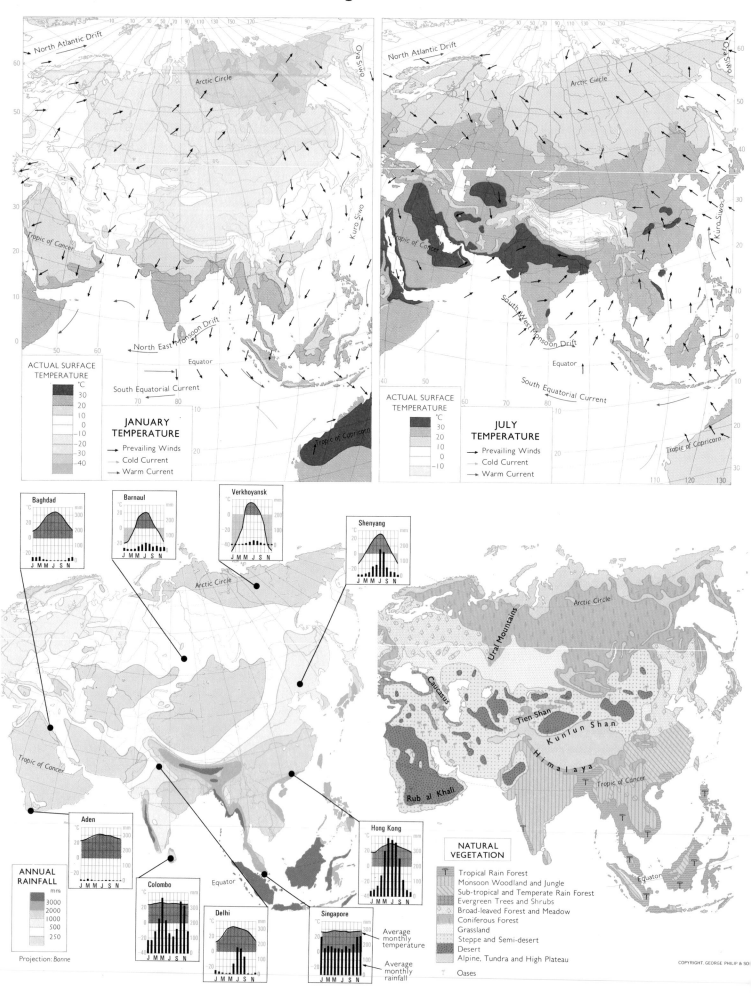

ACTUAL SURFACE TEMPERATURE

°C
30
20
10
0
-10
-20
-30
-40

JANUARY TEMPERATURE

→ Prevailing Winds
→ Cold Current
→ Warm Current

ACTUAL SURFACE TEMPERATURE

°C
30
20
10
0
-10

JULY TEMPERATURE

→ Prevailing Winds
→ Cold Current
→ Warm Current

Baghdad

Barnaul

Verkhoyansk

Shenyang

Aden

Colombo

Delhi

Hong Kong

Singapore

ANNUAL RAINFALL

mm
3000
2000
1000
500
250

Projection: Bonne

Average monthly temperature

Average monthly rainfall

NATURAL VEGETATION

T Tropical Rain Forest
Monsoon Woodland and Jungle
Sub-tropical and Temperate Rain Forest
Evergreen Trees and Shrubs
Broad-leaved Forest and Meadow
Coniferous Forest
Grassland
Steppe and Semi-desert
Desert
Alpine, Tundra and High Plateau

Y Oases

Ural Mountains

Caucasus

Tien Shan

Kunlun Shan

Himalaya

Rub al Khali

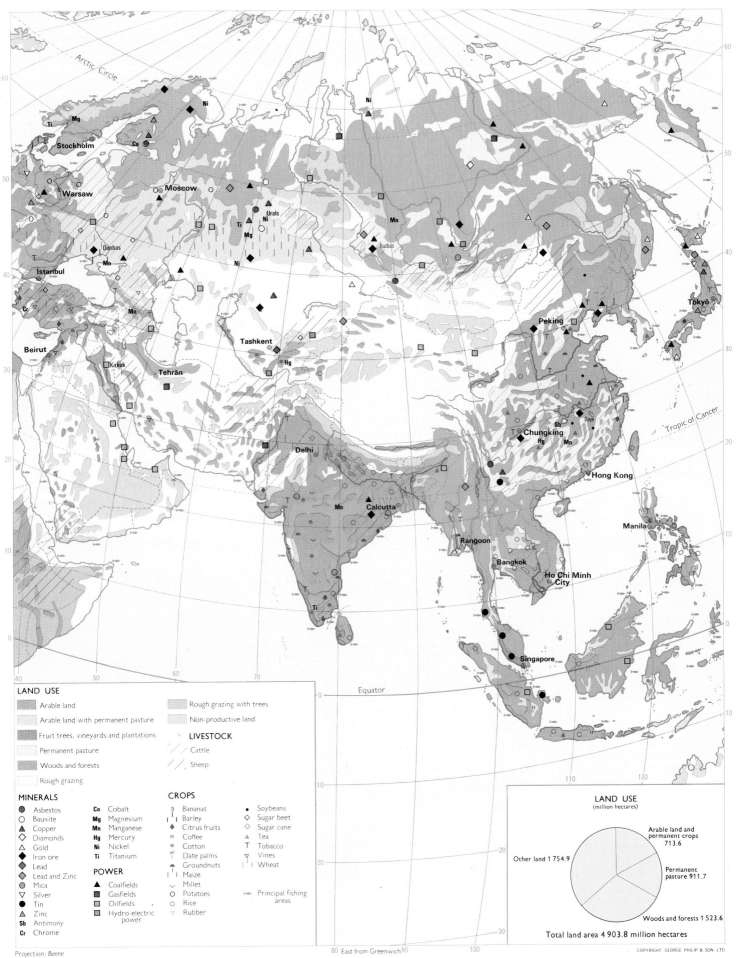

1:50 000 000

500   0   500   1000   1500   2000 km

Projection: Bonne

80 East from Greenwich 90   100

COPYRIGHT GEORGE PHILIP & SON LTD

LAND USE

	Arable land
	Arable land with permanent pasture
	Fruit trees, vineyards and plantations
	Permanent pasture
	Woods and forests
	Rough grazing
	Rough grazing with trees
	Non-productive land

LIVESTOCK

/ Cattle
// Sheep

MINERALS

- Asbestos
- Bauxite
- Copper
- Diamonds
- Gold
- Iron ore
- Lead
- Lead and Zinc
- Mica
- Silver
- Tin
- Zinc
- **Sb** Antimony
- **Cr** Chrome

Co Cobalt
Mg Magnesium
Mn Manganese
Hg Mercury
Ni Nickel
Ti Titanium

POWER

- Coalfields
- Gasfields
- Oilfields
- Hydro-electric power

CROPS

- Bananas
- Barley
- Citrus fruits
- Coffee
- Cotton
- Date palms
- Groundnuts
- Maize
- Millet
- Potatoes
- Rice
- Rubber
- Soybeans
- Sugar beet
- Sugar cane
- Tea
- Tobacco
- Vines
- Wheat
- Principal fishing areas

LAND USE
(million hectares)

Arable land and permanent crops 713.6

Permanent pasture 911.7

Woods and forests 1 523.6

Other land 1 754.9

Total land area 4 903.8 million hectares

Stockholm
Warsaw
Moscow
Urals
Donbas
Istanbul
Beirut
Kirkuk
Tehrān
Tashkent
Kuzbas
Peking
Tōkyō
Chungking
Daye
Hong Kong
Delhi
Calcutta
Rangoon
Bangkok
Ho Chi Minh City
Manila
Singapore

Arctic Circle
Tropic of Cancer
Equator

	Population								Land			Agriculture		
	Total	Density	Birth Rate	Death Rate	Life Expectancy	Growth 1965-80	Growth 1980-86	Urban	Area	Arable	Forest	Agricultural Population	Index of Production	Food Intake
	th.	persons per km²	per th. popn.	per th. popn.	yrs.	av. % per annum	av. % per annum	%	th. km²	th. km²	th. km²	% of total popn.	1979-81 = 100	calories per day
Afghanistan	18614	29	48	22	37	2.4	2.6	19	648	81	19	57	99	2055
Bangladesh	100616	751	45	18	50	2.7	2.6	12	134	91	21	71	118	1899
Burma	39411	60	31	11	59	2.3	2	30	658	101	322	49	142	2547
Cambodia	7492	42	46	20	43	0.3	2.9	16	177	31	134	72	163	1922
China	1072218	115	19	7	69	2.2	1.2	21	9326	1009	1379	70	134	2602
Cyprus	673	74	21	9	74		1.2	50	9	4.3	1.7	23	96	3378
Hong Kong	5533	5533	14	5	76	2.1	1.2	92	1	0.1	0.1	1.5	161	2698
India	766135	258	34	12	57	2.3	2.2	26	2973	1690	671	68	124	2189
Indonesia	166940	92	32	13	57	2.3	2.2	25	1812	209	1215	52	134	2533
Iran	49765	28	43	12	59	3.2	2.8	55	1636	148	180	31	117	3122
Iraq	16450	38	44	9	63	3.4	3.6	71	434	55	19	24	147	2926
Israel	4296	215	23	7	75	2.8	1.7	91	20	4.2	1.1	5	116	3060
Japan	121492	327	12	6	78	1.2	0.7	77	371	48	252	8	111	2856
Jordan	3656	38	45	8	65	2.6	3.7	64	97	4.2	0.7	7.4	125	2947
Korea, North	20883	174	31	6	68	2.7	2.5	64	120	24	90	37	123	3151
Korea, South	41569	424	23	6	69	1.9	1.4	65	98	21	66	29	117	2841
Laos	4218	18	41	16	50	1.4	2	16	231	9	132	73	147	2228
Lebanon	2707	270	29	9	65	1.6	-0.01	80	10	3	0.8	11	129	2995
Malaysia	16109	49	31	7	69	2.5	2.7	32	329	44	201	36	130	2684
Mongolia	1940	1.2	36	8	64	3	2.8	56	1565	14	152	34	113	2807
Nepal	17131	125	42	18	47	2.4	2.6	6	137	23	23	92	112	2034
Pakistan	99163	127	42	10	52	3.1	3.1	30	779	205	31	52	124	2159
Philippines	56004	188	33	8	63	2.9	2.5	40	298	79	114	49	110	2341
Saudi Arabia	12006	5.6	42	9	63	4.6	4.1	73	2150	12	12	43	260	3128
Singapore	2586	4310	16	5	73	1.6	1.1	74	0.6	0.05	0.03	1.2	96	2771
Sri Lanka	16117	248	24	6	70	1.8	1.5	21	65	22	24	52	101	2385
Syria	10612	58	47	9	64	3.4	3.5	47	184	56	5.2	27	123	3168
Taiwan	19300	536	20	5	73				36	8.9	1.9	18	104	2811
Thailand	52654	103	28	8	64	2.7	2	16	512	196	150	67	118	2462
Turkey	50301	65	30	9	65	2.4	2.5	48	771	275	202	52	116	3167
Vietnam	60919	187	31	10	65	3.1	2.6	20	325	68	131	63	134	2240
Yemen, North	7046	36	49	18	46	2.8	2.5	20	195	14	16	65	140	2337
Yemen, South	2365	7.1	47	17	50	2	3.1	40	333	2	16	35	98	2250
U.S.S.R. †														
Oceania														
Australia	15974	2.1	15	7	78	1.8	1.4	86	7618	486	1060	5.7	108	3389
New Zealand	3248	12	16	8	74	1.3	0.9	83	269	5	108	9.9	110	3386
Papua New Guinea	3400	7.5	39	13	52	2.3	2.1	14	452	3.8	383	71	114	2181

† See pages 32–33.

Population. This is the United Nations' estimate for the mid-year 1986 (thousands)

Population Density. This is the quoted population total divided by the quoted land area (persons per square kilometre).

Birth Rates and Death Rates. These are the registered or United Nations' estimated rates per thousand population.

Life Expectancy. This figure indicates the number of years that a child born today can expect to live if the levels of death of today last throughout its life. The figure is the average of that for men and women. The figure for women is usually higher than that for men (U.K. Male 72, female 78 years).

Population Growth. This shows the average annual percentage change in population for two periods, 1965–1980 and 1980–1986.

Urbanization. This is the percentage of the total population living in urban areas. The definition of urban is that of the individual nation and usually includes quite small towns.

Land Area. This is the total area of the country minus the area covered by major lakes and rivers (thousand square kilometres).

Arable Land and Permanent Crops. This excludes fallow land but includes temporary pasture (thousand square kilometres).

Forest and Woodland. This includes natural and planted woodland and land recently cleared of timber which will be replanted (thousand square kilometres).

Agricultural Population. This is the percentage of the economically active population working in agriculture. It also includes those people working also in forestry, hunting and fishing.

Index of Agricultural Population. The base period for this index is 1979–1981 and it shows the level of production in each country in 1986 in comparison with that of the earlier period. Only edible crops and meat are included.

Food Supply. The figures are the average intake per person in calories per day for the year 1985.

Trade		Education		Health	Energy	Consumer Price Index	G.N.P.		G.D.P.		Loans & Debt		
Imports	Exports	Primary	Secondary					Growth per capita	Part formed by Agric.	Part formed by Indust.			
US$ per capita	US$ per capita	% of age group	% of age group	Popn. per doctor	Consumption in kg of oil equiv. per capita	1980 = 100	US$ per capita	% per year 1965-86	%	%	end 1986 US$ millions	as % of G.N.P.	
75	30	35	12	16730	71				63	20			Afghanistan
27	9	60	18	7810	46	182	160	0.4	47	14	7282	48	Bangladesh
16	8	100	24	4680	76	135	200	2.3	48	13	3664	45	Burma
				20000	60								Cambodia
40	29	100	39	1740	532		300	5.1	33	47	17193	6.3	China
2067	871	84		1060	2000	144	3720		9	17			Cyprus
6392	6405	100	69	1210	1260	168	6910	6.2	0	29	251	0.7	Hong Kong
21	15	92	35	3690	208	184	290	1.8	32	29	31913	14	India
80	89	100	39	11530	213	168	490	4.6	24	36	31901	44	Indonesia
234	270	100	46	6090	958	207			18	26			Iran
	619	100	55	1800	734				7	60			Iraq
2499	1661	99	76	370	1944	40th	6210	2.6	4	23	15938	56	Israel
1050	1735	100	96	780	3186	115	12840	3.3	3	41	5761	0.4	Japan
665	200	99	79	900	767		1540	5.5	8	28	3079	69	Jordan
		100		430	2174								Korea, North
760	835	96	94	440	1408	149	2370	6.7	12	42	29108	31	Korea, South
16	4.6	97	18	20000	37								Laos
814	185	100	58	540	846				9	18	211		Lebanon
672	861	99	53	4000	762	127	1830	4.3	20	31	16759	66	Malaysia
388	258	100	88	450	1195		1500		15	29			Mongolia
27	8	79	25	30060	23	185	150	1.9	62	12	711	28	Nepal
54	34	47	17	3480	205	160	350	2.4	24	28	11764	36	Pakistan
96	85	100	65	7970	180	266	560	1.9	26	32	19828	66	Philippines
1592	1673	69	42	1670	3336	97	6950	4	4	50			Saudi Arabia
9865	8699	100	71	1150	1851	116	7410	7.6	1	38	2120	12	Singapore
121	75	100	63	7170	139	205	400	2.9	26	27	3448	54	Sri Lanka
255	125	100	61	2240	914	251	1570	3.7	22	21	3060	18	Syria
1147	1592	100	95	1242			2570		9	34			Taiwan
174	167	97	30	7100	327	134	810	4	17	30	11023	27	Thailand
219	159	100	42	1630	750	528	1110	2.7	18	36	23309	41	Turkey
		100	43	4190	87		170						Vietnam
147	3	67	10	11670	102		550	4.7	34	16	2052	41	Yemen, North
652	272	66	19	7120	714		470		19	27	1927	190	Yemen, South
													† U.S.S.R.
													Oceania
1634	1416	100	95	560	4710	176	11920	1.7	5	34	817	0.4	Australia
1857	1810	100	85	640	4127	231	7460	1.5	11	33	73	0.3	New Zealand
332	304	64	14	13590	244	145	720	0.5	34	26	1147	48	Papua New Guinea

Bahrain, Land 0.6/Popn. 412; Bhutan 47/1447; Brunei 5.3/244; Kuwait 17.8/1791; Macau 0.02/392; Maldives 0.3/189; Oman 212.5/2000; Qatar 11/335; U.A.E. 83.6/1384.
American Samoa 0.2/32; Cocos Is. 0.01/0.6; Cook Is. 0.2/20; Fed. States of Micronesia 0.7/73; Fiji 18.3/703; Fr. Polynesia 3.7/166; Guam 0.6/116; Kiribati 0.7/65; Nauru 0.02/8; New Caledonia 18.8/156; Niue I. 0.26/3; Norfolk I. 0.036/2; Northern Marianas 0.5/16.8; Palau 0.5/12; Samoa 2.9/164; Solomon Is. 27.5/281; Tokelau 0.01/2.0; Tonga 0.7/97; Tuvalu 0.2/8; Vanuatu 14.8/140; Wallis & Futuna 0.2/12.

Trade. The trade figures are for the year 1986. The total trade figures have been divided by the population and are a measure of the country's external trade (U.S. $ per capita).

Education. The ages of primary school are taken to be 6–11 years and secondary school 12–17 years. The percentage of total school age group in this type of education is shown.

Energy. All forms of energy have been converted to their equivalent in oil. Firewood and other traditional forms used in developing countries are not included and so the energy consumption in those countries is understated (kilograms of oil equivalent per capita).

Consumer Price Index. The base year is 1980 which is 100 and the level of consumer prices in 1986 or 1987 are shown in relation to the base year. It is a measure of inflation.

G.N.P. (Gross National Product) This figure is an estimate of the average production per person measured in U.S. dollars and for 1986. The G.N.P. measures the value of goods and services produced in a country, plus the balance, positive or negative, of income from abroad, for example investments, interest on capital, money returned from foreign labour, etc. The rate of change is the average annual percentage change during the period 1965–1986 in the G.N.P. The G.D.P. (Gross Domestic Product) is the G.N.P. minus the foreign balances. The adjoining two columns show the percentage contribution to the G.D.P. made by the agricultural and mining and manufacturing sectors.

Loans and Debts. This figure in millions of U.S. dollars shows the external public debt at the end of 1986. This is then shown as a percentage of the annual G.N.P. The figures in red show official development assistance made by the developed countries and also as a percentage of the donor country's G.N.P.

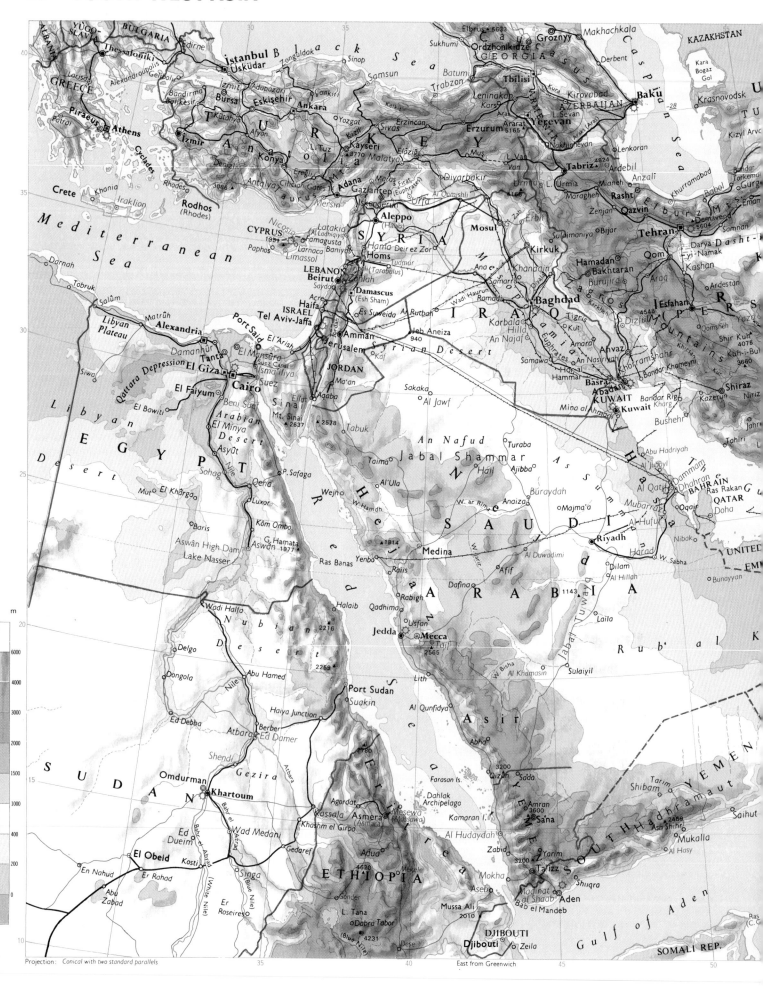

1:15 000 000

100 0 100 200 300 400 500 600 km

CHINA

S. S. R.

Tashauz UZBEK Samarkand
S. Amu Darya Bukhara Karshi TADZHIKISTAN Pamir
MENISTAN Chardzhou Dushanbe Gilgit Kashmir
Kara Kum Kerkio Termez Kholm Chitral Srinagar
Ashkhabad Mary Kushka Mazar-i-Sharif Baghlan Charikar U Rawalpindi
Nishapur Kunduz Kabul Jalalabad Peshawar Sialkot
Mashhad Herat Maimana Ghazni Khyber Pass Kohat Lahore
Sabzawar Gharian 3787 Lora Bannu Dera Ismail Khan Multan
Gunabad Farah Daulatabad Qalat Fort Sandeman Sutlej
Birjand Girishk Registan Pishin Quetta Bahawalpur
Kerman Zabul Helmand Bolan Pass Sibi Dera Ghazi Khan
Saguch Zahidan Nushki Kalat Jacobabad
Saidabad Bam Kuh-i-Taftan 4042 Shikarpur Sukkur INDIA
Khanu Bampur Panjgur Nawabshah
Bandar Abbas Minab Fanuch Bela Hyderabad
Qishm Kuhran 2163 Dasht Karachi

Str. of Hormuz Jask Gwadar Pasni

Gulf of Oman Arabian Sea

Abu Dhabi As Sohar Matrah Tropic of Cancer
ARAB Al Khabura Muscat
J. ash Sham 3019 Izki Sur Ras al Hadd
OMAN W. Batha W. Ardam

Gulf of Masira
Al Khalaf Dawwah Al Masira
Rishon Le-Zion
Dhofar Ras al Madraka
Saugra Bay
1678 Kuria Muria Is.
Salala Marbat

Socotra (South Yemen)
The Brothers

East from Greenwich 55 30 35

LEBANON · SYRIA · ISRAEL · JORDAN

BEIRUT (Bayrut) Djounie (Juniyah) Mts. J. Sannini 2628 Ba'labakk (Baalbek)
Bikfaiya Zahlah
Aley 2462
Sayda (Sidon) Jezzine Khirbat Qanafar Damascus (Esh Sham)
Nabatiye el Tahta 2814 Qatana Zabdani
Tyre (Sur) Litani Al Khiyam Kiswe
Tibnin Qiryat Shemona SYRIA
Nahariya Me'ona 1208 Al Qunaytirah
Acre B. of Haifa GALILEE Capernaum Sanamein
Haifa Qiryat Yam Migdal Kinneret (Sea of Galilee) 209
Tirat Karmel 546 Qiryat Ata Tiberias
Nazareth Dar'a
Daliyat el Karmel Afula 515 Samar
Caesarea Taiyiba Megiddo Irbid
Pardes Hanna Umm el Fahm Janin Beit Shean Ramtha
Hadera SAMARIA Yabis 1198
Netanya Tubas Jebel 'Ajlun 1247
Tul Karm 940 Jacob's Well Ajlun Jarash
Ra'anana 881 Nabulus Zarqa Al Mafraq
Herzliya Kefar Sava Damiya
TEL AVIV-JAFFA Petah Tiqva Shilo JORDAN Az Zarqa
Ramat Gan 1016 1113 As Salt
Holon Wadi es Sir Amman
Bat Yam Lod (Lydda) Na'ar
Ramla Jericho Hussein Br.
Rehovot Ram Allah 802 Madaba
Ashdod Gedera Jerusalem
Yavne Qumran Ma'daba
Ashqelon Bethlehem Heidan
JUDAEA Dead Sea
Qiryat Gat 1020 Hebron (El Khalil) 395
Gaza (Ghazzah) Az Zahiriya Mujib
Gaza Strip Masada Al Mazra
Khan Yunis Mishmar Ha Negev Arad Al Karak
Rafah Wilderness of Judaea Dhiban
EGYPT Beersheba Qatrana
NEGEV Dimona
716
Qeziot

THE HOLY LAND

Armistice boundaries between Arab States
and Israel, 1949-1974

1:1 500 000

10 0 10 20 30 40 50 km

COPYRIGHT GEORGE PHILIP & SON LTD.

U.S.S.R.

PERSIA (IRAN)

AFGHANISTAN

HERAT · Herat · Obeh
BADGHIS
FARYAB · Maimana
JOUZJAN · BALKH · SAMANGAN · BADAKHSHAN
GHOR · BAMIAN · TAKHAR
URUZGAN · KABUL · Kabul
GHAZNI · LOGAR · NANGARHAR · Peshawar · Khyber Pass
PAKTYA · WARDAK
PAKTIKA · ZABUL
Qandahar · QANDAHAR
NIMRUZ · HELMAND
Khash Desert · Dasht-i-Margo · Registan
Chagai Hills

HINDU KUSH
Chitral · Dir · KUNAR
Srinagar · JAMMU AND KASHMIR
Karakoram Range
K2 8611 · Karakoram Pass
Gilgit · Nanga Parbat 8126
LINE OF SMLA AGREEMENT 1972
Leh · LADAKH · ZASKAR Range

Rawalpindi · Islamabad
Jammu · Sialkot · Pathankot · HIMACHAL PRADESH
Gujrat · Gujranwala · Amritsar · Jullundur · Simla
Lahore · Kasur · Ludhiana · Chandigarh
Faisalabad (Lyallpur) · Ferozepore · PUNJAB · Ambala
Jhang Maghiana · Okara · Sahiwal · Fazilka · Patiala · Dehra Dun
Sargodha · Multan · Bhatinda · HARYANA · Hardwar
Khanewal · Ganganagar · Hissar · Saharanpur · Karnal · Najibabad
Bahawalpur · Sirsa · Panipat · Meerut · Moradabad
Ahmadpur · Bikaner · Churu · DELHI · Rampur
Rahimyar-Khan · Ratangarh · Ghaziabad · Bulandshahr
Nagaur · Sikar · Alwar · Mathura · Aligarh
Sukkur · Khairpur · Jodhpur · Ajmer · Jaipur · Bharatpur · Agra · Firozabad
RAJASTHAN · Dholpur · Gwalior
Nawabshah · Tonk · Kota · Jhansi
SIND · Hyderabad · Udaipur · Bhilwara · Bundi · Guna · Lalitpur
Tando Adam · Barmer · Pali · Gandhi Sagar Dam
KARACHI · Mirpur Khas · Deesa · Palanpur
INDUS · Rann of Kutch
Bhuj · GUJARAT · Mehsana · MADHYA
Gulf of Kutch · Ahmadabad · BHARAT
Jamnagar · Rajkot · Nadiad · Godhra · Ujjain · Bhopal
Porbandar · Amreli · Vadodara · Dhar · Indore
Junagadh · Bhavnagar · Bharuch · Khandwa · Nagpur
Veraval · Surat · Navsari · Burhanpur · Amravati · Wardha
Diu · Dhule · Jalgaon · Akola
DAMAN, DADRA NAGAR HAVELI · Malegaon · Bhusawal · Ajanta Range
Gulf of Cambay · Nasik · Aurangabad · MAHARASHTRA · Nander
Thana · Ulhasnagar · Ahmadnagar · Jalna · Parbhani · Nizamabad
BOMBAY · Pune (Poona) · Latur
Satara · Solapur · Gulbarga · Hyderabad · ANDHRA PRADESH
Ratnagiri · Pandharpur · WARANGAL
Kolhapur · Sangli · Miraj · Bijapur · Raichur
Belgaum · Gadag · GOA · Bellary · Kurnool

ARABIAN SEA

Tropic of Cancer

KARNATAKA
GOA · Dharwad · Kurnool · Adoni
Gadag · Bellary · Erramala Hills
Davangere · Proddatur · Ongole
Shimoga · Anantapur · Cuddapah · Nellore
Sagar · Bhadravati · Tirupati · Pulicat Lake
Mangalore · Tumkur · Chittoor
Bangalore · Kolar Gold Fields · Vellore · MADRAS
Hassan · Mandya · Kanchipuram
Mysore · Pondicherry
Cannanore · TAMIL NADU · Cuddalore
Calicut (Kozhikode) · Coimbatore · Salem · Thanjavur
Palghat · Tiruppur · Erode · Nagappattinam
Trichur · Pollachi · Tiruchchirappalli · Kumbakonam
KERALA · Dindigul · Karaikkudi
Cochin · Madurai
Mattancheri · Rajapalaiyam · Palk Strait
Alleppey · Tuticorin · Jaffna · Mannar
Quilon · Tirunelveli · Gulf of Mannar
Trivandrum · Nagercoil · Cape Comorin
Palk Bay · Trincomalee · Foul Pt.
Anuradhapura · Puttalam · Batticaloa
SRI LANKA
Kurunegala · Kandy · Adam's Peak 2243
Colombo · Moratuwa · Badulla
Kalutara · Galle · Matara · Dondra Head

Coromandel Coast · Malabar Coast · Western Ghats · Eastern Ghats

Continuation Southwards on same scale

Projection: Conical with two standard parallels

1 : 10 000 000

100   0   100   200   300   400 km

CHINESE   REPUBLIC

X I N J I A N G

Kun   Lun   Shan

Hoh   Xil   Shan

Q I N G H A I

Bayan   Har   Shan

Ngoring Hu

Gyaring Hu

Maqên Gangri 6282   Maqên

Dogai Coring

T I B E T

T   Tanglha

Tang Pass 5180

Range

Nyenchen   Tanglha   Range

S I C H U A N

Gerze

Siling Co

Nagqu

Dêngqên

Qamdo

Baiyü

Yushu

Garzê

Yajiang

Kangri

Tangra Yumco

Gyaring Co

Xainza

Nam Co

Lhari

Bomi

Cogên

Lhasa

7088

Lhünzhub

7756

Zhamog

Salween

Mekong

Yangtze

Ngangla

Mapam Yumco

Burang

Gangdise Shan

Namja Pass 4944

7059

Zhongba

Saga

Maquan

Yarlung Zangbo Jiang

Xigazê

Lhazê

Gyangzê

Gamba

Lhünzê

Gomai

Cona

Subansiri

Nizamghat

Dong

Jido

Sang

Zayu

5500

Zhangmu

A R U N A C H A L   P R A D E S H

Dihang

Dibrugarh

North Lakhimpur

Sibsagar

Hpungan Pass 3072   Putao

Chaukan Pass 2432

Bumhpa Bum

K A C H I N   S T A T E

Mandeldhura

Mustang

Dhaulagiri 8221

Muktinath

Gya Pass 5602

Gurkha

8013   Nyalam

Mt Everest 8848

Kanchenjunga 8598

7314

7564

Thimphu

Punakha

B H U T A N

Dibrugarh

Jorhat

Hukawng Valley

Parkai Bum

3411

Kumon Bum

Thala Pass 5881

Miputung

Zhanglung

Y U N N A N

Lakhimpur

Bahraich

Balrampur

Gonda

Basti

Gorakhpur

Bettiah

Motihari

Gandak

Darbhanga

Muzaffarpur

Siliguri

Jalpaiguri

Kurseong

Darjeeling

W   B E N G A L

Alipur Duar

Cooch-Behar

Barpeta

Gauhati

A S S A M

Nowgong

Tezpur

Mokokchung

N A G A L A N D

Kohima 3824

Magaung

Myitkyina

Tengchong

Baoshan

Lucknow

Faizabad

Rae Bareli

Fatehpur

Jaunpur

Ghazipur

Patna

Arrah

Chapra

Siwan

Azamgarh

Ghaghara

Darbhanga

Purnea

Katihar

Kishanganj

Dinajpur

Saidpur

Rangpur

Dhubri

Dhuburi

Turu

M E G H A L A Y A   1412

1924   Shillong

Barail Range

Silchar

M A N I P U R

Imphal

Thaungdut

Homalin

Indaw

Shwebo

Varanasi (Banaras)

Mirzapur

Allahabad

Jamuna

Satna

Rewa

690

Bihar

Monghyr

Bhagalpur

Jamalpur

Deoghar

Gaya

Aurangabad

Giridih

Ranchi

B I H A R

Balurghat

English Bazar

Rajshahi

Bogra

Sirajganj

Pabna

Berhampore

DACCA (Dhaka)

Comilla

Agartala

T R I P U R A

Belonia

M I Z O R A M

2704

Aijal

C H I N S

Karnaphuli Res

Kyaukpyu

Homalin

Shwegu

Mangin Range

Mawlaik

Kalewa

Kulewa

2299

Shweli

Namtu

Lashio

Hsenwi

M A D H Y A

Hazaribagh

Dhanbad 1366

Asansol

Durgapur

WEST BENGAL

Bankura

Purulia

Burdwan

Krishnanagar

Narayanganj

Khulna

Barisal

Chittagong

Cox's Bazar

Mt Victoria 3053

Palerwa

B U R M A

Monywa

Mandalay

2693

Ambikapur

Lohardaga

Ramgarh

Chakradharpur

Jamshedpur

Midnapore

Serampore

Haora

CALCUTTA

Bhatpara

Jessore

Sundarbans

Lakshmikantpur

Patuakhali

Mouths   of   the   Ganges

Mong Hsu

Keng Tung

S H A N   S T A T E

Bilaspur

Kawardha

Raigarh

Sambalpur 1187

Hirakud Dam

Raurkela

Balasore

Kharagpur

Subarnarekha

Mouths   of   the   Meghna R.

Myingyan

2519

Meiktila

Yamethin

Inle Lake

Mong Nai

Loi Kaw

Taunggyi

2160

Chiang Rai

Raipur

Durg

Dhamtari

Bolangir

Dhenkanal

Mahanadi

Brahmani

Denkanal

Cuttack

Bhubaneswar

Puri

Chilka Lake

Berhampur

Sittwe (Akyab)

Ramree I.

Taungup

Cheduba I.

Taungup Pass 1168

Minbu

Magwe

Thayetmyo

Prome

Pyu

Toungoo

K A Y A H

7262

Lamphun

2576

Chiengmai

T H A I L A N D   (S I A M)

1001

Jagdalpur

Jeypore

1240

Salar

Bobbili

1501

Vizianagram

Vishakhapatnam

Anakapalle

B A Y   O F   B E N G A L

Arakan Coast

Arakan Yoma

Henzada

Pegu Yoma

Bassein

Insein

Rangoon

Pegu

Moulmein

Thaton

Pa-an

Dawna Range

Tak (Raheng)

2080

Mae Klong

Rajahmundry

Godavari Point

Kakinada (Cocanada)

Bhimavaram

Machilipatnam (Bandar)

Gulf of Martaban

Myaungmya

Pyapon

Yandoon

Myanaung

Mouths   of   the   Irrawaddy

C. Negrais

Preparis I. (Burma)

Moscos Islands

Tavoy

I N D I A N   O C E A N

Gt. Coco Island (Burma)

COPYRIGHT GEORGE PHILIP & SON. LTD

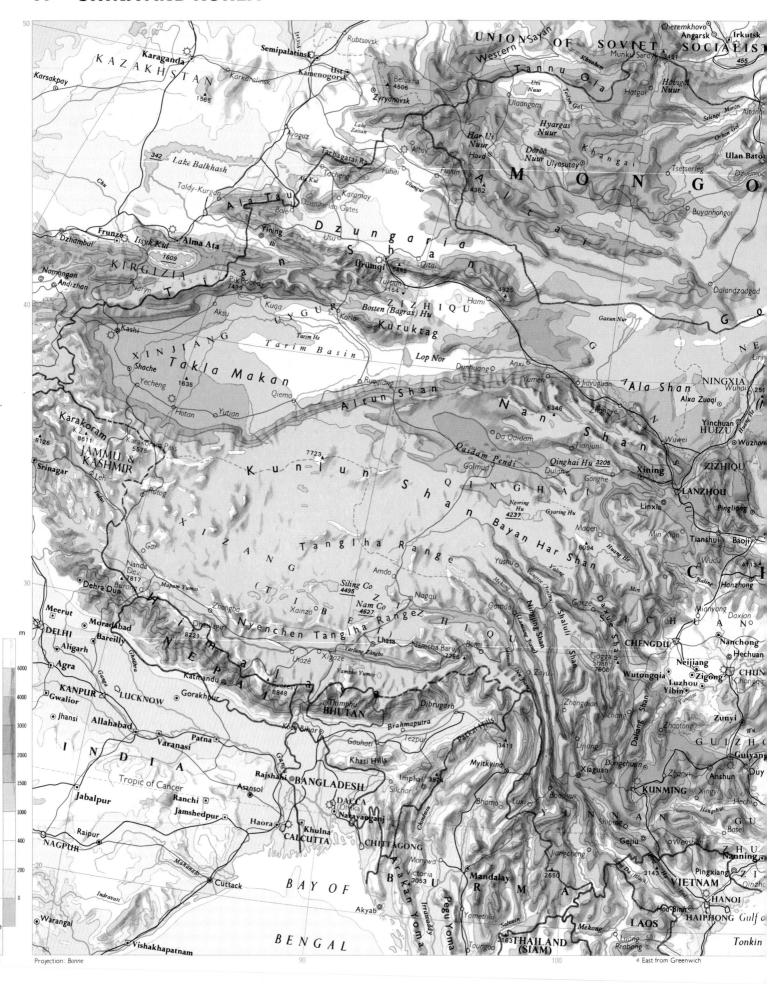

East from Greenwich

1:15 000 000

100   0   100   200   300   400   500   600 km

ze Baykal   Chita
Yablonovyy Ranges
an Ude
Nerchinsk
Borzya
Manzhouli
Hulun Nur
Choybalsan
Kerulen
Buir Nur
Svobodny
Chegdomyn
Amur
Aleksandrovsk
C. Terpeniya
Sakhalin
Blagoveshchensk
Aihui
Little Khingan Mts
Birobidzhan
Khabarovsk
Poronaysk
Yuzhno-Sakhalinsk
MONGOLIA
Saynshand
Dzamin Uud
Erenhot
Abagnar Qi
Nenjiang
Hailar
Butha Qi
Bei'an
Yichun
HEILONGJIANG
Qiqihar
Anda
Suihua
Jiamusi
Hegang
Shuangyashan
Bikin
La Perouse Str.
Wakkanai
Asahigawa
2290
Hokkaido
Otaru
SAPPORO
Kushiro
C. Erimo
Hakodate
INNER MONGOLIA
LIA
Horqin Youyi Qianqi
Tao'an
Manchuria
HARBIN
Mudanjiang
Jixi
Mishan
Lake Khanka
Ussuriysk
Sikhote Alin Ra.
Hohhot
Jining
Zhangjiakou
Xuanhua
1949
Chifeng
JILIN
CHANGCHUN
Shuangliao
Jilin
Liaoyuan
Songhua Lake
Yanji
Vladivostok
Nakhodka
Datong
Qinghuangdao
Tongliao
Siping
Fuxin
FUSHUN
SHENYANG
(Mukden)
Tonghua
Chongjin
SEA OF
JAPAN
Aomori
Hachinohe
Morioka
Akita
Tsugaru Strait
Sado
PEKING
(Beijing)
Baoding
3058
HEBEI
TIENTSIN (Tianjin)
Tangshan
Chengde
Chaoyang
Jinzhou
Liaoyang
Benxi
ANSHAN
Yingkou
Dandong
Qinhuangdao
G. of Liaodong
Korea Bay
Liaodong Pen.
PYONGYANG
Hungnam
Wonsan
NORTH
Talu
Niigata
Sendai
Koriyama
Utsunomiya
Toyama
Kanazawa
TAIYUAN
Yangquan
Yuci
Fenyang
Shijiazhuang
Handan
Anyang
Dezhou
Cangzhou
G. of Chihli
(Bo Hai)
Yantai
Weihai
Ye Xian
Weifang
Zibo
JINAN
Tai'an
Jining
Haeju
Kaesong
SEOUL
INCHON
Taejon
SOUTH
KOREA
TAEGU
Masan
PUSAN
Kanazawa
TOKYO
NAGOYA
KYOTO
KOBE
OSAKA
Sakai
Wakayama
Fuji-san 3776
Yokohama
Shizuoka
Hamamatsu
KAWASAKI
YOKOHAMA
SHANXI
Changzhi
Tongchuan
Sanmenxia
Luoyang
ZHENGZHOU
HENAN
Kaifeng
Shangqiu
Xuzhou
Qingjiang
Lianyungang
QINGDAO
YELLOW
SEA
Kwangju
1915
Hiroshima
Shimonoseki
Okayama
KOBE
Kochi
Matsuyama
Shikoku
SIAN
(Xi'an)
Nanyang
Pingdingshan
Zhumadian
Shangshui
Bengbu
Hongze Hu
NANKING
(Nanjing)
Zhenjiang
Changzhou
Nantong
Wuxi
Suzhou
Hefei
ANHUI
JIANGSU
Cheju Do
1950
Sasebo
Kumamoto
Nagasaki
KITAKYUSHU
FUKUOKA
Kyushu
Kagoshima
Tanega
Han Shui
Xiangfan
Yichang
Shashi
HUBEI
WUHAN
Huangshi
Anqing
Tongling
Wuhu
SHANGHAI
Dabie Shan
Changde
Yiyang
Dongting L.
Tunxi
Shaoxing
Ningbo
Hangzhou
Hangzhou Wan
EAST CHINA
SEA
Amami-ō-Shima
Guilin
Nan Ling
Hengyang
Shaoyang
Xiangtan
Zhuzhou
Changsha
HUNAN
Nanchang
JIANGXI
Jian
Shangrao
Jingdezhen
Jinhua
ZHEJIANG
Wenzhou
2120
Wu Shan
Nanping
Min
Sanming
Fuzhou
FUJIAN
Ryukyu Islands
Sakishima Gunto
Okinawa
Naha
PACIFIC
Tropic of Cancer
Ganzhou
Shaoguan
Zhangzhou
Quanzhou
Mei Xian
Chao'an
Xiamen
(Amoy)
Chiai
Yu Shan
3997
TAIWAN
Chilung
TAIPEI
Taichung
Sakishima Gunto
Formosa Strait
Wuzhou
GUANGDONG
Foshan
CANTON
(Guangzhou)
Shantou
Tainan
KAOHSIUNG
OCEAN
Maoming
Zhanjiang
Jiangmen
Macau
(Port.)
HONG KONG (Br.)
Batan Is.
Haikou
Hainan Str.
1879
Hainan
SOUTH CHINA
SEA
Babuyan Is.

COPYRIGHT GEORGE PHILIP & SON LTD

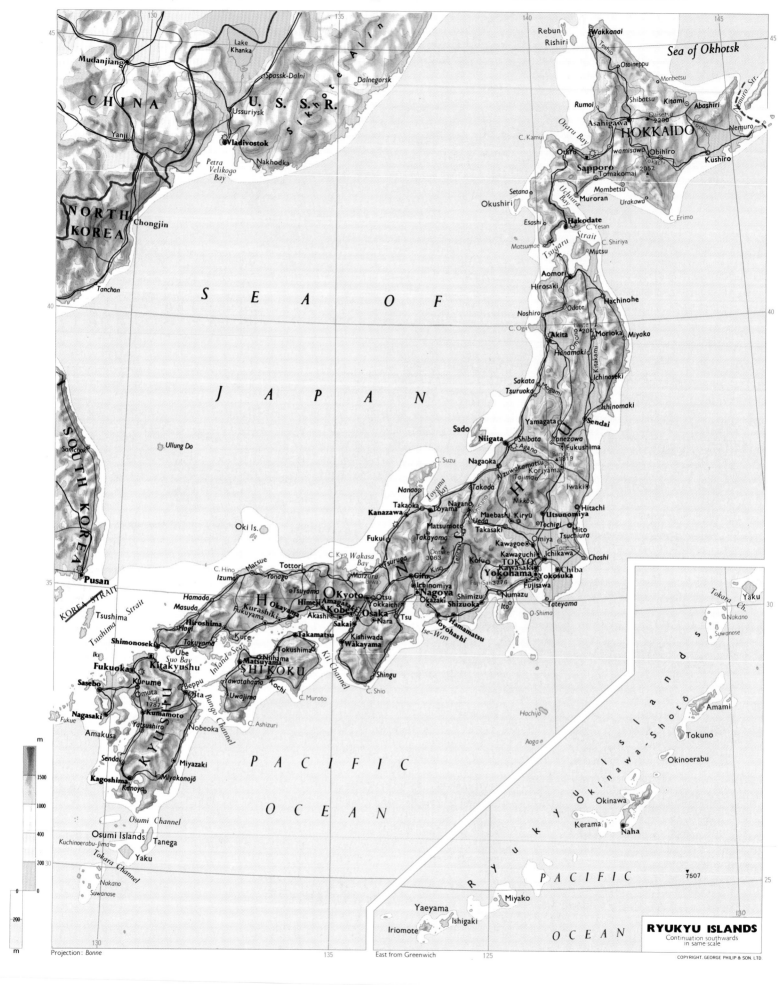

50 0 50 100 150 200 250 300 km

62 JAPAN

CHINA

U.S.S.R.

Sikhote Alin

Mudanjiang

Lake Khanka

Spassk-Dalni

Dalnegorsk

Ussuriysk

Yanji

Vladivostok

Nakhodka

Petra Velikogo Bay

Rebun
Rishiri

Wakkanai

Teshio

Sea of Okhotsk

NORTH
KOREA

Chongjin

Tanchon

S E A   O F

J A P A N

Otoineppu

Monbetsu

Shibatsu Kitami

Rumoi

Asahigawa Daisetsu 2290

HOKKAIDO

Otaru Bay

C. Kamui

Otaru

Iwamizawa Obihiro

Kushiro

Tokachi

Abashiri

C. Erimo

Nemuro Str.

Nemuro

Sapporo Tomakomai 2052

Setana

Uchiura Bay

Muroran

Mombetsu

Okushiri

Urakawa

Esashi

Hakodate

C. Yesan

Matsumae Tsugaru Strait

C. Shiriya

Mutsu

Aomori

Hirosaki

Noshiro Odate Hachinohe

C. Oga

Akita Iwate 2041 Miyako
Onoma **Morioka**

Hanamaki Kitakami

Sakata Ichinoseki

Tsuruoka Mogami

Ishinomaki

Yamagata **Sendai**

Sado

Niigata Shibata Yonezawa Fukushima
Agano Aizuwakamatsu Bandai 1819

Nagaoka Koriyama

C. Suzu Tajima Iwaki

Nanao Toyama Bay Takada Nikko Hitachi

Takaoka Toyama Nagano

Kanazawa Matsumoto Maebashi Kiryu **Utsunomiya**

Fukui Takayama Ueda Tochigi Mito
Takasaki Tsuchiura

Ontake 3063 Omiya Choshi
Kawagoe Tone
Ullung Do C. Kyo Wakasa Bay Kofu **TOKYO** Chiba
Tsuruga **Kawasaki** Yokosuka

Oki Is. Maizuru Gifu Fuji-San 3776 **Yokohama** Yokosuka
Biwa Ichinomiya Fujisawa

SOUTH KOREA C. Hino Matsue Yonago Otsu **Nagoya** Numazu
Tottori **Kyoto** Okazaki Tateyama
Pusan Izumo Tsuyama Yokkaichi Shimizu O-Shima
C. Hino Himeji Amaga- Shizuoka
Hokayama Akashi **Kobe** Nara Ito
KOREA STRAIT Hamada Kurashiki **Osaka** Tsu **Hamamatsu**
Tsushima Strait Masuda Fukuyama Sakai Toyohashi
Tsushima **Hiroshima** Kure **Takamatsu** Kishiwada Ise-Wan
Hagi Tokuyama Inland Sea Tokushima **Wakayama**
Shimonoseki Niihama Kii Channel Shingu

Fukuoka Ube Suo Bay Matsuyama Kochi C. Shio
Iki **Kitakyushu** **SHIKOKU**
Sasebo Kurume Beppu Yawatahama
Omuta Oita Uwajima C. Muroto
Kuju 1787
Nagasaki **Kumamoto** Bungo Channel
Fukue Yatsushiro Nobeoka C. Ashizuri

Amakusa **KYUSHU** Miyazaki
Senda Hachijo

Kagoshima Miyakonojo
Kanoya Aoga

Osumi Channel

Osumi Islands Tanega

Kuchinoerabu-Jima Yaku

Tokara Channel

Nakano

Suwanose

P A C I F I C

O C E A N

East from Greenwich

Projection: Bonne

(Ryukyu Islands inset:)

Tokara Ch. Yaku
Nakano
Suwanose
Amami
Tokuno
Okinoerabu
RYUKYU ISLANDS
Okinawa-Shoto
Okinawa
Kerama
Naha
Miyako
Yaeyama
Ishigaki 7507
Iriomote

RYUKYU ISLANDS
Continuation southwards
in same scale

COPYRIGHT. GEORGE PHILIP & SON. LTD

m
1500
1000
400
200
0

m

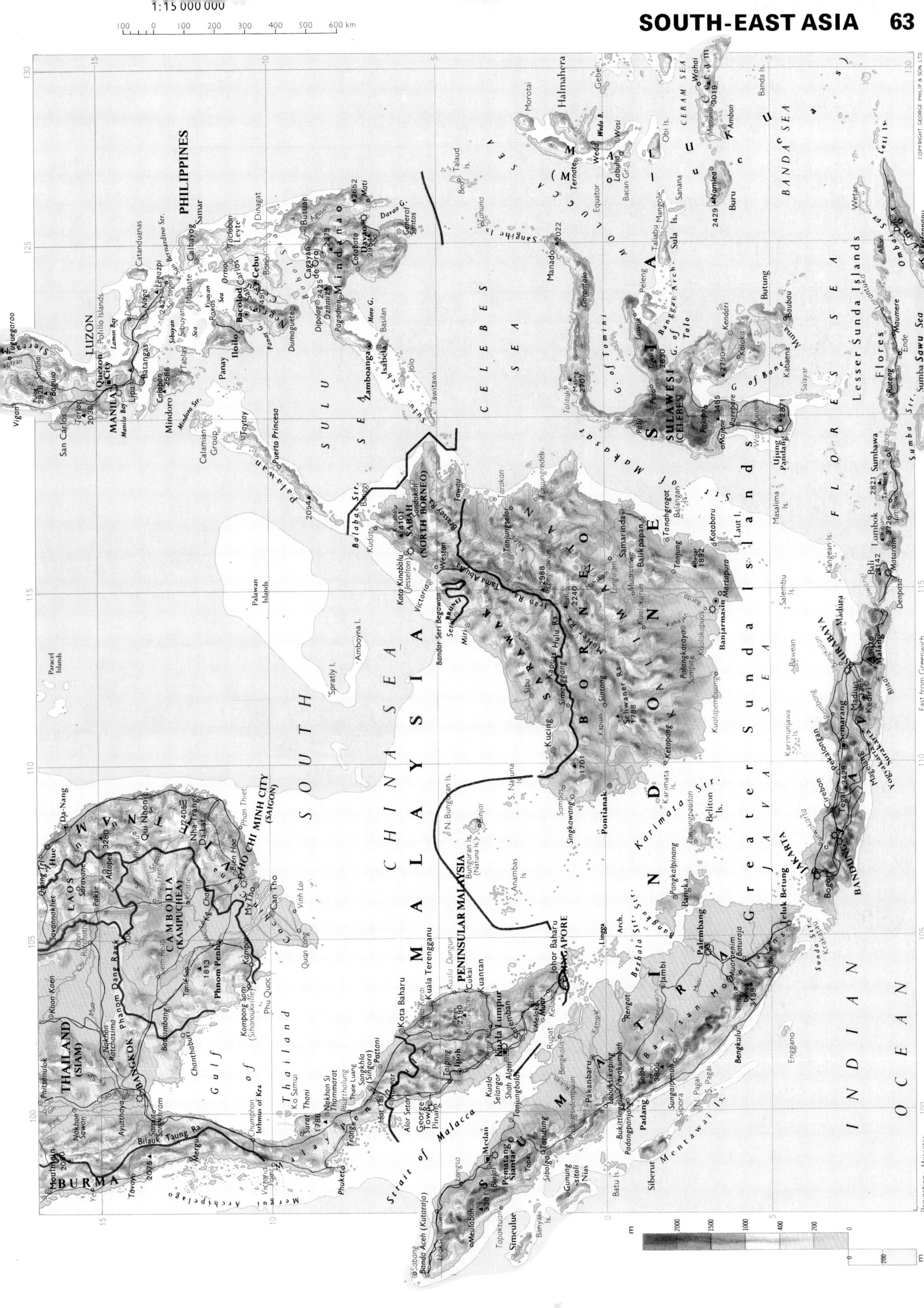

1:15 000 000

100 0 100 200 300 400 500 600 km

COPYRIGHT GEORGE PHILIP & SON LTD

PHILIPPINES

LUZON

MANILA
Quezon City

Manila Bay

Mindoro

Panay

Cebu

Samar

Leyte

Mindanao

CELEBES SEA

SOUTH CHINA SEA

SULU SEA

MOLUCCA SEA

Halmahera

Morotai

CERAM SEA

Buru

BANDA SEA

SULAWESI (CELEBES)

Manado

G. of Tomini

G. of Bone

Ujung Pandang

FLORES SEA

Lesser Sunda Islands

Flores

Sumbawa

Lombok

Bali

Sumba

Sawu Sea

Kupang

SABAH (NORTH BORNEO)

Kota Kinabalu (Jesselton)

Bandar Seri Begawan

SARAWAK

Kuching

B O R N E O

K A L I M A N T A N

Samarinda

Balikpapan

Banjarmasin

Pontianak

JAVA SEA

Greater Sunda Islands

JAKARTA

Bandung

SURABAYA

Semarang

J A V A

Madura

Indian Ocean

VIETNAM

LAOS

THAILAND (SIAM)

CAMBODIA (KAMPUCHEA)

Phnom Penh

BANGKOK

HO CHI MINH CITY (SAIGON)

Da-Nang

Hue

BURMA

Gulf of Thailand

MALAYSIA

PENINSULAR MALAYSIA

Kuala Lumpur

SINGAPORE

Johor Baharu

Strait of Malacca

S U M A T R A

Medan

Padang

Palembang

Banda Aceh (Kutaraja)

INDIAN OCEAN

East from Greenwich

Projection Mercator

m 2000 1500 1000 400 200 0

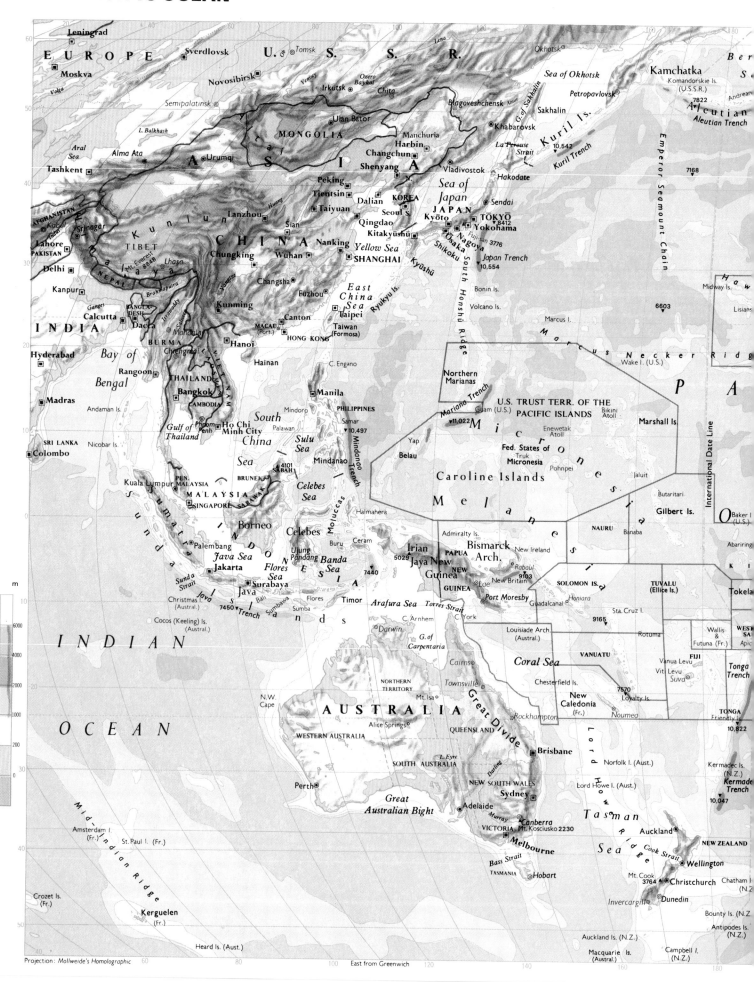

Projection: Mollweide's Homolographic

ALASKA

▲6050 Juneau

Gulf of Alaska

Bristol Bay

Prince of Wales I.

Queen Charlotte Is.

Prince Rupert

Kitimat

ROCKY

CANADA

NORTH AMERICA

GREENLAND

C. Farewell

Hudson Bay

Labrador

NORTH

Newfoundland

Edmonton

Vancouver

Vancouver I.

Victoria

Seattle

Portland

Calgary

Regina

Winnipeg

L. Winnipeg

L. Superior

Montréal

St. Lawrence

Quebec

Pr. Edward I.

Saint John

Mountains

Missouri

Minneapolis

L. Huron

L. Michigan

Ottawa

Toronto

L. Ontario

L. Erie

Buffalo

Detroit

Pittsburgh

Boston

C. Sable

CHICAGO

NEW YORK

C. Mendocino

Boise

Snake

Salt Lake City

Denver

Kansas

St. Louis

Cincinnati

Philadelphia

Baltimore

Washington

Appalachian Mts.

ATLANTIC

▼6741

San Francisco

4418

Colorado

UNITED STATES

Oklahoma

Memphis

Atlanta

C. Hatteras

Los Angeles

San Diego

Ciudad Juarez

Dallas

Mississippi

Jacksonville

40

Bermuda (U.K.)

6225

Sierra Madre

San Antonio

Houston

New Orleans

Gulf of Mexico

Miami

OCEAN

Tropic of Cancer

Hawaiian Is. (U.S.A.)

Honolulu

Oahu

Hawaii

Ridge

ston I. (U.S.)

IFIC

M E X I C O

Gulf of California

Monterrey

México

Guadalajara

Puebla

5700

Acapulco

Revilla Gigedo Is. (Mexico)

Florida Strait

Havana

CUBA

BAHAMAS

Yucatán Channel

Mérida

7680

West Indies

Hispaniola

DOM. REP.

9200

HAITI

JAMAICA

Kingston

PUERTO RICO

Leeward Is.

BELIZE

GUATEMALA

Guatemala

Caribbean Sea

Clipperton I. (Fr.)

HONDURAS

Salvador

EL SALVADOR

NICARAGUA

Managua

CENTRAL AMERICA

San José

COSTA RICA

Colón

PANAMA

Panama Canal

Barranquilla

Maracaibo

Windward Is.

BARBADOS

TRINIDAD & TOBAGO

Caracas

Orinoco

VENEZUELA

Cocos I.

Medellín

Bogota

Cali

COLOMBIA

Palmyra Is. (U.S.)

Teraina

Tabuaeran

Kiritimati

E

Christmas Island Ridge

Jarvis I. (U.S.)

N

Equator

Galápagos (Ecuador)

Guayaquil

Quito

ECUADOR

C. Parinas

Iquitos

Manaus

Amazon

BRAZIL

SOUTH

Trujillo

bury I.

enix Is.

KIRIBATI

Malden I.

Starbuck I.

6369

PERU

Lima

AMERICA

Marquesas Is.

Tongareva Penrhyn Is.

Manihiki

Suwarrow Is.

Vostok I.

Caroline I.

Flint I.

Cuzco

L. Titicaca

Arequipa

Illampu & Ancohuma

6550

Leeward Is.

Society Is.

Cook Islands

Manuae

Windward Is.

Tahiti

Tuamotu Archipelago

Tuamotu Ridge

FRENCH POLYNESIA

Peru–

6866

La Paz

BOLIVIA

Rarotonga

Austral

Seamount Chain

Tubuai Is. (Austral Is.)

Rapa Iti

Pitcairn I. (U.K.)

Ducie I.

Tropic of Capricorn

Sala-y-Gomez (Chile)

Easter Is. (Chile)

San Félix (Chile)

San Ambrosio (Chile)

Iquique

Chile

8050

Antofagasta Trench

PARAGUAY

Asunción

Tucumán

Pto. Alegre

Arch. de Juan Fernández (Chile)

6960

Valparaíso

Santiago

Córdoba

Rosario

Buenos Aires

URUGUAY

Montevideo

Río de la Plata

East Pacific Ridge

Concepcion

ARGENTINA

Chile Rise

SOUTH

Chonos Arch.

Patagonian Andes

ATLANTIC

Pacific–Antarctic Ridge

G. of Penas

6212

OCEAN

Punta Arenas

Falkland Is. (U.K.)

South Georgia

Str. of Magellan

Tierra del Fuego

C. Horn

West from Greenwich

COPYRIGHT. GEORGE PHILIP & SON, LTD

Projection: Bonne

East from Greenwich

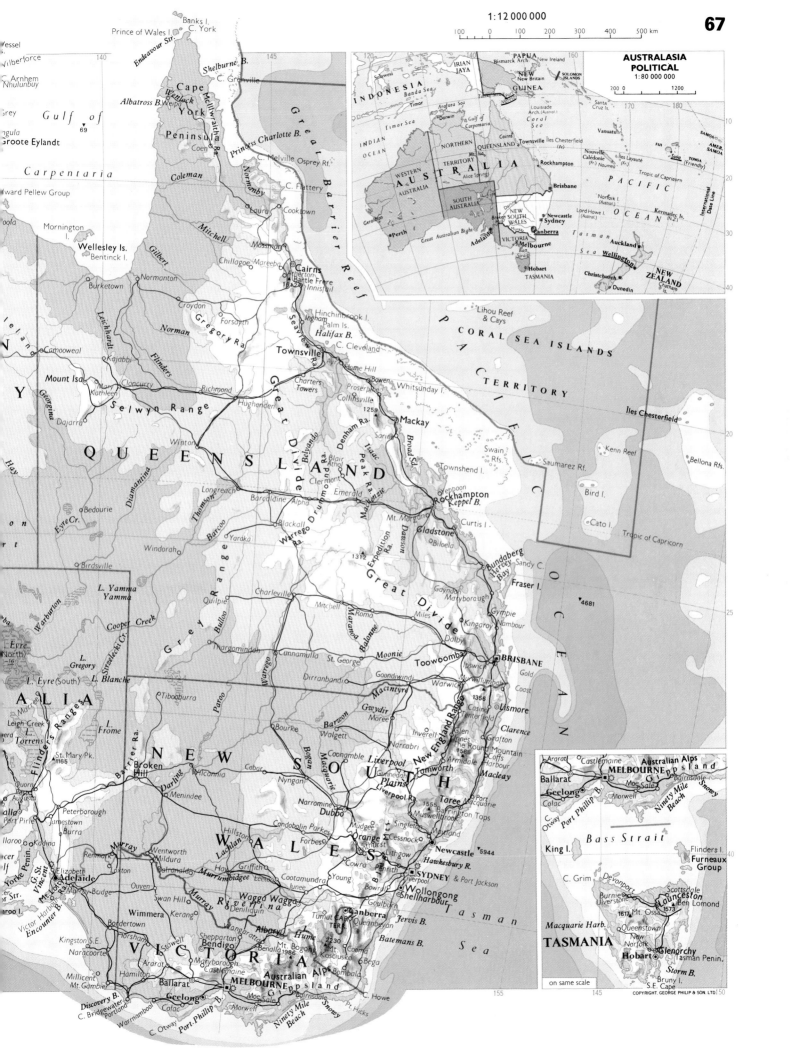

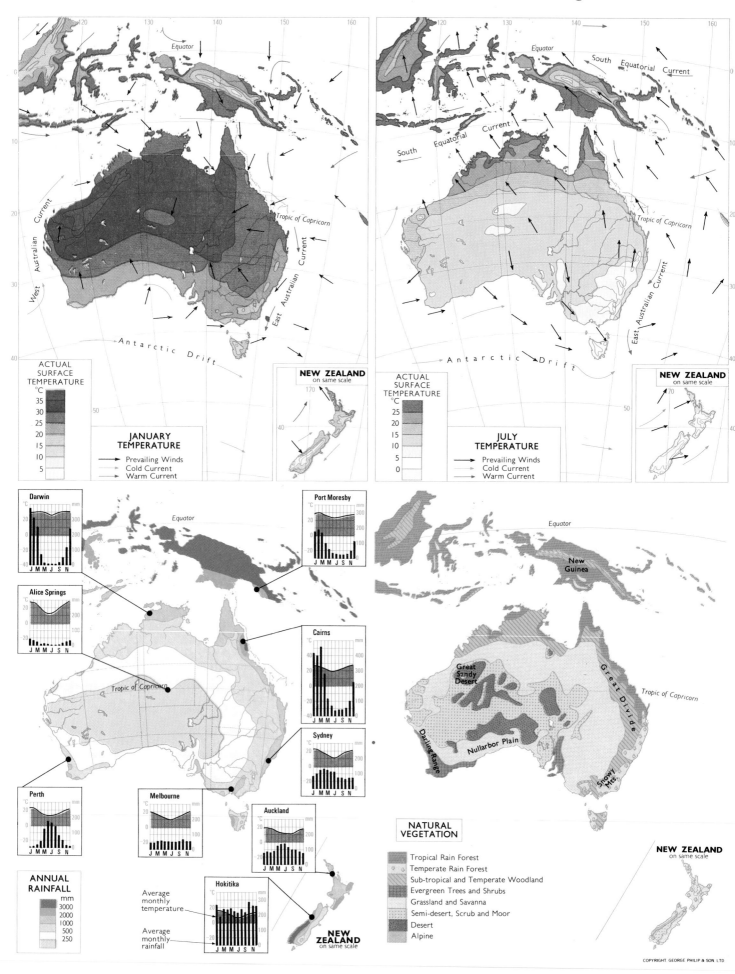

ACTUAL SURFACE TEMPERATURE °C
35
30
25
20
15
10
5

JANUARY TEMPERATURE
→ Prevailing Winds
→ Cold Current
→ Warm Current

NEW ZEALAND on same scale

ACTUAL SURFACE TEMPERATURE °C
25
20
15
10
5
0

JULY TEMPERATURE
→ Prevailing Winds
→ Cold Current
→ Warm Current

NEW ZEALAND on same scale

Darwin
Port Moresby
Alice Springs
Cairns
Sydney
Perth
Melbourne
Auckland
Hokitika

Average monthly temperature
Average monthly rainfall

ANNUAL RAINFALL mm
3000
2000
1000
500
250

New Guinea
Great Sandy Desert
Great Divide
Tropic of Capricorn
Darling Range
Nullarbor Plain
Snowy Mts.

NATURAL VEGETATION
Tropical Rain Forest
Temperate Rain Forest
Sub-tropical and Temperate Woodland
Evergreen Trees and Shrubs
Grassland and Savanna
Semi-desert, Scrub and Moor
Desert
Alpine

NEW ZEALAND on same scale

NEW ZEALAND on same scale

1:20 000 000

200   0   200   400   600   800 km

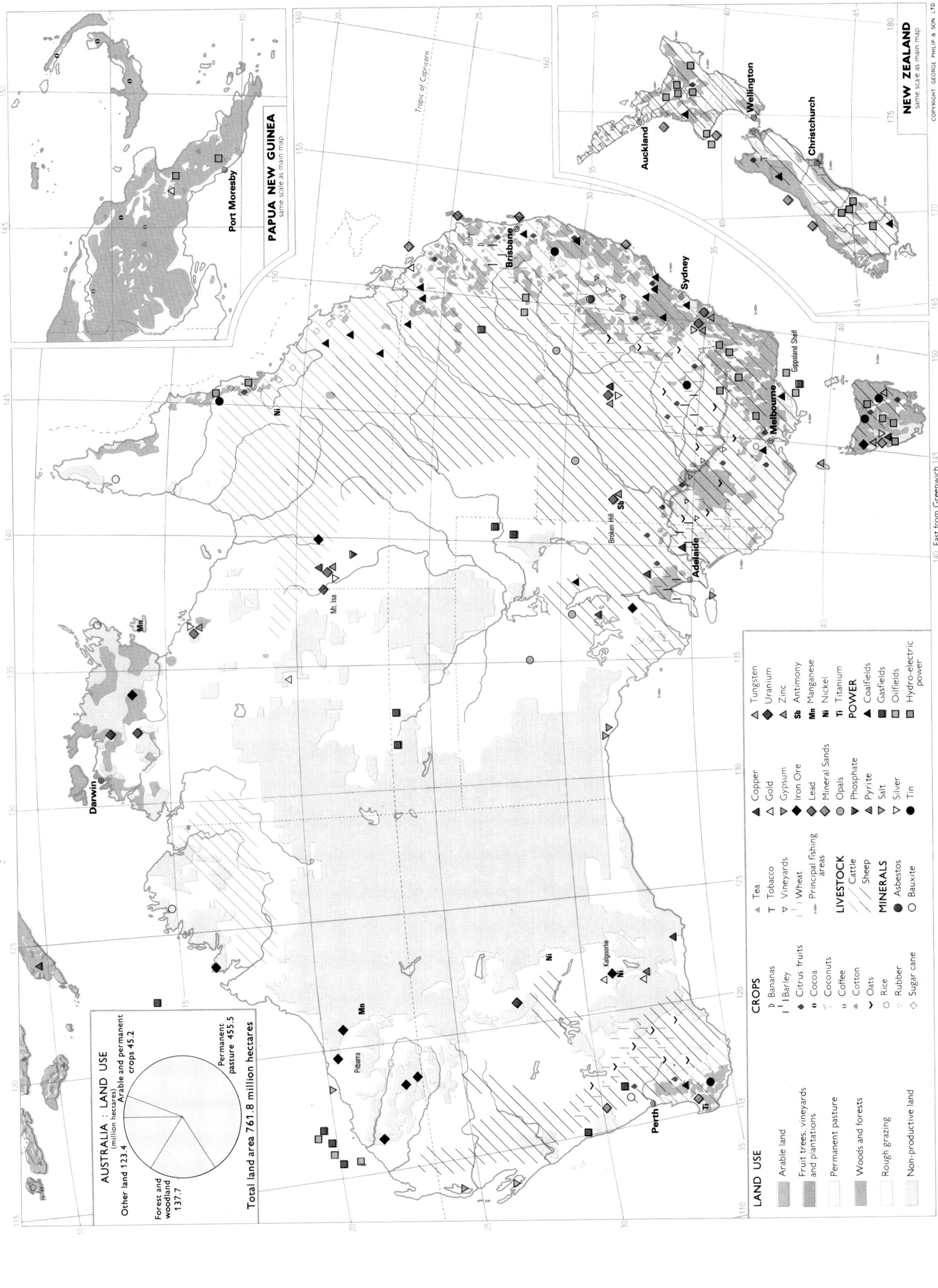

PAPUA NEW GUINEA
same scale as main map

Port Moresby

NEW ZEALAND
same scale as main map

COPYRIGHT GEORGE PHILIP & SON LTD

Auckland

Wellington

Christchurch

Tropic of Capricorn

Brisbane

Sydney

Gippsland Shelf

Melbourne

Broken Hill

Adelaide

Mt. Isa

Sb

Ni

Darwin

Mn

Kalgoorlie
Ni
Ni

Mn
Pilbara

Perth

East from Greenwich

Projection: Bonne

AUSTRALIA : LAND USE
(million hectares)

Arable and permanent
crops 45.2

Other land 123.4

Permanent
pasture 455.5

Forest and
woodland
137.7

Total land area 761.8 million hectares

LAND USE

Arable land

Fruit trees, vineyards
and plantations

Permanent pasture

Woods and forests

Rough grazing

Non-productive land

CROPS

⊅ Bananas
I I Barley
◆ Citrus fruits
o Cocoa
⌢ Coconuts
◒ Coffee
◒ Cotton
〉 Oats
○ Rice
◇ Rubber
◇ Sugar cane
◁ Tea
T Tobacco
▽ Vineyards
I I Wheat
⊢ Principal fishing
areas

LIVESTOCK

Cattle

Sheep

MINERALS

● Asbestos
○ Bauxite

◀ Copper
△ Gold
▽ Gypsum
◆ Iron Ore
◆ Lead
◆ Mineral Sands
◉ Opals
▼ Phosphate
◀ Pyrite
▽ Salt
▽ Silver
● Tin

◁ Tungsten
△ Uranium
△ Zinc
Sb Antimony
Mn Manganese
Ni Nickel
Ti Titanium

POWER

▲ Coalfields
▣ Gasfields
▣ Oilfields
▣ Hydro-electric
power

1:4 500 000

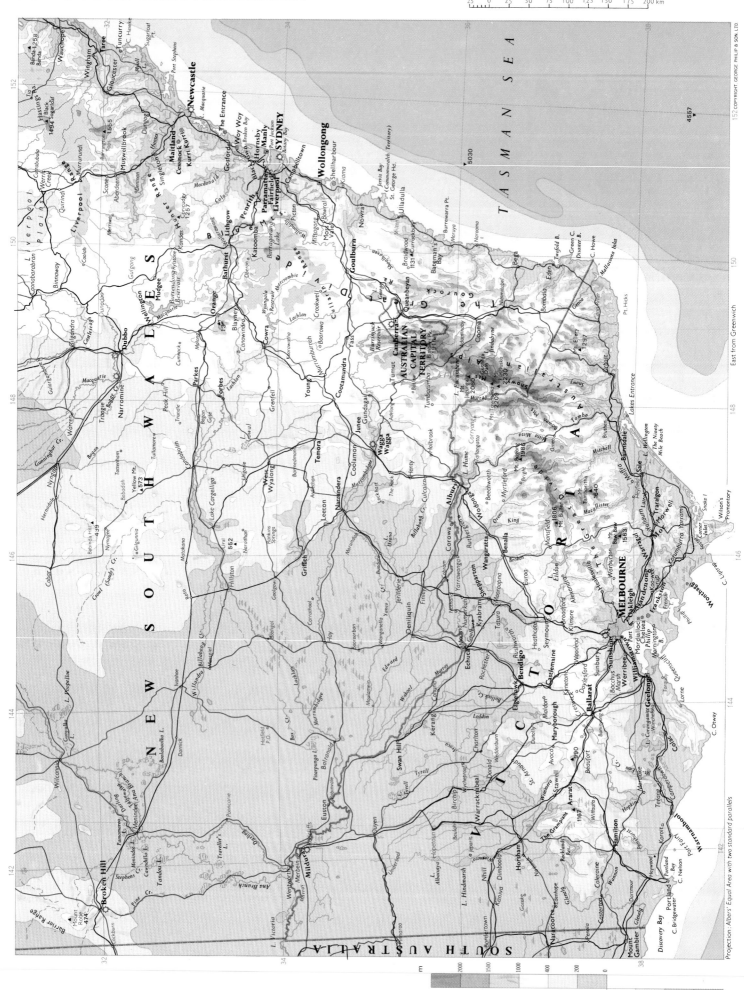

Projection: Alders' Equal Area with two standard parallels

COPYRIGHT GEORGE PHILIP & SON LTD

1 : 6 000 000

50 0 50 100 150 200 250 km

NEW ZEALAND & DEPENDENCIES

1 : 60 000 000

0 500 1000 1500 km

New Zealand Territory
Self-governing Territory

Inset (top left — Pacific dependencies)

Tokelau or Union Group
WESTERN SAMOA
Rotuma (Fiji)
Vanua Levu
FIJI
Viti Levu
Fiji Is.
Lau or Eastern Group
Savaii
Upolu
AMERICAN SAMOA
TONGA (Friendly Is.)
Niue
Pukapuka (Danger)
Nassau
Suwarrow
Rakahanga
Manihiki
Tongareva (Penrhyn) I.
Northern Group
Cook Is.
Palmerston Atoll
Lower Group
Rarotonga
Aitutaki
Mitiaro
Mauke
Mangaia
Îles de la Société
Tropic of Capricorn
PACIFIC OCEAN
Raoul (Sunday) I.
Macauley
Curtis
Kermadec Is.
Three Kings Is.
Auckland
NORTH I.
NEW ZEALAND
SOUTH I.
Wellington
Christchurch
Chatham Is.
Dunedin
Bounty Is.
Antipodes Is.
Tasman Sea
Stewart I.
Snares
Campbell I.
Auckland Is.
Macquarie I. (Austr.)
SOUTHERN OCEAN

Projection: Conical with two standard parallels

North Island

Three Kings Is.
North C.
C. Maria van Diemen
Houhora
Doubtless Bay
Mangonui
Kaitaia
Opua
C. Brett
Rawene
Kaikohe
Hikurangi
NORTHLAND
Whangarei
Dargaville
Waipu
Bream Hd.
Gt. Barrier I.
Kaipara Harb.
C. Colville
Hauraki Gulf
Helensville
Coromandel
CENTRAL AUCKLAND
Takapuna
Devonport
AUCKLAND
Manukau
Thames
Onehunga
Waiuku
Pukekohe
Waihi
Waikato
Mt. Maunganui
NORTH ISLAND
Huntly
Paeroa
Aroha
Bay of Plenty
Raglan
Waiapu
Tauranga
Cambridge
C. Runaway
Hamilton
SOUTH AUCKLAND
BAY OF PLENTY
Whakatane
Opotiki
East C.
Te Awamutu
Patea
Rotorua
Raukumara Ra.
Hikurangi 1754
Te Kuiti
Tokoroa
Kawerau
Murupara
EAST COAST
L. Taupo
Taumarunui
Taupo
Gisborne
North Taranaki Bight
Waitara
New Plymouth
Inglewood
Mt. Egmont 2518
Ruapehu 2797
Waioru
Wairoa
Mahia Peninsula
C. Egmont
Stratford
Eltham
Raetihi
Ohakune
Hawke Bay
Opunake
Hawera
Taihape
Napier
South Taranaki Bight
Patea
HAWKE'S BAY
Hastings
Wanganui
Marton
Feilding
Dannevirke
C. Kidnappers
Waipawa
Palmerston N.
Foxton
Woodville
Waipukurau
Levin
Pahiatua
Otaki
WELLINGTON
Up. Hutt
Masterton
Carterton
Porirua
Lr. Hutt
WELLINGTON
Eastbourne
Martinborough
Cook Strait

South Island

C. Farewell
Golden Bay
D'Urville I.
Collingwood
Tasman Bay
Takaka
Tasman Mts.
Motueka
Karamea Bight
Nelson
Richmond
Wairau
Westport
Lyell Ra.
MARLBOROUGH
Picton
Blenheim
Rototoa
Mt. Travers 2338
Kaikoura Ra.
Clarence
Runanga
Greymouth
Spenser Mts.
Tapuaenuku 2885
Reefton
Grey
Waiau
Kaikoura
L. Brunner
Hokitika
Hurunui
Waipara
Arthur's Pass
Oxford
Rangiora
Pegasus Bay
SOUTHERN ALPS
Coleridge
Waimakariri
New Brighton
Mt. Cook 3764
Methven
Riccarton
Christchurch
Westland Bight
WESTLAND
Lyttelton
Banks Peninsula
Mt. Aspiring 3027
Tekapo
Akaroa
Rakaia
L. Ellesmere
Milford Sd.
Fairlie
Ashburton Bight
Mt. Earnslaw 2819
Pukaki
Temuka
Canterbury Plain
Timaru
Ohau
Wanaka
Hawea
CANTERBURY
Queenstown
Kurow
Waimate
Wakatipu
Cromwell
OTAGO
Oamaru
Kingston
Alexandra
Roxburgh
Palmerston
Te Anau
Manapouri
Clutha
Port Chalmers
EYRE Mts.
GARVIE Mts.
Dunedin
Mosgiel
Secretary I.
Doubtful Sd.
Kelso
St. Kilda
Resolution I.
Mossburn
Winton
Gore
C. Saunders
SOUTHLAND
Milton
Balclutha
Riverton
Mataura
Nugget Pt.
Invercargill
Bluff
Ruapuke I.
Stewart I.
Foveaux Str.
Obah
Port Pegasus
S.W. Cape

SAMOA ISLANDS

1 : 12 000 000

WESTERN SAMOA
Savai'i
Apia
Upolu
AMERICAN SAMOA
Pago Pago
Tutuila
Manua Is.
Rose I.

FIJI AND TONGA ISLANDS

1 : 12 000 000

100 0 100 200 300 km

Futuna (Fr.)
Niuafo'ou (Tonga)
Thikombia
Lambasa
Yasawa Group
FIJI
Vanua Levu
Taveuni
Koro
Vanua Balavu
Lau or Eastern Group
Lautoka
Nadi
Viti Levu 1323
Levuka
Ovalau
Fiji Is.
Suva
Gau
Koro Sea
Moala
Lakemba
Vatoa
Kandavu
Vava'u
TONGA
Tonga (Friendly) Is.
Tofua
Ha'apai Group
Nuku'alofa
Tongatapu

Surrounding seas

PACIFIC OCEAN
TASMAN SEA
SOUTHERN OCEAN
Southland Bight
Pegasus Bay

m
4000
3000
2000
1000
400
200
0
200
m

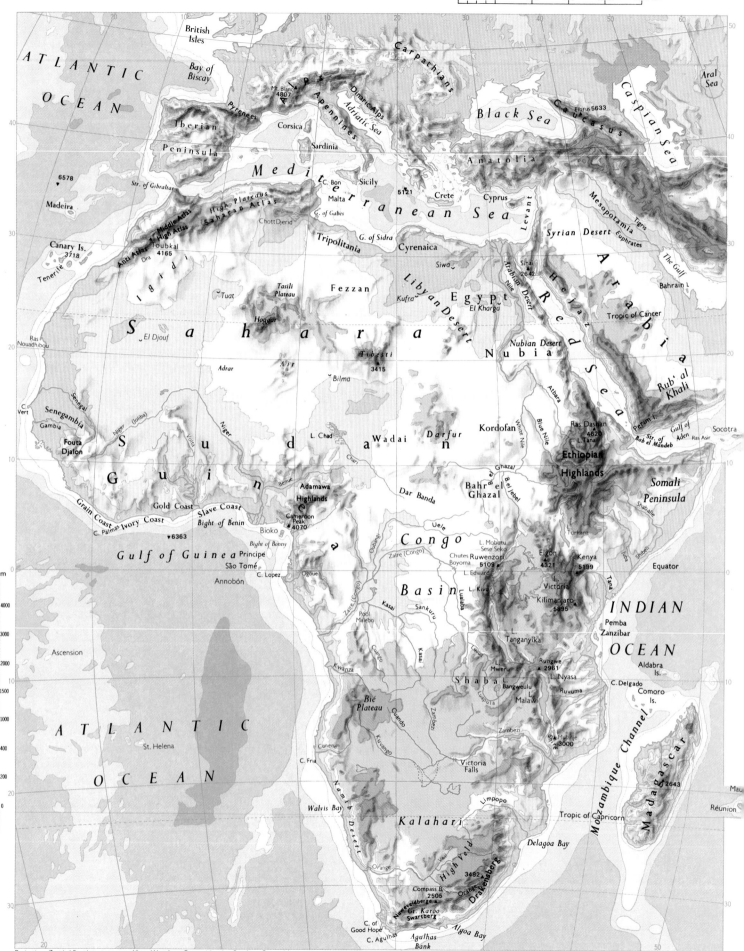

1:40 000 000

400　0　400　800　1200　1600 km

ATLANTIC OCEAN

British Isles

Bay of Biscay

Carpathians

Black Sea

Caucasus　Elbrus 5633

Caspian Sea

Aral Sea

Pyrenees　Mt Blanc 4807

Alps

Apennines

Dinaric Alps

Adriatic Sea

Anatolia

Iberian Peninsula

Corsica

Sardinia

6578

Str. of Gibraltar

Madeira

Mediterranean Sea

C. Bon　Sicily

Malta

Crete

Cyprus

5121

Levant

Mesopotamia

Tigris

Euphrates

The Gulf

Canary Is. 3718

Middle Atlas

High Atlas

Saharan Atlas

High plateaus

Anti Atlas

Toubkal 4165

Dra

Chott Djerid

G. of Gabes

G. of Sidra

Tripolitania

Cyrenaica

Siwa

Syrian Desert

Bahrain I.

Tropic of Cancer

Tenerife

Igidi

El Djouf

S　a　h　a　r　a

Tuat

Tasili Plateau

Fezzan

Libyan Desert

Egypt

Kufra

El Kharga

Arabian Desert

Nile

Sinai 2642

Red Sea

Hejaz

Arabia

Ras Nouadhibou

Adrar

Air

Hoggar

Tibesti 3415

Bilma

Nubian Desert

Nubia

Rub' al Khali

Petrum I.

Str. of Bab el Mandeb

Gulf of Aden

Ras Asir

Socotra

C. Vert

Senegambia

Senegal

Gambia

Fouta Djalon

Niger (Joliba)

Volta

Niger

L. Chad

Chari

Wadai

Darfur

Kordofan

White Nile

Blue Nile

Atbara

Ras Dashan 4620

L. Tana

Ethiopian Highlands

Somali Peninsula

S　u　d　a　n

Benue

Adamawa Highlands

Bahr el Ghazal

Dar Banda

Ghazal

Bahr el Jebel

Shabelle

G　u　i　n　e　a

Grain Coast

Gold Coast

Slave Coast

Ivory Coast

C. Palmas

Bight of Benin

Bioko

Cameroon Peak 4070

6363

Bight of Bonny

Uele

Ubangi

Zaire (Congo)

Congo Basin

L. Mobutu Sese Seko

Chutes Boyoma

Ruwenzori 5109

Elgon 4321

Kenya 5199

Equator

Gulf of Guinea

Principe

São Tomé

Annobón

C. Lopez

Ogoué

Zaire (Congo)

Pool Malebo

Kasai

Sankuru

Lualaba

L. Edward

L. Kivu

L. Victoria

Kilimanjaro 5895

INDIAN OCEAN

Pemba

Zanzibar

ATLANTIC OCEAN

Ascension

Kwanza

Cuango

Kasai

Kwango

Cuanza

Shaba

L. Mweru

L. Bangweulu

Luapula

Tanganyika

Luangwa

Rungwe 2961

L. Nyasa

L. Malawi

Ruvuma

C. Delgado

Comoro Is.

Aldabra Is.

St. Helena

Biè Plateau

Quando

Cunene

Kuvango

Zambezi

Zambezi

Shire

Muchinje 3000

Victoria Falls

Mozambique Channel

Madagascar 2643

C. Fria

Walvis Bay

Namib Desert

Kalahari

Orange

Limpopo

Victoria Falls

Vaal

High Veld 3482

Drakensberg

Orange

Delagoa Bay

Tropic of Capricorn

Mau

Réunion

Compass B 2505

Nieuveldberge

Gt. Karoo

Swartberg

C. of Good Hope

C. Agulhas

Agulhas Bank

Algoa Bay

m
4000
3000
2000
1500
1000
400
200
0
0
200
2000
4000
6000
m

Projection: Zenithal Equidistant.

10　West from Greenwich　0　East from Greenwich　10　20　30　40　50

COPYRIGHT GEORGE PHILIP & SON LTD

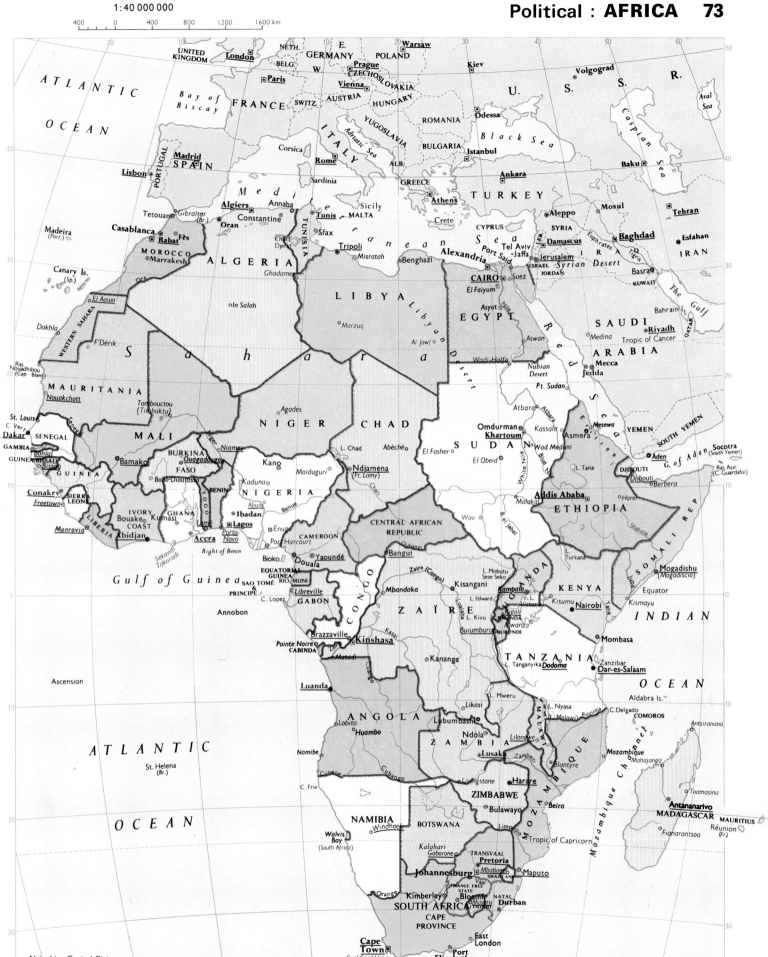

1:40 000 000

400   0   400   800   1200   1600 km

Projection: Zenithal Equidistant.

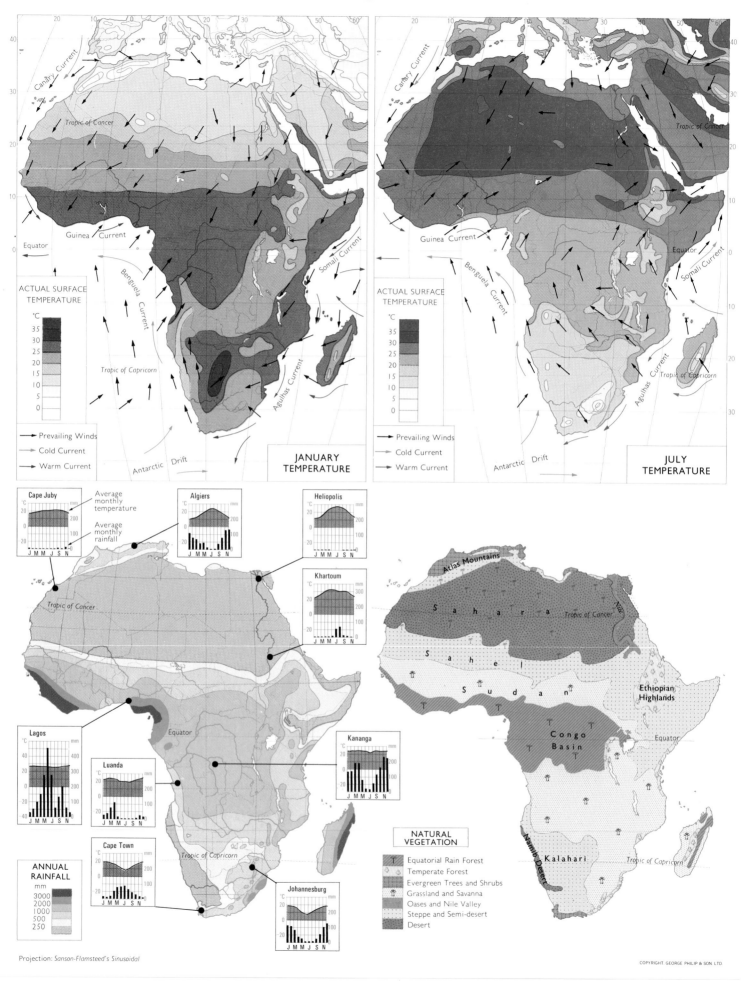

ACTUAL SURFACE
TEMPERATURE
°C
35
30
25
20
15
10
5
0

→ Prevailing Winds
→ Cold Current
→ Warm Current

JANUARY TEMPERATURE

ACTUAL SURFACE
TEMPERATURE
°C
35
30
25
20
15
10
5
0

→ Prevailing Winds
→ Cold Current
→ Warm Current

JULY TEMPERATURE

Cape Juby — Average monthly temperature
Algiers
Heliopolis
Average monthly rainfall
Khartoum
Lagos
Luanda
Kananga
Cape Town
Johannesburg

ANNUAL
RAINFALL
mm
3000
2000
1000
500
250

NATURAL VEGETATION

T   Equatorial Rain Forest
♧   Temperate Forest
     Evergreen Trees and Shrubs
♣   Grassland and Savanna
     Oases and Nile Valley
     Steppe and Semi-desert
     Desert

Atlas Mountains
S a h a r a
Tropic of Cancer
Nile
S a h e l
S u d a n
Ethiopian Highlands
Congo Basin
Equator
Namib Desert
Kalahari
Tropic of Capricorn

Projection: Sanson-Flamsteed's Sinusoidal

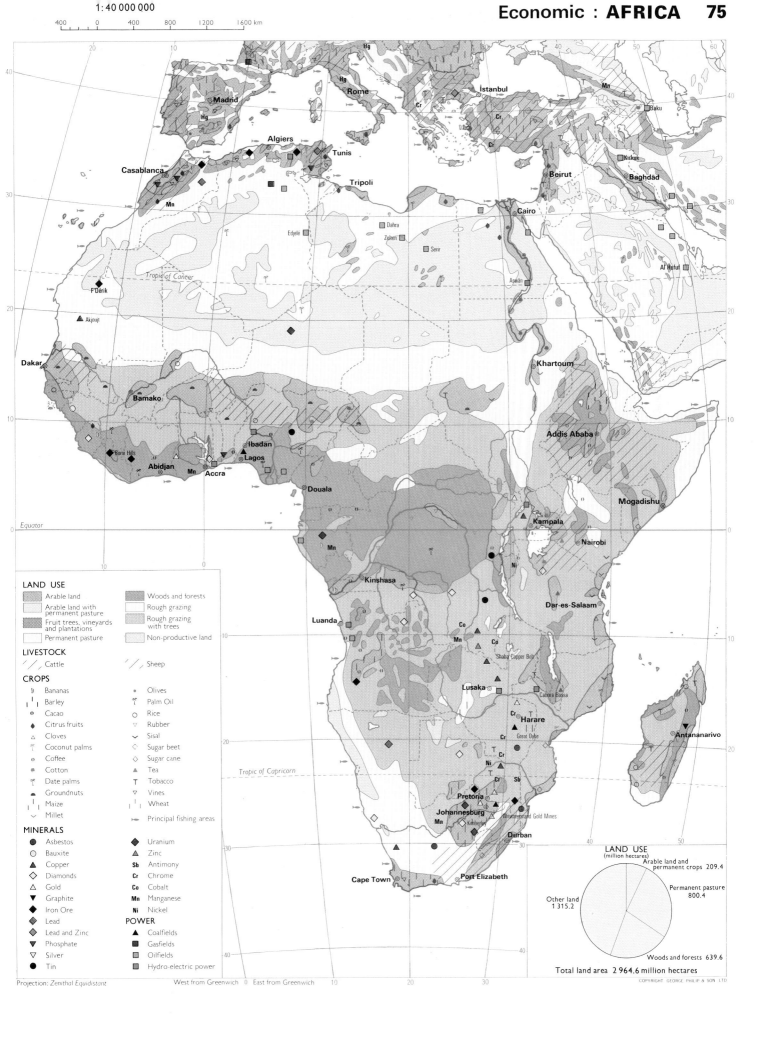

1:40 000 000

400   0   400   800   1200   1600 km

LAND USE
- Arable land
- Arable land with permanent pasture
- Fruit trees, vineyards and plantations
- Permanent pasture
- Woods and forests
- Rough grazing
- Rough grazing with trees
- Non-productive land

LIVESTOCK
- Cattle
- Sheep

CROPS
- Bananas
- Barley
- Cacao
- Citrus fruits
- Cloves
- Coconut palms
- Coffee
- Cotton
- Date palms
- Groundnuts
- Maize
- Millet
- Olives
- Palm Oil
- Rice
- Rubber
- Sisal
- Sugar beet
- Sugar cane
- Tea
- Tobacco
- Vines
- Wheat
- Principal fishing areas

MINERALS
- Asbestos
- Bauxite
- Copper
- Diamonds
- Gold
- Graphite
- Iron Ore
- Lead
- Lead and Zinc
- Phosphate
- Silver
- Tin
- Uranium
- Zinc
- Sb Antimony
- Cr Chrome
- Co Cobalt
- Mn Manganese
- Ni Nickel

POWER
- Coalfields
- Gasfields
- Oilfields
- Hydro-electric power

LAND USE
(million hectares)

Arable land and permanent crops 209.4

Permanent pasture 800.4

Other land 1 315.2

Woods and forests 639.6

Total land area 2 964.6 million hectares

Projection: *Zenithal Equidistant*   West from Greenwich 0 East from Greenwich   COPYRIGHT GEORGE PHILIP & SON LTD

	Population								Land			Agriculture		
	Total	Density	Birth Rate	Death Rate	Life Expectancy	Growth 1965-80	Growth 1980-86	Urban	Area	Arable	Forest	Agricultural Population	Index of Production	Food Intake
	th.	persons per km²	per th. popn.	per th. popn.	yrs.	av. % per annum	av. % per annum	%	th. km²	th. km²	th. km²	% of total popn.	1979-81 =100	calories per day
Algeria	22421	9.4	40	11	62	3.1	3.1	67	2382	76	44	26	125	2677
Angola	8981	7.2	47	22	44	2.8	2.6	25	1247	35	533	71	102	1969
Benin	4042	36	51	21	50	2.7	3.2	39	111	18	37	65	139	2173
Botswana	1128	1.9	50	13	59	3.5	3.5	19	585	14	9.6	66	99	2219
Burkina Faso	6754	25	48	20	47	2	2.5	8	274	26	69	85	146	1924
Burundi	4852	187	47	19	48	1.9	2.7	3	26	13	0.6	92	115	2116
Cameroon	10446	22	43	16	56	2.7	3.2	42	469	70	251	65	111	2089
Central Africa	2740	4.4	45	22	50	1.8	2.5	46	623	20	359	67	108	2050
Chad	5139	4.1	44	21	45	2	2.3	22	1259	32	131	78	122	1504
Congo	1787	5.2	45	19	58	2.7	3.3	40	342	6.8	213	61	108	2549
Egypt	49609	50	38	9	61	2.4	2.7	47	995	25	0.02	43	120	3263
Ethiopia	44927	41	50	23	46	2.7	2.4	18	1101	139	276	77	102	1688
Gabon	1172	4.5	34	18	52	3.5	4.4	41	258	4.5	200	71	107	2763
Gambia	656	66	48	29	43		1.9	21	10	1.7	1.9	82	136	2251
Ghana	14045	61	47	15	54	2.2	3.5	40	230	28	84	52	138	1747
Guinea	6225	25	47	24	42	1.9	2.4	22	246	16	102	77	108	1728
Guinea-Bissau	906	32	41	22	39		1.9	27	28	3.2	11	80	148	2505
Ivory Coast	10165	32	46	16	52	4.2	4.2	43	318	41	74	60	122	2505
Kenya	21163	37	55	14	57	3.6	4.1	17	569	24	37	79	119	2151
Lesotho	1559	52	42	17	55	2.3	2.7	6	30	3	0	82	93	2358
Liberia	2221	23	49	17	54	3	3.3	40	96	3.7	38	72	118	2311
Libya	3742	2.1	38	11	61	4.6	3.9	65	1760	21	6.5	14	178	3612
Madagascar	10303	18	45	17	53	2.5	3.3	22	582	30	151	78	114	2469
Malawi	7279	77	49	25	45	2.9	3.2	12	94	24	45	79	106	2448
Mali	8438	6.9	43	18	47	2.1	2.3	21	1220	21	86	83	122	1788
Mauritania	1946	1.9	50	21	47	2.3	2.6	35	1030	2	150	67	110	2078
Morocco	22476	50	36	11	60	2.5	2.5	44	446	84	52	40	137	2678
Mozambique	14174	18	45	20	48	2.5	2.7	19	784	31	152	83	101	1678
Namibia	1595	1.9	45	17	48		2.7	51	823	6.6	184	38	100	2197
Niger	6698	5.3	51	23	44	2.7	3	16	1267	38	26	89	108	2250
Nigeria	98517	108	50	17	51	2.5	3.3	23	911	311	149	66	129	2038
Rwanda	6275	251	52	19	48	3.3	3.3	5	25	10	5.1	92	106	1919
Senegal	6614	34	46	21	47	2.5	2.9	42	192	52	59	79	117	2342
Sierra Leone	3670	51	47	30	41	2	2.4	28	72	18	21	65	112	1817
Somalia	4760	7.6	48	23	47	2.7	2.9	34	627	11	89	72	108	2072
South Africa	33221	27	39	14	61	2.4	2.2	56	1221	132	45	15	99	2979
Sudan	22178	9.3	46	17	49	3	2.8	29	2376	125	474	65	123	1737
Swaziland	670	26	47	17	55		3	26	17	1.8	1	70	113	2553
Tanzania	22462	25	50	15	53	3.3	3.5	15	886	52	427	83	114	2335
Togo	3052	57	45	16	53	3	3.4	20	54	14	15	71	100	2235
Tunisia	7234	47	33	10	63	2.1	2.3	57	155	49	5.6	28	120	2836
Uganda	16018	80	50	17	48	2.9	3.1	14	200	66	58	83	152	2083
Zaire	30850	14	45	16	52	2.8	3.1	44	2268	66	1760	68	117	2154
Zambia	6896	9.3	48	15	53	3.1	3.5	50	741	52	294	71	118	2137
Zimbabwe	8406	22	47	12	58	3.1	3.7	25	387	27	238	70	122	2054

For explanations see pages 54–55 or 86–87.

Imports US$ per capita	Exports US$ per capita	Primary % of age group	Secondary % of age group	Popn. per doctor	Consumption in kg of oil equiv. per capita	Consumer Price Index 1980 = 100	US$ per capita	Growth per capita % per year 1965-86	Part formed by Agric. %	Part formed by Indust. %	end 1986 US$ millions	as % of G.N.P.	
453	351	94	51	2630	1034	136	2590	3.5	12	44	14777	25	Algeria
120	198	93	13		202								Angola
95	45	65	20	16980	46		270	0.2	49	13	781	57	Benin
		100	29	7378	430	174	840	8.8	4	58	355	36	Botswana
48	17	32	5	48510	18	109	150	1.3	45	22	616	42	Burkina Faso
43	34	53	4	45020	21		240	1.8	58	17	528	44	Burundi
145	197	100	23	13990	142	181	910	3.9	22	35	2267	21	Cameroon
80	47	73	13	26750	30		290	-0.6	41	12	393	42	Central Africa
40	23	38	6	47640	30		80	-2.3	41	17	172	21	Chad
352	377		69	5510	225	170	990	3.6	8	54	2861	152	Congo
192	93	85	62	970	577	239	760	3.1	20	29	22788	56	Egypt
25	10	36	12	69390	21	130	120	0	48	15	1989	36	Ethiopia
811	898			2560	1141	168	3080	1.9	10	35	1095	37	Gabon
156	75			11632	230	188	230	1.1					Gambia
56	61	66	39	7160	131	1132	390	-1.7	45	17	1413	26	Ghana
56	72	30	12	17110	59		320	0.8	40	22	1421	70	Guinea
59	14			7306	50		180	-1.5					Guinea-Bissau
199	315	78	20	15234	175	140	730	1.2	36	24	6500	73	Ivory Coast
78	57	94	20	7890	100	215	300	1.9	30	20	3438	52	Kenya
		100	22	18640		229	370	5.6	21	27	182	33	Lesotho
106	182	66	20	8550	166	123	460	-1.4	37	28	1002	99	Liberia
1205	1605	100	87	660	2259		7170	-1.3	4	57			Libya
38	32	121	36	10220	40	330	230	-1.7	43	16	2635	106	Madagascar
36	33	62	4	41460	43	211	160	1.5	37	18	910	79	Malawi
52	45	23	7	22130	23	147	180	1.1	50	13	1566	96	Mali
187	215	33	10	14500	114		420	-0.3	34	24	1637	210	Mauritania
169	109	81	31	10750	246	174	590	1.9	21	30	14610	104	Morocco
34	11	84	7	39140	86		210		35	12			Mozambique
							1760	1.8	6	46			Namibia
65	49	28	6	38790	42	139	260	-2.2	46	16	1026	51	Niger
46	67	92	29	12550	134	249	640	1.9	41	29	21496	44	Nigeria
55	30	64	2	31340	42		290	1.5	40	23	412	22	Rwanda
154	93	55	13	13780	116	186	420	-0.6	22	27	2456	69	Senegal
42	39	40	12	17520	77	1403	310	0.2	45	22	459	37	Sierra Leone
92	19	25	18	15630	82		280	-0.3	58	9	1415	54	Somalia
391	555			1906	2470	265	1850	0.4	6	46			South Africa
51	22	49	19	8930	58		320	-0.2	35	15	7057	96	Sudan
				7000		253	670	2.7	20	24			Swaziland
47	15	72	3	17740	35		250	-0.3	59	10	3650	82	Tanzania
94	90	95	21	18100	52	138	250	0.2	32	20	882	94	Togo
400	243	100	39	3690	499	133	1140	3.8	16	33	5001	59	Tunisia
21	25	60	8	26810	26		230	-2.6	76	6	929	27	Uganda
48	60	98	57	13940	73		160	-2.2	29	36	5430	97	Zaire
104	100	103	19	7670	381	384	300	-1.7	11	48	3575	241	Zambia
135	155	100	43	5900	517	230	620	1.2	11	46	1712	32	Zimbabwe

Cape Verde, Land 4.0/Popn. 333; Comoros 2.2/476; Djibouti 22/456; Eq. Guinea 28/401; Mauritius 1.9/1029; Reunion 2.5/538; St. Helena 0.3/6; Sao Tome 0.9/110; Seychelles 0.3/66; Western Sahara 266/160.

NORTH ATLANTIC

OCEAN

SPAIN

Cádiz Málaga
Str. of Gibraltar Gibraltar (Br.)
Tangier Ceuta (Sp.)
Tétouan Melilla
Ksar er Kebir Oujda
Kenitra Fès Taza
Salé Meknès
Rabat
CASABLANCA
El Jadida Khouribga
Settat
Safi M O R O C C O
Essaouira Marrakesh
Agadir
Anti Atlas
Middle Atlas
High Atlas

ALGIERS (Alger)
Tizi-Ouzou
Blida Constantine
Medéa Sétif
Mostaganem Ech Cheliff Batna
Oran Mascara Biskra
Sidi Bel Abbès Tiaret Djelfa
Tlemcen Saïda
Laghouat Touggourt El Oued
Ghardaïa Ouargla
Chott Djerid
TUNISIA
Gabès

Madeira (Port.) Funchal

Canary Is. (Span.)
Palma Lanzarote
Tenerife Fuerteventura
Gomera Sta. Cruz
Hierro Gran Canaria Las Palmas
C. Juby Tarfaya (Villa Bens)
El Aaiún
C. Bojador

A L G E R I A
Plateau du Tademaït
Adrar
In Salah
Zaouiet Reggane
Bordj Omar Driss
Ilizi

WESTERN SAHARA

Dakhla
Pta. Durnford

Nouadhibou (Port Etienne)
Nouadhibou
Atar Chinguetti
Akjoujt

M A U R I T A N I A
El Djouf
Fdérik Zouérate

Araouane

Tanezrouft
Poste Maurice Cortier (Bidon 5)
Tessalit
Adrar

A ï r (Azbine)
Tamgak Mts.
Agadès

Nouakchott
Boutilimit
Tidjikdja
Moudjéria
Kiffa
Néma
Goundam
Tombouctou (Timbuktu)
Bamba Bourem
Kidal
Gao Ménaka
Ansongo

M A L I

St. Louis
Louga
Linguéré
Thiès DAKAR
Kaolack
GAMBIA Banjul
Ziguinchor
GUINEA BISSAU
Bissau
Bissagos Is.

SENEGAL
Diourbel
Kayes
Tambacounda
Kolda

Didiéni
Kita
Bamako
Koulikoro
Ségou San
Djenné
Mopti
Douentza
Tahoua
Filingué

Nioro Sokolo
Nara

BURKINA FASO
Ouahigouya
Niamey
Dori Téra
Dosso

N I G E R

Sokoto
Gusau
Maradi Zinder
Katsina
Kano
Zaria

NIGERIA

GUINEA
Conakry
Kankan
Labé
Fouta Djalon

SIERRA LEONE
Freetown
Makeni Magburaka
Bo Kenema

LIBERIA
Monrovia
Buchanan

IVORY COAST
Man
Daloa
Bouaké
Korhogo
Gagnoa
Abidjan

GHANA
Tamale
Kumasi
Accra
Cape Coast
Sekondi-Takoradi

BURKINA FASO
Ouagadougou
Koudougou
Bobo-Dioulasso
Bolgatanga
Wa

TOGO
Sokodé
Lomé

BENIN
Natitingou
Parakou
Abomey
Porto Novo
Cotonou

NIGERIA
Ilorin
Ogbomosho
Ibadan
Abeokuta
LAGOS
Oshogbo
Benin City
Onitsha
Abuja
Kaduna
Minna
Bida
Lokoja
Makurdi
Enugu
Calabar
Port Harcourt

CAMEROON
Douala

Bight of Benin

EQUATORIAL GUINEA
Rey Malabo
Bioko

1 : 15 000 000

100 0 100 200 300 400 500 600 km

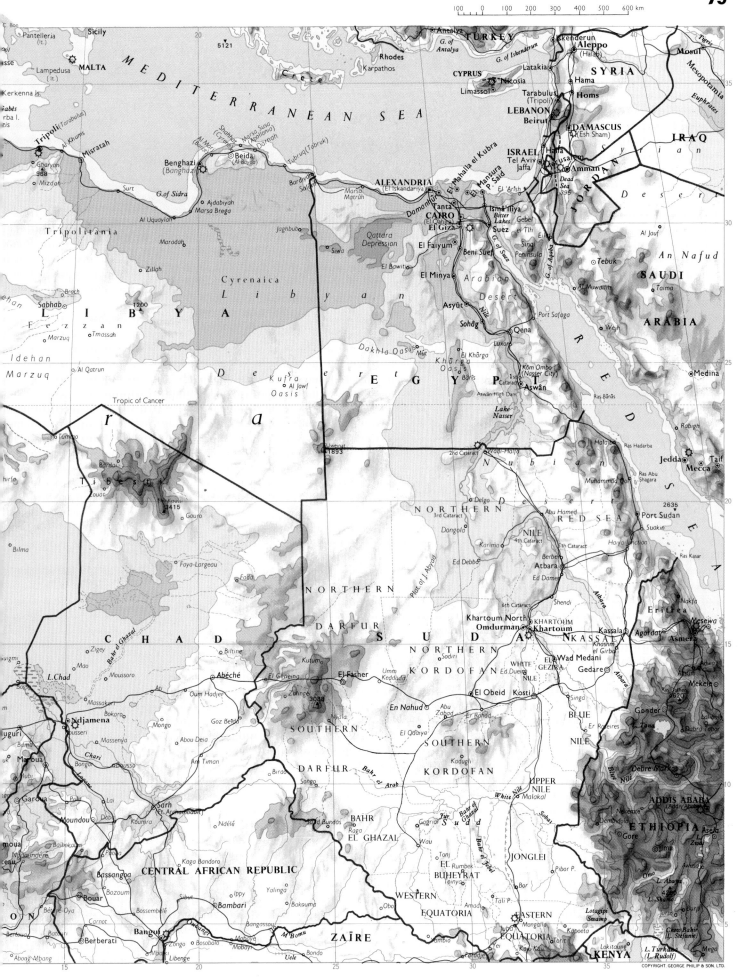

MEDITERRANEAN SEA

MALTA

Sicily

Pantelleria (It.)

Lampedusa (It.)

Kerkenna Is.

5121

Antalya

TURKEY

Rhodes

Karpathos

Crete

G. of Antalya

CYPRUS

Nicosia

Limassol

Latakia

Iskenderun

Aleppo (Halab)

Mosul

G. of Iskenderun

SYRIA

Hama

Homs

Mesopotamia

Euphrates

Tigris

LEBANON

Beirut

Tarabulus (Tripoli)

DAMASCUS (Esh Sham)

IRAQ

ISRAEL

Tel Aviv

Jaffa

Haifa

Jerusalem

Amman

JORDAN

Dead Sea -396

Desert

Tripoli (Tarabulus)

Al Khums

Misratah

Gharyan

968

Mizdah

Surt

G. of Sidra

Ajdabiyah

Marsa Brega

Al Uquaylah

Benghazi (Banghazi)

Beida (Al Bayda)

Shahhat (Cyrene)

Marsa Susa (Apollonia)

Darnah

Al Mirj (Barce)

Tubruq (Tobruk)

Bardiyah

Sallum

Marsa Matruh

El Daba

ALEXANDRIA (El Iskandariya)

El Alamein

Damanhur

Tanta

El Mahalla el Kubra

Mansura

P. Said

El 'Arish

Ismailiya

Bitter Lakes

Gebel

Suez

Gebel el Tih

Sinai Peninsula

G. of Aqaba

Al Jauf

An Nafud

Tebuk

SAUDI

Tripolitania

Cyrenaica

LIBYA

Jaghbub

Qattara Depression

Siwa

El Bawiti

CAIRO (El Qahira)

El Giza

El Faiyum

Beni Suef

El Minya

Arabian

Al Muwailih

Taima

ARABIA

Sabhab

1200

Marzuq

Zillah

Maradah

El Khârga

Asyût

Sohâg

Qena

Luxor

Port Safaga

Wejh

Desert

Nile

Medina

Fezzan

Broch

Tmassah

Idehan

Marzuq

Al Qatrun

Dakhla Oasis

Mût

Kharga Oasis

Bâris

Kôm Ombo (Nasser City)

Aswân

Aswân High Dam

1st Cataract

Ras Bânas

Rabigh

Jedda

Taif

Mecca

Tropic of Cancer

Tümmo

Kufra Oasis

Al Jawf

EGYPT

Lake Nasser

2nd Cataract

Wadi Halfa

Uweinat 1893

Nubian

Halaib

Ras Hadarba

Muhammad Qol

Ras Abu Shagara

RED SEA

Tibesti

Emi Koussi 3415

Bardai

Zouar

Gouro

NORTHERN

3rd Cataract

Dongola

Delgo

Abu Hamed

RED SEA

2635

Port Sudan

Suakin

Ras Kasar

Desert

Bilma

Faya-Largeau

Fada

NORTHERN

NILE

Karima

4th Cataract

5th Cataract

Ed Debba

Berber

Atbara

Ed Damer

Haiya Junction

Eritrea

Nakfa

Mesewa

CHAD

Zigey

Biltine

DARFUR

Kutum

Sodiri

6th Cataract

Shendi

Khartoum North

Omdurman

KHARTOUM

Kassala

Khashm el Girba

Agordat

Asmera

L. Chad

Mao

Moussoro

Abéché

El Geneina

El Fasher

Umm Keddada

NORTHERN KORDOFAN

Ed Dueim

WHITE NILE

El Obeid

Wad Medani

EL GEZIRA

Gedaref

Adwa

Aksum

Mekele

1620

Ndjamena

Bokoro

Ati

Oum Hadjer

Zalingei

3088

Myala

Abu Zabad

En Nahud

Er Rahad

Kosti

Singa

BLUE NILE

Er Roseires

Gonder

L. Tana

Gonder

Maroua

Bongor

Abou Deia

Am Timan

SOUTHERN

DARFUR

Nyala

El Odaiya

SOUTHERN

KORDOFAN

Kadugli

Malakal

UPPER NILE

White Nile

Blue Nile

Debre Markos

ETHIOPIA

ADDIS ABABA (Addis Abeba)

Garoua

Lai

Sarh (Ft. Archambault)

Kounra

Ndélé

Birao

Songo

Bahr el Arab

Bahr el Ghazal

Wau

Gogrial

Raga

Jur

BAHR EL GHAZAL

Tonj

Rumbek

EL BUHEYRAT

Bor

Pibor P.

Sobat

Gore

Nekemte

Jima

L. Abaya

L. Shamo

Asela

CENTRAL AFRICAN REPUBLIC

Bouar

Bozoum

Bossangoa

Sibut

Ippy

Yalinga

Bakouma

Bambari

WESTERN EQUATORIA

Obo

Amadi

Tali P.

Juba

EASTERN EQUATORIA

Mongalla

Kapoeta

Lotagipi Swamp

Chew Bahir (L. Stefanie)

Berberati

Bangui

Mobaye

M'Bomu

Uele

ZAÏRE

Bondo

Faradje

Kajo Kaji

Juba

KENYA

L. Turkana (L. Rudolf)

Mega

Moundou

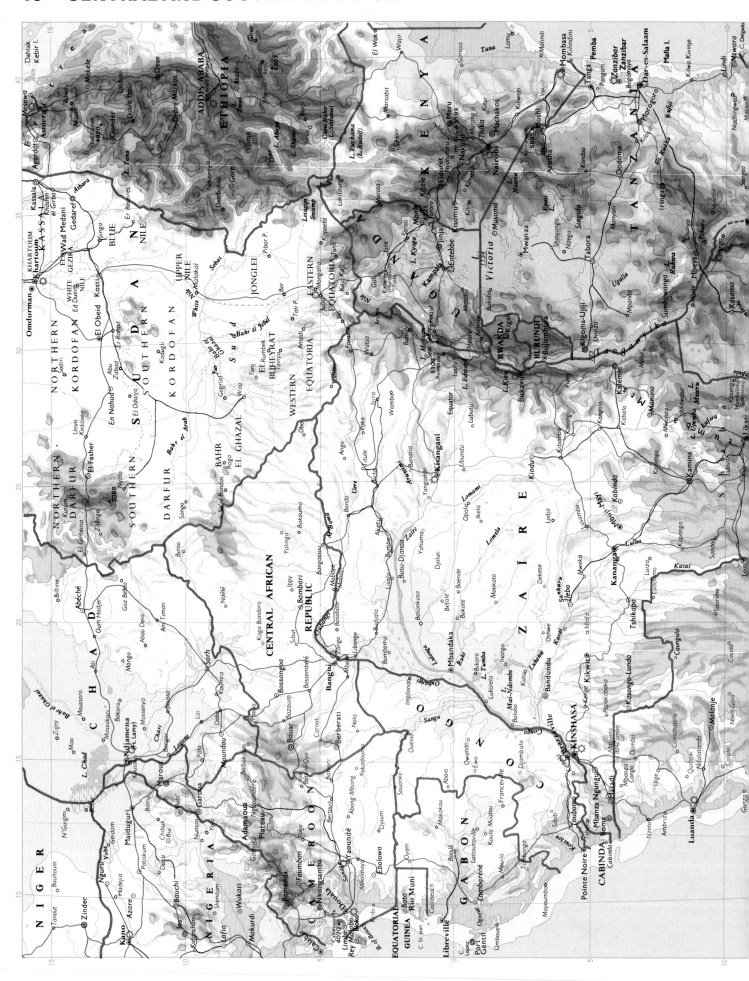

1:15 000 000

100 0 100 200 300 400 500 600 km

INDIAN   OCEAN

MADAGASCAR
On same scale as General Map

COPYRIGHT GEORGE PHILIP & SON LTD

MOZAMBIQUE

INDIAN   OCEAN

Tropic of Capricorn

Is. Glorieuses (Réunion)

5349 ▼

Ile Europa (Réunion)

Bassas da India (Réunion)

Antsiranana

Vohimarina

C. d'Ambre

Nosy Bé
Andoany

C. Masoala

Antalaha

Nossi Bé
Andoany

C. St. Sébastien

2876 △

Sofia

Maroantsetra

Nosy-Varika

Mahajanga

Morovoay

Ambatondrazoka

Toamasina (Tananarive)

Antananarivo (Tananarive)

Morafenobe

Mandritsara

Maevatanana

Ambatolampy

Mandoto

2643 △

Ambositra

Fianarantsoa

2658 △

Maintirano

Miandrivazo

Mahabo

Barren Is.

Belo-Tsiribihina

Morondava

Morombé

C. St. André

C. St. Vincent

Besalampy

Manakara

Farafangana

Vangaindrano

Ranotsara

Ihosy

Ambalavao

Betroka

Faradofay

Toliara

Ampanihy

Betioky

Onilahy

C. Ste. Marie

ZAMBIA

Lichinga

Marrupa

Pemba

Montepuez

Mueda

Nacala

Nampula

Mozambique

Angoche

Quelimane

Beira

Chinde

INDIAN   OCEAN

ZIMBABWE

Harare (Salisbury)

Bulawayo

BOTSWANA

Gaborone

Pretoria

JOHANNESBURG

TRANSVAAL

SWAZI LAND

Maputo (Lourenço Marques)

ORANGE FREE STATE

LESOTHO

Maseru

NATAL

Durban

Pietermaritzburg

CAPE PROVINCE

Port Elizabeth

East London

SOUTH AFRICA

CAPE TOWN

C. of Good Hope

NAMIBIA (SOUTH WEST AFRICA)

Windhoek

Walvis Bay

Lüderitz

Kalahari

Namaqualand

ATLANTIC   OCEAN

Tropic of Capricorn

5283 ▼

ANGOLA

Benguela

Lobito

Namibe

Lubango

East from Greenwich

Projection: Sanson Flamsteed's Sinusoidal

m
6000
4000
3000
2000
1500
1000
400
200
0
200
m

1:35 000 000

400   0   400   800   1200 km

ARCTIC OCEAN

Asia

Wrangel I.

Bering Strait

St. Lawrence I.

Bering Sea

Nunivak I.

Kodiak I.

Alaska Pen.

Gulf of Alaska

Brooks Range

Yukon

Porcupine

Alaska Range

Mt. McKinley 6194

Alexander Archipelago

Queen Charlotte Islands

Queen Charlotte Sound

Vancouver I.

Juan de Fuca Strait

C. Flattery

Mt. Waddington 4042

Beaufort Sea

C. Barrow

C. Bathurst

Banks I.

Victoria I.

Prince of Wales

Melville I.

Viscount Melville Sound

M'Clure Strait

N. Bathurst I.

Magnetic

Axel Heiberg Land

Sverdrup Is.

3800

Parry Is.

Queen Elizabeth Islands

Ellesmere I.

Kane Basin

Thule

Devon I.

Lancaster Sound

Somerset I.

Bylot I.

Gulf of Boothia

Boothia Pen.

Melville Pen.

Foxe Basin

Southampton I.

Foxe Channel

Chesterfield Inlet

Back

Great Bear L.

Arctic Circle

Mackenzie Mts.

Mackenzie

Liard

Great Slave L.

Athabasca

Dubawnt

Reindeer L.

Nelson

Churchill

Peace

Athabasca

Edmonton

Mt. Robson 3954

Yellowhead Pass

Kicking Horse Pass

Calgary

Crowsnest Pass

N. Saskatchewan

S. Saskatchewan

Regina

Winnipeg

Lake Winnipeg

Baffin Bay

Baffin Island

2591

Cumberland Sound

Frobisher Bay

Resolution I.

Chidley

Hudson Strait

Ungava Peninsula

Labrador

1676

Hamilton Inlet

Hudson Bay

James Bay

Eastmain

Belcher Is.

Henrietta Maria

Laurentian Plateau

Greenland

Peary Land 3400

Gunnbjorn's Fjeld 3700

Denmark Strait

Iceland

Hekla 1447

C. Farewell

Julianehåb

Godthåb

Disko I.

Davis Strait

Narcs Str.

Kane Basin

Anticosti I.

Gulf of St. Lawrence

Newfoundland

St. John's

C. Race

Belle Isle Strait

C. Charles

Sable I.

Prince Edward I.

C. Breton I.

Nova Scotia

Saint John

Bay of Fundy

C. Sable

Montreal

Quebec

Ottawa

Toronto

Hamilton

Niagara Falls

L. Ontario

L. Erie

L. Huron

Georgian Bay

L. Michigan

L. Superior

Detroit

Chicago

Minneapolis

Mississippi

Missouri

St. Louis

Kansas City

Ozark Plateau

Cumberland Plateau

Memphis

Atlanta

Alabama

New Orleans

Mississippi Delta

Red

Dallas

Houston

Rio Grande

Llano Estacado

Gila

Colorado

Colorado Plateau

Grand Canyon

Mt. Whitney 4418

Mt. Shasta 4317

San Francisco

Los Angeles

Sacramento

Sierra Nevada

Great Basin

Great Salt Lake

Mt. Elbert 4399

Denver

S. Platte

N. Platte

Arkansas

Pecos

Wasatch Range

Smoky

Rocky Mountains

Western Sierra Madre

Eastern Sierra Madre

Mexican Plateau

Monterrey

Guadalajara

Santiago

Mexico

Puebla

Popocatepetl 5452

Orizaba

Isthmus of Tehuantepec

G. of Tehuantepec

Guadalupe

Acapulco

Balsas

C. Corrientes

C. San Lucas

Gulf of California

Lower California

Revilla Gigedo Is.

6225

Tropic of Cancer

Mendocino Seascarp

C. Blanco

C. Mendocino

Murray Seascarp

PACIFIC OCEAN

Clarion Fracture Zone

Columbia

Portland

Seattle

Mt. Rainier 4392

Coast Range

Cascade Range

Snake

Columbia

Fraser

Vancouver I.

Vancouver

Bonneville

Gulf of Campeche

Yucatán

Yucatán Strait

C. Catoche

Yucatán Peninsula

Yucatán Basin

Gulf of Mexico

Florida

C. Sable

Florida Strait

Havana

Cuba

Bahama Islands

Bermuda

Washington

Philadelphia

New York

Long I.

Nantucket I.

C. Cod

Chesapeake Bay

C. Hatteras

Mt. Washington 1917

Lake Champlain

APPALACHIAN MTS.

Allegheny Mts.

Cumberland

6399

ATLANTIC OCEAN

Haiti

Hispaniola

Milwaukee Deep 9200

Puerto Rico

Greater Antilles

Jamaica

Port-au-Prince

Caribbean Sea

Colombian Basin

Lesser Antilles

Venezuelan Basin

Cayman Trough 7680

Gulf of Honduras

Gracias á Dios

Guatemala

4220

L. Nicaragua

Panama Canal

G. of Panama

G. of Darien

G. of Venezuela

Maracaibo

L. Maracaibo

Sa. Nevada de Sta. Marta 5800

Andes

Sierra de Mérida

Magdalena

Guatemala Trench 6662

Great Plains

Great Lakes

m
4000
2000
1000
400
200
0
0
200
2000
4000
6000
8000
m

Projection: Bonne

120   110   West from Greenwich   100   90   80

COPYRIGHT. GEORGE PHILIP & SON. LTD.

1 : 35 000 000

400   0   400   800   1200 km

Projection : Bonne

West from Greenwich

Washington   Capital Cities

C	CONNECTICUT	N.H.	NEW HAMPSHIRE
D.	DELAWARE	N.J.	NEW JERSEY
D.C.	DISTRICT OF COLUMBIA	R.I.	RHODE ISLAND
M.	MARYLAND	VER.	VERMONT
MASS.	MASSACHUSETTS	SPM	ST. PIERRE ET MIQUELON

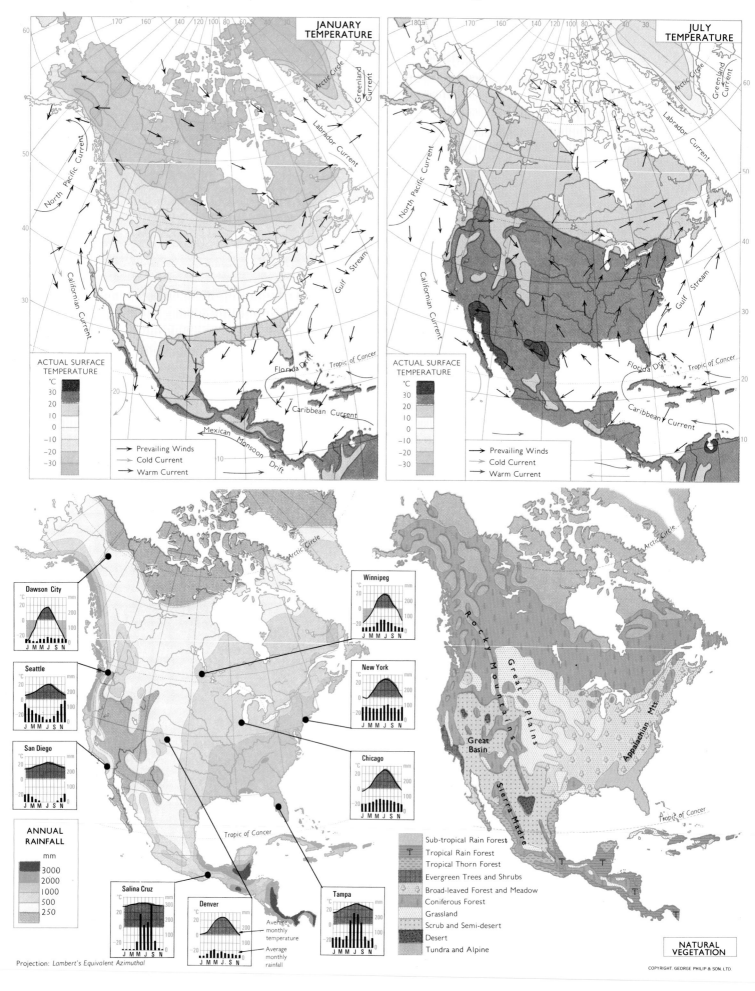

JANUARY TEMPERATURE

ACTUAL SURFACE TEMPERATURE
°C
30
20
10
0
-10
-20
-30

→ Prevailing Winds
→ Cold Current
→ Warm Current

Greenland Current
Labrador Current
North Pacific Current
Californian Current
Gulf Stream
Florida Drift
Caribbean Current
Mexican Monsoon Drift
Tropic of Cancer
Arctic Circle

JULY TEMPERATURE

ACTUAL SURFACE TEMPERATURE
°C
30
20
10
0
-10
-20
-30

→ Prevailing Winds
→ Cold Current
→ Warm Current

Greenland Current
Labrador Current
North Pacific Current
Californian Current
Gulf Stream
Florida Drift
Caribbean Current
Tropic of Cancer
Arctic Circle

Dawson City
Seattle
San Diego
Winnipeg
New York
Chicago
Salina Cruz
Denver
Tampa

ANNUAL RAINFALL
mm
3000
2000
1000
500
250

Average monthly temperature
Average monthly rainfall

Tropic of Cancer
Arctic Circle

Rocky Mountains
Great Plains
Great Basin
Sierra Madre
Appalachian Mts.

Sub-tropical Rain Forest
Tropical Rain Forest
Tropical Thorn Forest
Evergreen Trees and Shrubs
Broad-leaved Forest and Meadow
Coniferous Forest
Grassland
Scrub and Semi-desert
Desert
Tundra and Alpine

NATURAL VEGETATION

Projection: Lambert's Equivalent Azimuthal

1:32 000 000

400   0   400   800   1200 km

170   160   150   140   130   120   110   100   90   80   70   60   50   40   30

Arctic Circle

Prudhoe Bay

Mayo

Mo

Pine Point

Scheffervile

Wabush

Flin Flon

Ti

Edmonton

Vancouver   Mo

Seattle

Shoshone

Winnipeg

Timmins

Co

Mesabi

Ni

Montréal

Toronto   Niagara

Ti

Detroit

New York

Salt Lake City

Chicago

Washington

Bingham

San Francisco   Hg

St. Louis

Mo

Los Angeles

San Diego

Dallas

Hurricane Creek

New Orleans

Houston

San Antonio   Mg

Monterrey

Havana

Sb

Veracruz

Guadalajara

Mexico

Chiapas Tabasco

Tropic of Cancer

LAND USE
- Arable land
- Arable land with grazing
- Market gardening, fruit trees, bushes and orchard land
- Permanent pasture
- Woods and forests
- Woods and forests with grazing land
- Rough grazing
- Non-productive land

LIVESTOCK
- Beef cattle   Sheep
- Dairy cattle

CROPS
▷	Bananas	∨	Sisal
♦	Citrus fruits	•	Soybeans
◌	Coffee	◇	Sugar cane
⬤	Cotton	T	Tobacco
•	Fruit	▼	Vegetables
⌓	Groundnuts	‖	Wheat
⫿	Maize		
•	Olives		Principal fishing areas
○	Rice		

MINERALS
◑	Asbestos	Sb	Antimony
○	Bauxite	Co	Cobalt
▲	Copper	Mg	Magnesium
△	Gold	Hg	Mercury
◆	Iron ore	Mo	Molybdenum
◈	Lead	Ni	Nickel
◈	Lead and Zinc	Ti	Titanium
⬤	Mica		
▽	Phosphate	**POWER**	
▽	Silver	▲	Coalfields
◇	Uranium	▣	Gasfields
△	Zinc	▢	Oilfields
		▦	HEP

LAND USE
(million hectares)

Arable land and permanent crops 271.5

Permanent pasture 346.7

Other land 803.9

Woods and forests 718.3

Total land area 2 140.5 million hectares

West from Greenwich

Projection: Polyconic

COPYRIGHT GEORGE PHILIP & SON LTD

	Population								Land			Agriculture		
	Total	Density	Birth Rate	Death Rate	Life Expectancy	Growth 1965-80	Growth 1980-86	Urban	Area	Arable	Forest	Agricultural Population	Index of Production	Food Intake
	th.	persons per km²	per th. popn.	per th. popn.	yrs.	av. % per annum	av. % per annum	%	th. km²	th. km²	th. km²	% of total popn.	1979-81 = 100	calories per day
Bahamas	236	24	24	5	70		1.9		10	0.1	3.2	7.1		2200
Barbados	253	633	16	8	70		0.3	42	0.4	0.3	0	7.8	92	3020
Canada	25612	2.8	15	7	76	1.3	1.1	75	9221	468	3261	4	124	3432
Costa Rica	2666	52	31	4	74	2.6	2.4	46	51	6.1	16	26	109	2803
Cuba	10246	92	16	6	75	1.5	0.9	72	111	32	27	21	113	3122
Dominican Rep.	6416	134	33	8	66	2.7	2.4	56	48	15	6.3	40	111	2461
El Salvador	4913	234	30	6	61	2.7	1.2	43	21	7.3	1.1	40	100	2148
Guadeloupe	333	185	20	7	71		0.1	46	1.8	0.4	0.7	12	128	2512
Guatemala	8195	76	38	7	61	2.8	2.9	41	108	18	42	54	112	2294
Haiti	5358	191	41	14	54	2	1.8	28	28	9.1	0.5	66	110	1855
Honduras	4514	40	44	12	64	3.2	3.6	40	112	18	37	57	110	2211
Jamaica	2372	216	23	5	73	1.5	1.5	54	11	2.7	1.9	29	108	2585
Martinique	328	298	18	6	71		0.1	71	1.1	0.2	0.3	9.7	133	2673
Mexico	79563	41	34	5	68	3.1	2.2	70	1923	248	452	33	113	3177
Nicaragua	3384	28	44	10	61	3.1	3.4	59	119	13	39	42	91	2425
Panama	2227	29	27	5	72	2.6	2.2	52	76	5.7	40	28	106	2419
Puerto Rico	3502	393	19	7	73		1.6	67	8.9	1.3	1.8	3.2	91	
Trinidad and Tobago	1204	236	29	7	70	1.3	1.5	23	5.1	1.2	2.3	8.5	103	3006
U.S.A.	241596	26	16	9	75	1	1	74	9167	1899	2652	2.7	104	3663
Argentina	31030	11	24	8	70	1.6	1.6	85	2737	361	597	11	109	3221
Bolivia	6547	6	47	18	53	2.5	2.7	44	1084	34	559	43	104	2146
Brazil	138493	16	31	8	65	2.4	2.2	73	8457	758	5629	27	119	2633
Chile	12327	16	22	6	71	1.8	1.7	83	749	55	155	14	116	2602
Colombia	29188	28	31	8	65	2.2	1.9	67	1039	57	491	30	110	2574
Ecuador	9647	35	37	8	66	3.1	2.9	48	277	25	124	34	120	2054
Guyana	971	4.9	28	7	66		2	32	197	5	164	24	91	2359
Paraguay	3807	9.6	36	7	67	2.8	3.2	42	397	22	204	47	116	2796
Peru	20207	16	36	10	60	2.8	2.3	67	1280	37	697	37	112	2171
Surinam	380	2.4	28	7	66		0.1	46	161	0.6	156	18	129	2524
Uruguay	2983	17	18	10	71	0.4	0.4	85	174	14	6.3	14	102	2695
Venezuela	17791	20	29	5	70	3.5	2.9	86	882	38	316	13	110	2583

Population. This is the United Nations' estimate for the mid-year 1986 (thousands)

Population Density. This is the quoted population total divided by the quoted land area (persons per square kilometre).

Birth Rates and Death Rates. These are the registered or United Nations' estimated rates per thousand population.

Life Expectancy. This figure indicates the number of years that a child born today can expect to live if the levels of death of today last throughout its life. The figure is the average of that for men and women. The figure for women is usually higher than that for men (U.K. Male 72, female 78 years).

Population Growth. This shows the average annual percentage change in population for two periods, 1965–1980 and 1980–1986.

Urbanization. This is the percentage of the total population living in urban areas. The definition of urban is that of the individual nation and usually includes quite small towns.

Land Area. This is the total area of the country minus the area covered by major lakes and rivers (thousand square kilometres).

Arable Land and Permanent Crops. This excludes fallow land but includes temporary pasture (thousand square kilometres).

Forest and Woodland. This includes natural and planted woodland and land recently cleared of timber which will be replanted (thousand square kilometres).

Agricultural Population. This is the percentage of the economically active population working in agriculture. It also includes those people working also in forestry, hunting and fishing.

Index of Agricultural Population. The base period for this index is 1979–1981 and it shows the level of production in each country in 1986 in comparison with that of the earlier period. Only edible crops and meat are included.

Food Supply. The figures are the average intake per person in calories per day for the year 1985.

Trade		Education		Health	Energy	Consumer Price Index	G.N.P.		G.D.P.		Loans & Debt		
Imports	Exports	Primary	Secondary					Growth per capita	Part formed by Agric.	Part formed by Indust.			
US$ per capita	US$ per capita	% of age group	% of age group	Popn. per doctor	Consumption in kg of oil equiv. per capita	1980 = 100	US$ per capita	% per year 1965-86	%	%	end 1986 US$ millions	as % of G.N.P.	
13152	10361	99	1200	1200	5400	141	7070	-0.5	4	12			Bahamas
2636	1564	100		1300	1060	152	4630	2.3	6	13			Barbados
3321	3522	100	100	550	8945	156	14120	2.6	3	36	1606	0.4	Canada
430	422	100	41	1460	565	582	1480	1.6	21	29	3582	90	Costa Rica
815	618	100	85	720	1086		1400		4	43			Cuba
223	112	100	50	2410	337	233	710	2.5	17	30	2609	53	Dominican Rep.
184	154	70	24	3220	216	327	820	-0.3	20	21	1463	38	El Salvador
1855	261			1000	860	170	4330	4.7	7	7			Guadaloupe
110	127	76	17	8610	171	163	930	1.4	25	16	2187	30	Guatemala
94	70	78	18	8200	50	141	330	0.6	32	17	585	27	Haiti
189	194	100	36	3120	192	139	740	0.3	27	25	2342	69	Honduras
406	251	100	58	2830	844	246	840	-1.4	6	40	2993	144	Jamaica
1960	318			900	900	179	4270	3.3	6	5			Martinique
151	204	100	55	2000	1235	4626	1860	2.6	9	39	74962	63	Mexico
228	73	100	39	1800	259		790	-2.2	23	33	5343	198	Nicaragua
1327	1083	100	59	980	653	118	2330	2.4	9	18	3439	67	Panama
2930	3055	82		4000	2500	120	2890	0.8	2	41			Puerto Rico
1125	1143	95	76	1360	4778	216	5360	1.6	5	35	1154	24	Trinidad and Tobago
1602	899	100	99	520	7193	138	17480	1.6	2	31	9395	0.4	U.S.A.
152	221	100	70	430	1427	593th	2350	0.2	13	44	38453	46	Argentina
109	86	91	37	2000	255	6.8mill	600	-0.4	24	23	3523	79	Bolivia
112	162	100	35	1600	830	16.5th	1810	4.3	11	39	82523	32	Brazil
279	343	100	69	1930	812	376	1320	-0.2	6	31	15109	101	Chile
132	175	100	50	1710	728	404	1230	2.8	20	25	11437	37	Colombia
188	226	100	55	760	575	462	1160	3.5	14	42	7919	74	Ecuador
639	97	95		9000	700	209	500	-0.2	20	15			Guyana
152	61	100	31	1310	224		1000	3.6	27	26	1752	49	Paraguay
140	124	100	65	1390	478	11.2th	1090	0.1	11	38	11049	45	Peru
1274	686	100		1700	3160	166	2580	3.4	9	21			Surinam
275	365	100	70	540	742	223	1900	1.4	12	33	2759	46	Uruguay
538	564	100	45	990	2502	124	2920	0.4	9	37	24485	51	Venezuela

Antigua & Barbuda, Land 0.4/Popn. 81; Belize 23/171; Bermuda 0.05/56; Br. Virgin Is. 0.2/13; Cayman Is. 0.3/22; Dominica 0.8/77; Greenland 342/54; Grenada 0.3/113; Montserrat 0.1/12; Netherlands Antilles 1/190; St. Christopher-Nevis 0.4/47; St. Lucia 0.6/132; St. Pierre & M. 0.2/6; St. Vincent 0.3/105; Turks & Caicos Is. 0.4/8; U.S. Virgin Is. 0.3/103. Falkland Is. 12/2; Fr. Guiana 89/84.

Trade. The trade figures are for the year 1986. The total trade figures have been divided by the population and are a measure of the country's external trade (U.S. $ per capita).

Education. The ages of primary school are taken to be 6–11 years and secondary school 12–17 years. The percentage of total school age group in this type of education is shown.

Energy. All forms of energy have been converted to their equivalent in oil. Firewood and other traditional forms used in developing countries are not included and so the energy consumption in those countries is understated (kilograms of oil equivalent per capita).

Consumer Price Index. The base year is 1980 which is 100 and the level of consumer prices in 1986 or 1987 are shown in relation to the base year. It is a measure of inflation.

G.N.P. (Gross National Product) This figure is an estimate of the average production per person measured in U.S. dollars and for 1986. The G.N.P. measures the value of goods and services produced in a country, plus the balance, positive or negative, of income from abroad, for example investments, interest on capital, money returned from foreign labour, etc. The rate of change is the average annual percentage change during the period 1965–1986 in the G.N.P. The G.D.P. (Gross Domestic Product) is the G.N.P. minus the foreign balances. The adjoining two columns show the percentage contribution to the G.D.P. made by the agricultural and mining and manufacturing sectors.

Loans and Debts. This figure in millions of U.S. dollars shows the external public debt at the end of 1986. This is then shown as a percentage of the annual G.N.P. The figures in red show official development assistance made by the developed countries and also as a percentage of the donor country's G.N.P.

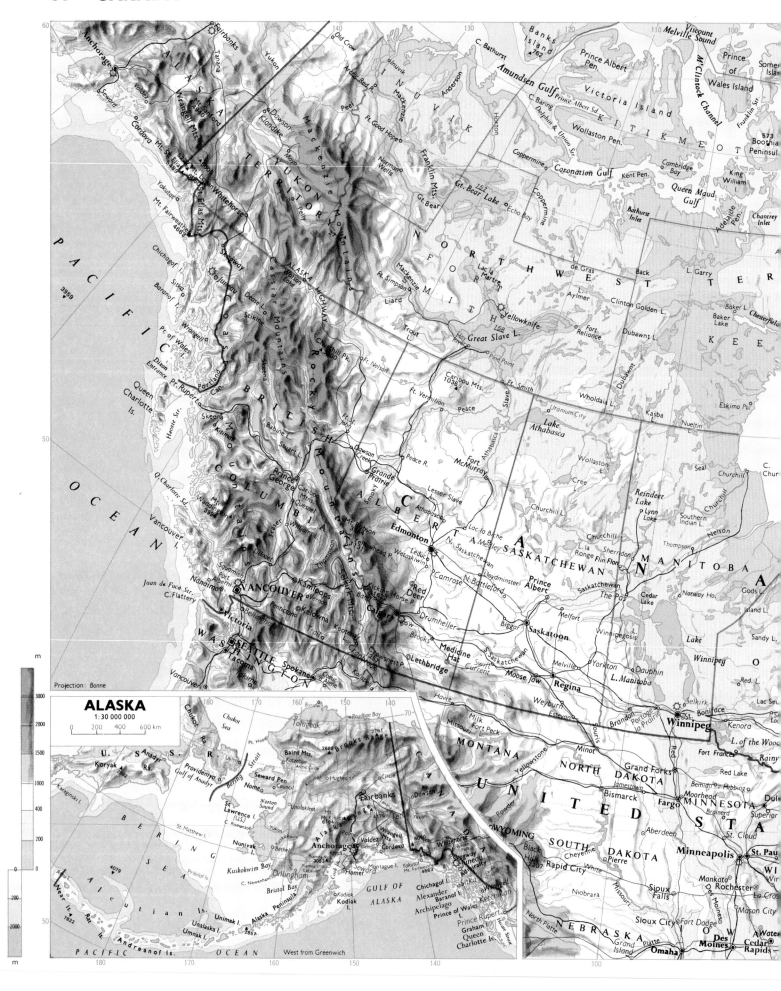

ALASKA
1:30 000 000
0   200   400   600 km

Projection: Bonne

West from Greenwich

1:15 000 000

100   0   100   200   300   400   500   600 km

Devon Island
Lancaster Sound
2134
Bylot I.
Pond Inlet
2136
Svartenhuk Peninsula

Baffin Bay

Brodeur Peninsula
C. Hewett
Home B.
Disko I.
C. Dyer

G R E E N L A N D

Angmagssalik

hia

B a f f i n

2591
Cumberland Peninsula
C. Mercy
Cumberland Sd.

Davis Strait

King Frederick VI Coast

Sondre Stromfjord
Godthåb

Frederikshaab
Julianehaab Sydproven

A T L A N T I C

Committee B.
Melville Peninsula
Foxe
Prince Charles I.
Basin
Nettilling L.
Amadjuak L.
Frobisher Bay

Foxe Channel
Wager B.
C. Dorchester
Foxe Penin.
Frobisher Bay
Resolution I.

C. Farewell

Southampton I.
Roes Welcome Sd.
Coats I.
Mansel I.
Hudson Strait
C. Chidley

Ivujivik
Maricourt (Wakeham Bay)
Koartac
Akpatok I.
Ungava Bay

3809

Hudson
Ottawa Is.
257

Peninsula
Payne
Payne L.
Bellin (Payne Bay)
Port Nouveau-Quebec (George R.)

Nain

N E W

Bay

Kuujjuaq
Leaf
Koksoak
George
L. Minto
Kaniapiskau

C. Harrison
Indian Harbour
Hopedale

F O U

King George Is.

Clearwater L.
Lac Bienville

Schefferville
Petitsikapau L.

Michikamau
Rigolet   Melville
Cartwright
Happy Valley Goose Bay
Battle Harb.

N D L A

Belcher Is.
C. Henrietta Maria

A   Poste de la Baleine (Great Whale River)

L A B R A D O R

Churchill

Str. of Belle Isle

Grand Gander
Falls
Bonavista

N D

Severn
Winisk
D
Ft. George

1128
Labrador City
Gagnon

Q U E B E C

Natashquan

NEWFOUNDLAND
Corner B.
Grand Falls
Carbonear
St. John's
C. Race

Big Trout L.
James Bay
Akimiski I.

Eastmain
Manicouagan

Mingan
Anticosti
Sept Iles
Port Cartier

Corner Brook
Channel Port aux Basques
Ray

Attawapiskat
T A R I O
Albany
St. Joseph
Fort Rupert (Rupert House)
Rupert
Mistassini L.
Chibougamau

Gulf of St. Lawrence
Cabot Str.
Cape Breton I.
ST. PIERRE & MIQUELON (Fr.)
Glace Bay

Missinaibi
Moosonee
Harricanaw
Gouin Reservoir

Baie Comeau
R. St. Lawrence
Matane
Gaspé Pen.
Gaspé
C. Gaspé

Geraldton
Hearst
Oba
L. Abitibi
Val d'Or
La Tuque
Saguenay
Rimouski
Campbellton
Bathurst
Chatham

Glace Bay
Sydney
New Glasgow

Nipigon
Mattagami
Timmins
Rouyn
Kirkland Lake
Jonquière
Chicoutimi
Shawinigan
Trois Rivieres
Quebec
Edmundston
Rivière du Loup
NEW BRUNSWICK
Moncton
Amherst
Truro
Sable I. (Nova Scotia)

Thunder Bay
Lake Superior
Sault Ste. Marie
Sudbury
North Bay
Cabonga Reservoir
MONTREAL
St. Hyacinthe
Sherbrooke
Thetford Mines
Fredericton
Saint John
N O V A   S C O T I A
Dartmouth
Halifax
Bridgewater
C. Sable

Marquette
Sault Ste. Marie
Espanola
Georgian Bay
North Ottawa
Hull
Ottawa
Cornwall
M A I N E
Bangor
B. of Fundy
Kentville
Yarmouth

Lake Huron
Orillia
Peterboro
Kingston
Burlington
Champlain
Lewiston
Portland
Concord   Manchester
NEW HAMPSHIRE

Wausau Green Bay
Appleton
Traverse City
Owen Sound
Oshawa
Ontario
TORONTO
Rochester
Syracuse
Albany
Springfield
MASS.   BOSTON
C. Cod
Providence

Saginaw
Kitchener
Niagara Falls
Hamilton
NEW YORK
Binghamton
Scranton
CONN.   ODE I.
New Haven

MILWAUKEE
London
Sarnia
BUFFALO
Y O R K
New York

Grand Rapids
DETROIT
Windsor
Erie
PENNSYLVANIA
Newark
NEW JERSEY

CHICAGO
Gary
INDIANA
OHIO
Toledo
CLEVELAND
Akron
Allentown

West from Greenwich   60
COPYRIGHT. GEORGE PHILIP & SON. LTD.

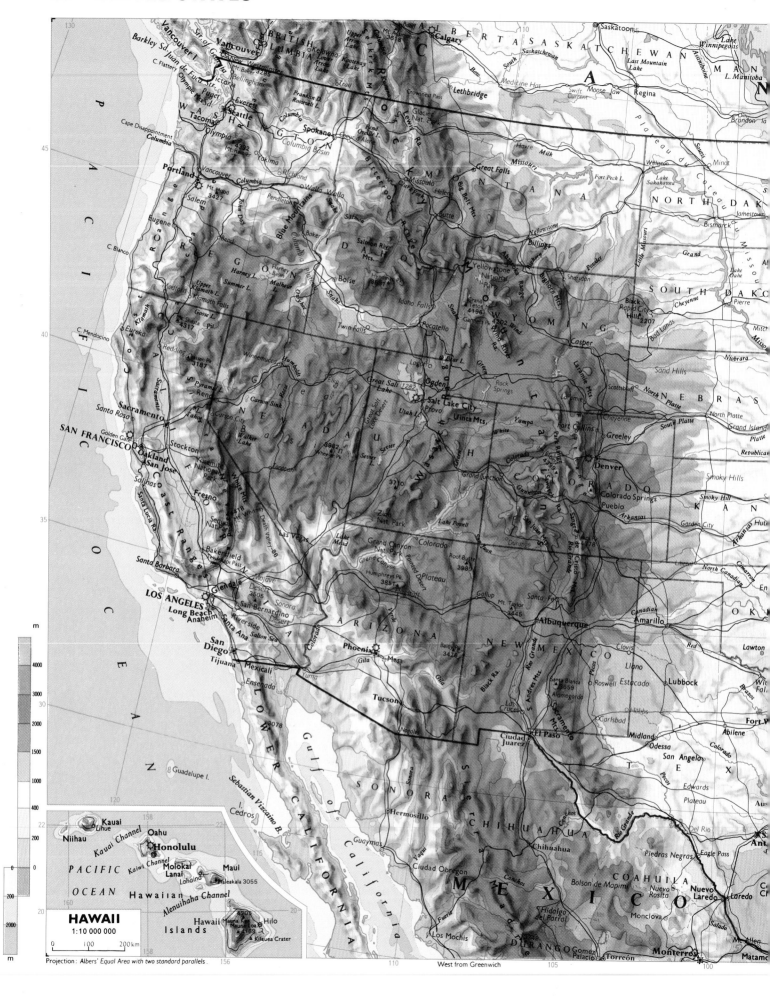

HAWAII
1:10 000 000

0   100   200 km

PACIFIC
OCEAN   Hawaiian

Islands

Kauai
Niihau   Lihue
Oahu
Honolulu
Molokai
Lanai   Maui
Lahaina
Haleakala 3055
Mauna Loa
4169   Hilo
4205
Kilauea Crater

Projection : Albers' Equal Area with two standard parallels

West from Greenwich

100 0 100 200 300 400 500 km

C A N A D A

Lake Winnipeg
Winnipeg
Lake of the Woods
Kenora
Thunder Bay
I. Royale
Lake Superior
183 above S.L.
Duluth
MINNESOTA
Bemidji
Brainerd
St. Cloud
Minneapolis St. Paul
WISCONSIN
Madison
Milwaukee
Green Bay
Appleton
Eau Claire
La Crosse
Rochester
IOWA
Des Moines
Council Bluffs
Waterloo
Cedar Rapids
Dubuque
Iowa City
Davenport
Rockford
Aurora
CHICAGO
Evanston
Kenosha
Racine
ILLINOIS
Peoria
Springfield
Decatur
Champaign
Bloomington
St. Louis
MISSOURI
Kansas City
St. Joseph
Columbia
Jefferson City
Springfield
Joplin
Tulsa
OKLAHOMA CITY
Fort Smith
ARKANSAS
Little Rock
Pine Bluff
Fayetteville
Boston Mts.
Ouachita Mts.
TEXAS
Dallas
Tyler
Longview
Texarkana
Sherman
Shreveport
Monroe
LOUISIANA
Alexandria
Lake Charles
Beaumont
Port Arthur
Houston
Pasadena
Galveston
Baton Rouge
Lafayette
New Orleans
Houma
Biloxi
Mobile
Pensacola
MISSISSIPPI
Jackson
Vicksburg
Hattiesburg
Meridian
ALABAMA
Tuscaloosa
Birmingham
Montgomery
Columbus
GEORGIA
Atlanta
Macon
Columbus
Albany
Savannah
Jacksonville
Tallahassee
Gainesville
Daytona Beach
Orlando
FLORIDA
Tampa
St. Petersburg
Sarasota
Lakeland
Ft. Myers
L. Okeechobee
West Palm Beach
Fort Lauderdale
Miami
Everglades
Key West
Florida Keys
Florida Bay
C. Sable

GULF OF MEXICO

Delta of the Mississippi

BAHAMAS
Grand Bahama I.
Freeport
Gt. Abaco
Nassau
New Providence
Eleuthera I.
Exuma Sound
Cat I.
Andros
Long I.

ATLANTIC OCEAN

TENNESSEE
Memphis
Nashville
Chattanooga
Knoxville 2037
Jonesboro
Florence
Huntsville
Rome
KENTUCKY
Louisville
Lexington
Owensboro
Bowling Green
Clarksville
Paducah
Cape Girardeau
Evansville
INDIANA
Indianapolis
Terre Haute
Lafayette
Muncie
Ft. Wayne
South Bend
Gary
Hammond
Kalamazoo
Grand Rapids
MICHIGAN
Lansing
Flint
Saginaw
Bay City
Cadillac
Ann Arbor
DETROIT
Windsor
Toledo
OHIO
Columbus
Dayton
Cincinnati
Covington
Lima
Mansfield
Akron
Cleveland
Euclid
Lorain
Canton
Youngstown
WEST VIRGINIA
Charleston
Huntington
Parkersburg
Wheeling
PENNSYLVANIA
Pittsburgh
Altoona
Harrisburg
Williamsport
Scranton
Wilkes Barre
Allentown
Reading
PHILADELPHIA
Camden
Trenton
NEW JERSEY
NEW YORK
Buffalo
Niagara Falls
Rochester
Syracuse
Utica
Binghamton
Albany
Troy
Schenectady
Catskill Mts.
Adirondack Mts.
Watertown
Jamestown
NEW YORK
Newark
Jersey City
Long I.
Atlantic City
Delaware Bay
C. May
MARYLAND
Baltimore
Washington D.C.
Annapolis
Wilmington
VIRGINIA
Richmond
Norfolk
Newport News
Portsmouth
Lynchburg
Roanoke
Danville
Charlottesville
Chesapeake Bay
C. Charles
Albemarle Sd.
C. Hatteras
Pamlico
NORTH CAROLINA
Raleigh
Durham
Greensboro
Winston Salem
Charlotte
Asheville
Fayetteville
Wilmington
C. Fear
Rocky Mount
Neuse
SOUTH CAROLINA
Columbia
Charleston
Greenville
Anderson
Florence
Santee
Augusta

CONNECTICUT
New Haven
Hartford
Bridgeport
Providence
RHODE ISLAND
MASSACHUSETTS
Boston
Worcester
Springfield
Cambridge
Lowell
Fall River
Martha's Vineyard
C. Cod
VERMONT
NEW HAMPSHIRE
Concord
Manchester
Portland
MAINE
Bangor
Augusta
Lewiston
White Mts. 1917
Burlington
L. Champlain
MONTREAL
Ottawa
Hull
Quebec
Trois-Rivières
Sherbrooke
NEW BRUNSWICK
Edmundston
Presque Isle
Moosehead L.
St. Lawrence
Rimouski
Matane
Chicoutimi
St. John
Gull L.
Gouin Res.
La Tuque
Baskatong Res.
Cabonga Res.
Algonquin Park
North Bay
Sudbury
L. Nipissing
Sault Ste. Marie
Marquette
Escanaba
Menominee
Manitoulin
Georgian Bay
Owen Sound
Barrie Simcoe
TORONTO
Hamilton
Kitchener
London
Sarnia
Lake Huron 177 above S.L.
Lake Erie
Lake Ontario
Kingston
Peterborough
Oshawa
Timmins
Hearst
Longlac
Nipigon
Wawa
Chapleau
Kapuskasing
Cochrane
Moose
Abitibi Lake
Rouyn
Kenogami
Matagami
Missinaibi
Albany
Sioux Lookout
Lake Nipigon
Lake Seul

COPYRIGHT. GEORGE PHILIP & SON. LTD.

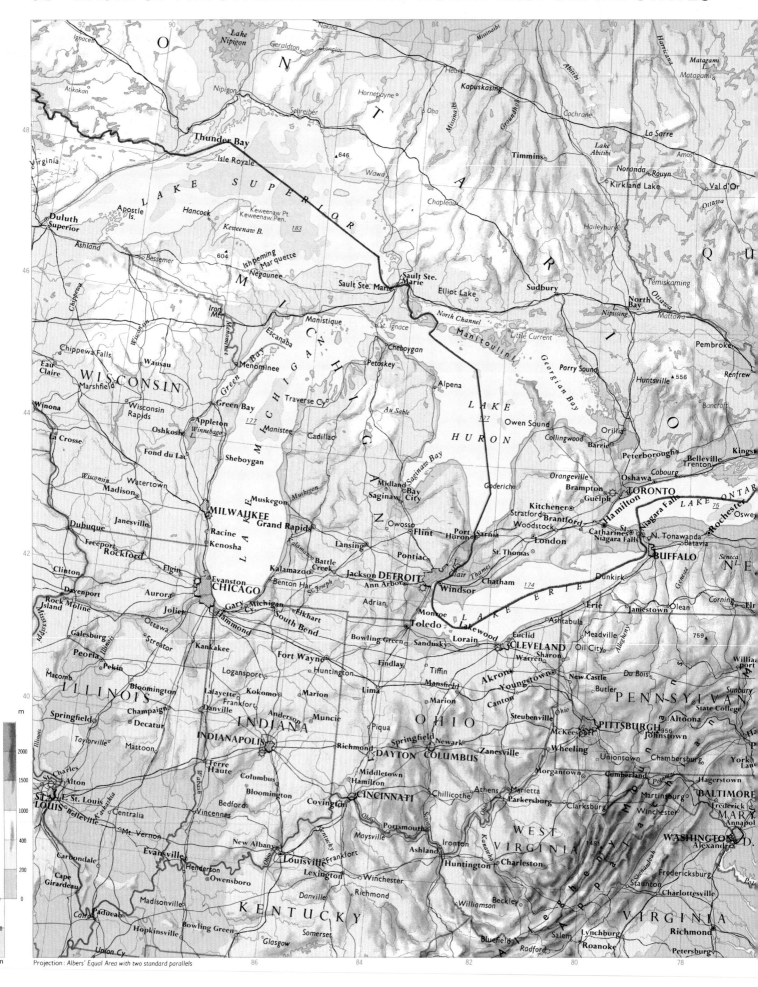

Projection: Albers' Equal Area with two standard parallels

1 : 6 000 000

50 0 50 100 150 200 250 km

Chibougamau
556 ▲ *Chibougamau L.*
Pipmuacan L.
Port Cartier
West Pt. *Anticosti I.*
Jupiter
Heath Pt.
▼ 572

Dolbeau
Pentecôte
Cap Chat
1310 *Gaspé*
Shickshock Mts.
C. Gaspé
GULF OF
ST. LAWRENCE

Gouin Res.
St. Félicien
Lac St-Jean
Chicoutimi
Roberval
Jonquière
Saguenay
Rimouski
Matane
Gaspé Peninsula

Magdalen Is.
(Quebec)
C. North

La Tuque
Baie St. Paul
Rivière du Loup
Campbellton
Dalhousie
Chaleur Bay
Bathurst
NEW
819
Tignish
PRINCE EDWARD
ISLAND
532
Cape Breton Island
Glace Bay
Sydney

B E C
Montmagny
Quebec
Levis
Edmundston
Grand Falls
BRUNSWICK
Newcastle
Miramichi B.
North Pt.
Chatham
Summerside
Charlottetown
Northumberland Str.
East Pt.
Bras d'Or L.

Grand'Mère
Shawinigan
Trois Rivières
Victoriaville
Thetford Mines
Presque Isle
Chipman
Moncton
Springhill
Stellarton
New Glasgow
Chedabucto B.
Canso

960 ▲
Joliette
Sorel
Drummondville
St. Jérôme
St. Hyacinthe
Mégantic
Mt. Katahdin
1606
Houlton
Grand L.
Fredericton
Sussex
Saint John
Truro
Dartmouth
N O V A   S C O T I A

Ottawa
MONTREAL
Sherbrooke
St. Jean
Magog
Moosehead L.
St. Stephen
St. John
Digby
L. Rossignol
Bridgewater
Halifax

Cornwall
Ogdensburg
Newport
MAINE
Bangor
Penobscot
Grand Manan I.
Bay of Fundy
Kentville

Plattsburg
L. Champlain
Burlington
Berlin
Waterville
Mt. Desert I.
Yarmouth
Shelburne
C. Sable

Watertown
Montpelier
Barre
Augusta
1917
Auburn Lewiston
Rockland

1629
L. George
Rutland
HAMPSHIRE
Laconia
Portland
Biddeford

Adirondack Mts.
Glen Falls
Concord
Rochester
Dover
Portsmouth

oneida L.
Rome
Utica
Schenectady
Troy
Keene Manchester
Bennington Fitchburg
Nashua
Lawrence
Lowell
Salem
Massachusetts Bay

YORK
Albany
Pittsfield
MASS.
Worcester
Newton
BOSTON
Quincy
C. Cod

Binghamton Mts.
1281
Catskill
Springfield
Holyoke
Cambridge
Brockton
Cape Cod B.

Hartford
Woonsocket
Pawtucket
Providence
Fall River
New Bedford

Poughkeepsie
Newburgh
New Britain
Waterbury
Meriden
R.I.
Newport
Nantucket Sd.

Middletown
Wilkes Barre
Hazleton
Bridgeport
New Haven
New London
Block I.
Martha's Vineyard
Nantucket I.

Paterson
Yonkers
Long Island

Bethlehem
Newark
Jersey City
NEW YORK
Allentown
Elizabeth
Reading
Edison

ELPHIA
Trenton
Camden
NEW JERSEY

Wilmington
Vineland
Atlantic City
DELAWARE
Dover
Cape May

A T L A N T I C

O C E A N

Cape Charles

PANAMA CANAL
1:1 000 000
0   10   20km

JAMAICA
1:5 000 000
0   50 km

TRINIDAD AND TOBAGO
1:5 000 000
0   50 km

LEEWARD ISLANDS
1:5 000 000
0   50 km

WINDWARD ISLANDS
1:5 000 000
0   50 km

Projection: Bonne

1:15 000 000

100 0 100 200 300 400 500 600 km

ATLANTIC OCEAN

Bermuda
Hamilton

Atlanta
Macon
lombus Charleston
Savannah
Albany
llahassee
Jacksonville
Daytona Beach
Orlando C. Canaveral
Tampa
etersburg
West Palm Beach
L. Okeechobee Grand
Bahama
I. Freeport Gt. Abaco I.
Miami Fort
Lauderdale New Providence I.
C. Sable Eleuthera I.
Key West Nassau Cat I. S. Salvador
Andros I. BAHAMAS
Havana Matanzas Sagua la Grande Long I. Tropic of Cancer
Rio Sta. Clara Mayaguana
C Cardenas Caicos I. (Br.)
Cienfuegos U Camagüey Acklins
I. de Juventud Sancti Spiritus B Gt. Inagua Turks Is.(Br.)
Ciego de Avila Holguin I.
Manzanillo A 2000 Guantánamo Cap Haitien Santiago PUERTO RICO (U.S.A.)
G Bayamo San Francisco St. Thomas (U.S.A.)
Grand Cayman Santiago Windward Passage de Macoris St. Juan Charlotte Amalie Anguilla (Fr. & Neth.)
(Br.) R de Cuba Gonaives DOMINICAN La Romana Virgin Is. (Br.) St. Martin
E 1375 REP. Caguas St. Croix ST. CHRISTOPHER-NEVIS
Montego Bay A 2280 Ponce (U.S.A.) (St. Kitts)
JAMAICA T Port au Prince Bani Barahona Santo Domingo Mayagüez 1338 ANTIGUA &
Kingston E H Les Cayes Hispaniola St. John's BARBUDA
R A N Montserrat Guadeloupe (Fr.)
I ANTILLES Leeward Pointe à Pitre
Caratasca Lagoon T Islands DOMINICA
oco I LESSER
C. Gracias á Dios L Martinique (Fr.)
E Fort de France
S ANTILLES ST. LUCIA
CARIBBEAN SEA Windward BARBADOS
Providencia ST. VINCENT Bridgetown
(Col.) Pta. Gallinas Aruba (Neth.) &
Bluefields San Andrés Venezuela Antilles (Neth.) THE GRENADINES Islands GRENADA
agua (Col.) Pen. de la Curaçao (Neth.) La Blanquilla
Juan Guajira Gulf of Willemstad (Ven.)
Santa Marta Pen de Bonaire (Neth.) Tobago
Barranquilla Paraguaná Margarita Port of Spain
pa Coast Punta Coro La Tortuga Carúpano TRINIDAD & TOBAGO
Mosquito 5800 Fijo (Ven.) Cumaná G. of San Fernando
Limón Sierra Nevada Maracaibo Cumaná Paria Delta of the
Cartagena de Santa Marta L. de Caracas Barcelona 2596 Maturin Orinoco
RICA Sincelejo Cabimas Maracay
Colón G. of Maracaibo Barquisimeto Valencia El Tigre
Vol Barú Darién Valera Orinoco Ciudad
3374 PANAMA Cauca Cord. de Mérida San Fernando Guayana
Panama Cúcuta 5007 de Apure Ciudad El Callao
David 4760 San Cristóbal Apure Bolívar Georgetown
Azuero G. of Barrancabermeja Arauca Arauca Caura Paragua 2560 New
Coiba Pen. Panama Medellín VENEZUELA Roraima Amsterdam
Atrato Bucaramanga Meta 2810
Quibdó 3960 2285 Pto. Aydcucho Sierra Pacaraima Cuyuni GUYANA
Manizales COLOMBIA Caura SURINAM
Pereira Bogotá Sa. Acurima 1280 Essequibo
Tolima 5215 Girardot Corentine
Buenaventura Armenia Guaviare Casiquiare
Cali 5750 Popayán Magdalena BRAZIL
4646

West from Greenwich 80 75 70 65 COPYRIGHT. GEORGE PHILIP & SON. LTD

1:30 000 000

200   0   200   400   600   800 1000 km

Sa. Nevada de Santa Marta
Barranquilla
▲5800
Maracaibo
G. of
Darien
Margarita
Tobago I.
Caracas
Trinidad
5994 ▼

Panama
Canal
L. Maracaibo
Cord. de Mérida
ATLANTIC

Orinoco
Georgetown

Medellín
Bogotá
L. Meta
Llanos
Guiana
Highlands
2810
▲Roraima
Sierra Pacaraima
OCEAN

Cali
Guaviare
Casiquiare
Essequibo
Courantyne
Serra de
Tumucumaque
C. Orange

C. de San Francisco
Guaviare
Branco
Negro
Equator

Quito
Cotopaxi
▲5897
Caquetá
Putumayo
Japurá
Amazon
Marajó I.
Pará
Belém

Chimborazo
6267▲
Napo
Amazon
Manaus
Fortaleza
C.
São Roque

Guayaquil
Marañón
Juruá
Purus
Madeira
Tapajós
Tocantins
Paraiba

G. of Guayaquil
Ucayali
Roosevelt
Aripuaná
Teles Pires
Araguaia
Plateau of
Borborema

Pta. Pariñas
Pta. Aguja
Madre de Dios
Guaporé
Arinos
São Francisco
Recife

Lobos Is.
Huascarán
6768
Mamoré
Plateau of
Mato Grosso
C.
Branco

Lima
L.
Titicaca
Ancohuma & Illampu
▲6550
La Paz
Brasília
Salvador

Chincha Is.
Bolivian Plateau
L. Poopó
Belo
Horizonte
2890
Pico da
Bandeira
Abrolhos Bank

Tropic of Capricorn
Atacama Desert
8050
Gran Chaco
Pilcomayo
Paraguay
Paraná
São Paulo
Serra da Mantiqueira
C. Frio

S. Félix
S. Ambrosio
Ojos del Salado
6863
Tucumán
Salado
Asunción
Iguaçu Falls
Rio de Janeiro

Arch. de Juan Fernández
Salinas
Grandes
Entre Rios
Uruguay
Pôrto Alegre

Córdoba
L. Mar
Chiquita
Paraná
Serra do Mar
Lagoa dos Patos

Aconcagua
▲6960
Uspallata Pass
Sierra de Córdoba
Rosario

Valparaíso
Santiago
Buenos Aires
Montevideo
Río de la Plata

Chiloé I.
Colorado
Negro
Bahía Blanca
Pta. Mogotes
SOUTH

G. of San Matias
Valdés Peninsula
ATLANTIC

Chonos
Archipelago
G. of San Jorge
Argentine
Basin
OCEAN

Taitao
Peninsula
▲4058
S. Valentin

Wellington I.
6212 ▼

Madre de Dios I.
Falkland Islands

Magellan's Strait
West Falkland
East Falkland

Santa Inés I.
Cockburn Chan.
Tierra del Fuego
Staten I.

Beagle
Chan.
C. Horn
60   West from Greenwich

Projection: Lambert's Equivalent Azimuthal
COPYRIGHT GEORGE PHILIP & SON. LTD

m
6000
4000
3000
2000
1000
400
200
0
0
200
2000
4000
6000
8000
m

1:30 000 000

200 0 200 400 600 800 1000 km

NORTH
ATLANTIC
OCEAN

COSTA
RICA
San José
PANAMA
Colón
Panamá
G. of
Darién
G. of
Panama

Barranquilla
Cartagena
Ciénaga
Maracaibo
Cabimas
Barquisimeto
Cúcuta
San
Cristóbal
Monteria
Medellín
Manizales
Pereira
Buenaventura
Cali
Popayán
Pasto
Bucaramanga
Bogotá
Ibagué

Valencia
Caracas
Cumaná
Maturín
Orinoco
Ciudad Guayana
Ciudad Bolivar

TRINIDAD AND
TOBAGO
Port of Spain

VENEZUELA

Georgetown
Paramaribo
Cayenne
GUYANA
SURINAM
FRENCH
GUIANA
C. Orange

COLOMBIA

Orinoco
Branco

ECUADOR
Quito
Guayaquil
Cuenca
G. de Guayaquil

Putumayo
Japurá
Negro
Iquitos
Benjamim
Constant
Marañón
Piura
Chiclayo
Trujillo
Chimbote

Juruá
Purus

Amazon
Manaus
Santarem
Macapá
Ilha de
Marajó
Belém
(Pará)

Equator
São Luís
Bacabal
Teresina
Fortaleza (Ceara)
C. de São Roque
Natal
João Pessoa
(Paraiba)
Recife
(Pernambuco)
Maceió
Aracaju

PERU
Callao
Lima
Ica
Cuzco
Huancayo

Madeira
Madre de Dios
Tapajós
Xingu
Tocantins
Araguaia
Parnaíba
Juazeiro do
Norte
São Francisco

Rio Branca
Pôrto Velho
Guaporé

B R A Z I L

Titicaca
La Paz
Arequipa
BOLIVIA
Oruro
Cochabamba
Sucre
Santa Cruz
Mamoré
Cuiabá
Corumbá

Brasília
Goiânia
Montes Claros
Salvador
(Bahía)

Arica
Iquique
Antofagasta

Campo Grande

Gov. Valadares
Uberaba
Belo
Horizonte
Ribeirão
Prêto
Bauru
Londrina
Juiz de Fora
Campos
Vitória

Tropic of Capricorn
San Felix
(Chile)
San Ambrosio
(Chile)

PARAGUAY
Pilcomayo
Asunción
Paraná
Ponta Grossa
SÃO
PAULO
Campinas
Santos
Niterói
RIO DE JANEIRO

Salta
San Miguel
de Tucumán
Resistencia
Posadas
Corrientes
Uruguay
Curitiba
Florianópolis

Santiago
del Estero
Salado
Paraná

SOUTH

PACIFIC OCEAN

Juan Fernández
(Chile)
Valparaíso
Viña del Mar
Santiago
Talcahuano
Concepción

CHILE

ARGENTINA
Córdoba
San Juan
Mendoza
Mercedes
Santa Fe
Rosario
Paraná
URUGUAY

Pôrto
Alegre
Lagoa dos Patos
Pelotas

ATLANTIC
OCEAN

Talca
Valdivia
Puerto Montt

BUENOS
AIRES
La
Plata
Rio de la Plata
Montevideo
Colorado
Bahía Blanca
Mar del Plata
Negro
Viedma

Chiloé
Chonos
Arch.
San Carlos
de Bariloche
Chubut
Trelew
Península
Valdés

Golfo
San Jorge
Comodoro Rivadavia

I. Wellington

FALKLAND ISLANDS
(ISLAS MALVINAS)
(U.K.)
Stanley

Río Gallegos
Punta
Arenas
Strait of Magellan
Tierra
del
Fuego
Cape Horn

Projection: Lambert's Equivalent Azimuthal

West from Greenwich

BUENOS AIRES Capital Cities

COPYRIGHT. GEORGE PHILIP & SON. LTD.

1:70 000 000

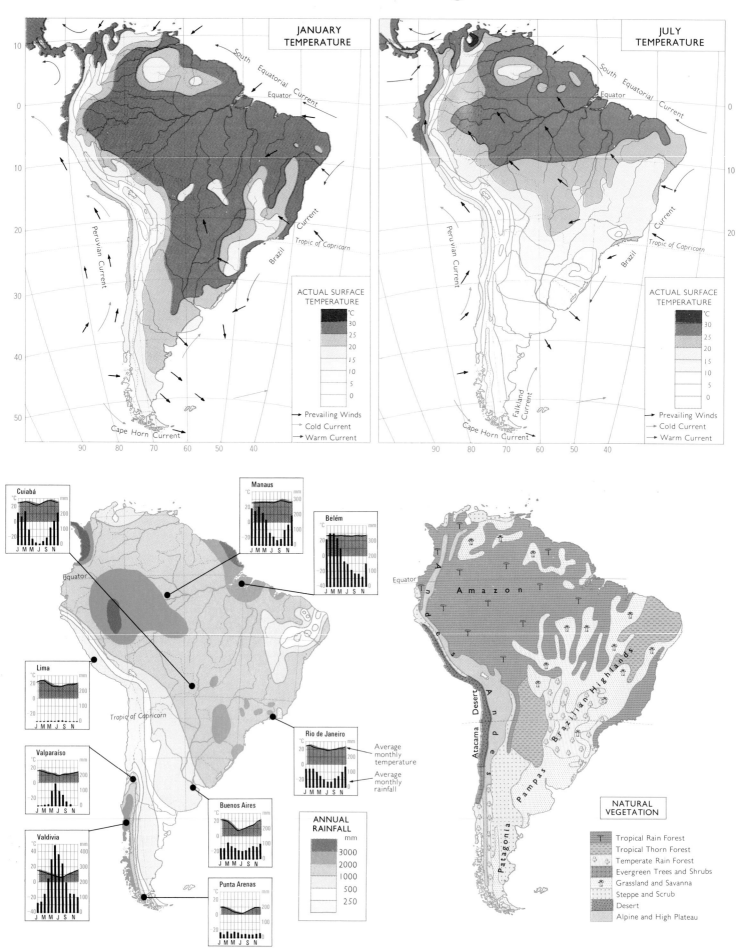

JANUARY TEMPERATURE

JULY TEMPERATURE

South Equatorial Current

Equator

South Equatorial Current

Equator

Peruvian Current

Tropic of Capricorn

Brazil Current

Peruvian Current

Tropic of Capricorn

Brazil Current

Falkland Current

Cape Horn Current

Cape Horn Current

ACTUAL SURFACE TEMPERATURE

°C
30
25
20
15
10
5
0

→ Prevailing Winds
→ Cold Current
→ Warm Current

Cuiabá

Manaus

Belém

Lima

Valparaíso

Valdivia

Buenos Aires

Rio de Janeiro

Average monthly temperature

Average monthly rainfall

Punta Arenas

Equator

Tropic of Capricorn

ANNUAL RAINFALL

mm
3000
2000
1000
500
250

Equator

Amazon

Andes

Atacama Desert

Brazilian Highlands

Pampas

Patagonia

NATURAL VEGETATION

Tropical Rain Forest
Tropical Thorn Forest
Temperate Rain Forest
Evergreen Trees and Shrubs
Grassland and Savanna
Steppe and Scrub
Desert
Alpine and High Plateau

Projection: Lambert's Equivalent Azimuthal

COPYRIGHT. GEORGE PHILIP & SON.

1 : 30 000 000

200   0   200   400   600   800   1000 km

LAND USE
(million hectares)

Other land 283.5

Arable land and permanent crops 104.1

Permanent pasture 441.8

Woods and forests 924.3

Total land area 1 753.7 million hectares

Maracaibo Caracas Oficina Cerro Bolivar Moengo **Mn** Serra do Navio

Bogotá

Quito

Equator

Cerro de Pasco **Mn** Urucum Ni Brasília Cr Recife

Lima Marcona Toquepala La Paz Colquiri **Sb** Potosi Itabira Morro Velho **Mn** Rio de Janeiro

Chuquicamata Itaipu São Paulo

Tropic of Capricorn Asunción

El Romeral

Santiago **Mo** El Teniente Buenos Aires Montevideo

Concepción

El Chocón

Comodoro Rivadavia

Projection: Lambert's Equivalent Azimuthal   West from Greenwich

COPYRIGHT. GEORGE PHILIP & SON LTD.

LAND USE
- Arable land
- Fruit trees, vineyards and plantations
- Permanent pasture
- Woods and forests
- Rough grazing
- Non-productive land

LIVESTOCK
- / / / Cattle
- / / / Sheep

CROPS
Ɒ	Bananas	◇	Sugar cane
₀	Cacao	▲	Tea
◆	Citrus fruits	T	Tobacco
₀	Coffee	▽	Vines
✳	Cotton	⊔	Wheat
⊔	Maize		
○	Rice	⊢	Fisheries

MINERALS
○	Bauxite	**Cr**	Chrome
▲	Copper	**Mn**	Manganese
◇	Diamonds	**Mo**	Molybdenum
△	Gold	**Ni**	Nickel
◆	Iron ore		**POWER**
◈	Lead and zinc	▲	Coalfields
◇	Saltpetre	◻	Oilfields
▽	Silver	◼	Gasfields
●	Tin	◻	Hydro-electric power stations
Sb	Antimony		

Projection: Sanson-Flamsteed's Sinusoidal

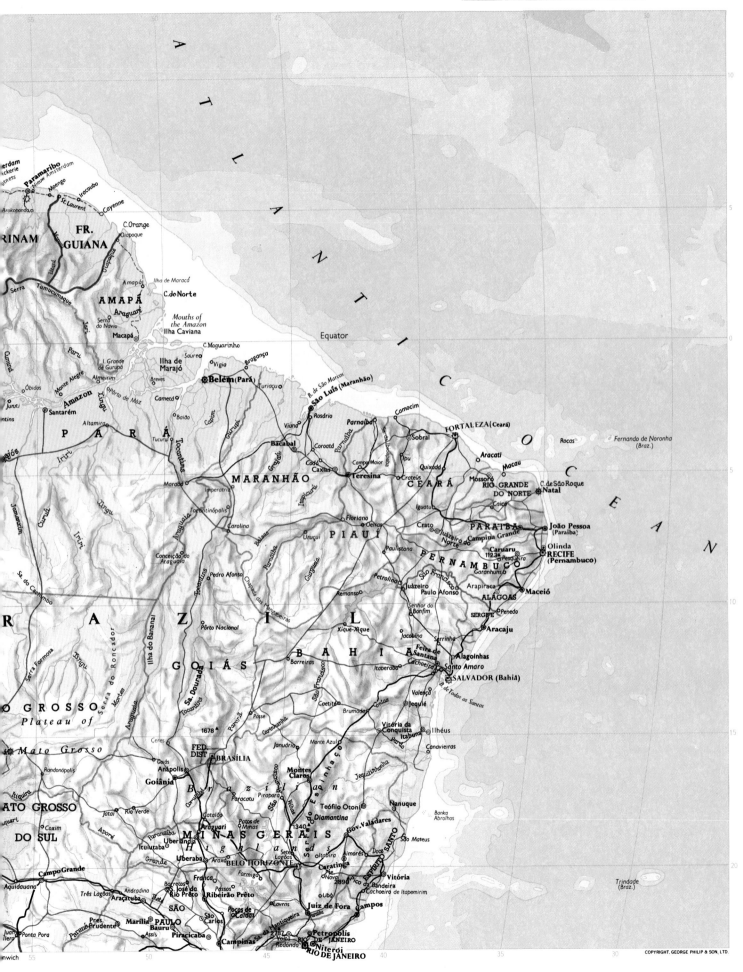

200 100 0 200 400 600 km

A T L A N T I C

Paramaribo
Nieuw Amsterdam
Brokopondo
St. Laurent
Cayenne

FR.
GUIANA

C. Orange
Oiapoque

SURINAM

AMAPÁ

C. do Norte

Macapá

Mouths of
the Amazon
Ilha Caviana

Equator

C. Maguarinho

Ilha de Marajó

Belém (Pará)

São Luís (Maranhão)

Bragança
Vigia

Breves

Cametá
Baião

Rosário

B. de São Marcos

Camocim

Santarém

Altamira

Viana

Parnaíba

FORTALEZA (Ceará)

Amazon

PARÁ

Tucuruí

Bacabal
Coroatá

Sobral

Ipu

Aracati
Macau

Rocas

Fernando de Noronha
(Braz.)

Marabá

Imperatriz

MARANHÃO

Codó
Caxias

Teresina

Campo Maior

Crateús

Quixadá

RIO GRANDE
DO NORTE

Mossoró

C. de São Roque
Natal

O C E A N

Tocantinópolis

Carolina

Floriano
Oeiras

Iguatu

Crato

Caicó

Uruçuí

PIAUÍ

Juazeiro do
Norte

Campina Grande

PARAÍBA

João Pessoa
(Paraíba)

Pedro Afonso

Paulistana

PERNAMBUCO

Caruaru

Olinda
RECIFE
(Pernambuco)

Conceição do
Araguaia

Petrolina

Juàzeiro
Paulo Afonso

São Francisco

Garanhuns

Pôrto Nacional

Remanso

Arapiraca

ALAGOAS

Maceió

Xique-Xique

Jacobina

Senhor do
Bonfim

SERGIPE

Penedo

B R A Z I L

GOIÁS

BAHIA

Barreiras

Feira de
Santana

Serrinha

Aracaju

Alagoinhas

Santo Amaro

Itaberaba
Cachoeira

SALVADOR (Bahia)

Posse

Valença

Jequié

B. de Todos os Santos

Brasília

FED.
DIST

Anápolis

Goiânia

Montes
Claros

Vitória da
Conquista
Itabuna

Ilhéus

Canavieiras

Banka
Abrolhos

MINAS GERAIS

Paracatu

Diamantina

Teófilo Otoni

Nanuque

MATO GROSSO
DO SUL

Uberlândia

BELO HORIZONTE

Caratinga

Gov. Valadares

Vitória

Campo Grande

Ribeirão Prêto

Juiz de Fora

Campos

SÃO PAULO

Campinas

Petrópolis

Niterói
RIO DE JANEIRO

1:16 000 000

200 100 0 200 400 600 km

m
6000
4000
3000
2000
1500
1000
400
200
0
200
2000
4000
6000
8000
m

Peru–Chile Trench

Richard's Deep

Tropic of Capricorn

Loa
Tocopilla
Mejillones
8050
Antofagasta
Taltal
Chañaral
Copiapó
Vallenar
La Serena
Coquimbo
Ovalle
Illapel
Viña del Mar
Valparaíso
SANTIAGO
San Antonio
Rancagua
Curicó
Talca
Linares
Talcahuano
Concepción
Lota
Coronel
Angol
Los Angeles
Victoria
Temuco
Valdivia
Osorno
L. Llanquihue
Puerto Montt
Ancud
Castro
I. de Chiloé
Chonos Arch.
I. Wellington
Pen. de Taitao
C. Tres Montes
G. de Penas
Concepción Chan.
Queen Adelaide Arch.
I. Santa Inés
I. Hoste
C. Horn

Atacama Desert
Calama
5970
Oran
S. Salvador de Jujuy
Salta
Llullaillaco 6723
5500
San Miguel de Tucumán
6722
Ojos del Salado 6863
Co. del Toro 6380
La Rioja
San Juan
Aconcagua 6800
Mendoza
Puente del Inca
San Rafael
Gral. Alvear
Malal
Neuquén
Zapala
S. C. de Bariloche
Tronador
Maquinchao
Valcheta
Esquel
José de San Martín
L. Colhué Huapi
Sarmiento
Coihaique
Pto. Aisén
Cerro Valentín 4058
Lago Buenos Aires
San Lorenzo 3700
L. S. Martín
L. O'Higgins
Murallón 3600
Lago Argentino
Calafate
Pto. Natales
Punta Arenas
Porvenir
Tierra del Fuego 2449
Ushuaia
Beagle Channel
I. Navarino
Islas Wollaston

PARAGUAY
Chaco Boreal
Tarija
Villa Montes
Tupiza
Yacuiba
La Quiaca
Tartagal
Tabacal
Joaquín V. Gonzalez
Metán
Santiago del Estero
Catamarca
Frías
Añatuya
La Banda
Campo Gallo
Salado
Dean Funes
Cruz del Eje
Córdoba
Alta Gracia
Va. Dolores
Villa María
Río Cuarto
San Luis
Mercedes
Venado Tuerto
Gral. Pico
Gral. Acha
Santa Rosa
Pehuajó
Olavarría
Azul
Tandil
Balcarce
Cor. Pringles
Tres Arroyos
Bahía Blanca
Punta Alta
Neuquén
Gral. Roca
Colorado
Negro
San Antonio Oeste
Viedma
Pta. Rasa
Golfo San Matías
Pto. Madryn
Golfo Nuevo
Trelew
Rawson
Península Valdés
C. Dos Bahías
Golfo San Jorge
Comodoro Rivadavia
Las Heras
Deseado
C. Tres Puntas
Pto. Deseado
San Julián
Santa Cruz
Bahía Grande
Río Gallegos
C. Vírgenes
Magellan's Str.

PARANÁ
Asunción
Villarrica
Caazapá
Formosa
Concepción
Pto. Pinasco
Apa
Pedro Juan Caballero
Ponta Porã
Horqueta
San Pedro
Paraguari
Pres. R. S. Peña
Pilar
Resistencia
Corrientes
Barranqueras
Bella Vista
Goya
Curuzú Cuatiá
Mercedes
Reconquista
S. Cristóbal
Santa Fe
Paraná
Rafaela
S. Francisco
Concepción del Urug.
Rosario
San Nicolás
Pergamino
Junín
Lincoln
Chivilcoy
BUENOS AIRES
La Plata
Dolores
C. S. Antonio
Necochea
Mar del Plata
Sta. Gertrudis

MATO GROSSO DO SUL
Confuso
Guaira
Encarnación
Posadas
S. Ignacio
Sto. Tomé
Uruguaiana
Cruz Alta
Santa Maria
Cachoeira do Sul
S. Gabriel
Bagé
Melo
Treinta y Tres
Florida
Minas
Rocha
Maldonado
MONTEVIDEO
Río de la Plata
URUGUAY
Fray Bentos
Mercedes
Paysandú
Salto
Concordia
Artigas
Rivera
Tacuarembó
Durazno
S. José de Mayo
Paso de los Toros
Lagoa Mirim

Araçatuba
Tietê
Marília
Assis
Londrina
Maringá
Pres. Prudente
Ribeirão Prêto
Poços de Caldas
São Carlos
Campinas
Jundiaí
Taubaté
RIO DE JANEIRO
SÃO PAULO
Sorocaba
Santo André
Santos
Sa. do Mar
Ponta Grossa
Guarapuava
Curitiba
Paranaguá
União da Vitória
Iguaçu Falls
Mafra
Joinvile
Itajaí
Blumenau
SANTA CATARINA
Lajes
Florianópolis
Tubarão
Criciúma
Erechim
Passo Fundo
Caxias do Sul
S. Leopoldo
PÔRTO ALEGRE
RIO GRANDE DO SUL
Lagoa dos Patos
Pelotas
Rio Grande
BRAZIL

SOUTH ATLANTIC OCEAN

FALKLAND ISLANDS
(ISLAS MALVINAS)
(Br.)
West Falkland
East Falkland
Stanley
Port Darwin
Falkland Sound
705
700

South Georgia
(Br.)

Projection: Sanson-Flamsteed's Sinusoidal

West from Greenwich

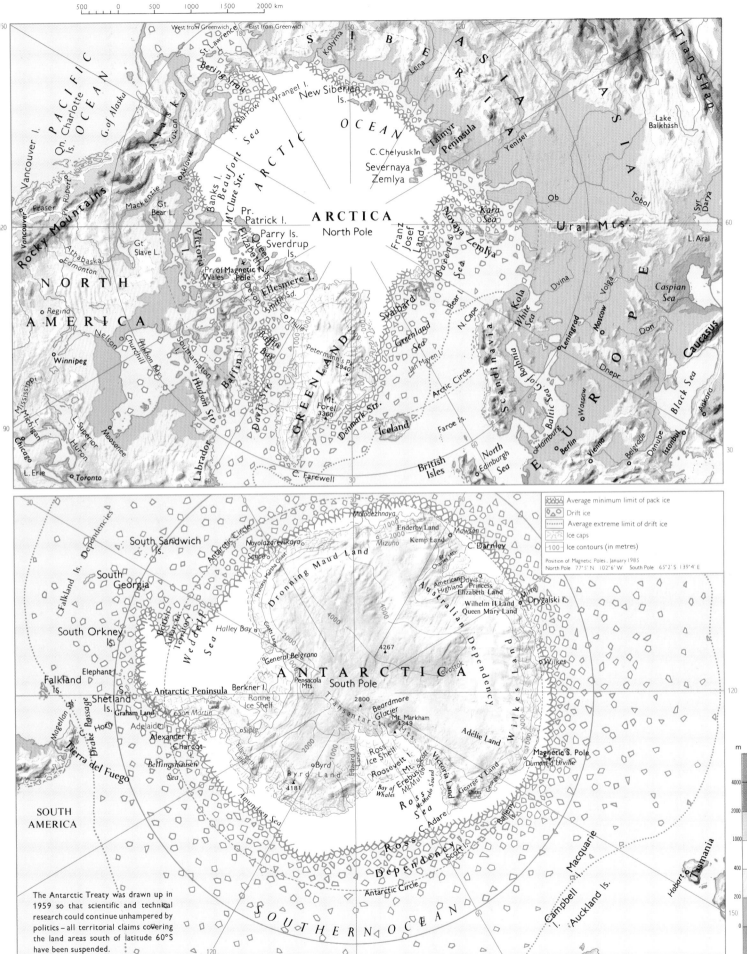

1:50 000 000

500   0   500   1000   1500   2000 km

ARCTICA
North Pole

PACIFIC OCEAN

ARCTIC OCEAN

SIBERIA

ASIA

Tian Shan

Lake Balkhash

Vancouver I.
Qn. Charlotte Is.
G. of Alaska
Alaska
Pt. Barrow
Bering Strait
St. Lawrence I.
Wrangel I.
New Siberian Is.
Kolyma
Lena
Taimyr Peninsula
C. Chelyuskin
Severnaya Zemlya
Yenisei
Ob
Tobol
Syr Darya

Vancouver
Fraser
Rupert
Yukon
Mackenzie
Oxflord
Beaufort Sea
Banks I.
M'Clure Str.
Pr. Patrick I.
Parry Is.
Sverdrup Is.
Queen Elizabeth Is.
Kara Sea
Novaya Zemlya
Ural Mts.

ROCKY MOUNTAINS

Edmonton
Athabaska
Gt. Bear L.
Gt. Slave L.
Victoria I.
Pr. of Wales I.
Magnetic N. Pole
Devon I.
Ellesmere I.
Smith Sd.
Thule
Franz Josef Land
Bear I.
Svalbard
N. Cape
L. Aral
Caspian Sea

NORTH AMERICA

Regina
Nelson
Churchill
Winnipeg
L. Superior
Moosonee
Hudson Bay
Southampton I.
Baffin I.
Baffin Bay
Davis Str.
Petermann's Pk. 2940
Greenland Sea
Jan Mayen I.
Scandinavia
Kola
White Sea
Dvina
Leningrad
Moscow
Volga
Don
Caspian Sea

GREENLAND

Mt. Forel 3360
Denmark Str.
Iceland
Faroe Is.
Arctic Circle
Gulf of Bothnia
Baltic Sea
Hamburg
Berlin
Warsaw
Vienna
Dnepr
Black Sea
Caucasus
Ankara
Istanbul
Danube
Belgrade

L. Erie
L. Michigan
Chicago
Mississippi
Toronto
L. Huron
Labrador
C. Farewell
British Isles
North Sea
Edinburgh

EUROPE

ANTARCTICA
South Pole

Molodezhnaya
Enderby Land
Mawson
Kemp Land
C. Darnley
Mizuho
Mirny
Drygalski I.

South Sandwich Is.
Antarctic Circle
Novolazarevskaya
Sanae
Princess Martha Coast
Dronning Maud Land
Charles Mts.
American Highland
Davis
Princess Elizabeth Land
Wilhelm II Land
Queen Mary Land

South Georgia
British Antarctic Territory
Halley Bay
Coats Land
4267
Wilkes

South Orkney Is.
Elephant I.
Weddell Sea
General Belgrano
Vostok
Australian Dependency
Wilkes Land

Falkland Is.
Shetland Is.
Graham Land
San Martin
Palmer Land
Berkner I.
Pensacola Mts.
Ronne Ice Shelf
2800
Beardmore Glacier
Mt. Markham 4349
Adélie Land
Magnetic S. Pole
Dumont d'Urville

Transantarctic

Adelaide
Alexander I.
Charcot
Siple
Ellsworth Land
Edward VII
Ross Ice Shelf
Roosevelt I.
Mt. Scott
Mt. Erebus
McMurdo Sound
Victoria Land
George V Land
Oates Land

Drake Passage
Horn
Bellingshausen Sea
Byrd
Byrd Land
4181
Bay of Whales
Ross Sea
C. Adare
Balleny Is.

Tierra del Fuego
Magellan

SOUTH AMERICA

Amundsen Sea
Ross Dependency
Scott
C. Adare
Macquarie I.
Campbell I.
Auckland Is.
Hobart
Tasmania

Antarctic Circle

SOUTHERN OCEAN

West from Greenwich 180 East from Greenwich

Legend:
⬡ Average minimum limit of pack ice
◇ Drift ice
····· Average extreme limit of drift ice
Ice caps
—100— Ice contours (in metres)

Position of Magnetic Poles, January 1985
North Pole 77°5′ N 102°6′ W   South Pole 65°2′ S 139°4′ E

m
4000
2000
1000
400
200
150
0

The Antarctic Treaty was drawn up in 1959 so that scientific and technical research could continue unhampered by politics – all territorial claims covering the land areas south of latitude 60°S have been suspended.

Projection: Zenithal Equidistant

COPYRIGHT. GEORGE PHILIP & SON. LTD.

Projection: Hammer Equal Area

HEIGHT OF LAND
in metres

Above 6 000
4 000–6 000
2 000–4 000
1000–2 000
200–1000
0–200
Below Sea-Level

DEPTH OF SEA
in metres

0–200
200–4000
4000–8000
Below 8000

ARCTIC OCEAN

New Siberian Is.

Severnaya Zemlya

Novaya Zemlya

N. Cape

Scandinavia

Baltic Sea

North European Plain

Rhine

Carpathians

ALPS

Apennines

Balkan Pen.

Danube

Mediterranean Sea

Black Sea

Anatolia

Caucasus

Elbrus 5633

Caspian Sea

Aral Sea

Ural Mts.

Ob

West Siberian Plain

Yenisey

Lr. Tunguska

Siberia

Lena

Aldan

Angara

Irtysh

Sayan Mts.

Altai

L. Balkhash

Syr Darya

Amu Darya

Tian Shan

Pamirs

Hindu Kush

Sulaiman Ra.

Karakoram

Kunlun

Plateau of Tibet

Himalaya

Mt. Everest 8848

Nan Shan

Gobi

Huang

North China Plain

Stanovoy Ra.

Amur

Sea of Okhotsk

Sakhalin

Hokkaido

Sea of Japan

Honshu

Mt. Fuji 3776

Yellow Sea

East China Sea

Taiwan

L. Baikal

PACIFIC OCEAN

Mariana Is.

Wake I.

Guam

Marshall Is.

Caroline Islands

Gilbert Is.

Nauru

Libyan Desert

Nile

Red Sea

The Gulf

Tigris

Euphrates

Arabia

Rub 'al Khali

Socotra

C. Guardafui

Tibesti

L. Chad

oggar

Cameroon Pk. 4070

Uele

(Congo)

Zaire

Kasai

L. Turkana

Ethiopian Highlands

Mt. Kenya 5199

L. Victoria

Kilimanjaro 5895

L. Tanganyika

Comoro Is.

Mozambique Chan.

Madagascar

Kalahari Desert

Orange

Zambezi

Cubango

L. Malawi

Drakensberg

C. of Good Hope

Thar Desert

Indus

Ganges

Deccan

W. Ghats

E. Ghats

Arabian Sea

C. Comorin

Ceylon

Bay of Bengal

Xi

Yangtze

Salween

Mekong

Hainan

Philippine Is.

South China Sea

Kinabalu 4101

Borneo

Celebes

Celebes Sea

Moluccas

Banda Sea

Timor

Java Sea

Java

Sumatra

Str. of Malacca

Sunda Is.

Seychelles

INDIAN OCEAN

Cocos or Keeling Is.

Mauritius

Réunion

Crozet Is.

Kerguelen Is.

New Guinea

Bismarck Arch.

Solomon Is.

Ellice Is.

Fiji Is.

New Hebrides

New Caledonia

Coral Sea

Gt. Barrier Reef

C. York

Torres Str.

Hamersley Ra.

Macdonnell Ra.

Great Victoria Desert

Great Australian Bight

C. Leeuwin

Great Divide

Darling

Murray

Australian Alps Mt. Kosciusko 2230

Bass Str.

Tasmania

North I.

New Zealand

Mt. Cook 3764

South I.

SOUTHERN OCEAN

Enderby Land

Queen Mary Coast

Wilkes Land

Adélie Land

South Magnetic Pole

Victoria Land

Queen Maud Land

from Greenwich

STRUCTURE

1 : 95 000 000

Structural Regions of the Land

Pre-Cambrian shields

Sedimentary cover on Pre-Cambrian shields

Palæozoic (Caledonian and Hercynian) folding

Sedimentary cover on Palæozoic folding

Mesozoic folding

Sedimentary cover on Mesozoic folding

Cainozoic folding

Sedimentary cover on Cainozoic folding

Intensive Mesozoic and Cainozoic vulcanism

Oceanic-type crust raised above sea level

Structural Regions of the Oceans

Regions of continental-type crust

Limit of continental shelf

Oceanic marginal troughs

Mid-oceanic volcanic ridges

Rift valleys in mid-oceanic ridges

Principal faults

Frontal line of overthrust folds

GEOLOGICAL TIME SCALE

Era	System	Orogeny	Millions of years before present
Cainozoic (Tertiary, Quaternary)	Quaternary / Pliocene		
	Miocene	ALPINE FOLDING	
	Oligocene		
	Eocene		50
	Paleocene	LARAMIDE FOLDING	
Mesozoic (Secondary)	Cretaceous		100
	Jurassic		150
	Triassic		200
Upper Palæozoic (Primary)	Permian		250
	Carboniferous	HERCYNIAN FOLDING	300
	Devonian		350
	Silurian	CALEDONIAN FOLDING	400
	Ordovician		450
Lower Palæozoic (Primary)	Cambrian		500 / 550
Pre-Cambrian	Pre-Cambrian		600

Canadian Shield

Rocky Mountains

Appalachians

Northern Mid-A

Sierra Madre

East Pacific Ridge

Guiana Shield

Amazonian Shield

Pacific-Antarctic Ridge

VOLCANOES

Equatorial Scale 1:280 00

EURASIAN PLATE

Hekla
Horney

Azores

Vesuvius

Etna

Katmai

Klyuchevskoi

Rainier
Mt. Helens

Fujiyama

AMERICAN PLATE

Tenerife

Mauna Loa

Paricuti

AFRICAN PLATE

Mt. Pelée
La Soufrière

Mt. Cameroon

Kilimanjaro

Taala

El Chichon

Paracé

Dempo

Galapagos

Galapagos
Cotopaxi

Krakatoa

PACIFIC

El Misti

INDIAN PLATE

PLATE

Ojos del Sado

Tristan da Cunha

Ruapehu

ANTARCTIC PLATE

Erebus

Projection: Interrupted Mollweide's Homolographic

- ● Land volcanoes active since 1700
- ○ Land volcanoes inactive since 1700
- · Submarine volcanoes
- + Geysers
- —— Plate boundaries
- —— Andesite line (boundary be sial continental crust and oceanic crust in the Pacific

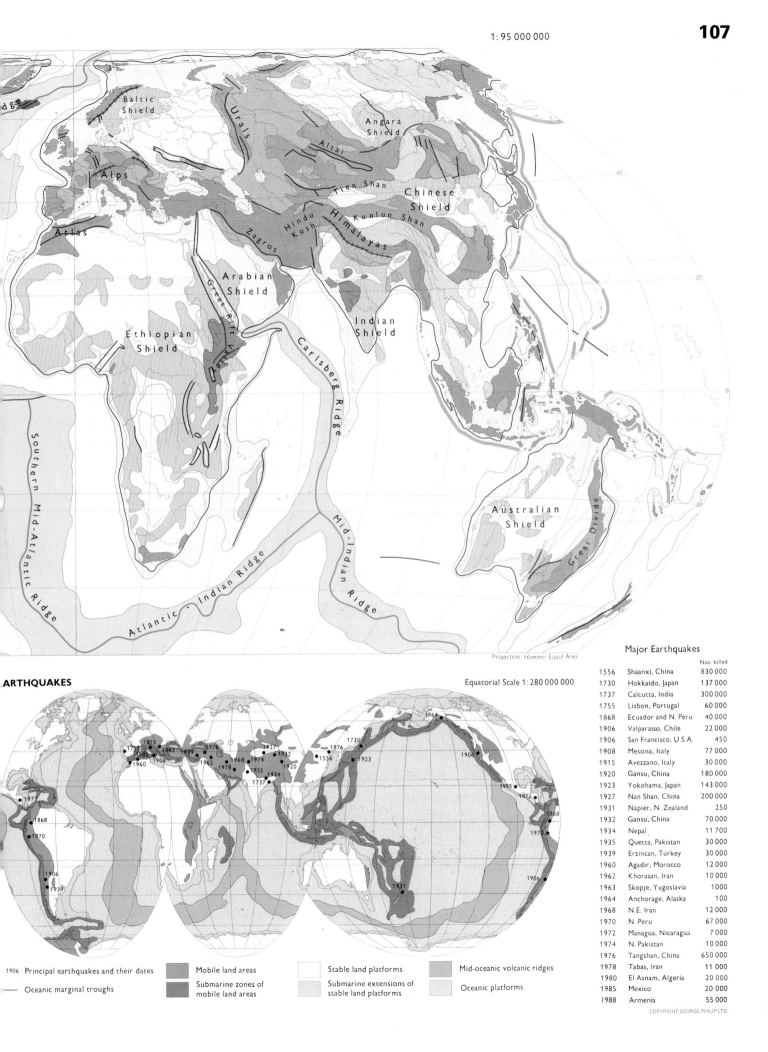

Baltic
Shield

Angara
Shield

Urals

Altai

Alps

Tien Shan

Chinese
Shield

Atlas

Hindu
Kush

Zagros

Himalayas

Kunlun Shan

Arabian
Shield

Great Rift Valley

Indian
Shield

Ethiopian
Shield

Carlsberg Ridge

Southern Mid-Atlantic Ridge

Atlantic – Indian Ridge

Mid-Indian Ridge

Australian
Shield

Great Divide

Projection: Hammer Equal Area

EARTHQUAKES

Equatorial Scale 1 : 280 000 000

1906 Principal earthquakes and their dates

Oceanic marginal troughs

Mobile land areas

Submarine zones of
mobile land areas

Stable land platforms

Submarine extensions of
stable land platforms

Mid-oceanic volcanic ridges

Oceanic platforms

Major Earthquakes

		Nos. killed
1556	Shaanxi, China	830 000
1730	Hokkaido, Japan	137 000
1737	Calcutta, India	300 000
1755	Lisbon, Portugal	60 000
1868	Ecuador and N. Peru	40 000
1906	Valparaiso, Chile	22 000
1906	San Francisco, U.S.A.	450
1908	Messina, Italy	77 000
1915	Avezzano, Italy	30 000
1920	Gansu, China	180 000
1923	Yokohama, Japan	143 000
1927	Nan Shan, China	200 000
1931	Napier, N. Zealand	250
1932	Gansu, China	70 000
1934	Nepal	11 700
1935	Quetta, Pakistan	30 000
1939	Erzincan, Turkey	30 000
1960	Agadir, Morocco	12 000
1962	Khorasan, Iran	10 000
1963	Skopje, Yugoslavia	1 000
1964	Anchorage, Alaska	100
1968	N.E. Iran	12 000
1970	N. Peru	67 000
1972	Managua, Nicaragua	7 000
1974	N. Pakistan	10 000
1976	Tangshan, China	650 000
1978	Tabas, Iran	11 000
1980	El Asnam, Algeria	20 000
1985	Mexico	20 000
1988	Armenia	55 000

CLIMATES

after Köppen

Climatic group		Climate	Temperature	Rainfall
A TROPICAL RAINY CLIMATES	**Af**	RAIN-FOREST CLIMATE	All mean monthly temperatures above 18°C	
	Am	MONSOON CLIMATE		
	Aw	SAVANNA CLIMATE		
B DRY CLIMATES	**BS**	STEPPE CLIMATE	Mean annual temperature	
			h = above 18°C	
	BW	DESERT CLIMATE	**k** = below 18°C	
C WARM TEMPERATE RAINY CLIMATES	**Cw**	DRY WINTER CLIMATE	Mean temperature of the coldest month between −3°C to 18°C	**a** Mean temperature of hottest month above 22°C, and with more than 4 months of over 10°C
	Cs	DRY SUMMER CLIMATE (Mediterranean)		**b** Mean temperature of hottest month below 22°C and with more than 4 months of over 10°C
	Cf	CLIMATE WITH NO DRY SEASON		**s** Rainfall of the driest month of the hot season is less than one-third of the rainfall of the wet-test month of the cold season and less than 40mm.
D COLD TEMPERATE RAINY CLIMATES	**Dw**	DRY WINTER CLIMATE	Mean temperature of the coldest month below −3°C	**c** Mean temperature of hottest month below 22°C, but with less than 4 months of over 10°C
	Df	CLIMATE WITH NO DRY SEASON		**d** Mean temperature of hottest month below 22°C, and of the coldest month below −38°C
E POLAR CLIMATES	**ET**	TUNDRA CLIMATE	Mean temperature of the hottest month below 10°C / Mean temperature of the hottest month between 0°C and 10°C	**H** More than 1500m above sea level
	EF	PERPETUAL FROST	Mean temperature of the hottest month between 0°C and 10°C	

w dry winter — Rainfall of the driest month of the cold season is one-tenth or less of the rainfall of the wettest month of the hot season

f with no dry season — Rainfall does not correspond to w or s climates

Rainfall during the driest month (mm) — Af, Aw, Am — *Annual rainfall (mm)* 1000 2000 3000

BW/BS Boundary — BW BS — BS/ Wet Climates Boundary — Wet Climates A, C, D — *Mean annual temperature (°C)* — *Annual rainfall (mm)* 0 200 400 600

— — — summer rainfall
– – – winter rainfall
–·–·– rainfall evenly distributed

SOIL REGIONS

1:240 000 000

after Glinka, Stremme, Marbut, and others

- Tundra Soil
- Podzols
- Brown Forest Soil
- Lightly leached Dry Forest Soil
- Red and yellow Sub-tropical Forest Soil
- Reddish Savanna Soil and Tropical Red Earths
- Laterites
- Chernozem
- Degraded Chernozem
- Black Savanna Soil
- Chestnut Steppe Soil
- Grey, light brown and red brown Desert Steppe Soils
- Alluvium
- Mountain and High Plateau Soils
- Oases Soil
- Tropical and Mangrove Swamp

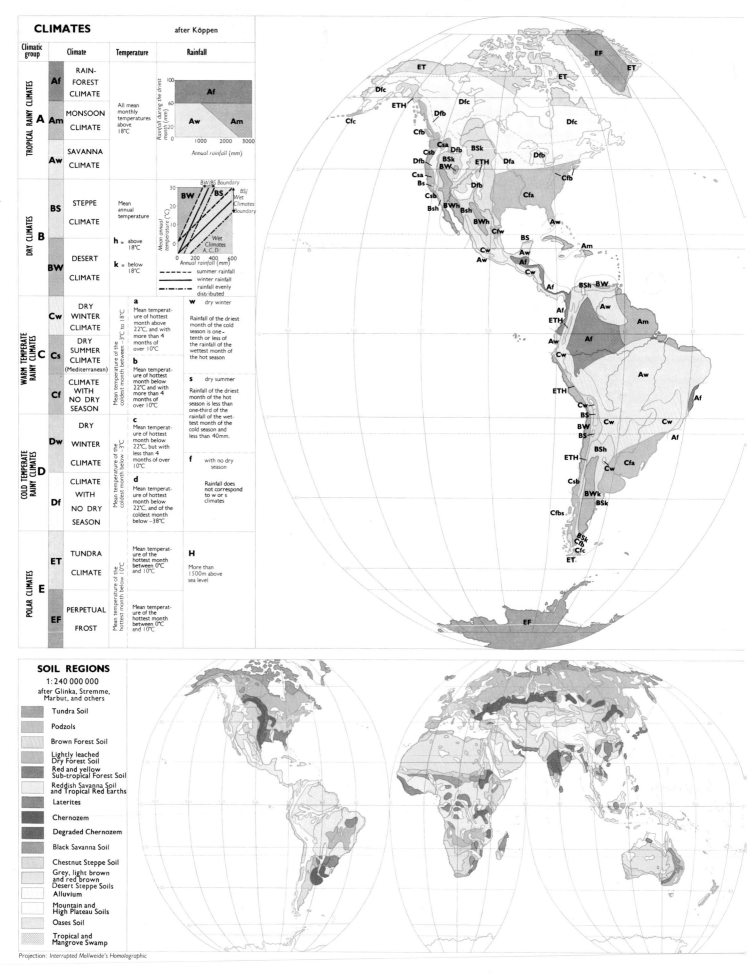

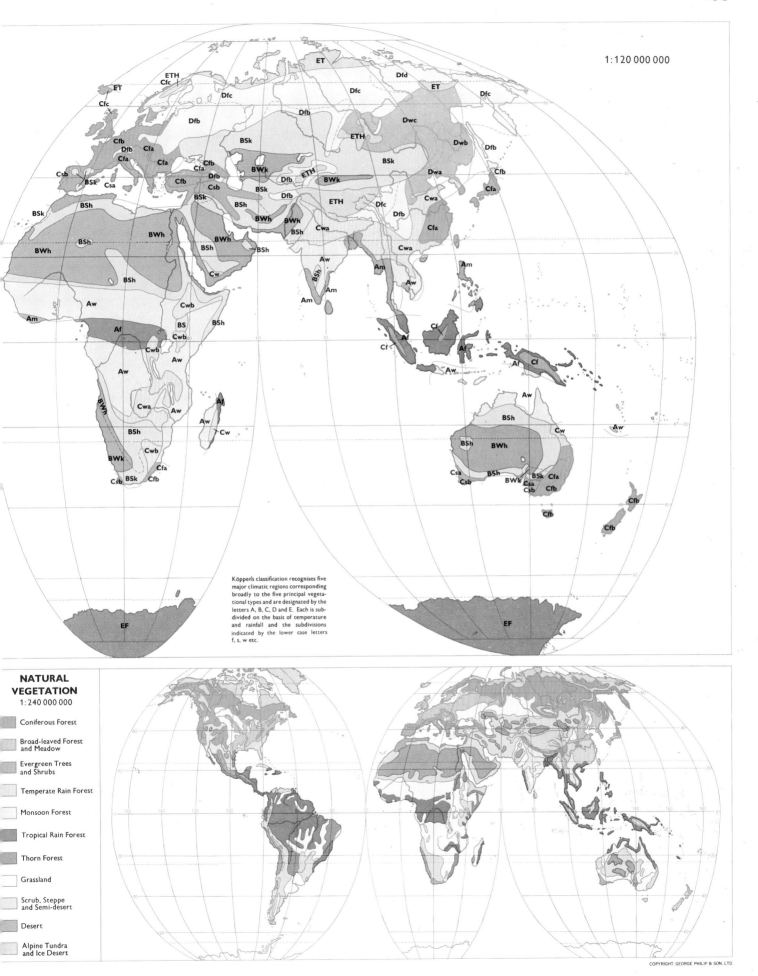

1:120 000 000

Köppen's classification recognises five major climatic regions corresponding broadly to the five principal vegetational types and are designated by the letters A, B, C, D and E. Each is subdivided on the basis of temperature and rainfall and the subdivisions indicated by the lower case letters f, s, w etc.

NATURAL VEGETATION

1:240 000 000

- Coniferous Forest
- Broad-leaved Forest and Meadow
- Evergreen Trees and Shrubs
- Temperate Rain Forest
- Monsoon Forest
- Tropical Rain Forest
- Thorn Forest
- Grassland
- Scrub, Steppe and Semi-desert
- Desert
- Alpine Tundra and Ice Desert

These four pages give temperature and precipitation statistics for over 80 stations, which are arranged by listing the continents and the places within each continent in alphabetical order. The elevation of each station, in metres above mean sea level, is stated beneath its name. The average monthly temperature, in degrees Celsius, and the average monthly precipitation, in millimetres, are given. To the right, the average yearly rainfall, the average yearly temperature, and the annual range of temperature (the difference between the warmest and the coldest months) are also stated.

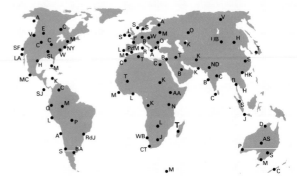

AFRICA

		Jan.	Feb.	Mar.	Apr.	May	June	July	Aug.	Sept.	Oct.	Nov.	Dec.	Year	Annual Range
Addis Ababa, Ethiopia	Precipitation	<3	3	25	135	213	201	206	239	102	28	<3	0	1 151	
2 450 m	Temperature	19	20	20	20	19	18	18	19	21	22	21	20	20	4
Cairo, Egypt	Precipitation	5	5	5	3	3	<3	0	0	<3	<3	3	5	28	
116 m	Temperature	13	15	18	21	25	28	28	28	26	24	20	15	22	15
Cape Town, South Africa	Precipitation	15	8	18	48	79	84	89	66	43	31	18	10	508	
17 m	Temperature	21	21	20	17	14	13	12	13	14	16	18	19	17	9
Casablanca, Morocco	Precipitation	53	48	56	36	23	5	0	<3	8	38	66	71	404	
50 m	Temperature	13	13	14	16	18	20	22	23	22	19	16	13	18	10
Johannesburg, South Africa	Precipitation	114	109	89	38	25	8	8	8	23	56	107	125	709	
1 665 m	Temperature	20	20	18	16	13	10	11	13	16	18	19	20	16	10
Khartoum, Sudan	Precipitation	<3	<3	<3	<3	3	8	53	71	18	5	<3	0	158	
390 m	Temperature	24	25	28	31	33	34	32	31	32	32	28	25	29	9
Kinshasa, Zaïre	Precipitation	135	145	196	196	158	8	3	3	31	119	221	142	1 354	
325 m	Temperature	26	26	27	27	26	24	23	24	25	26	26	26	25	4
Lagos, Nigeria	Precipitation	28	46	102	150	269	460	279	64	140	206	69	25	1 836	
3 m	Temperature	27	28	29	28	28	26	26	25	26	26	28	28	27	4
Lusaka, Zambia	Precipitation	231	191	142	18	3	<3	<3	0	<3	10	91	150	836	
1 277 m	Temperature	21	22	21	21	19	16	16	18	22	24	23	22	21	8
Monrovia, Liberia	Precipitation	31	56	97	216	516	973	996	373	744	772	236	130	5 138	
23 m	Temperature	26	26	27	27	26	25	24	25	25	25	26	26	26	3
Nairobi, Kenya	Precipitation	38	64	125	211	158	46	15	23	31	53	109	86	958	
1 820 m	Temperature	19	19	19	19	18	16	16	16	18	19	18	18	18	3
Tananarive, Madagascar	Precipitation	300	279	178	53	18	8	8	10	18	61	135	287	1 356	
1 372 m	Temperature	21	21	21	19	18	15	14	15	17	19	21	21	19	7
Timbuktu, Mali	Precipitation	<3	<3	3	<3	5	23	79	81	38	3	<3	<3	231	
301 m	Temperature	22	24	28	32	34	35	32	30	32	31	28	23	29	13
Tunis, Tunisia	Precipitation	64	51	41	36	18	8	3	8	33	51	48	61	419	
66 m	Temperature	10	11	13	16	19	23	26	27	25	20	16	11	18	17
Walvis Bay, South Africa	Precipitation	<3	5	8	3	3	<3	<3	3	<3	<3	<3	<3	23	
7 m	Temperature	19	19	19	18	17	16	15	14	14	15	17	18	18	5

AMERICA, NORTH

		Jan.	Feb.	Mar.	Apr.	May	June	July	Aug.	Sept.	Oct.	Nov.	Dec.	Year	Annual Range
Anchorage, Alaska, U.S.A.	Precipitation	20	18	15	10	13	18	41	66	66	56	25	23	371	
40 m	Temperature	−11	−8	−5	2	7	12	14	13	9	2	−5	−11	2	25
Cheyenne, Wyo., U.S.A.	Precipitation	10	15	25	48	61	41	53	41	31	25	13	13	376	
1 871 m	Temperature	−4	−3	1	5	10	16	19	19	14	7	1	−2	7	23
Chicago, Ill., U.S.A.	Precipitation	51	51	66	71	86	89	84	81	79	66	61	51	836	
251 m	Temperature	−4	−3	2	9	14	20	23	22	19	12	5	−1	10	27
Churchill, Man., Canada	Precipitation	15	13	18	23	32	44	46	58	51	43	39	21	402	
13 m	Temperature	−28	−26	−20	−10	−2	6	12	11	5	−2	−12	−22	−7	40

		Jan.	Feb.	Mar.	Apr.	May	June	July	Aug.	Sept.	Oct.	Nov.	Dec.	Year	Annual range
Edmonton, Alta., Canada															
	Precipitation	25	19	19	22	43	77	89	78	39	17	16	25	466	
676 m	Temperature	−15	−10	−5	4	11	15	17	16	11	6	−4	−10	3	32
Honolulu, Hawaii, U.S.A.															
	Precipitation	104	66	79	48	25	18	23	28	36	48	64	104	643	
12 m	Temperature	23	18	19	20	22	24	25	26	26	24	22	19	22	8
Houston, Tex., U.S.A.															
	Precipitation	89	76	84	91	119	117	99	99	104	94	89	109	1 171	
12 m	Temperature	12	13	17	21	24	27	28	29	26	22	16	12	21	17
Kingston, Jamaica															
	Precipitation	23	15	23	31	102	89	38	91	99	180	74	36	800	
34 m	Temperature	25	25	25	26	26	28	28	28	27	27	26	26	26	3
Los Angeles, Calif., U.S.A.															
	Precipitation	79	76	71	25	10	3	<3	<3	5	15	31	66	381	
95 m	Temperature	13	14	14	16	17	19	21	22	21	18	16	14	17	9
Mexico City, Mexico															
	Precipitation	13	5	10	20	53	119	170	152	130	51	18	8	747	
2 309 m	Temperature	12	13	16	18	19	19	17	18	18	16	14	13	16	7
Miami, Fla., U.S.A.															
	Precipitation	71	53	64	81	173	178	155	160	203	234	71	51	1 516	
8 m	Temperature	20	20	22	23	25	27	28	28	27	25	22	21	24	8
Montreal, Que., Canada															
	Precipitation	72	65	74	74	66	82	90	92	88	76	81	87	946	
57 m	Temperature	−10	−9	−3	−6	13	18	21	20	15	9	2	−7	6	31
New York, N.Y., U.S.A.															
	Precipitation	94	97	91	81	81	84	107	109	86	89	76	91	1 092	
96 m	Temperature	−1	−1	3	10	16	20	23	23	21	15	7	2	8	24
St. Louis, Mo., U.S.A.															
	Precipitation	58	64	89	97	114	114	89	86	81	74	71	64	1 001	
173 m	Temperature	0	1	7	13	19	24	26	26	22	15	8	2	14	26
San Francisco, Calif., U.S.A.															
	Precipitation	119	97	79	38	18	3	<3	<3	8	25	64	112	561	
16 m	Temperature	10	12	13	13	14	15	15	15	17	16	14	11	14	7
San José, Costa Rica															
	Precipitation	15	5	20	46	229	241	211	241	305	300	145	41	1 798	
1 146 m	Temperature	19	19	21	21	22	21	21	21	21	20	20	19	20	2
Vancouver, B.C., Canada															
	Precipitation	154	115	101	60	52	45	32	41	67	114	150	182	1113	
14 m	Temperature	3	5	6	9	12	15	17	17	14	10	6	4	10	14
Washington, D.C., U.S.A.															
	Precipitation	86	76	91	84	94	99	112	109	94	74	66	79	1 064	
22 m	Temperature	1	2	7	12	18	23	25	24	20	14	8	3	13	24

AMERICA, SOUTH

		Jan.	Feb.	Mar.	Apr.	May	June	July	Aug.	Sept.	Oct.	Nov.	Dec.	Year	Annual range
Antofagasta, Chile															
	Precipitation	0	0	0	<3	<3	3	5	3	<3	3	<3	0	13	
94 m	Temperature	21	21	20	18	16	15	14	14	15	16	18	19	17	7
Buenos Aires, Argentina															
	Precipitation	79	71	109	89	76	61	56	61	79	86	84	99	950	
27 m	Temperature	23	23	21	17	13	9	10	11	13	15	19	22	16	14
Caracas, Venezuela															
	Precipitation	23	10	15	33	79	102	109	109	107	109	94	46	836	
1 042 m	Temperature	19	19	20	21	22	21	21	21	21	21	20	20	21	3
Lima, Peru															
	Precipitation	3	<3	<3	<3	5	5	8	8	8	3	3	<3	41	
120 m	Temperature	23	24	24	22	19	17	17	16	17	18	19	21	20	8
Manaus, Brazil															
	Precipitation	249	231	262	221	170	84	58	38	46	107	142	203	1 811	
44 m	Temperature	28	28	28	27	28	28	28	28	29	29	29	28	28	2
Paraná, Brazil															
	Precipitation	287	236	239	102	13	<3	3	5	28	127	231	310	1 582	
260 m	Temperature	23	23	23	23	23	21	21	22	24	24	24	23	23	3
Quito, Ecuador															
	Precipitation	99	112	142	175	137	43	20	31	69	112	97	79	1 115	
2 879 m	Temperature	15	15	15	15	15	14	14	15	15	15	15	15	15	1
Rio de Janeiro, Brazil															
	Precipitation	125	122	130	107	79	53	41	43	66	79	104	137	1 082	
61 m	Temperature	26	26	25	24	22	21	21	21	21	22	23	25	23	5
Santiago, Chile															
	Precipitation	3	3	5	13	64	84	76	56	31	15	8	5	358	
520 m	Temperature	21	20	18	15	12	9	9	10	12	15	17	19	15	12

ASIA

		Jan.	Feb.	Mar.	Apr.	May	June	July	Aug.	Sept.	Oct.	Nov.	Dec.	Year	Annual range
Bahrain															
	Precipitation	8	18	13	8	<3	0	0	0	0	0	18	18	81	
5 m	Temperature	17	18	21	25	29	32	33	34	31	28	24	19	26	16
Bangkok, Thailand															
	Precipitation	8	20	36	58	198	160	160	175	305	206	66	5	1 397	
2 m	Temperature	26	28	29	30	29	29	28	28	28	28	26	25	28	5
Beirut, Lebanon															
	Precipitation	191	158	94	53	18	3	<3	<3	5	51	132	185	892	
34 m	Temperature	14	14	16	18	22	24	27	28	26	24	19	16	21	14
Bombay, India															
	Precipitation	3	3	3	<3	18	485	617	340	264	64	13	3	1 809	
11 m	Temperature	24	24	26	28	30	29	27	27	27	28	27	26	27	6
Calcutta, India															
	Precipitation	10	31	36	43	140	297	325	328	252	114	20	5	1 600	
6 m	Temperature	20	22	27	30	30	30	29	29	29	28	23	19	26	11
Colombo, Sri Lanka															
	Precipitation	89	69	147	231	371	224	135	109	160	348	315	147	2 365	
7 m	Temperature	26	26	27	28	28	27	27	27	27	27	26	26	27	2
Harbin, China															
	Precipitation	5	5	10	23	43	94	112	104	46	33	8	5	488	
160 m	Temperature	−18	−15	−5	6	13	19	22	21	14	4	−6	−16	3	40
Ho Chi Minh City, Vietnam															
	Precipitation	15	3	13	43	221	330	315	269	335	269	114	56	1 984	
9 m	Temperature	26	27	29	30	29	28	28	28	27	27	27	26	28	4
Jakarta, Indonesia															
	Precipitation	300	300	211	147	114	97	64	43	66	112	142	203	1 798	
8 m	Temperature	26	26	27	27	27	27	27	27	27	27	27	26	27	1
Hong Kong															
	Precipitation	33	46	74	137	292	394	381	361	257	114	43	31	2 162	
33 m	Temperature	16	15	18	22	26	28	28	28	27	25	21	18	23	13
Kabul, Afghanistan															
	Precipitation	31	36	94	102	20	5	3	3	<3	15	20	10	338	
1 815 m	Temperature	−3	−1	6	13	18	22	25	24	20	14	7	3	12	28
Karachi, Pakistan															
	Precipitation	13	10	8	3	3	18	81	41	13	<3	3	5	196	
4 m	Temperature	19	20	24	28	30	31	30	29	28	28	24	20	26	12
New Delhi, India															
	Precipitation	23	18	13	8	13	74	180	172	117	10	3	10	640	
218 m	Temperature	14	17	23	28	33	34	31	30	29	26	20	15	25	20
Shanghai, China															
	Precipitation	48	58	84	94	94	180	147	142	130	71	51	36	1 135	
7 m	Temperature	4	5	9	14	20	24	28	28	23	19	12	7	16	24
Singapore															
	Precipitation	252	173	193	188	173	173	170	196	178	208	254	257	2 413	
10 m	Temperature	26	27	28	28	28	28	28	27	27	27	27	27	27	2
Tehran, Iran															
	Precipitation	46	38	46	36	13	3	3	3	3	8	20	31	246	
1 220 m	Temperature	2	5	9	16	21	26	30	29	25	18	12	6	17	28
Tokyo, Japan															
	Precipitation	48	74	107	135	147	165	142	152	234	208	97	56	1 565	
6 m	Temperature	3	4	7	13	17	21	25	26	23	17	11	6	14	23
Ulan Bator, Mongolia															
	Precipitation	<3	<3	3	5	10	28	76	51	23	5	5	3	208	
1 325 m	Temperature	−26	−21	−13	−1	6	14	16	14	8	−1	−13	−22	−3	42

AUSTRALIA, NEW ZEALAND and ANTARCTICA

		Jan.	Feb.	Mar.	Apr.	May	June	July	Aug.	Sept.	Oct.	Nov.	Dec.	Year	Annual range
Alice Springs, Australia															
	Precipitation	43	33	28	10	15	13	8	8	8	18	31	38	252	
579 m	Temperature	29	28	25	20	15	12	12	14	18	23	26	28	21	17
Christchurch, New Zealand															
	Precipitation	56	43	48	48	66	66	69	48	46	43	48	56	638	
10 m	Temperature	16	16	14	12	9	6	6	7	9	12	14	16	11	10
Darwin, Australia															
	Precipitation	386	312	254	97	15	3	<3	3	13	51	119	239	1 491	
30 m	Temperature	29	29	29	29	28	26	25	26	28	29	30	29	28	5
Mawson, Antarctica															
	Precipitation	11	30	20	10	44	180	4	40	3	20	0	0	362	
14 m	Temperature	0	−5	−10	−14	−15	−16	−18	−18	−19	−13	−5	−1	−11	18

		Jan.	Feb.	Mar.	Apr.	May	June	July	Aug.	Sept.	Oct.	Nov.	Dec.	Year	Annual Range
Melbourne, Australia															
	Precipitation	48	46	56	58	53	53	48	48	58	66	58	58	653	
35 m	Temperature	20	20	18	15	13	10	9	11	13	14	16	18	15	11
Perth, Australia															
	Precipitation	8	10	20	43	130	180	170	149	86	56	20	13	881	
60 m	Temperature	23	23	22	19	16	14	13	13	15	16	19	22	18	10
Sydney, Australia															
	Precipitation	89	102	127	135	127	117	117	76	73	71	73	73	1 181	
42 m	Temperature	22	22	21	18	15	13	12	13	15	18	19	21	17	10

EUROPE and U.S.S.R.

		Jan.	Feb.	Mar.	Apr.	May	June	July	Aug.	Sept.	Oct.	Nov.	Dec.	Year	Annual Range
Archangel, U.S.S.R.															
	Precipitation	31	19	25	29	42	52	62	56	63	63	47	41	530	
13 m	Temperature	−16	−14	−9	0	7	12	15	14	8	2	−4	−11	0	31
Athens, Greece															
	Precipitation	62	37	37	23	23	14	6	7	15	51	56	71	402	
107 m	Temperature	10	10	12	16	20	25	28	28	24	20	15	11	18	18
Berlin, Germany															
	Precipitation	46	40	33	42	49	65	73	69	48	49	46	43	603	
55 m	Temperature	−1	0	4	9	14	17	19	18	15	9	5	1	9	20
Istanbul, Turkey															
	Precipitation	109	92	72	46	38	34	34	30	58	81	103	119	816	
114 m	Temperature	5	6	7	11	16	20	23	23	20	16	12	8	14	18
Kazalinsk, U.S.S.R.															
	Precipitation	10	10	13	13	15	5	5	8	8	10	13	15	125	
63 m	Temperature	−12	−11	−3	6	18	23	25	23	16	8	−1	−7	7	37
Lisbon, Portugal															
	Precipitation	111	76	109	54	44	16	3	4	33	62	93	103	708	
77 m	Temperature	11	12	14	16	17	20	22	23	21	18	14	12	17	12
London, U.K.															
	Precipitation	54	40	37	37	46	45	57	59	49	57	64	48	593	
5 m	Temperature	4	5	7	9	12	16	18	17	15	11	8	5	11	14
Málaga, Spain															
	Precipitation	61	51	62	46	26	5	1	3	29	64	64	62	474	
33 m	Temperature	12	13	15	17	19	29	25	26	23	20	16	13	18	17
Moscow, U.S.S.R.															
	Precipitation	39	38	36	37	53	58	88	71	58	45	47	54	624	
156 m	Temperature	−13	−10	−4	6	13	16	18	17	12	6	−1	−7	4	31
Odessa, U.S.S.R.															
	Precipitation	57	62	30	21	34	34	42	37	37	13	35	71	473	
64 m	Temperature	−3	−1	2	9	15	20	22	22	18	12	9	1	10	25
Omsk, U.S.S.R.															
	Precipitation	15	8	8	13	31	51	51	51	28	25	18	20	318	
85 m	Temperature	−22	−19	−12	−1	10	16	18	16	10	1	−11	−18	−1	40
Palma de Mallorca, Spain															
	Precipitation	39	34	51	32	29	17	3	25	55	77	47	40	449	
10 m	Temperature	10	11	12	15	17	21	24	25	23	18	14	11	17	15
Paris, France															
	Precipitation	56	46	35	42	57	54	59	64	55	50	51	50	619	
75 m	Temperature	3	4	8	11	15	18	20	19	17	12	7	4	12	17
Rome, Italy															
	Precipitation	71	62	57	51	46	37	15	21	63	99	129	93	744	
17 m	Temperature	8	9	11	14	18	22	25	25	22	17	13	10	16	17
Shannon, Irish Republic															
	Precipitation	94	67	56	53	61	57	77	79	86	86	96	117	929	
2 m	Temperature	5	5	7	9	12	14	16	16	14	11	8	6	10	11
Stavanger, Norway															
	Precipitation	93	56	45	70	49	84	93	118	142	129	125	126	1 130	
85 m	Temperature	1	1	3	6	10	13	15	15	13	9	6	3	8	14
Stockholm, Sweden															
	Precipitation	43	30	25	31	34	45	61	76	60	48	53	48	554	
44 m	Temperature	−3	−3	−1	5	10	15	18	17	12	7	3	0	7	21
Verkhoyansk, U.S.S.R.															
	Precipitation	5	5	3	5	8	23	28	25	13	8	8	5	134	
100 m	Temperature	−50	−45	−32	−15	0	12	14	9	2	−15	−38	−48	−17	64
Warsaw, Poland															
	Precipitation	27	32	27	37	46	69	96	65	43	38	31	44	555	
110 m	Temperature	−3	−3	2	7	14	17	19	18	14	9	3	0	8	22

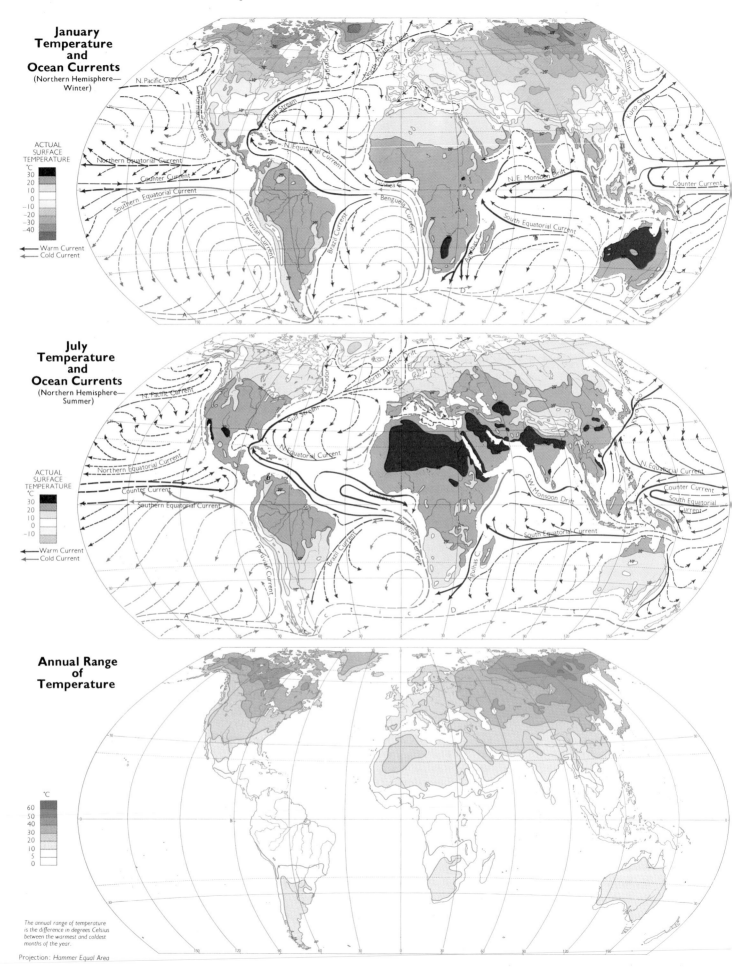

January Temperature and Ocean Currents
(Northern Hemisphere— Winter)

ACTUAL SURFACE TEMPERATURE
°C
30
20
10
0
-10
-20
-30
-40

→ Warm Current
→ Cold Current

July Temperature and Ocean Currents
(Northern Hemisphere— Summer)

ACTUAL SURFACE TEMPERATURE
°C
30
20
10
0
-10

→ Warm Current
→ Cold Current

Annual Range of Temperature

°C
60
50
40
30
20
10
5
0

The annual range of temperature is the difference in degrees Celsius between the warmest and coldest months of the year.

Projection: Hammer Equal Area

1:190 000 000

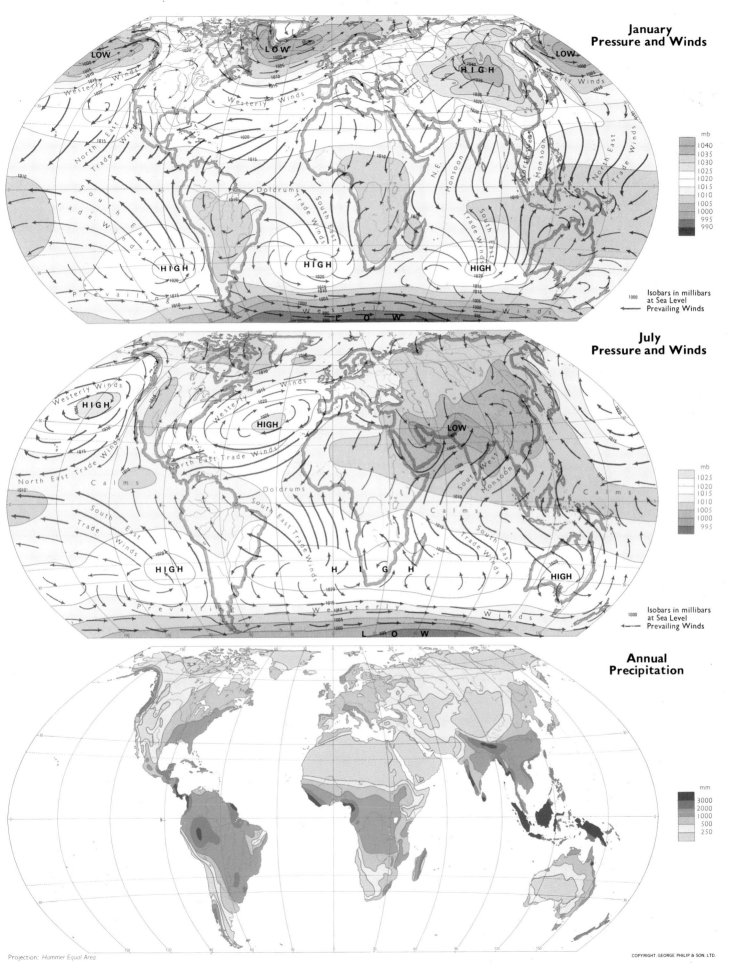

January Pressure and Winds

July Pressure and Winds

Annual Precipitation

mb
1040
1035
1030
1025
1020
1015
1010
1005
1000
995
990

1000 Isobars in millibars at Sea Level
Prevailing Winds

mb
1025
1020
1015
1010
1005
1000
995

1000 Isobars in millibars at Sea Level
Prevailing Winds

mm
3000
2000
1000
500
250

Projection: Hammer Equal Area

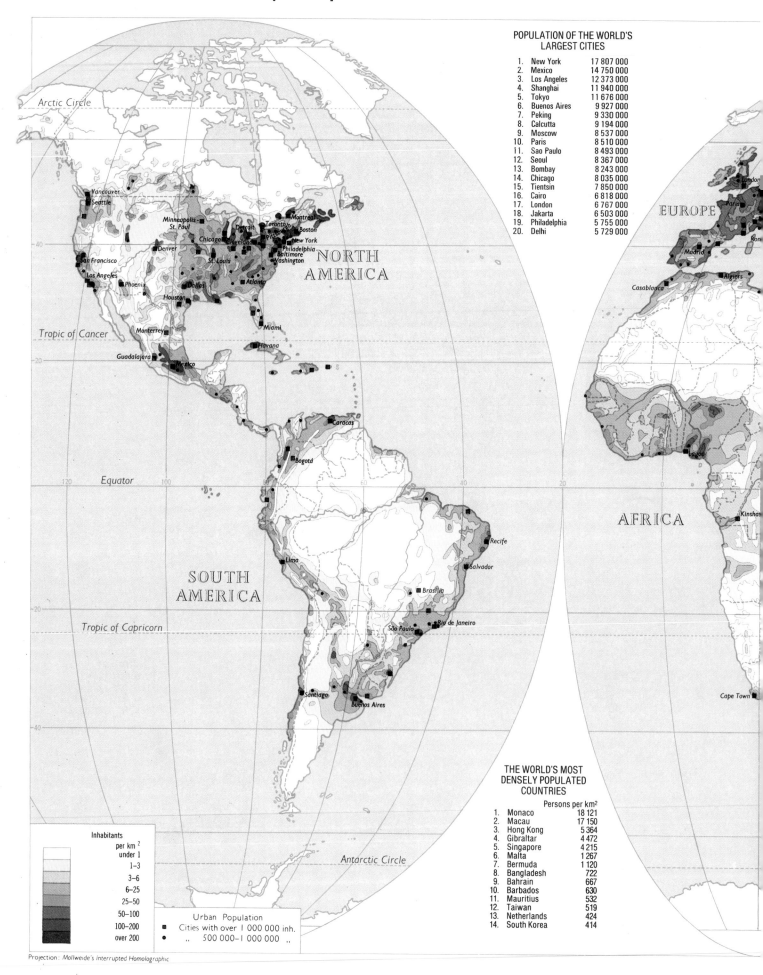

POPULATION OF THE WORLD'S LARGEST CITIES

1.	New York	17 807 000
2.	Mexico	14 750 000
3.	Los Angeles	12 373 000
4.	Shanghai	11 940 000
5.	Tokyo	11 676 000
6.	Buenos Aires	9 927 000
7.	Peking	9 330 000
8.	Calcutta	9 194 000
9.	Moscow	8 537 000
10.	Paris	8 510 000
11.	Sao Paulo	8 493 000
12.	Seoul	8 367 000
13.	Bombay	8 243 000
14.	Chicago	8 035 000
15.	Tientsin	7 850 000
16.	Cairo	6 818 000
17.	London	6 767 000
18.	Jakarta	6 503 000
19.	Philadelphia	5 755 000
20.	Delhi	5 729 000

THE WORLD'S MOST DENSELY POPULATED COUNTRIES

		Persons per km²
1.	Monaco	18 121
2.	Macau	17 150
3.	Hong Kong	5 364
4.	Gibraltar	4 472
5.	Singapore	4 215
6.	Malta	1 267
7.	Bermuda	1 120
8.	Bangladesh	722
9.	Bahrain	667
10.	Barbados	630
11.	Mauritius	532
12.	Taiwan	519
13.	Netherlands	424
14.	South Korea	414

Inhabitants per km²

- under 1
- 1–3
- 3–6
- 6–25
- 25–50
- 50–100
- 100–200
- over 200

Urban Population

- ■ Cities with over 1 000 000 inh.
- ● „ 500 000– 1 000 000 „

Projection: Mollweide's Interrupted Homolographic

Arctic Circle

Stockholm • Leningrad • Sverdlovsk
Moscow • Gorki • Novosibirsk
Warsaw • Kiev • Kuybyshev
Budapest • Kharkov
Bucharest • Baku • Tashkent
Istanbul
Ankara • Tehran
Damascus • Baghdad
Alexandria • Cairo

Harbin
Shenyang
Peking • Tientsin • Seoul
Lanzhou • Pusan • Tokyo
Wuhan • Shanghai
Changking
Taipei
Dacca • Canton
Hanoi • Hong Kong

ASIA

Lahore
Delhi
Karachi
Ahmadabad • Calcutta
Bombay
Hyderabad • Rangoon
Madras • Bangkok
Ho Chi Minh City

Tropic of Cancer

Addis Ababa

Colombo

Manila

Singapore

Equator

Jakarta

AUSTRALIA

Tropic of Capricorn

Johannesburg

Sydney

Melbourne

Antarctic Circle

THE WORLD'S MOST DENSELY POPULATED COUNTRIES

Continuation		Persons per km²
15.	Puerto Rico	382
16.	Grenada	373
17.	San Marino	367
18.	Saint Vincent	347
19.	Belgium	329
20.	Japan	323
21.	Martinique	297
22.	Lebanon	264
23.	El Salvador	257
24.	India	251
25.	West Germany	251
26.	Sri Lanka	240
27.	Rwanda	236
28.	UK	230

Some of the lesser islands have high densities but have been omitted from this table.

For comparison the London urban area has a density of 4 270 persons per km².

The population figures used are from censuses or more recent estimates and are given in thousands for towns and cities over 200,000 (over 250,000 in Brazil and Japan and 500,000 in China, India, United States and U.S.S.R.). Where possible the population of the metropolitan area is given e.g. Greater London, Greater New York etc.

AFRICA

ALGERIA (1977)
Algiers	1 740
Oran	543
Constantine	379
Annaba	246
Tizi-Ouzou	224

ANGOLA (1982)
Luanda	700

BENIN (1982)
Cotonou	487
Porto-Novo	208

BURKINA FASO (1982)
Ouagadougou	286

CAMEROON (1983)
Douala	708
Yaoundé	485

CANARY ISLANDS (1981)
Las Palmas	360

CENTRAL AFRICAN REPUBLIC (1981)
Bangui	387

CHAD (1979)
Ndjamena	303

CONGO (1980)
Brazzaville	422

EGYPT (1976)
Cairo	6 818
Alexandria	2 318
El Giza	1 230
Shubra el Kheima	394
El Mahalla el Kubra	292
Tanta	285
Port Said	263
El Mansûra	259
Asyût	214
Zagazig	203

ETHIOPIA (1983)
Addis Ababa	1 478
Asmera	491

GABON (1983)
Libreville	350

GHANA (1984)
Accra	965
Kumasi	489

GUINEA (1980)
Conakry	763

IVORY COAST (1982)
Abidjan	1 850
Bouaké	640
Man-Danane	450
Korhogo	280

KENYA (1983)
Nairobi (1985)	1 200
Mombasa	410

LIBERIA (1984)
Monrovia	425

LIBYA (1982)
Tripoli	980
Benghazi	650
Misrâtah	285

MADAGASCAR (1978)
Antananarivo	400

MALAWI (1977)
Blantyre	219

MALI (1976)
Bamako	419

MOROCCO (1981)
Casablanca	2 409
Rabat-Salé	842
Fès	562
Marrakesh	549
Meknès	487
Oujda	470
Kénitra	450
Tétouan	372
Tangier	304
Safi	256
Agadir	246
Khouribga	229
Béni-Mellal	204

MOZAMBIQUE (1970)
Maputo	384

NIGER (1977)
Niamey	225

NIGERIA (1975)
Lagos	1 477
Ibadan	847
Ogbomosho	432
Kano	399
Ilorin	282
Oshogbo	282
Abeokuta	253
Port Harcourt	242
Ilesha	224
Zaria	224
Onitsha	220
Iwo	214
Ado-Ekiti	213
Kaduna	202

SENEGAL (1979)
Dakar	799

SIERRA LEONE (1982)
Freetown	316

SOMALI REP. (1982)
Mogadishu	600

SOUTH AFRICA (1980)
Johannesburg	1 726
Cape Town	1 491
Durban	961
Pretoria	739
Port Elizabeth	585
Vanderbijlpark/ Vereeniging	448

SUDAN (1983)
Omdurman	526
Khartoum	476
Khartoum North	341
Port Sudan	207

TANZANIA (1978)
Dar-es-Salaam	757

TOGO (1980)
Lomé	283

TUNISIA (1984)
Tunis	774
Sfax	232

UGANDA (1975)
Kampala	332

ZAÏRE (1976)
Kinshasa	2 444
Kananga	704
Lubumbashi	451
Mbuji Mayi	383
Kisangani	339
Bukavu	209

ZAMBIA (1980)
Lusaka	538
Kitwe	315
Ndola	282

ZIMBABWE (1983)
Harare	681
Bulawayo	429
Chitungwiza	202

ASIA

AFGHANISTAN (1982)
Kābul	1 127

BANGLADESH (1982)
Dacca	3 459
Chittagong	1 388
Khulna	623
Narayanganj	298

BURMA (1977)
Rangoon (1983)	2 459
Mandalay	458
Kanbe (1973)	254

CAMBODIA (KAMPUCHEA) (1983)
Phnom Penh	500

CHINA (1982)
Shanghai	11 940
Peking	9 330
Tientsin	7 850
Shenyang	4 080
Wuhan	3 280
Canton	3 160
Chungking	2 690
Harbin	2 560
Chengdu	2 510
Zibo	2 264
Sian	2 220
Nanking	2 170
Taiyuan	1 790
Changchun	1 770
Dalian	1 520
Zhengzhou	1 517
Lanzhou	1 430
Jinan	1 360
Tangshan	1 351
Guiyang	1 330
Kunming	1 320
Anshan	1 240
Qiqihar	1 232
Qingdao	1 210
Hangzhou	1 201
Fushun	1 200
Fuzhou	1 142
Changsha	1 100
Jilin	1 099
Shijiazhuang	1 098
Nanchang	1 061
Baotou	1 051
Huainan	1 017
Ürümqi	944
Xuzhou	793
Suzhou (1970)	730
Wuxi (1970)	650
Hefei (1970)	630
Benxi (1970)	600
Luoyang (1970)	580
Nanning (1970)	550
Hohhot (1970)	530
Xining (1970)	500

HONG KONG (1981)
Kowloon	2 450
Hong Kong	1 184
Tsuen Wan	599

INDIA (1981)
Calcutta	9 194
Bombay	8 243
Delhi	5 729
Madras	4 289
Bangalore	2 922
Ahmadabad	2 548
Hyderabad	2 546
Pune	1 686
Kanpur	1 639
Nagpur	1 302
Jaipur	1 015
Lucknow	1 008
Coimbatore	920
Patna	919
Surat	914
Madurai	908
Indore	829
Varanasi	797
Jabalpur	757
Agra	747
Vadodara	744
Cochin	686
Dhanbad	678
Bhopal	671
Jamshedpur	670
Allahabad	650
Ulhasnagar	649
Tiruchchirappalli	610
Ludhiana	606
Srinagar	606
Vishakhapatnam	604
Amritsar	595
Gwalior	556
Calicut	546
Vijayawada	543
Meerut	537
Dharwad	527
Trivandrum	520
Salem	519
Solapur	515
Jodhpur	506
Ranchi	503

INDONESIA (1980)
Jakarta	6 503
Surabaya	2 028
Bandung	1 462
Medan	1 379
Semarang	1 026
Palembang	787
Ujung Pandang	709
Malang	512
Padang	481
Surakarta	470
Yogyakarta	399
Banjarmasin	381
Pontianak	305
Tanjung Karang	284
Balikpapan	281
Samarinda	265
Bogor	247
Jambi	230
Cirebon	224
Kediri	222
Manado	217
Ambon	209

IRAN (1976)
Tehrān	4 589
Esfahān	842
Mashhad	743
Tabrīz	715
Shirāz	448
Ahvāz	340
Bākhtarān	336
Abadan	308
Qom	247
Hamadan	230
Karaj	214

IRAQ (1970)
Baghdād	2 969
Basra	371
Mosul	293
Kirkūk	208

ISRAEL (1983)
Jerusalem	429
Tel Aviv-Jaffa	327
Haifa	226

JAPAN (1982)
Tōkyō	11 676
Yokohama	2 848
Ōsaka	2 623
Nagoya	2 093
Kyōto	1 480
Sapporo	1 465
Kobe	1 383
Fukuoka	1 121
Kitakyūshū	1 065
Kawasaki	1 055
Hiroshima	898
Sakai	809
Chiba	756
Sendai	662
Okayama	551
Kumamoto	522
Kagoshima	514
Amagasaki	510
Higashiōsaka	501
Hamamatsu	500
Funabashi	488
Shizuoka	462
Niigata	458
Sagamihara	455
Nagasaki	449
Hameji	448
Yokosuka	429
Matsuyama	413
Kanazawa	412
Matsudo	411
Kurashiki	410
Nishinoyama	410
Gifu	409
Wakayama	404
Toyonaka	397
Hachiōji	395
Kawaguchi	391
Utsunomiya	389
Ichikawa	374
Hirakata	368
Oita	367
Urawa	366
Omiya	361
Asahikawa	359
Fukuyama	353
Iwaki	352
Takatsuki	340
Suita	333
Nagano	328
Hakodate	321
Takamatsu	320
Fujisawa	313
Toyohashi	311
Nara	309
Toyama	308
Kōchi	305
Naha	302
Machida	301
Aomori	291
Akita	290
Kōriyama	290
Toyota	287
Maebashi	271
Okazaki	269
Shimonoseki	269
Miyazaki	267
Yao	266
Fukushima	265
Kawagoe	265
Yokkaichi	258
Akashi	257
Neyagawa	255
Ichinomiya	253
Sasebo	253
Tokushima	251

JORDAN (1981)
'Ammān	681
Az-Zarqā	234

KOREA, NORTH (1972)
Pyŏngyang	1 500
Hamhung	420
Chongjin	265
Kimchaek	265

KOREA, SOUTH (1980)
Seoul	8 367
Pusan	3 160
Taegu	1 607
Inchŏn	1 085
Kwangju	728
Taejon	652
Ulsan	418
Masan	387
Songnam	376
Chonju	367
Suwŏn	311

KUWAIT (1980)
Kuwait	775

LEBANON (1980)
Beirut	702

MACAU (1981)
Macau	250

MALAYSIA (1980)
Kuala Lumpur	938
Ipoh	301
Pinang	251

MONGOLIA (1980)
Ulan Bator	419

NEPAL (1981)
Katmandu	235

PAKISTAN (1981)
Karachi	5 103
Lahore	2 922
Faisalabad	1 092
Rawalpindi	806
Hyderabad	795
Multan	730
Gujranwala	597
Peshawar	555
Sialkot	296
Sargodha	294
Quetta	243
Islamabad	201

PHILIPPINES (1980)
Manila	1 630
Quezon City	1 166
Davao	610
Cebu	490
Caloocan	468
Zamboanga	344
Pasay	288
Bacolod	262
Iloilo	245
Cagayan de Oro	227

SAUDI ARABIA (1974)
Riyadh	667
Jedda	561
Mecca	367
Taif	205

SINGAPORE (1983)
Singapore	2 517

SRI LANKA (1982)
Colombo	1 412

SYRIA (1982)
Damascus	1 112
Aleppo	985
Homs	354

TAIWAN (1981)
Taipei	2 271
Kaohsiung	1 227
Taichung	607
Tainan	595
Chilung	348
Sanchung	335
Chiai	252
Hsinchu	243
Fengshan	227
Chunli	215
Yungho	214

THAILAND (1980)
Bangkok (1982)	5 468

TURKEY (1982)
İstanbul	2 949
Ankara	2 276
İzmir	1 083
Adana	864
Konya	691
Bursa	658
Gaziantep	526
Mersin	440
Kayseri	394
Diyarbakir	390
Samsun	354
Balikesir	352
Eskişehir	352
İzmit	328
Zonguldak	321
Erzurum	292
Maras	292
Antalya	290
Urfa	285
Sivas	279
Malatya	245
Denizli	211

UNITED ARAB EMIRATES (1980)
Dubai	266
Abu Dhabi	243

VIETNAM (1973)
Ho Chi Minh City (1979)	3 420
Hanoi (1979)	2 571
Haiphong (1979)	1 279
Da-Nang	492
Nha-Trang	216
Qui-Nhon	214
Hue	209

YEMEN, NORTH (1981)
Sana'	278

YEMEN, SOUTH (1981)
Aden	264

AUSTRALIA AND NEW ZEALAND

AUSTRALIA (1983)
Sydney	3 335
Melbourne	2 865
Brisbane	1 138
Adelaide	969
Perth	969
Newcastle	414
Canberra	256
Wollongong	235

NEW ZEALAND (1983)
Auckland	864
Wellington	343
Christchurch	322

EUROPE

ALBANIA (1982)
Tiranë	202

AUSTRIA (1984)
Vienna	1 531
Graz	243

BELGIUM (1983)
Brussels	989
Antwerp	491
Ghent	237
Charleroi	216
Liège	207

BULGARIA (1984)
Sofia	1 094
Plovdiv	373
Varna	295

CZECHOSLOVAKIA (1984)
Prague	1 190
Bratislava	409
Brno	383
Ostrava	325
Kosice	218

DENMARK (1984)
Copenhagen	1 366

FINLAND (1983)
Helsinki	932
Turku	257
Tampere	250

FRANCE (1982)
Paris	8 510
Lyons	1 170
Marseilles	1 080
Lille	935
Bordeaux	628
Toulouse	523
Nantes	465
Nice	449
Toulon	410
Grenoble	392
Rouen	380
Strasbourg	373
Valenciennes	337
Lens	323
St-Étienne	317
Grasse-Cannes	296
Nancy	278
Clermont-Ferrand	256
Le Havre	255
Tours	255
Rennes	234
Montpellier	221
Mulhouse	220
Orléans	220
Dijon	209
Douai	202

GERMANY, EAST (1982)
East Berlin	1 173
Leipzig	557
Dresden	521
Karl-Marx-Stadt	320
Magdeburg	288
Rostock	239
Halle	235
Erfurt	213

GERMANY, WEST (1983)
West Berlin	1 860
Hamburg	1 618
Munich	1 284
Cologne	953
Essen	635
Frankfurt	615
Dortmund	595
Düsseldorf	580
Stuttgart	571
Bremen	545
Duisburg	542
Hanover	524
Nuremberg	476
Bochum	391
Wuppertal	386
Bielefeld	308
Mannheim	300
Gelsenkirchen	295

Bonn	293
Munster	273
Wiesbaden	273
Karlsruhe	270
Mönchengladbach	258
Braunschweig	257
Kiel	248
Augsburg	247
Aachen	244
Oberhausen	226
Krefeld	222
Lübeck	216
Hagen	212

GREECE (1981)
Athens	3 027
Thessaloníki	871

HUNGARY (1984)
Budapest	2 064
Miskolc	211

IRISH REPUBLIC (1981)
Dublin	915

ITALY (1983)
Rome	2 831
Milan	1 561
Naples	1 209
Turin	1 069
Genoa	747
Palermo	712
Bologna	448
Florence	441
Catánia	380
Bari	370
Venice	341
Messina	264
Verona	262
Trieste	246
Táranto	243
Padua	231
Cágliari	225
Bréscia	204

NETHERLANDS (1984)
Rotterdam	1 025
Amsterdam	994
The Hague	672
Utrecht	501
Eindhoven	374
Arnhem	291
Heerlen-Kerkrade	266
Enschede-Hengelo	248
Tilburg	234
Nijmegen	222
Haarlem	217
Groningen	207

NORWAY (1984)
Oslo	643
Bergen	208

POLAND (1984)
Warsaw	1 649
Łodz	849
Kraków	740
Wrocław	636
Poznań	574
Gdansk	467
Szczecin	391
Katowice	363
Bydgoszcz	361
Lublin	324
Sosnowiec	254
Częstochowa	247
Białystok	245
Gdynia	243
Bytom	238
Radom	213
Gliwice	206

PORTUGAL (1981)
Lisbon	1 612
Oporto	1 315

ROMANIA (1982)
Bucharest	1 979
Braşov	334
Constanţa	307
Timişoara	302
Cluj-Napoca	301
Iaşi	295
Galaţi	279
Craiova	253
Ploieşti	228
Brăila	225
Oradea	201

SPAIN (1981)
Madrid	3 188
Barcelona	1 755
Valencia	752
Seville	654
Zaragoza	591
Málaga	503
Bilbao	433
Valladolid	330
Palma de Mallorca	304
Hospitalet	294
Murcia	289
Córdoba	285
Granada	262
Vigo	259
Gijón	256
Alicante	251
La Coruña	232
Badalona	228

SWEDEN (1983)
Stockholm	1 420
Göteborg	699
Malmö	455

SWITZERLAND (1983)
Zürich	840
Geneva	372
Basle	365
Bern	301
Lausanne	225

U.S.S.R. (1983-84)
Moscow	8 537
Leningrad	4 827
Kiev	2 409
Tashkent	1 986
Baku	1 661
Kharkov	1 536
Minsk	1 442
Gorki	1 392
Novosibirsk	1 384
Sverdlovsk	1 286
Kuybyshev	1 250
Dnepropetrovsk	1 140
Tbilisi	1 140
Yerevan	1 114
Odessa	1 113
Omsk	1 094
Chelyabinsk	1 086
Donetsk	1 064
Perm	1 048
Ufa	1 048
Alma-Ata	1 046
Kazan	1 039
Rostov	983
Volgograd	969
Saratov	893
Riga	875
Krasnoyarsk	857
Zaporozhye	844
Voronezh	840
Lvov	728
Krivoy Rog	680
Yaroslavl	623
Karaganda	608
Kishinev	605
Krasnodar	603
Ustinov	603
Frunze	590
Vladivostok	590
Irkutsk	589
Novokuznetsk	572
Barnaul	568
Khabarovsk	568
Dushanbe	539
Vilnius	535
Tula	529
Ulyanovsk	524
Penza	522
Zhdanov	520
Samarkand	515
Orenburg	513

UNITED KINGDOM (1981)
London (1985)	6 767
Birmingham (1985)	1 007
Glasgow	762
Liverpool	510
Leeds	449
Manchester	449
Sheffield	447
Edinburgh	419
Bristol	388
Belfast	374
Coventry	314
Leicester	283

Bradford	281
Cardiff	274
Nottingham	271
Hull	268
Stoke-on-Trent	252
Wolverhampton	252
Plymouth	244
Derby	216
Southampton	204

YUGOSLAVIA (1981)
Belgrade	1 407
Zagreb	1 175
Skopje	507
Sarajevo	449
Ljubljana	305
Novi Sad	258
Split	236
Niš	231
Priština	216

NORTH AMERICA

CANADA (1983)
Toronto	3 067
Montréal	2 862
Vancouver	1 311
Ottawa	738
Edmonton	699
Calgary	634
Winnipeg	601
Québec	580
Hamilton	548
St. Catherines	304
Kitchener	294
London	287
Halifax	281
Windsor	245
Victoria	240

COSTA RICA (1984)
San José	245

CUBA (1982)
Havana	1 951
Santiago de Cuba	349
Camagüey	251

DOMINICAN REP. (1981)
Santo Domingo	1 313
Santiago	279

EL SALVADOR (1983)
San Salvador	884

GUATEMALA (1983)
Guatemala	1 300

HAITI (1982)
Port-au-Prince	888

HONDURAS (1982)
Tegucigalpa	534
San Pedro Sula	398

JAMAICA (1980)
Kingston	671

MEXICO (1979)
Mexico	14 750
Guadalajara	2 468
Netzahualcóyotl	2 331
Monterrey	2 019
Puebla	711
Ciudad Juárez	625
León	625
Tijuana	566
Acapulco	462
Torreón	407
Tampico	390
Chihuahua	386
Mexicali	349
San Luis Potosi	327
Culiacán	324
Hermosillo	319
Veracruz	307
Mérida	270
Saltillo	258
Aguascalientes	257
Morelia	251
Toluca	242
Cuernavaca	241
Reynosa	231
Durango	229
Nuevo Laredo	224
Jalapa	201

NICARAGUA (1981)
Managua	615

PANAMA (1981)
Panama	655

PUERTO RICO (1980)
San Juan	1 086
Ponce	253
Bayamón	209

UNITED STATES (1984)
New York	17 807
Los Angeles	12 373
Chicago	8 035
Philadelphia	5 755
San Francisco	5 685
Detroit	4 577
Boston	4 027
Houston	3 566
Washington	3 429
Dallas	3 348
Miami	2 799
Cleveland	2 788
St. Louis	2 398
Atlanta	2 380
Pittsburgh	2 372
Baltimore	2 245
Minneapolis-St. Paul	2 231
Seattle	2 208
San Diego	2 064
Tampa	1 811
Denver	1 791
Phoenix	1 715
Cincinnati	1 673
Milwaukee	1 568
Kansas City	1 477
Portland	1 341
New Orleans	1 319
Columbus	1 279
Sacramento	1 220
Buffalo	1 205
Indianapolis	1 195
San Antonio	1 188
Providence	1 095
Norfolk	1 026
Salt Lake City	1 025
Rochester	989
Louisville	963
Oklahoma	963
Memphis	935
Dayton	930
Birmingham	895
Nashville-Davidson	890
Greensboro	886
Albany	843
Orlando	824
Honolulu	805
Richmond	796
Jacksonville	795
Hartford	729
Scranton	727
Tulsa	726
West Palm Beach	692
Syracuse	650
Charlotte	647
Austin	645
Allentown	635
Grand Rapids	626
Toledo	611
Raleigh	609
Omaha	607
Greenville	593
Knoxville	589
Fresno	565
Baton Rouge	538
Las Vegas	536
Tucson	531
El Paso	526
Youngstown	518
Springfield	516

SOUTH AMERICA

ARGENTINA (1980)
Buenos Aires	9 927
Córdoba	982
Rosario	955
Mendoza	597
La Plata	560
San Miguel de Tucuman	497
Mar del Plata	407
San Juan	290
Santa Fé	287
Salta	260
Bahia Blanca	221
Resistencia	218

BOLIVIA (1982)
La Paz	881
Santa Cruz	377
Cochabamba	282

BRAZIL (1980)
São Paulo	8 493
Rio de Janeiro	5 091
Belo Horizonte	1 781
Salvador	1 502
Fortaleza	1 308
Recife	1 204
Brasilia	1 177
Pôrto Alegre	1 125
Nova Iguaçu	1 095
Curitiba	1 025
Belém	933
Goiánia	717
Campinas	665
Manaus	633
São Gonçalo	615
Duque de Caxias	576
Santo André	553
Guarulhos	533
Osasco	474
São Luis	449
São Bernardo do Campo	426
Natal	417
Santos	417
Maceió	399
São João de Meriti	399
Niterói	397
Teresina	378
Campos	348
Jaboatao	330
João Pessoa	330
Ribeirão Preto	318
Juiz de Fora	307
Londrina	302
Aracaju	293
Campo Grande	292
Feira de Santana	292
São José dos Campos	288
Olinda	282
Sorocaba	269
Pelotas	260
Jundiaí	259

CHILE (1983)
Santiago	4 132
Viña del Mar	299
Valparaiso	268
Talcahuano	213
Concepción	210

COLOMBIA (1980)
Bogotá	4 486
Medellin	1 812
Cali	1 232
Barranquilla	900
Bucaramanga	459
Cartagena	368
Pereira	309
Manizales	302
Cucuta	272
Ibagué	238

ECUADOR (1982)
Guayaquil	1 301
Quito	1 110

PARAGUAY (1983)
Asunción	708

PERU (1981)
Lima (1983)	5 258
Arequipa	447
Callao	441
Trujillo	355
Chiclayo	280
Chimbote	216

URUGUAY (1981)
Montevideo	1 362

VENEZUELA (1980)
Caracas	2 944
Maracaibo	901
Valencia	506
Barquisimento	489
Maracay	344
Barcelona-Puerto La Cruz	275
San Cristóbal	272
Ciudad Guayana	206

1:105 000 000

LANGUAGES

1	Slavic
2	Germanic
3	Celtic
4	Romance
5	Greek
6	Albanian
7	Iranian
8	Indo-Aryan
9	Armenian

10	Caucasian
11	Basque
12	Burushaskis

13	Semitic
14	Kushit
15	Berber

16	Khoisan
17	Bantu
18	Sudanese
19	E & C Sudan
20	Nilotic

21	Ural

22	Turkic
23	Mongolian
24	Tungus-Manchu
25	Japanese/Korean

26	Sinitic and other
27	Tibeto-Burman
28	Vietnamese

29	Mon-Khmer
30	Munda

31	Dravidian
32	Andamanese

33	Indonesian
34	Polynesian
35	Melanesian

36	Papuan
37	Australian Abor.
•38•	Ainu
39	Paleoasiatic
40	Eskimo-Aleut
41	Amerindian

RELIGIONS

▲	Roman Catholicism
	Orthodox and other Eastern Churches
•	Protestantism
	Sunni Islam

	Shiah Islam
	Buddhism
	Hinduism
	Confucianism

✡	Judaism
	Shintoism
	Primitive religions

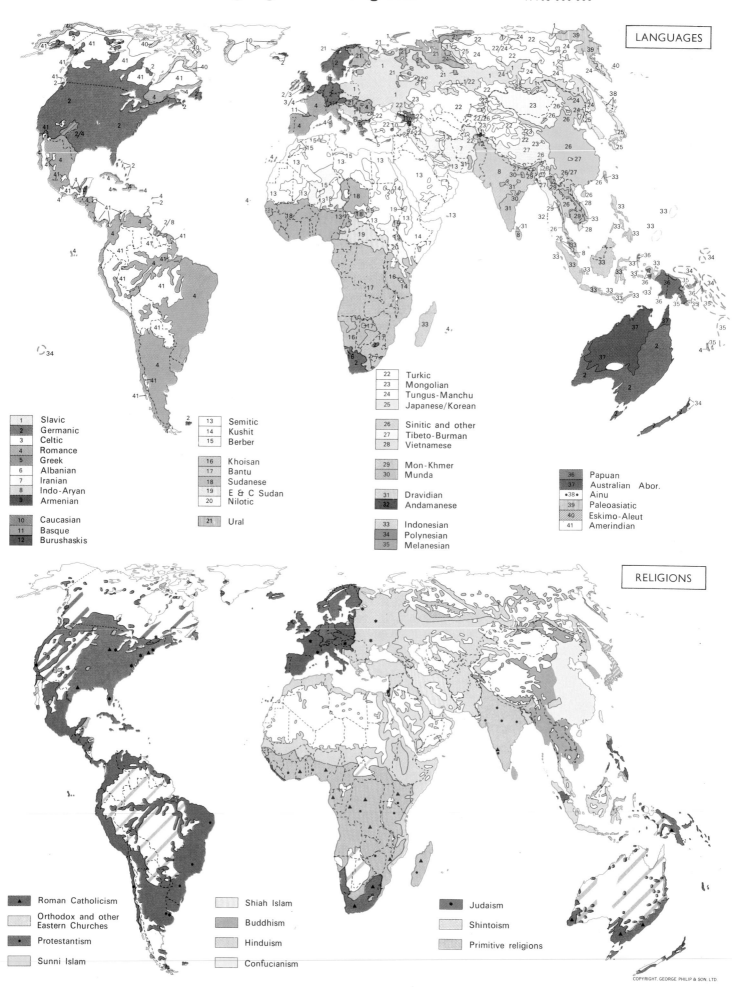

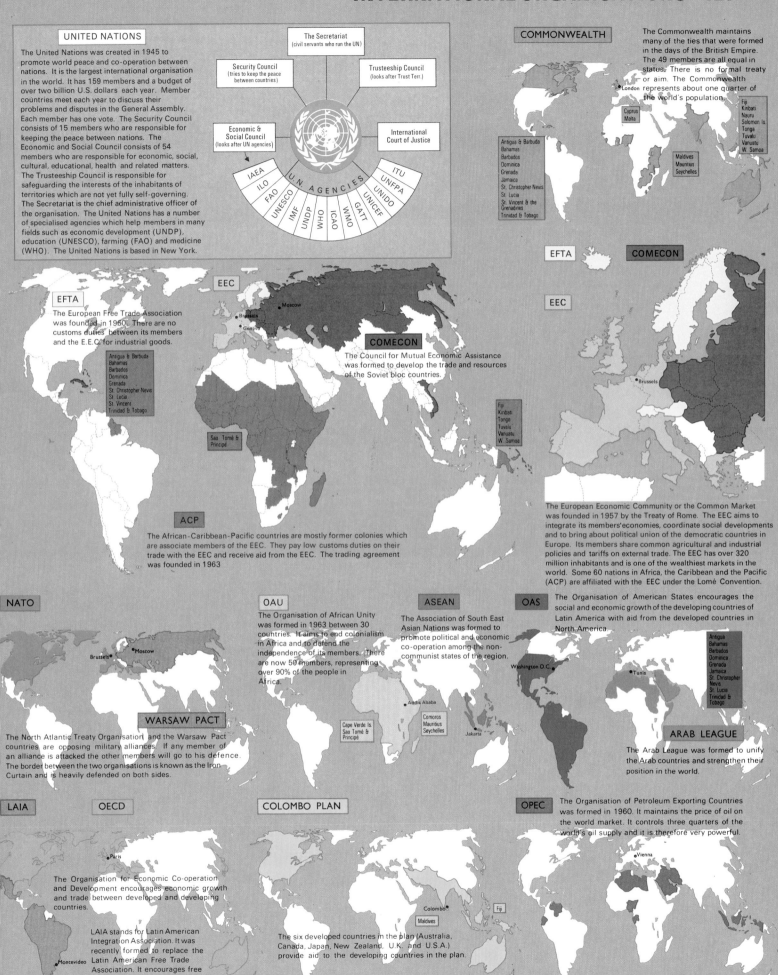

UNITED NATIONS

The United Nations was created in 1945 to promote world peace and co-operation between nations. It is the largest international organisation in the world. It has 159 members and a budget of over two billion U.S. dollars each year. Member countries meet each year to discuss their problems and disputes in the General Assembly. Each member has one vote. The Security Council consists of 15 members who are responsible for keeping the peace between nations. The Economic and Social Council consists of 54 members who are responsible for economic, social, cultural, educational, health and related matters. The Trusteeship Council is responsible for safeguarding the interests of the inhabitants of territories which are not yet fully self-governing. The Secretariat is the chief administrative officer of the organisation. The United Nations has a number of specialised agencies which help members in many fields such as economic development (UNDP), education (UNESCO), farming (FAO) and medicine (WHO). The United Nations is based in New York.

The Secretariat
(civil servants who run the UN)

Security Council
(tries to keep the peace between countries)

Trusteeship Council
(looks after Trust Terr.)

Economic & Social Council
(looks after UN agencies)

International Court of Justice

U.N. AGENCIES
IAEA, ILO, FAO, UNESCO, IMF, UNDP, OHW, ICAO, WMO, GATT, UNICEF, UNIDO, UNFPA, ITU

COMMONWEALTH

The Commonwealth maintains many of the ties that were formed in the days of the British Empire. The 49 members are all equal in status. There is no formal treaty or aim. The Commonwealth represents about one quarter of the world's population.

London, Cyprus, Malta

Antigua & Barbuda, Bahamas, Barbados, Dominica, Grenada, Jamaica, St. Christopher Nevis, St. Lucia, St. Vincent & the Grenadines, Trinidad & Tobago

Maldives, Mauritius, Seychelles

Fiji, Kiribati, Nauru, Solomon Is., Tonga, Tuvalu, Vanuatu, W. Samoa

EFTA

The European Free Trade Association was founded in 1960. There are no customs duties between its members and the E.E.C. for industrial goods.

Antigua & Barbuda, Bahamas, Barbados, Dominica, Grenada, St. Christopher Nevis, St. Lucia, St. Vincent, Trinidad & Tobago

EEC

Moscow, Brussels, Geneva

COMECON

The Council for Mutual Economic Assistance was formed to develop the trade and resources of the Soviet bloc countries.

Sao Tomé & Principé

Fiji, Kiribati, Tonga, Tuvalu, Vanuatu, W. Samoa

EFTA

COMECON

EEC

Brussels

The European Economic Community or the Common Market was founded in 1957 by the Treaty of Rome. The EEC aims to integrate its members' economies, coordinate social developments and to bring about political union of the democratic countries in Europe. Its members share common agricultural and industrial policies and tariffs on external trade. The EEC has over 320 million inhabitants and is one of the wealthiest markets in the world. Some 60 nations in Africa, the Caribbean and the Pacific (ACP) are affiliated with the EEC under the Lomé Convention.

ACP

The African-Caribbean-Pacific countries are mostly former colonies which are associate members of the EEC. They pay low customs duties on their trade with the EEC and receive aid from the EEC. The trading agreement was founded in 1963

NATO

Brussels, Moscow

WARSAW PACT

The North Atlantic Treaty Organisation and the Warsaw Pact countries are opposing military alliances. If any member of an alliance is attacked the other members will go to his defence. The border between the two organisations is known as the Iron Curtain and is heavily defended on both sides.

OAU

The Organisation of African Unity was formed in 1963 between 30 countries. It aims to end colonialism in Africa and to defend the independence of its members. There are now 50 members, representing over 90% of the people in Africa.

Addis Ababa

Cape Verde Is., Sao Tomé & Principé

Comoros, Mauritius, Seychelles

ASEAN

The Association of South East Asian Nations was formed to promote political and economic co-operation among the non-communist states of the region.

Jakarta

OAS

The Organisation of American States encourages the social and economic growth of the developing countries of Latin America with aid from the developed countries in North America.

Washington D.C., Tunis

Antigua, Bahamas, Barbados, Dominica, Grenada, Jamaica, St. Christopher Nevis, St. Lucia, Trinidad & Tobago

ARAB LEAGUE

The Arab League was formed to unify the Arab countries and strengthen their position in the world.

LAIA

OECD

Paris

The Organisation for Economic Co-operation and Development encourages economic growth and trade between developed and developing countries.

LAIA stands for Latin American Integration Association. It was recently formed to replace the Latin American Free Trade Association. It encourages free trade between its members.

Montevideo

COLOMBO PLAN

Colombo, Maldives, Fiji

The six developed countries in the plan (Australia, Canada, Japan, New Zealand, U.K. and U.S.A.) provide aid to the developing countries in the plan.

OPEC

The Organisation of Petroleum Exporting Countries was formed in 1960. It maintains the price of oil on the world market. It controls three quarters of the world's oil supply and it is therefore very powerful.

Vienna

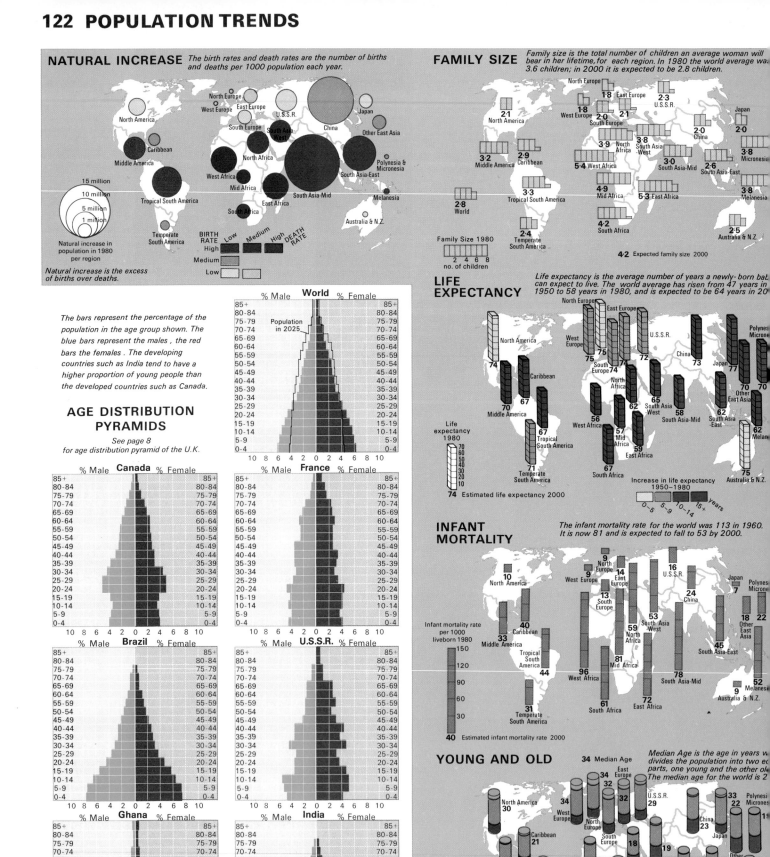

NATURAL INCREASE

The birth rates and death rates are the number of births and deaths per 1000 population each year.

Natural increase in population in 1980 per region

Natural increase is the excess of births over deaths.

BIRTH RATE: Low, Medium, High — DEATH RATE: High, Medium, Low

FAMILY SIZE

Family size is the total number of children an average woman will bear in her lifetime, for each region. In 1980 the world average was 3.6 children; in 2000 it is expected to be 2.8 children.

Family Size 1980 — no. of children
4·2 Expected family size 2000

AGE DISTRIBUTION PYRAMIDS

The bars represent the percentage of the population in the age group shown. The blue bars represent the males , the red bars the females . The developing countries such as India tend to have a higher proportion of young people than the developed countries such as Canada.

See page 8
for age distribution pyramid of the U.K.

(Pyramids: World, Canada, France, Brazil, U.S.S.R., Ghana, India)

LIFE EXPECTANCY

Life expectancy is the average number of years a newly-born baby can expect to live. The world average has risen from 47 years in 1950 to 58 years in 1980, and is expected to be 64 years in 2000.

Life expectancy 1980
74 Estimated life expectancy 2000
Increase in life expectancy 1950–1980: 0–5, 5–9, 10–14, 15+ years

INFANT MORTALITY

The infant mortality rate for the world was 113 in 1960. It is now 81 and is expected to fall to 53 by 2000.

Infant mortality rate per 1000 liveborn 1980
40 Estimated infant mortality rate 2000

YOUNG AND OLD

Median Age is the age in years which divides the population into two equal parts, one young and the other old. The median age for the world is 2...

34 Median Age

Age structure 1980: 100%, 75%, 50%, 25%

65+, 15–64, –15 years

35% of the world's population is under 15 years of age whilst 6% is over 65.

See page 125 for maps of Population Growth and Urbanisation

POPULATION BY COUNTRY

See map on pages 116-117 for greater detail.

The most populous country (China) contains a quarter of the world's population. The four most populous countries (China, India, U.S.S.R., and U.S.A.) contain half, and the first eighteen (all those countries named in larger type on the map) contain over three-quarters of the world's population. The remaining 150 countries contain only one quarter.

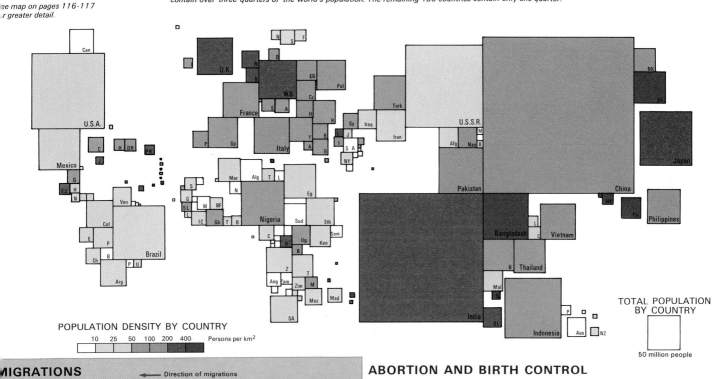

POPULATION DENSITY BY COUNTRY

10   25   50   100   200   400   Persons per km²

TOTAL POPULATION BY COUNTRY

50 million people

MIGRATIONS

← Direction of migrations

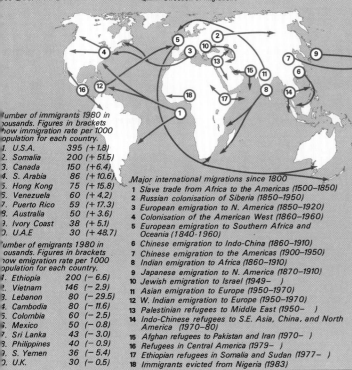

Number of immigrants 1980 in thousands. Figures in brackets show immigration rate per 1000 population for each country.

1. U.S.A.	395	(+ 1.8)
2. Somalia	200	(+ 51.5)
3. Canada	150	(+6.4)
4. S. Arabia	86	(+ 10.6)
5. Hong Kong	75	(+ 15.8)
6. Venezuela	60	(+ 4.2)
7. Puerto Rico	59	(+ 17.3)
8. Australia	50	(+ 3.6)
9. Ivory Coast	38	(+ 5.1)
10. U.A.E	30	(+ 48.7)

Number of emigrants 1980 in thousands. Figures in brackets show emigration rate per 1000 population for each country.

1. Ethiopia	200	(− 6.6)
2. Vietnam	146	(− 2.9)
3. Lebanon	80	(− 29.5)
4. Cambodia	80	(− 11.6)
5. Colombia	60	(− 2.5)
6. Mexico	50	(− 0.8)
7. Sri Lanka	43	(− 3.0)
8. Philippines	40	(− 0.9)
9. S. Yemen	36	(− 5.4)
10. U.K.	30	(− 0.5)

Major international migrations since 1800
1 Slave trade from Africa to the Americas (1500–1850)
2 Russian colonisation of Siberia (1850–1950)
3 European emigration to N. America (1850–1920)
4 Colonisation of the American West (1860–1960)
5 European emigration to Southern Africa and Oceania (1840-1960)
6 Chinese emigration to Indo-China (1860–1910)
7 Chinese emigration to the Americas (1900–1950)
8 Indian emigration to Africa (1860–1910)
9 Japanese emigration to N. America (1870–1910)
10 Jewish emigration to Israel (1949–   )
11 Asian emigration to Europe (1950–1970)
12 W. Indian emigration to Europe (1950–1970)
13 Palestinian refugees to Middle East (1950–   )
14 Indo-Chinese refugees to S.E. Asia, China, and North America (1970–80)
15 Afghan refugees to Pakistan and Iran (1970–   )
16 Refugees in Central America (1979–   )
17 Ethiopian refugees in Somalia and Sudan (1977–   )
18 Immigrants evicted from Nigeria (1983)

Until comparatively recently there was little increase in the population of the world. It is thought there were about 200 million in 600 B.C., 300 million in 1000 A.D. and 500 million by 1600 A.D.. This diagram shows how the world's population has increased since then at an ever increasing rate. 90% of this increase has been in the less developed regions. The world population of 1950 will have doubled by 1990 and if present trends continue it will have trebled by 2020.

POPULATION INCREASE SINCE 1650

ABORTION AND BIRTH CONTROL

Poland 75 %
France 79 %
China 69 %
U.S.A. 65%
Mexico 39%
Egypt 24 %
India 28 %
Indonesia 53 %
Nigeria 6 %

Status of Abortion
- Abortion legal
- Legal only for certain medical or juridical reasons
- Abortions illegal
- No data

Percentage of married women using contraception, for selected countries.

Legally induced abortions per 1000 live births. Total abortions in thousands are in brackets.

Bulgaria	1216	(152)	Canada	175 (66)
U.S.A.	347	(1 158)	New Zealand	133 (7)
France	207	(171)	Tunisia	77 (16)
Poland	192	(141)	India	27 (346)
Great Britain	189	(137)		

POPULATION IN 2000 A.D.

Percentage of world total is given in brackets.

World	6 119		
South Asia	2 075 (34%)	U.S.S.R.	310 (5%)
East Asia	1 475 (24%)	Europe	512 (8.5%)
Oceania	30 (0.5%)		
Africa	853 (14%)		
South America	566 (9%)		
N. America	299 (5%)		

6000 m
5000 m
4000 m
South Asia
Oceania
3000 m
2000 m
Africa
East Asia
South America
1000 m
North America

Asia pre 1925
Europe pre 1925
U.S.S.R.
Europe

1700   1750   1800   1850   1900   1925   1950   1975   2000

NATURAL DISASTERS

EARTHQUAKES AND VOLCANOES

○ Major earthquakes with dates

▲ Major volcanoes

▨ Earthquake zones (land and sea)

STORMS AND FLOODS

✳ Major storms and floods with dates

⇨ Paths of winter blizzards

⇨ Paths of tropical storms

⬛ Areas liable to flood

PESTS

⠿ Locust invasion areas

▨ Main tsetse fly areas

MAJOR FAMINES

◉ Sahel 1973

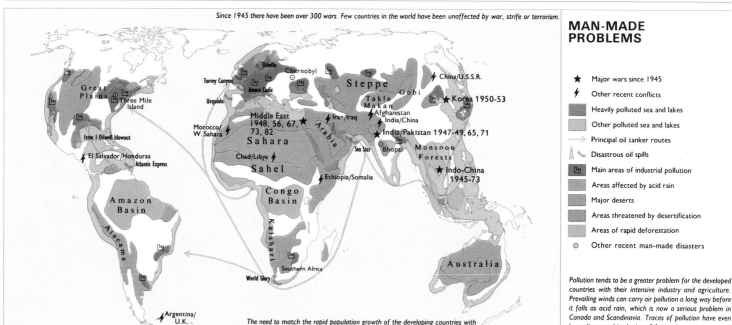

Famine is by far the most destructive of these disasters. Over a quarter million starved to death in the Sahel during the drought of 1968–1973. Famine is usually the result of prolonged drought but it can also be caused by war, flood, disease or pests.

Since 1945 there have been over 300 wars. Few countries in the world have been unaffected by war, strife or terrorism.

MAN-MADE PROBLEMS

★ Major wars since 1945

⚡ Other recent conflicts

⬛ Heavily polluted sea and lakes

⬛ Other polluted sea and lakes

→ Principal oil tanker routes

⚓ Disastrous oil spills

⬛ Main areas of industrial pollution

⬛ Areas affected by acid rain

⬛ Major deserts

⬛ Areas threatened by desertification

⬛ Areas of rapid deforestation

⊙ Other recent man-made disasters

Pollution tends to be a greater problem for the developed countries with their intensive industry and agriculture. Prevailing winds can carry air pollution a long way before it falls as acid rain, which is now a serious problem in Canada and Scandinavia. Traces of pollution have even been discovered in the ice of Antarctica.

The need to match the rapid population growth of the developing countries with increased production of food and fuel has led to overfarming and the destruction of the vegetation cover and the soil.

MEDICAL CARE

Persons per doctor in each country

over 25000	1000–5000
10000–25000	less than 1000
5000–10000	

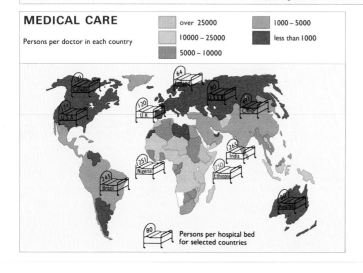

Persons per hospital bed for selected countries

NUTRITION

Calorie intake as a percentage of needs per person

less than 80%	100–110%
80–90%	110–120%
90–100%	over 120%

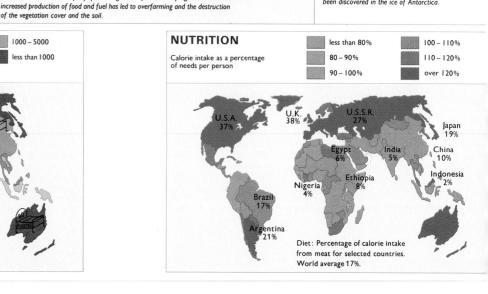

Diet: Percentage of calorie intake from meat for selected countries. World average 17%.

STANDARDS OF LIVING

THE RICH

Countries with more than four times the world's average income

Countries with more than twice the world's average income

Countries with incomes just above the world's average

THE POOR

Countries with incomes just below the world's average

Countries with less than half of the world's average income

Countries with less than one quarter of the world's average income

Data not available

The world's average income is just under 2200 US$ per annum. The richest country on a per capita basis is Kuwait with an income over 200 times that of the poorest country, Mali.

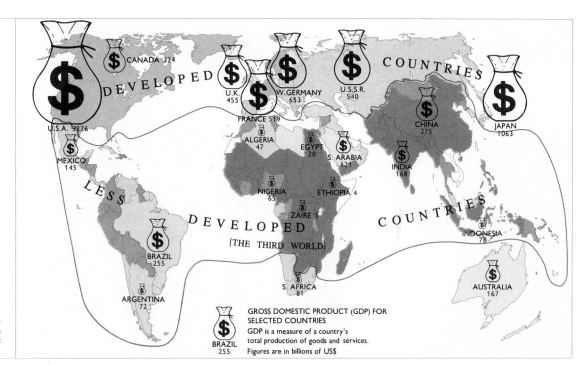

DEVELOPED COUNTRIES

CANADA 324
U.K. 455
W.GERMANY 653
U.S.S.R. 540
U.S.A. 3276
FRANCE 519
CHINA 275
JAPAN 1063
MEXICO 145
ALGERIA 47
EGYPT 28
S. ARABIA 121
INDIA 168

LESS DEVELOPED COUNTRIES
(THE THIRD WORLD)

NIGERIA 65
ETHIOPIA 4
ZAIRE 5
INDONESIA 78

BRAZIL 255
S. AFRICA 81
AUSTRALIA 167
ARGENTINA 72

GROSS DOMESTIC PRODUCT (GDP) FOR SELECTED COUNTRIES

GDP is a measure of a country's total production of goods and services. Figures are in billions of US$

BRAZIL 255

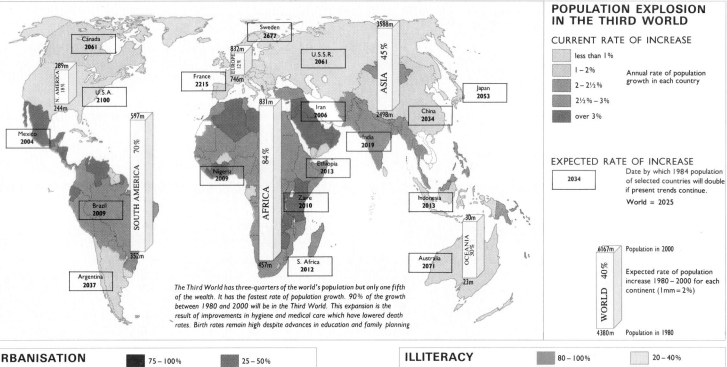

POPULATION EXPLOSION IN THE THIRD WORLD

CURRENT RATE OF INCREASE

less than 1%

1 – 2%

2 – 2½%

2½% – 3%

over 3%

Annual rate of population growth in each country

EXPECTED RATE OF INCREASE

2034

Date by which 1984 population of selected countries will double if present trends continue.

World = 2025

6167m — Population in 2000

WORLD 40%

Expected rate of population increase 1980 – 2000 for each continent (1mm = 2%)

4380m — Population in 1980

Canada 2061
N. AMERICA 18% 289m
U.S.A. 2100 244m
Mexico 2004 597m
SOUTH AMERICA 70%
Brazil 2009 352m
Argentina 2037
Sweden 2677
EUROPE 12% 832m
France 2215 746m
U.S.S.R. 2061
AFRICA 84% 831m
Iran 2006
Nigeria 2009
Ethiopia 2013
Zaire 2010
S. Africa 2012 457m
ASIA 45% 3588m
India 2019
China 2034 2498m
Japan 2053
Indonesia 2013
Australia 2071
OCEANIA 30% 30m 23m

The Third World has three-quarters of the world's population but only one fifth of the wealth. It has the fastest rate of population growth. 90% of the growth between 1980 and 2000 will be in the Third World. This expansion is the result of improvements in hygiene and medical care which have lowered death rates. Birth rates remain high despite advances in education and family planning

URBANISATION

Percentage of population living in towns and cities in each country

75 – 100%
50 – 75%
25 – 50%
0 – 25%

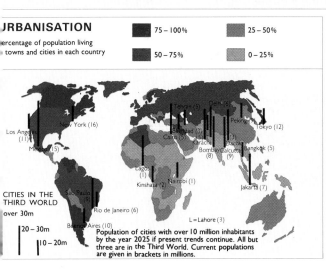

Tehran (5)
New York (16)
Delhi (6)
Los Angeles (11)
Baghdad (3)
Peking (9)
Tokyo (12)
Mexico (15)
Cairo (5)
Karachi (3)
Dacca (3)
Bombay (8)
Calcutta (9)
Bangkok (5)
Lagos (1)
Kinshasa (2)
Nairobi (1)
Jakarta (7)
Sao Paulo (9)
Rio de Janeiro (6)
L = Lahore (3)
Buenos Aires (10)

CITIES IN THE THIRD WORLD
over 30m
20 – 30m
10 – 20m

Population of cities with over 10 million inhabitants by the year 2025 if present trends continue. All but three are in the Third World. Current populations are given in brackets in millions.

ILLITERACY

Percentage of population in each country who are illiterate

80 – 100%
60 – 80%
40 – 60%
20 – 40%
0 – 20%

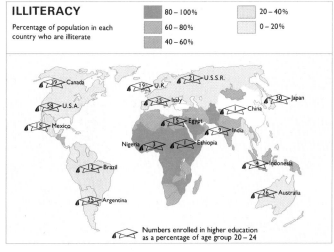

39 Canada
19 U.K.
21 U.S.S.R.
58 U.S.A.
25 Italy
30 Japan
15 Mexico
15 Egypt
1 China
9 India
Nigeria 3
Ethiopia
12 Brazil
4 Indonesia
25 Argentina
26 Australia

Numbers enrolled in higher education as a percentage of age group 20 – 24

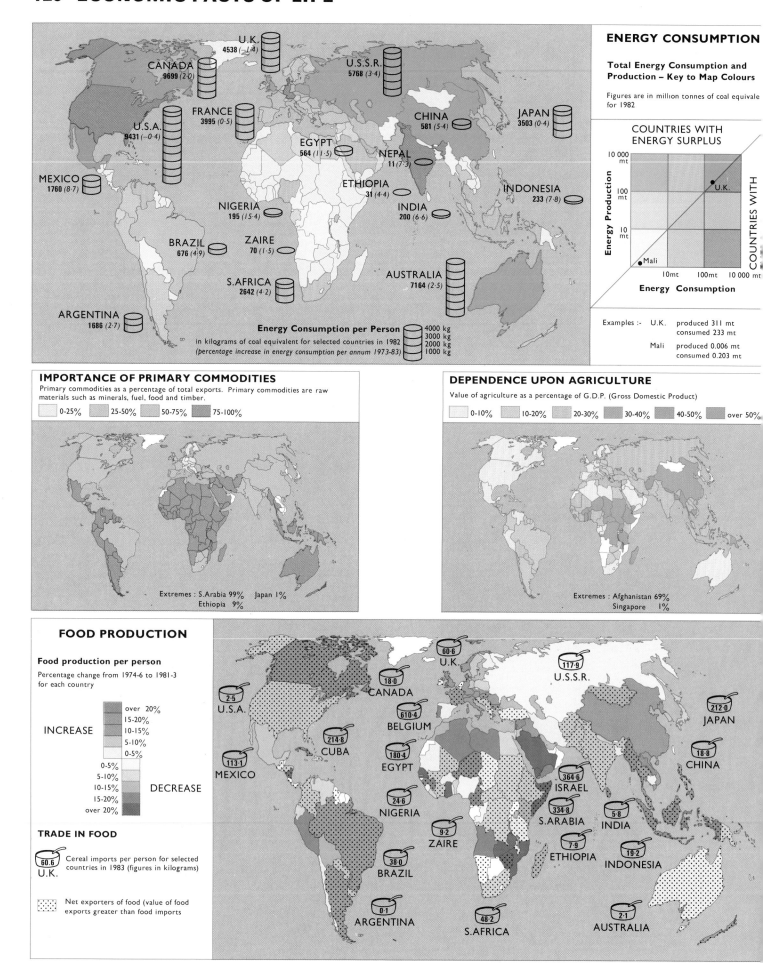

ENERGY CONSUMPTION

Total Energy Consumption and Production – Key to Map Colours

Figures are in million tonnes of coal equivalent for 1982

COUNTRIES WITH ENERGY SURPLUS

CANADA 9699 (2·0)
U.K. 4538 (–1·4)
U.S.S.R. 5768 (3·4)
FRANCE 3995 (0·5)
CHINA 581 (5·4)
JAPAN 3503 (0·4)
U.S.A. 9431 (–0·4)
EGYPT 564 (11·5)
NEPAL 11 (7·3)
MEXICO 1760 (8·7)
ETHIOPIA 31 (4·4)
INDONESIA 233 (7·8)
NIGERIA 195 (15·4)
INDIA 200 (6·6)
BRAZIL 676 (4·9)
ZAIRE 70 (1·5)
S.AFRICA 2642 (4·2)
AUSTRALIA 7164 (2·5)
ARGENTINA 1686 (2·7)

Energy Consumption per Person
in kilograms of coal equivalent for selected countries in 1982
(percentage increase in energy consumption per annum 1973-83)

4000 kg
3000 kg
2000 kg
1000 kg

Examples :- U.K. produced 311 mt
consumed 233 mt

Mali produced 0.006 mt
consumed 0.203 mt

IMPORTANCE OF PRIMARY COMMODITIES

Primary commodities as a percentage of total exports. Primary commodities are raw materials such as minerals, fuel, food and timber.

0-25% 25-50% 50-75% 75-100%

Extremes : S.Arabia 99% Japan 1%
Ethiopia 9%

DEPENDENCE UPON AGRICULTURE

Value of agriculture as a percentage of G.D.P. (Gross Domestic Product)

0-10% 10-20% 20-30% 30-40% 40-50% over 50%

Extremes : Afghanistan 69%
Singapore 1%

FOOD PRODUCTION

Food production per person

Percentage change from 1974-6 to 1981-3 for each country

INCREASE
over 20%
15-20%
10-15%
5-10%
0-5%

0-5%
5-10%
10-15%
15-20%
over 20%
DECREASE

TRADE IN FOOD

Cereal imports per person for selected countries in 1983 (figures in kilograms)
U.K. 60·6

Net exporters of food (value of food exports greater than food imports)

U.K. 60·6
U.S.S.R. 117·9
CANADA 18·0
U.S.A. 2·5
JAPAN 212·0
BELGIUM 610·4
CUBA 214·8
EGYPT 180·4
CHINA 18·8
MEXICO 113·1
ISRAEL 364·6
NIGERIA 24·6
S.ARABIA 334·8
INDIA 5·8
ZAIRE 9·2
ETHIOPIA 7·9
INDONESIA 19·2
BRAZIL 38·0
ARGENTINA 0·1
S.AFRICA 48·2
AUSTRALIA 2·1

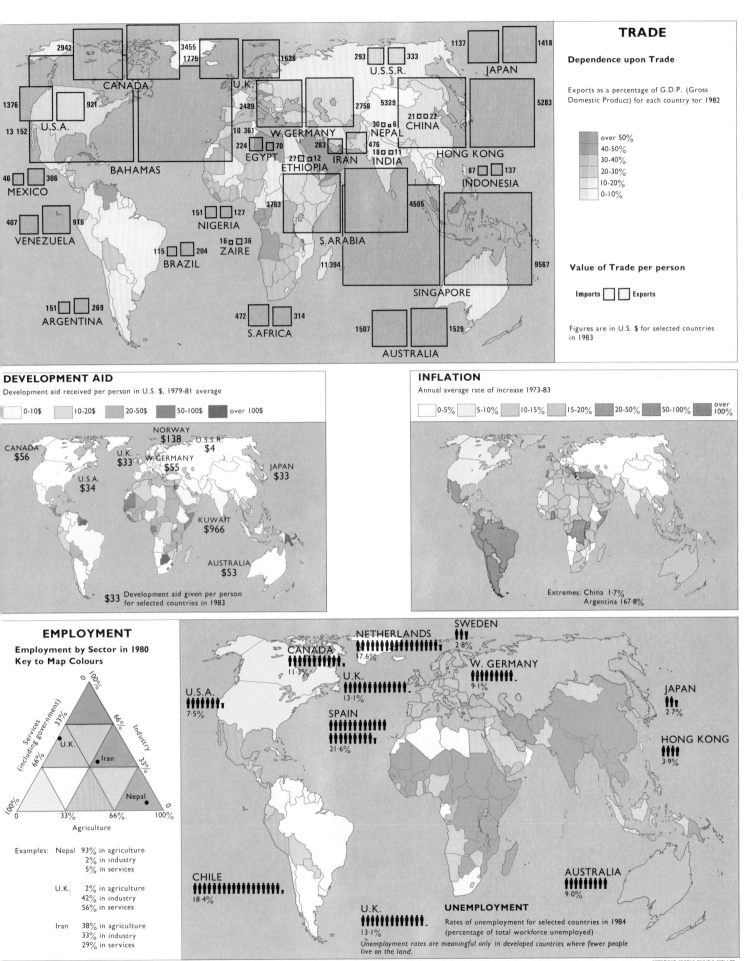

TRADE

Dependence upon Trade

Exports as a percentage of G.D.P. (Gross Domestic Product) for each country for 1982

over 50%
40-50%
30-40%
20-30%
10-20%
0-10%

Value of Trade per person

Imports [ ] [ ] Exports

Figures are in U.S. $ for selected countries in 1983

CANADA 2942
3455
1775
U.K. 1628
U.S.S.R. 293 333
JAPAN 1137 1418
1376 921
U.S.A. 13 152
2489
2758 5329
W.GERMANY 10 361
CHINA 21 □□ 22
JAPAN 5283
NEPAL 30 □ 6
224 □ 70
EGYPT
283
IRAN 476
INDIA 18 □ 11
27 □ 12
ETHIOPIA
HONG KONG
INDONESIA 87 □ 137
BAHAMAS
MEXICO 46 306
NIGERIA 151 127
3763
S.ARABIA 4505
SINGAPORE 9567
VENEZUELA 407 915
BRAZIL 115 204
ZAIRE 16 □ 36
11 394
ARGENTINA 151 269
S.AFRICA 472 314
AUSTRALIA 1507 1529

DEVELOPMENT AID

Development aid received per person in U.S. $, 1979-81 average

0-10$ 10-20$ 20-50$ 50-100$ over 100$

CANADA $56
NORWAY $138
U.S.S.R. $4
U.K. $33
W.GERMANY $55
JAPAN $33
U.S.A. $34
KUWAIT $966
AUSTRALIA $53
$33 Development aid given per person for selected countries in 1983

INFLATION

Annual average rate of increase 1973-83

0-5% 5-10% 10-15% 15-20% 20-50% 50-100% over 100%

Extremes: China 1·7%
Argentina 167·8%

EMPLOYMENT

**Employment by Sector in 1980
Key to Map Colours**

Services (including government)
Industry
Agriculture

Examples: Nepal 93% in agriculture
2% in industry
5% in services

U.K. 2% in agriculture
42% in industry
56% in services

Iran 38% in agriculture
33% in industry
29% in services

SWEDEN 2·8%
NETHERLANDS 17·6%
CANADA 11·3%
W.GERMANY 9·1%
U.K. 13·1%
JAPAN 2·7%
U.S.A. 7·5%
SPAIN 21·6%
HONG KONG 3·9%
CHILE 18·4%
AUSTRALIA 9·0%
U.K. 13·1%

UNEMPLOYMENT

Rates of unemployment for selected countries in 1984 (percentage of total workforce unemployed)

Unemployment rates are meaningful only in developed countries where fewer people live on the land.

Principal Air Routes
Distances in km

Polar Routes

Pacific
Routes

Pacific
Routes

180   160   140   120   100   80   60   40   20

Queen Elizabeth Is.

GREENLAND

Victoria I.

Baffin I.

ICELAND

Anchorage

Churchill

Hudson
Bay

UNITED
KINGDOM
Glasgow
IRELAND   Lon

Edmonton

C A N A D A

Newfoundland

Vancouver

Calgary

Winnipeg

Seattle

Quebec
Montreal

40

FRA

San Francisco

Denver   St. Louis

Chicago

Detroit   Toronto
Boston

PORTUGAL   Mad

UNITED   STATES

New York
Washington

Azores   Lisbon   SPA

Los Angeles

Dallas

New Orleans

Casablanca   MORO CO

Houston

Hawaiian
Islands
(U.S.)

Tropic of Cancer

Gulf of
Mexico

Miami

ATLANTIC

Canary Is.

A

20

MEXICO

BAHAMAS

MAURITANIA

M

Havana   C U B A

West Indies

Mexico

JAMAICA   HAITI   DOMINICAN REP.
PUERTO
RICO

C. Verde Is.

SENEGAL

Palmyra Is.
(U.S.)

BELIZE
GUATEMALA   HONDURAS
EL SALVADOR
NICARAGUA

Caribbean
Sea

GAMBIA
GUINEA-BISSAU

M

GUINEA

Tabuaeran

COSTA
RICA   PANAMA

Caracas

SIERRA
LEONE   IVORY
COAST

Kiritimati

P A C I F I C

Equator

Galapagos Is.
(Ecuador)

VENEZUELA   GUYANA   SURINAM
FR.
GUIANA

LIBERIA

0

Phoenix Is.

Quito
ECUADOR

Bogota

COLOMBIA

Belém

Manaus

O C E A N

Tokelau Is.
(N.Z.)

PERU

B R A Z I L

Recife

Ascension
(Br.)

Samoan Is.

Lima

Salvador

St. Helena
(Br.)

O C E A N

Brasilia

Society Is.
(Fr.)

Tuamotu
Archipelago
(Fr.)

La Paz
BOLIVIA

Rio de Janeiro

Tonga

20

Tubuai Is.
(Fr.)

Tropic of Capricorn

Easter I.

PARAGUAY

São Paulo

Asunción

Kermadec Is.
(N.Z.)

C
H
I
L
E

A
R
G
E
N
T
I
N
A

URUGUAY

Montevideo

Tristan da
Cunha
(Br.)

Santiago

Buenos
Aires

40

Chatham Is.
(N.Z.)

Falkland Is.

Tierra del Fuego

S. Georgia

FALKLAND   IS.   DEPENDENCIES(Br.)

60

ROSS DEPENDENCY

BRITISH ANTARCTIC TERRITORY

NORW

80   60   40   20

140   120   100   80

West from Greenwi

180   160

Projection: Hammer Equal Area

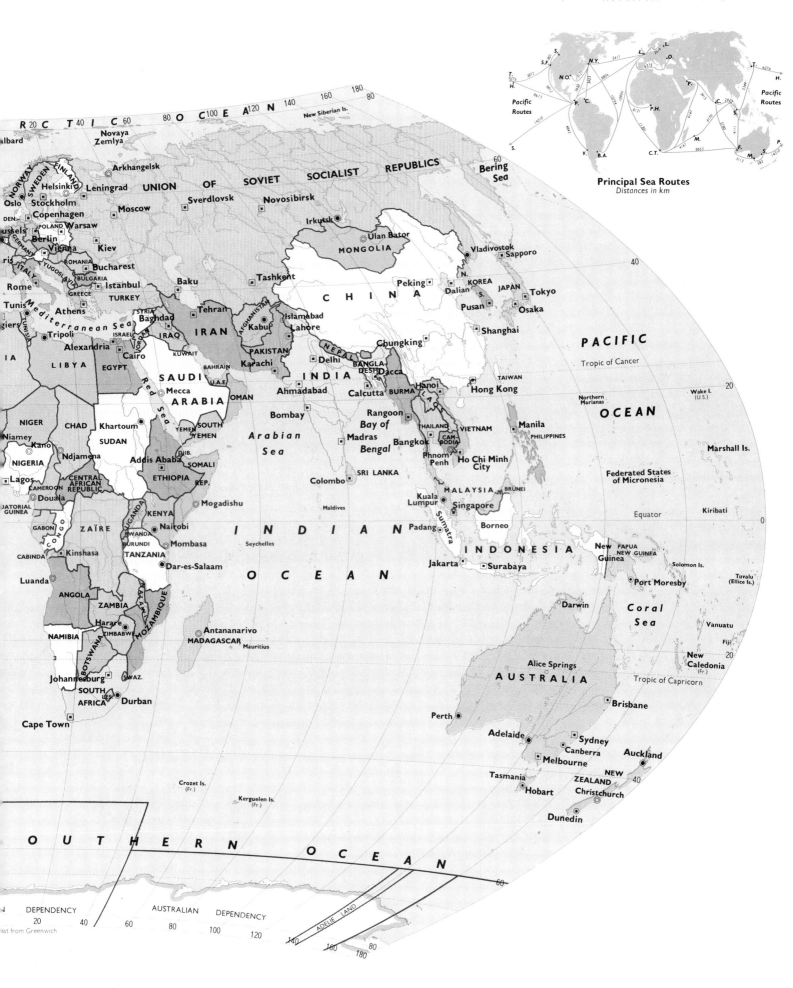

ARCTIC OCEAN

R 20 40 60 80 100 120 N 140 160 180 80

New Siberian Is.

Ibard

Novaya
Zemlya

NORWAY
SWEDEN FINLAND
Helsinki
Oslo Stockholm   Arkhangelsk
DEN. Copenhagen   Leningrad   UNION   OF   SOVIET   SOCIALIST   REPUBLICS   Bering
ussels POLAND Warsaw   Moscow   Sverdlovsk   Novosibirsk   Sea
Berlin GERMANY   Kiev   60
ris Vienna ROMANIA Bucharest   Irkutsk   Vladivostok Sapporo
Rome ITALY YUGOSL. BULGARIA   Baku   Tashkent   MONGOLIA   Ulan Bator   N. KOREA   40
Tunis GREECE Istanbul   Tehran   Peking   Dalian   JAPAN Tokyo
Athens TURKEY   SYRIA Baghdad   AFGHANISTAN   Pusan   Osaka
Tripoli Alexandria   Mediterranean Sea ISRAEL IRAQ IRAN   Kabul Islamabad   CHINA   Shanghai
giers TUNISIA   JORDAN   Lahore
Cairo   KUWAIT PAKISTAN   Delhi   Chungking   PACIFIC
IA LIBYA EGYPT   BAHRAIN Karachi   NEPAL   Hanoi   Hong Kong   OCEAN
SAUDI   U.A.E.   Ahmadabad   BANGLA-DESH Dacca   Tropic of Cancer
Mecca ARABIA OMAN   INDIA   Calcutta   BURMA   TAIWAN   Wake I.   20
NIGER CHAD Khartoum   SOUTH Arabian   Bombay   Rangoon   VIETNAM   (U.S.)
Niamey   YEMEN YEMEN Sea   Madras Bay of   THAILAND   Manila   Northern Marianas
Kano SUDAN   Bengal   Bangkok   CAM-   PHILIPPINES   Marshall Is.
NIGERIA Ndjamena   DJIB. Addis Ababa SOMALI   Phnom   BODIA   Federated States
Lagos CENTRAL   ETHIOPIA REP.   Colombo   SRI LANKA   Penh Ho Chi Minh   of Micronesia
Douala AFRICAN   Mogadishu   Maldives   City
ATORIAL REPUBLIC   UGANDA KENYA   MALAYSIA   BRUNEI
GUINEA CAMEROON   RWANDA Nairobi   Kuala   Equator   Kiribati
GABON ZAIRE   BURUNDI   INDIAN   Lumpur Singapore   Borneo
CONGO CABINDA Kinshasa   TANZANIA Mombasa   Padang Sumatra   New PAPUA
Dar-es-Salaam   Seychelles   INDONESIA   Guinea NEW GUINEA
Luanda   OCEAN   Jakarta Surabaya   Solomon Is.   Tuvalu
ANGOLA ZAMBIA   Port Moresby   (Ellice Is.)
NAMIBIA   MOZAMBIQUE   Darwin   Coral
Harare   Antananarivo   Vanuatu
ZIMBABWE   MADAGASCAR Mauritius   Sea
BOTSWANA   Alice Springs   New
Johannesburg SWAZ.   AUSTRALIA   Tropic of Capricorn   Caledonia   20
SOUTH LES.   (Fr.)
AFRICA Durban   Fiji
Cape Town   Perth   Brisbane   New
Adelaide   Sydney   20
Crozet Is.   Canberra Auckland
(Fr.)   Melbourne   NEW
Kerguelen Is.   Tasmania ZEALAND   40
(Fr.)   Hobart Christchurch
Dunedin

OUTHERN   OCEAN   60

N DEPENDENCY   AUSTRALIAN   DEPENDENCY
20 40   60   80   100   120   ADELIE LAND   140
ast from Greenwich   160 80 180

Principal Sea Routes
Distances in km

Pacific
Routes

Pacific
Routes

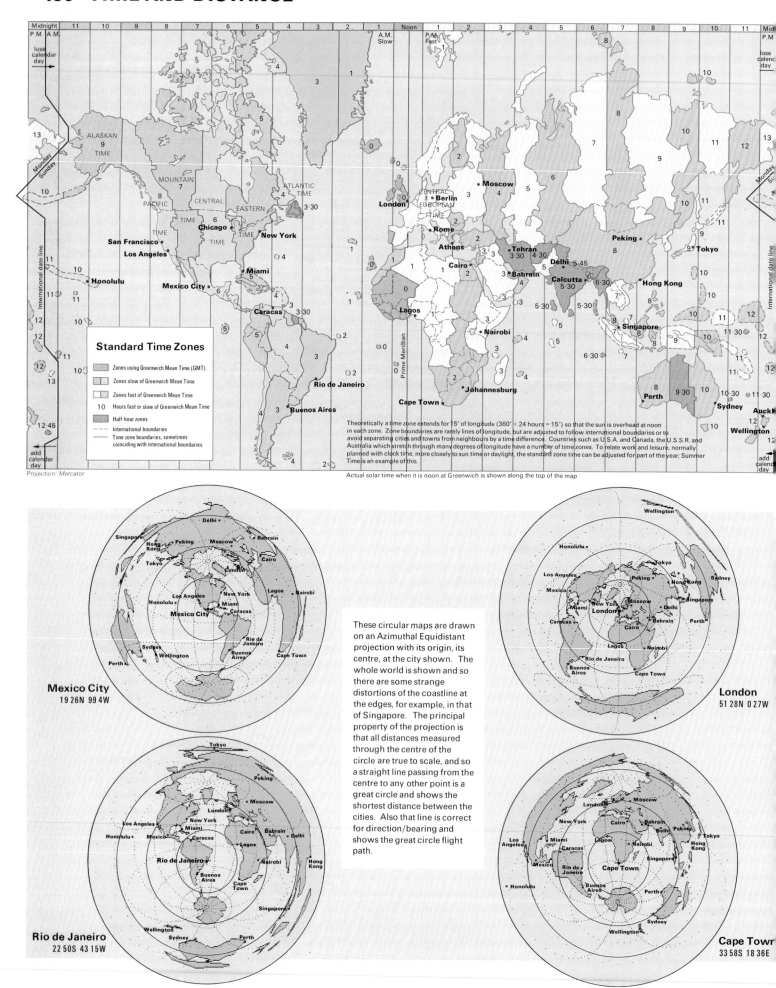

Standard Time Zones

- Zones using Greenwich Mean Time (GMT)
- Zones slow of Greenwich Mean Time
- Zones fast of Greenwich Mean Time
- 10 Hours fast or slow of Greenwich Mean Time
- Half-hour zones
- --- International boundaries
- — Time zone boundaries, sometimes coinciding with international boundaries

Theoretically a time zone extends for 15° of longitude (360° ÷ 24 hours = 15°) so that the sun is overhead at noon in each zone. Zone boundaries are rarely lines of longitude, but are adjusted to follow international boundaries or to avoid separating cities and towns from neighbours by a time difference. Countries such as U.S.A. and Canada, the U.S.S.R. and Australia which stretch through many degrees of longitude have a number of time zones. To relate work and leisure, normally planned with clock time, more closely to sun time or daylight, the standard zone time can be adjusted for part of the year; Summer Time is an example of this.

Projection: *Mercator*

Actual solar time when it is noon at Greenwich is shown along the top of the map

Mexico City
19 26N 99 4W

London
51 28N 0 27W

These circular maps are drawn on an Azimuthal Equidistant projection with its origin, its centre, at the city shown. The whole world is shown and so there are some strange distortions of the coastline at the edges, for example, in that of Singapore. The principal property of the projection is that all distances measured through the centre of the circle are true to scale, and so a straight line passing from the centre to any other point is a great circle and shows the shortest distance between the cities. Also that line is correct for direction/bearing and shows the great circle flight path.

Rio de Janeiro
22 50S 43 15W

Cape Town
33 58S 18 36E

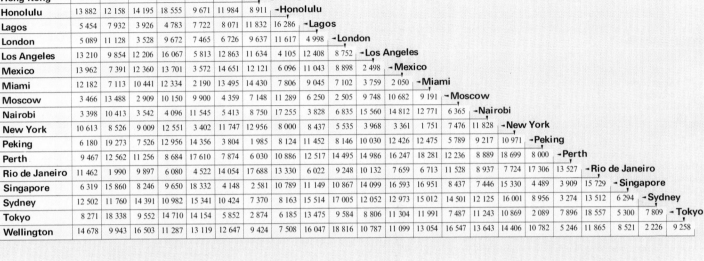

These distances are in kilometres and are the great circle distances between the cities (international airports).   Great circle distances are the shortest distances between two points on the globe. They are the normal flight paths for aircraft where they are free from the restrictions of air corridors or national airspace.

	Bahrain	Buenos Aires	Cairo	Cape Town	Caracas	Delhi	Hong Kong	Honolulu	Lagos	London	Los Angeles	Mexico	Miami	Moscow	Nairobi	New York	Peking	Perth	Rio de Janeiro	Singapore	Sydney	Tokyo
Buenos Aires	13 291																					
Cairo	1 927	11 845																				
Cape Town	7 496	6 880	7 246																			
Caracas	12 121	5 124	10 200	10 254																		
Delhi	2 618	15 784	4 400	9 278	14 186																	
Hong Kong	6 387	18 442	8 121	11 852	16 340	3 768																
Honolulu	13 882	12 158	14 195	18 555	9 671	11 984	8 911															
Lagos	5 454	7 932	3 926	4 783	7 722	8 071	11 832	16 286														
London	5 089	11 128	3 528	9 672	7 465	6 726	9 637	11 617	4 998													
Los Angeles	13 210	9 854	12 206	16 067	5 813	12 863	11 634	4 105	12 408	8 752												
Mexico	13 962	7 391	12 360	13 701	3 572	14 651	12 121	6 096	11 043	8 898	2 498											
Miami	12 182	7 113	10 441	12 334	2 190	13 495	14 430	7 806	9 045	7 102	3 759	2 050										
Moscow	3 466	13 488	2 909	10 150	9 900	4 359	7 148	11 289	6 250	2 505	9 748	10 682	9 191									
Nairobi	3 398	10 413	3 542	4 096	11 545	5 413	8 750	17 255	3 828	6 835	15 560	14 812	12 771	6 365								
New York	10 613	8 526	9 009	12 551	3 402	11 747	12 956	8 000	8 437	5 535	3 968	3 361	1 751	7 476	11 828							
Peking	6 180	19 273	7 526	12 956	14 356	3 804	1 985	8 124	11 452	8 146	10 030	12 426	12 475	5 789	9 217	10 971						
Perth	9 467	12 562	11 256	8 684	17 610	7 874	6 030	10 886	12 517	14 495	14 986	16 247	18 281	12 236	8 889	18 699	8 000					
Rio de Janeiro	11 462	1 990	9 897	6 080	4 522	14 054	17 688	13 330	6 022	9 248	10 132	7 659	6 713	11 528	8 937	7 724	17 306	13 527				
Singapore	6 319	15 860	8 246	9 650	18 332	4 148	2 581	10 789	11 149	10 867	14 099	16 593	16 951	8 437	7 446	15 330	4 489	3 909	15 729			
Sydney	12 502	11 760	14 391	10 982	15 341	10 424	7 370	8 163	15 514	17 005	12 052	12 973	15 012	14 501	12 125	16 001	8 956	3 274	13 512	6 294		
Tokyo	8 271	18 338	9 552	14 710	14 154	5 852	2 874	6 185	13 475	9 584	8 806	11 304	11 991	7 487	11 243	10 869	2 089	7 896	18 557	5 300	7 809	
Wellington	14 678	9 943	16 503	11 287	13 119	12 647	9 424	7 508	16 047	18 816	10 787	11 099	13 054	16 547	13 643	14 406	10 782	5 246	11 865	8 521	2 226	9 258

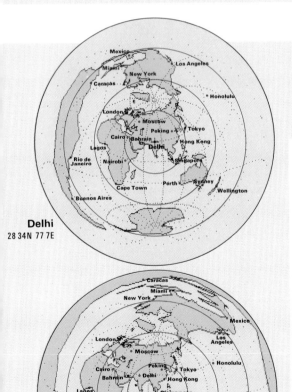

Delhi
28 34N 77 7E

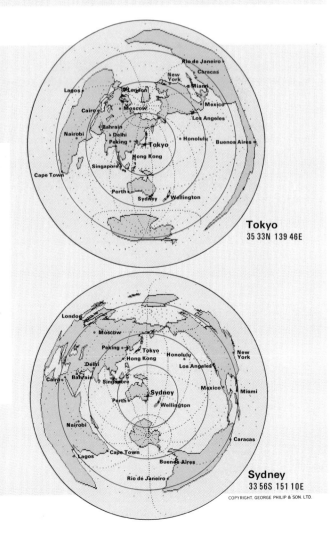

Tokyo
35 33N 139 46E

The three circles are drawn at radius 5 000, 10 000 and 15 000 km from the central city

• Cities shown on the distance table

The co-ordinates given are for the airport of each city

Singapore
1 21N 103 54E

Sydney
33 56S 151 10E

INDEX

The number in bold type which follows each name in the index refers to the number of the page where that feature or place will be found.

The geographical co-ordinates which follow the place name are sometimes only approximate but are close enough for the place name to be located.

An open square ☐ signifies that the name refers to an administrative division of a country while a solid square ■ follows the name of a country.

Rivers have been indexed to their mouth or to their confluence.

The alphabetical order of names composed of two or more words is governed primarily by the first word and then by the second. This is an example of the rule:

> West Wyalong
> West Yorkshire
> Westbourne
> Westbury
> Westbury-on-Severn
> Western Australia

Names composed of a proper name (Gibraltar) and a description (Strait of) are positioned alphabetically by the proper name. All river names are followed by �. If the same word occurs in the name of a town and a geographical feature, the town name is listed first followed by the name or names of the geographical features.

Names beginning with M', Mc are all indexed as if they were spelled Mac.

If the same place name occurs twice or more in the index and the places are in different countries they will be followed by the country names and the latter in alphabetical order.

> Sydney, Australia
> Sydney, Canada

In the index each placename is followed by its geographical co-ordinates which allow the reader to find the place on the map. These co-ordinates give the latitude and longitude of a particular place.

The latitude (or parallel) is the distance of a point north or south of the Equator measured as an angle with the centre of the earth. The Equator is latitude 0°, the North Pole is 90°N and the South Pole 90°S. On a globe the lines could be drawn as concentric circles parallel to the Equator, decreasing in diameter from the Equator until they become a point at the Poles. On the maps these lines of latitude are usually represented as lines running across the map from East to West in smooth curves. They are numbered on the sides of the map; north of the Equator the numbers increase northwards, to the south they increase southwards. The degree interval between them depends on the scale of the map. On a large scale map (for example, 1:2 000 000) the interval is one degree, but on a small scale (for example 1:50 000 000) it will be ten degrees.

Lines of longitude (or meridians) cut the latitude lines at right angles on the globe and intersect with one another at the Poles. Longitude is measured by the angle at the centre of the earth between it and the meridian of origin which runs through Greenwich (0°). It may be a measurement East or West of this line and from 0° to 180° in each direction. The longitude line of 180° runs North – South through the Pacific Ocean. On a particular map the interval between the lines of longitude is always the same as that between the lines of latitude and normally they are drawn vertically. They are numbered in the top and bottom margins and a note states East or West from Greenwich.

The unit of measurement for latitude and longitude is the degree and it is subdivided into 60 minutes. An index entry states the position of a place in degrees and minutes, a space being left between the degrees and minutes. The latitude is followed by N(orth) or S(outh) and the longitude by E(ast) or W(est).

The diagram illustrates how the reader has to estimate the required distance from the nearest line of latitude or longitude. In the diagram there is one degree, or 60 minutes between the lines and so to find the position of Calais an estimate has to be made, 57 parts of 60 north of the 50 degree latitude line and 50 parts of 60, or 50 minutes east of the one degree longitude line.

Where the map is smaller in scale it is more difficult to calculate the position of a place because there are five or ten degree intervals between the lines.

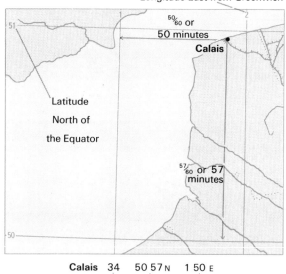

Scale 1 : 2 000 000

Calais 34   50 57 N   1 50 E

page   latitude   longitude

The following is a list of the principal abbreviations used in the Index.

A.S.S.R. – Autonomous Soviet Socialist Republic	Col. – Colombia	I. – Island (Isle, Ile, Isla)	P.N.G. – Papua New Guinea
Afg. – Afghanistan	Cont. – Continent	Ill. – Illinois	P.R. – Puerto Rico
Afr. – Africa	Cr. – Creek	Ind. – Indies	Pac. Oc. – Pacific Ocean
Alb. – Albania	Cur. – Curaçao	Kor. – Korea	Pan. – Panama
Alg. – Algeria	Dom. – Dominica	Kuw. – Kuwait	Par. – Paraguay
Am. – America	Dom. Rep. – Dominican Republic	L. – Lake (Lac, Loch, Lough, Lago)	Pen. – Peninsula
Ant. – Antarctica	E. – East	Leb. – Lebanon	Pk. – Peak
Arch. – Archipelago	Eq. Guin. – Equatorial Guinea	Les. – Lesotho	Pt. – Point (Pointe, Punta)
Arg. – Argentina	Eth. – Ethiopia	Lib. – Liberia	Ra. – Range
Atl. Oc. – Atlantic Ocean	Falk. – Falkland Is.	Mart. – Martinique	Rom. – Romania
B. – Bay	Fr. – France	Mass. – Massachusetts	S. – South
B. Faso – Burkina Faso	Fr. G. – French Guiana	Maurit. – Mauritania	S. Oc. – Southern Ocean
Barb. – Barbados	G. – Gulf (Golf, Golfo)	Minn. – Minnesota	Sd. – Sound
Berm. – Bermuda	Ga. – Georgia	Miss. – Mississippi	Sene. – Senegal
Bol. – Bolivia	Ger. – Germany	Mong. – Mongolia	Si. Arab. – Saudi Arabia
Bots. – Botswana	Gr. – Great	Mor. – Morocco	Som. – Somalia
Bulg. – Bulgaria	Green. – Greenland	Mt. – Mountain (Mount, Mont, Monte, Monti, Montana)	St. L. – St. Lucia
Bur. – Burma	Gren. – Grenada	N. – North	Str. – Strait
C. – Cape (Cap, Cabo)	Guad. – Guadeloupe	N. Cal. – New Caledonia	Swaz. – Swaziland
C.A.R. – Central African Republic	Guat. – Guatemala	Nam. – Namibia	Tanz. – Tanzania
C.R. – Costa Rica	Guin. – Guinea	Nic. – Nicaragua	U.A.E. – United Arab Emirates
Cam. – Cameroon	Guy. – Guyana	Nig. – Nigeria	Ven. – Venezuela
Carib. – Caribbean Sea	Hond. – Honduras	Nor. – Norway	W. – West
Chan. – Channel	Hr. – Harbour	Oc. – Oceania	Yem. – Yemen
	Hts. – Heights		Zam. – Zambia
			Zim. – Zimbabwe

A

Aachen, *W. Ger.* **36** 50 47N 6 4 E
Aalborg, *Den.* **45** 57 2N 9 54 E
Aalst, *Belg.* **36** 50 56N 4 2 E
Aarhus, *Den.* **45** 56 8N 10 11 E
Ābādān, *Iran* **56** 30 22N 48 20 E
Abbey Town, *U.K.* **18** 54 50N 3 18W
Abbots Bromley, *U.K.* **14** 52 50N 1 52W
Abbots Langley, *U.K.* **15** 51 43N 0 25W
Abbotsbury, *U.K.* **14** 50 40N 2 36W
Abéché, *Chad* **79** 13 50N 20 35 E
Aberaeron, *U.K.* **17** 52 15N 4 16W
Aberdare, *U.K.* **17** 51 43N 3 27W
Aberdeen, *U.K.* **23** 57 9N 2 6W
Aberdour, *U.K.* **21** 56 2N 3 18W
Aberdovey, *U.K.* **17** 52 33N 4 3W
Aberfeldy, *U.K.* **23** 56 37N 3 50W
Aberfoyle, *U.K.* **20** 56 10N 4 23W
Abergavenny, *U.K.* **17** 51 49N 3 1W
Abergele, *U.K.* **17** 53 17N 3 35W
Aberlady, *U.K.* **21** 56 0N 2 51W
Abernethy, *U.K.* **21** 56 19N 3 18W
Aberporth, *U.K.* **17** 52 8N 4 32W
Abersoch, *U.K.* **17** 52 50N 4 30W
Abersychan, *U.K.* **17** 51 44N 3 3W
Abertillery, *U.K.* **17** 51 44N 3 9W
Aberystwyth, *U.K.* **17** 52 25N 4 6W
Abidjan, *Ivory C.* **78** 5 26N 3 58W
Abingdon, *U.K.* **14** 51 40N 1 17W
Abington, *U.K.* **21** 55 30N 3 42W
Aboyne, *U.K.* **23** 57 4N 2 48W
Abū Dhabī, *U.A.E.* **57** 24 28N 54 36 E
Acapulco, *Mex.* **94** 16 51N 99 56W
Accra, *Ghana* **78** 5 35N 0 6W
Accrington, *U.K.* **18** 53 46N 2 22W
Achill Hd., *Ire.* **24** 53 59N 10 15W
Achill I., *Ire.* **24** 53 58N 10 5W
Achinsk, *U.S.S.R.* **49** 56 20N 90 20 E
Achnasheen, *U.K.* **22** 57 35N 5 5W
Acklins I., *Baham.* **95** 22 30N 74 0W
Acle, *U.K.* **15** 52 38N 1 32 E
Aconcagua, Cerro, *Arg.* **102** 32 39S 70 0W
Acre, *Isr.* **57** 32 55N 35 4 E
Acton Burnell, *U.K.* **14** 52 37N 2 41W
Adamaoua Plateau, *Cam.* **80** 7 20N 12 20 E
Adam's Bridge, *Sri L.* **58** 9 15N 79 40 E
Adana, *Turk.* **47** 37 0N 35 16 E
Adapazarı, *Turk.* **47** 40 48N 30 25 E
Addis Ababa, *Eth.* **79** 9 2N 38 42 E
Addlestone, *U.K.* **15** 51 22N 0 30W
Adelaide, *Austral.* **67** 34 52S 138 30 E
Adélie Land, *Ant.* **103** 68 0S 140 0 E
Aden, *S. Yem.* **56** 12 45N 45 0 E
Aden, G. of, *Asia* **56** 13 0N 50 0 E
Adirondack Mts., *U.S.A.* **93** 44 0N 74 15W
Admiralty Is., *P.N.G.* **64** 2 0S 147 0 E
Adrar, *Alg.* **78** 27 51N 0 11W
Adriatic Sea, *Europe* **40** 43 0N 16 0 E
Adwick le Street, *U.K.* **19** 53 35N 1 12W
Ægean Sea, *Europe* **41** 37 0N 25 0 E
Afghanistan ■, *Asia* **57** 33 0N 65 0 E
Agadès, *Niger* **78** 16 58N 7 59 E
Agadir, *Mor.* **78** 30 28N 9 35W
Agartala, *India* **59** 23 50N 91 23 E
Agra, *India* **58** 27 17N 77 58 E
Agrigento, *It.* **40** 37 19N 13 33 E
Aguascalientes, *Mex.* **94** 21 53N 102 12W
Ahmadabad, *India* **58** 23 0N 72 40 E
Ahvāz, *Iran* **56** 31 20N 48 40 E
Ahvenanmaa = Åland, *Fin.* **45** 60 15N 20 0 E
Ailsa Craig, *U.K.* **20** 55 15N 5 7W
Ainsdale, *U.K.* **18** 53 37N 3 2W
Airdrie, *U.K.* **21** 55 53N 3 57W
Aire →, *U.K.* **19** 53 42N 0 55W
Aisgill, *U.K.* **18** 54 23N 2 21W
Aix-en-Provence, *Fr.* **35** 43 32N 5 27 E
Ajaccio, *Fr.* **35** 41 55N 8 40 E
Akashi, *Jap.* **62** 34 45N 135 0 E
Akita, *Jap.* **62** 39 45N 140 7 E
Akranes, *Ice.* **44** 64 19N 21 58W
Akron, *U.S.A.* **92** 41 7N 81 31W
Aktyubinsk, *U.S.S.R.* **47** 50 17N 57 10 E
Akure, *Nig.* **78** 7 15N 5 5 E
Akureyri, *Ice.* **44** 65 40N 18 6W
Al Ḩudaydah, *Yem.* **56** 14 50N 43 0 E
Al Hūfuf, *Si. Arab.* **56** 25 25N 49 45 E
Al Jawf, *Si. Arab.* **56** 29 55N 39 40 E
Al Qaṭīf, *Si. Arab.* **56** 26 35N 50 0 E
Al Qunaytirah, *Syria* **57** 32 55N 35 45 E
Alabama □, *U.S.A.* **91** 33 0N 87 0W
Åland, *Fin.* **45** 60 15N 20 0 E
Alaska □, *U.S.A.* **88** 65 0N 150 0W
Alaska, G. of, *Pac. Oc.* **88** 58 0N 145 0W
Alaska Pen., *U.S.A.* **88** 56 0N 160 0W
Alaska Range, *U.S.A.* **88** 62 50N 151 0W
Alba Iulia, *Rom.* **43** 46 8N 23 39 E
Albacete, *Sp.* **37** 39 0N 1 50W
Albania ■, *Europe* **41** 41 0N 20 0 E
Albany, *Austral.* **66** 35 1S 117 58 E
Albany, *Ga., U.S.A.* **90** 31 40N 84 10W
Albany, *N.Y., U.S.A.* **93** 42 35N 73 47W
Albany →, *Canada* **89** 52 17N 81 31W
Alberta □, *Canada* **88** 54 40N 115 0W
Albrighton, *U.K.* **14** 52 38N 2 17W
Albuquerque, *U.S.A.* **90** 35 5N 106 47W
Albury, *Austral.* **70** 36 3S 146 56 E
Alcalá de Henares, *Sp.* **37** 40 28N 3 22W
Alcester, *U.K.* **14** 52 13N 1 52W
Aldan →, *U.S.S.R.* **49** 63 28N 129 35 E
Aldborough, *U.K.* **19** 54 6N 1 21W
Aldbourne, *U.K.* **14** 51 28N 1 38W
Aldbrough, *U.K.* **19** 53 50N 0 7W
Aldeburgh, *U.K.* **15** 52 9N 1 35 E
Alderbury, *U.K.* **14** 51 4N 1 45W
Alderley Edge, *U.K.* **18** 53 18N 2 15W
Alderney, *U.K.* **34** 49 42N 2 12W
Aldershot, *U.K.* **15** 51 15N 0 43W
Aldingham, *U.K.* **18** 54 8N 3 3W
Aleppo, *Syria* **56** 36 10N 37 15 E
Alessándria, *It.* **40** 44 54N 8 37 E
Ålesund, *Nor.* **44** 62 28N 6 12 E
Aleutian Is., *Pac. Oc.* **88** 52 0N 175 0W
Alexander Arch., *U.S.A.* **88** 57 0N 135 0W
Alexandria, *Egypt* **79** 31 0N 30 0 E
Alexandria, *U.K.* **20** 55 59N 4 40W
Alexandria, *U.S.A.* **90** 31 20N 92 30W
Alford, *Grampian, U.K.* **23** 57 13N 2 42W
Alford, *Lincs., U.K.* **19** 53 16N 0 10 E
Alfreton, *U.K.* **19** 53 6N 1 22W
Alfriston, *U.K.* **15** 50 48N 0 10 E
Algarve, *Port.* **37** 36 58N 8 20W
Algeciras, *Sp.* **37** 36 9N 5 28W
Algeria ■, *Africa* **78** 35 10N 3 11 E
Algiers, *Alg.* **78** 36 42N 3 8 E
Alicante, *Sp.* **37** 38 23N 0 30W
Alice Springs, *Austral.* **66** 23 40S 133 50 E
Aligarh, *India* **58** 27 55N 78 10 E
Alkmaar, *Neth.* **36** 52 37N 4 45 E
Allahabad, *India* **59** 25 25N 81 58 E
Allegheny Mts., *U.S.A.* **92** 38 0N 80 0W
Allen →, *U.K.* **21** 54 53N 2 13W
Allen, Bog of, *Ire.* **25** 53 15N 7 0W
Allen, L., *Ire.* **24** 54 12N 8 5W
Allendale, *U.K.* **21** 54 55N 2 15W
Allenheads, *U.K.* **21** 54 49N 2 12W
Allentown, *U.S.A.* **93** 40 36N 75 30W
Alloa, *U.K.* **21** 56 7N 3 49W
Allonby, *U.K.* **18** 54 45N 3 27W
Alma Ata, *U.S.S.R.* **48** 43 15N 76 57 E
Almelo, *Neth.* **36** 52 22N 6 42 E
Almería, *Sp.* **37** 36 52N 2 27W
Almond →, *U.K.* **21** 56 27N 3 27W
Almondsbury, *U.K.* **14** 51 33N 2 34W
Aln →, *U.K.* **21** 55 27N 1 32W
Alness, *U.K.* **23** 57 41N 4 15W
Alnmouth, *U.K.* **21** 55 24N 1 37W
Alnwick, *U.K.* **19** 55 25N 1 42W
Alphen, *Neth.* **36** 51 29N 4 58 E
Alphington, *U.K.* **16** 50 41N 3 32W
Alps, *Europe* **42** 47 0N 8 0 E
Alrewas, *U.K.* **14** 52 43N 1 44W
Alsager, *U.K.* **18** 53 7N 2 20W
Alston, *U.K.* **18** 54 48N 2 26W
Altai Mts., *Asia* **60** 46 40N 92 45 E
Altarnun, *U.K.* **16** 50 35N 4 30W
Altay, *China* **60** 47 48N 88 10 E
Alton, *U.K.* **15** 51 8N 0 59W
Altoona, *U.S.A.* **92** 40 32N 78 24W
Altrincham, *U.K.* **18** 53 25N 2 21W
Altun Shan, *China* **60** 38 30N 88 0 E
Alva, *U.K.* **21** 56 9N 3 49W
Alvechurch, *U.K.* **14** 52 22N 1 58W
Alwinton, *U.K.* **21** 55 20N 2 7W
Alyth, *U.K.* **23** 56 38N 3 15W
Amadjuak L., *Canada* **89** 65 0N 71 8W
Amagasaki, *Jap.* **62** 34 42N 135 20 E
Amarillo, *U.S.A.* **90** 35 14N 101 46W
Amazon →, *S. Am.* **100** 0 5S 50 0W
Amazonas □, *Brazil* **101** 4 0S 62 0W
Amble, *U.K.* **21** 55 20N 1 36W
Ambleside, *U.K.* **18** 54 26N 2 58W
Ambon, *Indon.* **63** 3 35S 128 20 E
American Samoa ■, *Pac. Oc.* **65** 14 20S 170 40W
Amersfoort, *Neth.* **36** 52 9N 5 23 E
Amersham, *U.K.* **15** 51 40N 0 38W
Amesbury, *U.K.* **14** 51 10N 1 46W
Amiens, *Fr.* **34** 49 54N 2 16 E
Amlwch, *U.K.* **17** 53 24N 4 21W
'Ammān, *Jord.* **57** 31 57N 35 52 E
Ammanford, *U.K.* **17** 51 48N 4 0W
Amoy = Xiamen, *China* **61** 24 25N 118 4 E
Ampleforth, *U.K.* **19** 54 13N 1 8W
Ampthill, *U.K.* **15** 52 3N 0 30W
Amravati, *India* **58** 20 55N 77 45 E
Amritsar, *India* **58** 31 35N 74 57 E
Amsterdam, *Neth.* **36** 52 23N 4 54 E
Amudarya →, *U.S.S.R.* **48** 43 40N 59 0 E
Amundsen Gulf, *Canada* **88** 71 0N 124 0W
Amundsen Sea, *Ant.* **103** 72 0S 115 0W
Amur →, *U.S.S.R.* **49** 52 56N 141 10 E
An Nafūd, *Si. Arab.* **56** 28 15N 41 0 E
An Najaf, *Iraq* **56** 32 3N 44 15 E
An Uaimh, *Ire.* **24** 53 39N 6 40W
Anadyr, G. of, *U.S.S.R.* **49** 64 0N 180 0 E
Anaheim, *U.S.A.* **90** 33 50N 118 0W
Anápolis, *Brazil* **101** 16 15S 48 50W
Anatolia, *Turk.* **47** 38 0N 30 0 E
Ancaster, *U.K.* **19** 52 59N 0 32W
Ancholme →, *U.K.* **19** 53 42N 0 32W
Anchorage, *U.S.A.* **88** 61 10N 149 50W
Ancona, *It.* **40** 43 37N 13 30 E
Ancrum, *U.K.* **21** 55 31N 2 35W
Anda, *China* **61** 46 24N 125 19 E
Andalusia, Reg., *Sp.* **37** 37 35N 5 0W
Andaman Is., *India* **51** 12 30N 92 30 E
Anderlecht, *Belg.* **36** 50 50N 4 19 E
Andes, *S. Am.* **96** 20 0S 68 0W
Andhra Pradesh □, *India* **58** 16 0N 79 0 E
Andizhan, *U.S.S.R.* **48** 41 10N 72 0 E
Andorra ■, *Europe* **35** 42 30N 1 30 E
Andover, *U.K.* **14** 51 13N 1 29W
Andreanof Is., *Pac. Oc.* **88** 52 0N 178 0W
Andreas, *U.K.* **18** 54 23N 4 25W
Ándria, *It.* **40** 41 13N 16 17 E
Andropov, *U.S.S.R.* **46** 58 5N 38 50 E
Andros I., *Baham.* **95** 24 30N 78 0W
Angara →, *U.S.S.R.* **49** 58 30N 97 0 E
Angarsk, *U.S.S.R.* **49** 52 30N 104 0 E
Angers, *Fr.* **34** 47 30N 0 35W
Anglesey, *U.K.* **17** 53 17N 4 20W
Angmagssalik, *Green.* **89** 65 40N 37 20W
Angmering, *U.K.* **15** 50 48N 0 28W
Angola ■, *Africa* **81** 12 0S 18 0 E
Angoulême, *Fr.* **35** 45 39N 0 10 E
Anguilla, *W. Ind.* **94** 18 14N 63 5W
Angus, Braes of, *U.K.* **23** 56 51N 3 10W
Anhui □, *China* **61** 32 0N 117 0 E
Anjou, *Fr.* **34** 47 20N 0 15W
Ankara, *Turk.* **47** 40 0N 32 54 E
Ann Arbor, *U.S.A.* **92** 42 17N 83 45W
Annaba, *Alg.* **78** 36 50N 7 46 E
Annalee →, *Ire.* **24** 54 3N 7 15W
Annan, *U.K.* **21** 55 0N 3 17W
Annan →, *U.K.* **21** 54 58N 3 18W
Annandale, *U.K.* **21** 55 10N 3 25W
Annecy, *Fr.* **35** 45 55N 6 8 E
Annfield Plain, *U.K.* **19** 54 52N 1 45W
Annobón, *Atl. Oc.* **73** 1 25S 5 36 E
Anshan, *China* **61** 41 5N 122 58 E
Anshun, *China* **60** 26 18N 105 57 E
Anstey, *U.K.* **14** 52 41N 1 14W
Anstruther, *U.K.* **21** 56 14N 2 40W
Antalya, *Turk.* **47** 36 52N 30 45 E
Antananarivo, *Madag.* **81** 18 55S 47 31 E
Antarctic Pen., *Ant.* **103** 67 0S 60 0W
Antarctica, *Cont.* **103** 90 0S 0 0 E
Anticosti, I. d', *Canada* **93** 49 30N 63 0W
Antigua & Barbuda ■, *W. Ind.* **94** 17 20N 61 48W
Antofagasta, *Chile* **102** 23 50S 70 30W
Antony, *U.K.* **16** 50 22N 4 13W
Antrim, *U.K.* **24** 54 43N 6 13W
Antrim □, *U.K.* **24** 54 55N 6 20W
Antrim, Mts. of, *U.K.* **24** 54 57N 6 8W
Antsiranana, *Madag.* **81** 12 25S 49 20 E
Antwerp, *Belg.* **36** 51 13N 4 25 E
Anyang, *China* **61** 36 5N 114 21 E
Anzhero-Sudzhensk, *U.S.S.R.* **48** 56 10N 86 0 E
Aomori, *Jap.* **62** 40 45N 140 45 E
Apeldoorn, *Neth.* **36** 52 13N 5 57 E
Apennines, *It.* **40** 44 20N 10 20 E
Appalachian Mts., *U.S.A.* **91** 38 0N 80 0W
Appleby, *U.K.* **18** 54 35N 2 29W
Appledore, *Devon, U.K.* **16** 51 3N 4 12W
Appledore, *Kent, U.K.* **15** 51 2N 0 47 E
Arabia, *Asia* **50** 25 0N 45 0 E
Arabian Desert, *Egypt* **79** 26 0N 33 30 E
Arabian Sea, *Ind. Oc.* **50** 16 0N 65 0 E
Aracaju, *Brazil* **101** 10 55S 37 4W
Araçatuba, *Brazil* **101** 21 10S 50 30W
Arad, *Rom.* **43** 46 10N 21 20 E
Arafura Sea, *E. Ind.* **64** 9 0S 135 0 E
Aragón □, *Sp.* **37** 41 25N 1 0W
Araguaia →, *Brazil* **101** 5 21S 48 41W
Arakan Yoma, *Burma* **59** 20 0N 94 40 E
Aral Sea, *U.S.S.R.* **48** 44 30N 60 0 E
Aralsk, *U.S.S.R.* **48** 46 50N 61 20 E
Aran I., *Ire.* **24** 55 0N 8 30W
Aran Is., *Ire.* **25** 53 5N 9 42W
Arapiraca, *Brazil* **101** 9 45S 36 39W
Ararat, *Austral.* **70** 37 16S 143 0 E
Arbroath, *U.K.* **23** 56 34N 2 35W
Arctic Ocean, *Arctic* **103** 78 0N 160 0W
Arctic Red River, *Canada* **88** 67 15N 134 0W
Ardbeg, *U.K.* **20** 55 38N 6 6W
Ardchyle, *U.K.* **20** 56 26N 4 24W
Ardee, *Ire.* **24** 53 51N 6 32W
Ardennes, *Belg.* **36** 50 0N 5 10 E
Ardentinny, *U.K.* **20** 56 3N 4 56W
Ardgour, *U.K.* **22** 56 45N 5 25W
Ardingly, *U.K.* **15** 51 3N 0 3W
Ardlui, *U.K.* **20** 56 19N 4 43W
Ardmore Pt., *U.K.* **20** 55 40N 6 0W
Ardnamurchan, Pt. of, *U.K.* **22** 56 44N 6 14W
Ardnave Pt., *U.K.* **20** 55 54N 6 20W
Ardrishaig, *U.K.* **20** 56 0N 5 27W
Ardrossan, *U.K.* **20** 55 39N 4 50W
Ards □, *U.K.* **24** 54 35N 5 30W
Ards Pen., *U.K.* **24** 54 30N 5 25W
Ardvasar, *U.K.* **22** 57 5N 5 52W
Arendal, *Nor.* **45** 58 28N 8 46 E
Arequipa, *Peru* **100** 16 20S 71 30W
Argentina ■, *S. Am.* **102** 35 0S 66 0W
Argyll, *U.K.* **20** 56 14N 5 10W
Arica, *Chile* **100** 18 32S 70 20W
Arima, *Trin. & Tob.* **94** 10 38N 61 17W
Arinagour, *U.K.* **20** 56 38N 6 31W
Arisaig, *U.K.* **22** 56 55N 5 50W
Arizona □, *U.S.A.* **90** 34 20N 111 30W
Arkaig, L., *U.K.* **22** 56 58N 5 10W
Arkansas □, *U.S.A.* **91** 35 0N 92 30W
Arkansas →, *U.S.A.* **91** 33 48N 91 4W
Arkhangelsk, *U.S.S.R.* **46** 64 40N 41 0 E
Arkle →, *U.K.* **18** 54 25N 1 55W
Arklow, *Ire.* **25** 52 48N 6 10W
Arles, *Fr.* **35** 43 41N 4 40 E
Arlon, *Belg.* **36** 49 42N 5 49 E
Armadale, *U.K.* **21** 55 54N 3 42W
Armagh, *U.K.* **24** 54 22N 6 40W
Armagh □, *U.K.* **24** 54 18N 6 37W
Armenia, *Col.* **100** 4 35N 75 45W
Armenia □, *U.S.S.R.* **47** 40 0N 41 0 E
Armidale, *Austral.* **67** 30 30S 151 40 E
Arnhem, *Neth.* **36** 51 58N 5 55 E
Arnhem Land, *Austral.* **66** 13 10S 134 30 E
Arnold, *U.K.* **19** 53 0N 1 8W
Arnside, *U.K.* **18** 54 12N 2 49W
Arran, *U.K.* **20** 55 34N 5 12W
Arras, *Fr.* **34** 50 17N 2 46 E
Arrochar, *U.K.* **20** 56 12N 4 45W
Arrow, L., *Ire.* **24** 54 3N 8 20W
Arun →, *U.K.* **15** 50 48N 0 33W
Arunachal Pradesh □, *India* **59** 28 0N 95 0 E
Arundel, *U.K.* **15** 50 52N 0 32W
Arusha, *Tanz.* **80** 3 20S 36 40 E
As Salt, *Jord.* **57** 32 2N 35 43 E
As Summān, *Si. Arab.* **56** 25 0N 47 0 E
Asahigawa, *Jap.* **62** 43 46N 142 22 E
Asansol, *India* **59** 23 40N 87 1 E
Ascension I., *Atl. Oc.* **128** 8 0S 14 15W
Ascot, *U.K.* **15** 51 24N 0 41W
Asfordby, *U.K.* **15** 52 45N 0 57W
Ash, *Kent, U.K.* **15** 51 17N 1 16 E
Ash, *Surrey, U.K.* **15** 51 14N 0 43W
Ashbourne, *U.K.* **19** 53 2N 1 44W
Ashburton, *N.Z.* **71** 43 53S 171 48 E
Ashburton, *U.K.* **16** 50 31N 3 45W
Ashburton →, *Austral.* **66** 21 40S 114 56 E
Ashby-de-la-Zouch, *U.K.* **14** 52 45N 1 29W
Ashchurch, *U.K.* **14** 52 0N 2 7W
Ashdown Forest, *U.K.* **15** 51 4N 0 2 E
Ashford, *Derby, U.K.* **19** 53 13N 1 43W
Ashford, *Kent, U.K.* **15** 51 8N 0 53 E
Ashington, *U.K.* **21** 55 12N 1 35W
Ashkhabad, *U.S.S.R.* **48** 38 0N 57 50 E
Ashq'elon, *Isr.* **57** 31 42N 34 35 E
Ashton-in-Makerfield, *U.K.* **18** 53 29N 2 39W
Ashton-under-Lyne, *U.K.* **18** 53 30N 2 8W
Ashurstwood, *U.K.* **15** 51 6N 0 2 E
Ashwater, *U.K.* **16** 50 43N 4 18W
Ashwick, *U.K.* **14** 51 13N 2 31W
'Asīr □, *Si. Arab.* **56** 18 40N 42 30 E
Asir, Ras, *Som.* **73** 11 55N 51 10 E
Askrigg, *U.K.* **18** 54 19N 2 6W
Aslackby, *U.K.* **19** 52 53N 0 23W
Asmera, *Eth.* **79** 15 19N 38 55 E
Aspatria, *U.K.* **18** 54 45N 3 20W
Assam □, *India* **59** 26 0N 93 0 E
Assen, *Neth.* **36** 53 0N 6 35 E
Assynt, L., *U.K.* **22** 58 25N 5 15W
Asti, *It.* **40** 44 54N 8 11 E
Aston Clinton, *U.K.* **15** 51 48N 0 44W
Astrakhan, *U.S.S.R.* **47** 46 25N 48 5 E
Astwood Bank, *U.K.* **14** 52 15N 1 55W
Asunción, *Par.* **102** 25 10S 57 30W
Aswân, *Egypt* **79** 24 4N 32 57 E
Atacama, Desierto de, *Chile* **102** 24 0S 69 20W
Atbara, *Sudan* **79** 17 42N 33 59 E
Athabasca, L., *Canada* **88** 59 15N 109 15W
Athboy, *Ire.* **24** 53 37N 6 55W
Athenry, *Ire.* **25** 53 18N 8 45W
Athens, *Greece* **41** 37 58N 23 46 E
Atherstone, *U.K.* **14** 52 35N 1 32W
Atherton, *U.K.* **18** 53 32N 2 30W
Athínai = Athens, *Greece* **41** 37 58N 23 46 E
Athlone, *Ire.* **24** 53 26N 7 57W
Atholl, Forest of, *U.K.* **23** 56 51N 3 50W
Athy, *Ire.* **25** 53 0N 7 0W
Atlanta, *U.S.A.* **91** 33 50N 84 24W
Atlantic City, *U.S.A.* **93** 39 25N 74 25W
Atlantic Ocean **128** 0 0 20 0W
Atlas Mts., *Mor.* **72** 32 30N 5 0W
Attleborough, *U.K.* **15** 52 32N 1 1 E
Auchencairn, *U.K.* **21** 54 51N 3 52W
Auchinleck, *U.K.* **20** 55 28N 4 18W
Auchterarder, *U.K.* **21** 56 18N 3 43W
Auchterderran, *U.K.* **21** 56 8N 3 16W
Auchtermuchty, *U.K.* **21** 56 18N 3 15W
Auchtertyre, *U.K.* **22** 57 17N 5 35W
Auckland, *N.Z.* **71** 36 52S 174 46 E
Audlem, *U.K.* **18** 52 59N 2 31W
Aughnacloy, *U.K.* **24** 54 25N 6 58W
Augsburg, *W. Ger.* **42** 48 22N 10 54 E
Augusta, *U.S.A.* **90** 33 29N 81 59W
Aurangabad, *India* **58** 19 50N 75 23 E
Aurora, *U.S.A.* **92** 41 42N 88 12W
Austin, *U.S.A.* **90** 30 20N 97 45W
Australia ■, *Oc.* **66** 23 0S 135 0 E
Australian Alps, *Austral.* **70** 36 30S 148 30 E
Australian Cap. Terr. □, *Austral.* **70** 35 30S 149 0 E
Austria ■, *Europe* **42** 47 0N 14 0 E
Auxerre, *Fr.* **34** 47 48N 3 32 E

Avebury, *U.K.* 14 51 25N 1 52W
Avellino, *It.* 40 40 54N 14 46 E
Aveton Gifford, *U.K.* 16 50 17N 3 51W
Avich, L., *U.K.* 20 56 17N 5 25W
Aviemore, *U.K.* 23 57 11N 3 50W
Avignon, *Fr.* 35 43 57N 4 50 E
Ávila, *Sp.* 37 40 39N 4 43W
Avoca, *Ire.* 25 52 52N 6 13W
Avon □, *U.K.* 14 51 30N 2 40W
Avon →, *Avon, U.K.* 14 51 30N 2 43W
Avon →, *Hants., U.K.* 14 50 44N 1 45W
Avon →, *Warwick, U.K.* 14 52 0N 2 9W
Avonmouth, *U.K.* 14 51 30N 2 42W
Awe, L., *U.K.* 20 56 15N 5 15W
Axbridge, *U.K.* 14 51 17N 2 50W
Axe →, *U.K.* 14 51 17N 2 52W
Axe Edge, *U.K.* 18 53 14N 1 59W
Axholme, Isle of, *U.K.* 19 53 30N 0 55W
Axminster, *U.K.* 16 50 47N 3 1W
Axmouth, *U.K.* 16 50 43N 3 2W
Ayers Rock, *Austral.* 66 25 23S 131 5 E
Aylesbury, *U.K.* 15 51 48N 0 49W
Aylesford, *U.K.* 15 51 18N 0 29 E
Aylsham, *U.K.* 15 52 48N 1 16 E
Aynho, *U.K.* 14 51 59N 1 15W
Ayr, *U.K.* 20 55 28N 4 37W
Ayr →, *U.K.* 20 55 29N 4 40W
Ayr, Heads of, *U.K.* 20 55 25N 4 43W
Ayre, Pt. of, *U.K.* 18 54 27N 4 21W
Aysgarth, *U.K.* 18 54 18N 2 0W
Ayton, *Borders, U.K.* 21 55 51N 2 6W
Ayton, *N. Yorks., U.K.* 19 54 15N 0 29W
Az Zarqā, *Jord.* 57 32 5N 36 4 E
Azores, *Atl. Oc.* 128 38 44N 29 0W
Azov Sea, *U.S.S.R.* 47 46 0N 36 30 E
Azuero, Pen. de, *Pan.* 95 7 30N 80 30W

B

Bābol, *Iran* 56 36 40N 52 50 E
Bacabal, *Brazil* 101 4 15S 44 45W
Bacău, *Rom.* 43 46 35N 26 55 E
Back, *U.K.* 22 58 17N 6 20W
Bacolod, *Phil.* 63 10 40N 122 57 E
Bacton, *U.K.* 15 52 50N 1 29 E
Bacup, *U.K.* 18 53 42N 2 12W
Badajoz, *Sp.* 37 38 50N 6 59W
Badalona, *Sp.* 37 41 26N 2 15 E
Baffin B., *Canada* 89 72 0N 64 0W
Baffin I., *Canada* 89 68 0N 75 0W
Bagenalstown = Muine Bheag, *Ire.* 25 52 42N 6 57W
Baggy Pt., *U.K.* 16 51 11N 4 12W
Baghdād, *Iraq* 56 33 20N 44 30 E
Bagshot, *U.K.* 15 51 22N 0 41W
Bahamas ■, *Atl. Oc.* 95 24 0N 75 0W
Bahawalpur, *Pak.* 58 29 24N 71 40 E
Bahía = Salvador, *Brazil* 101 13 0S 38 30W
Bahía Blanca, *Arg.* 102 38 35S 62 13W
Bahrain ■, *Asia* 56 26 0N 50 35 E
Baia Mare, *Rom.* 43 47 40N 23 35 E
Baildon, *U.K.* 19 53 52N 1 46W
Baile Atha Cliath = Dublin, *Ire.* 24 53 20N 6 18W
Bain →, *U.K.* 19 53 10N 0 15W
Bainbridge, *U.K.* 18 54 18N 2 7W
Bakersfield, *U.S.A.* 90 35 25N 119 0W
Bakewell, *U.K.* 19 53 13N 1 40W
Bākhtarān, *Iran* 56 34 23N 47 0 E
Baku, *U.S.S.R.* 47 40 25N 49 45 E
Bala, *U.K.* 17 52 54N 3 36W
Bala, L. = Tegid, L., *U.K.* 17 52 53N 3 38W
Balallan, *U.K.* 22 58 5N 6 35W
Balaton, *Hung.* 43 46 50N 17 40 E
Balbeggie, *U.K.* 21 56 26N 3 19W
Balboa, *Pan.* 94 9 0N 79 30W
Balbriggan, *Ire.* 24 53 35N 6 10W
Balderton, *U.K.* 19 53 3N 0 46W
Baldock, *U.K.* 15 51 59N 0 11W
Balearic Is., *Sp.* 37 39 30N 3 0 E
Balfron, *U.K.* 20 56 4N 4 20W
Bali □, *Indon.* 63 8 20S 115 0 E
Balikesir, *Turk.* 47 39 35N 27 58 E
Balikpapan, *Indon.* 63 1 10S 116 55 E
Balkan Mts., *Bulg.* 41 43 15N 23 0 E
Balkan Pen., *Europe* 26 42 0N 22 0 E
Balkhash, L., *U.S.S.R.* 48 46 0N 74 50 E
Ballachulish, *U.K.* 22 56 40N 5 10W
Ballantrae, *U.K.* 20 55 6N 5 0W
Ballarat, *Austral.* 70 37 33S 143 50 E
Ballasalla, *U.K.* 18 54 7N 4 36W
Ballater, *U.K.* 23 57 2N 3 2W
Ballaugh, *U.K.* 18 54 20N 4 32W
Ballina, *Mayo, Ire.* 24 54 7N 9 10W
Ballina, *Tipp., Ire.* 25 52 49N 8 27W
Ballinasloe, *Ire.* 25 53 20N 8 12W
Ballinrobe, *Ire.* 24 53 36N 9 13W
Ballinskelligs B., *Ire.* 25 51 46N 10 11W
Balloch, *U.K.* 20 56 0N 4 35W
Ballycastle, *U.K.* 24 55 12N 6 15W
Ballyclare, *U.K.* 24 54 46N 6 0W
Ballymena, *U.K.* 24 54 53N 6 18W
Ballymena □, *U.K.* 24 54 53N 6 18W
Ballymoney, *U.K.* 24 55 5N 6 30W
Ballymoney □, *U.K.* 24 55 5N 6 23W
Ballynahinch, *U.K.* 24 54 24N 5 55W
Ballyshannon, *Ire.* 24 54 30N 8 10W
Balmaclellan, *U.K.* 21 55 6N 4 5W
Balmoral, *U.K.* 23 57 3N 3 13W
Balquhidder, *U.K.* 20 56 22N 4 22W
Balsas →, *Mex.* 94 17 55N 102 10W
Baltic Sea, *Europe* 45 56 0N 20 0 E
Baltimore, *Ire.* 25 51 29N 9 22W
Baltimore, *U.S.A.* 92 39 18N 76 37W
Baluchistan □, *Pak.* 58 27 30N 65 0 E
Balurghat, *India* 59 25 15N 88 44 E
Balvicar, *U.K.* 20 56 17N 5 38W
Bamako, *Mali* 78 12 34N 7 55W
Bamberg, *W. Ger.* 42 49 54N 10 53 E
Bamburgh, *U.K.* 21 55 36N 1 42W
Bamenda, *Cam.* 80 5 57N 10 11 E
Bamford, *U.K.* 19 53 21N 1 41W
Bampton, *Devon, U.K.* 16 50 59N 3 29W
Bampton, *Oxon., U.K.* 14 51 44N 1 33W
Banaras = Varanasi, *India* 59 25 22N 83 0 E
Banbridge, *U.K.* 24 54 21N 6 17W
Banbridge □, *U.K.* 24 54 21N 6 16W
Banbury, *U.K.* 14 52 4N 1 21W
Banchory, *U.K.* 23 57 3N 2 30W
Banda Aceh, *Indon.* 63 5 35N 95 20 E
Banda Sea, *Indon.* 63 6 0S 130 0 E
Bandār 'Abbās, *Iran* 57 27 15N 56 15 E
Bandar Seri Begawan, *Brunei* 63 4 52N 115 0 E
Bandon, *Ire.* 25 51 44N 8 45W
Bandon →, *Ire.* 25 51 40N 8 41W
Bandundu, *Zaïre* 80 3 15S 17 22 E
Bandung, *Indon.* 63 6 54S 107 36 E
Banff, *U.K.* 23 57 40N 2 32W
Bangalore, *India* 58 12 59N 77 40 E
Bangka, Selat, *Indon.* 63 2 30S 105 30 E
Bangkok, *Thai.* 63 13 45N 100 35 E
Bangladesh ■, *Asia* 59 24 0N 90 0 E
Bangor, *N. Ireland, U.K.* 24 54 40N 5 40W
Bangor, *Wales, U.K.* 17 53 13N 4 9W
Bangor, *U.S.A.* 93 44 48N 68 42W
Bangui, *C.A.R.* 80 4 23N 18 35 E
Banham, *U.K.* 15 52 27N 1 3 E
Banjarmasin, *Indon.* 63 3 20S 114 35 E
Banjul, *Gambia* 78 13 28N 16 40W
Bankend, *U.K.* 21 55 2N 3 31W
Bankfoot, *U.K.* 21 56 30N 3 31W
Banks I., *Canada* 88 73 15N 121 30W
Banks Pen., *N.Z.* 71 43 45S 173 15 E
Bann →, *Down, U.K.* 24 54 30N 6 31W
Bann →, *Londonderry, U.K.* 24 55 10N 6 34W
Bannockburn, *U.K.* 21 56 5N 3 55W
Bantry, *Ire.* 25 51 40N 9 28W
Bantry, B., *Ire.* 25 51 35N 9 50W
Banwell, *U.K.* 14 51 19N 2 51W
Baoding, *China* 61 38 50N 115 28 E
Baoji, *China* 60 34 20N 107 5 E
Baotou, *China* 61 40 32N 110 2 E
Barbados ■, *W. Ind.* 94 13 0N 59 30W
Barcaldine, *Austral.* 67 23 43S 145 6 E
Barcelona, *Sp.* 37 41 21N 2 10 E
Bardney, *U.K.* 19 53 13N 0 19W
Bardsey I., *U.K.* 17 52 46N 4 47W
Bareilly, *India* 58 28 22N 79 27 E
Barents Sea, *Arctic* 48 73 0N 39 0 E
Barford, *U.K.* 14 52 15N 1 35W
Bargoed, *U.K.* 17 51 42N 3 22W
Barham, *U.K.* 15 51 12N 1 10 E
Bari, *It.* 40 41 6N 16 52 E
Bari Doab, *Pak.* 58 30 20N 73 0 E
Barisal, *Bangla.* 59 22 45N 90 20 E
Barisan Mts., *Indon.* 63 3 30S 102 15 E
Barking, *U.K.* 15 51 31N 0 10 E
Barkly Tableland, *Austral.* 67 17 50S 136 40 E
Barlborough, *U.K.* 19 53 17N 1 17W
Barlby, *U.K.* 19 53 48N 1 3W
Barletta, *It.* 40 41 20N 16 17 E
Barmby Moor, *U.K.* 19 53 55N 0 47W
Barmoor Castle, *U.K.* 21 55 38N 2 0W
Barmouth, *U.K.* 17 52 44N 4 3W
Barnard Castle, *U.K.* 18 54 33N 1 55W
Barnaul, *U.S.S.R.* 48 53 20N 83 40 E
Barnet, *U.K.* 15 51 37N 0 15W
Barnetby le Wold, *U.K.* 19 53 34N 0 24W
Barnoldswick, *U.K.* 18 53 55N 2 11W
Barnsley, *U.K.* 19 53 33N 1 29W
Barnstaple, *U.K.* 16 51 5N 4 3W
Barnstaple B., *U.K.* 16 51 5N 4 25W
Baroda = Vadodara, *India* 58 22 20N 73 10 E
Barquísimeto, *Ven.* 100 10 4N 69 19W
Barr, *U.K.* 20 55 13N 4 44W
Barra, *U.K.* 22 57 0N 7 30W
Barra, Sd. of, *U.K.* 22 57 4N 7 25W
Barra Hd., *U.K.* 22 56 47N 7 40W
Barrancabermeja, *Col.* 100 7 0N 73 50W
Barranquilla, *Col.* 100 11 0N 74 50W
Barrhead, *U.K.* 20 55 48N 4 23W
Barrhill, *U.K.* 20 55 7N 4 46W
Barrow →, *Ire.* 25 52 10N 6 57W
Barrow-in-Furness, *U.K.* 18 54 8N 3 15W
Barrow upon Humber, *U.K.* 19 53 41N 0 22W
Barrowford, *U.K.* 18 53 51N 2 14W
Barry, *S. Glam., U.K.* 17 51 23N 3 19W
Barry, *Tayside, U.K.* 21 56 29N 2 45W
Barton, *U.K.* 19 54 28N 1 38W
Barton-upon-Humber, *U.K.* 19 53 41N 0 27W
Barvas, *U.K.* 22 58 21N 6 31W
Barwell, *U.K.* 14 52 35N 1 22W
Basildon, *U.K.* 15 51 34N 0 29 E
Basingstoke, *U.K.* 14 51 15N 1 5W
Basle, *Switz.* 42 47 35N 7 35 E
Basra, *Iraq* 56 30 30N 47 50 E
Bass Rock, *U.K.* 21 56 5N 2 40W
Bass Str., *Austral.* 67 39 15S 146 30 E
Basse-Terre, *Guad.* 94 16 0N 61 40W
Bassein, *Burma* 59 16 45N 94 30 E
Bassenthwaite, L., *U.K.* 18 54 40N 3 14W
Basseterre, *Guad.* 94 17 17N 62 43W
Bastia, *Fr.* 35 42 40N 9 30 E
Baston, *U.K.* 15 52 43N 0 19W
Bata, *Eq. Guin.* 80 1 57N 9 50 E
Batangas, *Phil.* 63 13 35N 121 10 E
Bath, *U.K.* 14 51 22N 2 22W
Bathford, *U.K.* 14 51 23N 2 18W
Bathgate, *U.K.* 21 55 54N 3 38W
Bathurst, *Austral.* 70 33 25S 149 31 E
Bathurst, *Canada* 93 47 37N 65 43W
Batley, *U.K.* 19 53 43N 1 38W
Batna, *Alg.* 78 35 34N 6 15 E
Baton Rouge, *U.S.A.* 91 30 30N 91 5W
Battle, *U.K.* 15 50 55N 0 30 E
Batumi, *U.S.S.R.* 47 41 30N 41 30 E
Bauru, *Brazil* 101 22 10S 49 0W
Bavaria □, *W. Ger.* 42 49 7N 11 30 E
Bawdsey, *U.K.* 15 52 1N 1 27 E
Bawtry, *U.K.* 19 53 25N 1 1W
Bayamo, *Cuba* 95 20 20N 76 40W
Bayan Har Shan, *China* 60 34 0N 98 0 E
Bayeux, *Fr.* 34 49 17N 0 42W
Baykal, L., *U.S.S.R.* 49 53 0N 108 0 E
Bayonne, *Fr.* 35 43 30N 1 28W
Beachley, *U.K.* 14 51 37N 2 39W
Beachy Head, *U.K.* 15 50 44N 0 16 E
Beaconsfield, *U.K.* 15 51 36N 0 39W
Beadnell, *U.K.* 21 55 33N 1 38W
Beagle, Canal, *S. Am.* 102 55 0S 68 30W
Beaminster, *U.K.* 14 50 48N 2 44W
Bear I., *Ire.* 25 51 38N 9 50W
Beardmore Glacier, *Ant.* 103 84 30S 170 0 E
Bearsden, *U.K.* 20 55 55N 4 21W
Bearsted, *U.K.* 15 51 15N 0 35 E
Beattock, *U.K.* 21 55 19N 3 27W
Beaufort Sea, *Arctic* 103 72 0N 140 0W
Beaulieu, *U.K.* 14 50 49N 1 27W
Beauly, *U.K.* 23 57 29N 4 27W
Beauly →, *U.K.* 23 57 26N 4 28W
Beaumaris, *U.K.* 17 53 16N 4 7W
Beaumont, *U.S.A.* 91 30 5N 94 8W
Beauvais, *Fr.* 34 49 25N 2 8 E
Bebington, *U.K.* 18 53 23N 3 1W
Beccles, *U.K.* 15 52 27N 1 33 E
Béchar, *Alg.* 78 31 38N 2 18W
Beckermet, *U.K.* 18 54 26N 3 31W
Beckfoot, *U.K.* 18 54 50N 3 25W
Beckingham, *U.K.* 19 53 24N 0 49W
Bedale, *U.K.* 19 54 18N 1 35W
Beddgelert, *U.K.* 17 53 2N 4 8W
Bedford, *U.K.* 15 52 8N 0 29W
Bedford □, *U.K.* 15 52 4N 0 28W
Bedford Level, *U.K.* 15 52 25N 0 5 E
Bedlington, *U.K.* 21 55 8N 1 35W
Bedworth, *U.K.* 14 52 28N 1 29W
Beeford, *U.K.* 19 53 58N 0 18W
Beer, *U.K.* 16 50 41N 3 5W
Beersheba, *Isr.* 57 31 15N 34 48 E
Beeston, *U.K.* 19 52 55N 1 11W
Bei'an, *China* 61 48 10N 126 20 E
Beighton, *U.K.* 19 53 21N 1 21W
Beijing = Peking, *China* 61 39 55N 116 20 E
Beira, *Mozam.* 81 19 50S 34 52 E
Beira-Baixa, *Port.* 37 40 2N 7 30W
Beirut, *Leb.* 57 33 53N 35 31 E
Beith, *U.K.* 20 55 45N 4 38W
Bejaïa, Golfe de, *Alg.* 78 36 42N 5 13 E
Belbroughton, *U.K.* 14 52 23N 2 5W
Belcher Is., *Canada* 89 56 15N 78 45W
Belém, *Brazil* 101 1 20S 48 30W
Belfast, *U.K.* 24 54 35N 5 56W
Belfast □, *U.K.* 24 54 35N 5 56W
Belfast L., *U.K.* 24 54 40N 5 50W
Belford, *U.K.* 21 55 36N 1 50W
Belfort, *Fr.* 34 47 38N 6 50 E
Belgium ■, *Europe* 36 50 30N 5 0 E
Belgorod, *U.S.S.R.* 47 50 35N 36 35 E
Belgrade, *Yug.* 41 44 50N 20 37 E
Beliton, Is., *Indon.* 63 3 10S 107 50 E
Belize ■, *Cent. Am.* 94 17 0N 88 30W
Belize City, *Belize* 94 17 25N 88 0W
Bell Rock = Inchcape Rock, *U.K.* 21 56 26N 2 24W
Bellary, *India* 58 15 10N 76 56 E
Belle-Ile, *Fr.* 34 47 20N 3 10W
Belle Isle, Str. of, *Canada* 89 51 30N 56 30W
Belleville, *Canada* 92 44 10N 77 23W
Bellingham, *U.K.* 21 55 9N 2 16W
Belmopan, *Belize* 94 17 18N 88 30W
Belmullet, *Ire.* 24 54 13N 9 58W
Belo Horizonte, *Brazil* 101 19 55S 43 56W
Beloye More, *U.S.S.R.* 46 66 30N 38 0 E
Belper, *U.K.* 19 53 2N 1 29W
Belsay, *U.K.* 21 55 6N 1 53W
Belton, *Humberside, U.K.* 19 53 33N 0 49W
Belton, *Norfolk, U.K.* 15 52 35N 1 39 E
Belturbet, *Ire.* 24 54 6N 7 28W
Bembridge, *U.K.* 14 50 41N 1 4W
Ben Bheigeir, *U.K.* 20 55 43N 6 6W
Ben Chonzie, *U.K.* 21 56 27N 4 0W
Ben Cruachan, *U.K.* 20 56 26N 5 8W
Ben Dearg, *U.K.* 23 57 47N 4 58W
Ben Dorain, *U.K.* 20 56 30N 4 42W
Ben Hope, *U.K.* 23 58 24N 4 36W
Ben Lawers, *U.K.* 23 56 33N 4 13W
Ben Lomond, *U.K.* 20 56 12N 4 39W
Ben Lui, *U.K.* 20 56 24N 4 50W
Ben Macdhui, *U.K.* 23 57 4N 3 40W
Ben Mhor, *U.K.* 22 57 16N 7 21W
Ben More, *Central, U.K.* 20 56 23N 4 31W
Ben More, *Strathclyde, U.K.* 20 56 26N 6 2W
Ben More Assynt, *U.K.* 23 58 7N 4 51W
Ben Nevis, *U.K.* 22 56 48N 5 0W
Ben Venue, *U.K.* 20 56 13N 4 28W
Ben Vorlich, *U.K.* 20 56 22N 4 15W
Ben Wyvis, *U.K.* 23 57 40N 4 35W
Benalla, *Austral.* 70 36 30S 146 0 E
Benares = Varanasi, *India* 59 25 22N 83 0 E
Benbecula, *U.K.* 22 57 26N 7 21W
Bendigo, *Austral.* 70 36 40S 144 15 E
Beneraird, *U.K.* 20 55 4N 4 57W
Benevento, *It.* 40 41 7N 14 45 E
Bengal, Bay of, *Ind. Oc.* 59 18 0N 90 0 E
Bengbu, *China* 61 32 58N 117 20 E
Benghazi, *Libya* 79 32 11N 20 3 E
Beni Suef, *Egypt* 79 29 5N 31 6 E
Benin ■, *Africa* 78 10 0N 2 0 E
Benin, Bight of, *W. Afr.* 78 5 0N 3 0 E
Benin City, *Nig.* 78 6 20N 5 31 E
Benington, *U.K.* 19 52 59N 0 5 E
Bennane Hd., *U.K.* 20 55 9N 5 2W
Benoni, *S. Afr.* 81 26 11S 28 18 E
Benson, *U.K.* 14 51 37N 1 6W
Bentley, *Hants., U.K.* 15 51 12N 0 52W
Bentley, *S. Yorks., U.K.* 19 53 33N 1 9W
Benue →, *Nig.* 78 7 48N 6 46 E
Benxi, *China* 61 41 20N 123 48 E
Berbera, *Som.* 73 10 30N 45 2 E
Berbérati, *C.A.R.* 80 4 15N 15 40 E
Bere Alston, *U.K.* 16 50 29N 4 11W
Bere Regis, *U.K.* 14 50 45N 2 13W
Berezniki, *U.S.S.R.* 46 59 24N 56 46 E
Bérgamo, *It.* 40 45 42N 9 40 E
Bergen, *Nor.* 45 60 23N 5 20 E
Bergen-op-Zoom, *Neth.* 36 51 30N 4 18 E
Bergerac, *Fr.* 35 44 51N 0 30 E
Bergisch-Gladbach, *W. Ger.* 36 50 59N 7 9 E
Berhampore, *India* 59 24 2N 88 27 E
Berhampur, *India* 59 19 15N 84 54 E
Bering Sea, *Pac. Oc.* 88 58 0N 167 0 E
Bering Str., *N. Am.* 103 66 0N 170 0W
Berkeley, *U.K.* 14 51 41N 2 28W
Berkhamsted, *U.K.* 15 51 45N 0 33W
Berkshire □, *U.K.* 14 51 30N 1 20W
Berkshire Downs, *U.K.* 15 51 30N 1 30W
Berlin, *Ger.* 42 52 32N 13 24 E
Bermuda ■, *Atl. Oc.* 95 32 45N 65 0W
Bern, *Switz.* 42 46 57N 7 28 E
Berry Hd., *U.K.* 16 50 24N 3 29W
Berwick-upon-Tweed, *U.K.* 19 55 47N 2 0W
Berwyn Mts., *U.K.* 17 52 54N 3 26W
Besançon, *Fr.* 34 47 15N 6 0 E
Bethesda, *U.K.* 17 53 11N 4 3W
Bethlehem, *Jord.* 57 31 43N 35 12 E
Bethlehem, *U.S.A.* 93 40 39N 75 24W
Béthune, *Fr.* 34 50 30N 2 38 E
Betws-y-Coed, *U.K.* 17 53 4N 3 49W
Beverley, *U.K.* 19 53 52N 0 26W
Beverwijk, *Neth.* 36 52 28N 4 38 E
Bewdley, *U.K.* 14 52 23N 2 19W
Bexhill, *U.K.* 15 50 51N 0 29 E
Bexley, *U.K.* 15 51 26N 0 10 E
Béziers, *Fr.* 35 43 20N 3 12 E
Bhagalpur, *India* 59 25 10N 87 0 E
Bhatinda, *India* 58 30 15N 74 57 E
Bhatpara, *India* 59 22 50N 88 25 E
Bhavnagar, *India* 58 21 45N 72 10 E
Bhimavaram, *India* 59 16 30N 81 30 E
Bhopal, *India* 58 23 20N 77 30 E
Bhubaneshwar, *India* 59 20 15N 85 50 E
Bhutan ■, *Asia* 59 27 25N 90 30 E
Bialystok, *Pol.* 43 53 10N 23 10 E
Biarritz, *Fr.* 34 43 29N 1 33W
Bibury, *U.K.* 14 51 46N 1 50W
Bicester, *U.K.* 14 51 53N 1 9W
Bicton, *U.K.* 14 52 43N 2 47W
Biddenden, *U.K.* 15 51 7N 0 40 E
Biddulph, *U.K.* 18 53 8N 2 11W
Bideford, *U.K.* 16 51 1N 4 13W
Bideford Bay, *U.K.* 16 51 5N 4 20W
Bidford on Avon, *U.K.* 14 52 9N 1 53W
Bié Plateau, *Angola* 81 12 0S 16 0 E
Biel, *Switz.* 42 47 8N 7 14 E
Bielefeld, *W. Ger.* 42 52 2N 8 31 E
Bigbury, *U.K.* 16 50 17N 3 52W
Bigbury B., *U.K.* 16 50 18N 3 58W
Biggar, *U.K.* 21 55 38N 3 31W
Biggleswade, *U.K.* 15 52 6N 0 16W
Bighorn Mts., *U.S.A.* 90 44 30N 107 30W
Bihar □, *India* 59 25 0N 86 0 E
Bikaner, *India* 58 28 2N 73 18 E

Bikini Atoll, *Pac. Oc.* **64** 12 0N 167 30 E
Bilbao, *Sp.* **37** 43 16N 2 56W
Billericay, *U.K.* **15** 51 38N 0 25 E
Billesdon, *U.K.* **15** 52 38N 0 56W
Billingham, *U.K.* **19** 54 36N 1 18W
Billinghay, *U.K.* **19** 53 5N 0 17W
Billings, *U.S.A.* **90** 45 43N 108 29W
Billingshurst, *U.K.* **15** 51 2N 0 28W
Bilston, *U.K.* **14** 52 34N 2 5W
Binbrook, *U.K.* **19** 53 26N 0 9W
Bingham, *U.K.* **19** 52 57N 0 55W
Binghamton, *U.S.A.* **93** 42 9N 75 54W
Bingley, *U.K.* **18** 53 51N 1 50W
Bioko, *Eq. Guin.* **80** 3 30N 8 40 E
Birch, *U.K.* **15** 51 50N 0 54 E
Birchington, *U.K.* **15** 51 22N 1 18 E
Birdlip, *U.K.* **14** 51 50N 2 7W
Birkdale, *U.K.* **18** 53 38N 3 2W
Birkenhead, *U.K.* **18** 53 24N 3 1W
Birmingham, *U.K.* **14** 52 30N 1 55W
Birmingham, *U.S.A.* **91** 33 31N 86 50W
Birr, *Ire.* **25** 53 7N 7 55W
Birtley, *Northumberland, U.K.* **21** 55 5N 2 12W
Birtley, *Tyne & Wear, U.K.* **21** 54 53N 1 34W
Biscay, B. of, *Atl. Oc.* **35** 45 0N 2 0W
Bishop Auckland, *U.K.* **19** 54 40N 1 40W
Bishop's Castle, *U.K.* **14** 52 29N 3 0W
Bishop's Cleeve, *U.K.* **14** 51 56N 2 3W
Bishop's Frome, *U.K.* **14** 52 8N 2 29W
Bishops Lydeard, *U.K.* **14** 51 4N 3 12W
Bishop's Nympton, *U.K.* **16** 50 58N 3 44W
Bishop's Stortford, *U.K.* **15** 51 52N 0 11 E
Bishop's Waltham, *U.K.* **14** 50 57N 1 13W
Bishopsteignton, *U.K.* **16** 50 32N 3 32W
Bishopstoke, *U.K.* **14** 50 58N 1 19W
Biskra, *Alg.* **78** 34 50N 5 44 E
Bismarck Arch., *P.N.G.* **64** 2 30S 150 0 E
Bissau, *Guin.-Biss.* **78** 11 45N 15 45W
Bitola, *Yug.* **41** 41 5N 21 10 E
Bitton, *U.K.* **14** 51 25N 2 27W
Biwa-Ko, *Jap.* **62** 35 15N 136 10 E
Biysk, *U.S.S.R.* **48** 52 40N 85 0 E
Blaby, *U.K.* **14** 52 34N 1 10W
Black Combe, *U.K.* **18** 54 16N 3 20W
Black Esk →, *U.K.* **21** 55 14N 3 13W
Black Forest, Mts., *W. Ger.* **42** 48 0N 8 0 E
Black Hd., *U.K.* **16** 50 1N 5 6W
Black Mt. = Mynydd Du, *U.K.* **17** 51 45N 3 45W
Black Mts., *U.K.* **17** 51 52N 3 5W
Black Sea, *Europe* **47** 43 30N 35 0 E
Black Volta →, *Africa* **78** 8 41N 1 33W
Blackall, *Austral.* **67** 24 25S 145 45 E
Blackburn, *U.K.* **18** 53 44N 2 30W
Blackdown Hills, *U.K.* **14** 50 57N 3 15W
Blackford, *U.K.* **21** 56 15N 3 48W
Blackmoor Gate, *U.K.* **16** 51 9N 3 55W
Blackmoor Vale, *U.K.* **14** 50 54N 2 28W
Blackpool, *U.K.* **18** 53 48N 3 3W
Blacksod B., *Ire.* **24** 54 6N 10 0W
Blacktown, *Austral.* **70** 33 48S 150 55 E
Blackwater →, *Ire.* **25** 51 55N 7 50W
Blackwater →, *Essex, U.K.* **15** 51 44N 0 53 E
Blackwater →, *N. Ireland, U.K.* **24** 54 31N 6 35W
Blackwood, *U.K.* **21** 55 40N 3 56W
Blaenau Ffestiniog, *U.K.* **17** 53 0N 3 57W
Blaenavon, *U.K.* **17** 51 46N 3 5W
Blagdon, *U.K.* **14** 51 19N 2 42W
Blagoveshchensk, *U.S.S.R.* **49** 50 20N 127 30 E
Blair Athol, *Austral.* **67** 22 42S 147 31 E
Blair Atholl, *U.K.* **23** 56 46N 3 50W
Blairgowrie, *U.K.* **23** 56 36N 3 20W
Blakeney, *Gloucs., U.K.* **14** 51 45N 2 29W
Blakeney, *Norfolk, U.K.* **15** 52 57N 1 1 E
Blanc, Mont, *Europe* **35** 45 48N 6 50 E
Blandford Forum, *U.K.* **14** 50 52N 2 10W
Blantyre, *Malawi* **81** 15 45S 35 0 E
Blarney, *Ire.* **25** 51 57N 8 35W
Blaydon, *U.K.* **19** 54 56N 1 47W
Bleadon, *U.K.* **14** 51 18N 2 57W
Blean, *U.K.* **15** 51 18N 1 3 E
Bleasdale Moors, *U.K.* **18** 53 57N 2 40W
Blenheim, *N.Z.* **71** 41 38S 173 57 E
Bletchingdon, *U.K.* **14** 51 51N 1 16W
Bletchley, *U.K.* **15** 51 59N 0 44W
Blisworth, *U.K.* **15** 52 11N 0 56W
Blockley, *U.K.* **14** 52 1N 1 45W
Bloemfontein, *S. Afr.* **81** 29 6S 26 14 E
Blofield, *U.K.* **15** 52 38N 1 25 E
Blois, *Fr.* **34** 47 35N 1 20 E
Bloody Foreland, *Ire.* **24** 55 10N 8 18W
Bloxham, *U.K.* **14** 52 1N 1 22W
Blue Mts., *Austral.* **70** 33 40S 150 0 E
Blue Mts., *U.S.A.* **90** 45 15N 119 0W
Blue Nile →, *Sudan* **79** 12 30N 34 30 E
Blue Ridge Mts., *U.S.A.* **91** 36 30N 80 15W
Blue Stack Mts., *Ire.* **24** 54 46N 8 5W
Blumenau, *Brazil* **102** 27 0S 49 0W
Blundeston, *U.K.* **15** 52 33N 1 42 E
Blyth, *Northumberland, U.K.* **19** 55 8N 1 32W
Blyth, *Notts., U.K.* **19** 53 22N 1 2W
Blyth →, *U.K.* **21** 55 8N 1 30W
Blyth Bridge, *U.K.* **21** 55 41N 3 22W
Blyton, *U.K.* **19** 53 25N 0 42W
Bobo-Dioulasso, *B. Faso* **78** 11 8N 4 13W
Bocholt, *W. Ger.* **36** 51 50N 6 35 E
Bochum, *W. Ger.* **36** 51 28N 7 12 E
Bodenham, *U.K.* **14** 52 9N 2 41W
Bodensee, *W. Ger.* **42** 47 35N 9 25 E
Bodiam, *U.K.* **15** 51 1N 0 33 E
Bodinnick, *U.K.* **16** 50 20N 4 37W
Bodmin, *U.K.* **16** 50 28N 4 44W
Bodmin Moor, *U.K.* **16** 50 33N 4 36W
Bodø, *Nor.* **44** 67 17N 14 24 E
Bogan →, *Austral.* **67** 29 59S 146 17 E
Boggeragh Mts., *Ire.* **25** 52 2N 8 55W
Bognor Regis, *U.K.* **15** 50 47N 0 40W
Bogor, *Indon.* **63** 6 36S 106 48 E
Bogota, *Col.* **100** 4 34N 74 0W
Bohemian Forest, *Czech.* **42** 49 20N 13 0 E
Boise, *U.S.A.* **90** 43 43N 116 9W
Bolgatanga, *Ghana* **78** 10 44N 0 53W
Bolivia ■, *S. Am.* **100** 17 6S 64 0W
Bolivian Plateau, *S. Am.* **96** 20 0S 67 30W
Bollington, *U.K.* **18** 53 18N 2 8W
Bolney, *U.K.* **15** 50 59N 0 11W
Bologna, *It.* **40** 44 30N 11 20 E
Bolshevik, I., *U.S.S.R.* **49** 78 30N 102 0 E
Bolshezemelskaya Tundra, *U.S.S.R.* **46** 67 0N 56 0 E
Bolsover, *U.K.* **19** 53 14N 1 18W
Bolt Head, *U.K.* **16** 50 13N 3 48W
Bolt Tail, *U.K.* **16** 50 13N 3 55W
Bolton, *U.K.* **18** 53 35N 2 26W
Bolton Abbey, *U.K.* **18** 53 59N 1 53W
Bolton by Bowland, *U.K.* **18** 53 56N 2 21W
Bolton le Sands, *U.K.* **18** 54 7N 2 49W
Bolungavík, *Ice.* **44** 66 9N 23 15W
Bolzano, *It.* **40** 46 30N 11 20 E
Boma, *Zaïre* **80** 5 50S 13 4 E
Bombay, *India* **58** 18 55N 72 50 E
Bonaparte Archipelago, *Austral.* **66** 14 0S 124 30 E
Bonarbridge, *U.K.* **23** 57 53N 4 20W
Bonchester Bridge, *U.K.* **21** 55 23N 2 36W
Bonchurch, *U.K.* **14** 50 36N 1 11W
Bo'ness, *U.K.* **21** 56 0N 3 38W
Bonifacio, Str. of, *Fr.* **40** 41 12N 9 15 E
Bonn, *W. Ger.* **36** 50 43N 7 6 E
Bonnyrigg, *U.K.* **21** 55 52N 3 8W
Boot, *U.K.* **18** 54 24N 3 18W
Boothia, Gulf of, *Canada* **89** 71 0N 90 0W
Boothia Pen., *Canada* **88** 71 0N 94 0W
Bootle, *Cumbria, U.K.* **18** 54 17N 3 24W
Bootle, *Merseyside, U.K.* **18** 53 28N 3 1W
Borås, *Swed.* **45** 57 43N 12 56 E
Bordeaux, *Fr.* **35** 44 50N 0 36W
Borders □, *U.K.* **21** 55 35N 2 50W
Bordon, *U.K.* **15** 51 6N 0 52W
Borehamwood, *U.K.* **15** 51 40N 0 15W
Boreland, *U.K.* **21** 55 12N 3 16W
Borgarnes, *Ice.* **44** 64 32N 21 55W
Borneo, *E. Ind.* **63** 1 0N 115 0 E
Bornholm, *Den.* **45** 55 10N 15 0 E
Boroughbridge, *U.K.* **19** 54 6N 1 23W
Borrowdale, *U.K.* **18** 54 31N 3 10W
Borth, *U.K.* **17** 52 29N 4 3W
Bosbury, *U.K.* **14** 52 5N 2 27W
Boscastle, *U.K.* **16** 50 42N 4 42W
Bosham, *U.K.* **15** 50 50N 0 51W
Bosporus, *Turk.* **47** 41 10N 29 10 E
Boston, *U.K.* **19** 52 59N 0 2W
Boston, *U.S.A.* **93** 42 20N 71 0W
Botany Bay, *Austral.* **70** 34 0S 151 14 E
Bothel, *U.K.* **18** 54 43N 3 16W
Bothnia, G. of, *Europe* **44** 63 0N 20 0 E
Botswana ■, *Africa* **81** 22 0S 24 0 E
Bottesford, *U.K.* **19** 52 57N 0 48W
Bottrop, *W. Ger.* **36** 51 34N 6 59 E
Bouaké, *Ivory C.* **78** 7 40N 5 2W
Bouar, *C.A.R.* **80** 6 0N 15 40 E
Boulogne-sur-Mer, *Fr.* **34** 50 42N 1 36 E
Bourges, *Fr.* **34** 47 9N 2 25 E
Bourgogne, *Fr.* **34** 47 0N 4 50 E
Bourke, *Austral.* **67** 30 8S 145 55 E
Bourne, *U.K.* **15** 52 46N 0 22W
Bournemouth, *U.K.* **14** 50 43N 1 53W
Bourton-on-the-Water, *U.K.* **14** 51 53N 1 45W
Bovey Tracey, *U.K.* **16** 50 36N 3 40W
Bowen, *Austral.* **67** 20 0S 148 16 E
Bowes, *U.K.* **18** 54 31N 1 59W
Bowland, Forest of, *U.K.* **18** 54 0N 2 30W
Bowmore, *U.K.* **20** 55 45N 6 18W
Bowness, *Solway, U.K.* **18** 54 57N 3 13W
Bowness, *Windermere, U.K.* **18** 54 22N 2 56W
Box, *U.K.* **14** 51 24N 2 16W
Box Hill, *U.K.* **15** 51 16N 0 16W
Boxley, *U.K.* **15** 51 17N 0 34 E
Boyle, *Ire.* **24** 53 58N 8 19W
Boyne →, *Ire.* **24** 53 43N 6 15W
Bozeat, *U.K.* **15** 52 14N 0 41W
Bracadale, L., *U.K.* **22** 57 20N 6 30W
Bracebridge Heath, *U.K.* **19** 53 13N 0 32W
Brackley, *U.K.* **14** 52 3N 1 9W
Bracknell, *U.K.* **15** 51 24N 0 45W
Braco, *U.K.* **21** 56 16N 3 55W
Bradda Hd., *U.K.* **18** 54 6N 4 46W
Bradford, *U.K.* **19** 53 47N 1 45W
Bradford-on-Avon, *U.K.* **14** 51 20N 2 15W
Brading, *U.K.* **14** 50 41N 1 9W
Bradwell-on-Sea, *U.K.* **15** 51 44N 0 55 E
Bradworthy, *U.K.* **16** 50 54N 4 22W
Braemar, *U.K.* **23** 57 2N 3 20W
Braga, *Port.* **37** 41 35N 8 25W
Brahmaputra →, *India* **59** 24 2N 90 59 E
Braich-y-pwll, *U.K.* **17** 52 47N 4 46W
Brăila, *Rom.* **43** 45 19N 27 59 E
Brailsford, *U.K.* **19** 52 58N 1 35W
Braintree, *U.K.* **15** 51 53N 0 34 E
Bramford, *U.K.* **15** 52 5N 1 6 E
Brampton, *Canada* **92** 43 45N 79 45W
Brampton, *Cambs., U.K.* **15** 52 19N 0 13W
Brampton, *Cumbria, U.K.* **18** 54 56N 2 43W
Bramshott, *U.K.* **15** 51 5N 0 47W
Brancaster, *U.K.* **15** 52 58N 0 40 E
Branco →, *Brazil* **100** 1 20S 61 50W
Brander, Pass of, *U.K.* **20** 56 25N 5 10W
Brandon, *Canada* **88** 49 50N 99 57W
Brandon, *Durham, U.K.* **19** 54 46N 1 37W
Brandon, *Suffolk, U.K.* **15** 52 27N 0 37 E
Brandon, Mt., *Ire.* **25** 52 15N 10 15W
Brandon B., *Ire.* **25** 52 17N 10 8W
Branston, *U.K.* **19** 53 13N 0 28W
Brantford, *Canada* **92** 43 10N 80 15W
Brasília, *Brazil* **101** 15 47S 47 55 E
Braşov, *Rom.* **43** 45 38N 25 35 E
Brasted, *U.K.* **15** 51 16N 0 8 E
Bratislava, *Czech.* **43** 48 10N 17 7 E
Bratsk, *U.S.S.R.* **49** 56 10N 101 30 E
Braunton, *U.K.* **16** 51 6N 4 9W
Bray, *Ire.* **25** 53 12N 6 6W
Bray, *U.K.* **15** 51 30N 0 42W
Brazil ■, *S. Am.* **101** 10 0S 50 0W
Brazilian Highlands, *Brazil* **101** 18 0S 46 30W
Brazzaville, *Congo* **80** 4 9S 15 12 E
Breadalbane, *U.K.* **20** 56 30N 4 15W
Breage, *U.K.* **16** 50 6N 5 17W
Breamish →, *U.K.* **21** 55 30N 1 55W
Brechin, *U.K.* **23** 56 44N 2 40W
Breckland, *U.K.* **15** 52 30N 0 40 E
Brecon, *U.K.* **17** 51 57N 3 23W
Brecon Beacons, *U.K.* **17** 51 53N 3 27W
Brede, *U.K.* **15** 50 56N 0 37 E
Bredon Hill, *U.K.* **14** 52 3N 2 2W
Breiðafjörður, *Ice.* **44** 65 15N 23 15W
Bremen, *W. Ger.* **42** 53 4N 8 47 E
Bremerhaven, *W. Ger.* **40** 53 34N 8 35 E
Brendon Hills, *U.K.* **14** 51 6N 3 25W
Brenner Pass, *Alps* **42** 47 0N 11 30 E
Brent, *U.K.* **15** 51 33N 0 18W
Brentwood, *U.K.* **15** 51 37N 0 19 E
Bréscia, *It.* **40** 45 33N 10 13 E
Breslau = Wrocław, *Pol.* **43** 51 5N 17 5 E
Bressay I., *U.K.* **22** 60 10N 1 5W
Brest, *Fr.* **34** 48 24N 4 31W
Brest, *U.S.S.R.* **46** 52 10N 23 40 E
Bretagne, *Fr.* **34** 48 0N 3 0W
Brewood, *U.K.* **14** 52 41N 2 10W
Brezhnev, *U.S.S.R.* **46** 55 42N 52 19 E
Bride, *U.K.* **18** 54 24N 4 23W
Bridestowe, *U.K.* **16** 50 41N 4 7W
Bridge, *U.K.* **15** 51 14N 1 8 E
Bridge of Allan, *U.K.* **21** 56 9N 3 57W
Bridge of Earn, *U.K.* **21** 56 20N 3 25W
Bridge of Orchy, *U.K.* **20** 56 29N 4 48W
Bridge of Weir, *U.K.* **20** 55 51N 4 35W
Bridgend, *Islay, U.K.* **20** 55 46N 6 15W
Bridgend, *Mid Glam., U.K.* **17** 51 30N 3 35W
Bridgeport, *U.S.A.* **93** 41 12N 73 12W
Bridgetown, *Barb.* **94** 13 0N 59 30W
Bridgnorth, *U.K.* **14** 52 33N 2 25W
Bridgwater, *U.K.* **14** 51 7N 3 0W
Bridgwater B., *U.K.* **14** 51 15N 3 15W
Bridlington, *U.K.* **19** 54 6N 0 11W
Bridlington B., *U.K.* **19** 54 4N 0 10W
Bridport, *U.K.* **14** 50 43N 2 45W
Brierfield, *U.K.* **18** 53 49N 2 15W
Brierley Hill, *U.K.* **14** 52 29N 2 7W
Brigg, *U.K.* **19** 53 33N 0 30W
Brighouse, *U.K.* **19** 53 42N 1 47W
Brighstone, *U.K.* **15** 50 38N 1 23W
Brightlingsea, *U.K.* **15** 51 49N 1 1 E
Brighton, *U.K.* **15** 50 50N 0 9W
Brigstock, *U.K.* **15** 52 27N 0 38W
Brill, *U.K.* **15** 51 49N 1 3W
Brimfield, *U.K.* **14** 52 18N 2 42W
Bríndisi, *It.* **41** 40 39N 17 55 E
Brinklow, *U.K.* **14** 52 25N 1 22W
Brinkworth, *U.K.* **14** 51 33N 1 59W
Brisbane, *Austral.* **67** 27 25S 153 2 E
Bristol, *U.K.* **14** 51 26N 2 35W
Bristol Channel, *U.K.* **16** 51 18N 4 30W
Briston, *U.K.* **15** 52 52N 1 4 E
British Columbia □, *Canada* **88** 55 0N 125 15W
British Guiana = Guyana ■, *S. Am.* **100** 5 0N 59 0W
British Isles, *Europe* **4** 55 0N 4 0W
Briton Ferry, *U.K.* **17** 51 37N 3 50W
Brittany = Bretagne, *Fr.* **34** 48 0N 3 0W
Brixham, *U.K.* **16** 50 24N 3 31W
Brixworth, *U.K.* **15** 52 20N 0 54W
Brize Norton, *U.K.* **14** 51 46N 1 35W
Brno, *Czech.* **42** 49 10N 16 35 E
Broad B., *U.K.* **22** 58 14N 6 16W
Broad Chalke, *U.K.* **14** 51 2N 1 54W
Broad Haven, *Ire.* **24** 54 20N 9 55W
Broad Law, *U.K.* **21** 55 30N 3 22W
Broad Sd., *U.K.* **16** 49 56N 6 19W
Broadclyst, *U.K.* **16** 50 46N 3 27W
Broadford, *U.K.* **22** 57 14N 5 55W
Broadhembury, *U.K.* **16** 50 49N 3 16W
Broads, The, *U.K.* **15** 52 45N 1 30 E
Broadstairs, *U.K.* **15** 51 21N 1 28 E
Broadway, *U.K.* **14** 52 2N 1 51W
Broadwindsor, *U.K.* **14** 50 49N 2 49W
Brockenhurst, *U.K.* **14** 50 49N 1 34W
Brockton, *U.S.A.* **93** 42 25N 79 26W
Brockworth, *U.K.* **14** 51 51N 2 9W
Brodick, *U.K.* **20** 55 34N 5 9W
Broken Hill, *Austral.* **70** 31 58S 141 29 E
Bromborough, *U.K.* **18** 53 20N 3 0W
Bromfield, *U.K.* **14** 52 25N 2 45W
Bromham, *U.K.* **14** 51 23N 2 3W
Bromley, *U.K.* **15** 51 20N 0 5 E
Brompton, *U.K.* **19** 54 22N 1 25W
Bromsgrove, *U.K.* **14** 52 20N 2 3W
Bromyard, *U.K.* **14** 52 12N 2 30W
Brooks, *Canada* **88** 50 35N 111 55W
Brooks Ra., *U.S.A.* **88** 68 40N 147 0W
Broom, L., *U.K.* **22** 57 55N 5 15W
Broomfield, *U.K.* **14** 51 46N 0 28 E
Broomhill, *U.K.* **21** 55 19N 1 36W
Brora, *U.K.* **23** 58 0N 3 50W
Brora →, *U.K.* **23** 58 4N 3 52W
Broseley, *U.K.* **14** 52 36N 2 30W
Brosna →, *Ire.* **25** 53 8N 8 0W
Brothertoft, *U.K.* **19** 53 0N 0 5W
Brotton, *U.K.* **19** 54 34N 0 55W
Brough, *Cumbria, U.K.* **18** 54 32N 2 19W
Brough, *Humberside, U.K.* **19** 53 44N 0 35W
Broughton, *Borders, U.K.* **21** 55 37N 3 25W
Broughton, *Humberside, U.K.* **19** 53 33N 0 36W
Broughton, *N. Yorks., U.K.* **19** 54 26N 1 8W
Broughton, *Northants., U.K.* **15** 52 22N 0 45W
Broughton-in-Furness, *U.K.* **18** 54 17N 3 12W
Broughty Ferry, *U.K.* **21** 56 29N 2 50W
Brown Willy, *U.K.* **16** 50 35N 4 34W
Brownhills, *U.K.* **14** 52 38N 1 57W
Broxburn, *U.K.* **21** 55 56N 3 23W
Bruay-en-Artois, *Fr.* **34** 50 29N 2 33 E
Bruce, Mt., *Austral.* **66** 22 37S 118 8 E
Brue →, *U.K.* **14** 51 10N 2 59W
Bruges, *Belg.* **36** 51 13N 3 13 E
Brunei ■, *E. Ind.* **63** 4 50N 115 0 E
Brunswick, *W. Ger.* **42** 52 17N 10 28 E
Brunton, *U.K.* **21** 55 2N 2 6W
Brussels, *Belg.* **36** 50 51N 4 21 E
Bruton, *U.K.* **14** 51 6N 2 28W
Bryansk, *U.S.S.R.* **46** 53 13N 34 25 E
Bryher I., *U.K.* **16** 49 57N 6 21W
Brynamman, *U.K.* **17** 51 49N 3 52W
Brynmawr, *U.K.* **17** 51 48N 3 11W
Bucaramanga, *Col.* **100** 7 0N 73 0W
Buchan, *U.K.* **23** 57 32N 2 8W
Buchan Ness, *U.K.* **23** 57 29N 1 48W
Bucharest, *Rom.* **43** 44 27N 26 10 E
Buchlyvie, *U.K.* **20** 56 7N 4 20W
Buckden, *U.K.* **15** 52 17N 0 16W
Buckfastleigh, *U.K.* **16** 50 28N 3 47W
Buckhaven, *U.K.* **21** 56 10N 3 2W
Buckie, *U.K.* **23** 57 40N 2 58W
Buckingham, *U.K.* **15** 52 0N 0 59W
Buckingham □, *U.K.* **15** 51 50N 0 55W
Buckland Brewer, *U.K.* **16** 50 56N 4 14W
Buckland Newton, *U.K.* **14** 50 45N 2 25W
Buckley, *U.K.* **17** 53 10N 3 5W
Budapest, *Hung.* **43** 47 29N 19 5 E
Buddon Ness, *U.K.* **21** 56 29N 2 42W
Bude, *U.K.* **16** 50 49N 4 33W
Bude Bay, *U.K.* **16** 50 50N 4 40W
Budle B., *U.K.* **21** 55 37N 1 45W
Budleigh Salterton, *U.K.* **16** 50 37N 3 19W
Buenaventura, *Col.* **100** 3 53N 77 4W
Buenos Aires, *Arg.* **102** 34 30S 58 20W
Buffalo, *U.S.A.* **92** 42 55N 78 50W
Bug →, *Pol.* **43** 52 31N 21 5 E
Bug →, *U.S.S.R.* **47** 46 59N 31 58 E
Buglawton, *U.K.* **18** 53 12N 2 11W
Bugle, *U.K.* **16** 50 23N 4 46W
Buie L., *U.K.* **20** 56 20N 5 55W
Builth Wells, *U.K.* **17** 52 10N 3 26W
Bujumbura, *Bur.* **80** 3 16S 29 18 E
Bukavu, *Zaïre* **80** 2 20S 28 52 E
Bukhara, *U.S.S.R.* **48** 39 48N 64 25 E
Bulawayo, *Zimb.* **81** 20 7S 28 32 E
Bulford, *U.K.* **14** 51 11N 1 45W
Bulgaria ■, *Europe* **41** 42 35N 25 30 E
Bulwell, *U.K.* **19** 53 1N 1 12W
Bunbury, *Austral.* **66** 33 20S 115 35 E
Buncrana, *Ire.* **24** 55 8N 7 28W
Bundaberg, *Austral.* **67** 24 54S 152 22 E
Bundoran, *Ire.* **24** 54 24N 8 17W

Bunessan, *U.K.* **20** 56 18N 6 15W
Bungay, *U.K.* .... **15** 52 27N 1 26 E
Buntingford, *U.K.* **15** 51 57N 0 1W
Bunwell, *U.K.* .... **15** 52 30N 1 9 E
Buraydah, *Si. Arab.* ... **56** 26 20N 44 8 E
Burbage, *Derby, U.K.* . **18** 53 15N 1 55W
Burbage, *Leics., U.K.* . **14** 52 31N 1 20W
Burbage, *Wilts., U.K.* . **14** 51 21N 1 40W
Burdwan, *India* ...... **59** 23 14N 87 39 E
Bure →, *U.K.* .... **15** 52 38N 1 45 E
Burford, *U.K.* **14** 51 48N 1 38W
Burgas, *Bulg.* .... **41** 42 33N 27 29 E
Burgess Hill, *U.K.* **15** 50 57N 0 7W
Burgh-le-Marsh, *U.K.* . **19** 53 10N 0 15 E
Burgos, *Sp.* **37** 42 21N 3 41W
Burgundy = Bourgogne, *Fr.* ..... **34** 47 0N 4 50 E
Burkina Faso ■, *Africa* **78** 12 0N 1 0W
Burley, *Hants., U.K.* .. **14** 50 49N 1 41W
Burley, *N. Yorks., U.K.* **19** 53 55N 1 46W
Burlington, *U.S.A.* **93** 44 27N 73 14W
Burma ■, *Asia* .... **59** 21 0N 96 30 E
Burnham, *Essex, U.K.* . **15** 51 37N 0 50 E
Burnham, *Somerset, U.K.* **14** 51 14N 3 0W
Burnham Market, *U.K.* **15** 52 57N 0 43 E
Burnie, *Austral.* ...... **67** 41 4S 145 56 E
Burnley, *U.K.* **18** 53 47N 2 15W
Burnmouth, *U.K.* **21** 55 50N 2 4W
Burntisland, *U.K.* **21** 56 4N 3 14W
Burrelton, *U.K.* **21** 56 30N 3 16W
Burrow Hd., *U.K.* **20** 54 40N 4 23W
Burry Port, *U.K.* **17** 51 41N 4 17W
Bursa, *Turk.* .... **47** 40 15N 29 5 E
Burstwick, *U.K.* **19** 53 43N 0 6W
Burton, *U.K.* **18** 54 10N 2 43W
Burton Agnes, *U.K.* ... **19** 54 4N 0 18W
Burton Bradstock, *U.K.* **14** 50 41N 2 43W
Burton Fleming, *U.K.* . **19** 54 8N 0 20W
Burton Latimer, *U.K.* .. **15** 52 23N 0 41W
Burton upon Stather, *U.K.* **19** 53 39N 0 41W
Burton-upon-Trent, *U.K.* **14** 52 48N 1 39W
Burundi ■, *Africa* .... **80** 3 15S 30 0 E
Burwash, *U.K.* .... **15** 50 59N 0 24 E
Burwell, *U.K.* .... **15** 52 17N 0 20 E
Bury, *U.K.* **18** 53 36N 2 19W
Bury St. Edmunds, *U.K.* **15** 52 15N 0 42 E
Buryat A.S.S.R. □, *U.S.S.R.* .... **49** 53 0N 110 0 E
Būshehr, *Iran* .... **56** 28 20N 51 45 E
Bushey, *U.K.* **15** 51 38N 0 20W
Bushmills, *U.K.* **24** 55 14N 6 32W
Bute, *U.K.* **20** 55 48N 5 2W
Bute, Kyles of, *U.K.* .. **20** 55 55N 5 10W
Bute, Sd. of, *U.K.* **20** 55 43N 5 8W
Buttermere, *U.K.* **18** 54 32N 3 17W
Butuan, *Phil.* .... **63** 8 57N 125 33 E
Buxton, *U.K.* **18** 53 16N 1 54W
Buzău, *Rom.* .... **43** 45 10N 26 50 E
Bydgoszcz, *Pol.* ...... **43** 53 10N 18 0 E
Byfield, *U.K.* **14** 52 10N 1 15W
Byrd Land, *Ant.* **103** 79 30S 125 0W
Byrrang Mts., *U.S.S.R.* **49** 75 0N 100 0 E
Bytom, *Pol.* .... **43** 50 25N 18 54 E

C

Cabimas, *Ven.* **100** 10 23N 71 25W
Cabinda □, *Angola* ... **80** 5 0S 12 30 E
Čačak, *Yug.* .... **41** 43 54N 20 20 E
Cáceres, *Sp.* **37** 39 26N 6 23W
Cachoeira do Sul, *Brazil* **102** 30 3S 52 53W
Cader Idris, *U.K.* **17** 52 43N 3 56W
Cádiz, *Sp.* **37** 36 30N 6 20W
Caen, *Fr.* **34** 49 10N 0 22W
Caenby Corner, *U.K.* .. **19** 53 23N 0 32W
Caernarfon, *U.K.* **17** 53 8N 4 17W
Caernarfon B., *U.K.* ... **17** 53 4N 4 40W
Caerphilly, *U.K.* **17** 51 34N 3 13W
Caersws, *U.K.* **17** 52 32N 3 27W
Cagayan de Oro, *Phil.* **63** 8 30N 124 40 E
Cágliari, *It.* .... **40** 39 15N 9 6 E
Caha Mts., *Ire.* **25** 51 45N 9 40W
Caher, *Ire.* **25** 52 23N 7 56W
Cahersiveen, *Ire.* **25** 51 57N 10 13W
Cahore Pt., *Ire.* **25** 52 34N 6 11W
Caicos Is., *W. Ind.* ... **95** 21 40N 71 40W
Cairn Gorm, *U.K.* **23** 57 7N 3 40W
Cairn Table, *U.K.* **21** 55 30N 4 0W
Cairn Toul, *U.K.* **23** 57 3N 3 44W
Cairngorm Mts., *U.K.* . **23** 57 6N 3 42W
Cairnryan, *U.K.* **20** 54 59N 5 0W
Cairns, *Austral.* ...... **67** 16 57S 145 45 E
Cairo, *Egypt* .... **79** 30 1N 31 14 E
Caister-on-Sea, *U.K.* .. **15** 52 38N 1 43 E
Caistor, *U.K.* **19** 53 29N 0 20W
Caithness, Ord of, *U.K.* **23** 58 9N 3 37W
Cajamarca, *Peru* **100** 7 5S 78 28W
Calabar, *Nig.* .... **78** 4 57N 8 20 E
Calábria □, *It.* .... **40** 39 24N 16 30 E
Calais, *Fr.* .... **34** 50 57N 1 50 E
Calbayog, *Phil.* ...... **63** 12 4N 124 38 E
Calcutta, *India* ...... **59** 22 36N 88 24 E
Caldbeck, *U.K.* **18** 54 45N 3 3W
Calder →, *U.K.* **19** 53 44N 1 21W
Calder Bridge, *U.K.* ... **18** 54 27N 3 31W
Caldew →, *U.K.* **18** 54 54N 2 59W
Caledonian Canal, *U.K.* **23** 56 50N 5 6W
Calf of Man, *U.K.* **18** 54 4N 4 48W
Calgary, *Canada* **88** 51 0N 114 10W
Calgary, *U.K.* **20** 56 34N 6 17W
Cali, *Col.* **100** 3 25N 76 35W
Caliach Pt., *U.K.* **20** 56 37N 6 20W
Calicut, *India* .... **58** 11 15N 75 43 E
California □, *U.S.A.* ... **90** 37 25N 120 0W
California, G. of, *N. Am.* **94** 27 0N 111 0W
Callan, *Ire.* **25** 52 33N 7 25W
Callander, *U.K.* **20** 56 15N 4 14W
Callao, *Peru* **100** 12 0S 77 0W
Calne, *U.K.* **14** 51 26N 2 0W
Calshot, *U.K.* **14** 50 49N 1 18W
Calstock, *U.K.* **16** 50 30N 4 13W
Caltanissetta, *It.* ..... **40** 37 30N 14 3 E
Cam →, *U.K.* .... **15** 52 21N 0 16 E
Camagüey, *Cuba* **95** 21 20N 78 0W
Camargue, *Fr.* .... **35** 43 34N 4 34 E
Cambay, G. of, *India* .. **58** 20 45N 72 30 E
Camberley, *U.K.* **15** 51 20N 0 44W
Cambo, *U.K.* **21** 55 9N 1 57W
Cambodia ■, *Asia* ... **63** 12 15N 105 0 E
Camborne, *U.K.* **16** 50 13N 5 18W
Cambrian Mts., *U.K.* .. **17** 52 25N 3 52W
Cambridge, *U.K.* ..... **15** 52 13N 0 8 E
Cambridge, *U.S.A.* ... **93** 42 20N 71 8W
Cambridge Bay, *Canada* **88** 69 10N 105 0W
Cambridgeshire □, *U.K.* **15** 52 12N 0 7 E
Camden, *U.K.* **15** 51 33N 0 10W
Camden, *U.S.A.* **93** 39 57N 75 7W
Camel →, *U.K.* **16** 50 28N 4 49W
Camelford, *U.K.* **16** 50 37N 4 41W
Cameroon ■, *Africa* .. **80** 6 0N 12 30 E
Campbellton, *Canada* . **93** 49 17N 54 56W
Campbelltown, *Austral.* **70** 34 53S 138 40 E
Campbeltown, *U.K.* ... **20** 55 25N 5 36W
Campeche, *Mex.* **94** 19 50N 90 32W
Campeche, G. of, *Mex.* **94** 19 30N 93 0W
Campina Grande, *Brazil* **101** 7 20S 35 47W
Campinas, *Brazil* **102** 22 50S 47 0W
Campo Grande, *Brazil* **101** 20 25S 54 40W
Campos, *Brazil* **101** 21 50S 41 20W
Campsie Fells, *U.K.* .. **20** 56 2N 4 20W
Camrose, *Canada* **88** 53 0N 112 50W
Can Tho, *Viet.* .... **63** 10 2N 105 46 E
Canada ■, *N. Am.* **88** 60 0N 100 0W
Canary Is., *Atl. Oc.* ... **78** 29 30N 17 0W
Canaveral, C., *U.S.A.* . **91** 28 28N 80 31W
Canberra, *Austral.* ... **70** 35 15S 149 8 E
Canik Mts., *Turk.* ..... **47** 40 30N 38 0 E
Canna, *U.K.* **22** 57 3N 6 33W
Cannes, *Fr.* .... **35** 43 32N 7 0 E
Cannington, *U.K.* **14** 51 8N 3 4W
Cannock, *U.K.* **14** 52 42N 2 2W
Cannock Chase, *U.K.* . **14** 52 43N 2 0W
Canonbie, *U.K.* **21** 55 4N 2 58W
Cantabrian Mts., *Sp.* .. **37** 43 0N 5 10W
Canterbury, *U.K.* ..... **15** 51 17N 1 5 E
Canterbury Plains, *N.Z.* **71** 43 55S 171 22 E
Canton = Guangzhou, *China* .... **61** 23 5N 113 10 E
Canton, *U.S.A.* **92** 40 47N 81 22W
Canvey, *U.K.* .... **15** 51 32N 0 35 E
Caoles, *U.K.* **20** 56 32N 6 43W
Caolisport, Loch, *U.K.* **20** 55 54N 5 40W
Cape Breton I., *Canada* **93** 46 0N 60 30W
Cape Coast, *Ghana* .. **78** 5 5N 1 15W
Cape Province □, *S. Afr.* .... **81** 32 0S 23 0 E
Cape Town, *S. Afr.* ... **81** 33 55S 18 22 E
Cape Verde Is. ■, *Atl. Oc.* **128** 17 10N 25 20W
Cape York Peninsula, *Austral.* .... **67** 12 0S 142 30 E
Capel, *U.K.* **15** 51 8N 0 18W
Caracas, *Ven.* **100** 10 30N 66 55W
Caratinga, *Brazil* **101** 19 50S 42 10W
Carbost, *U.K.* **22** 57 19N 6 21W
Cardiff, *U.K.* **17** 51 28N 3 11W
Cardigan, *U.K.* **17** 52 6N 4 41W
Cardigan B., *U.K.* **17** 52 30N 4 30W
Cardington, *U.K.* **15** 52 7N 0 23W
Carey, L., *Austral.* ... **66** 29 0S 122 15 E
Caribbean Sea **95** 15 0N 75 0W
Carisbrooke, *U.K.* **14** 50 42N 1 19W
Cark, *U.K.* **18** 54 11N 2 59W
Carleton Rode, *U.K.* .. **15** 52 30N 1 6 E
Carlingford, L., *Ire.* ... **24** 54 0N 6 5W
Carlisle, *U.K.* **18** 54 54N 2 55W
Carlops, *U.K.* **21** 55 47N 3 20W
Carlow, *Ire.* **25** 52 50N 6 58W
Carlow □, *Ire.* **25** 52 43N 6 50W
Carloway, *U.K.* **22** 58 17N 6 48W
Carlton, *U.K.* **19** 52 58N 1 6W
Carlton Colville, *U.K.* .. **15** 52 27N 1 41 E
Carlton Miniott, *U.K.* .. **19** 54 13N 1 22W
Carluke, *U.K.* **21** 55 44N 3 50W
Carmarthen, *U.K.* **17** 51 52N 4 20W
Carmarthen B., *U.K.* .. **17** 51 40N 4 30W
Carnarvon, *Austral.* ... **66** 24 51S 113 42 E
Carndonagh, *Ire.* **24** 55 15N 7 16W
Carnegie, L., *Austral.* . **66** 26 5S 122 30 E
Carnforth, *U.K.* **18** 54 8N 2 47W
Carno, *U.K.* **17** 52 34N 3 31W
Carnoustie, *U.K.* **21** 56 30N 2 41W
Carnsore Pt., *Ire.* **25** 52 10N 6 20W
Carnwath, *U.K.* **21** 55 42N 3 38W
Caroline Is., *Pac. Oc.* . **64** 8 0N 150 0 E
Carpathians, Mts., *Europe* .... **43** 49 50N 21 0 E
Carpentaria, G. of, *Austral.* .... **67** 14 0S 139 0 E
Carradale, *U.K.* **20** 55 35N 5 30W
Carrauntoohill, Mt., *Ire.* **25** 52 0N 9 49W
Carrick, *U.K.* **20** 55 12N 4 38W
Carrick-on-Shannon, *Ire.* **24** 53 57N 8 7W
Carrick-on-Suir, *Ire.* .. **25** 52 22N 7 30W
Carrickfergus, *U.K.* ... **24** 54 43N 5 50W
Carrickfergus □, *U.K.* . **24** 54 43N 5 49W
Carrickmacross, *Ire.* .. **24** 54 0N 6 43W
Carron →, *U.K.* **22** 57 30N 5 30W
Carron, L., *U.K.* **22** 57 22N 5 35W
Carronbridge, *U.K.* ... **21** 55 16N 3 46W
Carse of Gowrie, *U.K.* . **21** 56 30N 3 10W
Carsphairn, *U.K.* **20** 55 13N 4 15W
Carstairs, *U.K.* **21** 55 42N 3 41W
Cartagena, *Col.* **100** 10 25N 75 33W
Cartagena, *Sp.* **37** 37 38N 0 59W
Cartmel, *U.K.* **18** 54 13N 2 57W
Caruaru, *Brazil* **101** 8 15S 35 55W
Carúpano, *Ven.* **100** 10 39N 63 15W
Casablanca, *Mor.* **78** 33 36N 7 36W
Cascade Ra., *U.S.A.* .. **90** 47 0N 121 30W
Cashel, *Ire.* **25** 52 31N 7 53W
Casper, *U.S.A.* **90** 42 52N 106 20W
Caspian Sea, *U.S.S.R.* **47** 43 0N 50 0 E
Castellón □, *Sp.* **37** 40 15N 0 5W
Castle Acre, *U.K.* .... **15** 52 42N 0 42 E
Castle Cary, *U.K.* **14** 51 5N 2 32W
Castle Donington, *U.K.* **14** 52 50N 1 20W
Castle Douglas, *U.K.* .. **21** 54 57N 3 57W
Castle Eden, *U.K.* **19** 54 45N 1 20W
Castlebar, *Ire.* **24** 53 52N 9 17W
Castlebay, *U.K.* **22** 56 57N 7 30W
Castleblaney, *Ire.* **24** 54 7N 6 44W
Castleford, *U.K.* **19** 53 43N 1 21W
Castlereagh, *Ire.* **24** 53 47N 8 30W
Castlereagh □, *U.K.* .. **24** 54 33N 5 53W
Castlereagh →, *Austral.* .... **70** 30 12S 147 32 E
Castleside, *U.K.* **18** 54 50N 1 52W
Castleton, *Derby, U.K.* **19** 53 20N 1 47W
Castleton, *N. Yorks., U.K.* **19** 54 27N 0 57W
Castletown, *U.K.* **18** 54 4N 4 40W
Castletown Bearhaven, *Ire.* **25** 51 40N 9 54W
Castries, *St. Lucia* **94** 14 0N 60 50W
Catánia, *It.* .... **40** 37 31N 15 4 E
Catanzaro, *It.* .... **40** 38 54N 16 38 E
Catcleugh, *U.K.* **21** 55 19N 2 22W
Caterham, *U.K.* **15** 51 16N 0 4W
Caton, *U.K.* **18** 54 5N 2 41W
Catrine, *U.K.* **20** 55 30N 4 20W
Catsfield, *U.K.* .... **15** 50 53N 0 28 E
Catterick, *U.K.* **19** 54 23N 1 38W
Catterick Camp, *U.K.* . **19** 54 22N 1 43W
Catton, *U.K.* **21** 54 56N 2 16W
Caucasus, *U.S.S.R.* ... **47** 43 0N 44 0 E
Caulkerbush, *U.K.* **21** 54 54N 3 40W
Cavan, *Ire.* **24** 54 0N 7 22W
Cavan □, *Ire.* **24** 53 58N 7 10W
Cawood, *U.K.* **19** 53 50N 1 7W
Cawston, *U.K.* .... **15** 52 47N 1 10 E
Caxias, *Brazil* **101** 4 55S 43 20W
Caxias do Sul, *Brazil* . **102** 29 10S 51 10W
Cayenne, *Fr. G.* **101** 5 0N 52 18W
Ceanannus Mor, *Ire.* .. **24** 53 42N 6 53W
Cebu, *Phil.* .... **63** 10 18N 123 54 E
Cedar Rapids, *U.S.A.* . **90** 42 0N 91 38W
Celbridge, *Ire.* **25** 53 20N 6 33W
Celebes = Sulawesi □, *Indon.* .... **63** 2 0S 120 0 E
Celebes Sea, *E. Ind.* .. **63** 3 0N 123 0 E
Cemaes Bay, *U.K.* **17** 53 24N 4 27W
Central □, *U.K.* **20** 56 10N 4 30W
Central African Republic ■, *Africa* .. **80** 7 0N 20 0 E
Central Russian Uplands, *U.S.S.R.* .. **26** 54 0N 36 0 E
Central Siberian Plateau, *U.S.S.R.* ... **49** 65 0N 105 0 E
Cephalonia = Kefallinía, *Greece* .... **41** 38 20N 20 30 E
Ceram, *Indon.* .... **63** 3 10S 129 0 E
Ceres, *U.K.* **21** 56 18N 2 57W
Cerignola, *It.* .... **40** 41 17N 15 53 E
Cerne Abbas, *U.K.* ... **14** 50 49N 2 29W
Cerrig-y-drudion, *U.K.* **17** 53 2N 3 34W
Cessnock, *Austral.* ... **70** 32 50S 151 21 E
Ceuta, *Mor.* **78** 35 52N 5 18W
Cévennes, *Fr.* .... **34** 44 10N 3 50 E
Ceylon = Sri Lanka ■, *Asia* .... **58** 7 30N 80 50 E
Chacewater, *U.K.* **16** 50 15N 5 8W
Chad ■, *Africa* ...... **78** 15 0N 17 15 E
Chad, L., *Chad* ...... **79** 13 30N 14 30 E
Chagford, *U.K.* **16** 50 40N 3 50W
Chale, *U.K.* **14** 50 35N 1 19W
Chalfont St. Peter, *U.K.* **15** 51 36N 0 33W
Châlons-sur-Marne, *Fr.* **34** 48 58N 4 20 E
Chambéry, *Fr.* .... **35** 45 34N 5 55 E
Champagne, *Fr.* ..... **34** 48 40N 4 20 E
Champlain, L., *U.S.A.* . **93** 44 30N 73 20W
Chandigarh, *India* .... **58** 30 43N 76 47 E
Chandler's Ford, *U.K.* . **14** 50 59N 1 23W
Changchun, *China* ... **61** 43 58N 125 19 E
Changde, *China* ..... **61** 29 4N 111 35 E
Changsha, *China* ..... **61** 28 5N 113 1 E
Changzhou, *China* ... **61** 31 47N 119 58 E
Channel Is., *U.K.* **34** 49 30N 2 40W
Chao Phraya →, *Thai.* **63** 13 32N 100 36 E
Chapel-en-le-Frith, *U.K.* **18** 53 19N 1 54W
Chapel St. Leonards, *U.K.* .... **19** 53 13N 0 19 E
Chard, *U.K.* **14** 50 52N 2 59W
Chardzhou, *U.S.S.R.* .. **48** 39 6N 63 34 E
Charing, *U.K.* .... **15** 51 12N 0 49 E
Charlbury, *U.K.* **14** 51 52N 1 29W
Charleroi, *Belg.* ...... **36** 50 24N 4 27 E
Charleston, *U.S.A.* **91** 32 47N 79 56W
Charleville = Rath Luirc, *Ire.* **25** 52 21N 8 40W
Charleville, *Austral.* ... **67** 26 24S 146 15 E
Charleville-Mézières, *Fr.* **34** 49 44N 4 40 E
Charlotte, *U.S.A.* **91** 35 16N 80 46W
Charlottenburg, *W. Ger.* **42** 52 31N 13 15 E
Charlottetown, *Canada* **93** 46 14N 63 8W
Charlton Kings, *U.K.* .. **14** 51 52N 2 3W
Charlwood, *U.K.* **15** 51 8N 0 12W
Charminster, *U.K.* **14** 50 43N 2 28W
Charmouth, *U.K.* **14** 50 45N 2 54W
Charnwood Forest, *U.K.* **14** 52 43N 1 18W
Charters Towers, *Austral.* .... **67** 20 5S 146 13 E
Chartham, *U.K.* ...... **15** 51 14N 1 1 E
Chartres, *Fr.* .... **34** 48 29N 1 30 E
Châteauroux, *Fr.* ..... **34** 46 50N 1 40 E
Chatham, *U.K.* ...... **15** 51 22N 0 32 E
Chattanooga, *U.S.A.* .. **91** 35 2N 85 17W
Chatteris, *U.K.* .... **15** 52 27N 0 3 E
Chatton, *U.K.* **21** 55 34N 1 55W
Cheadle, *Gr. Manchester, U.K.* **18** 53 23N 2 14W
Cheadle, *Staffs., U.K.* . **18** 52 59N 1 59W
Cheadle Hulme, *U.K.* . **18** 53 22N 2 12W
Cheboksary, *U.S.S.R.* . **46** 56 8N 47 12 E
Cheddar, *U.K.* **14** 51 16N 2 47W
Cheddleton, *U.K.* **18** 53 5N 2 2W
Chelmarsh, *U.K.* **14** 52 29N 2 25W
Chelmer →, *U.K.* .... **15** 51 45N 0 42 E
Chelmsford, *U.K.* ..... **15** 51 44N 0 29 E
Cheltenham, *U.K.* **14** 51 55N 2 5W
Chelyabinsk, *U.S.S.R.* . **48** 55 10N 61 24 E
Chenab →, *Pak.* ..... **58** 30 23N 71 2 E
Chengdu, *China* ..... **60** 30 38N 104 2 E
Chepstow, *U.K.* **17** 51 38N 2 40W
Cherbourg, *Fr.* **34** 49 39N 1 40W
Cheremkhovo, *U.S.S.R.* **49** 53 8N 103 1 E
Cherepovets, *U.S.S.R.* **46** 59 5N 37 55 E
Cheriton, *U.K.* **14** 51 3N 1 9W
Cheriton Fitzpaine, *U.K.* **16** 50 51N 3 38W
Cherkassy, *U.S.S.R.* .. **47** 49 27N 32 4 E
Chernigov, *U.S.S.R.* .. **46** 51 28N 31 20 E
Chernovtsy, *U.S.S.R.* . **47** 48 15N 25 52 E
Chertsey, *U.K.* **15** 51 23N 0 30W
Cherwell →, *U.K.* **14** 51 46N 1 18W
Chesapeake Bay, *U.S.A.* **92** 38 0N 76 12W
Chesham, *U.K.* **15** 51 42N 0 36W
Cheshire □, *U.K.* **18** 53 14N 2 30W
Cheshunt, *U.K.* **15** 51 42N 0 1W
Chesil Beach, *U.K.* ... **14** 50 37N 2 33W
Chester, *U.K.* **18** 53 12N 2 53W
Chester-le-Street, *U.K.* **19** 54 53N 1 34W
Chesterfield, *U.K.* **19** 53 14N 1 26W
Chesterfield Inlet, *Canada* **88** 63 30N 90 45W
Cheviot, The, *U.K.* **19** 55 29N 2 8W
Cheviot Hills, *U.K.* **19** 55 20N 2 30W
Chew Magna, *U.K.* ... **14** 51 21N 2 37W
Chiai, *China* .... **61** 23 29N 120 25 E
Chiba, *Jap.* .... **62** 35 30N 140 7 E
Chicago, *U.S.A.* **92** 41 53N 87 40W
Chichester, *U.K.* **15** 50 50N 0 47W
Chiclayo, *Peru* **100** 6 42S 79 50W
Chicoutimi, *Canada* ... **93** 48 28N 71 5W
Chiddingfold, *U.K.* **15** 51 6N 0 37W
Chidley, C., *Canada* .. **89** 60 23N 64 26W
Chieti, *It.* .... **40** 42 22N 14 10 E
Chihli, G. of, *China* ... **61** 38 30N 119 0 E
Chihuahua, *Mex.* **94** 28 40N 106 3W
Chile ■, *S. Am.* **102** 35 0S 72 0W
Chilham, *U.K.* .... **15** 51 15N 0 59 E
Chillán, *Chile* **102** 36 40S 72 10W
Chilpancingo, *Mex.* ... **94** 17 30N 99 30W
Chiltern Hills, *U.K.* ... **15** 51 44N 0 42W
Chilung, *Taiwan* ..... **61** 25 3N 121 45 E
Chimborazo, *Ecuad.* .. **100** 1 29S 78 55W
Chimbote, *Peru* **100** 9 0S 78 35W
Chimkent, *U.S.S.R.* ... **48** 42 18N 69 36 E
China ■, *Asia* .... **60** 30 0N 110 0 E
Chincha Alta, *Peru* ... **100** 13 25S 76 7W
Chingola, *Zam.* ...... **81** 12 31S 27 53 E
Chipata, *Zam.* .... **81** 13 38S 32 28 E
Chippenham, *U.K.* **14** 51 27N 2 7W
Chipping Campden, *U.K.* **14** 52 4N 1 48W
Chipping Norton, *U.K.* . **14** 51 56N 1 32W
Chipping Ongar, *U.K.* . **15** 51 43N 0 15 E
Chipping Sodbury, *U.K.* **14** 51 31N 2 23W
Chirbury, *U.K.* **14** 52 35N 3 6W
Chirnside, *U.K.* **21** 55 47N 2 11W
Chiseldon, *U.K.* **14** 51 30N 1 44W
Chita, *U.S.S.R.* ...... **49** 52 0N 113 35 E
Chittagong, *Bangla.* .. **59** 22 19N 91 48 E

Chollerton, *U.K.* 21 55 4N 2 7W
Cholsey, *U.K.* 14 51 34N 1 10W
Chongjin, *N. Kor.* 61 41 47N 129 50 E
Chongqing = Chungking, *China* 60 29 35N 106 25 E
Chorley, *U.K.* 18 53 39N 2 39W
Chorrera, La, *Pan.* 94 8 50N 79 50W
Chorzów, *Pol.* 43 50 18N 18 57 E
Choybalsan, *Mong.* 61 48 4N 114 30 E
Christchurch, *N.Z.* 71 43 33S 172 47 E
Christchurch, *U.K.* 14 50 44N 1 33W
Chudleigh, *U.K.* 16 50 35N 3 36W
Chulmleigh, *U.K.* 16 50 55N 3 52W
Chungking, *China* 60 29 35N 106 25 E
Chur, *Switz.* 42 46 52N 9 32 E
Church Stretton, *U.K.* 14 52 32N 2 49W
Churchdown, *U.K.* 14 51 53N 2 9W
Churchill →, *Canada* 88 58 47N 94 12W
Ciénaga, *Col.* 100 11 1N 74 15W
Cienfuegos, *Cuba* 95 22 10N 80 30W
Cincinnati, *U.S.A.* 92 39 10N 84 26W
Cinderford, *U.K.* 14 51 49N 2 30W
Cirencester, *U.K.* 14 51 43N 1 59W
Citlaltépetl, *Mex.* 94 19 0N 97 20W
Ciudad Bolívar, *Ven.* 100 8 5N 63 36W
Ciudad Guayana, *Ven.* 100 8 0N 62 30W
Ciudad Juárez, *Mex.* 94 31 40N 106 28W
Ciudad Madero, *Mex.* 94 22 19N 97 50W
Ciudad Obregón, *Mex.* 94 27 28N 109 59W
Ciudad Real, *Sp.* 37 38 59N 3 55W
Ciudad Victoria, *Mex.* 94 23 41N 99 9W
Clabhach, *U.K.* 20 56 38N 6 36W
Clach Leathad, *U.K.* 20 56 36N 7 52W
Clachan, *U.K.* 20 55 45N 5 35W
Clackmannan, *U.K.* 21 56 10N 3 50W
Clacton-on-Sea, *U.K.* 15 51 47N 1 10 E
Cladich, *U.K.* 20 56 21N 5 5W
Clara, *Ire.* 25 53 20N 7 38W
Clare, *U.K.* 15 52 5N 0 36 E
Clare □, *Ire.* 25 52 20N 9 0W
Clare →, *Ire.* 24 53 22N 9 5W
Clare I., *Ire.* 24 53 48N 10 0W
Claremorris, *Ire.* 24 53 45N 9 0W
Clarksville, *U.S.A.* 90 36 32N 87 20W
Clatteringshaws L., *U.K.* 20 55 3N 4 17W
Claverley, *U.K.* 14 52 32N 2 19W
Clay Cross, *U.K.* 19 53 11N 1 26W
Clay Hd., *U.K.* 18 54 13N 4 23W
Claydon, *U.K.* 15 52 6N 1 7 E
Clear, C., *Ire.* 25 51 26N 9 30W
Clear I., *Ire.* 25 51 26N 9 30W
Cleator Moor, *U.K.* 18 54 30N 3 32W
Clee Hills, *U.K.* 14 52 26N 2 35W
Cleethorpes, *U.K.* 19 53 33N 0 2W
Cleeve Cloud, *U.K.* 14 51 56N 2 0W
Clent, *U.K.* 14 52 25N 2 6W
Cleobury Mortimer, *U.K.* 14 52 23N 2 28W
Clermont-Ferrand, *Fr.* 34 45 46N 3 4 E
Clevedon, *U.K.* 14 51 26N 2 52W
Cleveland, *U.S.A.* 92 41 28N 81 43W
Cleveland □, *U.K.* 19 54 35N 1 8 E
Cleveland Hills, *U.K.* 19 54 25N 1 11W
Clew B., *Ire.* 24 53 54N 9 50W
Cley, *U.K.* 15 52 57N 1 3 E
Clifden, *Ire.* 24 53 30N 10 2W
Cliffe, *U.K.* 15 51 27N 0 31 E
Clifford, *U.K.* 14 52 6N 3 6W
Clipston, *U.K.* 15 52 26N 0 58W
Clitheroe, *U.K.* 18 53 52N 2 23W
Clonakilty, *Ire.* 25 51 37N 8 53W
Clonakilty B., *Ire.* 25 51 33N 8 50W
Cloncurry, *Austral.* 67 20 40S 140 28 E
Clones, *Ire.* 24 54 10N 7 13W
Clonmel, *Ire.* 25 52 22N 7 42W
Closeburn, *U.K.* 21 55 13N 3 45W
Cloughton, *U.K.* 19 54 20N 0 27W
Clovelly, *U.K.* 16 51 0N 4 25W
Clowne, *U.K.* 19 53 18N 1 16W
Cluj-Napoca, *Rom.* 43 46 47N 23 38 E
Clun, *U.K.* 14 52 26N 3 2W
Clun Forest, *U.K.* 14 52 27N 3 7W
Clunbury, *U.K.* 14 52 25N 2 55W
Clwyd □, *U.K.* 17 53 5N 3 20W
Clwyd →, *U.K.* 17 53 20N 3 30W
Clyde →, *U.K.* 20 55 56N 4 29W
Clyde, Firth of, *U.K.* 20 55 20N 5 0W
Clydebank, *U.K.* 20 55 54N 4 25W
Clydesdale, *U.K.* 21 55 42N 3 50W
Coalbrookdale, *U.K.* 14 52 38N 2 30W
Coalburn, *U.K.* 21 55 35N 3 55W
Coalville, *U.K.* 14 52 43N 1 21W
Coast Mts., *Canada* 88 55 0N 129 0W
Coast Ranges, *U.S.A.* 90 41 0N 123 0W
Coatbridge, *U.K.* 21 55 52N 4 2W
Coatzacoalcos, *Mex.* 94 18 7N 94 25W
Cóbh, *Ire.* 25 51 50N 8 18W
Cobourg Pen., *Austral.* 66 11 20S 132 15 E
Cochabamba, *Bol.* 100 17 26S 66 10W
Cochin, *India* 58 9 59N 76 22 E
Cockburnspath, *U.K.* 21 55 56N 2 23W
Cockenzie, *U.K.* 21 55 58N 2 59W
Cockerham, *U.K.* 18 53 58N 2 49W
Cockermouth, *U.K.* 18 54 40N 3 22W
Cockfield, *U.K.* 15 52 8N 0 47 E
Cod, C., *U.S.A.* 93 42 8N 70 10W
Coddenham, *U.K.* 15 52 8N 1 8 E
Coffs Harbour, *Austral.* 67 30 16S 153 5 E
Coggeshall, *U.K.* 15 51 53N 0 41 E
Coimbatore, *India* 58 11 2N 76 59 E
Coimbra, *Port.* 37 40 15N 8 27W
Colac, *Austral.* 70 38 21S 143 35 E
Colby, *U.K.* 18 54 6N 4 42W
Colchester, *U.K.* 15 51 54N 0 55 E
Cold Fell, *U.K.* 18 54 54N 2 40W
Coldingham, *U.K.* 21 55 53N 2 10W
Coldstream, *U.K.* 21 55 39N 2 14W
Colebrooke, *U.K.* 16 50 45N 3 44W
Coleford, *U.K.* 14 51 46N 2 38W
Coleraine, *U.K.* 24 55 8N 6 40W
Coleraine □, *U.K.* 24 55 8N 6 40 E
Coleshill, *U.K.* 14 52 30N 1 42W
Colima, *Mex.* 94 19 14N 103 43W
Colinton, *U.K.* 21 55 54N 3 17W
Coll, *U.K.* 20 56 40N 6 35W
Collie, *Austral.* 66 33 22S 116 8 E
Collier Law Pk., *U.K.* 18 54 47N 1 59W
Collin, *U.K.* 21 55 4N 3 30W
Collingbourne, *U.K.* 14 51 16N 1 39W
Collooney, *Ire.* 24 54 11N 8 28W
Colmar, *Fr.* 34 48 5N 7 20 E
Colmonel, *U.K.* 20 55 8N 4 55W
Colne, *U.K.* 18 53 51N 2 11W
Colne →, *Essex, U.K.* 15 51 55N 0 50 E
Colne →, *Herts., U.K.* 15 51 36N 0 30W
Cologne, *W. Ger.* 36 50 56N 6 58 E
Colombia ■, *S. Am.* 100 3 45N 73 0W
Colombo, *Sri L.* 58 6 56N 79 58 E
Colón, *Mex.* 94 20 48N 100 3W
Colonsay, *U.K.* 20 56 4N 6 12W
Colorado □, *U.S.A.* 90 37 40N 106 0W
Colorado →, *Calif., U.S.A.* 90 34 45N 114 40W
Colorado →, *Tex., U.S.A.* 90 28 36N 95 58W
Colorado Plateau, *U.S.A.* 90 36 40N 110 30W
Colorado Springs, *U.S.A.* 90 38 55N 104 50W
Colstorworth, *U.K.* 15 52 48N 0 37W
Coltishall, *U.K.* 15 52 44N 1 21 E
Columbia, *Miss., U.S.A.* 90 31 16N 89 50W
Columbia, *S.C., U.S.A.* 91 34 0N 81 0W
Columbia →, *N. Am.* 90 46 15N 124 5W
Columbus, *Ga., U.S.A.* 91 32 30N 84 58W
Columbus, *Ohio, U.S.A.* 92 39 57N 83 1W
Colwell, *U.K.* 21 55 4N 2 4W
Colwich, *U.K.* 14 52 48N 1 58W
Colwyn Bay, *U.K.* 17 53 17N 3 44W
Colyton, *U.K.* 16 50 44N 3 4W
Combe Martin, *U.K.* 16 51 12N 4 2W
Comber, *U.K.* 24 54 33N 5 45W
Comeragh Mts., *Ire.* 25 52 17N 7 35W
Comilla, *Bangla.* 59 23 28N 91 10 E
Comino, *Malta* 40 36 0N 14 20 E
Communism Pk., *U.S.S.R.* 48 38 40N 72 20 E
Como, *It.* 40 45 48N 9 5 E
Como, L., *It.* 40 46 5N 9 17 E
Comodoro Rivadavia, *Arg.* 102 45 50S 67 40W
Comorin, C., *India* 58 8 3N 77 40 E
Comoro Is. ■, *Ind. Oc.* 73 12 10S 44 15 E
Compiègne, *Fr.* 34 49 24N 2 50 E
Comrie, *U.K.* 21 56 22N 4 0W
Conakry, *Guin.* 78 9 29N 13 49W
Concepción, *Chile* 102 36 50S 73 0W
Conchos →, *Mex.* 94 29 32N 104 25W
Concordia, *Arg.* 102 31 20S 58 2W
Condover, *U.K.* 14 52 39N 2 46W
Congleton, *U.K.* 18 53 10N 2 12W
Congo = Zaïre →, *Africa* 80 6 4S 12 24 E
Congo ■, *Africa* 80 1 0S 16 0 E
Congo Basin, *Africa* 72 0 10S 24 30 E
Congresbury, *U.K.* 14 51 20N 2 49W
Coningsby, *U.K.* 19 53 7N 0 9W
Conisbrough, *U.K.* 19 53 29N 1 12W
Coniston, *U.K.* 18 54 22N 3 6W
Coniston Water, *U.K.* 18 54 20N 3 5W
Conn, L., *Ire.* 24 54 3N 9 15W
Connacht, *Ire.* 24 53 23N 8 40W
Connah's Quay, *U.K.* 17 53 13N 3 6W
Connecticut □, *U.S.A.* 93 41 40N 72 40W
Connecticut →, *U.S.A.* 93 41 17N 72 21W
Connel, *U.K.* 20 56 27N 5 24W
Connel Park, *U.K.* 20 55 22N 4 15W
Connemara, *Ire.* 24 53 29N 9 45W
Conon →, *U.K.* 23 57 33N 4 28W
Cononbridge, *U.K.* 23 57 32N 4 30W
Consett, *U.K.* 18 54 52N 1 50W
Constance, L. = Bodensee, *W. Ger.* 42 47 35N 9 25 E
Constanţa, *Rom.* 43 44 14N 28 38 E
Constantine, *Alg.* 78 36 25N 6 42 E
Conwy, *U.K.* 17 53 17N 3 50W
Conwy →, *U.K.* 17 53 18N 3 50W
Cook, Mt., *N.Z.* 71 43 36S 170 9 E
Cook Is., *Pac. Oc.* 65 17 0S 160 0W
Cook Strait, *N.Z.* 71 41 15S 174 29 E
Cookham, *U.K.* 15 51 33N 0 42W
Cookstown, *U.K.* 24 54 40N 6 43W
Cookstown □, *U.K.* 24 54 40N 6 43W
Coolgardie, *Austral.* 66 30 55S 121 8 E
Cootamundra, *Austral.* 70 34 36S 148 1 E
Cootehill, *Ire.* 24 54 5N 7 5W
Copenhagen, *Den.* 45 55 41N 12 34 E
Coppermine, *Canada* 88 67 50N 115 5W
Coppermine →, *Canada* 88 67 49N 116 4W
Copythorne, *U.K.* 14 50 56N 1 34W
Coquet →, *U.K.* 19 55 18N 1 45W
Coquet, I., *U.K.* 21 55 21N 1 30W
Coral Sea, *Pac. Oc.* 64 15 0S 150 0 E
Coral Sea Islands Terr., *Austral.* 67 20 0S 155 0 E
Corbridge, *U.K.* 21 54 58N 2 0W
Corby, *U.K.* 15 52 29N 0 41W
Corby Glen, *U.K.* 15 52 49N 0 31W
Córdoba, *Arg.* 102 31 20S 64 10W
Córdoba, *Sp.* 37 37 50N 4 50W
Cordova, *U.S.A.* 88 60 36N 145 45W
Corfe Castle, *U.K.* 14 50 37N 2 3W
Corfe Mullen, *U.K.* 14 50 45N 2 0W
Corfu = Kérkira, *Greece* 41 39 38N 19 50 E
Corinth, G. of, *Greece* 41 38 16N 22 30 E
Cork, *Ire.* 25 51 54N 8 30W
Cork □, *Ire.* 25 51 50N 8 50W
Cork Harbour, *Ire.* 25 51 46N 8 16W
Corner Brook, *Canada* 89 48 57N 57 58W
Cornforth, *U.K.* 19 54 42N 1 28W
Cornwall □, *U.K.* 16 50 26N 4 40W
Cornwall, C., *U.K.* 16 50 8N 5 42W
Coro, *Ven.* 100 11 25N 69 41W
Coromandel Coast, *India* 58 12 30N 81 0 E
Coronation Gulf, *Canada* 88 68 25N 110 0W
Corpus Christi, *U.S.A.* 90 27 50N 97 28W
Corrib, L., *Ire.* 24 53 5N 9 10W
Corrie, *U.K.* 20 55 39N 5 10W
Corrientes, *Arg.* 102 27 30S 58 45W
Corringham, *U.K.* 19 53 25N 0 42W
Corryvreckan, G. of, *U.K.* 20 56 10N 5 44W
Corsewall Pt., *U.K.* 20 55 0N 5 10W
Corsham, *U.K.* 14 51 25N 2 11W
Corsica, I., *Medit. S.* 35 42 0N 9 0 E
Corsley, *U.K.* 14 51 12N 2 14W
Corsock, *U.K.* 21 55 54N 3 56W
Corton, *U.K.* 15 52 31N 1 46 E
Corumbá, *Brazil* 100 19 0S 57 30W
Coruña, La, *Sp.* 37 43 20N 8 25W
Corve →, *U.K.* 14 52 22N 2 43W
Coseley, *U.K.* 14 52 33N 2 6W
Cosenza, *It.* 40 39 17N 16 14 E
Cosham, *U.K.* 14 50 51N 1 3W
Costa Rica ■, *Cent. Am.* 95 10 0N 84 0W
Costessey, *U.K.* 15 52 40N 1 11 E
Côte d'Or, *Fr.* 34 47 10N 4 50 E
Cotherstone, *U.K.* 18 54 34N 1 59W
Cotonou, *Benin* 78 6 20N 2 25 E
Cotopaxi, Vol., *Ecuad.* 100 0 40S 78 30W
Cotswold Hills, *U.K.* 14 51 42N 2 10W
Cottbus, *E. Ger.* 42 51 44N 14 20 E
Cottenham, *U.K.* 15 52 18N 0 8 E
Cottingham, *U.K.* 19 53 47N 0 29W
Coulport, *U.K.* 20 56 3N 4 53W
Council Bluffs, *U.S.A.* 90 41 20N 95 50W
Coupar Angus, *U.K.* 21 56 33N 3 17W
Coventry, *U.K.* 14 52 25N 1 31W
Cover →, *U.K.* 18 54 14N 1 45W
Coverack, *U.K.* 16 50 2N 5 6W
Covington, *U.S.A.* 92 39 5N 84 30W
Cowal, *U.K.* 20 56 5N 5 8W
Cowan, L., *Austral.* 66 31 45S 121 45 E
Cowbridge, *U.K.* 17 51 28N 3 28W
Cowdenbeath, *U.K.* 21 56 7N 3 20W
Cowes, *U.K.* 14 50 45N 1 18W
Cowfold, *U.K.* 15 50 58N 0 16W
Cowley, *U.K.* 14 51 43N 1 12W
Cowpen, *U.K.* 21 55 8N 1 34W
Cowra, *Austral.* 70 33 49S 148 42 E
Craigavon □, *U.K.* 24 54 30N 6 25W
Craighouse, *U.K.* 20 55 50N 5 58W
Craignish, L., *U.K.* 20 56 11N 5 32W
Crail, *U.K.* 21 56 16N 2 38W
Craiova, *Rom.* 43 44 21N 23 48 E
Cramlington, *U.K.* 21 55 5N 1 36W
Cranborne, *U.K.* 14 50 55N 1 55W
Cranborne Chase, *U.K.* 14 50 56N 2 6W
Cranbrook, *Canada* 88 49 30N 115 46W
Cranbrook, *U.K.* 15 51 6N 0 33 E
Cranleigh, *U.K.* 15 51 8N 0 29W
Cranshaws, *U.K.* 21 55 51N 2 30W
Cranwell, *U.K.* 19 53 4N 0 29W
Craven Arms, *U.K.* 14 52 27N 2 49W
Crawford, *U.K.* 21 55 28N 3 40W
Crawley, *U.K.* 15 51 7N 0 10W
Credenhill, *U.K.* 14 52 6N 2 49W
Crediton, *U.K.* 16 50 47N 3 39W
Cree →, *U.K.* 20 54 51N 4 24W
Creeside, *U.K.* 20 55 4N 4 41W
Creetown, *U.K.* 20 54 54N 4 23W
Cremona, *It.* 40 45 8N 10 2 E
Crete, I., *Greece* 41 35 15N 25 0 E
Creusot, Le, *Fr.* 34 46 48N 4 24 E
Crewe, *U.K.* 18 53 6N 2 28W
Crewkerne, *U.K.* 14 50 53N 2 48W
Crianlarich, *U.K.* 20 56 24N 4 37W
Criccieth, *U.K.* 17 52 55N 4 15W
Crick, *U.K.* 14 52 22N 1 9W
Crickhowell, *U.K.* 17 51 52N 3 8W
Cricklade, *U.K.* 14 51 38N 1 50W
Crieff, *U.K.* 21 56 22N 3 50W
Criffell, *U.K.* 21 54 56N 3 38W
Crimea, *U.S.S.R.* 47 45 0N 34 0 E
Crinan, *U.K.* 20 56 6N 5 34W
Crinan Canal, *U.K.* 20 56 4N 5 30W
Croaghpatrick, *Ire.* 24 53 46N 9 40W
Crocketford, *U.K.* 21 55 3N 3 49W
Croglin, *U.K.* 18 54 50N 2 37W
Cromarty, *U.K.* 23 57 40N 4 2W
Cromarty Firth, *U.K.* 23 57 40N 4 15W
Cromer, *U.K.* 15 52 56N 1 18 E
Crondall, *U.K.* 15 51 13N 0 51W
Crook, *U.K.* 19 54 43N 1 45W
Crooklands, *U.K.* 18 54 16N 2 43W
Crosby, *Cumbria, U.K.* 18 54 45N 3 25W
Crosby, *Merseyside, U.K.* 18 53 30N 3 2W
Crosby Ravensworth, *U.K.* 18 54 34N 2 35W
Cross Fell, *U.K.* 18 54 44N 2 29W
Crosshaven, *Ire.* 25 51 48N 8 19W
Crosshill, *U.K.* 20 55 19N 4 39W
Crouch →, *U.K.* 15 51 37N 0 53 E
Crow Hd., *Ire.* 25 51 34N 10 9W
Crow Sound, *U.K.* 16 49 56N 6 16W
Crowborough, *U.K.* 15 51 3N 0 9 E
Crowland, *U.K.* 15 52 41N 0 10W
Crowle, *U.K.* 19 53 36N 0 49W
Croyde, *U.K.* 16 51 7N 4 13W
Croydon, *U.K.* 15 51 18N 0 5W
Crudgington, *U.K.* 14 52 46N 2 33W
Crummock Water, *U.K.* 18 54 33N 3 18W
Cruzeiro do Sul, *Brazil* 100 7 35S 72 35W
Cuba ■, *W. Ind.* 95 22 0N 79 0W
Cuckfield, *U.K.* 15 51 0N 0 8W
Cúcuta, *Col.* 100 7 54N 72 31W
Cudworth, *U.K.* 19 53 35N 1 25W
Cuenca, *Ecuad.* 100 2 50S 79 9W
Cuenca, *Sp.* 37 40 5N 2 10W
Cuernavaca, *Mex.* 94 18 55N 99 15W
Cuiabá, *Brazil* 101 15 30S 56 0W
Cuillin Hills, *U.K.* 22 57 14N 6 15W
Cuillin Sd., *U.K.* 22 57 4N 6 20W
Culiacán, *Mex.* 94 24 50N 107 23W
Cullen, *U.K.* 23 57 45N 2 50W
Culloden Moor, *U.K.* 23 57 29N 4 7W
Cullompton, *U.K.* 16 50 52N 3 23W
Culm →, *U.K.* 16 50 46N 3 31W
Culrain, *U.K.* 23 57 55N 4 25W
Culross, *U.K.* 21 56 4N 3 38W
Cumaná, *Ven.* 100 10 30N 64 5W
Cumberland Plateau, *U.S.A.* 91 36 0N 84 30W
Cumbrae Is., *U.K.* 20 55 46N 4 54W
Cumbria □, *U.K.* 18 54 35N 2 55W
Cumbrian Mts., *U.K.* 18 54 30N 3 0W
Cummertrees, *U.K.* 21 55 0N 3 20W
Cumnock, *U.K.* 20 55 27N 4 18W
Cumnor, *U.K.* 14 51 44N 1 20W
Cumwhinton, *U.K.* 18 54 51N 2 49W
Cúneo, *It.* 40 44 23N 7 31 E
Cunninghame, *U.K.* 20 55 38N 4 35W
Cupar, *U.K.* 21 56 20N 3 0W
Curitiba, *Brazil* 102 25 20S 49 10W
Currie, *U.K.* 21 55 53N 3 17W
Curry Rivel, *U.K.* 14 51 2N 2 52W
Cuttack, *India* 59 20 25N 85 57 E
Cuzco, *Peru* 100 13 32S 72 0W
Cwmbran, *U.K.* 17 51 39N 3 0W
Cyclades = Kikládhes, *Greece* 41 37 20N 24 30 E
Cyprus ■, *Medit. S.* 47 35 0N 33 0 E
Czechoslovakia ■, *Europe* 42 49 0N 17 0 E
Częstochowa, *Pol.* 43 50 49N 19 7 E

D

Da Lat, *Viet.* 63 11 56N 108 25 E
Da Nang, *Viet.* 63 16 4N 108 13 E
Dacca, *Bangla.* 59 23 43N 90 26 E
Daer →, *U.K.* 21 55 23N 3 39W
Dailly, *U.K.* 20 55 16N 4 44W
Daingean, *Ire.* 25 53 18N 7 15W
Dakar, *Sene.* 78 14 34N 17 29W
Dakhla, *W. Sah.* 78 23 50N 15 53W
Dalbeattie, *U.K.* 21 54 55N 3 50W
Dalian, *China* 61 38 50N 121 40 E
Dalkeith, *U.K.* 21 55 54N 3 5W
Dallas, *U.S.A.* 91 32 50N 96 50W
Dalmally, *U.K.* 20 56 25N 5 0W
Dalmatia, *Yug.* 41 43 20N 17 0 E
Dalmellington, *U.K.* 20 55 20N 4 25W
Daloa, *Ivory C.* 78 7 0N 6 30W
Dalry, *U.K.* 20 55 44N 4 42W
Dalrymple, *U.K.* 20 55 24N 4 36W
Dalton, *Cumbria, U.K.* 18 54 9N 3 11W
Dalton, *Dumf. & Gall., U.K.* 21 55 3N 3 22W
Dalton, *N. Yorks., U.K.* 19 54 28N 1 32W
Dalwhinnie, *U.K.* 23 56 56N 4 14W
Damascus, *Syria* 57 33 30N 36 18 E
Damerham, *U.K.* 14 50 57N 1 52W
Dampier, *Austral.* 66 20 41S 116 42 E
Dandenong, *Austral.* 70 38 0S 145 15 E
Dandong, *China* 61 40 10N 124 20 E
Dannevirke, *N.Z.* 71 40 12S 176 8 E
Danube →, *Europe* 42 45 20N 29 40 E
Dar-es-Salaam, *Tanz.* 80 6 50S 39 12 E
Dar'ā, *Syria* 57 32 36N 36 7 E
Dardanelles, *Turk.* 47 40 0N 26 0 E
Darent →, *U.K.* 15 51 22N 0 12 E

Dargaville, N.Z. 71 35 57S 173 52 E
Darién, G. del, Col. 95 9 0N 77 0W
Darlaston, U.K. 14 52 35N 2 1W
Darling —►, Austral. 70 34 4S 141 54 E
Darling Ra., Austral. 66 32 30S 116 0 E
Darlington, U.K. 19 54 33N 1 33W
Darmstadt, W. Ger. 42 49 51N 8 40 E
Dart —►, U.K. 16 50 24N 3 36W
Dartford, U.K. 15 51 26N 0 15 E
Dartington, U.K. 16 50 26N 3 42W
Dartmoor, U.K. 16 50 36N 4 0W
Dartmouth, Canada 93 44 40N 63 30W
Dartmouth, U.K. 16 50 21N 3 35W
Darton, U.K. 19 53 36N 1 32W
Darvel, U.K. 20 55 37N 4 20W
Darwen, U.K. 18 53 42N 2 29W
Darwin, Austral. 66 12 25S 130 51 E
Dasht-e Kavīr, Iran 57 34 30N 55 0 E
Dasht-e Lūt, Iran 57 31 30N 58 0 E
Datong, China 61 40 6N 113 18 E
Dauphin, Canada 88 51 9N 100 5W
Dauphiné, Fr. 35 45 15N 5 25 E
Davao, Phil. 63 7 0N 125 40 E
Davenport, U.S.A. 92 41 30N 90 40W
Daventry, U.K. 14 52 16N 1 10W
David, Pan. 95 8 30N 82 30W
Davis Str., N. Am. 89 65 0N 58 0W
Dawley, U.K. 14 52 40N 2 29W
Dawlish, U.K. 16 50 34N 3 28W
Dawson, Canada 88 64 10N 139 30W
Dawson Creek, Canada 88 55 45N 120 15W
Dayton, U.S.A. 92 39 45N 84 10W
De Aar, S. Afr. 81 30 39S 24 0 E
De Grey —►, Austral. 66 20 12S 119 13 E
Dead Sea, Asia 57 31 30N 35 30 E
Deal, U.K. 15 51 13N 1 25 E
Dean, Forest of, U.K. 14 51 50N 2 35W
Dearham, U.K. 18 54 43N 3 28W
Dease Lake, Canada 88 58 25N 130 6W
Death Valley, U.S.A. 90 36 19N 116 52W
Deben —►, U.K. 15 52 4N 1 19 E
Debenham, U.K. 15 52 14N 1 10 E
Debrecen, Hung. 43 47 33N 21 42 E
Deccan, India 58 18 0N 79 0 E
Deddington, U.K. 14 51 58N 1 19W
Dee —►, Scotland, U.K. 23 57 4N 2 7W
Dee —►, Wales, U.K. 17 53 15N 3 7W
Deeping St. Nicholas, U.K. 15 52 44N 0 11W
Deeping Fen, U.K. 15 52 45N 0 15W
Dehra Dun, India 58 30 20N 78 4 E
Delabole, U.K. 16 50 37N 4 45W
Delaware □, U.S.A. 93 39 0N 75 40W
Delaware —►, U.S.A. 93 39 20N 75 25W
Delft, Neth. 36 52 1N 4 22 E
Delhi, India 58 28 38N 77 17 E
Den Helder, Neth. 36 52 57N 4 45 E
Denbigh, U.K. 17 53 12N 3 26W
Denby Dale, U.K. 19 53 35N 1 40W
Deniliquin, Austral. 70 35 30S 144 58 E
Denizli, Turk. 47 37 42N 29 2 E
Denmark ■, Europe 45 55 30N 9 0 E
Denmark Str., Atl. Oc. 103 66 0N 30 0W
Denny, U.K. 21 56 1N 3 55W
Dent, U.K. 18 54 17N 2 28W
Denton, E. Sussex, U.K. 15 50 48N 0 5 E
Denton, Gr. Manchester, U.K. 18 53 26N 2 10W
Denton, Lincs., U.K. 19 52 52N 0 42W
Denver, U.S.A. 90 39 45N 105 0W
Derby, U.K. 19 52 55N 1 28W
Derby □, U.K. 19 52 55N 1 28W
Derg —►, U.K. 24 54 42N 7 26W
Derg, L., Ire. 25 53 0N 8 20W
Derry = Londonderry, U.K. 24 55 0N 7 20W
Derryveagh Mts., Ire. 24 55 0N 8 40W
Dervaig, U.K. 20 56 35N 6 13W
Derwent —►, Derby, U.K. 19 52 53N 1 17W
Derwent —►, N. Yorks., U.K. 19 53 45N 0 57W
Derwent —►, Tyne & Wear, U.K. 21 54 58N 1 40W
Derwent Water, L., U.K. 18 54 35N 3 9W
Des Moines, U.S.A. 91 41 35N 93 37W
Des Moines —►, U.S.A. 91 40 23N 91 25W
Desborough, U.K. 15 52 27N 0 50W
Desford, U.K. 14 52 38N 1 19W
Dessau, E. Ger. 42 51 49N 12 15 E
Detroit, U.S.A. 92 42 23N 83 5W
Deurne, Belg. 36 51 12N 4 24 E
Deventer, Neth. 36 52 15N 6 10 E
Deveron —►, U.K. 23 57 40N 2 31W
Devizes, U.K. 14 51 21N 2 0W
Devonport, N.Z. 71 36 49S 174 49 E
Devonport, U.K. 16 50 23N 4 11W
Devonshire □, U.K. 16 50 50N 3 40W
Dewsbury, U.K. 19 53 42N 1 38W
Dhanbad, India 59 23 50N 86 30 E
Dharwad, India 58 15 22N 75 15 E
Dhule, India 58 20 58N 74 50 E
Diamantina —►, Austral. 67 26 45S 139 10 E
Dibden, U.K. 14 50 53N 1 24W
Didcot, U.K. 14 51 36N 1 14W
Dieppe, Fr. 34 49 54N 1 4 E
Dijon, Fr. 34 47 20N 5 0 E
Dillingham, U.S.A. 88 59 5N 158 30W
Dinaric Alps, Yug. 40 44 0N 16 30 E
Dingle, Ire. 25 52 9N 10 17W
Dingle B., Ire. 25 52 3N 10 20W
Dingwall, U.K. 23 57 36N 4 26W
Diss, U.K. 15 52 23N 1 6 E
Distington, U.K. 18 54 35N 3 33W
Ditchingham, U.K. 15 52 28N 1 26 E
Ditchling Beacon, U.K. 15 50 49N 0 7W
Dittisham, U.K. 16 50 22N 3 36W
Ditton Priors, U.K. 14 52 30N 2 33W
Diyarbakir, Turk. 47 37 55N 40 18 E
Dizzard Pt., U.K. 16 50 46N 4 38W
Djibouti ■, Africa 56 12 0N 43 0 E
Dnepr —►, U.S.S.R. 46 46 30N 32 18 E
Dneprodzerzhinsk, U.S.S.R. 47 48 32N 34 37 E
Dnepropetrovsk, U.S.S.R. 47 48 30N 35 0 E
Dnestr —►, U.S.S.R. 47 46 18N 30 17 E
Docking, U.K. 15 52 55N 0 39 E
Doddington, Cambs., U.K. 15 52 29N 0 3 E
Doddington, Northumberland, U.K. 21 55 33N 2 0W
Dodecanese, Greece 41 36 35N 27 0 E
Dodman Pt., U.K. 16 50 13N 4 49W
Dodoma, Tanz. 80 6 8S 35 45 E
Dogger Bank, N. Sea 26 54 50N 2 0 E
Dolgarrog, U.K. 17 53 11N 3 50W
Dolgellau, U.K. 17 52 44N 3 53W
Dollar, U.K. 21 56 9N 3 41W
Dolomites, It. 40 46 30N 11 40 E
Dolphinton, U.K. 21 55 42N 3 28W
Dolton, U.K. 16 50 53N 4 2W
Dominica ■, W. Ind. 94 15 20N 61 20W
Dominican Rep. ■, W. Ind. 95 19 0N 70 30W
Don —►, Humberside, U.K. 19 53 41N 0 51W
Don —►, Grampian, U.K. 23 57 14N 2 5W
Don —►, U.S.S.R. 47 47 4N 39 18 E
Donaghadee, U.K. 24 54 38N 5 32W
Doncaster, U.K. 19 53 31N 1 9W
Dondra Head, Sri L. 58 5 55N 80 40 E
Donegal, Ire. 24 54 39N 8 8W
Donegal □, Ire. 24 54 53N 8 0W
Donegal B., Ire. 24 54 30N 8 35W
Donetsk, U.S.S.R. 47 48 0N 37 45 E
Dongting Hu, China 61 29 18N 112 45 E
Donhead, U.K. 14 51 1N 2 8W
Donington, U.K. 19 52 54N 0 12W
Donna Nook, Pt., U.K. 19 53 29N 0 9 E
Doon —►, U.K. 20 55 26N 4 41W
Doon, L., U.K. 20 55 15N 4 22W
Dorchester, Dorset, U.K. 14 50 42N 2 28W
Dorchester, Oxon., U.K. 14 51 38N 1 10W
Dordrecht, Neth. 36 51 48N 4 39 E
Dorking, U.K. 15 51 14N 0 20W
Dornoch, U.K. 23 57 52N 4 0W
Dornoch Firth, U.K. 23 57 52N 4 0W
Dorset □, U.K. 14 50 48N 2 25W
Dorstone, U.K. 14 52 4N 3 0W
Dortmund, W. Ger. 36 51 32N 7 28 E
Douai, Fr. 34 50 21N 3 4 E
Douala, Cam. 80 4 0N 9 45 E
Douglas, I. of M., U.K. 18 54 9N 4 29W
Douglas, Strathclyde, U.K. 21 55 33N 3 50W
Douglas Hd., U.K. 18 54 9N 4 28W
Doune, U.K. 21 56 12N 4 3W
Dounreay, U.K. 23 58 34N 3 44W
Douro —►, Port. 37 41 8N 8 40W
Dove —►, N. Yorks., U.K. 19 54 20N 0 55W
Dove —►, Staffs., U.K. 18 52 51N 1 36W
Dove Dale, U.K. 19 53 10N 1 47W
Dover, U.K. 15 51 7N 1 19 E
Dover, Str. of, Europe 34 51 0N 1 30 E
Doveridge, U.K. 18 52 54N 1 49 E
Dovey —►, U.K. 17 52 32N 4 0W
Down □, U.K. 24 54 20N 6 0W
Downham, U.K. 15 52 26N 0 15 E
Downham Market, U.K. 15 52 36N 0 22 E
Downpatrick, U.K. 24 54 20N 5 43W
Downpatrick Hd., Ire. 24 54 20N 9 21W
Downton, U.K. 14 51 0N 1 44W
Drake Passage, S. Oc. 103 58 0S 68 0W
Drakensberg, S. Afr. 81 31 0S 28 0 E
Drammen, Nor. 45 59 42N 10 12 E
Drava —►, Yug. 42 45 33N 18 55 E
Dreghorn, U.K. 20 55 36N 4 30W
Drenthe □, Neth. 36 52 52N 6 40 E
Dresden, E. Ger. 42 51 2N 13 45 E
Driffield, U.K. 19 54 0N 0 25W
Drina —►, Yug. 41 44 53N 19 21 E
Drogheda, Ire. 24 53 45N 6 20W
Droichead Nua, Ire. 25 53 11N 6 50W
Droitwich, U.K. 14 52 16N 2 10W
Dronfield, U.K. 19 53 18N 1 29W
Dronning Maud Land, Ant. 103 72 30S 12 0 E
Drumheller, Canada 88 51 25N 112 40W
Drumjohn, U.K. 20 55 14N 4 15W
Drummondville, Canada 93 45 55N 72 25W
Drummore, U.K. 20 54 41N 4 53W
Druridge B., U.K. 21 55 16N 1 32W
Drymen, U.K. 20 56 4N 4 28W
Dubai, U.A.E. 57 25 18N 55 20 E
Dubbo, Austral. 70 32 11S 148 35 E
Dubh Artach, U.K. 20 56 8N 6 40W
Dublin, Ire. 24 53 20N 6 18W
Dublin □, Ire. 24 53 24N 6 20W
Dublin B., Ire. 25 53 18N 6 5W
Dubrovnik, Yug. 41 42 39N 18 6 E
Duddington, U.K. 15 52 36N 0 32W
Duddon —►, U.K. 18 54 12N 3 15W
Dudley, U.K. 14 52 30N 2 5W
Duero —►, Sp. 37 41 8N 8 40W
Duffield, U.K. 19 52 59N 1 30W
Dufftown, U.K. 23 57 26N 3 9W
Duisburg, W. Ger. 36 51 27N 6 42 E
Dukinfield, U.K. 18 53 29N 2 7W
Duluth, U.S.A. 92 46 48N 92 10W
Dulverton, U.K. 14 51 2N 3 33W
Dumbarton, U.K. 20 55 58N 4 35W
Dumfries, U.K. 21 55 4N 3 37W
Dumfries & Galloway □, U.K. 21 55 0N 4 0W
Dun Laoghaire, Ire. 25 53 17N 6 9W
Dunans, U.K. 20 56 4N 5 9W
Dunbar, U.K. 21 56 0N 2 32W
Dunblane, U.K. 21 56 10N 3 58W
Duncansby Head, U.K. 23 58 39N 3 0W
Dunchurch, U.K. 14 52 21N 1 19W
Dundalk, Ire. 24 54 1N 6 25W
Dundalk Bay, Ire. 24 53 55N 6 15W
Dundee, U.K. 21 56 29N 3 0W
Dundrennan, U.K. 21 54 49N 3 56W
Dundrum, U.K. 24 54 17N 5 50W
Dundrum B., U.K. 24 54 12N 5 40W
Dunedin, N.Z. 71 45 50S 170 33 E
Dunfermline, U.K. 21 56 5N 3 28W
Dungannon, U.K. 24 54 30N 6 47W
Dungannon □, U.K. 24 54 30N 6 55W
Dungarvan, Ire. 25 52 6N 7 40W
Dungarvan Bay, Ire. 25 52 5N 7 35W
Dungavel, U.K. 21 55 37N 4 7W
Dungeness, U.K. 15 50 54N 0 59 E
Dunkeld, U.K. 23 56 34N 3 36W
Dunkerque, Fr. 34 51 2N 2 20 E
Dunkery Beacon, U.K. 14 51 15N 3 37W
Dunkirk = Dunkerque, Fr. 34 51 2N 2 20 E
Dúnleary = Dun Laoghaire, Ire. 25 53 17N 6 9W
Dunlop, U.K. 20 55 43N 4 32W
Dunmanus B., Ire. 25 51 31N 9 50W
Dunmore Hd., Ire. 25 52 10N 10 35W
Dunnet Hd., U.K. 23 58 38N 3 22W
Dunning, U.K. 21 56 18N 3 37W
Dunoon, U.K. 20 55 57N 4 56W
Duns, U.K. 21 55 47N 2 20W
Dunscore, U.K. 21 55 8N 3 48W
Dunsford, U.K. 16 50 41N 3 40W
Dunstable, U.K. 15 51 53N 0 31W
Dunster, U.K. 14 51 11N 3 28W
Dunston, U.K. 14 52 46N 2 7W
Dunvegan, U.K. 22 57 26N 6 35W
Durango, Mex. 94 24 3N 104 39W
Durban, S. Afr. 81 29 49S 31 1 E
Düren, W. Ger. 36 50 48N 6 30 E
Durg, India 59 21 15N 81 22 E
Durgapur, India 59 23 30N 87 20 E
Durham, U.K. 19 54 47N 1 34W
Durham, U.S.A. 91 36 0N 78 55W
Durham □, U.K. 19 54 42N 1 45W
Durlston Hd., U.K. 14 50 35N 1 58W
Durness, U.K. 23 58 34N 4 45W
Durrësi, Alb. 41 41 19N 19 28 E
Durrington, U.K. 14 51 12N 1 47W
Dursley, U.K. 14 51 41N 2 21W
Dushanbe, U.S.S.R. 48 38 33N 68 48 E
Düsseldorf, W. Ger. 36 51 15N 6 46 E
Duyun, China 60 26 18N 107 29 E
Dvina, N. —►, U.S.S.R. 46 61 40N 45 30 E
Dyfed □, U.K. 17 52 0N 4 30W
Dymchurch, U.K. 15 51 2N 1 0 E
Dymock, U.K. 14 51 58N 2 27W
Dysart, U.K. 21 56 8N 3 8W
Dzerzhinsk, U.S.S.R. 46 56 14N 43 30 E
Dzhambul, U.S.S.R. 48 42 54N 71 22 E
Dzungaria, China 60 44 10N 88 0 E

E

Eaglesfield, U.K. 21 55 3N 3 12W
Eagleshan, U.K. 20 55 44N 4 18W
Eakring, U.K. 19 53 9N 0 59W
Ealing, U.K. 15 51 30N 0 19W
Earby, U.K. 18 53 55N 2 8W
Eardisland, U.K. 14 52 14N 2 50W
Eardisley, U.K. 14 52 8N 3 0W
Earith, U.K. 15 52 21N 0 1 E
Earl Shilton, U.K. 14 52 35N 1 20W
Earl Soham, U.K. 15 52 14N 1 15 E
Earls Barton, U.K. 15 52 16N 0 44W
Earl's Colne, U.K. 15 51 56N 0 43 E
Earlsferry, U.K. 21 56 11N 2 50W
Earlston, U.K. 21 55 39N 2 40W
Earn —►, U.K. 21 56 20N 3 19W
Earn, L., U.K. 20 56 23N 4 14W
Earsdon, U.K. 21 55 4N 1 30W
Easebourne, U.K. 15 51 0N 0 42W
Easington, Durham, U.K. 19 54 50N 1 24W
Easington, Humberside, U.K. 19 53 40N 0 7 E
Easington Colliery, U.K. 19 54 49N 1 19W
Easingwold, U.K. 19 54 8N 1 11W
East Anglian Hts., U.K. 15 52 10N 0 17 E
East Bergholt, U.K. 15 51 58N 1 2 E
East Brent, U.K. 14 51 14N 2 55W
East China Sea, Asia 61 30 5N 126 0 E
East Cowes, U.K. 14 50 45N 1 17W
East Dereham, U.K. 15 52 40N 0 57 E
East Fen, U.K. 19 53 4N 0 5 E
East Germany ■, Europe 42 52 0N 12 0 E
East Grinstead, U.K. 15 51 8N 0 1W
East Harling, U.K. 15 52 26N 0 55 E
East Ilsley, U.K. 14 51 33N 1 15W
East Indies, Asia 50 0 0N 120 0 E
East Kilbride, U.K. 20 55 46N 4 10W
East Kirkby, U.K. 19 53 5N 1 15W
East Linton, U.K. 21 56 0N 2 40W
East London, S. Afr. 81 33 0S 27 55 E
East Markham, U.K. 19 53 15N 0 53W
East Moor, U.K. 19 53 15N 1 30W
East Retford, U.K. 19 53 19N 0 55W
East Siberian Sea, U.S.S.R. 49 73 0N 160 0 E
East Sussex □, U.K. 15 51 0N 0 20 E
East Wemyss, U.K. 21 56 8N 3 5W
East Wittering, U.K. 15 50 46N 0 53W
East Woodhay, U.K. 14 51 21N 1 26W
Eastbourne, U.K. 15 50 46N 0 18 E
Eastchurch, U.K. 15 51 23N 0 53 E
Easter Islands, Pac. Oc. 65 27 0S 109 0W
Eastern Ghats, India 58 14 0N 78 50 E
Eastleigh, U.K. 14 50 58N 1 21W
Eastnor, U.K. 14 52 2N 2 22W
Easton, Avon, U.K. 14 51 28N 2 42W
Easton, Dorset, U.K. 14 50 32N 2 27W
Easton, Northants., U.K. 15 52 37N 0 31W
Eastry, U.K. 15 51 15N 1 19 E
Eastwood, U.K. 19 53 2N 1 17W
Eaton, U.K. 15 52 52N 0 46W
Eaton Socon, U.K. 15 52 13N 0 18W
Eau Claire, U.S.A. 92 44 46N 91 30W
Ebberston, U.K. 19 54 14N 0 35W
Ebbw Vale, U.K. 17 51 47N 3 12W
Ebro —►, Sp. 37 40 43N 0 54 E
Ecclefechan, U.K. 21 55 3N 3 18W
Eccleshall, U.K. 14 52 52N 2 14W
Ech Cheliff, Alg. 78 36 10N 1 20 E
Echo Bay, Canada 88 66 5N 117 55W
Echuca, Austral. 70 36 10S 144 20 E
Eck, L., U.K. 20 56 5N 5 0W
Eckington, U.K. 19 53 19N 1 21W
Ecuador ■, S. Am. 100 2 0S 78 0W
Edam, Neth. 36 52 31N 5 3 E
Eday, U.K. 23 59 11N 2 47W
Eddrachillis B., U.K. 22 58 16N 5 10W
Eddystone, U.K. 16 50 11N 4 16W
Ede, Neth. 36 52 4N 5 40 E
Eden —►, U.K. 18 54 57N 3 2W
Edenbridge, U.K. 15 51 12N 0 4 E
Edenderry, Ire. 25 53 21N 7 3W
Edge Hill, U.K. 14 52 7N 1 28W
Edinburgh, U.K. 21 55 57N 3 12W
Edington, U.K. 14 51 17N 2 6W
Edmondbyers, U.K. 18 54 50N 1 59W
Edmonton, Canada 88 53 30N 113 30W
Edmundston, Canada 93 47 23N 68 20W
Edward, L., Africa 80 0 25S 29 40 E
Egersund, Nor. 45 58 26N 6 1 E
Egham, U.K. 15 51 25N 0 33W
Egmont, Mt., N.Z. 71 39 17S 174 5 E
Egremont, U.K. 18 54 28N 3 33W
Egton, U.K. 19 54 27N 0 45W
Egypt ■, Africa 79 28 0N 31 0 E
Eifel, W. Ger. 36 50 10N 6 45 E
Eigg, U.K. 22 56 54N 6 10W
Eighty Mile Beach, Austral. 66 19 30S 120 40 E
Eil, L., U.K. 22 56 50N 5 15W
Eildon, L., Austral. 70 37 10S 146 0 E
Eindhoven, Neth. 36 51 26N 5 30 E
Eire ■, Europe 25 53 0N 8 0W
El Aaiún, W. Sah. 78 27 9N 13 12W
El Asnam = Ech Cheliff, Alg. 78 36 10N 1 20 E
El Faiyûm, Egypt 79 29 19N 30 50 E
El Fâsher, Sudan 79 13 33N 25 26 E
El Gîza, Egypt 79 30 0N 31 10 E
El Jadida, Mor. 78 33 11N 8 17W
El Mahalla el Kubra, Egypt 79 31 0N 31 0 E
El Mansûra, Egypt 79 31 0N 31 19 E
El Minyâ, Egypt 79 28 7N 30 33 E
El Obeid, Sudan 79 13 8N 30 10 E
El Paso, U.S.A. 90 31 50N 106 30W
El Qâhira = Cairo, Egypt 79 30 1N 31 14 E
El Salvador ■, Cent. Am. 94 13 50N 89 0W
Elba, It. 40 42 48N 10 15 E
Elbasani, Alb. 41 41 9N 20 9 E
Elbe —►, W. Ger. 42 53 50N 9 0 E
Elbląg, Pol. 43 54 10N 19 25 E
Elburz Mts., Iran 56 36 0N 52 0 E
Elche, Sp. 37 38 15N 0 42W
Eldoret, Kenya 80 0 30N 35 17 E
Eleuthera, Baham. 95 25 0N 76 20W
Elgin, U.K. 23 57 39N 3 20W
Elham, U.K. 15 51 9N 1 7 E
Elie, U.K. 21 56 11N 2 50W

Elishaw, U.K. 21 55 16N 2 14W
Elizabeth, Austral. 67 34 42S 138 41 E
Elizabeth, U.S.A. 93 40 37N 74 12W
Elland, U.K. 19 53 41N 1 49W
Ellen →, U.K. 18 54 44N 3 30W
Eller Beck Bridge, U.K. 19 54 23N 0 40W
Ellesmere, U.K. 18 52 55N 2 53W
Ellesmere I., Canada 103 79 30N 80 0W
Ellesmere Port, U.K. 18 53 17N 2 55W
Ellice Is. = Tuvalu ■, Pac. Oc. 64 8 0S 178 0 E
Ellington, U.K. 21 55 14N 1 34W
Ellon, U.K. 23 57 21N 2 5W
Elmira, U.S.A. 92 42 8N 76 49W
Elmswell, U.K. 15 52 14N 0 53 E
Eluru, India 59 16 48N 81 8 E
Ely, U.K. 15 52 24N 0 16 E
Emāmrūd, Iran 56 36 30N 55 0 E
Embleton, U.K. 21 55 30N 1 38W
Emden, W. Ger. 36 53 22N 7 12 E
Emerald, Austral. 67 23 32S 148 10 E
Emmeloord, Neth. 36 52 44N 5 46 E
Emmen, Neth. 36 52 48N 6 57 E
Ems →, W. Ger. 36 52 37N 9 26 E
Enard B., U.K. 22 58 5N 5 20W
Enderbury I., Pac. Oc. 64 3 8S 171 5W
Enderby, U.K. 14 52 35N 1 15W
Enderby Land, Ant. 103 66 0S 53 0 E
Enfield, U.K. 15 51 39N 0 4W
England □, U.K. 5 53 0N 2 0W
English Channel, Europe 15 50 0N 2 0W
Ennerdale Water, U.K. 18 54 32N 3 24W
Ennis, Ire. 25 52 51N 8 59W
Enniscorthy, Ire. 25 52 30N 6 35W
Enniskillen, U.K. 24 54 20N 7 40W
Ennistimon, Ire. 25 52 56N 9 18W
Enschede, Neth. 36 52 13N 6 53 E
Ensenada, Mex. 94 31 50N 116 50W
Enstone, U.K. 14 51 55N 1 25W
Entebbe, Uganda 80 0 4N 32 28 E
Enugu, Nig. 78 6 20N 7 30 E
Epping, U.K. 15 51 42N 0 8 E
Epping Forest, U.K. 15 51 40N 0 5 E
Epsom, U.K. 15 51 19N 0 16W
Epworth, U.K. 19 53 30N 0 50W
Equatorial Guinea ■, Africa 80 2 0S 8 0 E
Erebus, Mt., Ant. 103 77 35S 167 0 E
Erfurt, E. Ger. 42 50 58N 11 2 E
Eriboll, L., U.K. 23 58 28N 4 41W
Erie, U.S.A. 92 42 10N 80 7W
Erie, L., N. Am. 92 42 15N 81 0W
Eritrea □, Eth. 79 14 0N 41 0 E
Erlangen, W. Ger. 42 49 35N 11 0 E
Erne →, U.K. 24 54 30N 8 16W
Erne, Lough, U.K. 24 54 26N 7 46W
Erode, India 58 11 24N 77 45 E
Errigal, Mt., Ire. 24 55 2N 8 8W
Erris Hd., Ire. 24 54 19N 10 0W
Errol, U.K. 21 56 24N 3 13W
Erzurum, Turk. 47 39 57N 41 15 E
Esbjerg, Den. 45 55 29N 8 29 E
Esch, Neth. 36 51 37N 5 17 E
Eschweiler, W. Ger. 36 50 49N 6 14 E
Escrick, U.K. 19 53 53N 1 3W
Eşfahān, Iran 56 33 0N 53 0 E
Esk →, Cumbria, U.K. 18 54 23N 3 21W
Esk →, Dumf. & Gall., U.K. 21 54 58N 3 4W
Esk →, N. Yorks., U.K. 19 54 27N 0 36W
Eskdale, U.K. 21 55 12N 3 4W
Eskifjörður, Ice. 44 65 3N 13 55W
Eskilstuna, Swed. 45 59 22N 16 32 E
Eskimo Pt., Canada 88 61 10N 94 15W
Eskişehir, Turk. 47 39 50N 30 35 E
Esmeraldas, Ecuad. 100 1 0N 79 40W
Esperance, Austral. 66 33 45S 121 55 E
Espinhaço, Serra do, Brazil 101 17 30S 43 30W
Essen, W. Ger. 36 51 28N 6 59 E
Essex □, U.K. 15 51 48N 0 30 E
Eston, U.K. 19 54 33N 1 6W
Estonian S.S.R. □, U.S.S.R. 46 58 30N 25 30 E
Etchingham, U.K. 15 51 0N 0 27 E
Ethiopia ■, Africa 78 8 0N 40 0 E
Ethiopian Highlands, Eth. 72 10 0N 37 0 E
Etive, L., U.K. 20 56 30N 5 12W
Etna, It. 40 37 45N 15 0 E
Eton, U.K. 15 51 29N 0 37W
Ettington, U.K. 14 52 8N 1 38W
Ettrick Forest, U.K. 21 55 30N 3 0W
Ettrick Water →, U.K. 21 55 31N 2 55W
Eugene, U.S.A. 90 44 0N 123 8W
Euphrates →, Asia 56 31 0N 47 25 E
Euston, Austral. 70 34 30S 142 46 E
Euxton, U.K. 18 53 41N 2 42W
Evansville, U.S.A. 92 38 0N 87 35W
Evercreech, U.K. 14 51 8N 2 30W
Everest, Mt., Nepal 60 28 5N 86 58 E
Evesham, U.K. 14 52 6N 1 57W
Évora, Port. 37 38 33N 7 57W
Évreux, Fr. 34 49 0N 1 8 E
Évvoia, Greece 41 38 30N 24 0 E
Ewe, L., U.K. 22 57 49N 5 38W
Ewell, U.K. 15 51 20N 0 15W
Ewhurst, U.K. 15 51 9N 0 25W
Exe →, U.K. 16 50 38N 3 27W
Exeter, U.K. 16 50 43N 3 31W
Exford, U.K. 14 51 8N 3 39W
Exminster, U.K. 16 50 40N 3 29W
Exmoor, U.K. 16 51 10N 3 59W
Exmouth, Austral. 66 21 54S 114 10 E
Exmouth, U.K. 16 50 37N 3 26W
Exmouth G., Austral. 66 22 15S 114 15 E
Exton, U.K. 15 52 42N 0 38W
Eyam, U.K. 19 53 17N 1 40W
Eye, Cambs., U.K. 15 52 36N 0 11W
Eye, Suffolk, U.K. 15 52 19N 1 9 E
Eye Pen., U.K. 22 58 13N 6 10W
Eyemouth, U.K. 21 55 53N 2 5W
Eynsham, U.K. 14 51 47N 1 21W
Eyre, L., Austral. 67 29 30S 137 26 E
Eyre Cr. →, Austral. 67 26 40S 139 0 E
Eyre Pen., Austral. 66 33 30S 137 17 E

F

Fair Hd., U.K. 24 55 14N 6 10W
Fairbanks, U.S.A. 88 64 50N 147 50W
Fairfield, Austral. 70 33 53S 150 57 E
Fairford, U.K. 14 51 42N 1 48W
Fairlie, N.Z. 71 44 5S 170 49 E
Fairlie, U.K. 20 55 44N 4 52W
Fairlight, U.K. 15 50 53N 0 40 E
Faisalabad, Pak. 58 31 30N 73 5 E
Faizabad, India 59 26 45N 82 10 E
Fakenham, U.K. 15 52 50N 0 51 E
Faldingworth, U.K. 19 53 21N 0 22W
Falkenberg, Swed. 45 56 54N 12 30 E
Falkirk, U.K. 21 56 0N 3 47W
Falkland, U.K. 21 56 15N 3 13W
Falkland Is., Atl. Oc. 102 51 30S 59 0W
Fall River, U.S.A. 93 41 45N 71 5W
Falmouth, U.K. 16 50 9N 5 5W
Falmouth B., U.K. 16 50 7N 5 3W
Falstone, U.K. 21 55 10N 2 26W
Falun, Swed. 45 60 37N 15 37 E
Famagusta, Cyprus 47 35 8N 33 55 E
Fannich, L., U.K. 22 57 40N 5 0W
Fareham, U.K. 14 50 52N 1 11W
Faringdon, U.K. 14 51 39N 1 34W
Farnborough, U.K. 15 51 17N 0 46W
Farne Is., U.K. 19 55 38N 1 37W
Farnham, U.K. 15 51 13N 0 49W
Farnworth, U.K. 18 53 33N 2 24W
Faroe Is., Atl. Oc. 26 62 0N 7 0W
Farrar →, U.K. 23 57 30N 4 30W
Faslane, U.K. 20 56 3N 4 49W
Fastnet Rock, Ire. 25 51 22N 9 37W
Fauldhouse, U.K. 21 55 50N 3 44W
Faversham, U.K. 15 51 18N 0 54 E
Fawley, U.K. 14 50 49N 1 20W
Faya-Largeau, Chad 79 17 58N 19 6 E
Fayetteville, U.S.A. 91 35 0N 78 58W
Fazeley, U.K. 14 52 36N 1 42W
Fdérik, Maurit. 78 22 40N 12 45W
Feale →, Ire. 25 52 26N 9 40W
Feilding, N.Z. 71 40 13S 175 35 E
Feira de Santana, Brazil 101 12 15S 38 57W
Felixstowe, U.K. 15 51 58N 1 22 E
Felpham, U.K. 15 50 47N 0 38W
Felton, U.K. 21 55 18N 1 42W
Feltwell, U.K. 15 52 29N 0 32 E
Fenit, Ire. 25 52 17N 9 51W
Fenny Bentley, U.K. 19 53 4N 1 43W
Fenny Compton, U.K. 14 52 9N 1 20W
Fenny Stratford, U.K. 15 51 59N 0 42W
Fens, The, U.K. 15 52 45N 0 2 E
Fenwick, U.K. 20 55 38N 4 25W
Fergana, U.S.S.R. 48 40 23N 71 19 E
Fermanagh □, U.K. 24 54 21N 7 40W
Fermoy, Ire. 25 52 4N 8 18W
Fernhurst, U.K. 15 51 3N 0 43W
Ferrara, It. 40 44 50N 11 36 E
Ferryhill, U.K. 19 54 42N 1 32W
Fès, Mor. 78 34 0N 5 0W
Fetlar, U.K. 22 60 36N 0 52W
Ffestiniog, U.K. 17 52 58N 3 56W
Fianarantsoa, Madag. 81 21 26S 47 5 E
Fife □, U.K. 21 56 13N 3 2W
Fife Ness, U.K. 21 56 17N 2 35W
Fiji ■, Pac. Oc. 64 17 20S 179 0 E
Filby, U.K. 15 52 40N 1 39 E
Filey, U.K. 19 54 13N 0 18W
Filey B., U.K. 19 54 12N 0 15W
Filton, U.K. 14 51 29N 2 34W
Fincham, U.K. 15 52 38N 0 30 E
Findhorn →, U.K. 23 57 38N 3 38W
Findon, U.K. 15 50 53N 0 24W
Finedon, U.K. 15 52 20N 0 40W
Fingest, U.K. 15 51 35N 0 52W
Finisterre, C., Sp. 37 42 50N 9 19W
Finland ■, Europe 44 63 0N 27 0 E
Finland, G. of, Europe 45 60 0N 26 0 E
Finn →, Ire. 24 54 50N 7 55W
Finnart, U.K. 20 56 7N 4 48W
Finnmark fylke □, Nor. 44 69 30N 25 0 E
Finstown, U.K. 23 59 0N 3 8W
Fionnphort, U.K. 20 56 19N 6 23W
Firozabad, India 58 27 10N 78 25 E
Fishguard, U.K. 17 51 59N 4 59W
Fishtoft, U.K. 19 52 27N 0 2 E
Fitzroy →, Austral. 66 17 31S 123 35 E
Flamborough, U.K. 19 54 7N 0 7W
Flamborough Hd., U.K. 19 54 8N 0 4W
Flanders, Belg. 34 51 10N 3 15 E
Flatey, Ice. 44 65 22N 22 56W
Fleet, U.K. 15 51 16N 0 50W
Fleetwood, U.K. 18 53 55N 3 1W
Flensburg, W. Ger. 42 54 46N 9 28 E
Fletton, U.K. 15 52 34N 0 13W
Flimby, U.K. 18 54 42N 3 31W
Flinders →, Austral. 67 17 36S 140 36 E
Flinders Ranges, Austral. 67 31 30S 138 30 E
Flint, U.K. 17 53 15N 3 7W
Flint, U.S.A. 92 43 5N 83 40W
Flint →, U.S.A. 91 30 52N 84 38W
Flitwick, U.K. 15 51 59N 0 30W
Flodden, U.K. 19 55 37N 2 8W
Florence, It. 40 43 47N 11 15 E
Flores, Indon. 63 8 35S 121 0 E
Flores Sea, Indon. 63 6 30S 124 0 E
Florianópolis, Brazil 102 27 30S 48 30W
Florida □, U.S.A. 91 28 30N 82 0W
Florida, Straits of, U.S.A. 95 25 0N 80 0W
Florida Keys, U.S.A. 91 25 0N 80 40W
Florissant, U.S.A. 90 38 48N 90 20W
Flushing = Vlissingen, Neth. 36 51 26N 3 34 E
Fóggia, It. 40 41 28N 15 31 E
Folkestone, U.K. 15 51 5N 1 11 E
Fontainebleau, Fr. 34 48 24N 2 40 E
Forbach, Fr. 34 49 10N 6 52 E
Ford, U.K. 20 56 10N 5 27W
Fordham, U.K. 15 52 19N 0 23 E
Fordingbridge, U.K. 14 50 56N 1 48W
Forest Row, U.K. 15 51 6N 0 3 E
Forfar, U.K. 23 56 40N 2 53W
Formby, U.K. 18 53 34N 3 4W
Formby Pt., U.K. 18 53 33N 3 7W
Formosa = Taiwan ■, Asia 61 23 30N 121 0 E
Formosa Strait, Asia 61 24 40N 120 0 E
Forres, U.K. 23 57 37N 3 38W
Fort Augustus, U.K. 23 57 9N 4 40W
Fort Collins, U.S.A. 90 40 30N 105 4W
Fort-de-France, Mart. 94 14 36N 61 2W
Fort George, Canada 89 53 50N 79 0W
Fort Lauderdale, U.S.A. 91 26 10N 80 5W
Fort McMurray, Canada 88 56 44N 111 7W
Fort Smith, U.S.A. 90 35 25N 94 25W
Fort Wayne, U.S.A. 92 41 5N 85 10W
Fort William, U.K. 22 56 48N 5 8W
Fort Worth, U.S.A. 90 32 45N 97 25W
Fortaleza, Brazil 101 3 45S 38 35W
Forth, U.K. 21 55 45N 3 42W
Forth, Firth of, U.K. 21 56 5N 2 55W
Forth Bridge, U.K. 21 56 0N 3 24W
Fortrose, U.K. 23 57 35N 4 10W
Foshan, China 61 23 4N 113 5 E
Fothergill, U.K. 18 54 43N 3 30W
Fotheringhay, U.K. 15 52 32N 0 28W
Foulness I., U.K. 15 51 36N 0 55 E
Foulness Pt., U.K. 15 51 36N 0 59 E
Foulsham, U.K. 15 52 48N 1 1 E
Fountainhall, U.K. 21 55 45N 2 55W
Fountains Abbey, U.K. 19 54 8N 1 35W
Fovant, U.K. 14 51 4N 2 0W
Foveaux Str., N.Z. 71 46 42S 168 10 E
Fowey, U.K. 16 50 20N 4 39W
Fowey →, U.K. 16 50 20N 4 39W
Fownhope, U.K. 14 52 0N 2 37W
Foxdale, U.K. 18 54 12N 4 38W
Foxe Chan., Canada 89 65 0N 80 0W
Foyle, Lough, U.K. 24 55 6N 7 8W
Foynes, Ire. 25 52 37N 9 5W
Fraddon, U.K. 16 50 22N 4 55W
Framlingham, U.K. 15 52 14N 1 20 E
France ■, Europe 34 47 0N 3 0 E
Frankfurt am Main, W. Ger. 42 50 7N 8 40 E
Frankston, Austral. 70 38 8S 145 8 E
Frant, U.K. 15 51 5N 0 17 E
Franz Josef Land, U.S.S.R. 48 82 0N 55 0 E
Fraser →, Canada 88 49 7N 123 11W
Fraser I., Austral. 67 25 15S 153 10 E
Fraserburgh, U.K. 23 57 41N 2 0W
Fredericton, Canada 93 45 57N 66 40W
Frederikshavn, Den. 45 57 28N 10 31 E
Fredrikstad, Nor. 45 59 13N 10 57 E
Freetown, Sa. Leone 78 8 30N 13 17W
Freiburg, W. Ger. 42 48 0N 7 52 E
Fremantle, Austral. 66 32 7S 115 47 E
French Guiana ■, S. Am. 101 4 0N 53 0W
French Polynesia □, Pac. Oc. 65 20 0S 145 0 E
Freshwater, U.K. 14 50 42N 1 31W
Fresnillo, Mex. 94 23 10N 103 0W
Fresno, U.S.A. 90 36 47N 119 50W
Freuchie, U.K. 21 56 14N 3 8W
Fridaythorpe, U.K. 19 54 2N 0 40W
Friesland □, Neth. 36 53 5N 5 50 E
Frimley, U.K. 15 51 18N 0 43W
Frinton-on-Sea, U.K. 15 51 50N 1 16 E
Frisa, Loch, U.K. 20 56 34N 6 5W
Frisian Is., Europe 36 53 30N 6 0 E
Frizington, U.K. 18 54 33N 3 30W
Frobisher B., Canada 89 62 30N 66 0W
Frodsham, U.K. 18 53 17N 2 45W
Frome, U.K. 14 51 16N 2 17W
Frome →, U.K. 14 50 44N 2 5W
Frome, L., Austral. 67 30 45S 139 45 E
Frunze, U.S.S.R. 48 42 54N 74 46 E
Fuji-San, Jap. 62 35 22N 138 44 E
Fujian □, China 61 26 0N 118 0 E
Fukui, Jap. 62 36 0N 136 10 E
Fukuoka, Jap. 62 33 39N 130 21 E
Fukushima, Jap. 62 37 44N 140 28 E
Fukuyama, Jap. 62 34 35N 133 20 E
Fulwood, U.K. 18 53 47N 2 41W
Fundy, B. of, Canada 93 45 0N 66 0W
Furneaux Group, Austral. 66 40 10S 147 50 E
Furness, Pen., U.K. 18 54 12N 3 10W
Fürth, W. Ger. 42 49 29N 11 0 E
Fury and Hecla Str., Canada 89 69 56N 84 0W
Fushun, China 61 41 50N 123 56 E
Fuxin, China 61 42 5N 121 48 E
Fuzhou, China 61 26 5N 119 16 E
Fylde, U.K. 18 53 50N 2 58W
Fylingdales Moor, U.K. 19 54 22N 0 32W
Fyn, Den. 45 55 20N 10 30 E
Fyne, L., U.K. 20 56 0N 5 20W
Fyvie, U.K. 23 57 26N 2 24W

G

Gabès, Tunisia 78 33 53N 10 2 E
Gabon ■, Africa 80 0 10S 10 0 E
Gaborone, Bots. 81 24 45S 25 57 E
Gabrovo, Bulg. 41 42 52N 25 19 E
Gainesville, U.S.A. 90 29 38N 82 20W
Gainford, U.K. 19 54 34N 1 44W
Gainsborough, U.K. 19 53 23N 0 46W
Gairdner L., Austral. 66 31 30S 136 0 E
Gairloch, U.K. 22 57 42N 5 40W
Gairloch, L., U.K. 22 57 43N 5 45W
Galápagos, Pac. Oc. 65 0 0 89 0W
Galashiels, U.K. 21 55 37N 2 50W
Galaţi, Rom. 43 45 27N 28 2 E
Galgate, U.K. 18 53 59N 2 47W
Galilee, Sea of = Kinneret, Lake, Isr. 57 32 45N 35 35 E
Galle, Sri L. 58 6 5N 80 10 E
Galley Hd., Ire. 25 51 32N 8 56W
Gällivare, Swed. 44 67 9N 20 40 E
Galloway, U.K. 20 55 0N 4 25W
Galloway, Mull of, U.K. 20 54 38N 4 50W
Galmpton, U.K. 16 50 23N 3 32W
Galston, U.K. 20 55 36N 4 22W
Galty Mts., Ire. 25 52 22N 8 10W
Galtymore, Ire. 25 52 22N 8 12W
Galveston, U.S.A. 91 29 15N 94 48W
Galway, Ire. 25 53 16N 9 4W
Galway □, Ire. 24 53 16N 9 3W
Galway B., Ire. 25 53 10N 9 20W
Gambia ■, W. Afr. 78 13 25N 16 0W
Gamboa, Pan. 94 9 8N 79 42W
Gamlingay, U.K. 15 52 9N 0 11W
Gan Jiang →, China 61 29 15N 116 0 E
Ganga →, India 59 23 20N 90 30 E
Ganganagar, India 58 29 56N 73 56 E
Ganges = Ganga →, India 59 23 20N 90 30 E
Gansu □, China 60 36 0N 104 0 E
Gao, Mali 78 16 15N 0 5W
Gap, Fr. 34 44 33N 6 5 E
Garboldisham, U.K. 15 52 24N 0 57 E
Garda, L. di, It. 40 45 40N 10 40 E
Gare, L., U.K. 20 56 1N 4 50W
Garelochhead, U.K. 20 56 7N 4 50W
Garforth, U.K. 19 53 48N 1 22W
Gargrave, U.K. 18 53 58N 2 7W
Garlieston, U.K. 20 54 47N 4 22W
Garonne →, Fr. 35 45 2N 0 36W
Garoua, Cam. 80 9 19N 13 21 E
Garry →, U.K. 23 56 47N 3 47W
Garsdale Head, U.K. 18 54 19N 2 19W
Garstang, U.K. 18 53 53N 2 47W
Garston, U.K. 18 53 21N 2 55W
Garvald, U.K. 21 55 55N 2 39W
Garvellachs, Is., U.K. 20 56 14N 5 48W
Gary, U.S.A. 92 41 35N 87 20W
Garzê, China 60 31 39N 99 58 E
Gascony, Fr. 35 43 45N 0 20 E
Gascoyne →, Austral. 66 24 52S 113 37 E
Gaspé, Pén. de, Canada 93 48 45N 65 40W
Gatehouse of Fleet, U.K. 20 54 53N 4 10W
Gateshead, U.K. 19 54 57N 1 37W
Gatley, U.K. 18 53 25N 2 15W
Gatun, Pan. 94 9 16N 79 55W
Gatun, L., Pan. 94 9 7N 79 56W
Gävle, Swed. 45 60 40N 17 9 E
Gawthwaite, U.K. 18 54 16N 3 6W
Gaya, India 59 24 47N 85 4 E
Gayton, U.K. 15 52 45N 0 35 E
Gaywood, U.K. 15 52 46N 0 26 E
Gaza, Egypt 57 31 30N 34 28 E
Gaziantep, Turk. 47 37 6N 37 23 E
Gdańsk, Pol. 43 54 22N 18 40 E
Gdańsk Bay, Pol. 43 54 30N 19 20 E
Gdynia, Pol. 43 54 35N 18 33 E
Gedney, U.K. 15 52 47N 0 5 E
Geelong, Austral. 70 38 10S 144 22 E
Gejiu, China 60 23 20N 103 10 E
Gelderland □, Neth. 36 52 5N 6 10 E

Gelsenkirchen, *W. Ger.* **36** 51 30N 7 5 E
Geneva, *Switz.* **42** 46 12N 6 9 E
Geneva, L., *Switz.* **42** 46 26N 6 30 E
Genk, *Belg.* **36** 50 58N 5 32 E
Gennargentu, Mti. del, *It.* **40** 40 0N 9 10 E
Genoa, *It.* **40** 44 24N 8 56 E
Geographe Chan., *Austral.* **66** 24 30S 113 0 E
George, *S. Afr.* **81** 33 58S 22 29 E
George Town, *Malay.* **63** 5 25N 100 15 E
Georgetown, *Guy.* **100** 6 50N 58 12W
Georgia □, *U.S.A.* **91** 32 0N 82 0W
Georgia □, *U.S.S.R.* **47** 42 0N 43 0 E
Georgian B., *Canada* **92** 45 15N 81 0W
Gera, *E. Ger.* **42** 50 53N 12 11 E
Geraldton, *Austral.* **66** 28 48S 114 32 E
Germiston, *S. Afr.* **81** 26 15S 28 10 E
Gerona, *Sp.* **37** 41 58N 2 46 E
Gerrans B., *U.K.* **16** 50 12N 4 57W
Gerrards Cross, *U.K.* **15** 51 35N 0 32W
Ghaghara —►, *India* **59** 25 45N 84 40 E
Ghana ■, *W. Afr.* **78** 6 0N 1 0W
Ghaziabad, *India* **58** 28 42N 77 26 E
Ghent, *Belg.* **36** 51 2N 3 42 E
Giant's Causeway, *U.K.* **24** 55 15N 6 30W
Gibraltar, *Europe* **37** 36 7N 5 22W
Gibraltar, Str. of, *Medit. S.* **37** 35 55N 5 40W
Gibraltar Pt., *U.K.* **19** 53 6N 0 20 E
Gibson Desert, *Austral.* **66** 24 0S 126 0 E
Gifford, *U.K.* **21** 55 54N 2 45W
Gifu, *Jap.* **62** 35 30N 136 45 E
Giggleswick, *U.K.* **18** 54 5N 2 19W
Gigha, *U.K.* **20** 55 42N 5 45W
Gijón, *Sp.* **37** 43 32N 5 42W
Gilbert Is. = Kiribati ■, *Pac. Oc.* **65** 1 0N 176 0 E
Gillingham, *Dorset, U.K.* **14** 51 2N 2 15W
Gillingham, *Kent, U.K.* **15** 51 23N 0 34 E
Gilsland, *U.K.* **18** 55 0N 2 34W
Girdle Ness, *U.K.* **23** 57 9N 2 2W
Gironde —►, *Fr.* **35** 45 32N 1 7W
Girvan, *U.K.* **20** 55 15N 4 50W
Girvan —►, *U.K.* **20** 55 18N 4 51W
Gisborne, *N.Z.* **71** 38 39S 178 5 E
Gisburn, *U.K.* **18** 53 56N 2 16W
Gizhiga, *U.S.S.R.* **49** 62 3N 160 30 E
Gizhiga, G., *U.S.S.R.* **49** 61 0N 158 0 E
Gladstone, *Austral.* **67** 25 57S 114 17 E
Glanton, *U.K.* **21** 55 25N 1 54W
Glasgow, *U.K.* **20** 55 52N 4 14W
Glastonbury, *U.K.* **14** 51 9N 2 42W
Glemsford, *U.K.* **15** 52 6N 0 41 E
Glen —►, *U.K.* **15** 52 50N 0 7W
Glen Affric, *U.K.* **22** 57 15N 5 0W
Glen Almond, *U.K.* **21** 56 28N 3 50W
Glen Coe, *U.K.* **19** 56 40N 5 0W
Glen Etive, *U.K.* **20** 56 37N 5 0W
Glen Garry, *U.K.* **22** 57 3N 5 7W
Glen Helen, *U.K.* **18** 54 14N 4 35W
Glen Mor, *U.K.* **23** 57 12N 4 37 E
Glen Moriston, *U.K.* **22** 57 10N 4 58W
Glen Orchy, *U.K.* **20** 56 27N 4 52W
Glen Spean, *U.K.* **23** 56 53N 4 40W
Glenbarr, *U.K.* **20** 55 34N 5 40W
Glendale, *U.S.A.* **90** 34 7N 118 18W
Gleneagles, *U.K.* **21** 56 16N 3 44W
Glengarriff, *Ire.* **25** 51 45N 9 33W
Glenkens, The, *U.K.* **20** 55 10N 4 15W
Glenluce, *U.K.* **20** 54 53N 4 50W
Glenmaye, *U.K.* **18** 54 11N 4 42W
Glenorchy, *Austral.* **67** 31 55S 139 46 E
Glenrothes, *U.K.* **20** 56 12N 3 11W
Glenties, *Ire.* **24** 54 48N 8 18W
Glentrool Village, *U.K.* **20** 55 5N 4 30W
Gliwice, *Pol.* **43** 50 22N 18 41 E
Glossop, *U.K.* **18** 53 27N 1 56W
Gloucester, *U.K.* **14** 51 52N 2 15W
Gloucestershire □, *U.K.* **14** 51 44N 2 10W
Gnosall, *U.K.* **14** 52 48N 2 15W
Goa □, *India* **58** 15 33N 73 59 E
Goat Fell, *U.K.* **20** 55 37N 5 11W
Gobi, *Asia* **60** 44 0N 111 0 E
Godalming, *U.K.* **15** 51 12N 0 37W
Godavari —►, *India* **58** 16 25N 82 18 E
Godmanchester, *U.K.* **15** 52 19N 0 11W
Godshill, *U.K.* **14** 50 38N 1 13W
Godstone, *U.K.* **15** 51 15N 0 3W
Goiânia, *Brazil* **101** 16 43S 49 20W
Goil, L., *U.K.* **20** 56 8N 4 52W
Gold Coast, *Austral.* **67** 28 0S 153 25 E
Golden Vale, *Ire.* **25** 52 33N 8 17W
Golspie, *U.K.* **23** 57 58N 3 58W
Gomel, *U.S.S.R.* **46** 52 28N 31 0 E
Gometra I., *U.K.* **20** 56 30N 6 18W
Gómez Palacio, *Mex.* **94** 25 40N 104 0W
Gonder, *Eth.* **79** 12 39N 37 30 E
Good Hope, C. of, *S. Afr.* **81** 34 24S 18 30 E
Goodrich, *U.K.* **14** 51 52N 2 38W
Goodwood, *U.K.* **15** 50 53N 0 44W
Goole, *U.K.* **19** 53 42N 0 52W
Goondiwindi, *Austral.* **67** 28 30S 150 21 E
Gorakhpur, *India* **59** 26 47N 83 23 E
Gordon, *U.K.* **21** 55 41N 2 32W
Gorebridge, *U.K.* **21** 55 51N 3 2W
Gorey, *Ire.* **25** 52 41N 6 18W
Goring, *Oxon., U.K.* **14** 51 31N 1 8W
Goring, *W. Sussex, U.K.* **15** 50 49N 0 26W
Gorki, *U.S.S.R.* **46** 56 20N 44 0 E
Gorleston, *U.K.* **15** 52 35N 1 44 E
Görlitz, *E. Ger.* **42** 51 10N 14 59 E
Gort, *Ire.* **25** 53 4N 8 50W
Gorzów Wielkopolski, *Pol.* **42** 52 43N 15 15 E
Gosberton, *U.K.* **19** 52 52N 0 10W
Gosford, *Austral.* **70** 33 23S 151 18 E
Gosforth, *U.K.* **18** 54 24N 3 27W
Gosport, *U.K.* **14** 50 48N 1 8W
Göteborg, *Swed.* **45** 57 43N 11 59 E
Gotha, *E. Ger.* **42** 50 56N 10 42 E
Gotland, *Swed.* **45** 57 30N 18 33 E
Gouda, *Neth.* **36** 52 1N 4 42 E
Goudhurst, *U.K.* **15** 51 7N 0 28 E
Gouin, Rés., *Canada* **93** 48 35N 74 40W
Goulburn, *Austral.* **70** 34 44S 149 44 E
Gourock, *U.K.* **20** 55 58N 4 49W
Governador Valadares, *Brazil* **101** 18 15S 41 57W
Gower, The, *U.K.* **17** 51 35N 4 10W
Gowna, L., *Ire.* **24** 53 52N 7 35W
Gowrie, Carse of, *U.K.* **21** 56 30N 3 10W
Goya, *Arg.* **102** 29 10S 59 10W
Gozo, *Malta* **40** 36 0N 14 13 E
Grafham Water, *U.K.* **15** 52 18N 0 17W
Grafton, *Austral.* **67** 29 38S 152 58 E
Graham Bell, I., *U.S.S.R.* **48** 80 5N 70 0 E
Graham Land, *Ant.* **103** 65 0S 64 0W
Grainthorpe, *U.K.* **19** 53 27N 0 5 E
Grampian □, *U.K.* **23** 57 0N 3 0W
Grampian Mts., *U.K.* **23** 56 50N 4 0W
Gran Canaria, *Can. Is.* **78** 27 55N 15 35W
Gran Chaco, *S. Am.* **96** 25 0S 61 0W
Granada, *Sp.* **37** 37 10N 3 35W
Granard, *Ire.* **24** 53 47N 7 30W
Grand Bahama, *Baham.* **95** 26 40N 78 30W
Grand Canyon National Park, *U.S.A.* **90** 36 15N 112 20W
Grand Cayman, *W. Ind.* **95** 19 20N 81 20W
Grand Rapids, *U.S.A.* **92** 42 57N 86 40W
Grande de Santiago —►, *Mex.* **94** 21 36N 105 26W
Grande Prairie, *Canada* **88** 55 10N 118 50W
Grange-over-Sands, *U.K.* **18** 54 12N 2 55W
Grangemouth, *U.K.* **21** 56 1N 3 43W
Grangetown, *U.K.* **19** 54 36N 1 7W
Grantham, *U.K.* **19** 52 55N 0 39W
Grantown-on-Spey, *U.K.* **23** 57 19N 3 36W
Grantshouse, *U.K.* **21** 55 53N 2 17W
Grasmere, *U.K.* **18** 54 28N 3 2W
Grassington, *U.K.* **18** 54 5N 2 0W
Gravesend, *U.K.* **15** 51 25N 0 22 E
Grayrigg, *U.K.* **18** 54 22N 2 40W
Grays, *U.K.* **15** 51 28N 0 23 E
Graz, *Austria* **42** 47 4N 15 27 E
Great Abaco I., *Baham.* **95** 26 25N 77 10W
Great Australian Bight, *Austral.* **66** 33 30S 130 0 E
Great Ayton, *U.K.* **19** 54 29N 1 8W
Great Baddow, *U.K.* **15** 51 43N 0 31 E
Great Barrier Reef, *Austral.* **67** 18 0S 146 50 E
Great Basin, *U.S.A.* **90** 40 0N 116 30W
Great Bear L., *Canada* **88** 65 30N 120 0W
Great Bentley, *U.K.* **15** 51 51N 1 5 E
Great Blasket I., *Ire.* **25** 52 5N 10 30W
Great Britain, *Europe* **5** 54 0N 2 15W
Great Chesterford, *U.K.* **15** 52 4N 0 11 E
Great Clifton, *U.K.* **18** 54 39N 3 29W
Great Divide, The, *Austral.* **70** 35 0S 149 17 E
Great Dividing Ra., *Austral.* **67** 23 0S 146 0 E
Great Dunmow, *U.K.* **15** 51 52N 0 22 E
Great Falls, *U.S.A.* **90** 47 27N 111 12W
Great Harwood, *U.K.* **18** 53 43N 2 30W
Great Inagua I., *Baham.* **95** 21 0N 73 20W
Great Indian Desert = Thar Desert, *India* **58** 28 0N 72 0 E
Great Malvern, *U.K.* **14** 52 7N 2 19W
Great Massingham, *U.K.* **15** 52 47N 0 41 E
Great Missenden, *U.K.* **15** 51 42N 0 42W
Great Orme's Head, *U.K.* **17** 53 20N 3 52W
Great Ouse —►, *U.K.* **15** 52 47N 0 22 E
Great Plains, *N. Am.* **82** 47 0N 105 0W
Great Salt Lake, *U.S.A.* **90** 41 0N 112 30W
Great Sandy Desert, *Austral.* **66** 21 0S 124 0 E
Great Shefford, *U.K.* **14** 51 29N 1 27W
Great Shelford, *U.K.* **15** 52 9N 0 9 E
Great Shunner Fell, *U.K.* **18** 54 22N 2 16W
Great Slave L., *Canada* **88** 61 23N 115 38W
Great Stour = Stour —►, *U.K.* **15** 51 15N 1 20 E
Great Torrington, *U.K.* **16** 50 57N 4 9W
Great Victoria Desert, *Austral.* **66** 29 30S 126 30 E
Great Waltham, *U.K.* **15** 51 47N 0 29 E
Great Whernside, *U.K.* **18** 54 9N 1 59W
Great Wyrley, *U.K.* **14** 52 40N 2 1W
Great Yarmouth, *U.K.* **15** 52 40N 1 45 E
Great Yeldham, *U.K.* **15** 52 1N 0 33 E
Greater Antilles, *W. Ind.* **95** 17 40N 74 0W
Greater London □, *U.K.* **15** 51 30N 0 5W
Greater Manchester □, *U.K.* **18** 53 30N 2 15W
Greater Sunda Is., *Indon.* **63** 7 0S 112 0 E
Greatham, *U.K.* **19** 54 38N 1 14W
Greece ■, *Europe* **41** 40 0N 23 0 E
Greeley, *U.S.A.* **90** 40 30N 104 40W
Green B., *U.S.A.* **92** 45 0N 87 30W
Green Bay, *U.S.A.* **92** 44 30N 88 0W
Green Hammerton, *U.K.* **19** 54 2N 1 17W
Green Lowther, *U.K.* **21** 55 22N 3 44W
Greenhead, *U.K.* **21** 54 58N 2 31W
Greenland ■, *N. Am.* **89** 66 0N 45 0W
Greenland Sea, *Arctic* **103** 73 0N 10 0W
Greenlaw, *U.K.* **21** 55 42N 2 28W
Greenock, *U.K.* **20** 55 57N 4 46W
Greenodd, *U.K.* **18** 54 14N 3 3W
Greenore, *Ire.* **24** 54 2N 6 8W
Greenore Pt., *Ire.* **25** 52 15N 6 20W
Greensboro, *U.S.A.* **91** 36 7N 79 46W
Greenwich, *U.K.* **15** 51 28N 0 0 E
Grenada ■, *W. Ind.* **94** 12 10N 61 40W
Grenoble, *Fr.* **35** 45 12N 5 42 E
Greta —►, *U.K.* **18** 54 9N 2 36W
Gretna, *U.K.* **21** 54 59N 3 4W
Gretna Green, *U.K.* **21** 55 0N 3 3W
Gretton, *U.K.* **15** 52 33N 0 40W
Grey Range, *Austral.* **67** 27 0S 143 30 E
Greymouth, *N.Z.* **71** 42 29S 171 13 E
Greystoke, *U.K.* **18** 54 39N 2 52W
Gribbin Head, *U.K.* **16** 50 18N 4 41W
Griffith, *Austral.* **70** 34 18S 146 2 E
Grimsby, *U.K.* **19** 53 35N 0 5W
Gris-Nez, C., *Fr.* **34** 50 52N 1 35 E
Grizebeck, *U.K.* **18** 54 16N 3 10W
Grodno, *U.S.S.R.* **46** 53 42N 23 52 E
Groningen, *Neth.* **36** 53 15N 6 35 E
Groote Eylandt, *Austral.* **67** 14 0S 136 40 E
Groznyy, *U.S.S.R.* **47** 43 20N 45 45 E
Gruinard B., *U.K.* **22** 57 56N 5 35W
Guadalajara, *Mex.* **94** 20 40N 103 20W
Guadalajara, *Sp.* **37** 40 37N 3 12W
Guadalete —►, *Sp.* **37** 36 35N 6 13W
Guadeloupe ■, *W. Ind.* **94** 16 20N 61 40W
Guadiana —►, *Port.* **37** 37 14N 7 22W
Guadix, *Sp.* **37** 37 18N 3 11W
Gualeguay, *Arg.* **102** 33 10S 59 14W
Guam, *Pac. Oc.* **64** 13 27N 144 45 E
Guangdong □, *China* **61** 23 0N 113 0 E
Guangxi Zhuangzu Zizhiqu □, *China* **61** 24 0N 109 0 E
Guangzhou, *China* **61** 23 5N 113 10 E
Guantánamo, *Cuba* **95** 20 10N 75 14W
Guaporé —►, *Brazil* **100** 11 55S 65 4W
Guard Bridge, *U.K.* **21** 56 21N 2 52W
Guardafui, C. = Asir, Ras, *Som.* **73** 11 55N 51 10 E
Guatemala, *Guat.* **94** 14 40N 90 22W
Guatemala ■, *Cent. Am.* **94** 15 40N 90 30W
Guaviare —►, *Col.* **100** 4 3N 67 44W
Guayaquil, *Ecuad.* **100** 2 15S 79 52W
Guaymas, *Mex.* **94** 27 59N 110 54W
Guelph, *Canada* **92** 43 35N 80 20W
Guernsey, *U.K.* **34** 49 30N 2 35W
Guestling Green, *U.K.* **15** 50 53N 0 40 E
Guildford, *U.K.* **15** 51 14N 0 34W
Guilin, *China* **61** 25 18N 110 15 E
Guinea ■, *W. Afr.* **78** 10 20N 10 0W
Guinea, Gulf of, *Atl. Oc.* **72** 3 0N 2 30 E
Guinea-Bissau ■, *Africa* **78** 12 0N 15 0W
Guisborough, *U.K.* **19** 54 32N 1 2W
Guiyang, *China* **60** 26 32N 106 40 E
Guizhou □, *China* **60** 27 0N 107 0 E
Gujarat □, *India* **58** 23 20N 71 0 E
Gujranwala, *Pak.* **58** 32 10N 74 12 E
Gujrat, *Pak.* **58** 32 40N 74 2 E
Gulbarga, *India* **58** 17 20N 76 50 E
Gulf, The, *Asia* **56** 27 0N 50 0 E
Gullane, *U.K.* **21** 56 2N 2 50W
Guntur, *India* **59** 16 23N 80 30 E
Gurnard's Head, *U.K.* **16** 50 12N 5 37W
Guyana ■, *S. Am.* **100** 5 0N 59 0W
Gwalchmai, *U.K.* **17** 53 16N 4 23W
Gwalior, *India* **58** 26 12N 78 10 E
Gweebarra B., *Ire.* **24** 54 52N 8 21W
Gweedore, *Ire.* **24** 55 4N 8 15W
Gweek, *U.K.* **16** 50 6N 5 12W
Gwennap, *U.K.* **16** 50 12N 5 9W
Gwent □, *U.K.* **17** 51 45N 2 55W
Gweru, *Zimb.* **81** 19 28S 29 45 E
Gwynedd □, *U.K.* **17** 53 0N 4 0W
Gympie, *Austral.* **67** 26 11S 152 38 E
Györ, *Hung.* **43** 47 41N 17 40 E

H

Haarlem, *Neth.* **36** 52 23N 4 39 E
Hachinohe, *Jap.* **62** 40 30N 141 29 E
Hackney, *U.K.* **15** 51 33N 0 2W
Hackthorpe, *U.K.* **18** 54 37N 2 42W
Haddenham, *U.K.* **15** 51 46N 0 56W
Haddington, *U.K.* **21** 55 57N 2 48W
Hadleigh, *U.K.* **15** 52 3N 0 58 E
Hadley, *U.K.* **14** 52 42N 2 28W
Hadlow, *U.K.* **15** 51 12N 0 20 E
Hadrians Wall, *U.K.* **19** 55 0N 2 30W
Haeju, *N. Kor.* **61** 38 3N 125 45 E
Hafnarfjörður, *Ice.* **44** 64 4N 21 57W
Hagen, *W. Ger.* **36** 51 21N 7 29 E
Hags Hd., *Ire.* **25** 52 57N 9 30W
Haifa, *Isr.* **57** 32 46N 35 0 E
Haikou, *China* **61** 20 1N 110 16 E
Ḥā'il, *Si. Arab.* **56** 27 28N 41 45 E
Hailar, *China* **61** 49 12N 119 37 E
Hailsham, *U.K.* **15** 50 52N 0 17 E
Hainan, *China* **61** 19 0N 109 30 E
Hainton, *U.K.* **19** 53 21N 0 13W
Haiphong, *Viet.* **60** 20 47N 106 41 E
Haiti ■, *W. Ind.* **95** 19 0N 72 30W
Hakodate, *Jap.* **62** 41 45N 140 44 E
Halberton, *U.K.* **16** 50 55N 3 24W
Hale, *U.K.* **18** 53 24N 2 21W
Halesowen, *U.K.* **14** 52 27N 2 2W
Halesworth, *U.K.* **15** 52 21N 1 30 E
Halifax, *Canada* **93** 44 38N 63 35W
Halifax, *U.K.* **18** 53 43N 1 51W
Halifax B., *Austral.* **67** 18 50S 147 0 E
Halkirk, *U.K.* **23** 58 30N 3 30W
Halle, *Ger.* **42** 51 29N 12 0 E
Hallow, *U.K.* **14** 52 14N 2 15W
Hallworthy, *U.K.* **16** 50 38N 4 34W
Halmahera, *Indon.* **63** 0 40N 128 0 E
Halmstad, *Swed.* **45** 56 41N 12 52 E
Halstead, *U.K.* **15** 51 59N 0 39 E
Haltwhistle, *U.K.* **21** 54 58N 2 27W
Hamadān, *Iran* **56** 34 52N 48 32 E
Hamāh, *Syria* **56** 35 5N 36 40 E
Hamamatsu, *Jap.* **62** 34 45N 137 45 E
Hambledon, *U.K.* **14** 50 56N 1 6W
Hambleton Hills, *U.K.* **19** 54 17N 1 12W
Hamburg, *W. Ger.* **42** 53 32N 9 59 E
Hämeenlinna, *Fin.* **45** 61 0N 24 28 E
Hamersley Ra., *Austral.* **66** 22 0S 117 45 E
Hamilton, *Berm.* **95** 32 15N 64 45W
Hamilton, *Canada* **92** 43 15N 79 50W
Hamilton, *N.Z.* **71** 37 47S 175 19 E
Hamilton, *U.K.* **21** 55 47N 4 2W
Hamm, *W. Ger.* **36** 51 40N 7 49 E
Hammerfest, *Nor.* **44** 70 39N 23 41 E
Hammersmith, *U.K.* **15** 51 30N 0 15W
Hammond, *U.S.A.* **92** 41 40N 87 30W
Hampshire □, *U.K.* **14** 51 3N 1 20W
Hampshire Downs, *U.K.* **14** 51 10N 1 10W
Hampton in Arden, *U.K.* **14** 52 26N 1 42W
Hangzhou, *China* **61** 30 18N 120 11 E
Hanko, *Fin.* **45** 59 59N 22 57 E
Hanningfield Water, *U.K.* **15** 51 40N 0 30 E
Hanoi, *Viet.* **60** 21 5N 105 55 E
Hanover, *W. Ger.* **42** 52 23N 9 43 E
Haora, *India* **59** 22 37N 88 20 E
Happy Valley, *Canada* **89** 53 15N 60 20W
Harare, *Zimb.* **81** 17 43S 31 2 E
Harbin, *China* **61** 45 46N 126 51 E
Hardangerfjorden, *Nor.* **45** 60 15N 6 0 E
Harewood, *U.K.* **19** 53 54N 1 30W
Haringey, *U.K.* **15** 51 35N 0 7W
Harlech, *U.K.* **17** 52 52N 4 7W
Harleston, *U.K.* **15** 52 25N 1 18 E
Harlingen, *Neth.* **36** 53 11N 5 25 E
Harlow, *U.K.* **15** 51 47N 0 9 E
Harpenden, *U.K.* **15** 51 48N 0 20W
Harrietsham, *U.K.* **15** 51 15N 0 41 E
Harrington, *U.K.* **18** 54 37N 3 55W
Harris, *U.K.* **22** 57 50N 6 55W
Harris, Sd. of, *U.K.* **22** 57 44N 7 6W
Harrisburg, *U.S.A.* **93** 40 18N 76 52W
Harrogate, *U.K.* **19** 53 59N 1 32W
Harrow, *U.K.* **15** 51 35N 0 15W
Hartest, *U.K.* **15** 52 7N 0 41 E
Hartford, *U.S.A.* **93** 41 47N 72 41W
Harthill, *U.K.* **21** 55 52N 3 45W
Hartland, *U.K.* **16** 50 59N 4 29W
Hartland Pt., *U.K.* **16** 51 2N 4 32W
Hartlebury, *U.K.* **14** 52 20N 2 13W
Hartlepool, *U.K.* **19** 54 42N 1 11W
Hartley, *U.K.* **21** 55 5N 1 27W
Hartpury, *U.K.* **14** 51 55N 2 18W
Harwell, *U.K.* **14** 51 40N 1 17W
Harwich, *U.K.* **15** 51 56N 1 18 E
Harz, *Europe* **26** 51 40N 10 40 E
Hasa, *Si. Arab.* **56** 26 0N 49 0 E
Haslemere, *U.K.* **15** 51 5N 0 41W
Haslingden, *U.K.* **18** 53 43N 2 20W
Hasselt, *Belg.* **36** 50 56N 5 21 E
Hastings, *N.Z.* **71** 39 39S 176 52 E
Hastings, *U.K.* **15** 50 51N 0 36 E
Hatfield, *U.K.* **15** 51 46N 0 11W
Hatfield Broad Oak, *U.K.* **15** 51 48N 0 16 E
Hatherleigh, *U.K.* **16** 50 49N 4 4W
Hathersage, *U.K.* **19** 53 20N 1 39W
Hatteras, C., *U.S.A.* **91** 35 10N 75 30W
Haugh of Urr, *U.K.* **21** 55 0N 3 51W
Haughley, *U.K.* **15** 52 13N 0 59 E
Hauraki Gulf, *N.Z.* **71** 36 35S 175 5 E
Hauxley, *U.K.* **21** 55 21N 1 35W
Havana, *Cuba* **95** 23 8N 82 22W
Havant, *U.K.* **15** 50 51N 0 59W
Haverfordwest, *U.K.* **17** 51 48N 4 59W
Haverhill, *U.K.* **15** 52 6N 0 27 E
Haverigg, *U.K.* **18** 54 12N 3 16W
Havering, *U.K.* **15** 51 33N 0 20 E
Havre, Le, *Fr.* **34** 49 30N 0 5 E
Hawaiian Is., *Pac. Oc.* **90** 20 30N 156 0W
Hawera, *N.Z.* **71** 39 35S 174 19 E
Hawes, *U.K.* **18** 54 18N 2 12W
Haweswater, *U.K.* **18** 54 32N 2 48W
Hawick, *U.K.* **21** 55 25N 2 48W
Hawkchurch, *U.K.* **16** 50 47N 2 56W

Hawke B., *N.Z.* 71 39 25S 177 20 E
Hawkesbury Upton, *U.K.* 14 51 34N 2 19W
Hawkhurst, *U.K.* 15 51 2N 0 31 E
Hawkshead, *U.K.* 18 54 23N 3 0W
Haworth, *U.K.* 18 53 50N 1 57W
Hawsker, *U.K.* 19 54 27N 0 34W
Haxby, *U.K.* 19 54 1N 1 4W
Hay-on-Wye, *U.K.* 17 52 4N 3 9W
Hay River, *Canada* 88 60 51N 115 44W
Hayburn Wyke, *U.K.* 19 54 22N 0 28W
Haydon Bridge, *U.K.* 21 54 58N 2 15W
Hayle, *U.K.* 16 50 12N 5 25W
Hayton, *U.K.* 18 54 55N 2 45W
Haywards Heath, *U.K.* 15 51 0N 0 5W
Heacham, *U.K.* 15 52 55N 0 30 E
Headcorn, *U.K.* 15 51 10N 0 39 E
Heanor, *U.K.* 19 53 1N 1 20W
Heathfield, *U.K.* 15 50 58N 0 18 E
Hebburn, *U.K.* 21 54 59N 1 30W
Hebden Bridge, *U.K.* 18 53 45N 2 0W
Hebei □, *China* 61 39 0N 116 0 E
Hebrides, *U.K.* 22 57 30N 7 0W
Hechuan, *China* 60 30 2N 106 12 E
Heckington, *U.K.* 19 52 59N 0 17W
Hedmark fylke □, *Nor.* 44 61 17N 11 40 E
Hednesford, *U.K.* 14 52 43N 2 0W
Hedon, *U.K.* 19 53 44N 0 11W
Heerlen, *Neth.* 36 50 55N 6 0 E
Hefei, *China* 61 31 52N 117 18 E
Hegang, *China* 61 47 20N 130 19 E
Heidelberg, *W. Ger.* 42 49 23N 8 41 E
Heilbronn, *W. Ger.* 42 49 8N 9 13 E
Heilongjiang □, *China* 61 48 0N 126 0 E
Hekla, *Ice.* 44 63 56N 19 35W
Helensburgh, *U.K.* 20 56 0N 4 44W
Heligoland, *W. Ger.* 42 54 10N 7 51 E
Hellifield, *U.K.* 18 54 0N 2 13W
Helmond, *Neth.* 36 51 29N 5 41 E
Helmsdale, *U.K.* 23 58 7N 3 40W
Helmsley, *U.K.* 19 54 15N 1 2W
Helperby, *U.K.* 19 54 8N 1 20W
Helsby, *U.K.* 18 53 16N 2 47W
Helsingborg, *Swed.* 45 56 3N 12 42 E
Helsingør, *Den.* 45 56 2N 12 35 E
Helsinki, *Fin.* 45 60 15N 25 3 E
Helston, *U.K.* 16 50 7N 5 17W
Helvellyn, *U.K.* 18 54 31N 3 1W
Hemel Hempstead, *U.K.* 15 51 45N 0 28W
Hempton, *U.K.* 15 52 50N 0 49 E
Hemsworth, *U.K.* 19 53 37N 1 21W
Hemyock, *U.K.* 16 50 50N 3 15W
Henan □, *China* 61 34 0N 114 0 E
Henfield, *U.K.* 15 50 56N 0 17W
Hengelo, *Neth.* 36 52 16N 6 48 E
Hengyang, *China* 61 26 51N 112 30 E
Henley-in-Arden, *U.K.* 14 52 18N 1 47W
Henley-on-Thames, *U.K.* 15 51 32N 0 53W
Henlow, *U.K.* 15 52 2N 0 18W
Henstridge, *U.K.* 14 50 59N 2 24W
Henzada, *Burma* 59 17 38N 95 26 E
Herāt, *Afg.* 57 34 20N 62 7 E
Hereford, *U.K.* 14 52 4N 2 42W
Hereford and Worcester □, *U.K.* 14 52 10N 2 30W
Hermosillo, *Mex.* 94 29 4N 110 58W
Herne, *W. Ger.* 36 51 33N 7 12 E
Herne Bay, *U.K.* 15 51 22N 1 8 E
Herning, *Den.* 45 56 8N 8 58 E
Herstmonceux, *U.K.* 15 50 53N 0 21 E
Hertford, *U.K.* 15 51 47N 0 4W
Hertford □, *U.K.* 15 51 51N 0 5W
's-Hertogenbosch, *Neth.* 36 51 42N 5 17 E
Hesse □, *W. Ger.* 42 50 40N 9 20 E
Hessle, *U.K.* 19 53 44N 0 28 E
Hethersett, *U.K.* 15 52 35N 1 10 E
Hetton-le-Hole, *U.K.* 21 54 49N 1 26W
Hexham, *U.K.* 19 54 58N 2 7W
Heybridge, *U.K.* 15 51 44N 0 42 E
Heysham, *U.K.* 18 54 5N 2 53W
Heytesbury, *U.K.* 14 51 11N 2 7W
Heywood, *U.K.* 18 53 36N 2 13W
High Atlas, *Mor.* 72 32 30N 5 0W
High Bentham, *U.K.* 18 54 8N 2 31W
High Borrow Bridge, *U.K.* 18 54 26N 2 43W
High Ercall, *U.K.* 14 52 46N 2 37W
High Hesket, *U.K.* 18 54 47N 2 49W
High Pike, *U.K.* 18 54 43N 3 4W
High Willhays, *U.K.* 16 50 41N 3 59W
High Wycombe, *U.K.* 15 51 37N 0 45W
Higham Ferrers, *U.K.* 15 52 18N 0 36W
Highbridge, *U.K.* 14 51 13N 2 59W
Highclere, *U.K.* 14 51 20N 1 22W
Highland □, *U.K.* 22 57 30N 5 0W
Highley, *U.K.* 14 52 25N 2 23W
Hightae, *U.K.* 21 55 5N 3 27W
Highworth, *U.K.* 14 51 38N 1 42W
Hilgay, *U.K.* 15 52 34N 0 23 E
Hillingdon, *U.K.* 15 51 33N 0 29W
Hillsborough, *U.K.* 24 54 28N 6 6W
Hilo, *U.S.A.* 90 19 44N 155 5W
Hilpsford Pt., *U.K.* 18 54 4N 3 12W
Hilversum, *Neth.* 36 52 14N 5 10 E
Himachal Pradesh □, *India* 58 31 30N 77 0 E
Himalaya, Mts., *Asia* 60 29 0N 84 0 E
Himeji, *Jap.* 62 34 50N 134 40 E
Hinckley, *U.K.* 14 52 33N 1 21W
Hinderwell, *U.K.* 19 54 32N 0 45W
Hindhead, *U.K.* 15 51 6N 0 42W
Hindley, *U.K.* 18 53 32N 2 35W
Hindu Kush, *Asia* 57 36 0N 71 0 E
Hingham, *U.K.* 15 52 35N 0 59 E
Hinkley Pt., *U.K.* 14 50 59N 3 32W
Hinstock, *U.K.* 14 52 50N 2 28W
Hiroshima, *Jap.* 62 34 24N 132 30 E
Hispaniola, *W. Ind.* 95 19 0N 71 0W
Histon, *U.K.* 15 52 15N 0 6 E
Hitchin, *U.K.* 15 51 57N 0 16W
Ho Chi Minh City, *Viet.* 63 10 58N 106 40 E
Hobart, *Austral.* 66 42 50S 147 21 E
Hodder →, *U.K.* 18 53 57N 2 27W
Hoddesdon, *U.K.* 15 51 45N 0 1W
Hodge →, *U.K.* 19 54 14N 0 55W
Hoff, *U.K.* 18 54 34N 2 31W
Hoggar, Mts., *Alg.* 78 23 0N 6 30 E
Hog's Back, *U.K.* 15 51 13N 0 40W
Hohhot, *China* 61 40 52N 111 40 E
Hokitika, *N.Z.* 71 42 42S 171 0 E
Hokkaidō □, *Jap.* 62 43 30N 143 0 E
Holbeach, *U.K.* 15 52 48N 0 1 E
Holbeach Marsh, *U.K.* 15 52 52N 0 5 E
Holderness, *U.K.* 19 53 45N 0 5W
Holguín, *Cuba* 95 20 50N 76 20W
Holkham, *U.K.* 15 52 57N 0 48 E
Holland Fen, *U.K.* 19 53 0N 0 8W
Holland-on-Sea, *U.K.* 15 51 48N 1 12 E
Holme, *Humberside, U.K.* 19 53 50N 0 48W
Holme, *N. Yorks., U.K.* 18 53 34N 1 50W
Holmes Chapel, *U.K.* 18 53 13N 2 21W
Holmfirth, *U.K.* 19 53 34N 1 48W
Holmwood, *U.K.* 15 51 12N 0 19W
Holsworthy, *U.K.* 16 50 48N 4 21W
Holt, *U.K.* 15 52 55N 1 4 E
Holy I., *England, U.K.* 19 55 42N 1 48W
Holy I., *Scotland, U.K.* 20 55 31N 5 4W
Holy I., *Wales, U.K.* 17 53 17N 4 37W
Holyhead, *U.K.* 17 53 18N 4 38W
Holywell, *U.K.* 17 53 16N 3 14W
Holywood, *U.K.* 24 54 38N 5 50W
Homs, *Syria* 56 34 40N 36 45 E
Honduras ■, *Cent. Am.* 94 14 40N 86 30W
Honduras, G. de, *Cent. Am.* 94 16 50N 87 0W
Hong →, *Viet.* 60 20 17N 106 34 E
Hong Kong ■, *Asia* 61 22 11N 114 14 E
Honington, *U.K.* 19 52 58N 0 35W
Honiton, *U.K.* 16 50 48N 3 11W
Honolulu, *U.S.A.* 90 21 19N 157 52W
Honshū, *Jap.* 62 36 0N 138 0 E
Hoo, *U.K.* 15 51 25N 0 33 E
Hook, *U.K.* 15 51 17N 0 55W
Hook Hd., *Ire.* 25 52 8N 6 57W
Hoorn, *Neth.* 36 52 38N 5 4 E
Horden, *U.K.* 19 54 45N 1 17W
Horley, *U.K.* 15 51 10N 0 10W
Horn, C., *Chile* 102 55 50S 67 30W
Horn Head, *Ire.* 24 55 13N 8 0W
Horncastle, *U.K.* 19 53 13N 0 8W
Horndean, *U.K.* 15 50 50N 0 59W
Horningsham, *U.K.* 14 51 11N 2 16W
Hornsby, *Austral.* 70 33 42S 151 2 E
Hornsea, *U.K.* 19 53 55N 0 10W
Horsens, *Den.* 45 55 52N 9 51 E
Horsforth, *U.K.* 19 53 50N 1 39W
Horsham, *Austral.* 70 36 44S 142 13 E
Horsham, *U.K.* 15 51 4N 0 20W
Horsham St. Faith, *U.K.* 15 52 41N 1 15 E
Horsted Keynes, *U.K.* 15 51 2N 0 1W
Horton-in-Ribblesdale, *U.K.* 18 54 9N 2 19W
Horwich, *U.K.* 18 53 37N 2 33W
Hospitalet de Llobregat, *Sp.* 37 41 21N 2 6 E
Hotan, *China* 60 37 25N 79 55 E
Houghton-le-Spring, *U.K.* 19 54 51N 1 28W
Houghton Regis, *U.K.* 15 51 54N 0 32W
Hounslow, *U.K.* 15 51 29N 0 20W
Houston, *U.S.A.* 91 29 50N 95 20W
Hovd, *Mong.* 60 48 2N 91 37 E
Hove, *U.K.* 15 50 50N 0 10W
Hoveton, *U.K.* 15 52 45N 1 23 E
Hovingham, *U.K.* 19 54 10N 0 59W
Hövsgöl Nuur, *Mong.* 60 51 0N 100 30 E
Howden, *U.K.* 19 53 45N 0 52W
Howth Hd., *Ire.* 24 53 21N 6 0W
Hoxne, *U.K.* 15 52 22N 1 11 E
Hoy I., *U.K.* 23 58 50N 3 15W
Hoylake, *U.K.* 18 53 24N 3 11W
Hrádec Králové, *Czech.* 42 50 15N 15 50 E
Hron →, *Czech.* 43 47 49N 18 45 E
Huainan, *China* 61 32 39N 117 2 E
Huambo, *Angola* 81 12 42S 15 54 E
Huancayo, *Peru* 100 12 5S 75 12W
Huang He →, *China* 60 37 55N 118 50 E
Huangshi, *China* 61 30 10N 115 3 E
Huánuco, *Peru* 100 9 55S 76 15W
Hubei □, *China* 61 31 0N 112 0 E
Hucknall, *U.K.* 19 53 3N 1 12W
Huddersfield, *U.K.* 19 53 38N 1 49W
Hudson →, *U.S.A.* 93 40 42N 74 2W
Hudson Bay, *Canada* 89 52 51N 102 23W
Hudson Str., *Canada* 89 62 0N 70 0W
Hue, *Viet.* 63 16 30N 107 35 E
Huelva, *Sp.* 37 37 18N 6 57W
Huesca, *Sp.* 37 42 8N 0 25W
Hugh Town, *U.K.* 16 49 55N 6 19W
Hughenden, *Austral.* 67 20 52S 144 10 E
Hughes, *U.S.A.* 88 66 0N 154 20W
Hull, *Canada* 93 45 25N 75 44W
Hull = Kingston-upon-Hull, *U.K.* 19 53 45N 0 20W
Hull →, *U.K.* 19 53 43N 0 25W
Hullavington, *U.K.* 14 51 31N 2 9W
Hulme End, *U.K.* 18 53 8N 1 51W
Humber →, *U.K.* 19 53 40N 0 10W
Humber, Mouth of the, *U.K.* 19 53 32N 0 28W
Humberside □, *U.K.* 19 53 50N 0 30W
Humboldt →, *U.S.A.* 90 40 2N 118 31W
Hume, L., *Austral.* 70 36 0S 147 0 E
Humshaugh, *U.K.* 21 55 3N 2 8W
Húnaflói, *Ice.* 44 65 50N 20 50W
Hunan □, *China* 61 27 30N 111 30 E
Hungary ■, *Europe* 43 47 20N 19 20 E
Hungary, Plain of, *Europe* 26 47 0N 20 0 E
Hungerford, *U.K.* 14 51 25N 1 30W
Hŭngnam, *N. Kor.* 61 39 49N 127 45 E
Hunmanby, *U.K.* 19 54 12N 0 19W
Hunstanton, *U.K.* 15 52 57N 0 30 E
Hunter →, *Austral.* 70 32 52S 151 46 E
Hunterston, *U.K.* 20 55 43N 4 55W
Huntingdon, *U.K.* 15 52 20N 0 11W
Huntington, *U.S.A.* 92 38 20N 82 30W
Huntly, *U.K.* 23 57 27N 2 48W
Huntsville, *U.S.A.* 91 34 45N 86 35W
Hurlford, *U.K.* 20 55 35N 4 29W
Huron, L., *N. Am.* 92 45 0N 83 0W
Hursley, *U.K.* 14 51 1N 1 23W
Hurstbourne Tarrant, *U.K.* 14 51 17N 1 27W
Hurstpierpoint, *U.K.* 15 50 56N 0 11W
Húsavík, *Ice.* 44 66 3N 17 21W
Husband's Bosworth, *U.K.* 14 52 27N 1 3W
Huyton, *U.K.* 18 53 25N 2 52W
Hyde, *U.K.* 18 53 26N 2 6W
Hyderabad, *India* 58 17 22N 78 29 E
Hyderabad, *Pak.* 58 25 23N 68 24 E
Hynish, *U.K.* 20 56 27N 6 54W
Hynish B., *U.K.* 20 56 29N 6 40W
Hythe, *U.K.* 15 51 4N 1 5 E

I

Iaşi, *Rom.* 43 47 10N 27 40 E
Ibadan, *Nig.* 78 7 22N 3 58 E
Ibagué, *Col.* 100 4 20N 75 20W
Iberian Peninsula, *Europe* 26 40 0N 5 0W
Ibiza, *Sp.* 37 38 54N 1 26 E
Ibstock, *U.K.* 14 52 42N 1 23W
Icá, *Peru* 100 14 0S 75 48W
Iceland ■, *Atl. Oc.* 44 65 0N 19 0W
Ichinomiya, *Jap.* 62 35 18N 136 48 E
Idaho □, *U.S.A.* 90 44 10N 114 0W
Idar-Oberstein, *W. Ger.* 36 49 43N 7 19 E
Idle →, *U.K.* 19 53 27N 0 49W
Idmiston, *U.K.* 14 51 8N 1 43W
Idsworth, *U.K.* 15 50 56N 0 56W
Igarka, *U.S.S.R.* 49 67 30N 86 33 E
Iglésias, *It.* 40 39 19N 8 27 E
Iguaçu Falls, *Brazil* 102 25 41S 54 26W
IJsselmeer, *Neth.* 36 52 45N 5 20 E
Ilchester, *U.K.* 14 51 0N 2 41W
Île-de-France, *Fr.* 34 49 0N 2 20 E
Ilfracombe, *U.K.* 16 51 13N 4 8W
Ilhéus, *Brazil* 101 14 49S 39 2W
Ilkeston, *U.K.* 19 52 59N 1 19W
Ilkley, *U.K.* 18 53 56N 1 49W
Illinois □, *U.S.A.* 91 40 15N 89 30W
Ilminster, *U.K.* 14 50 55N 2 56W
Iloilo, *Phil.* 63 10 45N 122 33 E
Immingham, *U.K.* 19 53 37N 0 12W
Imphal, *India* 59 24 48N 93 56 E
Inari, *Fin.* 44 68 54N 27 5 E
Ince, *U.K.* 18 53 32N 2 38W
Inchcape Rock, *U.K.* 21 56 26N 2 24W
Inchkeith, I., *U.K.* 21 56 2N 3 8W
Inchon, *S. Kor.* 61 37 27N 126 40 E
Inchture, *U.K.* 21 56 26N 3 8W
Indaal, L., *U.K.* 20 55 44N 6 20W
India ■, *Asia* 58 20 0N 78 0 E
Indian Ocean 129 5 0S 75 0 E
Indiana □, *U.S.A.* 92 40 0N 86 0W
Indianapolis, *U.S.A.* 92 39 42N 86 10W
Indonesia ■, *Asia* 63 5 0S 115 0 E
Indore, *India* 58 22 42N 75 53 E
Indus →, *Pak.* 58 24 20N 67 47 E
Ingatestone, *U.K.* 15 51 40N 0 23 E
Ingleborough, *U.K.* 18 54 11N 2 23W
Ingleton, *U.K.* 18 54 9N 2 29W
Ingoldmells, Pt., *U.K.* 19 53 11N 0 21 E
Inishbofin, *Ire.* 24 53 35N 10 12W
Inishmore, *Ire.* 25 53 8N 9 45W
Inishowen, *Ire.* 24 55 14N 7 15W
Inkberrow, *U.K.* 14 52 13N 1 59W
Inkpen Beacon, *U.K.* 14 51 22N 1 28W
Inn →, *Austria* 40 48 35N 13 28 E
Innellan, *U.K.* 20 55 54N 4 58W
Inner Hebrides, *U.K.* 22 57 0N 6 30W
Inner Mongolia □, *China* 61 42 0N 112 0 E
Inner Sound, *U.K.* 22 57 30N 5 55W
Innerleithen, *U.K.* 21 55 37N 3 4W
Innsbruck, *Austria* 42 47 16N 11 23 E
Inny →, *Ire.* 25 53 30N 7 50W
Interlaken, *Switz.* 42 46 41N 7 50 E
Inuvik, *Canada* 88 68 16N 133 40W
Inveraray, *U.K.* 20 56 13N 5 5W
Inverbervie, *U.K.* 23 56 50N 2 17W
Invercargill, *N.Z.* 71 46 24S 168 24 E
Inverell, *Austral.* 67 29 45S 151 8 E
Invergarry, *U.K.* 23 57 5N 4 48W
Invergordon, *U.K.* 23 57 41N 4 10W
Invergowrie, *U.K.* 21 56 29N 3 5W
Inverkeithing, *U.K.* 21 56 2N 3 24W
Invermoriston, *U.K.* 23 57 13N 4 38W
Inverness, *U.K.* 23 57 29N 4 12W
Inverurie, *U.K.* 23 57 15N 2 21W
Iona, *U.K.* 20 56 20N 6 25W
Ionian Is., *Greece* 41 38 40N 20 0 E
Ionian Sea, *Greece* 41 37 30N 17 30 E
Iowa □, *U.S.A.* 91 42 18N 93 30W
Iowa City, *U.S.A.* 90 41 40N 91 35W
Ipoh, *Malay.* 63 4 35N 101 5 E
Ipswich, *U.K.* 15 52 4N 1 9 E
Iquique, *Chile* 100 20 19S 70 5W
Iquitos, *Peru* 100 3 45S 73 10W
Iráklion, *Greece* 41 35 20N 25 12 E
Iran ■, *Asia* 57 33 0N 53 0 E
Irapuato, *Mex.* 94 20 40N 101 30W
Iraq ■, *Asia* 56 33 0N 44 0 E
Irchester, *U.K.* 15 52 17N 0 40W
Ireland ■, *Europe* 24 53 0N 8 0W
Ireland's Eye, *Ire.* 24 53 25N 6 4W
Irian Jaya □, *Indon.* 64 4 0S 137 0 E
Iringa, *Tanz.* 80 7 48S 35 43 E
Irish Republic ■, *Europe* 25 53 0N 8 0W
Irish Sea, *Europe* 18 54 0N 5 0W
Irkutsk, *U.S.S.R.* 49 52 18N 104 20 E
Irlam, *U.K.* 18 53 26N 2 27W
Ironbridge, *U.K.* 14 52 38N 2 29W
Irrawaddy →, *Burma* 59 15 50N 95 6 E
Irt →, *U.K.* 18 54 24N 3 25W
Irthing →, *U.K.* 21 54 55N 2 55W
Irthlingborough, *U.K.* 15 52 20N 0 37W
Irtysh →, *U.S.S.R.* 48 61 4N 68 52 E
Irvine, *U.K.* 20 55 37N 4 40W
Irvine →, *U.K.* 20 55 35N 4 40W
Irvinestown, *U.K.* 24 54 28N 7 38W
Isabela, *Phil.* 63 10 12N 122 59 E
Ísafjörður, *Ice.* 44 66 5N 23 9W
Ishim →, *U.S.S.R.* 48 57 45N 71 10 E
İskenderun, *Turk.* 47 36 32N 36 10 E
Isla →, *U.K.* 23 56 32N 3 20W
Islamabad, *Pak.* 58 33 40N 73 10 E
Islay, *U.K.* 20 55 46N 6 10W
Islay Sound, *U.K.* 20 55 45N 6 5W
Isle of Whithorn, *U.K.* 20 54 42N 4 22W
Isle of Wight □, *U.K.* 14 50 40N 1 20W
Isleham, *U.K.* 15 52 21N 0 24 E
Islip, *U.K.* 14 51 49N 1 12W
Ismâ'ilîya, *Egypt* 79 30 37N 32 18 E
Israel ■, *Asia* 57 32 0N 34 50 E
İstanbul, *Turk.* 47 41 0N 29 0 E
Itabuna, *Brazil* 101 14 48S 39 16W
Italy ■, *Europe* 40 42 0N 13 0 E
Itchen →, *U.K.* 14 50 57N 1 20W
Ivanovo, *U.S.S.R.* 46 52 7N 25 29 E
Ivinghoe, *U.K.* 15 51 50N 0 38W
Ivory Coast ■, *Africa* 78 7 30N 5 0W
Ivugivik, *Canada* 89 62 24N 77 55W
Ivybridge, *U.K.* 16 50 24N 3 56W
Iwaki, *Jap.* 62 37 3N 140 55 E
Ixworth, *U.K.* 15 52 18N 0 50 E
Izhevsk = Ustinov, *U.S.S.R.* 46 56 51N 53 14 E
İzmir, *Turk.* 47 38 25N 27 8 E

J

Jabalpur, *India* 58 23 9N 79 58 E
Jackson, *U.S.A.* 91 32 20N 90 10W
Jacksonville, *U.S.A.* 91 30 15N 81 38W
Jaén, *Sp.* 37 37 44N 3 43W
Jaffna, *Sri L.* 58 9 45N 80 2 E
Jaipur, *India* 58 27 0N 75 50 E
Jakarta, *Indon.* 63 6 9S 106 49 E
Jamaica ■, *W. Ind.* 94 18 10N 77 30W
Jambi, *Indon.* 63 1 38S 103 30 E
James B., *Canada* 89 51 30N 80 0W
Jammu, *India* 58 32 43N 74 54 E
Jammu & Kashmir □, *India* 58 34 25N 77 0 E
Jamnagar, *India* 58 22 30N 70 6 E
Jamshedpur, *India* 59 22 44N 86 12 E
Japan ■, *Asia* 62 36 0N 136 0 E
Japan, Sea of, *Asia* 62 40 0N 135 0 E
Japurá →, *Brazil* 100 3 8S 64 46W
Jarrow, *U.K.* 21 54 58N 1 28W
Java, I., *Indon.* 63 7 0S 110 0 E
Java Sea, *E. Ind.* 63 4 35S 107 15 E
Jedburgh, *U.K.* 21 55 28N 2 33W
Jedda, *Si. Arab.* 56 21 29N 39 10 E
Jena, *E. Ger.* 42 50 56N 11 33 E
Jequié, *Brazil* 101 13 51S 40 5W
Jerez de la Frontera, *Sp.* 37 36 41N 6 7W
Jericho, *Jord.* 57 31 52N 35 27 E
Jersey, I., *U.K.* 34 49 13N 2 7W

Jersey City, U.S.A. 93 40 41N 74 8W
Jerusalem, Asia 57 31 47N 35 10 E
Jervaulx, U.K. 19 54 19N 1 41W
Jervis Bay, Austral. 70 35 8S 150 43 E
Jhansi, India 58 25 30N 78 36 E
Jhelum →, Pak. 58 31 20N 72 10 E
Jiamusi, China 61 46 40N 130 26 E
Ji'an, China 61 27 6N 114 59 E
Jiangsu □, China 61 33 0N 120 0 E
Jiangxi □, China 61 27 30N 116 0 E
Jilin, China 61 43 44N 126 30 E
Jilin □, China 61 44 0N 124 0 E
Jima, Eth. 79 7 40N 36 47 E
Jinan, China 61 36 38N 117 1 E
Jinja, Uganda 80 0 25N 33 12 E
Jinzhou, China 61 41 5N 121 3 E
Jixi, China 61 45 20N 130 50 E
João Pessoa, Brazil 101 7 10S 34 52W
Johannesburg, S. Afr. 81 26 10S 28 2 E
John o' Groats, U.K. 23 58 39N 3 3W
Johnstone, U.K. 20 55 50N 4 31W
Johnstown, U.S.A. 92 40 19N 78 53W
Johor Baharu, Malay. 63 1 28N 103 46 E
Jönköping, Swed. 45 57 45N 14 10 E
Jonquière, Canada 93 48 27N 71 14W
Jordan ■, Asia 57 31 0N 36 0 E
Jordan →, Asia 57 31 48N 35 32 E
Jos, Nig. 78 9 53N 8 51 E
Joseph Bonaparte G., Austral. 66 14 35S 128 50 E
Jotunheimen, Nor. 44 61 35N 8 25 E
Juan de Fuca Str., Canada 90 48 15N 124 0W
Juàzeiro do Norte, Brazil 101 7 10S 39 18W
Juiz de Fora, Brazil 101 21 43S 43 19W
Juliaca, Peru 100 15 25S 70 10W
Julianehåb, Green. 89 60 43N 46 0W
Jullundur, India 58 31 20N 75 40 E
Jundiaí, Brazil 102 24 30S 47 0W
Juneau, U.S.A. 88 58 20N 134 20W
Jura, U.K. 20 56 0N 5 50W
Jura, Mts., Europe 42 46 40N 6 5 E
Jura, Paps of, U.K. 20 55 55N 6 0W
Jura, Sd. of, U.K. 20 55 57N 5 45W
Jurby Hd., U.K. 18 54 23N 4 31W
Juruá →, Brazil 100 2 37S 65 44W
Jutland = Jylland, Den. 45 56 25N 9 30 E
Jylland, Den. 45 56 25N 9 30 E
Jyväskylä, Fin. 44 62 14N 25 50 E

K

Kābul, Afg. 57 34 28N 69 11 E
Kabwe, Zam. 81 14 30S 28 29 E
Kaduna, Nig. 78 10 30N 7 21 E
Kaesŏng, N. Kor. 61 37 58N 126 35 E
Kagoshima, Jap. 62 31 35N 130 33 E
Kaifeng, China 61 34 49N 114 30 E
Kaiserslautern, W. Ger. 36 49 30N 7 43 E
Kaitaia, N.Z. 71 35 8S 173 17 E
Kajaani, Fin. 44 64 17N 27 46 E
Kakinada, India 59 16 57N 82 11 E
Kalahari, Africa 81 24 0S 21 30 E
Kalamazoo, U.S.A. 92 42 20N 85 35W
Kalemie, Zaïre 80 5 55S 29 9 E
Kalgoorlie-Boulder, Austral. 66 30 40S 121 22 E
Kalimantan, Indon. 63 0 0 114 0 E
Kalinin, U.S.S.R. 46 56 55N 35 55 E
Kaliningrad, U.S.S.R. 46 54 42N 20 32 E
Kaluga, U.S.S.R. 46 54 35N 36 10 E
Kamchatka Pen., U.S.S.R. 49 57 0N 160 0 E
Kamensk Uralskiy, U.S.S.R. 48 56 25N 62 2 E
Kames, U.K. 20 55 53N 5 15W
Kamina, Zaïre 80 8 45S 25 0 E
Kamloops, Canada 88 50 40N 120 20W
Kampala, Uganda 80 0 20N 32 30 E
Kampuchea = Cambodia ■, Asia 63 12 15N 105 0 E
Kananga, Zaïre 80 5 55S 22 18 E
Kanazawa, Jap. 62 36 30N 136 38 E
Kanchenjunga, Nepal 59 27 50N 88 10 E
Kandy, Sri L. 58 7 18N 80 43 E
Kangaroo I., Austral. 67 35 45S 137 0 E
Kanin, Pen., U.S.S.R. 46 68 0N 45 0 E
Kankan, Guin. 78 10 23N 9 15W
Kano, Nig. 78 12 2N 8 30 E
Kanpur, India 58 26 28N 80 20 E
Kansas □, U.S.A. 90 38 40N 98 0W
Kansas City, Kans., U.S.A. 91 39 0N 94 40W
Kansas City, Mo., U.S.A. 91 39 3N 94 30W
Kansk, U.S.S.R. 49 56 20N 95 37 E
Kanturk, Ire. 25 52 10N 8 55W
Kaohsiung, Taiwan 61 22 35N 120 16 E
Kaolack, Sene. 78 14 5N 16 8W
Kara Bogaz Gol, Zaliv, U.S.S.R. 47 41 0N 53 30 E
Kara Kalpak A.S.S.R. □, U.S.S.R. 48 43 0N 60 0 E
Kara Kum, U.S.S.R. 48 39 30N 60 0 E
Kara Sea, U.S.S.R. 48 75 0N 70 0 E
Karachi, Pak. 58 24 53N 67 0 E
Karaganda, U.S.S.R. 48 49 50N 73 10 E
Karakoram Ra., Asia 58 35 30N 77 0 E
Karbalā, Iraq 56 32 36N 44 3 E
Karl-Marx-Stadt, E. Ger. 42 50 50N 12 55 E
Karlskrona, Swed. 45 56 10N 15 35 E
Karlsruhe, W. Ger. 42 49 3N 8 23 E
Karlstad, Swed. 45 59 23N 13 30 E
Karratha, Austral. 66 20 53S 116 40 E
Karsakpay, U.S.S.R. 48 47 55N 66 40 E
Karshi, U.S.S.R. 48 38 53N 65 48 E
Kāshān, Iran 56 34 5N 51 30 E
Kashi, China 60 39 30N 76 2 E
Kassala, Sudan 79 16 0N 36 0 E
Kassel, W. Ger. 42 51 19N 9 32 E
Katmandu, Nepal 59 27 45N 85 20 E
Katoomba, Austral. 70 33 41S 150 19 E
Katowice, Pol. 43 50 17N 19 5 E
Katrine, L., U.K. 20 56 15N 4 30W
Katsina, Nig. 78 13 0N 7 32 E
Kattegatt, Den. 45 57 0N 11 20 E
Kauai, U.S.A. 90 22 0N 159 30W
Kaunas, U.S.S.R. 46 54 54N 23 54 E
Kaválla, Greece 41 40 57N 24 28 E
Kawagoe, Jap. 62 35 55N 139 29 E
Kawasaki, Jap. 62 35 35N 139 42 E
Kawthoolei □, Burma 59 18 0N 97 30 E
Kayes, Mali 78 14 25N 11 30W
Kayseri, Turk. 47 38 45N 35 30 E
Kazakhstan □, U.S.S.R. 48 50 0N 70 0 E
Kazan, U.S.S.R. 46 55 48N 49 3 E
Kea, U.K. 16 50 13N 5 4W
Keady, U.K. 24 54 15N 6 42W
Keal, Loch na, U.K. 20 56 30N 6 5W
Kecskemét, Hung. 43 46 57N 19 42 E
Kediri, Indon. 63 7 51S 112 1 E
Keelby, U.K. 19 53 34N 0 15W
Keele, U.K. 18 53 0N 2 17W
Keeper Hill, Ire. 25 52 46N 8 17W
Keewatin, Canada 88 49 46N 94 34W
Kefallinía, Greece 41 38 20N 20 30 E
Keflavík, Ice. 44 64 2N 22 35W
Kegworth, U.K. 14 52 50N 1 17W
Keighley, U.K. 18 53 52N 1 54W
Keith, U.K. 23 57 33N 2 58W
Keld, U.K. 18 54 24N 2 11W
Kellerberrin, Austral. 66 31 36S 117 38 E
Kells = Ceanannus Mor, Ire. 24 53 42N 6 53W
Kells, Rhinns of, U.K. 20 55 9N 4 22W
Kelowna, Canada 88 49 50N 119 25W
Kelsale, U.K. 15 52 15N 1 30 E
Kelsall, U.K. 18 53 14N 2 44W
Kelso, U.K. 21 55 36N 2 27W
Kelvedon, U.K. 15 51 50N 0 43 E
Kemble, U.K. 14 51 40N 2 1W
Kemerovo, U.S.S.R. 48 55 20N 86 5 E
Kemi, Fin. 44 65 44N 24 34 E
Kempsey, U.K. 14 52 8N 2 11W
Kempston, U.K. 15 52 7N 0 30W
Ken, L., U.K. 21 55 0N 4 8W
Kendal, U.K. 18 54 19N 2 44W
Kenilworth, U.K. 14 52 22N 1 35W
Kenitra, Mor. 78 34 15N 6 40W
Kenmare, Ire. 25 51 52N 9 35W
Kenmare →, Ire. 25 51 40N 10 0W
Kennet →, U.K. 14 51 24N 0 58W
Kenninghall, U.K. 15 52 26N 1 0 E
Kenora, Canada 88 49 47N 94 29W
Kent □, U.K. 15 51 12N 0 40 E
Kentisbeare, U.K. 16 50 51N 3 18W
Kenton, U.K. 16 50 37N 3 28W
Kentucky □, U.S.A. 91 37 20N 85 0W
Kenya ■, Africa 80 1 0N 38 0 E
Kerala □, India 58 11 0N 76 15 E
Kerch, U.S.S.R. 47 45 20N 36 20 E
Kérkira, Greece 41 39 38N 19 50 E
Kermān, Iran 57 30 15N 57 1 E
Kerrera I., U.K. 20 56 24N 5 32W
Kerry □, Ire. 25 52 7N 9 35W
Kerry Hd., Ire. 25 52 26N 9 56W
Kessingland, U.K. 15 52 25N 1 41 E
Keswick, U.K. 18 54 35N 3 9W
Ketchikan, U.S.A. 88 55 25N 131 40W
Kettering, U.K. 15 52 24N 0 44W
Kettle Ness, U.K. 19 54 32N 0 41W
Kettlewell, U.K. 18 54 8N 2 2W
Keweenaw Pen., U.S.A. 92 47 30N 88 0W
Kexby, U.K. 19 53 21N 0 41W
Key West, U.S.A. 91 24 33N 82 0W
Keyingham, U.K. 19 53 42N 0 7W
Keymer, U.K. 15 50 55N 0 5W
Keynsham, U.K. 14 51 25N 2 30W
Keyworth, U.K. 14 52 52N 1 8W
Khabarovsk, U.S.S.R. 49 48 30N 135 5 E
Khaniá, Greece 41 35 30N 24 4 E
Kharagpur, India 59 22 20N 87 25 E
Kharkov, U.S.S.R. 47 49 58N 36 20 E
Khartoum, Sudan 79 15 31N 32 35 E
Khaskovo, Bulg. 41 41 56N 25 30 E
Kherson, U.S.S.R. 47 46 35N 32 35 E
Khíos, I., Greece 41 38 20N 26 0 E
Khorrāmshahr, Iran 56 30 29N 48 15 E
Khouribga, Mor. 78 32 58N 6 57W
Khulna, Bangla. 59 22 45N 89 34 E
Khulna □, Bangla. 59 22 25N 89 35 E
Khurasan, Iran 57 34 0N 57 0 E
Kibworth Beauchamp, U.K. 15 52 33N 0 59W
Kicking Horse Pass, Canada 88 51 28N 116 16W
Kidderminster, U.K. 14 52 24N 2 13W
Kidlington, U.K. 14 51 49N 1 18W
Kidsgrove, U.K. 18 53 6N 2 15W
Kidstones, U.K. 18 54 15N 2 2W
Kidwelly, U.K. 17 51 44N 4 20W
Kiel, W. Ger. 42 54 16N 10 8 E
Kielce, Pol. 43 50 52N 20 42 E
Kielder, U.K. 21 55 14N 2 35W
Kiev, U.S.S.R. 47 50 30N 30 28 E
Kigali, Rwanda 80 1 59S 30 4 E
Kigoma-Ujiji, Tanz. 80 4 55S 29 36 E
Kikládhes, Greece 41 37 20N 24 30 E
Kikwit, Zaïre 80 5 5S 18 45 E
Kilbirnie, U.K. 20 55 46N 4 42W
Kilbrannan Sd., U.K. 20 55 40N 5 23W
Kilcreggan, U.K. 20 55 59N 4 50W
Kildare, Ire. 25 53 10N 6 50W
Kildare □, Ire. 25 53 10N 6 50W
Kildonan, U.K. 23 58 10N 3 50W
Kilfinan, U.K. 20 55 57N 5 19W
Kilham, U.K. 19 54 4N 0 22W
Kilimanjaro, Tanz. 80 3 7S 37 20 E
Kilkee, Ire. 25 52 41N 9 40W
Kilkeel, U.K. 24 54 4N 6 0W
Kilkenny, Ire. 25 52 40N 7 17W
Kilkenny □, Ire. 25 52 35N 7 15W
Kilkhampton, U.K. 16 50 53N 4 30W
Kilkieran B., Ire. 25 53 18N 9 45W
Killala, Ire. 24 54 13N 9 12W
Killala B., Ire. 24 54 20N 9 12W
Killaloe, Ire. 25 52 48N 8 28W
Killarney, Ire. 25 52 2N 9 30W
Killarney, Lakes of, Ire. 25 52 0N 9 30W
Killary Harbour, Ire. 24 53 38N 9 52W
Killchianaig, U.K. 20 56 2N 5 48W
Killean, U.K. 20 55 38N 5 40W
Killiecrankie, Pass of, U.K. 23 56 44N 3 46W
Killin, U.K. 20 56 28N 4 20W
Killinghall, U.K. 19 54 1N 1 33W
Killybegs, Ire. 24 54 38N 8 26W
Kilmacolm, U.K. 20 55 54N 4 39W
Kilmarnock, U.K. 20 55 36N 4 30W
Kilmartin, U.K. 20 56 8N 5 29W
Kilmaurs, U.K. 20 55 37N 4 33W
Kilmelford, U.K. 20 56 16N 5 30W
Kilninver, U.K. 20 56 20N 5 30W
Kilrenny, U.K. 21 56 15N 2 40W
Kilrush, Ire. 25 52 39N 9 30W
Kilsby, U.K. 14 52 20N 1 11W
Kilsyth, U.K. 21 55 58N 4 3W
Kilwinning, U.K. 20 55 40N 4 41W
Kimberley, Austral. 66 16 20S 127 0 E
Kimberley, S. Afr. 81 28 43S 24 46 E
Kimbolton, U.K. 15 52 17N 0 23W
Kincardine, U.K. 21 56 4N 3 43W
Kindu, Zaïre 80 2 55S 25 50 E
Kineton, U.K. 14 52 10N 1 30W
King Frederick VI Coast, Green. 89 63 0N 43 0W
King Sd., Austral. 66 16 50S 123 20 E
Kingarth, U.K. 20 55 45N 5 2W
Kinghorn, U.K. 21 56 4N 3 10W
King's Lynn, U.K. 15 52 45N 0 25 E
King's Sutton, U.K. 14 52 1N 1 16W
King's Worthy, U.K. 14 51 6N 1 18W
Kingsbarns, U.K. 21 56 18N 2 40W
Kingsbridge, U.K. 16 50 17N 3 46W
Kingsbury, U.K. 14 52 33N 1 41W
Kingscourt, Ire. 24 53 55N 6 48W
Kingskerswell, U.K. 16 50 30N 3 34W
Kingsland, U.K. 14 52 15N 2 49W
Kingsteignton, U.K. 16 50 32N 3 35W
Kingston, Canada 92 44 14N 76 30W
Kingston, Jam. 94 18 0N 76 50W
Kingston, U.K. 14 51 18N 1 40W
Kingston-upon-Hull, U.K. 19 53 45N 0 20W
Kingston-upon-Thames, U.K. 15 51 23N 0 20W
Kingstown, St. Vinc. 94 13 10N 61 10W
Kingswear, U.K. 16 50 21N 3 33W
Kingswood, U.K. 14 51 26N 2 31W
Kington, U.K. 14 52 12N 3 2W
Kingussie, U.K. 23 57 5N 4 2W
Kinlochewe, U.K. 22 57 37N 5 20W
Kinlochleven, U.K. 22 56 42N 4 59W
Kinnairds Hd., U.K. 23 57 40N 2 0W
Kinneret, Lake, Isr. 57 32 45N 35 35 E
Kinross, U.K. 21 56 13N 3 25W
Kinsale, Ire. 25 51 42N 8 31W
Kinsale, Old Hd. of, Ire. 25 51 37N 8 32W
Kinshasa, Zaïre 80 4 20S 15 15 E
Kintyre, U.K. 20 55 30N 5 35W
Kintyre, Mull of, U.K. 20 55 17N 5 55W
Kippen, U.K. 20 56 8N 4 12W
Kippure, Ire. 25 53 11N 6 23W
Kirensk, U.S.S.R. 49 57 50N 107 55 E
Kirgizia □, U.S.S.R. 48 42 0N 75 0 E
Kirgiziya Steppe, U.S.S.R. 47 50 0N 55 0 E
Kiribati ■, Pac. Oc. 65 1 0N 176 0 E
Kirk Michael, U.K. 18 54 17N 4 35W
Kirkbean, U.K. 21 54 56N 3 35W
Kirkbride, U.K. 18 54 54N 3 13W
Kirkburton, U.K. 19 53 36N 1 42W
Kirkby, U.K. 18 53 29N 2 54W
Kirkby-in-Ashfield, U.K. 19 53 6N 1 15W
Kirkby Lonsdale, U.K. 18 54 13N 2 36W
Kirkby Malzeard, U.K. 19 54 10N 1 38W
Kirkby Stephen, U.K. 18 54 27N 2 23W
Kirkby Thore, U.K. 18 54 38N 2 34W
Kirkbymoorside, U.K. 19 54 16N 0 56W
Kirkcaldy, U.K. 21 56 7N 3 10W
Kirkcolm, U.K. 20 54 59N 5 4W
Kirkconnel, U.K. 21 55 23N 4 0W
Kirkcowan, U.K. 20 54 53N 4 38W
Kirkcudbright, U.K. 21 54 50N 4 3W
Kirkcudbright B., U.K. 21 54 46N 4 0W
Kirkham, U.K. 18 53 47N 2 52W
Kirkinner, U.K. 20 54 49N 4 28W
Kirkintilloch, U.K. 21 55 57N 4 10W
Kirkland Lake, Canada 92 48 9N 80 2W
Kirkliston, U.K. 21 55 55N 3 27W
Kirkoswald, U.K. 18 54 46N 2 41W
Kirkoswold, U.K. 20 55 19N 4 48W
Kirkstone P., U.K. 18 54 29N 2 55W
Kirkūk, Iraq 56 35 30N 44 21 E
Kirkwall, U.K. 23 58 59N 2 59W
Kirkwhelpington, U.K. 21 55 9N 2 0W
Kirov, U.S.S.R. 46 58 35N 49 40 E
Kirovabad, U.S.S.R. 47 40 45N 46 20 E
Kirovograd, U.S.S.R. 47 48 35N 32 20 E
Kirovsk, U.S.S.R. 46 48 35N 38 30 E
Kirriemuir, U.K. 23 56 41N 3 0W
Kirtling, U.K. 15 52 11N 0 27 E
Kirtlington, U.K. 14 51 54N 1 9W
Kirton, U.K. 19 52 56N 0 3W
Kirton-in-Lindsey, U.K. 19 53 29N 0 35W
Kiruna, Swed. 44 67 52N 20 15 E
Kisangani, Zaïre 80 0 35N 25 15 E
Kishinev, U.S.S.R. 47 47 0N 28 50 E
Kismayu, Som. 73 0 22S 42 32 E
Kisumu, Kenya 80 0 3S 34 45 E
Kitakyūshū, Jap. 62 33 50N 130 50 E
Kitchener, Canada 92 43 27N 80 29W
Kíthira, Greece 41 36 9N 23 0 E
Kitikmeot □, Canada 88 70 0N 110 0W
Kitimat, Canada 88 54 3N 128 38W
Kitwe, Zam. 81 12 54S 28 13 E
Klagenfurt, Austria 42 46 38N 14 20 E
Klerksdorp, S. Afr. 81 26 51S 26 38 E
Klondike, Canada 88 64 0N 139 26W
Knapdale, U.K. 20 55 55N 5 30W
Knaresborough, U.K. 19 54 1N 1 29W
Knebworth, U.K. 15 51 52N 0 11W
Knighton, U.K. 17 52 21N 3 2W
Knockmealdown Mts., Ire. 25 52 16N 8 0W
Knossos, Greece 41 35 16N 25 10 E
Knott End, U.K. 18 53 55N 3 0W
Knottingley, U.K. 19 53 42N 1 15W
Knowle, U.K. 14 52 23N 1 43W
Knoxville, U.S.A. 91 35 58N 83 57W
Knutsford, U.K. 18 53 18N 2 22W
Kōbe, Jap. 62 34 45N 135 10 E
København = Copenhagen, Den. 45 55 41N 12 34 E
Koblenz, W. Ger. 36 50 21N 7 36 E
Kodiak I., U.S.A. 88 57 30N 152 45W
Koforidua, Ghana 78 6 3N 0 17W
Kokand, U.S.S.R. 48 40 30N 70 57 E
Kokchetav, U.S.S.R. 48 53 20N 69 25 E
Kokkola, Fin. 44 63 50N 23 8 E
Kola Pen., U.S.S.R. 46 67 30N 38 0 E
Kolding, Den. 45 55 30N 9 29 E
Kolguyev, I., U.S.S.R. 46 69 20N 48 30 E
Kolomna, U.S.S.R. 46 55 8N 38 45 E
Kolwezi, Zaïre 80 10 40S 25 25 E
Kolyma →, U.S.S.R. 49 69 30N 161 0 E
Kolyma Ra., U.S.S.R. 49 63 0N 157 0 E
Komandorskiye, Is., U.S.S.R. 49 55 0N 167 0 E
Komsomolets I., U.S.S.R. 49 80 30N 95 0 E
Komsomolsk, U.S.S.R. 49 50 30N 137 0 E
Konya, Turk. 47 37 52N 32 35 E
Kópavogur, Ice. 44 64 6N 21 55W
Korce, Alb. 41 40 37N 20 50 E
Korea, North ■, Asia 61 40 0N 127 0 E
Korea, South ■, Asia 61 36 0N 128 0 E
Korea Strait, Asia 61 34 0N 129 30 E
Kōriyama, Jap. 62 37 24N 140 23 E
Korla, China 60 41 45N 86 4 E
Kortrijk, Belg. 36 50 50N 3 17 E
Koryak Range, U.S.S.R. 49 61 0N 171 0 E
Kos, Greece 41 36 50N 27 15 E
Košice, Czech. 43 48 42N 21 15 E
Kōstī, Sudan 79 13 8N 32 43 E
Kostroma, U.S.S.R. 46 57 50N 40 58 E
Kota, India 58 25 14N 75 49 E
Kota Baharu, Malay. 63 6 7N 102 14 E
Kota Kinabalu, Malay. 63 6 0N 116 4 E
Kotka, Fin. 45 60 28N 26 58 E
Kra, Isthmus of, Thai. 63 10 15N 99 30 E
Kragujevac, Yug. 41 44 2N 20 56 E
Krakatau, Indon. 63 6 10S 105 20 E
Kraków, Pol. 43 50 4N 19 57 E
Krasnodar, U.S.S.R. 47 45 5N 39 0 E
Krasnoturinsk, U.S.S.R. 46 59 46N 60 12 E
Krasnovodsk, U.S.S.R. 48 40 0N 52 52 E
Krasnoyarsk, U.S.S.R. 49 56 8N 93 0 E
Krefeld, W. Ger. 36 51 20N 6 32 E
Kremenchug, U.S.S.R. 47 49 5N 33 25 E
Krishna →, India 59 15 57N 80 59 E
Kristiansand, Nor. 45 58 9N 8 1 E
Kristianstad, Swed. 45 56 2N 14 9 E
Kristiansund, Nor. 44 63 7N 7 45 E
Krivoy Rog, U.S.S.R. 47 47 51N 33 20 E
Kroonstad, S. Afr. 81 27 43S 27 19 E
Krung Thep = Bangkok, Thai. 63 13 45N 100 35 E
Kruševac, Yug. 41 43 35N 21 28 E
Kuala Lumpur, Malay. 63 3 9N 101 41 E

Kuala Trengganu, *Malay.* **63** 5 20N 103 8 E
Kuangchou = Guangzhou, *China* **61** 23 5N 113 10 E
Kuantan, *Malay.* **63** 3 49N 103 20 E
Kucing, *Malay.* **63** 1 33N 110 25 E
Kueiyang = Guiyang, *China* **60** 26 32N 106 40 E
Kumanovo, *Yug.* **41** 42 9N 21 42 E
Kumasi, *Ghana* **78** 6 41N 1 38W
Kunlun Shan, *Asia* **60** 36 0N 86 30 E
Kunming, *China* **60** 25 1N 102 41 E
Kuopio, *Fin.* **44** 62 53N 27 35 E
Kura ➝, *U.S.S.R.* **47** 39 50N 49 20 E
Kurashiki, *Jap.* **62** 34 40N 133 50 E
Kure, *Jap.* **62** 34 14N 132 32 E
Kurgan, *U.S.S.R.* **48** 55 26N 65 18 E
Kuria Maria Is., *Ind. Oc.* **57** 17 30N 55 58 E
Kuril Is., *U.S.S.R.* **49** 45 0N 150 0 E
Kurnool, *India* **58** 15 45N 78 0 E
Kurri Kurri, *Austral.* **70** 32 50S 151 28 E
Kursk, *U.S.S.R.* **46** 51 42N 36 11 E
Kurume, *Jap.* **62** 33 15N 130 30 E
Kushiro, *Jap.* **62** 43 0N 144 25 E
Kustanay, *U.S.S.R.* **48** 53 10N 63 35 E
Kütahya, *Turk.* **47** 39 30N 30 2 E
Kutaisi, *U.S.S.R.* **47** 42 19N 42 40 E
Kutch, Gulf of, *India* **58** 22 50N 69 15 E
Kutch, Rann of, *India* **58** 24 0N 70 0 E
Kuwait, *Kuw.* **56** 29 30N 47 30 E
Kuwait ■, *Asia* **56** 29 30N 47 30 E
Kuybyshev, *U.S.S.R.* **46** 53 8N 50 6 E
Kwangju, *S. Kor.* **61** 35 9N 126 54 E
Kyle, *U.K.* **20** 55 32N 4 25W
Kyle of Lochalsh, *U.K.* **22** 57 17N 5 43W
Kyōto, *Jap.* **62** 35 0N 135 45 E
Kyūshū, *Jap.* **62** 33 0N 131 0 E
Kzyl-Orda, *U.S.S.R.* **48** 44 48N 65 28 E

L

Labe = Elbe ➝, *Ger.* **42** 53 50N 9 0 E
Labé, *Guin.* **78** 11 24N 12 16W
Labrador, Coast of □, *Canada* **89** 53 20N 61 0W
Labrador City, *Canada* **89** 52 57N 66 55W
Laccadive Is. = Lakshadweep Is., *Ind. Oc.* **51** 10 0N 72 30 E
Laceby, *U.K.* **19** 53 32N 0 10W
Lachlan ➝, *Austral.* **70** 34 22S 143 55 E
Lacock, *U.K.* **14** 51 24N 2 8W
Ladock, *U.K.* **16** 50 19N 4 58W
Ladoga, L., *U.S.S.R.* **46** 61 15N 30 30 E
Ladybank, *U.K.* **21** 56 16N 3 8W
Lafayette, *U.S.A.* **90** 30 18N 92 0W
Lagan ➝, *U.K.* **24** 54 35N 5 55W
Lagg, *U.K.* **20** 55 51N 5 50W
Laggan B., *U.K.* **20** 55 40N 6 20W
Lagos, *Nig.* **78** 6 25N 3 27 E
Lagos, *Port.* **37** 37 5N 8 41W
Lahore, *Pak.* **58** 31 32N 74 22 E
Lahti, *Fin.* **45** 60 58N 25 40 E
Lairg, *U.K.* **23** 58 1N 4 24W
Lake Charles, *U.S.A.* **90** 30 15N 93 10W
Lake District, *U.K.* **18** 54 30N 3 10W
Lakenheath, *U.K.* **15** 52 25N 0 30 E
Lakewood, *U.S.A.* **92** 41 28N 81 50W
Lakshadweep Is., *Ind. Oc.* **51** 10 0N 72 30 E
Lambay I., *Ire.* **24** 53 30N 6 0W
Lamberhurst, *U.K.* **15** 51 5N 0 21 E
Lambeth, *U.K.* **15** 51 27N 0 7W
Lambley, *U.K.* **21** 54 56N 2 30W
Lambourn, *U.K.* **14** 51 31N 1 31W
Lamlash, *U.K.* **20** 55 32N 5 8W
Lammermuir, *U.K.* **21** 55 50N 2 25W
Lammermuir Hills, *U.K.* **21** 55 50N 2 40W
Lampeter, *U.K.* **17** 52 6N 4 6W
Lanark, *U.K.* **21** 55 40N 3 48W
Lancashire □, *U.K.* **18** 53 40N 2 30W
Lancaster, *U.K.* **18** 54 3N 2 48W
Lancaster Sd., *Canada* **89** 74 13N 84 0W
Lanchester, *U.K.* **19** 54 50N 1 44W
Lancing, *U.K.* **15** 50 49N 0 19W
Landkey, *U.K.* **16** 51 2N 4 0W
Land's End, *U.K.* **16** 50 4N 5 43W
Langholm, *U.K.* **21** 55 9N 2 59W
Langness, *U.K.* **18** 54 3N 4 37W
Langport, *U.K.* **14** 51 2N 2 51W
Langstrothdale Chase, *U.K.* **18** 54 14N 2 13W
Langtoft, *U.K.* **15** 52 42N 0 19W
Langtree, *U.K.* **16** 50 55N 4 11W
Lansing, *U.S.A.* **92** 42 47N 84 40W
Lanzhou, *China* **60** 36 1N 103 52 E
Laoag, *Phil.* **63** 18 7N 120 34 E
Laois □, *Ire.* **25** 53 0N 7 20W
Laos ■, *Asia* **63** 17 45N 105 0 E
Lapford, *U.K.* **16** 50 52N 3 49W
Lapland, *Europe* **44** 68 7N 24 0 E
Laptev Sea, *U.S.S.R.* **49** 76 0N 125 0 E
Larbert, *U.K.* **21** 56 2N 3 50W
Laredo, *U.S.A.* **90** 27 34N 99 29W
Largs, *U.K.* **20** 55 48N 4 51W
Lárisa, *Greece* **41** 39 49N 22 28 E
Larkhall, *U.K.* **21** 55 44N 4 0W
Larne, *U.K.* **24** 54 52N 5 50W
Las Palmas, *Can. Is.* **78** 28 7N 15 26W
Las Vegas, *U.S.A.* **90** 36 10N 115 5W
Laskill, *U.K.* **19** 54 19N 1 6W
Lasswade, *U.K.* **21** 55 53N 3 8W
Latakia, *Syria* **56** 35 30N 35 45 E
Latina, *It.* **40** 41 26N 12 53 E
Latvia □, *U.S.S.R.* **46** 56 50N 24 0 E
Lauder, *U.K.* **21** 55 43N 2 45W
Lauderdale, *U.K.* **21** 55 43N 2 44W
Launceston, *Austral.* **67** 41 24S 147 8 E
Launceston, *U.K.* **16** 50 38N 4 21W
Laune ➝, *Ire.* **25** 52 5N 9 40W
Laurencekirk, *U.K.* **23** 56 50N 2 30W
Laurentian Plateau, *Canada* **82** 52 0N 70 0W
Laurieston, *U.K.* **21** 54 57N 4 2W
Lausanne, *Switz.* **42** 46 32N 6 38 E
Laval, *Fr.* **34** 48 4N 0 48W
Lavendon, *U.K.* **15** 52 11N 0 39W
Lavenham, *U.K.* **15** 52 7N 0 48 E
Lawers, *U.K.* **21** 56 31N 4 9W
Lawrence, *U.S.A.* **93** 42 40N 71 9W
Laxey, *U.K.* **18** 54 15N 4 23W
Laxfield, *U.K.* **15** 52 18N 1 23 E
Laxford, L., *U.K.* **22** 58 25N 5 10W
Lazonby, *U.K.* **18** 54 45N 2 42W
Lea, *U.K.* **19** 53 22N 0 45W
Lea ➝, *U.K.* **15** 51 30N 0 10W
Leadenham, *U.K.* **19** 53 5N 0 33W
Leadhills, *U.K.* **21** 55 25N 3 47W
Leamington, *U.K.* **14** 52 18N 1 32W
Leatherhead, *U.K.* **15** 51 18N 0 20W
Lebanon ■, *Asia* **56** 34 0N 36 0 E
Lecce, *It.* **41** 40 20N 18 10 E
Lechlade, *U.K.* **14** 51 42N 1 40W
Ledbury, *U.K.* **14** 52 3N 2 25W
Leduc, *Canada* **88** 53 15N 113 30W
Lee, *U.K.* **14** 50 47N 1 11W
Lee ➝, *Ire.* **25** 51 50N 8 30W
Leeds, *U.K.* **19** 53 48N 1 34W
Leek, *U.K.* **18** 53 7N 2 2W
Leer, *W. Ger.* **36** 53 13N 7 29 E
Leeton, *Austral.* **70** 34 33S 146 23 E
Leeuwarden, *Neth.* **36** 53 15N 5 48 E
Leeuwin, C., *Austral.* **66** 34 20S 115 9 E
Leghorn, *It.* **40** 43 32N 10 18 E
Legnica, *Pol.* **42** 51 12N 16 10 E
Leicester, *U.K.* **14** 52 39N 1 9W
Leicester □, *U.K.* **14** 52 40N 1 10W
Leiden, *Neth.* **36** 52 9N 4 30 E
Leigh, *Gr. Manchester, U.K.* **18** 53 29N 2 31W
Leigh, *Hereford & Worcs., U.K.* **14** 52 10N 2 21W
Leighton Buzzard, *U.K.* **15** 51 55N 0 39W
Leinster □, *Ire.* **25** 53 0N 7 10W
Leinster, Mt., *Ire.* **25** 52 38N 6 47W
Leintwardine, *U.K.* **14** 52 22N 2 51W
Leipzig, *E. Ger.* **42** 51 20N 12 23 E
Leiston, *U.K.* **15** 52 13N 1 35 E
Leith, *U.K.* **21** 55 59N 3 10W
Leith Hill, *U.K.* **15** 51 10N 0 23W
Leitholm, *U.K.* **21** 55 42N 2 16W
Leitrim, *Ire.* **24** 54 0N 8 5W
Leitrim □, *Ire.* **24** 54 8N 8 0W
Lek ➝, *Neth.* **36** 51 54N 4 35 E
Lelant, *U.K.* **16** 50 11N 5 26W
Lelystad, *Neth.* **36** 52 30N 5 25 E
Lena ➝, *U.S.S.R.* **49** 72 52N 126 40 E
Lendalfoot, *U.K.* **20** 55 12N 4 55W
Lenham, *U.K.* **15** 51 14N 0 44 E
Leninakan, *U.S.S.R.* **47** 40 47N 43 50 E
Leningrad, *U.S.S.R.* **46** 59 55N 30 20 E
Leninsk-Kuznetskiy, *U.S.S.R.* **48** 54 44N 86 10 E
Lennox Hills, *U.K.* **20** 56 3N 4 12W
Lennoxtown, *U.K.* **20** 55 58N 4 14W
Lens, *Fr.* **34** 50 26N 2 50 E
Leominster, *U.K.* **14** 52 15N 2 43W
León, *Mex.* **94** 21 7N 101 40W
León, *Sp.* **37** 42 38N 5 34W
Lérida, *Sp.* **37** 41 37N 0 39 E
Lerwick, *U.K.* **22** 60 10N 1 10W
Lesbos, I. = Lésvos, *Greece* **41** 39 10N 26 20 E
Lesbury, *U.K.* **21** 55 25N 1 37W
Leskovac, *Yug.* **41** 43 0N 21 58 E
Leslie, *U.K.* **21** 56 12N 3 12W
Lesmahagow, *U.K.* **21** 55 38N 3 55W
Lesotho ■, *Africa* **81** 29 40S 28 0 E
Lésvos, *Greece* **41** 39 10N 26 20 E
Leswalt, *U.K.* **20** 54 56N 5 6W
Letchworth, *U.K.* **15** 51 58N 0 13W
Lethbridge, *Canada* **88** 49 45N 112 45W
Letterkenny, *Ire.* **24** 54 57N 7 42W
Leuchars, *U.K.* **21** 56 23N 2 53W
Leven, *Fife, U.K.* **21** 56 12N 3 0W
Leven, *Humberside, U.K.* **19** 53 54N 0 18W
Leven ➝, *U.K.* **19** 54 27N 1 15W
Leven, L., *U.K.* **21** 56 12N 3 22W
Leverburgh, *U.K.* **22** 57 46N 7 0W
Leverkusen, *W. Ger.* **36** 51 2N 6 59 E
Lewes, *U.K.* **15** 50 53N 0 2 E
Lewis, *U.K.* **22** 58 10N 6 40W
Lewis, Butt of, *U.K.* **22** 58 30N 6 12W
Lewisham, *U.K.* **15** 51 27N 0 1W
Lexington, *U.S.A.* **92** 38 6N 84 30W
Leyburn, *U.K.* **19** 54 19N 1 50W
Leyland, *U.K.* **18** 53 41N 2 42W
Leysdown on Sea, *U.K.* **15** 51 23N 0 57 E
Lhasa, *China* **60** 29 50N 91 3 E
Liaodong, Gulf of, *China* **61** 40 20N 121 10 E
Liaoning □, *China* **61** 41 40N 122 30 E
Liaoyang, *China* **61** 41 15N 123 10 E
Liaoyüan, *China* **61** 42 55N 125 10 E
Liberia ■, *W. Afr.* **78** 6 30N 9 30W
Libreville, *Gabon* **80** 0 25N 9 26 E
Libya ■, *N. Afr.* **79** 27 0N 17 0 E
Libyan Desert, *Africa* **79** 25 0N 25 0 E
Lichfield, *U.K.* **14** 52 40N 1 50W
Lichinga, *Mozam.* **81** 13 13S 35 11 E
Liechtenstein ■, *Europe* **42** 47 8N 9 35 E
Liège, *Belg.* **36** 50 38N 5 35 E
Liepaja, *U.S.S.R.* **46** 56 30N 21 0 E
Liffey ➝, *Ire.* **25** 53 21N 6 20W
Lifford, *Ire.* **24** 54 50N 7 30W
Ligurian Sea, *It.* **40** 43 20N 9 0 E
Likasi, *Zaïre* **80** 10 55S 26 48 E
Lille, *Fr.* **34** 50 38N 3 3 E
Lille Bælt, *Den.* **45** 55 20N 9 45 E
Lillehammer, *Nor.* **45** 61 8N 10 30 E
Lilleshall, *U.K.* **14** 52 45N 2 22W
Lilongwe, *Malawi* **81** 14 0S 33 48 E
Lima, *Peru* **100** 12 0S 77 0W
Limassol, *Cyprus* **47** 34 42N 33 1 E
Limavady, *U.K.* **24** 55 3N 6 58W
Limavady □, *U.K.* **24** 55 0N 6 55W
Limburg □, *Neth.* **36** 51 20N 5 55 E
Limerick, *Ire.* **25** 52 40N 8 38W
Limerick □, *Ire.* **25** 52 30N 8 50W
Límnos, *Greece* **41** 39 50N 25 5 E
Limoges, *Fr.* **35** 45 50N 1 15 E
Limpopo ➝, *Mozam.* **81** 25 15S 33 30 E
Limpsfield, *U.K.* **15** 51 15N 0 1 E
Linares, *Sp.* **37** 38 10N 3 40W
Lincluden, *U.K.* **21** 55 5N 3 40W
Lincoln, *U.K.* **19** 53 14N 0 32W
Lincoln, *U.S.A.* **90** 40 50N 96 42W
Lincoln □, *U.K.* **19** 53 14N 0 32W
Lincoln Wolds, *U.K.* **19** 53 20N 0 5W
Lindale, *U.K.* **18** 54 14N 2 54W
Lingfield, *U.K.* **15** 51 11N 0 1W
Linkinhorne, *U.K.* **16** 50 31N 4 22W
Linköping, *Swed.* **45** 58 28N 15 36 E
Linlithgow, *U.K.* **21** 55 58N 3 38W
Linnhe, L., *U.K.* **20** 56 36N 5 25W
Linslade, *U.K.* **15** 51 55N 0 40W
Linton, *U.K.* **15** 52 6N 0 19 E
Linxia, *China* **60** 35 36N 103 10 E
Linz, *Austria* **42** 48 18N 14 18 E
Lion, G. du, *Fr.* **35** 43 0N 4 0 E
Lípari, Is., *It.* **40** 38 30N 14 50 E
Lipetsk, *U.S.S.R.* **46** 52 37N 39 35 E
Lisbon, *Port.* **37** 38 42N 9 10W
Lisburn, *U.K.* **24** 54 30N 6 9W
Liscannor, B., *Ire.* **25** 52 57N 9 24W
Liskeard, *U.K.* **16** 50 27N 4 29W
Lismore, *Austral.* **67** 28 44S 153 21 E
Lismore, *Ire.* **25** 52 8N 7 58W
Lismore I., *U.K.* **20** 56 30N 5 30W
Liss, *U.K.* **15** 51 3N 0 53W
Listowel, *Ire.* **25** 52 27N 9 30W
Litcham, *U.K.* **15** 52 43N 0 49 E
Litherland, *U.K.* **18** 53 29N 3 0W
Lithgow, *Austral.* **70** 33 25S 150 8 E
Lithuania □, *U.S.S.R.* **46** 55 30N 24 0 E
Little Minch, *U.K.* **22** 57 35N 6 45W
Little Ouse ➝, *U.K.* **15** 52 25N 0 50 E
Little Rock, *U.S.A.* **91** 34 41N 92 10W
Little Walsingham, *U.K.* **15** 52 53N 0 51 E
Littleborough, *U.K.* **18** 53 38N 2 8W
Littlehampton, *U.K.* **15** 50 48N 0 32W
Littleport, *U.K.* **15** 52 27N 0 18 E
Littlestone-on-Sea, *U.K.* **15** 50 59N 0 59 E
Liuzhou, *China* **61** 24 22N 109 22 E
Liverpool, *Austral.* **70** 33 54S 150 58 E
Liverpool, *U.K.* **18** 53 25N 3 0W
Liverpool Plains, *Austral.* **70** 31 15S 150 15 E
Livingston, *U.K.* **21** 55 52N 3 33W
Livingstone, *Zam.* **81** 17 46S 25 52 E
Lizard, *U.K.* **16** 49 58N 5 10W
Lizard Pt., *U.K.* **16** 49 57N 5 11W
Ljubljana, *Yug.* **40** 46 4N 14 33 E
Llandeilo, *U.K.* **17** 51 53N 4 0W
Llandovery, *U.K.* **17** 51 59N 3 49W
Llandrindod Wells, *U.K.* **17** 52 15N 3 23W
Llandudno, *U.K.* **17** 53 19N 3 51W
Llanelli, *U.K.* **17** 51 41N 4 11W
Llanerchymedd, *U.K.* **17** 53 20N 4 22W
Llanfair Caereinion, *U.K.* **17** 52 39N 3 20W
Llanfair Talhaiarn, *U.K.* **17** 53 13N 3 37W
Llanfairfechan, *U.K.* **17** 53 15N 3 58W
Llangefni, *U.K.* **17** 53 15N 4 20W
Llangollen, *U.K.* **17** 52 58N 3 10W
Llanidloes, *U.K.* **17** 52 28N 3 31W
Llanllyfni, *U.K.* **17** 53 2N 4 18W
Llanos, *S. Am.* **100** 5 0N 71 35W
Llanrhystyd, *U.K.* **17** 52 19N 4 9W
Llantrisant, *U.K.* **17** 51 33N 3 22W
Llantwit-Major, *U.K.* **17** 51 24N 3 29W
Llanwrtyd Wells, *U.K.* **17** 52 6N 3 39W
Llanyblodwel, *U.K.* **14** 52 47N 3 8W
Llanymynech, *U.K.* **14** 52 48N 3 6W
Lleyn Peninsula, *U.K.* **17** 52 55N 4 35W
Loanhead, *U.K.* **21** 55 53N 3 10W
Lobito, *Angola* **81** 12 18S 13 35 E
Lochaber, *U.K.* **22** 56 55N 5 0W
Lochans, *U.K.* **20** 54 52N 5 1W
Lochboisdale, *U.K.* **22** 57 10N 7 20W
Lochbuie, *U.K.* **20** 56 21N 5 52W
Lochcarron, *U.K.* **22** 57 25N 5 30W
Lochdonhead, *U.K.* **20** 56 27N 5 40W
Lochearnhead, *U.K.* **20** 56 24N 4 19W
Lochgelly, *U.K.* **21** 56 7N 3 18W
Lochgilphead, *U.K.* **20** 56 2N 5 37W
Lochgoilhead, *U.K.* **20** 56 10N 4 54W
Lochinver, *U.K.* **22** 58 9N 5 15W
Lochmaben, *U.K.* **21** 55 8N 3 27W
Lochmaddy, *U.K.* **22** 57 36N 7 10W
Lochnagar, *U.K.* **23** 56 57N 3 14W
Lochranza, *U.K.* **20** 55 42N 5 18W
Lochwinnoch, *U.K.* **20** 55 47N 4 39W
Lochy ➝, *U.K.* **22** 56 52N 5 3W
Lockerbie, *U.K.* **21** 55 7N 3 21W
Lod, *Isr.* **57** 31 57N 34 54 E
Loddon, *U.K.* **15** 52 32N 1 29 E
Łódź, *Pol.* **43** 51 45N 19 27 E
Lofoten, *Nor.* **44** 68 30N 15 0 E
Loftus, *U.K.* **19** 54 33N 0 52W
Logan, Mt., *Canada* **88** 60 31N 140 22W
Logroño, *Sp.* **37** 42 28N 2 27W
Loire ➝, *Fr.* **34** 47 16N 2 10W
Lolland, *Den.* **45** 54 45N 11 30 E
Lombardy □, *It.* **40** 45 35N 9 45 E
Lomé, *Togo* **78** 6 9N 1 20 E
Lomond, L., *U.K.* **20** 56 8N 4 38W
Lomza, *Pol.* **43** 53 10N 22 2 E
London, *Canada* **92** 42 59N 81 15W
London, *U.K.* **15** 51 30N 0 5W
London, Greater □, *U.K.* **15** 51 30N 0 5W
Londonderry, *U.K.* **24** 55 0N 7 20W
Londonderry □, *U.K.* **24** 55 0N 7 20W
Londrina, *Brazil* **102** 23 18S 51 10W
Long, L., *U.K.* **20** 56 4N 4 50W
Long Beach, *U.S.A.* **90** 33 46N 118 12W
Long Bennington, *U.K.* **19** 52 59N 0 45W
Long Clawson, *U.K.* **15** 52 51N 0 56W
Long Crendon, *U.K.* **15** 51 47N 1 0W
Long Eaton, *U.K.* **19** 52 54N 1 16W
Long I., *Baham.* **95** 23 20N 75 10W
Long I., *U.S.A.* **93** 40 50N 73 20W
Long Itchington, *U.K.* **14** 52 16N 1 24W
Long Melford, *U.K.* **15** 52 5N 0 44 E
Long Mynd, *U.K.* **14** 52 35N 2 50W
Long Preston, *U.K.* **18** 54 0N 2 16W
Long Sutton, *U.K.* **15** 52 47N 0 9 E
Longford, *Ire.* **24** 53 43N 7 50W
Longford, *U.K.* **14** 51 53N 2 14W
Longford □, *Ire.* **24** 53 42N 7 45W
Longforgan, *U.K.* **21** 56 28N 3 8W
Longframlington, *U.K.* **21** 55 18N 1 47W
Longhorsley, *U.K.* **21** 55 15N 1 46W
Longhoughton, *U.K.* **21** 55 26N 1 38W
Longridge, *U.K.* **18** 53 50N 2 37W
Longton, *U.K.* **18** 53 43N 2 48W
Longtown, *Cumbria, U.K.* **18** 55 1N 2 59W
Longtown, *Hereford & Worcs., U.K.* **14** 51 58N 2 59W
Löningen, *W. Ger.* **36** 52 43N 7 44 E
Looe, *U.K.* **16** 50 24N 4 25W
Loop Hd., *Ire.* **25** 52 34N 9 55W
Lop Nor, *China* **60** 40 20N 90 10 E
Lorca, *Sp.* **37** 37 41N 1 42W
Lorient, *Fr.* **34** 47 45N 3 23W
Lorn, *U.K.* **20** 56 26N 5 10W
Lorn, Firth of, *U.K.* **20** 56 20N 5 40W
Los Angeles, *Chile* **102** 37 28S 72 23W
Los Angeles, *U.S.A.* **90** 34 0N 118 10W
Los Mochis, *Mex.* **94** 25 45N 108 57W
Lossiemouth, *U.K.* **23** 57 43N 3 17W
Lostwithiel, *U.K.* **16** 50 24N 4 41W
Lothian □, *U.K.* **21** 55 50N 3 0W
Loughborough, *U.K.* **15** 52 46N 1 11W
Loughrea, *Ire.* **25** 53 11N 8 33W
Loughros More B., *Ire.* **24** 54 48N 8 30W
Louisiana □, *U.S.A.* **91** 30 50N 92 0W
Louisville, *U.S.A.* **92** 38 15N 85 45W
Lourdes, *Fr.* **35** 43 6N 0 3W
Louth, *Ire.* **24** 53 47N 6 33W
Louth, *U.K.* **19** 53 23N 0 0 E
Louth □, *Ire.* **24** 53 55N 6 30W
Louvière, La, *Belg.* **36** 50 27N 4 10 E
Lowell, *U.S.A.* **93** 42 38N 71 19W
Lower Beeding, *U.K.* **15** 51 2N 0 15W
Lower California, *Mex.* **94** 31 10N 115 12W
Lower Hutt, *N.Z.* **71** 41 10S 174 55 E
Lower Tunguska ➝, *U.S.S.R.* **49** 64 20N 93 0 E
Lowes Water L., *U.K.* **18** 54 35N 3 23W
Lowestoft, *U.K.* **15** 52 29N 1 44 E
Lowick, *U.K.* **21** 55 38N 1 57W
Lowther Hills, *U.K.* **21** 55 20N 3 40W
Luanda, *Angola* **80** 8 50S 13 15 E
Luanshya, *Zam.* **81** 13 3S 28 28 E
Lubbock, *U.S.A.* **90** 33 40N 101 53W
Lübeck, *W. Ger.* **42** 53 52N 10 41 E
Lublin, *Pol.* **43** 51 12N 22 38 E
Lubumbashi, *Zaïre* **81** 11 40S 27 28 E
Luce Bay, *U.K.* **20** 54 45N 4 48W
Lucknow, *India* **59** 26 50N 81 0 E
Lüda = Dalian, *China* **61** 38 50N 121 40 E
Ludgershall, *U.K.* **14** 51 15N 1 38W
Ludgvan, *U.K.* **16** 50 9N 5 30W
Ludhiana, *India* **58** 30 57N 75 56 E
Ludlow, *U.K.* **14** 52 23N 2 42W
Ludwigshafen, *W. Ger.* **42** 49 27N 8 27 E

Lugano, *Switz.* 42 46 0N 8 57 E
Lugnaquilla, *Ire.* 25 52 58N 6 28W
Lugo, *Sp.* 37 43 2N 7 35W
Lugwardine, *U.K.* 14 52 4N 2 38W
Luing I., *U.K.* 20 56 15N 5 40W
Luleå, *Swed.* 44 65 35N 22 10 E
Lundy, *U.K.* 16 51 10N 4 41W
Lune →, *U.K.* 18 54 0N 2 51W
Lünen, *W. Ger.* 36 51 36N 7 31 E
Luoyang, *China* 61 34 40N 112 26 E
Lurgan, *U.K.* 24 54 28N 6 20W
Lusaka, *Zam.* 81 15 28S 28 16 E
Luss, *U.K.* 20 56 6N 4 40W
Luton, *U.K.* 15 51 53N 0 24W
Lutterworth, *U.K.* 14 52 28N 1 12W
Luxembourg, *Lux.* 36 49 37N 6 9 E
Luxembourg ■, *Europe* 36 50 0N 6 0 E
Luzern, *Switz.* 42 47 3N 8 18 E
Luzhou, *China* 60 28 52N 105 20 E
Luzon, *Phil.* 63 16 0N 121 0 E
Lvov, *U.S.S.R.* 47 49 50N 24 0 E
Lyakhov Is., *U.S.S.R.* 49 73 40N 141 0 E
Lybster, *U.K.* 23 58 18N 3 16W
Lydd, *U.K.* 15 50 57N 0 56 E
Lydford, *U.K.* 16 50 38N 4 7W
Lydham, *U.K.* 14 52 31N 2 59W
Lyell Range, *N.Z.* 71 41 38S 172 20 E
Lyme Bay, *U.K.* 16 50 36N 2 55W
Lyme Regis, *U.K.* 16 50 44N 2 57W
Lyminge, *U.K.* 15 51 7N 1 6 E
Lymington, *U.K.* 14 50 46N 1 32W
Lymm, *U.K.* 18 53 23N 2 30W
Lympne, *U.K.* 15 51 4N 1 2 E
Lynchburg, *U.S.A.* 92 37 23N 79 10W
Lyndhurst, *U.K.* 14 50 53N 1 33W
Lyneham, *U.K.* 14 51 30N 1 57W
Lynemouth, *U.K.* 21 55 15N 1 29W
Lynmouth, *U.K.* 16 51 14N 3 50W
Lynn Lake, *Canada* 88 56 51N 101 3W
Lynton, *U.K.* 16 51 14N 3 50W
Lyons, *Fr.* 35 45 46N 4 50 E
Lytchett Minster, *U.K.* 14 50 44N 2 3W
Lytham St. Anne's, *U.K.* 18 53 45N 2 58W
Lythe, *U.K.* 19 54 30N 0 40W

M

Ma'ān, *Jord.* 56 30 12N 35 44 E
Maarianhamina, *Fin.* 45 60 5N 19 55 E
Maastricht, *Neth.* 36 50 50N 5 40 E
Mablethorpe, *U.K.* 19 53 21N 0 14 E
Macapá, *Brazil* 101 0 5N 51 4W
Macau ■, *Asia* 61 22 16N 113 35 E
Macclesfield, *U.K.* 18 53 16N 2 9W
McClure Str., *Canada* 103 75 0N 119 0W
Macdonnell Ranges, *Austral.* 66 23 40S 133 0 E
Macduff, *U.K.* 23 57 40N 2 30W
Macedonia □, *Greece* 41 40 39N 22 0 E
Macedonia □, *Yug.* 41 41 53N 21 40 E
Maceió, *Brazil* 101 9 40S 35 41W
Macgillycuddy's Reeks, *Ire.* 25 52 2N 9 45W
Machakos, *Kenya* 80 1 30S 37 15 E
Machala, *Ecuad.* 100 3 20S 79 57W
Machars, The, *U.K.* 20 54 46N 4 30W
Machrihanish, *U.K.* 20 55 25N 5 42W
Machynlleth, *U.K.* 17 52 36N 3 51W
Macintyre →, *Austral.* 67 28 37S 150 47 E
Mackay, *Austral.* 67 21 8S 149 11 E
Mackay, L., *Austral.* 66 22 30S 129 0 E
McKeesport, *U.S.A.* 92 40 21N 79 50W
Mackenzie →, *Austral.* 67 23 38S 149 46 E
Mackenzie →, *Canada* 88 69 10N 134 20W
Mackenzie Mts., *Canada* 88 64 0N 130 0W
McKinley, Mt., *U.S.A.* 88 63 2N 151 0W
M'Clintock Chan., *Canada* 88 72 0N 102 0W
Macon, *U.S.A.* 90 32 50N 83 37W
Macquarie →, *Austral.* 70 30 5S 147 30 E
Macquarie Harbour, *Austral.* 67 42 15S 145 23 E
Macquarie Is., *S. Oc.* 64 54 36S 158 55 E
Macroom, *Ire.* 25 51 54N 8 57W
Madadeni, *S. Afr.* 81 27 43S 30 3 E
Madagascar ■, *Africa* 81 20 0S 47 0 E
Madeira, *Atl. Oc.* 78 32 50N 17 0W
Madeira →, *Brazil* 100 3 22S 58 45W
Madeley, *Salop, U.K.* 14 52 38N 2 28W
Madeley, *Staffs., U.K.* 18 52 59N 2 20W
Madhya Pradesh □, *India* 59 21 50N 81 0 E
Madīnat ash Sha'b, *S. Yem.* 56 12 50N 45 0 E
Madison, *U.S.A.* 92 43 5N 89 25W
Madiun, *Indon.* 63 7 38S 111 32 E
Madley, *U.K.* 14 52 3N 2 51W
Madras, *India* 58 13 8N 80 19 E
Madre, L., *U.S.A.* 91 26 0N 97 40W
Madre, Sierra, *Mex.* 94 16 0N 93 0W
Madrid, *Sp.* 37 40 25N 3 45W
Madurai, *India* 58 9 55N 78 10 E
Maesteg, *U.K.* 17 51 36N 3 40W
Magadan, *U.S.S.R.* 49 59 38N 150 50 E
Magdalena →, *Col.* 100 11 6N 74 51W
Magdeburg, *E. Ger.* 42 52 8N 11 36 E
Magee, I., *U.K.* 24 54 48N 5 44W
Magelang, *Indon.* 63 7 29S 110 13 E
Magellan's Str., *Chile* 102 52 30S 75 0W
Maggiore, L., *It.* 40 46 0N 8 35 E
Magherafelt, *U.K.* 24 54 44N 6 37W
Maghull, *U.K.* 18 53 31N 2 56W
Magnitogorsk, *U.S.S.R.* 46 53 27N 59 4 E
Mahajanga, *Madag.* 81 17 0S 47 0 E
Maiden Bradley, *U.K.* 14 51 9N 2 18W
Maiden Newton, *U.K.* 14 50 46N 2 35W
Maidenhead, *U.K.* 15 51 31N 0 42W
Maidstone, *U.K.* 15 51 16N 0 31 E
Maiduguri, *Nig.* 79 12 0N 13 20 E
Main →, *U.K.* 24 54 49N 6 20W
Maine □, *U.S.A.* 93 45 20N 69 0W
Maine →, *Ire.* 25 52 10N 9 40W
Mainland, *Orkney, U.K.* 23 59 0N 3 10W
Mainland, *Shetland, U.K.* 22 60 15N 1 22W
Mainz, *W. Ger.* 36 50 0N 8 17 E
Maitland, *Austral.* 70 32 33S 151 36 E
Majorca, I. = Mallorca, *Sp.* 37 39 30N 3 0 E
Makasar, Str. of, *Indon.* 63 1 0S 118 20 E
Maker, *U.K.* 16 50 20N 4 10W
Makeyevka, *U.S.S.R.* 47 48 0N 38 0 E
Makhachkala, *U.S.S.R.* 47 43 0N 47 30 E
Makran Coast Range, *Pak.* 58 25 40N 64 0 E
Mal B., *Ire.* 25 52 50N 9 30W
Malabar Coast, *India* 58 11 0N 75 0 E
Malacca, Str. of, *Indon.* 63 3 0N 101 0 E
Málaga, *Sp.* 37 36 43N 4 23W
Malang, *Indon.* 63 7 59S 112 45 E
Malanje, *Angola* 80 9 36S 16 17 E
Mälaren, *Swed.* 45 59 30N 17 10 E
Malatya, *Turk.* 47 38 25N 38 20 E
Malawi ■, *Africa* 81 13 0S 34 0 E
Malay Pen., *Asia* 63 7 25N 100 0 E
Malaysia ■, *Asia* 63 5 0N 110 0 E
Maldives ■, *Ind. Oc.* 129 7 0N 73 0 E
Maldon, *U.K.* 15 51 43N 0 41 E
Malham Tarn, *U.K.* 18 54 6N 2 11W
Mali ■, *Africa* 78 15 0N 2 0W
Mallaig, *U.K.* 22 57 0N 5 50W
Mallorca, *Sp.* 37 39 30N 3 0 E
Mallow, *Ire.* 25 52 8N 8 40W
Malmédy, *Belg.* 36 50 25N 6 2 E
Malmesbury, *U.K.* 14 51 35N 2 5W
Malmö, *Swed.* 45 55 36N 12 59 E
Malpas, *U.K.* 18 53 3N 2 47W
Malta ■, *Europe* 40 35 50N 14 30 E
Maltby, *U.K.* 19 53 25N 1 12W
Malton, *U.K.* 19 54 9N 0 48W
Malvern, *U.K.* 14 52 7N 2 19W
Malvern Hills, *U.K.* 14 52 0N 2 19W
Malvern Wells, *U.K.* 14 52 4N 2 19W
Malvinas, Is. = Falkland Is., *Atl. Oc.* 102 51 30S 59 0W
Man, I. of, *U.K.* 18 54 15N 4 30W
Manaar, Gulf of, *Asia* 58 8 30N 79 0 E
Manacles, The, *U.K.* 16 50 3N 5 5W
Manado, *Indon.* 63 1 29N 124 51 E
Managua, *Nic.* 94 12 6N 86 20W
Manaus, *Brazil* 100 3 0S 60 0W
Manby, *U.K.* 19 53 22N 0 6 E
Manchester, *U.K.* 18 53 30N 2 15W
Manchester, *U.S.A.* 93 42 58N 71 29W
Manchuria, *China* 61 42 0N 125 0 E
Mandalay, *Burma* 59 22 0N 96 4 E
Manea, *U.K.* 15 52 29N 0 10 E
Mangalore, *India* 58 12 55N 74 47 E
Mangotsfield, *U.K.* 14 51 29N 2 29W
Manila, *Phil.* 63 14 40N 121 3 E
Manitoba □, *Canada* 88 55 30N 97 0W
Manizales, *Col.* 100 5 5N 75 32W
Manly, *Austral.* 70 33 48S 151 17 E
Mannheim, *W. Ger.* 42 49 28N 8 29 E
Manningtree, *U.K.* 15 51 56N 1 3 E
Mans, Le, *Fr.* 34 48 0N 0 10 E
Mansfield, *U.K.* 19 53 8N 1 12W
Mansfield, *U.S.A.* 92 40 45N 82 30W
Mansfield Woodhouse, *U.K.* 19 53 11N 1 11W
Mantes-la-Jolie, *Fr.* 34 49 0N 1 41 E
Manton, *U.K.* 15 52 37N 0 41W
Mantua, *It.* 40 45 20N 10 42 E
Manukau, *N.Z.* 71 37 1S 174 55 E
Manzhouli, *China* 61 49 35N 117 25 E
Maoming, *China* 61 21 50N 110 54 E
Maputo, *Mozam.* 81 25 58S 32 32 E
Mar del Plata, *Arg.* 102 38 0S 57 30W
Maracaibo, *Ven.* 100 10 40N 71 37W
Maracaibo, L., *Ven.* 100 9 40N 71 30W
Maracay, *Ven.* 100 10 15N 67 28W
Marajó, I. de, *Brazil* 101 1 0S 49 30W
Maranhão = São Luís, *Brazil* 101 2 39S 44 15W
Marañón →, *Peru* 100 4 30S 73 35W
Marazion, *U.K.* 16 50 8N 5 29W
March, *U.K.* 15 52 33N 0 5 E
Marden, *U.K.* 14 52 7N 2 42W
Maree L., *U.K.* 22 57 40N 5 30W
Mareeba, *Austral.* 67 16 59S 145 28 E
Mareham le Fen, *U.K.* 19 53 7N 0 3W
Marfleet, *U.K.* 19 53 45N 0 15W
Margarita I., *Ven.* 100 11 0N 64 0W
Margate, *U.K.* 15 51 23N 1 24 E
Maribor, *Yug.* 40 46 36N 15 40 E
Maricourt, *Canada* 89 56 34N 70 49W
Marie-Galante, *W. Ind.* 94 15 56N 61 16W
Marilia, *Brazil* 101 22 13S 50 0W
Maringá, *Brazil* 102 23 26S 52 2W
Mark, *U.K.* 20 55 2N 5 1W
Market Bosworth, *U.K.* 14 52 37N 1 24W
Market Deeping, *U.K.* 15 52 40N 0 20W
Market Drayton, *U.K.* 18 52 55N 2 30W
Market Harborough, *U.K.* 15 52 29N 0 55W
Market Lavington, *U.K.* 14 51 17N 1 59W
Market Rasen, *U.K.* 19 53 24N 0 20W
Market Weighton, *U.K.* 19 53 52N 0 40W
Markfield, *U.K.* 14 52 42N 1 18W
Markinch, *U.K.* 21 56 12N 3 9W
Marks Tey, *U.K.* 15 51 53N 0 48 E
Marlborough, *U.K.* 14 51 26N 1 44W
Marlborough □, *N.Z.* 71 41 45S 173 33 E
Marlborough Downs, *U.K.* 14 51 25N 1 55W
Marlow, *U.K.* 15 51 34N 0 47W
Marmara, Sea of, *Turk.* 47 40 45N 28 15 E
Marne →, *Fr.* 34 48 48N 2 24 E
Marnhull, *U.K.* 14 50 58N 2 20W
Maroua, *Cam.* 80 10 40N 14 20 E
Marple, *U.K.* 18 53 23N 2 5W
Marquesas Is., *Pac. Oc.* 65 9 30S 140 0W
Marrakech, *Mor.* 78 31 9N 8 0W
Marseilles, *Fr.* 35 43 18N 5 23 E
Marshall Is., *Pac. Oc.* 64 9 0N 171 0 E
Marshfield, *U.K.* 14 51 27N 2 18W
Marske by the Sea, *U.K.* 19 54 35N 1 0W
Marston Moor, *U.K.* 19 53 58N 1 17W
Martaban, G. of, *Burma* 59 16 5N 96 30 E
Martham, *U.K.* 15 52 42N 1 38 E
Martinique, *W. Ind.* 94 14 40N 61 0W
Martley, *U.K.* 14 52 14N 2 22W
Martock, *U.K.* 14 50 58N 2 47W
Mary Kathleen, *Austral.* 67 20 44S 139 48 E
Maryborough, *Austral.* 67 37 0S 143 44 E
Maryland □, *U.S.A.* 93 39 10N 76 40W
Maryport, *U.K.* 18 54 43N 3 30W
Marytavy, *U.K.* 16 50 34N 4 6W
Masan, *S. Kor.* 61 35 11N 128 32 E
Maseru, *Les.* 81 29 18S 27 30 E
Masham, *U.K.* 19 54 15N 1 40W
Mashhad, *Iran* 57 36 20N 59 35 E
Mask, L., *Ire.* 24 53 36N 9 24W
Massachusetts □, *U.S.A.* 93 42 25N 72 0W
Massif Central, *Fr.* 35 45 30N 3 0 E
Masterton, *N.Z.* 71 40 56S 175 39 E
Masvingo, *Zimb.* 81 20 8S 30 49 E
Matadi, *Zaïre* 80 5 52S 13 31 E
Matamoros, *Mex.* 94 25 33N 103 15W
Matera, *It.* 40 40 40N 16 37 E
Matlock, *U.K.* 19 53 8N 1 32W
Mato Grosso □, *Brazil* 101 14 0S 55 0W
Matsue, *Jap.* 62 35 25N 133 10 E
Matsuyama, *Jap.* 62 33 45N 132 45 E
Matterhorn, *Switz.* 42 45 58N 7 39 E
Maturín, *Ven.* 100 9 45N 63 11W
Maubeuge, *Fr.* 34 50 17N 3 57 E
Mauchline, *U.K.* 20 55 31N 4 23W
Maughold, *U.K.* 18 54 18N 4 17W
Maughold Hd., *U.K.* 18 54 18N 4 17W
Maui, *U.S.A.* 90 20 45N 156 20 E
Mauna Loa, *U.S.A.* 90 21 8N 157 10W
Mauritania ■, *Africa* 78 20 50N 10 0W
Mauritius ■, *Ind. Oc.* 129 20 0S 57 0 E
Mawgan, *U.K.* 16 50 4N 5 10W
Mawlaik, *Burma* 59 23 40N 94 26 E
Maxwellheugh, *U.K.* 21 55 35N 2 23W
May, I. of, *U.K.* 21 56 11N 2 32W
May Pen, *Jam.* 94 17 58N 77 15W
Maybole, *U.K.* 20 55 21N 4 41W
Mayfield, *Derby, U.K.* 19 53 1N 1 47W
Mayfield, *E. Sussex, U.K.* 15 51 1N 0 17 E
Maynooth, *Ire.* 24 53 22N 6 38W
Mayo □, *Ire.* 24 53 47N 9 7W
Mazar-e Sharīf, *Afg.* 57 36 41N 67 0 E
Mazatlán, *Mex.* 94 23 13N 106 25W
Mbabane, *Swaz.* 81 26 18S 31 6 E
Mbandaka, *Zaïre* 80 0 1N 18 18 E
Mbanza Ngungu, *Zaïre* 80 5 12S 14 53 E
Mbeya, *Tanz.* 80 8 54S 33 29 E
Mbini □, *Eq. Guin.* 80 1 30N 10 0 E
Mbuji-Mayi, *Zaïre* 80 6 9S 23 40 E
Mdantsane, *S. Afr.* 81 32 56S 27 46 E
Mealsgate, *U.K.* 18 54 46N 3 14W
Measham, *U.K.* 14 52 43N 1 30W
Meath □, *Ire.* 24 53 32N 6 40W
Mecca, *Si. Arab.* 56 21 30N 39 54 E
Mechelen, *Belg.* 36 50 58N 5 41 E
Medan, *Indon.* 63 3 40N 98 38 E
Medellín, *Col.* 100 6 15N 75 35W
Medicine Hat, *Canada* 88 50 0N 110 45W
Medina, *Si. Arab.* 56 24 35N 39 52 E
Mediterranean Sea, *Europe* 38 35 0N 15 0 E
Medley, *Canada* 88 54 25N 110 16W
Medstead, *U.K.* 14 51 7N 1 4W
Medway →, *U.K.* 15 51 28N 0 45 E
Meekatharra, *Austral.* 66 26 32S 118 29 E
Meerut, *India* 58 29 1N 77 42 E
Mei Xian, *China* 61 24 16N 116 6 E
Meknès, *Mor.* 78 33 57N 5 33W
Mekong →, *Asia* 63 9 30N 106 15 E
Melanesia, *Pac. Oc.* 64 4 0S 155 0 E
Melbourn, *U.K.* 15 52 5N 0 1 E
Melbourne, *Austral.* 70 37 50S 145 0 E
Melbourne, *U.K.* 14 52 50N 1 25W
Melfort, Loch, *U.K.* 20 56 13N 5 33W
Melitopol, *U.S.S.R.* 47 46 50N 35 22 E
Melksham, *U.K.* 14 51 22N 2 9W
Melmerby, *U.K.* 18 54 44N 2 35W
Melrose, *U.K.* 21 55 35N 2 44W
Melsonby, *U.K.* 19 54 28N 1 41W
Melton, *U.K.* 15 52 6N 1 20 E
Melton Constable, *U.K.* 15 52 52N 1 1 E
Melton Mowbray, *U.K.* 15 52 46N 0 52W
Melvich, *U.K.* 23 58 33N 3 55W
Melville I., *Austral.* 66 11 30S 131 0 E
Melville Pen., *Canada* 89 68 0N 84 0W
Memphis, *U.S.A.* 91 35 7N 90 0W
Menai Bridge, *U.K.* 17 53 14N 4 11W
Menai Strait, *U.K.* 17 53 14N 4 10W
Menan = Chao Phraya →, *Thai.* 63 13 32N 100 36 E
Mendip Hills, *U.K.* 14 51 17N 2 40W
Mendlesham, *U.K.* 15 52 15N 1 4 E
Mendoza, *Arg.* 102 32 50S 68 52W
Menindee, *Austral.* 70 32 20S 142 25 E
Menorca, *Sp.* 37 40 0N 4 0 E
Mere, *U.K.* 14 51 5N 2 16W
Mérida, *Mex.* 94 20 58N 89 37W
Mérida, *Ven.* 100 8 24N 71 8W
Meriden, *U.K.* 14 52 27N 1 36W
Merrick, *U.K.* 20 55 8N 4 30W
Merse, *U.K.* 21 55 40N 2 30W
Mersea I., *U.K.* 15 51 48N 0 55 E
Mersey →, *U.K.* 18 53 20N 2 56W
Merseyside □, *U.K.* 18 53 25N 2 55W
Mersin, *Turk.* 47 36 51N 34 36 E
Merthyr Tydfil, *U.K.* 17 51 45N 3 23W
Merton, *U.K.* 15 51 25N 0 13W
Meru, *Tanz.* 80 3 15S 36 46 E
Mesa, *U.S.A.* 90 33 20N 111 56W
Mesopotamia, *Asia* 56 33 30N 44 0 E
Messina, *It.* 40 38 10N 15 32 E
Messina, Str. of, *It.* 40 38 5N 15 35 E
Metheringham, *U.K.* 19 53 9N 0 22W
Methil, *U.K.* 21 56 10N 3 1W
Methven, *U.K.* 21 56 25N 3 35W
Methwold, *U.K.* 15 52 30N 0 33 E
Metz, *Fr.* 34 49 8N 6 10 E
Meuse →, *Europe* 34 50 45N 5 41 E
Mevagissey, *U.K.* 16 50 16N 4 48W
Mevagissey Bay, *U.K.* 16 50 15N 4 40W
Mexborough, *U.K.* 19 53 29N 1 18W
Mexicali, *Mex.* 94 32 40N 115 29W
México, *Mex.* 94 19 20N 99 10W
Mexico ■, *Cent. Am.* 94 20 0N 100 0W
Mexico, G. of, *Cent. Am.* 94 25 0N 90 0W
Miami, *U.S.A.* 91 25 45N 80 15W
Micheldever, *U.K.* 14 51 7N 1 17W
Michigan □, *U.S.A.* 92 44 40N 85 40W
Michigan, L., *U.S.A.* 92 44 0N 87 0W
Mickle Fell, *U.K.* 18 54 38N 2 16W
Mickleover, *U.K.* 19 52 55N 1 32W
Mickleton, *Durham, U.K.* 18 54 36N 2 3W
Mickleton, *Oxon., U.K.* 14 52 5N 1 45W
Micronesia, *Pac. Oc.* 64 11 0N 160 0 E
Mid Calder, *U.K.* 21 55 53N 3 23W
Mid Glamorgan □, *U.K.* 17 51 40N 3 25W
Middle Zoy, *U.K.* 14 51 5N 2 54W
Middleham, *U.K.* 19 54 17N 1 49W
Middlemarsh, *U.K.* 14 50 51N 2 29W
Middlesbrough, *U.K.* 19 54 35N 1 14W
Middleton, *Gr. Manchester, U.K.* 18 53 33N 2 12W
Middleton, *Norfolk, U.K.* 15 52 43N 0 29 E
Middleton Cheney, *U.K.* 14 52 4N 1 17W
Middleton-in-Teesdale, *U.K.* 18 54 38N 2 5W
Middleton on the Wolds, *U.K.* 19 53 56N 0 35W
Middlewich, *U.K.* 18 53 12N 2 28W
Midhurst, *U.K.* 15 50 59N 0 44W
Midland, *U.S.A.* 90 32 0N 102 3W
Midleton, *Ire.* 25 51 52N 8 12W
Midsomer Norton, *U.K.* 14 51 17N 2 29W
Midway Is., *Pac. Oc.* 64 28 13N 177 22W
Mieres, *Sp.* 37 43 18N 5 48W
Mikkeli, *Fin.* 44 61 43N 27 15 E
Milan, *It.* 40 45 28N 9 10 E
Milborne Port, *U.K.* 14 50 58N 2 28W
Mildenhall, *U.K.* 15 52 20N 0 30 E
Mildura, *Austral.* 70 34 13S 142 9 E
Milford Haven, *U.K.* 17 51 43N 5 2W
Milford Haven, B., *U.K.* 17 51 40N 5 10W
Milford on Sea, *U.K.* 14 50 44N 1 36W
Milk →, *U.S.A.* 90 48 5N 106 15W
Millbrook, *U.K.* 16 50 19N 4 12W
Milleur Pt., *U.K.* 20 55 2N 5 5W
Millom, *U.K.* 18 54 13N 3 16W
Millport, *U.K.* 20 55 45N 4 55W
Milltown Malbay, *Ire.* 25 52 51N 9 25W
Milnathort, *U.K.* 21 56 14N 3 25W
Milngavie, *U.K.* 20 55 57N 4 20W
Milnthorpe, *U.K.* 18 54 14N 2 47W
Milton, *Dumf. & Gall., U.K.* 20 55 18N 4 50W
Milton, *Hants., U.K.* 14 50 45N 1 40W
Milton, *Highland, U.K.* 23 57 18N 4 32W
Milton Abbot, *U.K.* 16 50 35N 4 16W
Milton Keynes, *U.K.* 15 52 3N 0 42W

Milverton, *U.K.* **14** 51 2N 3 15W
Milwaukee, *U.S.A.* **92** 43 9N 87 58W
Minas Gerais □, *Brazil* **101** 18 50S 46 0W
Minatitlán, *Mex.* **94** 17 59N 94 31W
Minchinghampton, *U.K.* **14** 51 42N 2 10W
Mindanao, *Phil.* **63** 8 0N 125 0 E
Mindoro, *Phil.* **63** 13 0N 121 0 E
Minehead, *U.K.* **14** 51 12N 3 29W
Minneapolis, *U.S.A.* **91** 44 58N 93 20W
Minnesota □, *U.S.A.* **91** 46 40N 94 0W
Minnigaff, *U.K.* **20** 54 58N 4 30W
Minorca = Menorca, *Sp.* **37** 40 0N 4 0 E
Minsk, *U.S.S.R.* **46** 53 52N 27 30 E
Minster, *U.K.* **15** 51 20N 1 20 E
Minster-on-Sea, *U.K.* **15** 51 25N 0 50 E
Minsterley, *U.K.* **14** 52 38N 2 56W
Mirfield, *U.K.* **19** 53 37N 1 54W
Mirzapur, *India* **59** 25 10N 82 34 E
Miskolc, *Hung.* **43** 48 7N 20 50 E
Misrãtah, *Libya* **79** 32 24N 15 3 E
Mississippi □, *U.S.A.* **91** 33 0N 90 0W
Mississippi ⟶, *U.S.A.* **91** 29 0N 89 15W
Mississippi, Delta of the, *U.S.A.* **91** 29 15N 90 30W
Missouri □, *U.S.A.* **91** 38 25N 92 30W
Missouri ⟶, *U.S.A.* **91** 38 50N 90 8W
Misterton, *Notts., U.K.* **19** 53 27N 0 49W
Misterton, *Somerset, U.K.* **14** 50 51N 2 46W
Mitcheldean, *U.K.* **14** 51 51N 2 29W
Mitchell ⟶, *Austral.* **67** 15 12S 141 35 E
Mitchelstown, *Ire.* **25** 52 16N 8 18W
Mittelland Kanal, *W. Ger.* **36** 52 23N 7 45 E
Mitumba, Mts., *Zaïre* **80** 6 0S 29 0 E
Miyazaki, *Jap.* **62** 31 56N 131 30 E
Mizen Hd., *Cork, Ire.* **25** 51 27N 9 50W
Mizen Hd., *Wicklow, Ire.* **25** 52 52N 6 4W
Mizoram □, *India* **59** 23 30N 92 40 E
Mmabatho, *S. Afr.* **81** 25 49S 25 30 E
Mo i Rana, *Nor.* **44** 66 15N 14 7 E
Mobile, *U.S.A.* **91** 30 41N 88 3W
Mobutu Sese Seko, L., *Africa* **80** 1 30N 31 0 E
Moçâmedes = Namibe, *Angola* **81** 15 7S 12 11 E
Modbury, *U.K.* **16** 50 21N 3 53W
Módena, *It.* **40** 44 39N 10 55 E
Moe, *Austral.* **70** 38 12S 146 19 E
Moffat, *U.K.* **21** 55 20N 3 27W
Mogadishu, *Som.* **73** 2 2N 45 25 E
Mogilev, *U.S.S.R.* **46** 53 55N 30 18 E
Moidart, L., *U.K.* **22** 56 47N 5 40W
Mojave Desert, *U.S.A.* **90** 35 0N 116 30W
Mold, *U.K.* **17** 53 10N 3 10W
Moldavia □, *U.S.S.R.* **47** 47 0N 28 0 E
Mole ⟶, *U.K.* **15** 51 13N 0 15W
Mollendo, *Peru* **100** 17 0S 72 0W
Mölndal, *Swed.* **45** 57 40N 12 3 E
Molokai, *U.S.A.* **90** 21 8N 157 0W
Moluccas, *Indon.* **63** 1 0S 127 0 E
Mombasa, *Kenya* **80** 4 2S 39 43 E
Mona Passage, *W. Ind.* **95** 18 0N 67 40W
Monach Is., *U.K.* **22** 57 32N 7 40W
Monaco ■, *Europe* **35** 43 46N 7 23 E
Monadhliath Mts., *U.K.* **23** 57 10N 4 4W
Monaghan, *Ire.* **24** 54 15N 6 58W
Monaghan □, *Ire.* **24** 54 10N 7 0W
Monastir = Bitola, *Yug.* **41** 41 5N 21 10 E
Monclova, *Mex.* **94** 26 50N 101 30W
Moncton, *Canada* **93** 46 7N 64 51W
Moneymore, *U.K.* **24** 54 42N 6 40W
Monghyr, *India* **59** 25 23N 86 30 E
Mongolia ■, *Asia* **60** 47 0N 103 0 E
Mongu, *Zam.* **81** 15 16S 23 12 E
Moniaive, *U.K.* **21** 55 11N 3 55W
Monifieth, *U.K.* **21** 56 30N 2 48W
Monkton, *U.K.* **20** 55 30N 4 37W
Monmouth, *U.K.* **17** 51 48N 2 43W
Monnow ⟶, *U.K.* **14** 51 54N 2 48W
Monroe, *U.S.A.* **90** 32 32N 92 4W
Monrovia, *Lib.* **78** 6 18N 10 47W
Mons, *Belg.* **36** 50 27N 3 58 E
Montana □, *U.S.A.* **90** 47 0N 110 0W
Montbéliard, *Fr.* **34** 47 31N 6 48 E
Montceau-les-Mines, *Fr.* **34** 46 40N 4 23 E
Monte-Carlo, *Monaco* **35** 43 46N 7 23 E
Montego Bay, *Jam.* **94** 18 30N 78 0W
Montería, *Col.* **100** 8 46N 75 53W
Monterrey, *Mex.* **94** 25 40N 100 30W
Montes Claros, *Brazil* **101** 16 30S 43 50W
Montevideo, *Urug.* **102** 34 50S 56 11W
Montgomery, *U.K.* **17** 52 34N 3 9W
Montgomery, *U.S.A.* **91** 32 20N 86 20W
Montluçon, *Fr.* **35** 46 22N 2 36 E
Montpelier, *U.S.A.* **93** 44 15N 72 38W
Montpellier, *Fr.* **35** 43 37N 3 52 E
Montréal, *Canada* **93** 45 31N 73 34W
Montrose, *U.K.* **23** 56 43N 2 28W
Montserrat, *W. Ind.* **94** 16 40N 62 10W
Moonie ⟶, *Austral.* **67** 29 19S 148 43 E
Moorfoot Hills, *U.K.* **21** 55 44N 3 8W
Moose Jaw, *Canada* **88** 50 24N 105 30W
Moosehead L., *U.S.A.* **93** 45 34N 69 40W
Mopti, *Mali* **78** 14 30N 4 0W
Moradabad, *India* **58** 28 50N 78 50 E
Morar L., *U.K.* **22** 56 57N 5 40W
Moray Firth, *U.K.* **23** 57 50N 3 30W
Morebattle, *U.K.* **21** 55 30N 2 20W
Morecambe, *U.K.* **18** 54 5N 2 52W
Morecambe B., *U.K.* **18** 54 7N 3 0W
Morelia, *Mex.* **94** 19 42N 101 7W
Morena, Sierra, *Sp.* **37** 38 20N 4 0W
Moreton-in-Marsh, *U.K.* **14** 51 59N 1 42W
Moretonhampstead, *U.K.* **16** 50 39N 3 45W
Morley, *U.K.* **19** 53 45N 1 36W
Morocco ■, *N. Afr.* **78** 32 0N 5 50W
Morogoro, *Tanz.* **80** 6 50S 37 40 E
Morpeth, *U.K.* **19** 55 11N 1 41W
Morte Bay, *U.K.* **16** 51 10N 4 13W
Morte Pt., *U.K.* **16** 51 13N 4 14W
Mortehoe, *U.K.* **16** 51 21N 4 12W
Mortimer's Cross, *U.K.* **14** 52 17N 2 50W
Morton Fen, *U.K.* **15** 52 45N 0 23W
Morvern, *U.K.* **22** 56 38N 5 44W
Morwell, *Austral.* **70** 38 10S 146 22 E
Morwenstow, *U.K.* **16** 50 53N 4 32W
Moscow, *U.S.S.R.* **46** 55 45N 37 35 E
Moselle ⟶, *Europe* **34** 50 22N 7 36 E
Moshi, *Tanz.* **80** 3 22S 37 18 E
Mossley, *U.K.* **18** 53 31N 2 1W
Mossoró, *Brazil* **101** 5 10S 37 15W
Mostaganem, *Alg.* **78** 35 54N 0 5 E
Mostar, *Yug.* **41** 43 22N 17 50 E
Mosul, *Iraq* **56** 36 15N 43 5 E
Motcombe, *U.K.* **14** 51 1N 2 12W
Motherwell, *U.K.* **21** 55 48N 4 0W
Mottisfont, *U.K.* **14** 51 2N 1 32W
Moulmein, *Burma* **59** 16 30N 97 40 E
Moulton, *U.K.* **15** 52 17N 0 51W
Mount Barker, *Austral.* **66** 34 38S 117 40 E
Mount Gambier, *Austral.* **70** 37 50S 140 46 E
Mount Isa, *Austral.* **67** 20 42S 139 26 E
Mount Lofty Ra., *Austral.* **67** 34 35S 139 5 E
Mountain Ash, *U.K.* **17** 51 42N 3 22W
Mountmellick, *Ire.* **25** 53 7N 7 20W
Mounts Bay, *U.K.* **16** 50 3N 5 27W
Mountsorrel, *U.K.* **14** 52 43N 1 9W
Mourne ⟶, *U.K.* **24** 54 45N 7 39W
Mourne Mts., *U.K.* **24** 54 10N 6 0W
Mouscron, *Belg.* **36** 50 45N 3 12 E
Moville, *Ire.* **24** 55 11N 7 3W
Moy ⟶, *Ire.* **24** 54 5N 8 50W
Moyle □, *U.K.* **24** 55 10N 6 15W
Mozambique ■, *Africa* **81** 19 0S 35 0 E
Mozambique Chan., *Africa* **81** 20 0S 39 0 E
Mu Us Shamo, *China* **61** 39 0N 109 0 E
Mubarraz, *Si. Arab.* **56** 25 29N 49 40 E
Much Dewchurch, *U.K.* **14** 51 58N 2 45W
Much Marcle, *U.K.* **14** 51 59N 2 27W
Much Wenlock, *U.K.* **14** 52 36N 2 34W
Muck, *U.K.* **22** 56 50N 6 15W
Mudanjiang, *China* **61** 44 38N 129 30 E
Mudgee, *Austral.* **70** 32 32S 149 31 E
Mufulira, *Zam.* **81** 12 32S 28 15 E
Muine Bheag, *Ire.* **25** 52 42N 6 57W
Muir of Ord, *U.K.* **23** 57 30N 4 35W
Muirdrum, *U.K.* **21** 56 31N 2 40W
Muirhead, *U.K.* **21** 55 54N 4 5W
Muirkirk, *U.K.* **21** 55 31N 4 6W
Mülheim, *W. Ger.* **36** 51 26N 6 53 E
Mulhouse, *Fr.* **34** 47 40N 7 20 E
Mull, *U.K.* **20** 56 27N 6 0W
Mull, Ross of, *U.K.* **20** 56 20N 6 15W
Mull, Sound of, *U.K.* **20** 56 30N 5 50W
Mullet Pen., *Ire.* **24** 54 10N 10 2W
Mullingar, *Ire.* **24** 53 31N 7 20W
Mullion, *U.K.* **16** 50 1N 5 15W
Multan, *Pak.* **58** 30 15N 71 36 E
Mumbles Hd., *U.K.* **17** 51 33N 4 0W
Munchen-Gladbach, *W. Ger.* **36** 51 12N 6 23 E
Mundesley, *U.K.* **15** 52 53N 1 24 E
Munich, *W. Ger.* **42** 48 8N 11 33 E
Münster, *W. Ger.* **36** 51 58N 7 37 E
Munster □, *Ire.* **25** 52 20N 8 40W
Murchison ⟶, *Austral.* **66** 27 45S 114 0 E
Murcia, *Sp.* **37** 38 20N 1 10W
Mureş ⟶, *Rom.* **43** 46 15N 20 13 E
Murmansk, *U.S.S.R.* **46** 68 57N 33 10 E
Murray ⟶, *S. Austral., Austral.* **70** 35 20S 139 22 E
Murray ⟶, *W. Austral., Austral.* **67** 32 33S 115 45 E
Murrumbidgee ⟶, *Austral.* **70** 34 43S 143 12 E
Murton, *U.K.* **19** 54 51N 1 22W
Murwillumbah, *Austral.* **67** 28 18S 153 27 E
Muscat, *Oman* **57** 23 40N 58 38 E
Musgrave Ras., *Austral.* **66** 26 0S 132 0 E
Musselburgh, *U.K.* **21** 55 57N 3 3W
Muswellbrook, *Austral.* **70** 32 16S 150 56 E
Mutare, *Zimb.* **81** 18 58S 32 38 E
Muthill, *U.K.* **21** 56 20N 3 50W
Muzaffarpur, *India* **59** 26 7N 85 23 E
Mwanza, *Tanz.* **80** 2 30S 32 58 E
Mweelrea, *Ire.* **24** 53 37N 9 48W
My Tho, *Viet.* **63** 10 29N 106 23 E
Myddle, *U.K.* **14** 52 49N 2 47W
Myitkyina, *Burma* **59** 25 24N 97 26 E
Mymensingh, *Bangla.* **59** 24 45N 90 24 E
Mynydd Du, *U.K.* **17** 51 45N 3 45W
Mynydd Prescelly, *U.K.* **17** 51 57N 4 48W
Mysore, *India* **58** 12 17N 76 41 E

N

Naas, *Ire.* **25** 53 12N 6 40W
Nābulus, *Jord.* **57** 32 14N 35 15 E
Nafferton, *U.K.* **19** 54 1N 0 24W
Nagaland □, *India* **59** 26 0N 94 30 E
Nagano, *Jap.* **62** 36 40N 138 10 E
Nagaoka, *Jap.* **62** 37 27N 138 51 E
Nagasaki, *Jap.* **62** 32 47N 129 50 E
Nagoya, *Jap.* **62** 35 10N 136 50 E
Nagpur, *India* **58** 21 8N 79 10 E
Naha, *Jap.* **62** 26 13N 127 42 E
Nailsea, *U.K.* **14** 51 25N 2 44W
Nailsworth, *U.K.* **14** 51 41N 2 12W
Nairn, *U.K.* **23** 57 35N 3 54W
Nairobi, *Kenya* **80** 1 17S 36 48 E
Nakuru, *Kenya* **80** 0 15S 36 4 E
Nalchik, *U.S.S.R.* **47** 43 30N 43 33 E
Nam Co, *China* **60** 30 30N 90 45 E
Namangan, *U.S.S.R.* **48** 41 0N 71 40 E
Namib Desert, *Nam.* **81** 22 30S 15 0 E
Namibe, *Angola* **81** 15 7S 12 11 E
Namibia ■, *Africa* **81** 22 0S 18 9 E
Nampula, *Mozam.* **81** 15 6N 39 15 E
Namur, *Belg.* **36** 50 27N 4 52 E
Nan Shan, *China* **60** 38 30N 99 0 E
Nanaimo, *Canada* **88** 49 10N 124 0W
Nanchang, *China* **61** 28 42N 115 55 E
Nanchong, *China* **60** 30 43N 106 2 E
Nancy, *Fr.* **34** 48 42N 6 12 E
Nanda Devi, *India* **58** 30 23N 79 59 E
Nanjing = Nanking, *China* **61** 32 2N 118 47 E
Nanking, *China* **61** 32 2N 118 47 E
Nanning, *China* **60** 22 48N 108 20 E
Nanping, *China* **61** 26 38N 118 10 E
Nantes, *Fr.* **34** 47 12N 1 33W
Nantong, *China* **61** 32 1N 120 52 E
Nantucket Sd., *U.S.A.* **93** 41 30N 70 15W
Nantwich, *U.K.* **18** 53 5N 2 31W
Napier, *N.Z.* **71** 39 30S 176 56 E
Naples, *It.* **40** 40 50N 14 17 E
Nappa, *U.K.* **18** 53 58N 2 14W
Nara, *Jap.* **62** 34 40N 135 49 E
Narayanganj, *Bangla.* **59** 23 40N 90 33 E
Narberth, *U.K.* **17** 51 48N 4 45W
Narborough, *U.K.* **14** 52 34N 1 12W
Nare Head, *U.K.* **16** 50 12N 4 55W
Narmada ⟶, *India* **58** 21 38N 72 36 E
Narrandera, *Austral.* **70** 34 42S 146 31 E
Narrogin, *Austral.* **66** 32 58S 117 14 E
Narromine, *Austral.* **70** 32 12S 148 12 E
Narvik, *Nor.* **44** 68 28N 17 26 E
Naseby, *U.K.* **15** 52 24N 0 59W
Nashua, *U.S.A.* **93** 42 50N 71 25W
Nashville, *U.S.A.* **91** 36 12N 86 46W
Nasik, *India* **58** 19 58N 73 50 E
Nassau, *Baham.* **95** 25 0N 77 20W
Nasser, L., *Egypt* **79** 23 0N 32 30 E
Nässjö, *Swed.* **45** 57 39N 14 42 E
Natal, *Brazil* **81** 5 47S 35 13W
Natal □, *S. Afr.* **101** 28 30S 30 30 E
Nauru ■, *Pac. Oc.* **64** 1 0S 166 0 E
Navan = An Uaimh, *Ire.* **24** 53 39N 6 40W
Navenby, *U.K.* **19** 53 7N 0 32W
Naver ⟶, *U.K.* **23** 58 34N 4 15W
Náxos, *Greece* **41** 37 8N 25 25 E
Nazareth, *Isr.* **57** 32 42N 35 17 E
Naze, The, *U.K.* **15** 51 53N 1 19 E
Ndjamena, *Chad* **79** 12 10N 14 59 E
Ndola, *Zam.* **81** 13 0S 28 34 E
Neagh, L., *U.K.* **24** 54 35N 6 25W
Neath, *U.K.* **17** 51 39N 3 49W
Nebraska □, *U.S.A.* **90** 41 30N 100 0W
Needham Market, *U.K.* **15** 52 9N 1 2 E
Needles, The, *U.K.* **14** 50 39N 1 35W
Negro ⟶, *Arg.* **102** 41 2S 62 47W
Negro ⟶, *Brazil* **100** 3 0S 60 0W
Negros, *Phil.* **63** 9 30N 122 40 E
Neijiang, *China* **60** 29 35N 104 55 E
Neilston, *U.K.* **20** 55 47N 4 27W
Neiva, *Col.* **100** 2 56N 75 18W
Nellore, *India* **58** 14 27N 79 59 E
Nelson, *N.Z.* **71** 41 18S 173 16 E
Nelson, *U.K.* **18** 53 50N 2 14W
Nelson ⟶, *Canada* **88** 54 33N 98 2W
Nelspruit, *S. Afr.* **81** 25 29S 30 59 E
Nenagh, *Ire.* **25** 52 52N 8 11W
Nene ⟶, *U.K.* **15** 52 38N 0 13 E
Nepal ■, *Asia* **59** 28 0N 84 30 E
Nephin, *Ire.* **24** 54 1N 9 21W
Ness, Loch, *U.K.* **23** 57 15N 4 30W
Neston, *U.K.* **18** 53 17N 3 3W
Netanya, *Isr.* **57** 32 20N 34 51 E
Nether Stowey, *U.K.* **14** 51 0N 3 10W
Netherbury, *U.K.* **14** 50 46N 2 45W
Netherlands ■, *Europe* **36** 52 0N 5 30 E
Netley, *U.K.* **14** 50 53N 1 21W
Netley Marsh, *U.K.* **14** 50 55N 1 32W
Nettlebed, *U.K.* **15** 51 34N 0 54W
Nettleham, *U.K.* **19** 53 15N 0 28W
Neuchâtel, *Switz.* **42** 47 0N 6 55 E
Neukirchen, *W. Ger.* **36** 54 52N 8 44 E
Neuss, *W. Ger.* **36** 51 12N 6 39 E
Neustadt, *W. Ger.* **36** 49 21N 8 10 E
Neuwied, *W. Ger.* **36** 50 26N 7 29 E
Nevada □, *U.S.A.* **90** 39 20N 117 0W
Nevada, Sierra, *Sp.* **37** 37 3N 3 15W
Nevada, Sierra, *U.S.A.* **90** 39 0N 120 30W
Nevers, *Fr.* **34** 47 0N 3 9 E
New Abbey, *U.K.* **21** 54 59N 3 38W
New Alresford, *U.K.* **14** 51 6N 1 10W
New Amsterdam, *Guy.* **101** 6 15N 57 36W
New Bedford, *U.S.A.* **93** 41 40N 70 52W
New Brighton, *N.Z.* **71** 43 29S 172 43 E
New Brighton, *U.K.* **18** 53 27N 3 2W
New Brunswick □, *Canada* **93** 46 50N 66 30W
New Caledonia, *Pac. Oc.* **64** 21 0S 165 0 E
New Castile, *Sp.* **37** 39 45N 3 20W
New Cumnock, *U.K.* **20** 55 24N 4 13W
New Forest, *U.K.* **14** 50 53N 1 40W
New Galloway, *U.K.* **21** 55 4N 4 10W
New Guinea, *Pac. Oc.* **64** 4 0S 136 0 E
New Hampshire □, *U.S.A.* **93** 43 40N 71 40W
New Haven, *U.S.A.* **93** 41 20N 72 54W
New Hebrides = Vanuatu ■, *Pac. Oc.* **64** 15 0S 168 0 E
New Holland, *U.K.* **19** 53 42N 0 22W
New Jersey □, *U.S.A.* **93** 40 30N 74 10W
New London, *U.S.A.* **93** 41 23N 72 8W
New Luce, *U.K.* **20** 54 57N 4 50W
New Mexico □, *U.S.A.* **90** 34 30N 106 0W
New Mills, *U.K.* **18** 53 22N 2 0W
New Orleans, *U.S.A.* **91** 30 0N 90 5W
New Plymouth, *N.Z.* **71** 39 4S 174 5 E
New Quay, *U.K.* **17** 52 13N 4 21W
New Radnor, *U.K.* **17** 52 15N 3 10W
New Romney, *U.K.* **15** 50 59N 0 57 E
New Ross, *Ire.* **25** 52 24N 6 58W
New Rossington, *U.K.* **19** 53 30N 1 4W
New Siberian Is., *U.S.S.R.* **49** 75 0N 142 0 E
New South Wales □, *Austral.* **70** 33 0S 146 0 E
New York □, *U.S.A.* **93** 42 40N 76 0W
New York City, *U.S.A.* **93** 40 45N 74 0W
New Zealand ■, *Pac. Oc.* **71** 40 0S 176 0 E
Newark, *U.S.A.* **93** 40 41N 74 12W
Newark-on-Trent, *U.K.* **19** 53 6N 0 48W
Newbiggin-by-the-Sea, *U.K.* **21** 55 12N 1 31W
Newbigging, *U.K.* **21** 55 42N 3 33W
Newburgh, *U.K.* **21** 56 21N 3 15W
Newburn, *U.K.* **21** 54 57N 1 45W
Newbury, *U.K.* **14** 51 24N 1 19W
Newby Bridge, *U.K.* **18** 54 16N 2 59W
Newcastle, *Austral.* **70** 33 0S 151 46 E
Newcastle, *U.K.* **24** 54 13N 5 54W
Newcastle Emlyn, *U.K.* **17** 52 2N 4 29W
Newcastle-under-Lyme, *U.K.* **18** 53 2N 2 15W
Newcastle-upon-Tyne, *U.K.* **19** 54 59N 1 37W
Newcastleton, *U.K.* **21** 55 10N 2 50W
Newent, *U.K.* **14** 51 56N 2 24W
Newfoundland □, *Canada* **89** 53 0N 58 0W
Newham, *U.K.* **15** 51 31N 0 2 E
Newhaven, *U.K.* **15** 50 47N 0 4 E
Newington, *Kent, U.K.* **15** 51 5N 1 8 E
Newington, *Kent, U.K.* **15** 51 21N 0 40 E
Newlyn, *U.K.* **16** 50 6N 5 33W
Newlyn East, *U.K.* **16** 50 22N 5 3W
Newman, *Austral.* **66** 23 18S 119 45 E
Newmarket, *Ire.* **25** 52 13N 9 0W
Newmarket, *Lewis, U.K.* **22** 58 14N 6 24W
Newmarket, *Suffolk, U.K.* **15** 52 15N 0 23 E
Newmilns, *U.K.* **20** 55 36N 4 20W
Newnham, *U.K.* **14** 51 48N 2 27W
Newport, *Dyfed, U.K.* **17** 52 1N 4 53W
Newport, *Essex, U.K.* **15** 51 58N 0 13 E
Newport, *Gwent, U.K.* **17** 51 35N 3 0W
Newport, *I. of W., U.K.* **14** 50 42N 1 18W
Newport, *Salop, U.K.* **14** 52 47N 2 22W
Newport News, *U.S.A.* **91** 37 2N 76 30W
Newport on Tay, *U.K.* **21** 56 27N 2 56W
Newport Pagnell, *U.K.* **15** 52 5N 0 42W
Newquay, *U.K.* **16** 50 24N 5 6W
Newry, *U.K.* **24** 54 10N 6 20W
Newry & Mourne □, *U.K.* **24** 54 10N 6 15W
Newton Abbot, *U.K.* **16** 50 32N 3 37W
Newton Arlosh, *U.K.* **18** 54 53N 3 15W
Newton-Aycliffe, *U.K.* **19** 54 36N 1 33W
Newton Ferrers, *U.K.* **16** 50 19N 4 3W
Newton le Willows, *U.K.* **18** 53 28N 2 40W
Newton St. Cyres, *U.K.* **16** 50 46N 3 35W
Newton Stewart, *U.K.* **20** 54 57N 4 30W
Newtongrange, *U.K.* **21** 55 52N 3 4W
Newtonmore, *U.K.* **23** 57 4N 4 7W
Newtown, *Wales, U.K.* **17** 52 31N 3 19W
Newtown St. Boswells, *Scotland, U.K.* **21** 55 34N 2 38W
Newtownabbey, *Ire.* **24** 54 40N 5 55W
Newtownabbey □, *U.K.* **24** 54 45N 6 0W
Newtownards, *U.K.* **24** 54 37N 5 41W
Nha Trang, *Viet.* **63** 12 16N 109 10 E
Niagara Falls, *Canada* **92** 43 7N 79 5W
Niagara Falls, *U.S.A.* **92** 43 5N 79 0W
Niamey, *Niger* **78** 13 27N 2 6 E
Nicaragua ■, *Cent. Am.* **94** 11 40N 85 30W
Nicaragua, L., *Nic.* **94** 12 0N 85 30W
Nice, *Fr.* **35** 43 42N 7 14 E
Nicobar Is., *Ind. Oc.* **51** 9 0N 93 0 E
Nicosia, *Cyprus* **47** 35 10N 33 25 E
Nicoya, Pen. de, *C.R.* **94** 9 45N 85 40W

Nidd —►, U.K. 19 54 1N 1 32W
Nidderdale, U.K. 19 54 5N 1 46W
Niger ■, W. Afr. 78 13 30N 10 0 E
Niger —►, W. Afr. 78 5 33N 6 33 E
Nigeria ■, W. Afr. 78 8 30N 8 0 E
Niigata, Jap. 62 37 58N 139 0 E
Niihau, U.S.A. 90 21 55N 160 10W
Nijmegen, Neth. 36 51 50N 5 52 E
Nikolayev, U.S.S.R. 47 46 58N 32 0 E
Nikolayevsk, U.S.S.R. 49 50 0N 45 35 E
Nile —►, Africa 79 30 10N 31 6 E
Nîmes, Fr. 35 43 50N 4 23 E
Ninety Mile Beach, The, Austral. 70 38 15S 147 24 E
Ninfield, U.K. 15 50 53N 0 26 E
Ningbo, China 61 29 51N 121 28 E
Ningxia Huizu Zizhiqu □, China 60 38 0N 106 0 E
Niort, Fr. 35 46 19N 0 29W
Nipigon, L., Canada 92 49 50N 88 30W
Niš, Yug. 41 43 19N 21 58 E
Niterói, Brazil 101 22 52S 43 0W
Nith —►, U.K. 21 55 20N 3 5W
Nithsdale, U.K. 21 55 14N 3 50W
Niton, U.K. 14 50 35N 1 14W
Nizhniy Tagil, U.S.S.R. 46 57 55N 59 57 E
Nkongsamba, Cam. 80 4 55N 9 55 E
Nobeoka, Jap. 62 32 36N 131 41 E
Nogales, Mex. 94 31 20N 110 56W
Nordelph, U.K. 15 52 34N 0 18 E
Nordhorn, W. Ger. 36 52 27N 7 4 E
Nordvik, U.S.S.R. 49 74 2N 111 32 E
Nore —►, Ire. 25 52 40N 7 20W
Norfolk, U.S.A. 91 36 40N 76 15W
Norfolk □, U.K. 15 52 39N 1 0 E
Norfolk Broads, U.K. 15 52 30N 1 15 E
Norfolk I., Pac. Oc. 64 28 58S 168 3 E
Norham, U.K. 21 55 44N 2 9W
Norilsk, U.S.S.R. 49 69 20N 88 6 E
Norman, U.S.A. 90 35 12N 97 30W
Normandy, Fr. 34 48 45N 0 10 E
Normanton, U.K. 19 53 41N 1 26W
Norrbotten □, Swed. 44 66 30N 22 30 E
Norrköping, Swed. 45 58 37N 16 11 E
Norrland □, Swed. 44 66 50N 18 0 E
Norseman, Austral. 66 32 8S 121 43 E
North Battleford, Canada 88 52 50N 108 17W
North Bay, Canada 92 46 20N 79 30W
North Berwick, U.K. 21 56 4N 2 44W
North Cape, Nor. 44 71 15N 25 40 E
North Carolina □, U.S.A. 91 35 30N 80 0W
North Cerney, U.K. 14 51 45N 1 58W
North Channel, U.K. 20 55 0N 5 30W
North Collingham, U.K. 19 53 8N 0 46W
North Dakota □, U.S.A. 90 47 30N 100 0W
North Dorset Downs, U.K. 14 50 50N 2 30W
North Down □, U.K. 24 54 40N 5 45W
North Downs, U.K. 15 51 17N 0 30 E
North Esk —►, U.K. 23 56 44N 2 25W
North European Plain 26 55 0N 20 0 E
North Foreland, U.K. 15 51 22N 1 28 E
North Hill, U.K. 16 50 33N 4 26W
North Hykeham, U.K. 19 53 10N 0 35W
North I., N.Z. 71 38 0S 175 0 E
North Minch, U.K. 22 58 5N 5 55W
North Molton, U.K. 16 51 3N 3 48W
North Petherton, U.K. 14 51 6N 3 1W
North Pole, Arctic 103 90 0N 0 0 E
North Queensferry, U.K. 21 56 1N 3 22W
North Rhine Westphalia □, W. Ger. 42 51 55N 7 0 E
North Ronaldsay, U.K. 23 59 20N 2 30W
North Sea, Europe 26 56 0N 4 0 E
North Somercotes, U.K. 19 53 28N 0 9 E
North Sunderland, U.K. 21 55 35N 1 40W
North Tawton, U.K. 16 50 48N 3 55W
North Thoresby, U.K. 19 53 27N 0 3W
North Tidworth, U.K. 14 51 14N 1 40W
North Tyne —►, U.K. 19 54 59N 2 7W
North Uist, U.K. 22 57 40N 7 15W
North Walsham, U.K. 15 52 49N 1 22 E
North West Highlands, U.K. 22 57 35N 5 2W
North West Territories □, Canada 89 67 0N 110 0W
North York Moors, U.K. 19 54 25N 0 50W
North Yorkshire □, U.K. 19 54 15N 1 25W
Northallerton, U.K. 19 54 20N 1 26W
Northam, Austral. 66 31 35S 116 42 E
Northam, U.K. 16 51 2N 4 13W
Northampton, U.K. 15 52 14N 0 54W
Northampton □, U.K. 15 52 16N 0 55W
Northern Ireland □, U.K. 24 54 45N 7 0W
Northern Marianas, Pac. Oc. 64 17 0N 145 0 E
Northern Territory □, Austral. 66 16 0S 133 0 E
Northfleet, U.K. 15 51 26N 0 20 E
Northiam, U.K. 15 50 59N 0 39 E
Northland □, N.Z. 71 35 30S 173 30 E
Northleach, U.K. 14 51 49N 1 50W
Northrepps, U.K. 15 52 53N 1 20 E
Northumberland □, U.K. 19 55 12N 2 0W
Northumberland Str., Canada 93 46 20N 64 0W
Northwich, U.K. 18 53 16N 2 30W
Northwold, U.K. 15 52 33N 0 37 E
Norton, N. Yorks., U.K. 19 54 9N 0 48W
Norton, Suffolk, U.K. 15 52 15N 0 52 E
Norton Fitzwarren, U.K. 14 51 1N 3 10W
Norway ■, Europe 44 63 0N 11 0 E
Norwegian Sea, Atl. Oc. 44 66 0N 1 0 E
Norwich, U.K. 15 52 38N 1 17 E
Noss Hd., U.K. 23 58 29N 3 4W
Nottingham, U.K. 19 52 57N 1 10W
Nottingham □, U.K. 19 53 10N 1 0W
Nouâdhibou, Maurit. 78 20 54N 17 0W
Nouakchott, Maurit. 78 18 9N 15 58W
Nouméa, N. Cal. 64 22 17S 166 30 E
Nova Scotia □, Canada 93 45 10N 63 0W
Novara, It. 40 45 27N 8 36 E
Novaya Zemlya, U.S.S.R. 48 75 0N 56 0 E
Novi Sad, Yug. 41 45 18N 19 52 E
Novocherkassk, U.S.S.R. 47 47 27N 40 5 E
Novokuznetsk, U.S.S.R. 48 53 45N 87 10 E
Novomoskovsk, U.S.S.R. 46 54 5N 38 15 E
Novorossiysk, U.S.S.R. 47 44 43N 37 46 E
Novoshakhtinsk, U.S.S.R. 47 47 46N 39 58 E
Novosibirsk, U.S.S.R. 48 55 0N 83 5 E
Nubian Desert, Sudan 79 21 30N 33 30 E
Nuevo Laredo, Mex. 94 27 30N 99 30W
Nullarbor Plain, Austral. 66 30 45S 129 0 E
Nuneaton, U.K. 14 52 32N 1 29W
Nunney, U.K. 14 51 13N 2 20W
Nuremburg, W. Ger. 42 49 26N 11 5 E
Nyasa, L., Africa 81 12 30S 34 30 E
Nyíregyháza, Hung. 43 47 58N 21 47 E
Nykøbing, Den. 45 56 48N 8 51 E

O

Oa, Mull of, U.K. 20 55 35N 6 20W
Oa, The, Pen., U.K. 20 55 36N 6 17W
Oadby, U.K. 14 52 37N 1 7W
Oahe L., U.S.A. 90 45 30N 100 25W
Oahu, U.S.A. 90 21 30N 158 0W
Oakengates, U.K. 14 52 42N 2 29W
Oakham, U.K. 15 52 40N 0 43W
Oakland, U.S.A. 90 37 50N 122 18W
Oakleigh, Austral. 70 37 54S 145 6 E
Oamaru, N.Z. 71 45 5S 170 59 E
Oaxaca, Mex. 94 17 2N 96 40W
Ob —►, U.S.S.R. 48 66 45N 69 30 E
Ob, G. of, U.S.S.R. 48 70 0N 73 0 E
Oban, U.K. 20 56 25N 5 30W
Oberhausen, W. Ger. 36 51 28N 6 50 E
Ochil Hills, U.K. 21 56 14N 3 40W
Ochiltree, U.K. 20 55 26N 4 23W
October Revolution I., U.S.S.R. 49 79 30N 97 0 E
Odense, Den. 45 55 22N 10 23 E
Odessa, U.S.A. 90 31 51N 102 23W
Odessa, U.S.S.R. 47 46 30N 30 45 E
Odiham, U.K. 15 51 16N 0 56W
Odra —►, Pol. 42 53 33N 14 38 E
Offaly □, Ire. 25 53 15N 7 30W
Offenbach, W. Ger. 42 50 6N 8 46 E
Ogbomosho, Nig. 78 8 1N 4 11 E
Ogden, U.S.A. 90 41 13N 112 1W
Ohio □, U.S.A. 92 40 20N 14 10 E
Ohio —►, U.S.A. 92 38 0N 86 0W
Ōita, Jap. 62 33 14N 131 36 E
Okavango Swamps, Bots. 81 18 45S 22 45 E
Okayama, Jap. 62 34 40N 133 54 E
Okazaki, Jap. 62 34 57N 137 10 E
Okehampton, U.K. 16 50 44N 4 1W
Okhotsk, U.S.S.R. 49 59 20N 143 10 E
Okhotsk, Sea of, Asia 49 55 0N 145 0 E
Oklahoma □, U.S.A. 90 35 20N 97 30W
Oklahoma City, U.S.A. 91 35 25N 97 30W
Ólafsfjörður, Ice. 44 66 4N 18 39W
Öland, Swed. 45 56 45N 16 38 E
Old Basing, U.K. 14 51 16N 1 3W
Old Castile, Sp. 37 41 55N 4 0W
Old Castle, Ire. 24 53 46N 7 10W
Old Kilpatrick, U.K. 20 55 56N 4 34W
Old Leake, U.K. 19 53 2N 0 6 E
Oldbury, Gloucs., U.K. 14 51 38N 2 30W
Oldbury, W. Midlands, U.K. 14 52 30N 2 0W
Oldenburg, W. Ger. 36 53 10N 8 10 E
Oldham, U.K. 18 53 33N 2 8W
Oldmeldrum, U.K. 23 57 20N 2 19W
Olekminsk, U.S.S.R. 49 60 25N 120 30 E
Olinda, Brazil 101 8 1S 34 51W
Ollerton, U.K. 19 53 12N 1 1W
Olney, U.K. 15 52 9N 0 42W
Olomouc, Czech. 42 49 38N 17 12 E
Olsztyn, Pol. 43 53 48N 20 29 E
Olympia, Greece 41 37 39N 21 39 E
Olympus, Mt., Greece 41 40 6N 22 23 E
Omagh, U.K. 24 54 36N 7 20W
Omagh □, U.K. 24 54 35N 7 15W
Omaha, U.S.A. 91 41 15N 96 0W
Oman ■, Si. Arab. 57 23 0N 58 0 E
Oman, G. of, Asia 57 24 30N 58 30 E
Ombersley, U.K. 14 52 17N 2 12W
Omdurmân, Sudan 79 15 40N 32 28 E
Ōmiya, Jap. 62 35 54N 139 38 E
Omsk, U.S.S.R. 48 55 0N 73 12 E
Ōmuta, Jap. 62 33 0N 130 26 E
Onchan, U.K. 18 54 11N 4 27W
Onega —►, U.S.S.R. 46 63 58N 37 55 E
Onega, G. of, U.S.S.R. 46 64 30N 37 0 E
Onega, L., U.S.S.R. 46 62 0N 35 30 E
Onehunga, N.Z. 71 36 55S 174 48 E
Onny —►, U.K. 14 52 30N 2 50W
Ontario □, Canada 88 52 0N 88 10W
Ontario, L., N. Am. 92 43 40N 78 0W
Opole, Pol. 43 50 42N 17 58 E
Oporto, Port. 37 41 8N 8 40W
Oradea, Rom. 43 47 2N 21 58 E
Oran, Alg. 78 35 45N 0 39W
Orange, Austral. 70 33 15S 149 7 E
Orange —►, S. Afr. 81 28 41S 16 28 E
Orange Free State □, S. Afr. 81 28 30S 27 0 E
Ord, Mt., Austral. 66 17 20S 125 34 E
Ordos = Mu Us Shamo, China 61 39 0N 109 0 E
Ordzhonikidze, U.S.S.R. 47 43 0N 44 35 E
Örebro, Swed. 45 59 20N 15 18 E
Oregon □, U.S.A. 90 44 0N 121 0W
Orekhovo-Zuyevo, U.S.S.R. 46 55 50N 38 55 E
Orel, U.S.S.R. 46 52 57N 36 3 E
Orenburg, U.S.S.R. 46 51 45N 55 6 E
Orense, Sp. 37 42 19N 7 55W
Orford, U.K. 15 52 6N 1 31 E
Orford Ness, U.K. 15 52 6N 1 31 E
Orinoco —►, Ven. 100 9 15N 61 30W
Orissa □, India 59 20 0N 84 0 E
Oristano, It. 40 39 54N 8 35 E
Orizaba, Mex. 94 18 51N 97 6W
Orkney □, U.K. 23 59 0N 3 0W
Orkney Is., U.K. 23 59 0N 3 0W
Orlando, U.S.A. 91 28 30N 81 25W
Orléans, Fr. 34 47 54N 1 52 E
Ormesby St. Margaret, U.K. 15 52 39N 1 42 E
Ormskirk, U.K. 18 53 35N 2 53W
Örnsköldsvik, Swed. 44 63 17N 18 40 E
Oronsay, Pass of, U.K. 20 56 0N 6 10W
Oronsay I., U.K. 20 56 0N 6 14W
Orsk, U.S.S.R. 46 51 12N 58 34 E
Orton Tebay, U.K. 18 54 28N 2 35W
Oruro, Bol. 100 18 0S 67 9W
Orwell —►, U.K. 15 52 2N 1 12 E
Ōsaka, Jap. 62 34 40N 135 30 E
Osh, U.S.S.R. 48 40 37N 72 49 E
Oshawa, Canada 92 43 50N 78 50W
Oshogbo, Nig. 78 7 48N 4 37 E
Osijek, Yug. 41 45 34N 18 41 E
Osizweni, S. Afr. 81 27 49S 30 7 E
Oslo, Nor. 45 59 55N 10 45 E
Oslo Fjord, Nor. 45 58 30N 10 0 E
Osmotherley, U.K. 19 54 22N 1 18W
Osnabrück, W. Ger. 36 52 16N 8 2 E
Osorno, Chile 102 40 25S 73 0W
Ossett, U.K. 19 53 40N 1 35W
Ostend, Belg. 36 51 15N 2 50 E
Östersund, Swed. 44 63 10N 14 38 E
Ostrava, Czech. 43 49 51N 18 18 E
Osumi, Is., Jap. 62 30 30N 130 45 E
Oswaldtwistle, U.K. 18 53 44N 2 27W
Oswestry, U.K. 14 52 52N 3 3W
Otago □, N.Z. 71 44 44S 169 10 E
Otaru, Jap. 62 43 10N 141 0 E
Otley, U.K. 19 53 54N 1 41W
Otranto, Str. of, It. 41 40 15N 18 40 E
Ōtsu, Jap. 62 35 0N 135 50 E
Ottawa, Canada 93 45 27N 75 42W
Ottawa —►, Canada 93 45 27N 74 8W
Otter —►, U.K. 16 50 47N 3 12W
Otter Ferry, U.K. 20 56 1N 5 20W
Otterburn, U.K. 21 55 14N 2 12W
Ottery St. Mary, U.K. 16 50 45N 3 16W
Ouagadougou, B. Faso 78 12 25N 1 30W
Oujda, Mor. 78 34 41N 1 55W
Oulton, U.K. 15 52 29N 1 40 E
Oulton Broad, U.K. 15 52 28N 1 43 E
Oulu, Fin. 44 65 1N 25 29 E
Oulu, L., Fin. 44 64 25N 27 0 E
Oundle, U.K. 15 52 28N 0 28W
Ouse —►, E. Sussex, U.K. 15 50 43N 0 3 E
Ouse —►, N. Yorks., U.K. 19 54 3N 0 7 E
Outer Hebrides, U.K. 22 57 30N 7 40W
Outwell, U.K. 15 52 36N 0 14 E
Over Wallop, U.K. 14 51 9N 1 35W
Overstand, U.K. 15 52 55N 1 20 E
Overton, U.K. 14 51 14N 1 16W
Oviedo, Sp. 37 43 25N 5 50W
Owston Ferry, U.K. 19 53 28N 0 47W
Ox Mts., Ire. 24 54 6N 9 0W
Oxford, U.K. 14 51 45N 1 15W
Oxford □, U.K. 14 51 45N 1 15W
Oykel —►, U.K. 23 57 55N 4 26W
Ozark Plateau, U.S.A. 91 37 20N 91 40W

P

Paarl, S. Afr. 81 33 45S 18 56 E
Pacaraima, Sierra, Ven. 100 4 0N 62 30W
Pachuca, Mex. 94 20 10N 98 40W
Pacific Ocean 64 10 0N 140 0W
Padang, Indon. 63 1 0S 100 20 E
Paddock Wood, U.K. 15 51 13N 0 24 E
Padiham, U.K. 18 53 48N 2 20W
Padstow, U.K. 14 50 33N 4 57W
Padstow Bay, U.K. 16 50 35N 4 58W
Padua, It. 40 45 24N 11 52 E
Pagalu = Annobón, Atl. Oc. 73 1 25S 5 36 E
Paignton, U.K. 16 50 26N 3 33W
Painswick, U.K. 14 51 47N 2 11W
Paisley, U.K. 20 55 51N 4 27W
Pakistan ■, Asia 58 30 0N 70 0 E
Palawan, Phil. 63 9 30N 118 30 E
Palembang, Indon. 63 3 0S 104 50 E
Palencia, Sp. 37 42 1N 4 34W
Palermo, It. 40 38 8N 13 20 E
Palgrave, U.K. 15 52 22N 1 7 E
Palk Strait, Asia 58 10 0N 79 45 E
Palma de Mallorca, Sp. 37 39 35N 2 39 E
Palmer —►, Austral. 66 24 46S 133 25 E
Palmerston North, N.Z. 71 40 21S 175 39 E
Palmira, Col. 100 3 32N 76 16W
Pamirs, U.S.S.R. 48 37 40N 73 0 E
Pamlico Sd., U.S.A. 91 35 20N 76 0W
Pampas, Arg. 96 35 0S 63 0W
Pamplona, Sp. 37 42 48N 1 38W
Panamá, Pan. 94 9 0N 79 25W
Panama ■, Cent. Am. 95 8 48N 79 55W
Panamá, G. de, Pan. 95 8 4N 79 20W
Panama Canal, Pan. 94 9 10N 79 37W
Panay, Phil. 63 11 10N 122 30 E
Pančevo, Yug. 41 44 52N 20 41 E
Pangbourne, U.K. 14 51 28N 1 5W
Pantelleria, It. 40 36 52N 12 0 E
Papua New Guinea ■, Oc. 64 8 0S 145 0 E
Pará □, Brazil 101 3 20S 52 0W
Paraguay ■, S. Am. 102 23 0S 57 0W
Paraguay —►, Par. 102 27 18S 58 38W
Paramaribo, Surinam 101 5 50N 55 10W
Paraná, Arg. 102 31 45S 60 30W
Paraná —►, Arg. 102 33 43S 59 15W
Parecis, Serra dos, Brazil 100 13 0S 60 0W
Parepare, Indon. 63 4 0S 119 40 E
Paris, Fr. 34 48 50N 2 20 E
Parkes, Austral. 70 33 9S 148 11 E
Parma, It. 40 44 50N 10 20 E
Parnaiba —►, Brazil 101 3 0S 41 50W
Parracombe, U.K. 16 51 11N 3 55W
Parramatta, Austral. 70 33 48S 151 1 E
Parrett —►, U.K. 14 51 7N 2 58W
Partney, U.K. 19 53 12N 0 7 E
Parton, U.K. 18 54 34N 3 35W
Passage West, Ire. 25 51 52N 8 20W
Pasto, Col. 100 1 13N 77 17W
Patagonia, Arg. 102 45 0S 69 0W
Patcham, U.K. 15 50 52N 0 9W
Pateley Bridge, U.K. 19 54 5N 1 45W
Paterson, U.S.A. 93 40 55N 74 10W
Patna, India 59 25 35N 85 12 E
Patna, U.K. 20 55 21N 4 30W
Pátrai, Greece 41 38 14N 21 47 E
Patrick, U.K. 18 54 13N 4 41W
Patrington, U.K. 19 53 41N 0 1W
Patterdale, U.K. 18 54 33N 2 55W
Pau, Fr. 35 43 19N 0 25W
Paull, U.K. 19 53 42N 0 12W
Pavia, It. 40 45 10N 9 10 E
Pavlodar, U.S.S.R. 48 52 33N 77 0 E
Pawtucket, U.S.A. 93 41 51N 71 22W
Paz, La, Bol. 100 16 20S 68 10W
Pazardzhik, Bulg. 41 42 12N 24 20 E
Peace —►, Canada 88 59 0N 111 25W
Peacehaven, U.K. 15 50 47N 0 1 E
Peak, The, U.K. 18 53 24N 1 53W
Peasenhall, U.K. 15 52 17N 1 24 E
Pechora —►, U.S.S.R. 46 68 13N 54 15 E
Pécs, Hung. 43 46 5N 18 15 E
Peebles, U.K. 21 55 40N 3 12W
Peel, U.K. 18 54 14N 4 40W
Peel Fell, U.K. 21 55 17N 2 35W
Pegasus Bay, N.Z. 71 43 20S 173 10 E
Pegswood, U.K. 21 55 12N 1 38W
Pegu, Burma 59 17 20N 96 29 E
Pegu Yoma, Burma 59 19 0N 96 0 E
Pegwell Bay, U.K. 15 51 18N 1 22 E
Pekanbaru, Indon. 63 0 30N 101 15 E
Peking, China 61 39 55N 116 20 E
Peloponnese □, Greece 41 37 10N 22 0 E
Pelotas, Brazil 102 31 42S 52 23W
Pelvoux, Massif de, Fr. 35 44 52N 6 20 E
Pematangsiantar, Indon. 63 2 57N 99 5 E
Pemba, Tanz. 80 5 0S 39 45 E
Pembridge, U.K. 14 52 13N 2 54W
Pembroke, U.K. 17 51 41N 4 57W
Pembury, U.K. 15 51 8N 0 20 E
Pen-y-Ghent, U.K. 18 54 10N 2 15W
Pen-y-groes, U.K. 17 53 3N 4 18W
Penang = Pinang, Malay. 63 5 25N 100 15 E
Penarth, U.K. 17 51 26N 3 11W
Pendeen, U.K. 16 50 11N 5 39W
Pendle Hill, U.K. 18 53 53N 2 18W
Penicuik, U.K. 21 55 50N 3 14W
Peninsular Malaysia □, Malay. 63 4 0N 102 0 E
Penistone, U.K. 19 53 31N 1 38W
Penkridge, U.K. 14 52 44N 2 8W
Pennines, U.K. 18 54 50N 2 20W
Pennsylvania □, U.S.A. 92 40 50N 78 0W
Penpont, U.K. 21 55 14N 3 49W

Penrith, *Austral.* 70 33 43S 150 38 E
Penrith, *U.K.* 18 54 40N 2 45W
Penryn, *U.K.* 16 50 10N 5 7W
Pensacola, *U.S.A.* 90 30 30N 87 10W
Penshurst, *U.K.* 15 51 10N 0 12 E
Pentire Pt., *U.K.* 16 50 35N 4 57W
Pentland Firth, *U.K.* 23 58 43N 3 10W
Pentland Hills, *U.K.* 21 55 48N 3 25W
Penwortham, *U.K.* 18 53 45N 2 44W
Penza, *U.S.S.R.* 46 53 15N 45 5 E
Penzance, *U.K.* 16 50 7N 5 32W
Peoria, *U.S.A.* 92 40 40N 89 40W
Pereira, *Col.* 100 4 49N 75 43W
Perm, *U.S.S.R.* 46 58 0N 57 10 E
Perouse Str., La, *Jap.* 64 45 40N 142 0 E
Perpignan, *Fr.* 35 42 42N 2 53 E
Perranporth, *U.K.* 16 50 21N 5 9W
Perranzabuloe, *U.K.* 16 50 18N 5 7W
Pershore, *U.K.* 14 52 7N 2 4W
Persian Gulf = Gulf, The, *Asia* 56 27 0N 50 0 E
Perth, *Austral.* 66 31 57S 115 52 E
Perth, *U.K.* 21 56 24N 3 27W
Peru ■, *S. Am.* 100 8 0S 75 0W
Perúgia, *It.* 40 43 6N 12 24 E
Pescara, *It.* 40 42 28N 14 13 E
Peshawar, *Pak.* 58 34 2N 71 37 E
Peterborough, *Canada* 92 44 20N 78 20W
Peterborough, *U.K.* 15 52 35N 0 14W
Peterchurch, *U.K.* 14 52 3N 2 57W
Peterhead, *U.K.* 23 57 30N 1 49W
Peterlee, *U.K.* 19 54 45N 1 18W
Petersfield, *U.K.* 15 51 0N 0 56W
Petropavlovsk, *U.S.S.R.* 48 54 53N 69 13 E
Petropavlovsk-Kamchatskiy, *U.S.S.R.* 49 53 3N 158 43 E
Petrópolis, *Brazil* 101 22 33S 43 9W
Petrozavodsk, *U.S.S.R.* 46 61 41N 34 20 E
Petworth, *U.K.* 15 50 59N 0 37W
Pevensey, *U.K.* 15 50 49N 0 20 E
Pevensey Levels, *U.K.* 15 50 50N 0 20 E
Pewsey, *U.K.* 14 51 20N 1 46W
Pewsey, Vale of, *U.K.* 14 51 20N 1 46W
Pforzheim, *W. Ger.* 42 48 53N 8 43 E
Philadelphia, *U.S.A.* 93 40 0N 75 10W
Philippines ■, *Asia* 63 12 0N 123 0 E
Phnom Penh, *Cambod.* 63 11 33N 104 55 E
Phoenix, *U.S.A.* 90 33 30N 112 10W
Phoenix Is., *Pac. Oc.* 65 3 30S 172 0W
Piacenza, *It.* 40 45 2N 9 42 E
Piatra Neamţ, *Rom.* 43 46 56N 26 21 E
Picardie, *Fr.* 34 49 50N 3 0 E
Picardy = Picardie, *Fr.* 34 49 50N 3 0 E
Pickering, *U.K.* 19 54 15N 0 46W
Pickering, Vale of, *U.K.* 19 54 0N 0 45W
Pidley, *U.K.* 15 52 33N 0 4W
Piedmont □, *It.* 40 45 0N 7 30 E
Piedras Negras, *Mex.* 94 28 42N 100 31W
Pierowall, *U.K.* 23 59 20N 3 0W
Pietermaritzburg, *S. Afr.* 81 29 35S 30 25 E
Pilbara, *Austral.* 66 21 15S 118 16 E
Pilcomayo →, *Par.* 102 25 21S 57 42W
Pilling, *U.K.* 18 53 55N 2 54W
Pilton, *U.K.* 14 51 0N 2 35W
Pinang, *Malay.* 63 5 25N 100 15 E
Pinchbeck, *U.K.* 15 52 48N 0 9W
Pindus Mts., *Greece* 41 40 0N 21 0 E
Pine Bluff, *U.S.A.* 90 34 10N 92 0W
Pingxiang, *China* 60 22 6N 106 46 E
Pinhoe, *U.K.* 16 50 44N 3 29W
Pinjarra, *Austral.* 66 32 37S 115 52 E
Pinwherry, *U.K.* 20 55 9N 4 50W
Piotrków Trybunalski, *Pol.* 43 51 23N 19 43 E
Piracicaba, *Brazil* 102 22 45S 47 40W
Piraiévs, *Greece* 41 37 57N 23 42 E
Pirbright, *U.K.* 15 51 17N 0 40W
Pirmasens, *W. Ger.* 36 49 12N 7 30 E
Pisa, *It.* 40 43 43N 10 23 E
Pistóia, *It.* 40 43 57N 10 53 E
Pitcairn I., *Pac. Oc.* 65 25 5S 130 5W
Piteşti, *Rom.* 43 44 52N 24 54 E
Pitlochry, *U.K.* 23 56 43N 3 43W
Pittenweem, *U.K.* 21 56 13N 2 43W
Pittsburgh, *U.S.A.* 92 40 25N 79 55W
Pittsfield, *U.S.A.* 93 42 28N 73 17W
Piura, *Peru* 100 5 15S 80 38W
Pladda, I., *U.K.* 20 55 25N 5 7W
Plata, La, *Arg.* 102 35 0S 57 55W
Plata, Río de la, *S. Am.* 102 34 45S 57 30W
Plauen, *E. Ger.* 42 50 29N 12 9 E
Plenty, Bay of, *N.Z.* 71 37 45S 177 0 E
Pleven, *Bulg.* 41 43 26N 24 37 E
Płock, *Pol.* 43 52 32N 19 40 E
Ploieşti, *Rom.* 43 44 57N 26 5 E
Plovdiv, *Bulg.* 41 42 8N 24 44 E
Plymouth, *U.K.* 16 50 23N 4 9W
Plymouth Sd., *U.K.* 16 50 20N 4 10W
Plympton, *U.K.* 16 50 24N 4 2W
Plymstock, *U.K.* 16 50 22N 4 6W
Plynlimon = Pumlumon Fawr, *U.K.* 17 52 29N 3 47W
Plzen, *Czech.* 42 49 45N 13 22 E
Po →, *It.* 40 44 57N 12 4 E
Pocklington, *U.K.* 19 53 56N 0 48W
Podolsk, *U.S.S.R.* 46 55 25N 37 30 E
Pointe-à-Pitre, *Guad.* 94 16 10N 61 30W
Pointe Noire, *Congo* 80 4 48S 11 53 E
Poitiers, *Fr.* 34 46 35N 0 20 E
Poland ■, *Europe* 43 52 0N 20 0 E
Polden Hills, *U.K.* 14 51 7N 2 50W
Polegate, *U.K.* 15 50 49N 0 15 E
Polesworth, *U.K.* 14 52 37N 1 37W
Polperro, *U.K.* 16 50 19N 4 31W
Polruan, *U.K.* 16 50 17N 4 36W
Poltava, *U.S.S.R.* 47 49 35N 34 35 E
Polynesia, *Pac. Oc.* 64 10 0S 162 0W
Ponce, *P.R.* 95 18 1N 66 37W
Pondicherry, *India* 58 11 59N 79 50 E
Ponta Grossa, *Brazil* 102 25 7S 50 10W
Pontardawe, *U.K.* 17 51 43N 3 51W
Pontardulais, *U.K.* 17 51 42N 4 3W
Pontchartrain, L., *U.S.A.* 90 30 12N 90 0W
Pontefract, *U.K.* 19 53 42N 1 19W
Ponteland, *U.K.* 21 55 7N 1 45W
Pontevedra, *Sp.* 37 42 26N 8 40W
Pontianak, *Indon.* 63 0 3S 109 15 E
Pontrilas, *U.K.* 14 51 56N 2 53W
Pontypool, *U.K.* 17 51 42N 3 1W
Pontypridd, *U.K.* 17 51 36N 3 21W
Poole, *U.K.* 14 50 42N 1 58W
Poole Harbour, *U.K.* 14 50 41N 2 0W
Pooley Bridge, *U.K.* 18 54 37N 2 49W
Poona = Pune, *India* 58 18 29N 73 57 E
Poopó, L., *Bol.* 100 18 30S 67 35W
Popayán, *Col.* 100 2 27N 76 36W
Popocatépetl, Volcán, *Mex.* 94 19 2N 98 38W
Pori, *Fin.* 45 61 29N 21 48 E
Porirua, *N.Z.* 71 41 8S 174 52 E
Porlock, *U.K.* 14 51 13N 3 36W
Porlock B., *U.K.* 14 51 14N 3 37W
Porlock Hill, *U.K.* 14 51 12N 3 40W
Porsangen Fjord, *Nor.* 44 70 45N 25 0 E
Port Antonio, *Jam.* 94 18 10N 76 30W
Port Arthur, *U.S.A.* 90 30 0N 94 0W
Port Askaig, *U.K.* 20 55 51N 6 8W
Port-au-Prince, *Haiti* 95 18 40N 72 20W
Port Augusta, *Austral.* 67 32 30S 137 50 E
Port Bannatyne, *U.K.* 20 55 51N 5 4W
Port Carlisle, *U.K.* 18 54 56N 3 12W
Port-Cartier, *Canada* 89 50 2N 66 50W
Port Charlotte, *U.K.* 20 55 44N 6 22W
Port Elizabeth, *S. Afr.* 81 33 58S 25 40 E
Port Ellen, *U.K.* 20 55 38N 6 10W
Port Erin, *U.K.* 18 54 5N 4 45W
Port-Gentil, *Gabon* 80 0 40S 8 50 E
Port Glasgow, *U.K.* 20 55 57N 4 40W
Port Harcourt, *Nig.* 78 4 40N 7 10 E
Port Hedland, *Austral.* 66 20 25S 118 35 E
Port Isaac, *U.K.* 16 50 35N 4 50W
Port Isaac B., *U.K.* 16 50 36N 4 50W
Port Laoise, *Ire.* 25 53 2N 7 20W
Port Logan, *U.K.* 20 54 42N 4 57W
Port Macquarie, *Austral.* 67 31 25S 152 25 E
Port Moresby, *P.N.G.* 64 9 24S 147 8 E
Port of Spain, *Trin. & Tob.* 94 10 40N 61 31W
Port Phillip B., *Austral.* 70 38 10S 144 50 E
Port Pirie, *Austral.* 67 33 10S 138 1 E
Port Said, *Egypt* 79 31 16N 32 18 E
Port St. Mary, *U.K.* 18 54 5N 4 45W
Port Sudan, *Sudan* 79 19 32N 37 9 E
Port Sunlight, *U.K.* 18 53 22N 3 0W
Port Talbot, *U.K.* 17 51 35N 3 48W
Port William, *U.K.* 20 54 46N 4 35W
Portadown, *U.K.* 24 54 27N 6 26W
Portaferry, *U.K.* 24 54 23N 5 32W
Portage La Prairie, *Canada* 88 49 58N 98 18W
Portarlington, *Ire.* 25 53 10N 7 10W
Porthcawl, *U.K.* 17 51 28N 3 42W
Porthleven, *U.K.* 16 50 5N 5 19W
Porthmadog, *U.K.* 17 52 55N 4 13W
Portishead, *U.K.* 14 51 29N 2 46W
Portland, *Austral.* 70 38 20S 141 35 E
Portland, *Maine, U.S.A.* 93 43 40N 70 15W
Portland, *Oreg., U.S.A.* 90 45 35N 122 40W
Portland Bill, *U.K.* 14 50 31N 2 27W
Portland, I. of, *U.K.* 14 50 32N 2 25W
Portnacroish, *U.K.* 20 56 34N 5 24W
Portnahaven, *U.K.* 20 55 40N 6 30W
Pôrto Alegre, *Brazil* 102 30 5S 51 10W
Porto Novo, *Benin* 78 6 23N 2 42 E
Pôrto Velho, *Brazil* 100 8 46S 63 54W
Porton, *U.K.* 14 51 8N 1 42W
Portovíejo, *Ecuad.* 100 1 7S 80 28W
Portpatrick, *U.K.* 20 54 50N 5 7W
Portree, *U.K.* 22 57 25N 6 11W
Portrush, *U.K.* 24 55 13N 6 40W
Portslade, *U.K.* 15 50 50N 0 11W
Portsmouth, *U.K.* 14 50 48N 1 6W
Portsmouth, *U.S.A.* 93 43 5N 70 45W
Portsoy, *U.K.* 23 57 41N 2 41W
Portstewart, *U.K.* 24 55 12N 6 43W
Portugal ■, *Europe* 37 40 0N 7 0W
Portumna, *Ire.* 25 53 5N 8 12W
Posadas, *Arg.* 102 27 30S 55 50W
Postbridge, *U.K.* 16 50 36N 3 54W
Potchefstroom, *S. Afr.* 81 26 41S 27 7 E
Potenza, *It.* 40 40 40N 15 50 E
Potomac →, *U.S.A.* 92 38 0N 76 23W
Potosí, *Bol.* 100 19 38S 65 50W
Potsdam, *E. Ger.* 42 52 23N 13 4 E
Potter Heigham, *U.K.* 15 52 44N 1 33 E
Potterne, *U.K.* 14 51 19N 2 0W
Potters Bar, *U.K.* 15 51 42N 0 11W
Potterspury, *U.K.* 15 52 5N 0 52W
Poulaphouca Res., *Ire.* 25 53 8N 6 30W
Poulton le Fylde, *U.K.* 18 53 51N 2 59W
Poundstock, *U.K.* 16 50 44N 4 34W
Powell, L., *U.S.A.* 90 37 25N 110 45W
Powick, *U.K.* 14 52 9N 2 15W
Powys □, *U.K.* 17 52 20N 3 20W
Poyang Hu, *China* 61 29 10N 116 10 E
Poznań, *Pol.* 42 52 25N 16 55 E
Prague, *Czech.* 42 50 5N 14 22 E
Prato, *It.* 40 43 53N 11 5 E
Prawle Pt., *U.K.* 16 50 13N 3 41W
Prees, *U.K.* 18 52 54N 2 40W
Preesall, *U.K.* 18 53 55N 2 58W
Prescot, *U.K.* 18 53 27N 2 49W
Preshute, *U.K.* 14 51 24N 1 45W
Presidente Prudente, *Brazil* 101 22 5S 51 25W
Presque Isle, *U.S.A.* 93 46 40N 68 0W
Prestatyn, *U.K.* 17 53 20N 3 24W
Prestbury, *U.K.* 14 51 54N 2 2W
Presteigne, *U.K.* 17 52 17N 3 0W
Preston, *Borders, U.K.* 21 55 48N 2 18W
Preston, *Dorset, U.K.* 14 50 38N 2 26W
Preston, *Lancs., U.K.* 18 53 46N 2 42W
Prestonpans, *U.K.* 21 55 58N 3 0W
Prestwich, *U.K.* 18 53 32N 2 18W
Prestwick, *U.K.* 20 55 30N 4 38W
Pretoria, *S. Afr.* 81 25 44S 28 12 E
Prince Albert, *Canada* 88 53 15N 105 50W
Prince Edward I. □, *Canada* 93 46 20N 63 20W
Prince George, *Canada* 88 53 55N 122 50W
Prince of Wales I., *Canada* 88 73 0N 99 0W
Prince Rupert, *Canada* 88 54 20N 130 20W
Princes Risborough, *U.K.* 15 51 43N 0 50W
Princess Charlotte B., *Austral.* 67 14 25S 144 0 E
Princetown, *U.K.* 16 50 33N 4 0W
Pripyat Marshes, *U.S.S.R.* 46 52 0N 28 10 E
Priština, *Yug.* 41 42 40N 21 13 E
Prizren, *Yug.* 41 42 13N 20 45 E
Probus, *U.K.* 16 50 17N 4 55W
Prokopyevsk, *U.S.S.R.* 48 54 0N 86 45 E
Prome, *Burma* 59 18 49N 95 13 E
Provence, *Fr.* 35 43 40N 5 46 E
Providence, *U.S.A.* 93 41 50N 71 28W
Prudhoe, *U.K.* 21 54 57N 1 52W
Prudhoe Bay, *U.S.A.* 88 70 20N 148 20W
Prut →, *Rom.* 41 46 3N 28 10 E
Przemyśl, *Pol.* 43 49 50N 22 45 E
Puddletown, *U.K.* 14 50 45N 2 21W
Pudsey, *U.K.* 19 53 47N 1 40W
Puebla, *Mex.* 94 19 3N 98 12W
Pueblo, *U.S.A.* 90 38 20N 104 40W
Puerto La Cruz, *Ven.* 100 10 13N 64 38W
Puerto Montt, *Chile* 102 41 28S 73 0W
Puerto Rico ■, *W. Ind.* 95 18 15N 66 45W
Pula, *It.* 40 39 0N 9 0 E
Pulborough, *U.K.* 15 50 58N 0 30W
Pulham Market, *U.K.* 15 52 25N 1 15 E
Pulham St. Mary, *U.K.* 15 52 25N 1 14 E
Pumlumon Fawr, *U.K.* 17 52 29N 3 47W
Pune, *India* 58 18 29N 73 57 E
Punjab □, *India* 58 31 0N 76 0 E
Punjab □, *Pak.* 58 30 0N 72 0 E
Punta Arenas, *Chile* 102 53 10S 71 0W
Punto Fijo, *Ven.* 100 11 50N 70 13W
Purbeck, Isle of, *U.K.* 14 50 40N 2 5W
Purfleet, *U.K.* 15 51 29N 0 15 E
Purley, *U.K.* 14 51 29N 1 4W
Purnia, *India* 59 25 45N 87 31 E
Purus →, *Brazil* 100 3 42S 61 28W
Pusan, *S. Kor.* 61 35 5N 129 0 E
Puy-de-Dôme, *Fr.* 35 45 46N 2 57 E
Pwllheli, *U.K.* 17 52 54N 4 26W
Pyŏngyang, *N. Kor.* 61 39 0N 125 30 E
Pyrenees, *Europe* 35 42 45N 0 18 E

Q

Qandahār, *Afg.* 57 31 32N 65 30 E
Qatar ■, *Asia* 56 25 30N 51 15 E
Qattâra Depression, *Egypt* 79 29 30N 27 30 E
Qazvin, *Iran* 56 36 15N 50 0 E
Qena, *Egypt* 79 26 10N 32 43 E
Qingdao, *China* 61 36 5N 120 20 E
Qinghai □, *China* 60 36 0N 98 0 E
Qinghai Hu, *China* 60 36 40N 100 10 E
Qingjiang, *China* 61 33 30N 119 2 E
Qiqihar, *China* 61 47 26N 124 0 E
Qom, *Iran* 56 34 40N 51 0 E
Quadring, *U.K.* 19 52 53N 0 9W
Quainton, *U.K.* 15 51 51N 0 53W
Quantock Hills, *U.K.* 14 51 8N 3 10W
Queanbeyan, *Austral.* 70 35 17S 149 14 E
Québec, *Canada* 93 46 52N 71 13W
Québec □, *Canada* 89 50 0N 70 0W
Queen Charlotte Is., *Canada* 88 53 20N 132 10W
Queen Elizabeth Is., *Canada* 103 76 0N 95 0W
Queen Maud G., *Canada* 88 68 15N 102 30W
Queenborough, *U.K.* 15 51 24N 0 46 E
Queensbury, *U.K.* 18 53 46N 1 50W
Queensferry, *U.K.* 21 56 0N 3 25W
Queensland □, *Austral.* 67 22 0S 142 0 E
Queenstown, *N.Z.* 71 45 1S 168 40 E
Queenstown, *S. Afr.* 81 31 52S 26 52 E
Querétaro, *Mex.* 94 20 36N 100 23W
Quetta, *Pak.* 58 30 15N 66 55 E
Quezon City, *Phil.* 63 14 38N 121 0 E
Qui Nhon, *Viet.* 63 13 40N 109 13 E
Quimper, *Fr.* 34 48 0N 4 9W
Quito, *Ecuad.* 100 0 15S 78 35W
Quorndon, *U.K.* 14 52 45N 1 10W

R

Raasay, *U.K.* 22 57 25N 6 4W
Raasay, Sd. of, *U.K.* 22 57 30N 6 8W
Rabat, *Malta* 40 35 53N 14 25 E
Rabat, *Mor.* 78 34 2N 6 48W
Rackheath, *U.K.* 15 52 41N 1 22 E
Radcliffe, *Gr. Manchester, U.K.* 18 53 35N 2 19W
Radcliffe, *Notts., U.K.* 19 52 57N 1 3W
Radley, *U.K.* 14 51 42N 1 14W
Radnor Forest, *U.K.* 17 52 17N 3 10W
Radom, *Pol.* 43 51 23N 21 12 E
Radstock, *U.K.* 14 51 17N 2 25W
Ragusa, *It.* 40 36 56N 14 42 E
Rainham, *U.K.* 15 51 22N 0 36 E
Rainworth, *U.K.* 19 53 8N 1 6W
Raipur, *India* 59 21 17N 81 45 E
Rajahmundry, *India* 59 17 1N 81 48 E
Rajasthan □, *India* 58 26 45N 73 30 E
Rajkot, *India* 58 22 15N 70 56 E
Raleigh, *U.S.A.* 91 35 47N 78 39W
Rame Head, *U.K.* 16 50 19N 4 14W
Rampside, *U.K.* 18 54 6N 3 10W
Rampur, *India* 58 28 50N 79 5 E
Ramree Kyun, *Burma* 59 19 0N 94 0 E
Ramsbottom, *U.K.* 18 53 36N 2 20W
Ramsbury, *U.K.* 14 51 26N 1 37W
Ramsey, *Cambs., U.K.* 15 52 27N 0 6W
Ramsey, *Essex, U.K.* 15 51 55N 1 12 E
Ramsey, *I. of M., U.K.* 18 54 20N 4 21W
Ramsey Bay, *U.K.* 18 54 23N 4 20W
Ramsgate, *U.K.* 15 51 20N 1 25 E
Rancagua, *Chile* 102 34 10S 70 50W
Ranchi, *India* 59 23 19N 85 27 E
Rangoon, *Burma* 59 16 45N 96 20 E
Rannoch, L., *U.K.* 23 56 41N 4 20W
Rannoch Moor, *U.K.* 20 56 38N 4 48W
Rasht, *Iran* 56 37 20N 49 40 E
Rath Luirc, *Ire.* 25 52 21N 8 40W
Rathdrum, *Ire.* 25 52 57N 6 13W
Rathfriland, *U.K.* 24 54 12N 6 12W
Rathkeale, *Ire.* 25 52 32N 8 57W
Rathlin I., *U.K.* 24 55 18N 6 14W
Rathlin O'Birne I., *Ire.* 24 54 40N 8 50W
Rattray Hd., *U.K.* 23 57 38N 1 50W
Raukumara Ra., *N.Z.* 71 38 5S 177 55 E
Raunds, *U.K.* 15 52 20N 0 32W
Raurkela, *India* 59 22 14N 84 50 E
Ravenglass, *U.K.* 18 54 21N 3 25W
Ravenna, *It.* 40 44 28N 12 15 E
Ravenstonedale, *U.K.* 18 54 26N 2 26W
Rawalpindi, *Pak.* 58 33 38N 73 8 E
Rawmarsh, *U.K.* 19 53 27N 1 20W
Rawtenstall, *U.K.* 18 53 42N 2 18W
Rayleigh, *U.K.* 15 51 36N 0 38 E
Reading, *U.K.* 15 51 27N 0 57W
Reading, *U.S.A.* 93 40 20N 75 53W
Recife, *Brazil* 101 8 0S 35 0W
Reculver, *U.K.* 15 51 22N 1 12 E
Red → = Hong *Viet.* 60 20 17N 106 34 E
Red →, *U.S.A.* 91 31 0N 91 40W
Red Deer, *Canada* 88 52 20N 113 50W
Red Dial, *U.K.* 18 54 48N 3 9W
Red Sea, *Asia* 56 25 0N 36 0 E
Redbridge, *U.K.* 15 51 35N 0 7 E
Redcar, *U.K.* 19 54 37N 1 4W
Redditch, *U.K.* 14 52 18N 1 57W
Rede →, *U.K.* 21 55 8N 2 12W
Redesmouth, *U.K.* 21 55 7N 2 12W
Redhill, *U.K.* 15 51 14N 0 10W
Redlynch, *U.K.* 14 50 59N 1 42W
Redmile, *U.K.* 19 52 54N 0 48W
Redmire, *U.K.* 18 54 19N 1 55W
Redruth, *U.K.* 16 50 14N 5 14W
Ree, L., *Ire.* 24 53 35N 8 0W
Reedham, *U.K.* 15 52 34N 1 33 E
Reepham, *U.K.* 15 52 46N 1 6 E
Reeth, *U.K.* 18 54 23N 1 56W
Regensburg, *W. Ger.* 42 49 1N 12 7 E
Réggio di Calábria, *It.* 40 38 7N 15 38 E
Réggio nell' Emilia, *It.* 40 44 42N 10 38 E
Regina, *Canada* 88 50 27N 104 35W
Reigate, *U.K.* 15 51 14N 0 11W
Reims, *Fr.* 34 49 15N 4 1 E
Reindeer L., *Canada* 88 57 15N 102 15W
Remscheid, *W. Ger.* 36 51 11N 7 12 E
Renfrew, *U.K.* 20 55 52N 4 24W
Renmark, *Austral.* 67 34 11S 140 43 E
Rennes, *Fr.* 34 48 7N 1 41W
Reno, *U.S.A.* 90 39 30N 119 50W
Repton, *U.K.* 14 52 50N 1 32W
Resistencia, *Arg.* 102 27 30S 59 0W
Reston, *U.K.* 21 55 51N 2 11W
Réthimnon, *Greece* 41 35 18N 24 30 E
Reykjavík, *Ice.* 44 64 10N 21 57W
Reynosa, *Mex.* 94 26 5N 98 18W

Rhayader, *U.K.* **17** 52 19N 3 30W
Rheidol →, *U.K.* **17** 52 25N 4 5W
Rhein →, *W. Ger.* **36** 51 52N 6 20 E
Rheine, *W. Ger.* **36** 52 17N 7 25 E
Rhine = Rhein →, *W. Ger.* **36** 51 52N 6 20 E
Rhineland-Palatinate □, *W. Ger.* **42** 50 0N 7 0 E
Rhins, The, *U.K.* **20** 54 52N 5 3W
Rhode Island □, *U.S.A.* **93** 41 38N 71 37W
Rhodes = Ródhos, *Greece* **41** 36 15N 28 10 E
Rhodesia = Zimbabwe ■, *Africa* **81** 20 0S 30 0 E
Rhodope Mts., *Bulg.* **41** 41 40N 24 20 E
Rhondda, *U.K.* **17** 51 39N 3 30W
Rhône →, *Fr.* **35** 43 28N 4 42 E
Rhosllanerchrugog, *U.K.* **17** 53 3N 3 4W
Rhossili, *U.K.* **17** 51 34N 4 18W
Rhum, *U.K.* **22** 57 0N 6 20W
Rhyl, *U.K.* **17** 53 19N 3 29W
Rhymney, *U.K.* **17** 51 32N 3 17W
Ribble →, *U.K.* **18** 54 13N 2 20W
Ribeirão Prêto, *Brazil* **101** 21 10S 47 50W
Riccall, *U.K.* **19** 53 50N 1 4W
Riccarton, *N.Z.* **71** 43 32S 172 37 E
Riccarton Junc., *U.K.* **21** 55 16N 2 43W
Richmond, *N. Yorks., U.K.* **19** 54 24N 1 43W
Richmond, *Surrey, U.K.* **15** 51 28N 0 18W
Richmond, *U.S.A.* **92** 37 33N 77 27W
Rickmansworth, *U.K.* **15** 51 38N 0 28W
Ridsdale, *U.K.* **21** 55 9N 2 8W
Rievaulx, *U.K.* **19** 54 16N 1 7W
Riga, *U.S.S.R.* **46** 56 53N 24 8 E
Riga, G. of, *U.S.S.R.* **46** 57 40N 23 45 E
Rijeka, *Yug.* **40** 45 20N 14 21 E
Rijswijk, *Neth.* **36** 52 4N 4 22 E
Rillington, *U.K.* **19** 54 10N 0 41W
Rímini, *It.* **40** 44 3N 12 33 E
Rîmnicu Vîlcea, *Rom.* **43** 45 9N 24 21 E
Rimouski, *Canada* **93** 48 27N 68 30W
Rineanna, *Ire.* **25** 52 42N 85 7W
Ringford, *U.K.* **21** 54 55N 4 3W
Ringmer, *U.K.* **15** 50 53N 0 5 E
Ringwood, *U.K.* **14** 50 50N 1 48W
Rio Branco, *Brazil* **100** 9 58S 67 49W
Río Cuarto, *Arg.* **102** 33 10S 64 25W
Rio de Janeiro, *Brazil* **101** 23 0S 43 12W
Río Gallegos, *Arg.* **102** 51 35S 69 15W
Rio Grande, *Brazil* **102** 32 0S 52 20W
Rio Grande →, *U.S.A.* **90** 25 57N 97 9W
Rio Grande do Norte □, *Brazil* **94** 5 40S 36 0W
Río Muni = Mbini □, *Eq. Guin.* **80** 1 30N 10 0 E
Riobamba, *Ecuad.* **100** 1 50S 78 45W
Ripley, *Derby, U.K.* **19** 53 3N 1 24W
Ripley, *N. Yorks., U.K.* **19** 54 3N 1 34W
Ripon, *U.K.* **19** 54 8N 1 31W
Risca, *U.K.* **17** 51 36N 3 6W
Rishton, *U.K.* **18** 53 46N 2 26W
Riverside, *U.S.A.* **90** 34 0N 117 22W
Riyadh, *Si. Arab.* **56** 24 41N 46 42 E
Roade, *U.K.* **15** 52 10N 0 53W
Roadhead, *U.K.* **18** 55 4N 2 44W
Roag, L., *U.K.* **22** 58 10N 6 55W
Roanne, *Fr.* **35** 46 3N 4 4 E
Roanoke, *U.S.A.* **92** 37 19N 79 55W
Robe →, *Ire.* **24** 53 38N 9 10W
Roberton, *U.K.* **21** 55 24N 2 53W
Robin Hood's Bay, *U.K.* **19** 54 26N 0 31W
Rocester, *U.K.* **18** 52 56N 1 50W
Rochdale, *U.K.* **18** 53 36N 2 10W
Roche, *U.K.* **16** 50 24N 4 50W
Rochelle, La, *Fr.* **35** 46 10N 1 9W
Rochester, *Kent, U.K.* **15** 51 22N 0 30 E
Rochester, *Northumberland, U.K.* **21** 55 16N 2 16W
Rochester, *Minn., U.S.A.* **90** 44 1N 92 28W
Rochester, *N.Y., U.S.A.* **92** 43 10N 77 40W
Rochford, *U.K.* **15** 51 36N 0 42 E
Rockall, *Atl. Oc.* **26** 57 37N 13 42W
Rockcliffe, *U.K.* **18** 54 58N 3 0W
Rockford, *U.S.A.* **92** 42 20N 89 0W
Rockhampton, *Austral.* **67** 23 22S 150 32 E
Rockingham, *U.K.* **15** 52 32N 0 43W
Rockingham Forest, *U.K.* **15** 52 28N 0 42W
Rocky Mts., *N. Am.* **90** 55 0N 121 0W
Ródhos, *Greece* **41** 36 15N 28 10 E
Roding →, *U.K.* **15** 51 31N 0 7 E
Roe →, *U.K.* **24** 55 10N 6 59W
Roeselare, *Belg.* **36** 50 57N 3 7 E
Rogaland fylke □, *Nor.* **45** 59 12N 6 20 E
Rogans Seat, *U.K.* **18** 54 25N 2 10W
Rogate, *U.K.* **15** 51 0N 0 51W
Roma, *Austral.* **67** 26 32S 148 49 E
Roma = Rome, *It.* **40** 41 54N 12 30 E
Romania ■, *Europe* **43** 46 0N 25 0 E
Rome, *It.* **40** 41 54N 12 30 E
Romney Marsh, *U.K.* **15** 51 0N 1 0 E
Romsey, *U.K.* **14** 51 0N 1 29W
Rona, *U.K.* **22** 57 33N 6 0W
Ronse, *Belg.* **36** 50 45N 3 35 E
Roosendaal, *Neth.* **36** 51 32N 4 29 E
Roper →, *Austral.* **67** 14 43S 135 27 E
Ropsley, *U.K.* **19** 52 53N 0 31W
Roraima, Mt., *Ven.* **101** 5 10N 60 40W
Rosario, *Arg.* **102** 33 0S 60 40W
Roscommon, *Ire.* **24** 53 38N 8 11W
Roscommon □, *Ire.* **24** 53 40N 8 15W
Roscrea, *Ire.* **25** 52 58N 7 50W
Roseau, *Dom.* **94** 15 20N 61 24W
Rosedale Abbey, *U.K.* **19** 54 22N 0 51W
Roskilde, *Den.* **45** 55 38N 12 3 E
Rosneath, *U.K.* **20** 56 1N 4 49W
Ross Ice Shelf, *Ant.* **103** 80 0S 180 0 E
Ross on Wye, *U.K.* **14** 51 55N 2 34W
Ross Sea, *Ant.* **103** 74 0S 178 0 E
Rossall Pt., *U.K.* **18** 53 55N 3 2W
Rossan Pt., *Ire.* **24** 54 42N 8 47W
Rosslare, *Ire.* **25** 52 17N 6 23W
Rostock, *E. Ger.* **42** 54 4N 12 9 E
Rostov, *U.S.S.R.* **47** 47 15N 39 45 E
Rosyth, *U.K.* **21** 56 2N 3 26W
Rothbury, *U.K.* **21** 55 19N 1 55W
Rothbury Forest, *U.K.* **21** 55 19N 1 50W
Rother →, *U.K.* **15** 50 59N 0 40 E
Rotherham, *U.K.* **19** 53 26N 1 21W
Rothes, *U.K.* **23** 57 31N 3 12W
Rothesay, *U.K.* **20** 55 50N 5 3W
Rothwell, *Northants., U.K.* **15** 52 25N 0 48W
Rothwell, *W. Yorks., U.K.* **19** 53 46N 1 29W
Rotorua, *N.Z.* **71** 38 9S 176 16 E
Rotorua, L., *N.Z.* **71** 38 5S 176 18 E
Rotterdam, *Neth.* **36** 51 55N 4 30 E
Rottingdean, *U.K.* **15** 50 48N 0 3W
Roubaix, *Fr.* **34** 50 40N 3 10 E
Rouen, *Fr.* **34** 49 27N 1 4 E
Rousay, *U.K.* **23** 59 10N 3 2W
Rowanburn, *U.K.* **21** 55 5N 2 54W
Rowrah, *U.K.* **18** 54 34N 3 26W
Roxburgh, *U.K.* **21** 55 34N 2 30W
Roxby, *U.K.* **19** 53 38N 0 37W
Royston, *U.K.* **15** 52 3N 0 1W
Royton, *U.K.* **18** 53 34N 2 7W
Ruahine Ra., *N.Z.* **71** 39 55S 176 2 E
Rub' al Khali, *Si. Arab.* **56** 18 0N 48 0 E
Rubery, *U.K.* **14** 52 24N 1 59W
Rubh a' Mhail, *U.K.* **20** 55 55N 6 10W
Rubha Hunish, *U.K.* **22** 57 42N 6 20W
Rudgwick, *U.K.* **15** 51 7N 0 54W
Rudston, *U.K.* **19** 54 6N 0 19W
Rufford, *U.K.* **18** 53 37N 2 50W
Rugby, *U.K.* **14** 52 23N 1 16W
Rugeley, *U.K.* **14** 52 47N 1 56W
Rum Jungle, *Austral.* **66** 13 0S 130 59 E
Runcorn, *U.K.* **18** 53 20N 2 44W
Ruse, *Bulg.* **41** 43 48N 25 59 E
Rushden, *U.K.* **15** 52 17N 0 37W
Ruskington, *U.K.* **19** 53 5N 0 23W
Russian S.F.S.R. □, *U.S.S.R.* **46** 62 0N 105 0 E
Rutherglen, *U.K.* **20** 55 50N 4 11W
Ruthin, *U.K.* **17** 53 7N 3 20W
Ruthwell, *U.K.* **21** 55 0N 3 24W
Rwanda ■, *Africa* **80** 2 0S 30 0 E
Ryan, L., *U.K.* **20** 55 0N 5 2W
Ryazan, *U.S.S.R.* **46** 54 40N 39 40 E
Rybinsk = Andropov, *U.S.S.R.* **46** 58 5N 38 50 E
Rybinsk Res., *U.S.S.R.* **46** 58 30N 38 0 E
Rydal, *U.K.* **18** 54 28N 2 59W
Ryde, *U.K.* **14** 50 44N 1 9W
Rye, *U.K.* **15** 50 57N 0 46 E
Rye →, *U.K.* **19** 54 12N 0 53W
Rye Bay, *U.K.* **15** 50 50N 0 50 E
Ryhope, *U.K.* **21** 54 52N 1 22W
Ryton, *Tyne & Wear, U.K.* **21** 54 58N 1 44W
Ryton, *Warwick, U.K.* **14** 52 23N 1 25W
Ryūkyū Is., *Jap.* **62** 26 0N 128 0 E
Rzeszów, *Pol.* **43** 50 5N 21 58 E

S

Saarbrücken, *W. Ger.* **36** 49 15N 6 58 E
Saaremaa, *U.S.S.R.* **46** 58 30N 22 30 E
Saarland □, *W. Ger.* **36** 49 15N 7 0 E
Saba, *W. Ind.* **94** 17 42N 63 26W
Sabadell, *Sp.* **37** 41 28N 2 7 E
Sabah □, *Malay.* **63** 6 0N 117 0 E
Sabhah, *Libya* **79** 27 9N 14 29 E
Sacramento, *U.S.A.* **90** 38 33N 121 30 E
Sacriston, *U.K.* **19** 54 49N 1 38W
Saddell, *U.K.* **20** 55 31N 5 30W
Saffron Walden, *U.K.* **15** 52 2N 0 15 E
Safi, *Mor.* **78** 32 18N 9 20W
Sagar, *India* **58** 14 14N 75 6 E
Saginaw, *U.S.A.* **92** 43 26N 83 55W
Saginaw B., *U.S.A.* **92** 43 50N 83 40W
Sahara, *Africa* **78** 23 0N 5 0 E
Saharan Atlas, *Alg.* **78** 34 9N 3 29 E
Saharanpur, *India* **58** 29 58N 77 33 E
Saigon = Ho Chi Minh City, *Viet.* **63** 10 58N 106 40 E
St. Abb's, *U.K.* **21** 55 54N 2 7W
St. Abb's Head, *U.K.* **21** 55 55N 2 10W
St. Agnes, *U.K.* **16** 50 18N 5 13W
St. Agnes Hd., *U.K.* **16** 50 19N 5 14W
St. Agnes I., *U.K.* **16** 49 53N 6 20W
St. Albans, *U.K.* **15** 51 44N 0 19W
St. Alban's Head, *U.K.* **14** 50 34N 2 3W
St. Andrews, *U.K.* **21** 56 20N 2 48W
St. Ann's, *U.K.* **21** 55 14N 3 28W
St. Asaph, *U.K.* **17** 53 15N 3 27W
St. Austell, *U.K.* **16** 50 20N 4 48W
St. Bees, *U.K.* **18** 54 29N 3 36W
St. Bee's Hd., *U.K.* **18** 54 30N 3 38 E
St. Blazey, *U.K.* **16** 50 22N 4 48W
St. Boniface, *Canada* **88** 49 53N 97 5W
St. Boswells, *U.K.* **21** 55 34N 2 39W
St. Briavels, *U.K.* **14** 51 44N 2 39W
St. Brides B., *U.K.* **17** 51 48N 5 15W
St.-Brieuc, *Fr.* **34** 48 30N 2 46W
St. Budeaux, *U.K.* **16** 50 23N 4 10W
St. Buryan, *U.K.* **16** 50 4N 5 34W
St. Catharines, *Canada* **92** 43 10N 79 15W
St. Catherine's Pt., *U.K.* **14** 50 34N 1 18W
St. Christopher-Nevis ■, *W. Ind.* **94** 17 20N 62 40W
St. Clair, L., *Canada* **92** 42 30N 82 45W
St.-Claude, *Fr.* **35** 46 22N 5 52 E
St. Clears, *U.K.* **17** 51 48N 4 30W
St. Columb Major, *U.K.* **16** 50 26N 4 56W
St. David's, *U.K.* **17** 51 54N 5 16W
St. David's Head, *U.K.* **17** 51 55N 5 16W
St. Dennis, *U.K.* **16** 50 23N 4 53W
St. Dominick, *U.K.* **16** 50 28N 4 15W
St. Elias Mts., *Canada* **88** 60 33N 139 28W
St. Endellion, *U.K.* **16** 50 33N 4 49W
St. Enoder, *U.K.* **16** 50 22N 4 57W
St. Erth, *U.K.* **16** 50 10N 5 26W
St.-Étienne, *Fr.* **35** 45 27N 4 22 E
St. Fillans, *U.K.* **21** 56 25N 4 7W
St. Gallen, *Switz.* **42** 47 25N 9 20 E
St. George's, *Gren.* **94** 12 5N 61 43W
St. George's Channel, *U.K.* **25** 52 0N 6 0W
St. Germans, *U.K.* **16** 50 24N 4 19W
St. Helena, *Atl. Oc.* **128** 15 55S 5 44W
St. Helena B., *S. Afr.* **81** 32 40S 18 10 E
St. Helens, *I. of W., U.K.* **14** 50 42N 1 6W
St. Helens, *Merseyside, U.K.* **18** 53 28N 2 44W
St. Helier, *U.K.* **34** 49 11N 2 6W
St-Hyacinthe, *Canada* **93** 45 40N 72 58W
St. Issey, *U.K.* **16** 50 30N 4 55W
St. Ives, *Cambs., U.K.* **15** 52 20N 0 5W
St. Ives, *Cornwall, U.K.* **16** 50 13N 5 29W
St. Ives Bay, *U.K.* **16** 50 15N 5 27W
St-Jean, L., *Canada* **93** 48 40N 72 0W
St-Jérôme, *Canada* **93** 45 47N 74 0W
St. John, *Canada* **93** 45 20N 66 8W
St. John's, *Antigua* **94** 17 6N 61 51W
St. John's, *Canada* **89** 47 35N 52 40W
St. John's, *U.K.* **18** 54 13N 4 38W
St. Johns Chapel, *U.K.* **18** 54 43N 2 10W
St. Joseph, *U.S.A.* **90** 39 46N 94 50W
St. Just, *U.K.* **16** 50 7N 5 41W
St. Keverne, *U.K.* **16** 50 3N 5 5W
St. Kew, *U.K.* **16** 50 34N 4 48W
St. Lawrence →, *Canada* **93** 49 30N 66 0W
St. Lawrence, Gulf of, *Canada* **89** 48 25N 62 0W
St. Leonards, *U.K.* **15** 50 51N 0 34 E
St. Levan, *U.K.* **16** 50 3N 5 36W
St.-Lô, *Fr.* **34** 49 7N 1 5W
St-Louis, *Sene.* **78** 16 8N 16 27W
St. Louis, *U.S.A.* **92** 38 40N 90 12W
St. Lucia ■, *W. Ind.* **94** 14 0N 60 50W
St. Maarten, *W. Ind.* **94** 18 0N 63 5W
St. Mabyn, *U.K.* **16** 50 30N 4 45W
St.-Malo, *Fr.* **34** 48 39N 2 1W
St. Margaret's-at-Cliffe, *U.K.* **15** 51 10N 1 23 E
St. Margaret's Hope, *U.K.* **23** 58 49N 2 58W
St-Martin, I., *W. Ind.* **94** 18 0N 63 0W
St. Martin's I., *U.K.* **16** 49 58N 6 16W
St. Mary Bourne, *U.K.* **14** 51 16N 1 24W
St. Mary's, *U.K.* **16** 49 55N 6 17W
St. Mary's Sd., *U.K.* **16** 49 53N 6 19W
St. Mawes, *U.K.* **16** 50 10N 5 1W
St. Merryn, *U.K.* **16** 50 31N 4 58W
St. Michael's Mt., *U.K.* **16** 50 7N 5 30W
St. Minver, *U.K.* **16** 50 34N 4 52W
St. Monance, *U.K.* **21** 56 13N 2 46W
St.-Nazaire, *Fr.* **34** 47 17N 2 12W
St. Neots, *U.K.* **15** 52 14N 0 16W
St-Niklaas, *Belg.* **36** 51 10N 4 8 E
St. Osyth, *U.K.* **15** 51 47N 1 4 E
St. Paul, *U.S.A.* **91** 44 54N 93 5W
St. Peter Port, *U.K.* **34** 49 27N 2 31W
St. Petersburg, *U.S.A.* **91** 27 45N 82 40W
St.-Pierre et Miquelon □, *N. Am.* **89** 46 55N 56 10W
St.-Quentin, *Fr.* **34** 49 50N 3 16 E
St. Stephen, *U.K.* **16** 50 20N 4 52W
St. Teath, *U.K.* **16** 50 34N 4 45W
St.-Tropez, *Fr.* **35** 43 17N 6 38 E
St. Tudy, *U.K.* **16** 50 33N 4 45W
St. Vincent and the Grenadines ■, *W. Ind.* **94** 13 0N 61 10W
Saintfield, *U.K.* **24** 54 28N 5 50W
Sakai, *Jap.* **62** 34 30N 135 30 E
Sakhalin, *U.S.S.R.* **49** 51 0N 143 0 E
Salado →, *Arg.* **102** 31 40S 60 41W
Salamanca, *Sp.* **37** 40 58N 5 39W
Salcombe, *U.K.* **16** 50 14N 3 47W
Salcombe Regis, *U.K.* **16** 50 41N 3 11W
Sale, *Austral.* **70** 38 6S 147 6 E
Sale, *U.K.* **18** 53 26N 2 19W
Salem, *India* **58** 11 40N 78 11 E
Salen, *U.K.* **20** 56 31N 5 57W
Salerno, *It.* **40** 40 48N 14 44 E
Salford, *U.K.* **18** 53 30N 2 17W
Salford Priors, *U.K.* **14** 52 10N 1 52W
Salisbury = Harare, *Zimb.* **81** 17 43S 31 2 E
Salisbury, *U.K.* **14** 51 4N 1 48W
Salisbury Plain, *U.K.* **14** 51 13N 1 50W
Salonica = Thessaloníki, *Greece* **41** 40 38N 22 58 E
Salop = Shropshire □, *U.K.* **14** 52 36N 2 45W
Salt Lake City, *U.S.A.* **90** 40 45N 111 58W
Salta, *Arg.* **102** 24 57S 65 25W
Saltash, *U.K.* **16** 50 25N 4 13W
Saltburn by the Sea, *U.K.* **19** 54 35N 0 58W
Saltcoats, *U.K.* **20** 55 38N 4 47W
Saltee Is., *Ire.* **25** 52 7N 6 37W
Saltergate, *U.K.* **19** 54 20N 0 40W
Saltfleet, *U.K.* **19** 53 25N 0 11 E
Saltfleetby, *U.K.* **19** 53 23N 0 10 E
Saltillo, *Mex.* **94** 25 25N 101 0W
Salto, *Urug.* **102** 31 27S 57 50W
Saltwood, *U.K.* **15** 51 4N 1 5 E
Salvador, *Brazil* **101** 13 0S 38 30W
Salween →, *Burma* **59** 16 31N 97 37 E
Salzburg, *Austria* **42** 47 48N 13 2 E
Salzgitter, *W. Ger.* **42** 52 13N 10 22 E
Samarinda, *Indon.* **63** 0 30S 117 9 E
Samarkand, *U.S.S.R.* **48** 39 40N 66 55 E
Sámos, *Greece* **41** 37 45N 26 50 E
Sampford Courtenay, *U.K.* **16** 50 47N 3 58W
Samsun, *Turk.* **47** 41 15N 36 22 E
San Angelo, *U.S.A.* **90** 31 30N 100 30W
San Antonio, *U.S.A.* **90** 29 30N 98 30W
San Bernardino, *U.S.A.* **90** 34 7N 117 18W
San Carlos, *Phil.* **63** 15 55N 120 20 E
San Cristóbal, *Ven.* **100** 16 50N 92 40W
San Diego, *U.S.A.* **90** 32 43N 117 10W
San Fernando, *Mex.* **94** 30 0N 115 10W
San Francisco, *U.S.A.* **90** 37 47N 122 30W
San Jorge, G., *Arg.* **102** 46 0S 66 0W
San José, *C.R.* **95** 10 0N 84 2W
San Jose, *U.S.A.* **90** 37 20N 121 53W
San Juan, *Arg.* **102** 31 30S 68 30W
San Juan, *P.R.* **95** 18 28N 66 8W
San Luis Potosí, *Mex.* **94** 22 9N 100 59W
San Marino ■, *Europe* **40** 43 56N 12 25 E
San Matías, G., *Arg.* **102** 41 30S 64 0W
San Miguel de Tucumán, *Arg.* **102** 26 50S 65 20W
San Pedro Sula, *Hond.* **94** 15 30N 88 0W
San Salvador, *El Salv.* **94** 13 40N 89 10W
San Salvador de Jujuy, *Arg.* **102** 24 10S 64 48W
San Sebastián, *Sp.* **37** 43 17N 1 58W
Sana', *Yem.* **56** 15 27N 44 12 E
Sanda I., *U.K.* **20** 55 17N 5 35W
Sanday, *U.K.* **23** 59 15N 2 30W
Sandbach, *U.K.* **18** 53 9N 2 23W
Sandbank, *U.K.* **20** 55 58N 4 57W
Sandgate, *U.K.* **15** 51 5N 1 9 E
Sandhead, *U.K.* **20** 54 48N 4 58W
Sandhurst, *U.K.* **15** 51 21N 0 48W
Sandness, *U.K.* **22** 60 18N 1 38W
Sandown, *U.K.* **14** 50 39N 1 9W
Sandringham, *U.K.* **15** 52 50N 0 30 E
Sandwich, *U.K.* **15** 51 16N 1 21 E
Sandy, *U.K.* **15** 52 8N 0 18W
Sangli, *India* **58** 16 55N 74 33 E
Sanquhar, *U.K.* **21** 55 21N 3 56W
Santa Ana, *Mex.* **94** 30 33N 111 7W
Santa Ana, *U.S.A.* **90** 33 48N 117 55W
Santa Clara, *Cuba* **95** 22 20N 80 0W
Santa Cruz, *Bol.* **100** 17 43S 63 10W
Santa Cruz de Tenerife, *Can. Is.* **78** 28 28N 16 15W
Santa Fe, *Arg.* **102** 31 35S 60 41W
Santa Fe, *U.S.A.* **90** 35 40N 106 0W
Santa Maria, *Brazil* **102** 29 40S 53 48W
Santa Marta, *Col.* **100** 11 15N 74 13W
Santander, *Sp.* **37** 43 27N 3 51W
Santarém, *Brazil* **101** 2 25S 54 42W
Santarém, *Port.* **37** 39 12N 8 42W
Santiago, *Chile* **102** 33 24S 70 40W
Santiago de Compostela, *Sp.* **37** 42 52N 8 37W
Santiago de Cuba, *Cuba* **95** 20 0N 75 49W
Santiago de los Cabelleros, *Dom. Rep.* **95** 19 30N 70 40W
Santo André, *Brazil* **102** 23 39S 46 29W
Santo Domingo, *Dom. Rep.* **95** 18 30N 64 54W
Santos, *Brazil* **102** 24 0S 46 20W
São Francisco →, *Brazil* **101** 10 30S 36 24W
São José do Rio Prêto, *Brazil* **101** 20 50S 49 20W
São Luís, *Brazil* **101** 2 39S 44 15W
São Paulo, *Brazil* **102** 23 32S 46 37W
São Roque, C. de, *Brazil* **101** 5 30S 35 16W
São Tomé & Principe ■, *Africa* **73** 0 12N 6 39 E
Saône →, *Fr.* **34** 45 44N 4 50 E
Sapporo, *Jap.* **62** 43 0N 141 21 E

Sarajevo, *Yug.* **41** 43 52N 18 26 E
Saransk, *U.S.S.R.* **46** 54 10N 45 10 E
Saratov, *U.S.S.R.* **46** 51 30N 46 2 E
Sarawak □, *Malay.* **63** 2 0N 113 0 E
Sardinia, I., *It.* **40** 40 0N 9 0 E
Sargodha, *Pak.* **58** 32 10N 72 40 E
Sarh, *Chad* **79** 9 5N 18 23 E
Sarnia, *Canada* **92** 42 58N 82 23W
Sasebo, *Jap.* **62** 33 10N 129 43 E
Saskatchewan □, *Canada* **88** 54 40N 106 0W
Saskatchewan →, *Canada* **88** 53 37N 100 40W
Saskatoon, *Canada* **88** 52 10N 106 38W
Sássari, *It.* **40** 40 44N 8 33 E
Satpura Ra., *India* **58** 21 25N 76 10 E
Satu Mare, *Rom.* **43** 47 46N 22 55 E
Sauðarkrókur, *Ice.* **44** 65 45N 19 40W
Saudi Arabia ■, *Asia* **56** 26 0N 44 0 E
Sault Ste. Marie, *Canada* **92** 46 30N 84 20W
Saundersfoot, *U.K.* **17** 51 43N 4 42W
Sava →, *Yug.* **41** 44 50N 20 26 E
Savanna la Mar, *Jam.* **94** 18 10N 78 10W
Savannah, *U.S.A.* **91** 32 4N 81 4W
Savona, *It.* **40** 44 19N 8 29 E
Savonlinna, *Fin.* **44** 61 52N 28 53 E
Sawbridgeworth, *U.K.* **15** 51 49N 0 10 E
Sawel, Mt., *U.K.* **24** 54 48N 7 5W
Sawston, *U.K.* **15** 52 7N 0 11 E
Sawtry, *U.K.* **15** 52 26N 0 17W
Saxilby, *U.K.* **19** 53 16N 0 40W
Saxlingham Nethergate, *U.K.* **15** 52 33N 1 16 E
Saxmundham, *U.K.* **15** 52 13N 1 29 E
Saydā, *Leb.* **57** 33 35N 35 25 E
Scafell Pikes, *U.K.* **18** 54 26N 3 14W
Scalasaig, *U.K.* **20** 56 4N 6 10W
Scalby, *U.K.* **19** 54 18N 0 26W
Scalby Ness, *U.K.* **19** 54 18N 0 25W
Scalloway, *U.K.* **22** 60 9N 1 16W
Scalpay, *U.K.* **22** 57 51N 6 40W
Scamblesby, *U.K.* **19** 53 17N 0 5W
Scandinavia, *Europe* **44** 64 0N 12 0 E
Scapa Flow, *U.K.* **23** 58 52N 3 6W
Scarba, I., *U.K.* **20** 56 10N 5 42W
Scarborough, *U.K.* **19** 54 17N 0 24W
Scarinish, *U.K.* **20** 56 30N 6 48W
Scarning, *U.K.* **15** 52 40N 0 53 E
Schefferville, *Canada* **89** 54 48N 66 50W
Schenectady, *U.S.A.* **93** 42 50N 73 58W
Schiedam, *Neth.* **36** 51 55N 4 25 E
Schleswig-Holstein □, *W. Ger.* **42** 54 10N 9 40 E
Schwerin, *E. Ger.* **42** 53 37N 11 22 E
Scilly, Isles of, *U.K.* **16** 49 55N 6 15W
Scole, *U.K.* **15** 52 22N 1 10 E
Scone, *U.K.* **21** 56 25N 3 26W
Scopwick, *U.K.* **19** 53 6N 0 24W
Scotland □, *U.K.* **20** 57 0N 4 0W
Scranton, *U.S.A.* **93** 41 22N 75 41W
Scremerston, *U.K.* **21** 55 44N 1 59W
Scridain, L., *U.K.* **20** 56 23N 6 7W
Scunthorpe, *U.K.* **19** 53 35N 0 38W
Seaford, *U.K.* **15** 50 46N 0 8 E
Seaham, *U.K.* **21** 54 51N 1 20W
Seahouses, *U.K.* **21** 55 35N 1 39W
Seamer, *U.K.* **19** 54 14N 0 27W
Seascale, *U.K.* **18** 54 24N 3 29W
Seaton, *Cumbria, U.K.* **18** 54 40N 3 31W
Seaton, *Devon, U.K.* **16** 50 42N 3 3W
Seaton Delaval, *U.K.* **21** 55 5N 1 33W
Seattle, *U.S.A.* **90** 47 41N 122 15W
Sedbergh, *U.K.* **18** 54 20N 2 31W
Sedgefield, *U.K.* **19** 54 40N 1 27W
Seend, *U.K.* **14** 51 20N 2 2W
Segovia, *Sp.* **37** 40 57N 4 10W
Seil, I., *U.K.* **20** 56 17N 5 37W
Seine →, *Fr.* **34** 49 26N 0 26 E
Sekondi-Takoradi, *Ghana* **78** 4 58N 1 45W
Selborne, *U.K.* **15** 51 5N 0 55W
Selby, *U.K.* **19** 53 47N 1 5W
Selkirk, *U.K.* **21** 55 33N 2 50W
Selsey, *U.K.* **15** 50 44N 0 47W
Selsey Bill, *U.K.* **15** 50 44N 0 47W
Selvas, *Brazil* **100** 6 30S 67 0W
Selwyn Ra., *Austral.* **67** 21 10S 140 0 E
Semarang, *Indon.* **63** 7 0S 110 26 E
Semipalatinsk, *U.S.S.R.* **48** 50 30N 80 10 E
Sendai, *Jap.* **62** 38 15N 140 53 E
Senegal ■, *W. Afr.* **78** 14 30N 14 30W
Senegal →, *W. Afr.* **78** 15 48N 16 32W
Sennen, *U.K.* **16** 50 4N 5 42W
Seoul, *S. Kor.* **61** 37 31N 126 58 E
Seph →, *U.K.* **19** 54 17N 1 9W
Sequoia Nat. Park, *U.S.A.* **90** 36 30N 118 30W
Serbia □, *Yug.* **41** 43 30N 21 0 E
Seremban, *Malay.* **63** 2 43N 101 53 E
Serena, La, *Chile* **102** 29 55S 71 10W
Serpukhov, *U.S.S.R.* **46** 54 55N 37 28 E
Sétif, *Alg.* **78** 36 9N 5 26 E
Settat, *Mor.* **78** 33 0N 7 40W
Settle, *U.K.* **18** 54 5N 2 18W
Setúbal, *Port.* **37** 38 30N 8 58W
Sevastopol, *U.S.S.R.* **47** 44 35N 33 30 E
Seven →, *U.K.* **19** 54 11N 0 51W
Sevenoaks, *U.K.* **15** 51 16N 0 11 E
Severn →, *U.K.* **14** 51 35N 2 38W
Severn Beach, *U.K.* **14** 51 34N 2 39W
Severn Stoke, *U.K.* **14** 52 5N 2 13W
Severnaya Zemlya, *U.S.S.R.* **49** 79 0N 100 0 E
Seville, *Sp.* **37** 37 23N 6 0W
Seward Pen., *U.S.A.* **88** 65 0N 164 0W
Seychelles ■, *Ind. Oc.* **129** 5 0S 56 0 E
Seyðisfjörður, *Ice.* **44** 65 16N 14 0W
Sfax, *Tunisia* **79** 34 49N 10 48 E
Shaanxi □, *China* **61** 35 0N 109 0 E
Shache, *China* **60** 38 20N 77 10 E
Shaftesbury, *U.K.* **14** 51 0N 2 12W
Shahjahanpur, *India* **58** 27 54N 79 57 E
Shakhty, *U.S.S.R.* **47** 47 40N 40 16 E
Shaldon, *U.K.* **16** 50 32N 3 31W
Shan □, *Burma* **59** 21 30N 98 30 E
Shandong □, *China* **61** 36 0N 118 0 E
Shanghai, *China* **61** 31 15N 121 26 E
Shangrao, *China* **61** 28 25N 117 59 E
Shanklin, *U.K.* **14** 50 39N 1 9W
Shannon →, *Ire.* **25** 52 35N 9 30W
Shantou, *China* **61** 23 18N 116 40 E
Shanxi □, *China* **61** 37 0N 112 0 E
Shaoguan, *China* **61** 24 48N 113 35 E
Shaoyang, *China* **61** 27 14N 111 25 E
Shap, *U.K.* **18** 54 32N 2 40W
Shapinsay, *U.K.* **23** 59 2N 2 50W
Shark B., *Austral.* **66** 11 20S 130 30 E
Sharpness, *U.K.* **14** 51 43N 2 28W
Shawbury, *U.K.* **14** 52 48N 2 40W
Shawinigan, *Canada* **93** 46 35N 72 50W
Shebbear, *U.K.* **16** 50 52N 4 12W
Sheelin, Lough, *Ire.* **24** 53 48N 7 20W
Sheep Haven, *Ire.* **24** 55 12N 7 55W
Sheerness, *U.K.* **15** 51 26N 0 47 E
Sheffield, *U.K.* **19** 53 23N 1 28W
Shefford, *U.K.* **15** 52 2N 0 20W
Shelekhov G., *U.S.S.R.* **49** 59 30N 157 0 E
Shellharbour, *Austral.* **70** 34 31S 150 51 E
Shelling Rocks, *Ire.* **25** 51 45N 10 35W
Shenfield, *U.K.* **15** 51 39N 0 21 E
Shenyang, *China* **61** 41 50N 123 25 E
Shepparton, *Austral.* **70** 36 23S 145 26 E
Sheppey, I. of, *U.K.* **15** 51 23N 0 50 E
Shepshed, *U.K.* **14** 52 47N 1 18W
Shepton Mallet, *U.K.* **14** 51 11N 2 31W
Sherborne, *U.K.* **14** 50 56N 2 31W
Sherborne St. John, *U.K.* **14** 51 18N 1 7W
Sherbrooke, *Canada* **93** 45 28N 71 57W
Sherburn, *N. Yorks., U.K.* **19** 54 12N 0 32W
Sherburn, *N. Yorks., U.K.* **19** 53 47N 1 15W
Shere, *U.K.* **15** 51 13N 0 28W
Sherfield English, *U.K.* **14** 51 1N 1 35W
Sheriff Hutton, *U.K.* **19** 54 5N 1 0W
Sheriff Muir, *U.K.* **21** 56 12N 3 53W
Sheringham, *U.K.* **15** 52 56N 1 11 E
Sherston, *U.K.* **14** 51 35N 2 13W
Sherwood Forest, *U.K.* **19** 53 5N 1 5W
Shetland □, *U.K.* **22** 60 30N 1 30W
Shetland Is., *U.K.* **22** 60 30N 1 30W
Shiel, L., *U.K.* **22** 56 48N 5 32W
Shieldaig, *U.K.* **22** 57 31N 5 39W
Shifnal, *U.K.* **14** 52 40N 2 23W
Shijiazhuang, *China* **61** 38 2N 114 28 E
Shikoku, *Jap.* **62** 33 30N 133 30 E
Shilbottle, *U.K.* **21** 55 23N 1 42W
Shildon, *U.K.* **19** 54 37N 1 39W
Shiliguri, *India* **59** 26 45N 88 25 E
Shillelagh, *Ire.* **25** 52 46N 6 32W
Shillingstone, *U.K.* **14** 50 54N 2 15W
Shillong, *India* **59** 25 35N 91 53 E
Shimonoseki, *Jap.* **62** 33 58N 131 0 E
Shin, L., *U.K.* **23** 58 7N 4 30W
Shipbourne, *U.K.* **15** 51 13N 0 19 E
Shipdham, *U.K.* **15** 52 38N 0 53 E
Shipley, *U.K.* **19** 53 50N 1 47W
Shipston-on-Stour, *U.K.* **14** 52 4N 1 38W
Shipton-under-Wychwood, *U.K.* **14** 51 51N 1 35W
Shīrāz, *Iran* **56** 29 42N 52 30 E
Shirebrook, *U.K.* **19** 53 13N 1 11W
Shizuoka, *Jap.* **62** 35 0N 138 24 E
Shkoder, *Alb.* **41** 42 6N 19 20 E
Shoeburyness, *U.K.* **15** 51 31N 0 49 E
Shoreham-by-Sea, *U.K.* **15** 50 50N 0 17W
Shotts, *U.K.* **21** 55 49N 3 47W
Shreveport, *U.S.A.* **91** 32 30N 93 50W
Shrewsbury, *U.K.* **14** 52 42N 2 45W
Shrewton, *U.K.* **14** 51 11N 1 55W
Shrivenham, *U.K.* **14** 51 36N 1 39W
Shropshire □, *U.K.* **14** 52 36N 2 45W
Shuangyashan, *China* **61** 46 28N 131 5 E
Siam = Thailand ■, *Asia* **63** 16 0N 102 0 E
Sian, *China* **61** 34 2N 109 0 E
Siberia, *U.S.S.R.* **50** 60 0N 100 0 E
Sibiu, *Rom.* **43** 45 45N 24 9 E
Sible Hedingham, *U.K.* **15** 51 58N 0 37 E
Sibsey, *U.K.* **19** 53 3N 0 1 E
Sichuan □, *China* **60** 31 0N 104 0 E
Sicily, *It.* **40** 37 30N 14 30 E
Sidbury, *U.K.* **16** 50 43N 3 12W
Sidlaw Hills, *U.K.* **21** 56 32N 3 10W
Sidlesham, *U.K.* **15** 50 46N 0 46W
Sidmouth, *U.K.* **16** 50 40N 3 13W
Sidon = Saydā, *Leb.* **57** 33 35N 35 25 E
Siegen, *W. Ger.* **36** 50 52N 8 2 E
Siena, *It.* **40** 43 20N 11 20 E
Sierra Leone ■, *W. Afr.* **78** 9 0N 12 0W
Sighty Crag, *U.K.* **21** 55 8N 2 37W
Siglufjörður, *Ice.* **44** 66 12N 18 55W
Sikhote Alin Ra., *U.S.S.R.* **49** 46 0N 136 0 E
Sikkim □, *India* **59** 27 50N 88 30 E
Silloth, *U.K.* **18** 54 53N 3 25W
Silsden, *U.K.* **18** 53 55N 1 55W
Silverstone, *U.K.* **14** 52 5N 1 3W
Silverton, *U.K.* **16** 50 49N 3 29W
Simferopol, *U.S.S.R.* **47** 44 55N 34 3 E
Simonsbath, *U.K.* **14** 51 8N 3 45W
Simonside, *U.K.* **21** 55 17N 2 0W
Simpson Desert, *Austral.* **67** 25 0S 137 0 E
Sinai Peninsula, *Egypt* **79** 29 30N 34 0 E
Sind Sagar Doab, *Pak.* **58** 32 0N 71 30 E
Singapore ■, *Asia* **63** 1 17N 103 51 E
Singleton, *U.K.* **15** 50 55N 0 45W
Sioux Falls, *U.S.A.* **91** 43 35N 96 40W
Siping, *China* **61** 33 25N 114 10 E
Siracusa, *It.* **40** 37 4N 15 17 E
Sittingbourne, *U.K.* **15** 51 20N 0 43 E
Sittwe, *Bur.* **59** 20 18N 92 45 E
Sivas, *Turk.* **47** 39 43N 36 58 E
Siwalik Range, *Nepal* **59** 28 0N 83 0 E
Sizewell, *U.K.* **15** 52 13N 1 38 E
Sjælland, *Den.* **45** 55 30N 11 30 E
Skagerrak, *Den.* **45** 57 30N 9 0 E
Skagway, *U.S.A.* **88** 59 23N 135 20W
Skegness, *U.K.* **19** 53 9N 0 20 E
Skellefteå, *Swed.* **44** 64 45N 20 58 E
Skellingthorpe, *U.K.* **19** 53 14N 0 37W
Skelmersdale, *U.K.* **18** 53 34N 2 49W
Skelmorlie, *U.K.* **20** 55 52N 4 53W
Skelton, *Cleveland, U.K.* **19** 54 33N 0 59W
Skelton, *Cumbria, U.K.* **18** 54 42N 2 50W
Skerries, The, *U.K.* **17** 53 27N 4 40W
Skibbereen, *Ire.* **25** 51 33N 9 16W
Skiddaw, *U.K.* **18** 54 39N 3 9W
Skien, *Nor.* **45** 59 12N 9 35 E
Skikda, *Alg.* **78** 36 50N 6 58 E
Skipness, *U.K.* **20** 55 46N 5 20W
Skipsea, *U.K.* **19** 53 58N 0 13W
Skipton, *U.K.* **18** 53 57N 2 1W
Skopje, *Yug.* **41** 42 1N 21 32 E
Skull, *Ire.* **25** 51 32N 9 40W
Skye, *U.K.* **22** 57 15N 6 10W
Slaidburn, *U.K.* **18** 53 57N 2 28W
Slaley, *U.K.* **21** 54 55N 2 4W
Slaney →, *Ire.* **25** 52 52N 6 45W
Sleaford, *U.K.* **19** 53 0N 0 22W
Sleat, Sd. of, *U.K.* **22** 57 5N 5 47W
Sledmere, *U.K.* **19** 54 4N 0 35W
Sleights, *U.K.* **19** 54 27N 0 40W
Slieve Aughty, *Ire.* **25** 53 4N 8 30W
Slieve Bloom, *Ire.* **25** 53 4N 7 40W
Slieve Donard, *U.K.* **24** 54 10N 5 57W
Slieve Gullion, *U.K.* **24** 54 8N 6 26W
Slieve Mish, *Ire.* **25** 52 12N 9 50W
Slievenamon, *Ire.* **25** 52 25N 7 37W
Sligo, *Ire.* **24** 54 17N 8 28W
Sligo □, *Ire.* **24** 54 10N 8 35W
Sligo B., *Ire.* **24** 54 20N 8 40W
Sliven, *Bulg.* **41** 42 42N 26 19 E
Slough, *U.K.* **15** 51 30N 0 35W
Slovenská Socialisticka Republika □, *Czech.* **43** 48 30N 20 0 E
Slyne Hd., *Ire.* **24** 53 25N 10 10W
Smederevo, *Yug.* **41** 44 40N 20 57 E
Smethwick, *U.K.* **14** 52 29N 1 58W
Smithfield, *U.K.* **18** 54 59N 2 51W
Smolensk, *U.S.S.R.* **46** 54 45N 32 0 E
Snaefell, *U.K.* **18** 54 18N 4 26W
Snainton, *U.K.* **19** 54 14N 0 33W
Snaith, *U.K.* **19** 53 42N 1 1W
Snake →, *U.S.A.* **90** 46 12N 119 2W
Snape, *U.K.* **15** 52 11N 1 29 E
Snettisham, *U.K.* **15** 52 52N 0 30 E
Snizort, L., *U.K.* **22** 57 33N 6 28W
Snowdon, *U.K.* **17** 53 4N 4 8W
Snowy Mts., *Austral.* **70** 36 30S 148 20 E
Sobral, *Brazil* **101** 3 50S 40 20W
Sochi, *U.S.S.R.* **47** 43 35N 39 40 E
Society Is., *Pac. Oc.* **65** 17 0S 151 0W
Socotra, *Ind. Oc.* **57** 12 30N 54 0 E
Söderhamn, *Swed.* **45** 61 18N 17 10 E
Sofia, *Bulg.* **41** 42 45N 23 20 E
Sogn og Fjordane fylke □, *Nor.* **44** 61 40N 6 0 E
Sognefjorden, *Nor.* **45** 61 10N 5 50 E
Sohâg, *Egypt* **79** 26 33N 31 43 E
Soham, *U.K.* **15** 52 20N 0 20 E
Sokoto, *Nig.* **78** 13 2N 5 16 E
Solapur, *India* **58** 17 43N 75 56 E
Solent, The, *U.K.* **14** 50 45N 1 25W
Solihull, *U.K.* **14** 52 26N 1 47W
Solimões → = Amazon →, *S. Am.* **100** 0 5S 50 0W
Solingen, *W. Ger.* **36** 51 10N 7 4 E
Solomon Is. ■, *Oc.* **64** 6 0S 155 0 E
Solway Firth, *U.K.* **18** 54 45N 3 38W
Somali Rep. ■, *E. Afr.* **73** 7 0N 47 0 E
Somerby, *U.K.* **14** 52 42N 0 49W
Somerset □, *U.K.* **14** 51 9N 3 0W
Somersham, *U.K.* **15** 52 24N 0 0 E
Somerton, *U.K.* **14** 51 3N 2 45W
Sompting, *U.K.* **15** 50 51N 0 20W
Søndre Strømfjord, *Green.* **89** 66 59N 50 40W
Sonning, *U.K.* **15** 51 28N 0 53W
Sorbie, *U.K.* **20** 54 46N 4 26W
Soria, *Sp.* **37** 41 43N 2 32W
Sorisdale, *U.K.* **20** 56 40N 6 28W
Sorn, *U.K.* **20** 55 31N 4 18W
Sorocaba, *Brazil* **102** 23 31S 47 27W
Sosnowiec, *Pol.* **43** 50 20N 19 10 E
Sousse, *Tunisia* **79** 35 50N 10 38 E
South Africa, Rep. of ■, *Africa* **81** 32 0S 17 0 E
South Australia □, *Austral.* **66** 32 0S 139 0 E
South Barrule, *U.K.* **18** 54 9N 4 36W
South Bend, *U.S.A.* **92** 41 38N 86 20W
South Benfleet, *U.K.* **15** 51 33N 0 34 E
South Brent, *U.K.* **16** 50 26N 3 50W
South Carolina □, *U.S.A.* **91** 33 45N 81 0W
South Cave, *U.K.* **19** 53 46N 0 37W
South China Sea, *Asia* **63** 10 0N 113 0 E
South Dakota □, *U.S.A.* **90** 45 0N 100 0W
South Dorset Downs, *U.K.* **14** 50 40N 2 26W
South Downs, *U.K.* **15** 50 53N 0 10W
South Elkington, *U.K.* **19** 53 22N 0 5W
South Esk →, *U.K.* **23** 56 44N 3 3W
South Foreland, *U.K.* **15** 51 7N 1 23 E
South Georgia, *Atl. Oc.* **102** 54 30S 37 0W
South Glamorgan □, *U.K.* **17** 51 30N 3 20W
South Hayling, *U.K.* **15** 50 47N 0 56W
South I., *N.Z.* **71** 44 0S 170 0 E
South Korea ■, *Asia* **61** 36 0N 128 0 E
South Molton, *U.K.* **16** 51 1N 3 50W
South Orkney Is., *Ant.* **103** 63 0S 45 0W
South Petherton, *U.K.* **14** 50 57N 2 49W
South Petherwin, *U.K.* **16** 50 35N 4 22W
South Platte →, *U.S.A.* **90** 41 7N 100 42W
South Pole, *Ant.* **103** 90 0S 0 0 E
South Ronaldsay, *U.K.* **23** 58 46N 2 58W
South Sandwich Is., *Ant.* **103** 57 0S 27 0W
South Shetland Is., *Ant.* **103** 62 0S 59 0W
South Shields, *U.K.* **19** 54 59N 1 26W
South Tawton, *U.K.* **16** 50 44N 3 55W
South Tyne →, *U.K.* **19** 54 46N 2 25W
South Uist, *U.K.* **22** 57 20N 7 15W
South West Africa = Namibia ■, *Africa* **81** 22 0S 18 9 E
South Woodham Ferrers, *U.K.* **15** 51 40N 0 37 E
South Yemen ■, *Asia* **56** 15 0N 48 0 E
South Yorkshire □, *U.K.* **19** 53 30N 1 20W
Southam, *U.K.* **14** 52 16N 1 24W
Southampton, *U.K.* **14** 50 54N 1 23W
Southampton I., *Canada* **89** 64 30N 84 0W
Southampton Water, *U.K.* **14** 50 52N 1 21W
Southborough, *U.K.* **15** 51 10N 0 15 E
Southend, *U.K.* **20** 55 18N 5 38W
Southend-on-Sea, *U.K.* **15** 51 32N 0 43 E
Southern Alps, *N.Z.* **71** 43 41S 170 11 E
Southern Ocean **103** 62 0S 60 0 E
Southern Uplands, *U.K.* **21** 55 30N 3 3W
Southery, *U.K.* **15** 52 32N 0 23 E
Southland □, *N.Z.* **71** 45 51S 168 13 E
Southminster, *U.K.* **15** 51 40N 0 51 E
Southport, *U.K.* **18** 53 38N 3 1W
Southwark, *U.K.* **15** 51 29N 0 5W
Southwell, *U.K.* **19** 53 4N 0 57W
Southwick, *U.K.* **15** 50 50N 0 14W
Southwold, *U.K.* **15** 52 19N 1 41 E
Sovetskaya Gavan, *U.S.S.R.* **49** 48 50N 140 0 E
Soviet Union ■ = Union of Soviet Socialist Republics ■, *Eurasia* **48** 60 0N 100 0 E
Sowerby, *U.K.* **19** 54 13N 1 19W
Soweto, *S. Afr.* **81** 26 14S 27 54 E
Spain ■, *Europe* **37** 40 0N 5 0W
Spalding, *U.K.* **15** 52 47N 0 9W
Spanish Town, *Jam.* **94** 18 0N 76 57W
Sparkford, *U.K.* **14** 51 2N 2 33W
Spean Bridge, *U.K.* **22** 56 53N 4 55W
Speke, *U.K.* **18** 53 21N 2 51W
Spelve, L., *U.K.* **20** 56 22N 5 45W
Spencer G., *Austral.* **67** 34 0S 137 20 E
Spennymoor, *U.K.* **19** 54 43N 1 35W
Sperrin Mts., *U.K.* **24** 54 50N 7 0W
Spey →, *U.K.* **23** 57 26N 3 25W
Spézia, La, *It.* **40** 44 8N 9 50 E
Spilsby, *U.K.* **19** 53 10N 0 6 E
Spithead, *U.K.* **15** 50 43N 1 5W
Spitzbergen = Svalbard, *Arctic* **103** 78 0N 17 0 E
Split, *Yug.* **40** 43 31N 16 26 E
Spofforth, *U.K.* **19** 53 57N 1 28W
Spokane, *U.S.A.* **90** 47 45N 117 25W
Springfield, *Ill., U.S.A.* **92** 39 48N 89 40W
Springfield, *Mass., U.S.A.* **93** 42 8N 72 37W
Springfield, *Mo., U.S.A.* **91** 37 15N 93 20W
Springfield, *Ohio, U.S.A.* **92** 39 58N 83 48W
Sproatley, *U.K.* **19** 53 46N 0 9W
Spurn Hd., *U.K.* **19** 53 34N 0 8 E
Sredinnyy Ra., *U.S.S.R.* **49** 57 0N 160 0 E
Srednekolymsk, *U.S.S.R.* **49** 67 27N 153 40 E
Sri Lanka ■, *Asia* **58** 7 30N 80 50 E
Srinagar, *India* **58** 34 5N 74 50 E

Place	Page	Lat.	Long.
Staffa, *U.K.*	**20**	56 26N	6 21W
Stafford, *U.K.*	**14**	52 49N	2 9W
Stafford □, *U.K.*	**14**	52 53N	2 10W
Staindrop, *U.K.*	**19**	54 35N	1 49W
Staines, *U.K.*	**15**	51 26N	0 30W
Stainforth, *U.K.*	**19**	53 37N	0 59W
Stainmore For., *U.K.*	**18**	54 29N	2 5W
Stainton, *U.K.*	**19**	53 17N	0 23W
Staithes, *U.K.*	**19**	54 33N	0 47W
Stalbridge, *U.K.*	**14**	50 57N	2 22W
Stalham, *U.K.*	**15**	52 46N	1 31 E
Stalingrad = Volgograd, *U.S.S.R.*	**47**	48 40N	44 25 E
Stallingborough, *U.K.*	**19**	53 36N	0 11W
Stalybridge, *U.K.*	**18**	53 29N	2 4W
Stamford, *U.K.*	**15**	52 39N	0 29W
Stamford, *U.S.A.*	**93**	41 5N	73 30W
Stamford Bridge, *U.K.*	**19**	53 59N	0 53W
Stamfordham, *U.K.*	**21**	55 3N	1 53W
Standish, *U.K.*	**18**	53 35N	2 39W
Standon, *U.K.*	**15**	51 53N	0 2 E
Stanford on Teme, *U.K.*	**14**	52 17N	2 26W
Stanhope, *U.K.*	**18**	54 45N	2 0W
Stanley, *Falk.*	**102**	51 40S	59 51W
Stanley, *Durham, U.K.*	**19**	54 53N	1 42W
Stanley, *Tayside, U.K.*	**21**	56 29N	3 28W
Stannington, *U.K.*	**21**	55 7N	1 41W
Stanovoy Ra., *U.S.S.R.*	**49**	55 0N	130 0 E
Stansted Mountfitchet, *U.K.*	**15**	51 54N	0 13 E
Stanwix, *U.K.*	**18**	54 54N	2 56W
Stapleford, *U.K.*	**19**	52 56N	1 16W
Staplehurst, *U.K.*	**15**	51 9N	0 35 E
Stara Zagora, *Bulg.*	**41**	42 26N	25 39 E
Start Bay, *U.K.*	**16**	50 15N	3 35W
Start Pt., *U.K.*	**16**	50 13N	3 38W
Staunton, *U.K.*	**14**	51 58N	2 19W
Stavanger, *Nor.*	**45**	58 57N	5 40 E
Staveley, *Cumbria, U.K.*	**18**	54 24N	2 49W
Staveley, *Derby, U.K.*	**19**	53 16N	1 20W
Stavropol, *U.S.S.R.*	**47**	45 5N	42 0 E
Stenhousemuir, *U.K.*	**21**	56 2N	3 46W
Sterlitamak, *U.S.S.R.*	**46**	53 40N	56 0 E
Stevenage, *U.K.*	**15**	51 54N	0 11W
Stevenston, *U.K.*	**20**	55 38N	4 46W
Stewart I., *N.Z.*	**71**	46 58S	167 54 E
Stewarton, *U.K.*	**20**	55 40N	4 30W
Steyning, *U.K.*	**15**	50 54N	0 19W
Stillington, *U.K.*	**19**	54 7N	1 5W
Stinchar →, *U.K.*	**20**	55 10N	4 50W
Stiperstones Mt., *U.K.*	**14**	52 36N	2 57W
Stirling, *U.K.*	**21**	56 7N	3 57W
Stobo, *U.K.*	**21**	55 38N	3 18W
Stockbridge, *U.K.*	**14**	51 7N	1 30W
Stockholm, *Swed.*	**45**	59 20N	18 3 E
Stockport, *U.K.*	**18**	53 25N	2 11W
Stocksbridge, *U.K.*	**19**	53 30N	1 36W
Stockton, *U.S.A.*	**90**	38 0N	121 20W
Stockton-on-Tees, *U.K.*	**19**	54 34N	1 20W
Stoke, *U.K.*	**15**	51 26N	0 41 E
Stoke Ferry, *U.K.*	**15**	52 34N	0 31 E
Stoke Fleming, *U.K.*	**16**	50 19N	3 36W
Stoke Mandeville, *U.K.*	**15**	51 46N	0 47W
Stoke-on-Trent, *U.K.*	**18**	53 1N	2 11W
Stoke Prior, *U.K.*	**14**	52 18N	2 5W
Stokenham, *U.K.*	**16**	50 15N	3 40W
Stokesley, *U.K.*	**19**	54 27N	1 12W
Stone, *Bucks., U.K.*	**15**	51 48N	0 52W
Stone, *Staffs., U.K.*	**18**	52 55N	2 10W
Stonehaven, *U.K.*	**23**	56 58N	2 11W
Stonehouse, *Gloucs., U.K.*	**14**	51 45N	2 18W
Stonehouse, *Strathclyde, U.K.*	**21**	55 42N	4 0W
Stonham Aspall, *U.K.*	**15**	52 11N	1 7 E
Stony Stratford, *U.K.*	**15**	52 4N	0 51W
Storm B., *Austral.*	**67**	43 10S	147 30 E
Stornoway, *U.K.*	**22**	58 12N	6 23W
Stort →, *U.K.*	**15**	51 50N	0 7 E
Stotfold, *U.K.*	**15**	52 2N	0 13W
Stour →, *Dorset, U.K.*	**14**	50 48N	2 7W
Stour →, *Hereford & Worcs., U.K.*	**14**	52 25N	2 13W
Stour →, *Kent, U.K.*	**15**	51 15N	1 20 E
Stour →, *Suffolk, U.K.*	**15**	51 55N	1 5 E
Stourbridge, *U.K.*	**14**	52 28N	2 8W
Stourport, *U.K.*	**14**	52 21N	2 18W
Stow, *U.K.*	**21**	55 41N	2 50W
Stow Bardolph, *U.K.*	**15**	52 38N	0 24 E
Stow-on-the-Wold, *U.K.*	**14**	51 55N	1 42W
Stowmarket, *U.K.*	**15**	52 11N	1 0 E
Strabane, *U.K.*	**24**	54 50N	7 28W
Strabane □, *U.K.*	**24**	54 45N	7 25W
Strachur, *U.K.*	**20**	56 10N	5 5W
Stradbroke, *U.K.*	**15**	52 19N	1 16 E
Stralsund, *E. Ger.*	**42**	54 17N	13 5 E
Strangford, L., *U.K.*	**24**	54 30N	5 37W
Stranraer, *U.K.*	**20**	54 54N	5 0W
Strasbourg, *Fr.*	**34**	48 35N	7 42 E
Stratford-on-Avon, *U.K.*	**14**	52 12N	1 42W
Stratford St. Mary, *U.K.*	**15**	51 58N	0 59 E
Strath Earn, *U.K.*	**21**	56 20N	3 50W
Strath Spey, *U.K.*	**23**	57 15N	3 40W
Strathaven, *U.K.*	**21**	55 40N	4 4W
Strathclyde □, *U.K.*	**20**	56 0N	4 50W
Strathmore, *U.K.*	**23**	56 40N	3 4W
Strathpeffer, *U.K.*	**23**	57 35N	4 32W
Strathy Pt., *U.K.*	**23**	58 35N	4 0W
Strathyre, *U.K.*	**20**	56 14N	4 20W
Stratmiglo, *U.K.*	**21**	56 16N	3 15W
Stratton, *Cornwall, U.K.*	**16**	50 49N	4 31W
Stratton, *Wilts., U.K.*	**14**	51 41N	1 45W
Stratton St. Margaret, *U.K.*	**14**	51 35N	1 45W
Streatley, *U.K.*	**14**	51 31N	1 9W
Street, *U.K.*	**14**	51 7N	2 43W
Strensall, *U.K.*	**19**	54 3N	1 2W
Stretford, *U.K.*	**18**	53 27N	2 19W
Stretton, *U.K.*	**18**	53 21N	2 34W
Strichen, *U.K.*	**23**	57 35N	2 5W
Striven, L., *U.K.*	**20**	55 58N	5 9W
Stromeferry, *U.K.*	**22**	57 20N	5 33W
Stromness, *U.K.*	**23**	58 58N	3 18W
Stronachlachar, *U.K.*	**20**	56 15N	4 35W
Strone, *U.K.*	**20**	55 59N	4 54W
Stronsay, *U.K.*	**23**	59 8N	2 38W
Stroud, *U.K.*	**14**	51 44N	2 12W
Studland, *U.K.*	**14**	50 39N	1 58W
Studley, *U.K.*	**14**	52 16N	1 54W
Sturminster Marshall, *U.K.*	**14**	50 48N	2 4W
Sturminster Newton, *U.K.*	**14**	50 56N	2 18W
Sturt Cr. →, *Austral.*	**66**	20 8S	127 24 E
Sturton, *U.K.*	**19**	53 22N	0 39W
Stuttgart, *W. Ger.*	**42**	48 46N	9 10 E
Subotica, *Yug.*	**41**	46 6N	19 49 E
Suck →, *Ire.*	**25**	53 17N	8 18W
Sucre, *Bol.*	**100**	19 0S	65 15W
Sudan ■, *Africa*	**78**	15 0N	30 0 E
Sudbury, *Canada*	**92**	46 30N	81 0W
Sudbury, *Derby, U.K.*	**19**	52 53N	1 43W
Sudbury, *Suffolk, U.K.*	**15**	52 2N	0 44 E
Suez, *Egypt*	**79**	29 58N	32 31 E
Suffolk □, *U.K.*	**15**	52 16N	1 0 E
Suir →, *Ire.*	**25**	52 15N	7 10W
Sukkur, *Pak.*	**58**	27 42N	68 54 E
Sulawesi □, *Indon.*	**63**	2 0S	120 0 E
Sulby, *U.K.*	**18**	54 18N	4 29W
Sullom Voe, *U.K.*	**22**	60 30N	1 20W
Sulu Sea, *E. Ind.*	**63**	8 0N	120 0 E
Sumatra □, *Indon.*	**63**	0 40N	100 20 E
Sumbawa, *Indon.*	**63**	8 26S	117 30 E
Sumburgh Hd., *U.K.*	**22**	59 52N	1 17W
Summer Is., *U.K.*	**22**	58 0N	5 27W
Sumy, *U.S.S.R.*	**47**	50 57N	34 50 E
Sunart, L., *U.K.*	**22**	56 42N	5 43W
Sunda Str., *Indon.*	**63**	6 20S	105 30 E
Sundarbans, The, *Asia*	**59**	22 0N	89 0 E
Sunderland, *U.K.*	**19**	54 54N	1 22W
Sundsvall, *Swed.*	**44**	62 23N	17 17 E
Sunk Island, *U.K.*	**19**	53 38N	0 7W
Sunninghill, *U.K.*	**15**	51 25N	0 40W
Sunshine, *Austral.*	**70**	37 48S	144 52 E
Superior, L., *N. Am.*	**92**	47 40N	87 0W
Sūr, *Leb.*	**57**	33 19N	35 16 E
Surabaya, *Indon.*	**63**	7 17S	112 45 E
Surakarta, *Indon.*	**63**	7 35S	110 48 E
Surat, *India*	**58**	21 12N	72 55 E
Surgut, *U.S.S.R.*	**48**	61 14N	73 20 E
Surinam ■, *S. Am.*	**101**	4 0N	56 0W
Surrey □, *U.K.*	**15**	51 16N	0 30W
Surtsey, *Ice.*	**44**	63 20N	20 30W
Sutlej →, *Pak.*	**58**	29 23N	71 3 E
Sutterton, *U.K.*	**19**	52 54N	0 8W
Sutton, *U.K.*	**15**	51 22N	0 13W
Sutton Bridge, *U.K.*	**15**	52 46N	0 12 E
Sutton Coldfield, *U.K.*	**14**	52 33N	1 50W
Sutton Courtenay, *U.K.*	**14**	51 39N	1 16W
Sutton-in-Ashfield, *U.K.*	**19**	53 7N	1 20W
Sutton-on-Sea, *U.K.*	**19**	53 18N	0 18 E
Sutton Scotney, *U.K.*	**14**	51 9N	1 20W
Suva, *Fiji*	**64**	18 6S	178 30 E
Suzhou, *China*	**61**	31 19N	120 38 E
Svalbard, *Arctic*	**103**	78 0N	17 0 E
Svendborg, *Den.*	**45**	55 4N	10 35 E
Sverdlovsk, *U.S.S.R.*	**46**	56 50N	60 30 E
Sverdrup Is., *Canada*	**103**	79 0N	97 0W
Swadlincote, *U.K.*	**14**	52 47N	1 34W
Swaffham, *U.K.*	**15**	52 38N	0 42 E
Swale →, *U.K.*	**19**	54 5N	1 20W
Swan Hill, *Austral.*	**70**	35 20S	143 33 E
Swanage, *U.K.*	**14**	50 36N	1 59W
Swansea, *U.K.*	**17**	51 37N	3 57W
Swaziland ■, *Africa*	**81**	26 30S	31 30 E
Sweden ■, *Europe*	**44**	57 0N	15 0 E
Swift Current, *Canada*	**88**	50 20N	107 45W
Swilly, L., *Ire.*	**24**	55 12N	7 35W
Swindon, *U.K.*	**15**	51 33N	1 47W
Swineshead, *U.K.*	**19**	52 56N	0 11W
Swinton, *Borders, U.K.*	**21**	55 43N	2 14W
Swinton, *Gr. Manchester, U.K.*	**18**	53 31N	2 21W
Swinton, *S. Yorks., U.K.*	**19**	53 28N	1 20W
Switzerland ■, *Europe*	**42**	46 30N	8 0 E
Swords, *Ire.*	**24**	53 27N	6 15W
Sydney, *Austral.*	**70**	33 53S	151 10 E
Sydney, *Canada*	**93**	46 7N	60 7W
Syktyvkar, *U.S.S.R.*	**46**	61 45N	50 40 E
Symington, *U.K.*	**21**	55 35N	3 36W
Symonds Yat, *U.K.*	**14**	51 50N	2 38W
Syracuse, *U.S.A.*	**93**	43 4N	76 11W
Syrdarya →, *U.S.S.R.*	**48**	46 3N	61 0 E
Syria ■, *Asia*	**56**	35 0N	38 0 E
Syrian Desert, *Asia*	**56**	31 0N	40 0 E
Syston, *U.K.*	**14**	52 42N	1 5W
Syzran, *U.S.S.R.*	**46**	53 12N	48 30 E
Szczecin, *Pol.*	**42**	53 27N	14 27 E
Szeged, *Hung.*	**43**	46 16N	20 10 E
Székesfehérvár, *Hung.*	**43**	47 15N	18 25 E
T			
Tabora, *Tanz.*	**80**	5 2S	32 50 E
Tabrīz, *Iran*	**56**	38 7N	46 20 E
Tabūk, *Si. Arab.*	**56**	28 23N	36 36 E
Tacna, *Peru*	**100**	18 0S	70 20W
Tacoma, *U.S.A.*	**90**	47 15N	122 30W
Tacuarembó, *Urug.*	**102**	31 45S	56 0W
Tadcaster, *U.K.*	**19**	53 53N	1 16W
Tadley, *U.K.*	**14**	51 21N	1 8W
Tadzhikistan □, *U.S.S.R.*	**48**	35 30N	70 0 E
Taegu, *S. Kor.*	**61**	35 50N	128 37 E
Taejŏn, *S. Kor.*	**61**	36 20N	127 28 E
Taganrog, *U.S.S.R.*	**47**	47 12N	38 50 E
Tagus = Tajo →, *Sp.*	**37**	38 40N	9 24W
Tahiti, *Pac. Oc.*	**65**	17 37S	149 27W
Taichung, *Taiwan*	**61**	24 10N	120 35 E
Taimyr Pen., *U.S.S.R.*	**49**	75 0N	100 0 E
Tain, *U.K.*	**23**	57 49N	4 4W
Tainan, *Taiwan*	**61**	23 17N	120 18 E
Taipei, *Taiwan*	**61**	25 2N	121 30 E
Taiwan ■, *Asia*	**61**	23 30N	121 0 E
Taiyuan, *China*	**61**	37 52N	112 33 E
Ta'izz, *Yem.*	**56**	13 35N	44 2 E
Tajo →, *Sp.*	**37**	38 40N	9 24W
Tak, *Thai.*	**59**	16 52N	99 8 E
Takamatsu, *Jap.*	**62**	34 20N	134 5 E
Takaoka, *Jap.*	**62**	36 47N	137 0 E
Takapuna, *N.Z.*	**71**	36 47S	174 47 E
Takasaki, *Jap.*	**62**	36 20N	139 0 E
Takeley, *U.K.*	**15**	51 52N	0 16 E
Takla Makan, *China*	**60**	39 0N	83 0 E
Talca, *Chile*	**102**	35 28S	71 40W
Talcahuano, *Chile*	**102**	36 40S	73 10W
Talgarth, *U.K.*	**17**	51 59N	3 15W
Tallahassee, *U.S.A.*	**91**	30 25N	84 15W
Tallinn, *U.S.S.R.*	**46**	59 22N	24 48 E
Tamar →, *U.K.*	**16**	50 33N	4 15W
Tambov, *U.S.S.R.*	**46**	52 45N	41 28 E
Tame →, *U.K.*	**14**	52 43N	1 45W
Tamerton Foliot, *U.K.*	**16**	50 25N	4 10W
Tamil Nadu □, *India*	**58**	11 0N	77 0 E
Tampa, *U.S.A.*	**91**	27 57N	82 38W
Tampere, *Fin.*	**44**	61 30N	23 50 E
Tampico, *Mex.*	**94**	22 20N	97 50W
Tamworth, *Austral.*	**67**	31 7S	150 58 E
Tamworth, *U.K.*	**14**	52 38N	1 41W
Tana, L., *Eth.*	**79**	13 5N	37 30 E
Tanami Desert, *Austral.*	**66**	18 50S	132 0 E
Tandragee, *U.K.*	**24**	54 22N	6 23W
Tanga, *Tanz.*	**80**	5 5S	39 2 E
Tanganyika, L., *E. Afr.*	**80**	6 40S	30 0 E
Tangier, *Mor.*	**78**	35 50N	5 49W
Tangshan, *China*	**61**	39 38N	118 10 E
Tanworth, *U.K.*	**14**	52 20N	1 50W
Tanzania ■, *E. Afr.*	**80**	6 40S	34 0 E
Tapajós →, *Brazil*	**101**	2 24S	54 41W
Tarābulus, *Leb.*	**56**	34 31N	35 50 E
Tarābulus, *Libya*	**79**	32 49N	13 7 E
Taranaki □, *N.Z.*	**71**	39 5S	174 51 E
Táranto, *It.*	**40**	40 30N	17 11 E
Táranto, G. di, *It.*	**40**	40 0N	17 15 E
Tarbat Ness, *U.K.*	**23**	57 52N	3 48W
Tarbert, *Strathclyde, U.K.*	**20**	55 55N	5 25W
Tarbert, *W. Isles, U.K.*	**22**	57 54N	6 49W
Tarbes, *Fr.*	**35**	43 15N	0 3 E
Tarbet, *U.K.*	**20**	56 13N	4 44W
Tarbolton, *U.K.*	**20**	55 30N	4 30W
Taree, *Austral.*	**70**	31 50S	152 30 E
Tarija, *Bol.*	**100**	21 30S	64 40W
Tarim Basin, *China*	**60**	40 0N	84 0 E
Tarleton, *U.K.*	**18**	53 41N	2 50W
Tarnów, *Pol.*	**43**	50 3N	21 0 E
Tarporley, *U.K.*	**18**	53 10N	2 42W
Tarragona, *Sp.*	**37**	41 5N	1 17 E
Tarrasa, *Sp.*	**37**	41 34N	2 1 E
Tashkent, *U.S.S.R.*	**48**	41 20N	69 10 E
Tasman B., *N.Z.*	**71**	40 59S	173 25 E
Tasman Sea, *Pac. Oc.*	**71**	36 0S	160 0 E
Tasmania □, *Austral.*	**67**	42 0S	146 30 E
Tatar A.S.S.R. □, *U.S.S.R.*	**46**	55 30N	51 30 E
Tattenhall, *U.K.*	**18**	53 7N	2 47W
Taunton, *U.K.*	**14**	51 1N	3 7W
Taupo, *N.Z.*	**71**	38 41S	176 7 E
Taupo, L., *N.Z.*	**71**	38 46S	175 55 E
Tauranga, *N.Z.*	**71**	37 42S	176 11 E
Taurus Mts., *Turk.*	**47**	37 0N	35 0 E
Tavistock, *U.K.*	**16**	50 33N	4 9W
Tavoy, *Burma*	**59**	14 2N	98 12 E
Taw →, *U.K.*	**16**	17 37S	177 55 E
Tay →, *U.K.*	**21**	56 37N	3 38W
Tay, Firth of, *U.K.*	**21**	56 25N	3 8W
Tay, L., *U.K.*	**21**	56 30N	4 10W
Tay Bridge, *U.K.*	**21**	56 28N	3 0W
Taynuilt, *U.K.*	**20**	56 25N	5 15W
Tayport, *U.K.*	**21**	56 27N	2 52W
Tayside □, *U.K.*	**21**	56 25N	3 30W
Tbilisi, *U.S.S.R.*	**47**	41 43N	44 50 E
Te Anau, L., *N.Z.*	**71**	45 15S	167 45 E
Te Aroha, *N.Z.*	**71**	37 32S	175 44 E
Tebay, *U.K.*	**18**	54 25N	2 35W
Tees →, *U.K.*	**19**	54 36N	1 25W
Teesdale, *U.K.*	**18**	54 37N	2 10W
Teesside, *U.K.*	**19**	54 37N	1 13W
Tegid, L., *U.K.*	**17**	52 53N	3 38W
Tegucigalpa, *Hond.*	**94**	14 5N	87 14W
Tehrān, *Iran*	**56**	35 44N	51 30 E
Tehuantepec, Gulf of, *Mex.*	**94**	15 50N	95 0W
Tehuantepec, Isthmus of, *Mex.*	**94**	17 0N	94 30W
Teifi →, *U.K.*	**17**	52 4N	4 14W
Teign →, *U.K.*	**16**	50 41N	3 42W
Teignmouth, *U.K.*	**16**	50 33N	3 30W
Tejo →, *Port.*	**37**	38 40N	9 24W
Tel Aviv-Jaffa, *Isr.*	**57**	32 4N	34 48 E
Telemark fylke □, *Nor.*	**45**	59 25N	8 30 E
Telford, *U.K.*	**14**	52 42N	2 31W
Teluk Betung, *Indon.*	**63**	5 20S	105 10 E
Tema, *Ghana*	**78**	5 41N	0 0 E
Teme →, *U.K.*	**14**	52 23N	2 15W
Temirtau, *U.S.S.R.*	**48**	50 5N	72 56 E
Temora, *Austral.*	**70**	34 30S	147 30 E
Temple Combe, *U.K.*	**14**	51 0N	2 25W
Temple Ewell, *U.K.*	**15**	51 9N	1 15 E
Temple Sowerby, *U.K.*	**18**	54 38N	2 33W
Templemore, *Ire.*	**25**	52 48N	7 50W
Tenbury, *U.K.*	**14**	52 18N	2 35W
Tenby, *U.K.*	**17**	51 40N	4 42W
Tenerife, *Can. Is.*	**78**	28 15N	16 35W
Tennessee □, *U.S.A.*	**91**	36 0N	86 30W
Tennessee →, *U.S.A.*	**91**	37 4N	88 34W
Tenterden, *U.K.*	**15**	51 4N	0 42 E
Teófilo Otoni, *Brazil*	**101**	17 50S	41 30W
Tepic, *Mex.*	**94**	21 30N	104 54W
Téramo, *It.*	**40**	42 40N	13 40 E
Teresina, *Brazil*	**101**	5 9S	42 45W
Terni, *It.*	**40**	42 34N	12 38 E
Terre Haute, *U.S.A.*	**92**	39 28N	87 24W
Teruel, *Sp.*	**37**	40 22N	1 8W
Test →, *U.K.*	**14**	51 7N	1 30W
Tetbury, *U.K.*	**14**	51 37N	2 9W
Tetlin, *U.S.A.*	**88**	63 14N	142 50W
Tetney, *U.K.*	**19**	53 30N	0 1W
Tétouan, *Mor.*	**78**	35 35N	5 21W
Tetovo, *Yug.*	**41**	42 1N	21 2 E
Tettenhall, *U.K.*	**14**	52 35N	2 7W
Teviot →, *U.K.*	**21**	55 21N	2 51W
Teviotdale, *U.K.*	**21**	55 25N	2 50W
Teviothead, *U.K.*	**21**	55 19N	2 55W
Tewkesbury, *U.K.*	**14**	51 59N	2 8W
Texas □, *U.S.A.*	**90**	31 40N	98 30W
Texel, *Neth.*	**36**	53 5N	4 50 E
Teynham, *U.K.*	**15**	51 19N	0 50 E
Thailand ■, *Asia*	**63**	16 0N	102 0 E
Thailand, G. of, *Asia*	**63**	11 30N	101 0 E
Thal Desert, *Pak.*	**58**	31 10N	71 30 E
Thame, *U.K.*	**15**	51 44N	0 58W
Thame →, *U.K.*	**15**	51 35N	1 8W
Thames →, *U.K.*	**15**	51 30N	0 35 E
Thanet, I. of, *U.K.*	**15**	51 21N	1 20 E
Thar Desert, *India*	**58**	28 0N	72 0 E
Thatcham, *U.K.*	**14**	51 24N	1 17W
Thaxted, *U.K.*	**15**	51 57N	0 20 E
The Entrance, *Austral.*	**70**	33 21S	151 30 E
The Grenadines, Is., *W. Ind.*	**94**	12 40N	61 20W
The Hague, *Neth.*	**36**	52 7N	4 17 E
The Pas, *Canada*	**88**	53 45N	101 15W
Theale, *U.K.*	**14**	51 26N	1 5W
Thessaloníki, *Greece*	**41**	40 38N	22 58 E
Thessaloniki, Gulf of, *Greece*	**41**	40 15N	22 45 E
Thessaly □, *Greece*	**41**	39 30N	22 0 E
Thetford, *U.K.*	**15**	52 25N	0 44 E
Thies, *Sene.*	**78**	14 50N	16 51W
Thimphu, *Bhutan*	**59**	27 31N	89 45 E
Thionville, *Fr.*	**34**	49 20N	6 10 E
Thirlmere, L., *U.K.*	**18**	54 32N	3 4W
Thirsk, *U.K.*	**19**	54 15N	1 20W
Thirston, *U.K.*	**21**	55 20N	1 34W
Thisted, *Den.*	**45**	56 58N	8 40 E
Thompson →, *Canada*	**88**	50 15N	121 24W
Thornaby on Tees, *U.K.*	**19**	54 36N	1 19W
Thornbury, *U.K.*	**14**	51 36N	2 31W
Thorndon, *U.K.*	**15**	52 16N	1 8 E
Thorne, *U.K.*	**19**	53 36N	0 56W
Thorney, *U.K.*	**15**	52 37N	0 8W
Thornham, *U.K.*	**15**	52 59N	0 35 E
Thornhill, *U.K.*	**21**	55 15N	3 46W
Thornthwaite, *U.K.*	**18**	54 36N	3 13W
Thornton, *U.K.*	**18**	53 52N	2 29W
Thornton Dale, *U.K.*	**19**	54 14N	0 41W
Thorpe, *U.K.*	**15**	52 38N	1 20 E
Thorpe le Soken, *U.K.*	**15**	51 50N	1 11 E
Thrace □, *Greece*	**41**	41 9N	25 30 E
Thrapston, *U.K.*	**15**	52 24N	0 32W
Threlkeld, *U.K.*	**18**	54 37N	3 2W
Threshfield, *U.K.*	**18**	54 5N	2 2W
Thule, *Green.*	**103**	77 40N	69 0W
Thunder Bay, *Canada*	**92**	48 20N	89 15W
Thurlby, *U.K.*	**15**	52 45N	0 21W
Thurles, *Ire.*	**25**	52 40N	7 53W
Thurmaston, *U.K.*	**14**	52 40N	1 8W
Thursby, *U.K.*	**18**	54 40N	3 3W
Thurso, *U.K.*	**23**	58 34N	3 31W
Tian Shan, *China*	**60**	43 0N	84 0 E
Tianshui, *China*	**60**	34 32N	105 40 E
Tiber →, *It.*	**40**	41 44N	12 14 E
Tiberias, *Isr.*	**57**	32 47N	35 32 E
Tibesti, *Chad*	**79**	21 0N	17 30 E
Ticehurst, *U.K.*	**15**	51 2N	0 23 E
Tickhill, *U.K.*	**19**	53 25N	1 8W
Tideswell, *U.K.*	**19**	53 17N	1 46W
Tientsin, *China*	**61**	39 10N	117 15 E
Tierra del Fuego □, *Arg.*	**102**	54 0S	67 45W
Tighnabruaich, *U.K.*	**20**	55 55N	5 13W
Tigris →, *Iraq*	**56**	37 0N	42 30 E

Tijuana, Mex. 94 32 30N 117 10W
Tiksi, U.S.S.R. 49 71 40N 128 45 E
Tilburg, Neth. 36 51 31N 5 6 E
Tilbury, U.K. 15 51 27N 0 24 E
Till →, U.K. 19 55 35N 2 3W
Tillicoultry, U.K. 21 56 9N 3 44W
Tilmanstone, U.K. 15 51 13N 1 18 E
Tilt →, U.K. 23 56 50N 3 50W
Timaru, N.Z. 71 44 23S 171 14 E
Timbuktu = Tombouctou, Mali 78 16 50N 3 0W
Timişoara, Rom. 43 45 43N 21 15 E
Timmins, Canada 92 48 28N 81 25W
Timor, Indon. 63 9 0S 125 0 E
Timor Sea, E. Ind. 66 10 0S 127 0 E
Tingewick, U.K. 14 51 59N 1 4W
Tintagel, U.K. 16 50 40N 4 45W
Tintagel Hd., U.K. 16 50 40N 4 46W
Tipperary, Ire. 25 52 28N 8 10W
Tipperary □, Ire. 25 52 37N 7 55W
Tipton, U.K. 14 52 32N 2 4W
Tiptree, U.K. 15 51 48N 0 46 E
Tiranë, Alb. 41 41 18N 19 49 E
Tiree, U.K. 20 56 31N 6 55W
Tiree, Passage of, U.K. 20 56 30N 6 30W
Tîrgu Mureş, Rom. 43 46 31N 24 38 E
Tiruchchirappalli, India 58 10 45N 78 45 E
Tisbury, U.K. 14 51 4N 2 4W
Tisza →, Hung. 43 46 8N 20 2 E
Titchfield, U.K. 14 50 51N 1 13W
Titicaca, L., Peru 100 15 30S 69 30W
Titograd, Yug. 41 42 30N 19 19 E
Tiverton, U.K. 16 50 54N 3 30W
Tizi-Ouzou, Alg. 78 36 42N 4 3 E
Toamasina, Madag. 81 18 10S 49 25 E
Tobago, W. Ind. 94 11 10N 60 30W
Tobermory, U.K. 20 56 37N 6 4W
Tobol →, U.S.S.R. 48 58 10N 68 12 E
Tocantins →, Brazil 101 1 45S 49 10W
Toddington, U.K. 15 51 57N 0 31W
Todmorden, U.K. 18 53 43N 2 7W
Togliatti, U.S.S.R. 46 53 32N 49 24 E
Togo ■, W. Afr. 78 6 15N 1 35 E
Tokelau Is., Pac. Oc. 64 9 0S 171 45W
Tōkyō, Jap. 62 35 45N 139 45 E
Tolageak, U.S.A. 88 70 2N 162 50W
Tolbukhin, Bulg. 41 43 37N 27 49 E
Toledo, Sp. 37 39 50N 4 2W
Toledo, U.S.A. 92 41 37N 83 33W
Toliara, Madag. 81 23 21S 43 40 E
Tollesbury, U.K. 15 51 46N 0 51 E
Toluca, Mex. 94 19 20N 99 40W
Tom Price, Austral. 66 22 40S 117 48 E
Tombouctou, Mali 78 16 50N 3 0W
Tomnavoulin, U.K. 23 57 19N 3 18W
Tomsk, U.S.S.R. 48 56 30N 85 5 E
Tonbridge, U.K. 15 51 12N 0 18 E
Tone →, U.K. 16 50 59N 3 15W
Tong, U.K. 14 52 39N 2 18W
Tonga ■, Pac. Oc. 64 19 50S 174 30W
Tonga Trench, Pac. Oc. 64 18 0S 175 0W
Tongue, U.K. 23 58 29N 4 25W
Tonkin, G. of, Asia 60 20 0N 108 0 E
Toowoomba, Austral. 67 27 32S 151 56 E
Topeka, U.S.A. 91 39 3N 95 40W
Topsham, U.K. 16 50 40N 3 27W
Tor Bay, U.K. 16 50 26N 3 31W
Torbay, U.K. 16 50 26N 3 31W
Torne älv →, Swed. 44 65 50N 24 12 E
Toronto, Canada 92 43 39N 79 20W
Torpoint, U.K. 16 50 23N 4 12W
Torquay, U.K. 16 50 27N 3 31W
Torran Rocks, U.K. 20 56 14N 6 24W
Torrens, L., Austral. 67 31 0S 137 50 E
Torreón, Mex. 94 25 33N 103 26W
Torridge →, U.K. 16 50 51N 4 10W
Torridon, L., U.K. 22 57 35N 5 50W
Torthorwald, U.K. 21 55 7N 3 30W
Tortosa, Sp. 37 40 49N 0 31 E
Toruń, Pol. 43 53 0N 18 39 E
Torver, U.K. 18 54 20N 3 7W
Tory I., Ire. 24 55 17N 8 12W
Totland, U.K. 14 50 41N 1 32W
Totley, U.K. 19 53 18N 1 32W
Totnes, U.K. 16 50 26N 3 41W
Totton, U.K. 14 50 55N 1 29W
Toulon, Fr. 35 43 10N 5 55 E
Toulouse, Fr. 35 43 37N 1 27 E
Tournai, Belg. 36 50 35N 3 25 E
Tours, Fr. 34 47 22N 0 40 E
Towcester, U.K. 15 52 7N 0 56W
Town Yetholm, U.K. 21 55 33N 2 19W
Townsville, Austral. 67 19 15S 146 45 E
Toyama, Jap. 62 36 40N 137 15 E
Toyohashi, Jap. 62 34 45N 137 25 E
Trabzon, Turk. 47 41 0N 39 45 E
Trail, Canada 88 49 5N 117 40W
Tralee, Ire. 25 52 16N 9 42W
Tralee B., Ire. 25 52 17N 9 55W
Tramore, Ire. 25 52 10N 7 10W
Tranent, U.K. 21 55 57N 2 58W
Transcaucasia, U.S.S.R. 47 42 0N 44 0 E
Transvaal □, S. Afr. 81 25 0S 29 0 E
Transylvanian Alps, Rom. 43 45 30N 25 0 E
Trápani, It. 40 38 1N 12 30 E
Traralgon, Austral. 70 38 12S 146 34 E
Trawsfynydd, U.K. 17 52 54N 3 55W
Tredegar, U.K. 17 51 47N 3 16W
Tregaron, U.K. 17 52 14N 3 56W
Trent →, U.K. 19 53 33N 0 44W
Trentham, U.K. 18 52 59N 2 12W
Trentino-Alto Adige □, It. 40 46 30N 11 0 E
Trento, It. 40 46 5N 11 8 E
Trenton, U.S.A. 93 40 15N 74 41W
Tresco I., U.K. 16 49 57N 6 20W
Treshnish Is., U.K. 20 56 30N 6 25W
Trevose Hd., U.K. 16 50 33N 5 3W
Trier, W. Ger. 36 49 45N 6 37 E
Trieste, It. 40 45 39N 13 45 E
Trim, Ire. 24 53 34N 6 48W
Trimdon, U.K. 19 54 43N 1 23W
Trimley, U.K. 15 51 59N 1 19 E
Trincomalee, Sri L. 58 8 38N 81 15 E
Trinidad, W. Ind. 94 10 30N 61 15W
Trinidad & Tobago ■, W. Ind. 94 10 30N 61 20W
Tripoli = Tarābulus, Leb. 56 34 31N 35 50 E
Tripoli = Tarābulus, Libya 79 32 49N 13 7 E
Tristan da Cunha, Atl. Oc. 128 37 6S 12 20W
Trivandrum, India 58 8 41N 77 0 E
Trois-Riviéres, Canada 93 46 25N 72 34W
Trollhättan, Swed. 45 58 17N 12 20 E
Troms fylke □, Nor. 44 68 56N 19 0 E
Tromsø, Nor. 44 69 40N 18 56 E
Trondheim, Nor. 44 63 36N 10 25 E
Troon, U.K. 20 55 33N 4 40W
Trossachs, The, U.K. 20 56 14N 4 24W
Trostan, U.K. 24 55 4N 6 10W
Trotternish, U.K. 22 57 32N 6 15W
Trowbridge, U.K. 14 51 18N 2 12W
Troy, U.S.A. 93 42 45N 73 39W
Troyes, Fr. 34 48 19N 4 3 E
Trujillo, Peru 100 8 6S 79 0W
Truk, Pac. Oc. 64 7 25N 151 46 E
Trull, U.K. 14 50 58N 3 8W
Trumpington, U.K. 15 52 11N 0 6 E
Truro, U.K. 16 50 17N 5 2W
Tselinograd, U.S.S.R. 48 51 10N 71 30 E
Tsimlyansk Res., U.S.S.R. 47 48 0N 43 0 E
Tsu, Jap. 62 34 45N 136 25 E
Tsugaru Str., Jap. 62 41 30N 140 30 E
Tuam, Ire. 24 53 30N 8 50W
Tuamotu Arch., Pac. Oc. 65 17 0S 144 0W
Tuath, Loch, U.K. 20 56 30N 6 15W
Tubuai Is., Pac. Oc. 65 25 0S 150 0W
Tucson, U.S.A. 90 32 14N 110 59W
Tula, U.S.S.R. 46 54 13N 37 38 E
Tulcán, Ecuad. 100 0 48N 77 43W
Tulla, L., U.K. 20 56 33N 4 47W
Tullamore, Ire. 25 53 17N 7 30W
Tullow, Ire. 25 52 48N 6 45W
Tulsa, U.S.A. 91 36 10N 96 0W
Tulua, Col. 100 4 6N 76 11W
Tumaco, Col. 100 1 50N 78 45W
Tummel, L., U.K. 23 56 43N 3 55W
Tunbridge Wells, U.K. 15 51 7N 0 16 E
Tuncurry, Austral. 70 32 17S 152 29 E
Tunis, Tunisia 78 36 50N 10 11 E
Tunisia ■, Africa 78 33 30N 9 10 E
Tunja, Col. 100 5 33N 73 25W
Tunstall, U.K. 15 52 7N 1 28 E
Tura, India 59 25 30N 90 16 E
Turfan Depression, China 50 42 40N 89 25 E
Turin, It. 40 45 4N 7 40 E
Turkana, L., Kenya 80 3 30N 36 5 E
Turkey ■, Eurasia 47 39 0N 36 0 E
Turkmenistan □, U.S.S.R. 48 39 0N 59 0 E
Turks Is., W. Ind. 95 21 20N 71 20W
Turku, Fin. 45 60 30N 22 19 E
Turnberry, U.K. 20 55 19N 4 50W
Turnu-Severin, Rom. 43 44 39N 22 41 E
Turriff, U.K. 23 57 32N 2 28W
Tuskar Rock, Ire. 25 52 12N 6 10W
Tutbury, U.K. 14 52 52N 1 41W
Tuticorin, India 58 8 50N 78 12 E
Tuvalu ■, Pac. Oc. 64 8 0S 178 0 E
Tuxford, U.K. 19 53 14N 0 52W
Tuxtla Gutiérrez, Mex. 94 16 50N 93 10W
Tuz Gölü, Turk. 47 38 45N 33 30 E
Tuzla, Yug. 41 44 34N 18 41 E
Twatt, U.K. 23 59 6N 3 15W
Tweed →, U.K. 21 55 42N 1 59W
Tweedmouth, U.K. 21 55 46N 2 1W
Tweedshawe, U.K. 21 55 26N 3 29W
Twenty, U.K. 15 52 43N 0 20W
Twyford, Berks., U.K. 15 51 29N 0 51W
Twyford, Hants., U.K. 14 51 1N 1 19W
Tychy, Pol. 43 50 9N 18 59 E
Tydd St. Mary, U.K. 15 52 45N 0 9 E
Tyldesley, U.K. 18 53 31N 2 29W
Tyler, U.S.A. 90 32 18N 95 18W
Tyndrum, U.K. 20 56 26N 4 41W
Tyne →, Tyne & Wear, U.K. 19 54 58N 1 28W
Tyne →, Lothian, U.K. 21 55 58N 2 45W
Tyne & Wear □, U.K. 19 54 55N 1 35W
Tynemouth, U.K. 19 55 1N 1 27W
Tyre = Sūr, Leb. 57 33 19N 35 16 E
Tyrol □, Austria 42 47 3N 10 43 E
Tyrrhenian Sea, Europe 40 40 0N 12 30 E
Tyumen, U.S.S.R. 48 57 11N 65 29 E
Tywardreath, U.K. 16 50 21N 4 40W
Tywi →, U.K. 17 51 48N 4 20W
Tywyn, U.K. 17 52 36N 4 5W

U

Ube, Jap. 62 33 56N 131 15 E
Uberaba, Brazil 101 19 50S 47 55W
Uberlândia, Brazil 101 19 0S 48 20W
Ucayali →, Peru 100 4 30S 73 30W
Uckfield, U.K. 15 50 58N 0 6 E
Udaipur, India 58 24 36N 73 44 E
Uddevalla, Swed. 45 58 21N 11 55 E
Uddingston, U.K. 21 55 50N 4 3W
Údine, It. 40 46 5N 13 10 E
Ufa, U.S.S.R. 46 54 45N 55 55 E
Uffculme, U.K. 16 50 54N 3 19W
Ufford, U.K. 15 52 6N 1 22 E
Uganda ■, E. Afr. 80 2 0N 32 0 E
Ugborough, U.K. 16 50 22N 3 53W
Uig, U.K. 22 57 35N 6 20W
Uitenhage, S. Afr. 81 33 40S 25 28 E
Ujung Pandang, Indon. 63 5 10S 119 20 E
Ukraine □, U.S.S.R. 47 49 0N 32 0 E
Ulan Bator, Mong. 60 47 55N 106 53 E
Ulan Ude, U.S.S.R. 49 51 45N 107 40 E
Ulceby Cross, U.K. 19 53 14N 0 6 E
Ulhasnagar, India 58 19 15N 73 10 E
Ullapool, U.K. 22 57 54N 5 10W
Ullswater, U.K. 18 54 35N 2 52W
Ulm, W. Ger. 42 48 23N 10 0 E
Ulster □, U.K. 24 54 35N 6 30W
Ulva, I., U.K. 20 56 30N 6 12W
Ulverston, U.K. 18 54 13N 3 7W
Ulyanovsk, U.S.S.R. 46 54 20N 48 25 E
Ulyasutay, Mong. 60 47 56N 97 28 E
Umbria □, It. 40 42 53N 12 30 E
Umeå, Swed. 44 63 45N 20 20 E
Umtata, S. Afr. 81 31 36S 28 49 E
Ungava B., Canada 89 59 30N 67 30W
Ungava Pen., Canada 89 60 0N 74 0W
Union of Soviet Socialist Republics ■, Eurasia 48 60 0N 100 0 E
United Arab Emirates ■, Asia 57 23 50N 54 0 E
United Kingdom ■, Europe 5 55 0N 3 0W
United States of America ■, N. Am. 90 37 0N 96 0W
United States Trust Terr. of the Pacific Is. □, Pac. Oc. 64 10 0N 160 0 E
Unst, U.K. 22 60 50N 0 55W
Upavon, U.K. 14 51 17N 1 49W
Upington, S. Afr. 81 28 25S 21 15 E
Upper Heyford, U.K. 14 51 54N 1 16W
Upper L. Erne, U.K. 24 54 14N 7 22W
Upper Volta ■ = Burkina Faso ■, Africa 78 12 0N 1 0W
Uppingham, U.K. 15 52 36N 0 43W
Uppsala, Swed. 45 59 53N 17 38 E
Upton, U.K. 18 53 14N 2 52W
Upton-upon-Severn, U.K. 14 52 4N 2 12W
Upwey, U.K. 14 50 40N 2 29W
Ural Mts., U.S.S.R. 46 60 0N 59 0 E
Uralsk, U.S.S.R. 46 51 20N 51 20 E
Uranium City, Canada 88 59 34N 108 37W
Ure →, U.K. 19 54 20N 1 25W
Urgench, U.S.S.R. 48 41 40N 60 41 E
Urmia, L., Iran 56 37 50N 45 30 E
Urmston, U.K. 18 53 28N 2 22W
Uruguay ■, S. Am. 102 32 30S 56 30W
Uruguay →, S. Am. 102 34 12S 58 18W
Ürümqi, China 60 43 45N 87 45 E
Usk →, U.K. 17 51 37N 2 56W
Üsküdar, Turk. 47 41 0N 29 5 E
Usselby, U.K. 19 53 25N 0 21W
Ust-Kamenogorsk, U.S.S.R. 48 50 0N 82 36 E
Ust Urt Plateau, U.S.S.R. 48 44 0N 55 0 E
Ustinov, U.S.S.R. 46 56 51N 53 14 E
Utah □, U.S.A. 90 39 30N 111 30W
Utica, U.S.A. 93 43 5N 75 18W
Utrecht, Neth. 36 52 5N 5 8 E
Utsunomiya, Jap. 62 36 30N 139 50 E
Uttar Pradesh □, India 58 27 0N 80 0 E
Uttoxeter, U.K. 18 52 53N 1 50W
Uzbekistan □, U.S.S.R. 48 41 30N 65 0 E

V

Vaasa, Fin. 44 63 6N 21 38 E
Vadodara, India 58 22 20N 73 10 E
Vadsø, Nor. 44 70 3N 29 50 E
Val d'Or, Canada 92 48 7N 77 47W
Valdez, U.S.A. 88 61 14N 146 17W
Valdivia, Chile 102 39 50S 73 14W
Valence, Fr. 35 44 57N 4 54 E
Valencia, Sp. 37 39 27N 0 23W
Valencia, Ven. 100 10 11N 68 0W
Valenciennes, Fr. 34 50 20N 3 34 E
Valentia Hr., Ire. 25 51 56N 10 17W
Valentia I., Ire. 25 51 54N 10 22W
Valladolid, Sp. 37 41 38N 4 43W
Valledupar, Col. 100 10 29N 73 15W
Valletta, Malta 40 35 54N 14 30 E
Valley, U.K. 17 53 17N 4 31W
Valparaíso, Chile 102 33 2S 71 40W
Van, L., Turk. 47 38 30N 43 0 E
Van Diemen G., Austral. 66 11 45S 132 0 E
Vancouver, Canada 88 49 15N 123 10W
Vancouver I., Canada 88 49 50N 126 0W
Vänern, Swed. 45 58 47N 13 30 E
Vanua Levu, Fiji 64 16 33S 179 15 E
Vanuatu ■, Pac. Oc. 64 15 0S 168 0 E
Varanasi, India 59 25 22N 83 0 E
Varangar Fjord, Nor. 44 70 3N 29 25 E
Vardar →, Yug. 41 40 35N 22 50 E
Värmlands län □, Swed. 45 60 0N 13 20 E
Varna, Bulg. 41 43 13N 27 56 E
Västerås, Swed. 45 59 37N 16 38 E
Västmanlands län □, Swed. 45 59 45N 16 20 E
Vatnajökull, Ice. 44 64 30N 16 48W
Vättern, Swed. 45 58 25N 14 30 E
Växjö, Swed. 45 56 52N 14 50 E
Vendée □, Fr. 34 46 50N 1 35W
Venezuela ■, S. Am. 100 8 0N 65 0W
Venice, It. 40 45 27N 12 20 E
Venlo, Neth. 36 51 22N 6 11 E
Ventnor, U.K. 14 50 35N 1 12W
Veracruz, Mex. 94 19 10N 96 10W
Vercelli, It. 40 45 19N 8 25 E
Vereeniging, S. Afr. 81 26 38S 27 57 E
Verkhoyansk, U.S.S.R. 49 67 35N 133 25 E
Verkhoyansk Ra., U.S.S.R. 49 66 0N 129 0 E
Vermont □, U.S.A. 93 43 40N 72 50W
Verona, It. 40 45 27N 11 0 E
Versailles, Fr. 34 48 48N 2 8 E
Verviers, Belg. 36 50 37N 5 52 E
Verwood, U.K. 14 50 53N 1 53W
Veryan, U.K. 16 50 13N 4 56W
Veryan Bay, U.K. 16 50 12N 4 51W
Vestmannaeyjar, Ice. 44 63 27N 20 15W
Vesuvius, Mt., It. 40 40 50N 14 22 E
Viborg, Den. 45 56 27N 9 23 E
Vickerstown, U.K. 18 54 8N 3 17W
Victoria, Canada 88 48 30N 123 25W
Victoria □, Austral. 70 37 0S 144 0 E
Victoria →, Austral. 66 15 10S 129 40 E
Victoria, L., Austral. 70 33 57S 141 15 E
Victoria, L., E. Afr. 80 1 0S 33 0 E
Victoria Falls, Zimb. 81 17 58S 25 52 E
Victoria I., Canada 88 71 0N 111 0W
Victoria Ld., Ant. 103 75 0S 160 0 E
Vienna, Austria 42 48 12N 16 22 E
Vientiane, Laos 51 17 58N 102 36 E
Vietnam ■, Asia 63 19 0N 106 0 E
Vigo, Sp. 37 42 12N 8 41W
Vijayawada, India 59 16 31N 80 39 E
Villahermosa, Mex. 94 17 59N 92 55W
Villefranche-sur-Saône, Fr. 35 45 59N 4 43 E
Vilnius, U.S.S.R. 46 54 38N 25 19 E
Vilyuysk, U.S.S.R. 49 63 40N 121 35 E
Viña del Mar, Chile 102 33 0S 71 30W
Vineland, U.S.A. 93 39 30N 75 0W
Vinnitsa, U.S.S.R. 47 49 15N 28 30 E
Virgin Is., W. Ind. 95 18 40N 64 30W
Virginia □, U.S.A. 91 37 45N 78 0W
Viscount Melville Sd., Canada 88 74 10N 108 0W
Vishakhapatnam, India 59 17 45N 83 20 E
Vistula = Wisła →, Pol. 43 54 22N 18 55 E
Vitebsk, U.S.S.R. 46 55 10N 30 15 E
Viterbo, It. 40 42 25N 12 8 E
Viti Levu, Fiji 64 17 30S 177 30 E
Vitim →, U.S.S.R. 49 59 26N 112 34 E
Vitória, Brazil 101 20 20S 40 22W
Vitoria, Sp. 37 42 50N 2 41W
Vitória da Conquista, Brazil 101 14 51S 40 51W
Vlaardingen, Neth. 36 51 55N 4 21 E
Vladimir, U.S.S.R. 46 56 15N 40 30 E
Vladivostok, U.S.S.R. 49 43 10N 131 53 E
Vlissingen, Neth. 36 51 26N 3 34 E
Vlóre, Alb. 41 40 32N 19 28 E
Voil, L., U.K. 20 56 20N 4 25W
Volga →, U.S.S.R. 46 48 30N 46 0 E
Volga Hts., U.S.S.R. 47 51 0N 46 0 E
Volgograd, U.S.S.R. 47 48 40N 44 25 E
Vologda, U.S.S.R. 46 59 10N 40 0 E
Vólos, Greece 41 39 24N 22 59 E
Volta, L., Ghana 78 7 30N 0 15 E
Volta Redonda, Brazil 101 22 31S 44 5W
Volzhskiy, U.S.S.R. 47 48 56N 44 46 E
Voorburg, Neth. 36 52 5N 4 24 E
Vorkuta, U.S.S.R. 46 67 48N 64 20 E
Voronezh, U.S.S.R. 46 51 40N 39 10 E
Voroshilovgrad, U.S.S.R. 47 48 38N 39 15 E
Vosges, Fr. 34 48 20N 7 10 E
Vryburg, S. Afr. 81 26 55S 24 45 E
Vyrnwy, L., U.K. 17 52 48N 3 30W

W

Waal →, Neth. 36 51 59N 4 30 E
Wabash →, U.S.A. 92 37 46N 88 2W
Waco, U.S.A. 91 31 33N 97 5W
Wâd Medanî, Sudan 79 14 28N 33 30 E
Waddenzee, Neth. 36 53 6N 5 10 E
Waddesdon, U.K. 15 51 50N 0 54W

Waddingham, *U.K.* **19** 53 28N 0 31W
Waddington, *U.K.* **19** 53 10N 0 31W
Waddington, Mt., *Canada* **88** 51 23N 125 15W
Wadebridge, *U.K.* **16** 50 31N 4 51W
Wadhurst, *U.K.* **15** 51 3N 0 21 E
Wagga Wagga, *Austral.* **70** 35 7S 147 24 E
Wagin, *Austral.* **66** 33 17S 117 25 E
Wainfleet All Saints, *U.K.* **19** 53 7N 0 16 E
Waipara, *N.Z.* **71** 43 3S 172 46 E
Waitaki →, *N.Z.* **71** 44 56S 171 7 E
Wakatipu, L., *N.Z.* **71** 45 5S 168 33 E
Wakayama, *Jap.* **62** 34 15N 135 15 E
Wakefield, *U.K.* **19** 53 41N 1 31W
Walberswick, *U.K.* **15** 52 18N 1 39 E
Wałbrzych, *Pol.* **42** 50 45N 16 18 E
Walbury Hill, *U.K.* **14** 51 22N 1 28W
Waldron, *U.K.* **15** 50 56N 0 13 E
Wales □, *U.K.* **17** 52 30N 3 30W
Walgett, *Austral.* **67** 30 0S 148 5 E
Wallachia, *Rom.* **43** 44 35N 25 0 E
Wallasey, *U.K.* **18** 53 26N 3 2W
Wallingford, *U.K.* **14** 51 40N 1 15W
Wallis & Futuna, *Pac. Oc.* **64** 13 18S 176 10W
Wallsend, *U.K.* **19** 54 59N 1 30W
Walmer, *U.K.* **15** 51 12N 1 23 E
Walney, Isle of, *U.K.* **18** 54 5N 3 15W
Walpole, *U.K.* **15** 52 44N 0 13 E
Walsall, *U.K.* **14** 52 36N 1 59W
Walsoken, *U.K.* **15** 52 41N 0 12 E
Waltham, *U.K.* **19** 53 32N 0 6W
Waltham Abbey, *U.K.* **15** 51 40N 0 1 E
Waltham Forest, *U.K.* **15** 51 37N 0 2 E
Waltham on the Wolds, *U.K.* **15** 52 49N 0 48W
Walton-on-the-Naze, *U.K.* **15** 51 52N 1 17 E
Walvis Bay, *S. Afr.* **81** 23 0S 14 28 E
Wanborough, *U.K.* **14** 51 33N 1 40W
Wandsworth, *U.K.* **15** 51 28N 0 15W
Wanganui, *N.Z.* **71** 39 56S 175 3 E
Wangaratta, *Austral.* **70** 36 21S 146 19 E
Wansbeck, *U.K.* **21** 55 12N 1 28W
Wantage, *U.K.* **14** 51 35N 1 25W
Warboys, *U.K.* **15** 52 25N 0 5W
Warburton →, *Austral.* **67** 28 4S 137 28 E
Wardington, *U.K.* **14** 52 8N 1 17W
Wardle, *U.K.* **18** 53 7N 2 35W
Ward's Stone, *U.K.* **18** 54 2N 2 39W
Ware, *U.K.* **15** 51 48N 0 2W
Wareham, *U.K.* **14** 50 41N 2 8W
Wark, *U.K.* **21** 55 5N 2 14W
Warkworth, *U.K.* **21** 55 22N 1 38W
Warley, *U.K.* **14** 52 30N 2 0W
Warminster, *U.K.* **14** 51 12N 2 11W
Warracknabeal, *Austral.* **70** 36 9S 142 26 E
Warrego →, *Austral.* **67** 30 24S 145 21 E
Warrenpoint, *U.K.* **24** 54 7N 6 15W
Warrington, *U.K.* **18** 53 25N 2 38W
Warrnambool, *Austral.* **70** 38 25S 142 30 E
Warsaw, *Pol.* **43** 52 13N 21 0 E
Warsop, *U.K.* **19** 53 13N 1 9W
Warta →, *Pol.* **43** 52 35N 14 39 E
Warthe = Warta →, *Pol.* **43** 52 35N 14 39 E
Warwick, *Austral.* **67** 28 10S 152 1 E
Warwick, *U.K.* **14** 52 17N 1 36W
Warwick □, *U.K.* **14** 52 20N 1 30W
Wasatch Ra., *U.S.A.* **90** 40 30N 111 15W
Wash, The, *U.K.* **19** 52 58N 0 20 E
Washford, *U.K.* **14** 51 9N 3 22W
Washington, *U.K.* **21** 54 55N 1 30W
Washington, *U.S.A.* **92** 38 52N 77 0W
Washington □, *U.S.A.* **90** 47 45N 120 30W
Wast Water, L., *U.K.* **18** 54 26N 3 18W
Watchet, *U.K.* **14** 51 10N 3 20W
Waterbeach, *U.K.* **15** 52 16N 0 11 E
Waterbury, *U.S.A.* **93** 41 32N 73 0W
Waterford, *Ire.* **25** 52 16N 7 8W
Waterford □, *Ire.* **25** 52 10N 7 40W
Waterford Harb., *Ire.* **25** 52 10N 6 58W
Watergate Bay, *U.K.* **16** 50 26N 5 4W
Waterloo, *U.K.* **18** 53 29N 3 2W
Watford, *U.K.* **15** 51 38N 0 23W
Wath, *U.K.* **19** 53 29N 1 20W
Watlington, *Norfolk, U.K.* **15** 52 40N 0 24 E
Watlington, *Oxon., U.K.* **15** 51 38N 1 0W
Watton, *U.K.* **15** 52 35N 0 50 E
Waveney →, *U.K.* **15** 52 24N 1 20 E
Waver →, *U.K.* **18** 54 50N 3 15W
Weald, The, *U.K.* **15** 51 7N 0 9 E
Wear →, *U.K.* **19** 54 55N 1 22W
Weardale, *U.K.* **18** 54 44N 2 5W
Wearhead, *U.K.* **18** 54 45N 2 14W
Weaver →, *U.K.* **18** 53 17N 2 35W
Weaverham, *U.K.* **18** 53 15N 2 30W
Weddell Sea, *Ant.* **103** 72 30S 40 0W
Wedmore, *U.K.* **14** 51 14N 2 50W
Wednesbury, *U.K.* **14** 52 33N 2 1W
Wednesfield, *U.K.* **14** 52 36N 2 3W
Weedon Bec, *U.K.* **14** 52 14N 1 6W
Weifang, *China* **61** 36 47N 119 10 E
Weldon, *U.K.* **21** 55 16N 1 46W
Welford, *Berks., U.K.* **14** 51 28N 1 24W
Welford, *Northants., U.K.* **14** 52 26N 1 5W
Welkom, *S. Afr.* **81** 28 0S 26 50 E
Welland →, *U.K.* **15** 52 43N 0 10W
Wellesley Is., *Austral.* **67** 16 42S 139 30 E
Wellingborough, *U.K.* **15** 52 18N 0 41W
Wellington, *Austral.* **70** 32 35S 148 59 E
Wellington, *N.Z.* **71** 41 19S 174 46 E
Wellington, *Salop, U.K.* **14** 52 42N 2 31W
Wellington, *Somerset, U.K.* **14** 50 58N 3 13W
Wellow, *U.K.* **14** 51 20N 2 22W
Wells, *Norfolk, U.K.* **15** 52 57N 0 51 E
Wells, *Somerset, U.K.* **14** 51 12N 2 39W
Welney, *U.K.* **15** 52 31N 0 15 E
Wels, *Austria* **42** 48 9N 14 1 E
Welshpool, *U.K.* **17** 52 40N 3 9W
Welton, *U.K.* **19** 53 19N 0 29W
Welwyn Garden City, *U.K.* **15** 51 49N 0 11W
Wem, *U.K.* **14** 52 52N 2 45W
Wembury, *U.K.* **16** 50 19N 4 6W
Wemyss Bay, *U.K.* **20** 55 52N 4 54W
Wendover, *U.K.* **15** 51 46N 0 45W
Wenhaston, *U.K.* **15** 52 17N 1 35 E
Wenlock Edge, *U.K.* **14** 52 30N 2 43W
Wensleydale, *U.K.* **18** 54 18N 2 0W
Wensum →, *U.K.* **15** 52 35N 1 20 E
Wenzhou, *China* **61** 28 0N 120 38 E
Weobley, *U.K.* **14** 52 9N 2 52W
Werribee, *Austral.* **70** 37 54S 144 40 E
Werrington, *U.K.* **16** 50 40N 4 22W
Weser →, *W. Ger.* **42** 53 33N 8 30 E
West Auckland, *U.K.* **19** 54 38N 1 42W
West Bengal □, *India* **59** 23 0N 88 0 E
West Bridgford, *U.K.* **19** 52 56N 1 8W
West Bromwich, *U.K.* **14** 52 32N 2 1W
West Calder, *U.K.* **21** 55 51N 3 34W
West Coker, *U.K.* **14** 50 55N 2 40W
West Fen, *U.K.* **19** 53 5N 0 5W
West Germany ■, *Europe* **42** 52 0N 9 0 E
West Glamorgan □, *U.K.* **17** 51 40N 3 55W
West Grinstead, *U.K.* **15** 50 58N 0 19W
West Haddon, *U.K.* **14** 52 21N 1 5W
West Kilbride, *U.K.* **20** 55 41N 4 50W
West Kirby, *U.K.* **18** 53 22N 3 11W
West Linton, *U.K.* **21** 55 45N 3 24W
West Lulworth, *U.K.* **14** 50 37N 2 14W
West Malling, *U.K.* **15** 51 16N 0 25 E
West Meon, *U.K.* **14** 51 2N 1 3W
West Mersea, *U.K.* **15** 51 46N 0 55 E
West Midlands □, *U.K.* **14** 52 30N 1 55W
West Moors, *U.K.* **14** 50 49N 1 50W
West Parley, *U.K.* **14** 50 46N 1 52W
West Rasen, *U.K.* **19** 53 23N 0 23W
West Schelde →, *Neth.* **36** 51 23N 3 50 E
West Siberian Plain, *U.S.S.R.* **48** 62 0N 75 0 E
West Sussex □, *U.K.* **15** 50 55N 0 30W
West Tarbert, L., *U.K.* **20** 55 58N 5 30W
West Virginia □, *U.S.A.* **92** 39 0N 81 0W
West Wyalong, *Austral.* **70** 33 56S 147 10 E
West Yorkshire □, *U.K.* **19** 53 45N 1 40W
Westbourne, *U.K.* **15** 50 53N 0 55W
Westbury, *Salop, U.K.* **14** 52 40N 2 57W
Westbury, *Wilts., U.K.* **14** 51 16N 2 11W
Westbury-on-Severn, *U.K.* **14** 51 49N 2 24W
Westerham, *U.K.* **15** 51 16N 0 5 E
Western Australia □, *Austral.* **66** 25 0S 118 0 E
Western Ghats, *India* **58** 14 0N 75 0 E
Western Isles □, *U.K.* **22** 57 30N 7 10W
Western Sahara ■, *Africa* **78** 25 0N 13 0W
Western Samoa ■, *Pac. Oc.* **64** 14 0S 172 0W
Westfield, *U.K.* **15** 50 53N 0 30 E
Westhoughton, *U.K.* **18** 53 34N 2 30W
Westland Bight, *N.Z.* **71** 42 55S 170 5 E
Westmeath □, *Ire.* **24** 53 30N 7 30W
Weston, *U.K.* **14** 52 51N 2 2W
Weston-super-Mare, *U.K.* **14** 51 20N 2 59W
Westport, *Ire.* **24** 53 44N 9 31W
Westport, *N.Z.* **71** 41 46S 171 37 E
Westray, *U.K.* **23** 59 18N 3 0W
Westruther, *U.K.* **21** 55 45N 2 34W
Westward Ho!, *U.K.* **16** 51 2N 4 16W
Wetherby, *U.K.* **19** 53 56N 1 23W
Wetwang, *U.K.* **19** 54 2N 0 35W
Wexford, *Ire.* **25** 52 20N 6 28W
Wexford □, *Ire.* **25** 52 20N 6 25W
Wexford Harb., *Ire.* **25** 52 20N 6 25W
Wey →, *U.K.* **15** 51 19N 0 29W
Weybourne, *U.K.* **15** 52 57N 1 9 E
Weybridge, *U.K.* **15** 51 22N 0 28W
Weymouth, *U.K.* **14** 50 36N 2 28W
Whakatane, *N.Z.* **71** 37 57S 177 1 E
Whaley Bridge, *U.K.* **18** 53 20N 2 0W
Whalley, *U.K.* **18** 53 49N 2 25W
Whalsay, *U.K.* **22** 60 22N 1 0W
Whalton, *U.K.* **21** 55 7N 1 46W
Whangarei, *N.Z.* **71** 35 43S 174 21 E
Whaplode, *U.K.* **15** 52 42N 0 3W
Wharfe →, *U.K.* **19** 53 55N 1 30W
Wharfedale, *U.K.* **18** 54 7N 2 4W
Whauphill, *U.K.* **20** 54 48N 4 31W
Wheatley Hill, *U.K.* **19** 54 45N 1 23W
Whernside, *U.K.* **18** 54 14N 2 24W
Whichham, *U.K.* **18** 54 14N 3 22W
Whimple, *U.K.* **16** 50 46N 3 21W
Whipsnade, *U.K.* **15** 51 51N 0 32W
Whissendine, *U.K.* **15** 52 43N 0 46W
Whiston, *U.K.* **18** 53 25N 2 45W
Whitburn, *U.K.* **21** 55 52N 3 41W
Whitby, *U.K.* **19** 54 29N 0 37W
Whitchurch, *Devon, U.K.* **16** 50 31N 4 7W
Whitchurch, *Hants., U.K.* **14** 51 14N 1 20W
Whitchurch, *Hereford & Worcs., U.K.* **14** 51 51N 2 41W
Whitchurch, *Salop, U.K.* **18** 52 58N 2 42W
White Esk →, *U.K.* **21** 55 14N 3 11W
White Horse Hill, *U.K.* **14** 51 35N 1 35W
White Nile →, *Sudan* **79** 15 38N 32 31 E
White Russia □, *U.S.S.R.* **46** 53 30N 27 0 E
White Sea, *U.S.S.R.* **46** 66 30N 38 0 E
Whiteadder Water →, *U.K.* **21** 55 47N 2 20W
Whitehaven, *U.K.* **18** 54 33N 3 35W
Whitehead, *U.K.* **24** 54 45N 5 42W
Whitehorse, *Canada* **88** 60 43N 135 3W
Whitehorse, Vale of, *U.K.* **14** 51 37N 1 30W
Whitekirk, *U.K.* **21** 56 2N 2 36W
Whitesand B., *U.K.* **16** 50 18N 4 20W
Whithorn, *U.K.* **20** 54 44N 4 25W
Whitley Bay, *U.K.* **21** 55 4N 1 28W
Whitney, Mt., *U.S.A.* **90** 36 35N 118 14W
Whitstable, *U.K.* **15** 51 21N 1 2 E
Whittington, *Derby, U.K.* **19** 53 17N 1 26W
Whittington, *Salop, U.K.* **14** 52 53N 3 0W
Whittlesey, *U.K.* **15** 52 34N 0 8W
Whittlesford, *U.K.* **15** 52 6N 0 9 E
Whitton, *U.K.* **19** 53 42N 0 39W
Whitwell, *Derby, U.K.* **19** 53 16N 1 11W
Whitwell, *I. of W., U.K.* **14** 50 35N 1 19W
Whitwick, *U.K.* **14** 52 45N 1 23W
Whitworth, *U.K.* **18** 53 40N 2 11W
Whixley, *U.K.* **19** 54 2N 1 19W
Whyalla, *Austral.* **67** 33 2S 137 30 E
Wichita, *U.S.A.* **91** 37 40N 97 20W
Wichita Falls, *U.S.A.* **90** 33 57N 98 30W
Wick, *U.K.* **23** 58 26N 3 5W
Wickford, *U.K.* **15** 51 37N 0 31 E
Wickham, *U.K.* **14** 50 54N 1 11W
Wickham Market, *U.K.* **15** 52 9N 1 21 E
Wicklow, *Ire.* **25** 53 0N 6 2W
Wicklow □, *Ire.* **25** 52 59N 6 25W
Wicklow Mts., *Ire.* **25** 53 0N 6 30W
Wickwar, *U.K.* **14** 51 35N 2 23W
Widdrington, *U.K.* **21** 55 15N 1 35W
Widecombe, *U.K.* **16** 50 34N 3 48W
Widemouth, *U.K.* **16** 50 45N 4 34W
Widnes, *U.K.* **18** 53 22N 2 44W
Wiesbaden, *W. Ger.* **36** 50 7N 8 17 E
Wigan, *U.K.* **18** 53 33N 2 38W
Wight, I. of, *U.K.* **14** 50 40N 1 20W
Wigmore, *U.K.* **14** 52 19N 2 51W
Wigston, *U.K.* **14** 52 35N 1 6W
Wigton, *U.K.* **18** 54 50N 3 9W
Wigtown, *U.K.* **20** 54 52N 4 27W
Wigtown B., *U.K.* **20** 54 46N 4 15W
Wilhelm II Land, *Ant.* **103** 68 0S 90 0 E
Wilhelmshaven, *W. Ger.* **42** 53 30N 8 9 E
Wilkes Barre, *U.S.A.* **93** 41 15N 75 52W
Wilkes Land, *Ant.* **103** 69 0S 120 0 E
Willemstad, *Cur.* **94** 12 5N 69 0W
Willenhall, *U.K.* **14** 52 36N 2 3W
Willesborough, *U.K.* **15** 51 8N 0 55 E
Williamstown, *Austral.* **70** 37 51S 144 52 E
Willingdon, *U.K.* **15** 50 47N 0 17 E
Williton, *U.K.* **14** 51 9N 3 20W
Willoughby, *U.K.* **19** 53 14N 0 12 E
Wilmington, *U.K.* **16** 50 46N 3 8W
Wilmington, *U.S.A.* **93** 39 45N 75 32W
Wilmslow, *U.K.* **18** 53 19N 2 14W
Wilnecote, *U.K.* **14** 52 36N 1 40W
Wilsons Promontory, *Austral.* **70** 38 55S 146 25 E
Wilton, *U.K.* **14** 51 5N 1 52W
Wiltshire □, *U.K.* **14** 51 20N 2 0W
Wimblington, *U.K.* **15** 52 31N 0 5 E
Wimborne Minster, *U.K.* **14** 50 48N 2 0W
Wimmera →, *Austral.* **70** 36 8S 141 56 E
Wincanton, *U.K.* **14** 51 3N 2 24W
Winchelsea, *U.K.* **15** 50 55N 0 43 E
Winchester, *U.K.* **14** 51 4N 1 19W
Windermere, *U.K.* **18** 54 24N 2 56W
Windermere, L., *U.K.* **18** 54 20N 2 57W
Windhoek, *Nam.* **81** 22 35S 17 4 E
Windrush →, *U.K.* **14** 51 48N 1 35W
Windsor, *Canada* **92** 42 18N 83 0W
Windsor, *U.K.* **15** 51 28N 0 36W
Windward Passage, *W. Ind.* **95** 20 0N 74 0W
Windygates, *U.K.* **21** 56 12N 3 1W
Wing, *U.K.* **15** 51 54N 0 41W
Wingham, *Austral.* **70** 31 48S 152 22 E
Wingham, *U.K.* **15** 51 16N 1 12 E
Winkleigh, *U.K.* **16** 50 49N 3 57W
Winnipeg, *Canada* **88** 49 54N 97 9W
Winnipeg, L., *Canada* **88** 52 0N 97 0W
Winsford, *U.K.* **18** 53 12N 2 31W
Winslow, *U.K.* **15** 51 57N 0 52W
Winster, *U.K.* **19** 53 9N 1 42W
Winston-Salem, *U.S.A.* **91** 36 7N 80 15W
Winterborne Abbas, *U.K.* **14** 50 43N 2 30W
Winterthur, *Switz.* **42** 47 30N 8 44 E
Winterton, *Humberside, U.K.* **19** 53 39N 0 37W
Winterton, *Norfolk, U.K.* **15** 52 43N 1 43 E
Wirksworth, *U.K.* **19** 53 5N 1 34W
Wirral, *U.K.* **18** 53 25N 3 0W
Wisbech, *U.K.* **15** 52 39N 0 10 E
Wisborough Green, *U.K.* **15** 51 2N 0 30W
Wisconsin □, *U.S.A.* **92** 44 30N 90 0W
Wishaw, *U.K.* **21** 55 46N 3 55W
Wiske →, *U.K.* **19** 54 26N 1 27W
Wisła →, *Pol.* **43** 54 22N 18 55 E
Witbank, *S. Afr.* **81** 25 51S 29 14 E
Witham, *U.K.* **15** 51 48N 0 39 E
Witham →, *U.K.* **19** 53 3N 0 8W
Withern, *U.K.* **19** 53 19N 0 9 E
Withernsea, *U.K.* **19** 53 43N 0 2 E
Witley, *U.K.* **15** 51 9N 0 39W
Witney, *U.K.* **14** 51 47N 1 29W
Witten, *W. Ger.* **36** 51 26N 7 19 E
Wittersham, *U.K.* **15** 51 1N 0 42 E
Wiveliscombe, *U.K.* **14** 51 2N 3 20W
Wivenhoe, *U.K.* **15** 51 51N 0 59 E
Włocławek, *Pol.* **43** 52 40N 19 3 E
Woburn, *U.K.* **15** 51 59N 0 37W
Woburn Sands, *U.K.* **15** 52 1N 0 38W
Wodonga, *Austral.* **70** 36 5S 146 50 E
Woking, *U.K.* **15** 51 18N 0 33W
Wokingham, *U.K.* **15** 51 25N 0 50W
Wolf Rock, *U.K.* **16** 49 56N 5 50W
Wolfsburg, *W. Ger.* **42** 52 27N 10 49 E
Wollongong, *Austral.* **70** 34 25S 150 54 E
Wolsingham, *U.K.* **18** 54 44N 1 52W
Wolverhampton, *U.K.* **14** 52 35N 2 6W
Wolverton, *U.K.* **15** 52 3N 0 48W
Wolviston, *U.K.* **19** 54 39N 1 25W
Wombwell, *U.K.* **19** 53 31N 1 23W
Wŏnsan, *N. Kor.* **61** 39 11N 127 27 E
Wonston, *U.K.* **14** 51 9N 1 18W
Woodbridge, *U.K.* **15** 52 6N 1 19 E
Woodbury, *U.K.* **16** 50 40N 3 24W
Woodhall Spa, *U.K.* **19** 53 10N 0 12W
Woodhouse, *U.K.* **19** 53 23N 1 21W
Woodley, *U.K.* **15** 51 26N 0 54W
Woods, L. of the, *Canada* **88** 49 15N 94 45W
Woodstock, *U.K.* **14** 51 51N 1 20W
Wookey, *U.K.* **14** 51 13N 2 41W
Wookey Hole, *U.K.* **14** 51 13N 2 41W
Wool, *U.K.* **14** 50 41N 2 13W
Woolacombe, *U.K.* **16** 51 10N 4 12W
Wooler, *U.K.* **21** 55 33N 2 0W
Wootton Bassett, *U.K.* **14** 51 32N 1 55W
Wootton Wawen, *U.K.* **14** 52 16N 1 47W
Worcester, *S. Afr.* **81** 33 39S 19 27 E
Worcester, *U.K.* **14** 52 12N 2 12W
Worcester, *U.S.A.* **93** 42 14N 71 49W
Worfield, *U.K.* **14** 52 34N 2 22W
Workington, *U.K.* **18** 54 39N 3 34W
Worksop, *U.K.* **19** 53 19N 1 9W
Wormit, *U.K.* **21** 56 26N 2 59W
Worms, *W. Ger.* **42** 49 37N 8 21 E
Worplesdon, *U.K.* **15** 51 16N 0 36W
Wortham, *U.K.* **15** 52 22N 1 3 E
Worthing, *U.K.* **15** 50 49N 0 21W
Wotton-under-Edge, *U.K.* **14** 51 37N 2 20W
Woy Woy, *Austral.* **70** 33 30S 151 19 E
Wragby, *U.K.* **19** 53 17N 0 18W
Wrangel I., *U.S.S.R.* **49** 71 0N 180 0 E
Wrangle, *U.K.* **19** 53 3N 0 9 E
Wrath, C., *U.K.* **22** 58 38N 5 0W
Wrekin, The, *U.K.* **14** 52 41N 2 35W
Wrentham, *U.K.* **15** 52 24N 1 39 E
Wrexham, *U.K.* **17** 53 5N 3 0W
Writtle, *U.K.* **15** 51 44N 0 27 E
Wrocław, *Pol.* **43** 51 5N 17 5 E
Wrotham, *U.K.* **15** 51 18N 0 20 E
Wroughton, *U.K.* **14** 51 31N 1 47W
Wroxham, *U.K.* **15** 52 42N 1 23 E
Wuhan, *China* **61** 30 31N 114 18 E
Wuhu, *China* **61** 31 22N 118 21 E
Wuppertal, *W. Ger.* **36** 51 15N 7 8 E
Würzburg, *W. Ger.* **42** 49 46N 9 55 E
Wutongqiao, *China* **60** 29 22N 103 50 E
Wuxi, *China* **61** 31 30N 120 30 E
Wuzhou, *China* **61** 23 30N 111 18 E
Wye, *U.K.* **15** 51 11N 0 56 E
Wye →, *U.K.* **14** 51 36N 2 40W
Wylye →, *U.K.* **14** 51 8N 1 53W
Wymondham, *Leics., U.K.* **15** 52 45N 0 42W
Wymondham, *Norfolk, U.K.* **15** 52 34N 1 7 E
Wyndham, *Austral.* **66** 15 33S 128 3 E
Wyoming □, *U.S.A.* **90** 42 48N 109 0W
Wyre →, *U.K.* **18** 53 52N 2 57W
Wyre Forest, *U.K.* **14** 52 24N 2 24W

X

Xiaguan, *China* **60** 25 32N 100 16 E
Xiamen, *China* **61** 24 25N 118 4 E
Xiangfan, *China* **61** 32 2N 112 8 E
Xiangtan, *China* **61** 27 51N 112 54 E
Xiangyang, *China* **61** 32 1N 112 8 E
Xingu →, *Brazil* **101** 1 30S 51 53W
Xining, *China* **60** 36 34N 101 40 E
Xinjiang Uygur Zizhiqu □, *China* **60** 42 0N 86 0 E
Xuzhou, *China* **61** 34 18N 117 10 E

Y

Yablonovy Ra., *U.S.S.R.* **49** 53 0N 114 0 E
Yakut A.S.S.R. □,
U.S.S.R. .... **49** 62 0N 130 0 E
Yakutsk, *U.S.S.R.* .... **49** 62 5N 129 50 E
Yamagata, *Jap.* ...... **62** 38 15N 140 15 E
Yamal, Peninsula,
U.S.S.R. .... **48** 71 0N 70 0 E
Yambol, *Bulg.* .... **41** 42 30N 26 36 E
Yamuna →, *India* ... **59** 25 30N 81 53 E
Yana →, *U.S.S.R.* ... **49** 71 30N 136 0 E
Yangtze Kiang →,
China .... **60** 31 40N 122 0 E
Yanji, *China* .... **61** 42 59N 129 30 E
Yantai, *China* .... **61** 37 34N 121 22 E
Yaoundé, *Cam.* ..... **80** 3 50N 11 35 E
Yarcombe, *U.K.* **16** 50 51N   3 6W
Yare →, *U.K.* .... **15** 52 36N   1 28 E
Yarm, *U.K.* **19** 54 31N   1 21W
Yarmouth, *U.K.* **14** 50 42N   1 29W
Yaroslavl, *U.S.S.R.* ... **46** 57 35N 39 55 E
Yarrow, *U.K.* **21** 55 32N   3 0W
Yate, *U.K.* **14** 51 32N   2 26W
Yatsushiro, *Jap.* .... **62** 32 30N 130 40 E
Yatton, *U.K.* **14** 51 23N   2 50W
Yaxley, *U.K.* **15** 52 31N   0 14W
Yazd, *Iran* .... **56** 31 55N 54 27 E
Yealmpton, *U.K.* **16** 50 21N   4 0W
Yell, *U.K.* **22** 60 35N   1 5W
Yell Sd., *U.K.* **22** 60 33N   1 15W

Yellow Sea, *China* .... **61** 35 0N 123 0 E
Yellowknife, *Canada* .. **88** 62 27N 114 29W
Yellowstone →, *U.S.A.* **90** 47 58N 103 59W
Yellowstone National
Park, *U.S.A.* **90** 44 35N 110 0W
Yemen ■, *Si. Arab.* ... **56** 15 0N 44 0 E
Yenisey →, *U.S.S.R.* .. **48** 71 50N 82 40 E
Yeo →, *U.K.* **14** 51 10N   3 0W
Yeovil, *U.K.* **14** 50 57N   2 38W
Yerevan, *U.S.S.R.* ... **47** 40 10N 44 31 E
Yes Tor, *U.K.* **16** 50 41N   3 59W
Yibin, *China* .... **60** 28 45N 104 32 E
Yichang, *China* ..... **61** 30 40N 111 20 E
Yichuan, *China* ...... **60** 36 2N 110 10 E
Yining, *China* .... **60** 43 58N 81 10 E
Yogyakarta, *Indon.* .. **63** 7 49S 110 22 E
Yokkaichi, *Jap.* ..... **62** 35 0N 136 38 E
Yokohama, *Jap.* ..... **62** 35 27N 139 28 E
Yokosuka, *Jap.* ..... **62** 35 20N 139 40 E
Yonkers, *U.S.A.* **93** 40 57N 73 51W
York, *U.K.* **19** 53 58N   1 7W
York, *U.S.A.* **92** 39 57N 76 43W
York, Vale of, *U.K.* **19** 54 15N   1 25W
Yorkshire Wolds, *U.K.* . **19** 54 0N   0 30W
Yosemite National Park,
U.S.A. **90** 38 0N 119 30W
Yoshkar Ola, *U.S.S.R.* . **46** 56 38N 47 55 E
Youghal, *Ire.* **25** 51 58N   7 51W
Youghal B., *Ire.* **25** 51 55N   7 50W
Youlgreave, *U.K.* **19** 53 12N   1 50W
Youngstown, *U.S.A.* .. **92** 41 7N 80 41W

Yoxall, *U.K.* **14** 52 45N   1 49W
Yoxford, *U.K.* .... **15** 52 16N   1 30 E
Ypres, *Belg.* .... **36** 50 51N   2 53 E
Ystalyfera, *U.K.* **17** 51 46N   3 48W
Ythan →, *U.K.* **23** 57 26N   2 0W
Yuan Jiang →, *China* **61** 28 55N 111 50 E
Yucatán, Península de,
Mex. **94** 19 30N 89 0W
Yucatan Str., *Carib.* .. **94** 22 0N 86 30W
Yugoslavia ■, *Europe* . **41** 44 0N 20 0 E
Yukon →, *N. Am.* ... **88** 65 30N 150 0W
Yukon Territory □,
Canada **88** 63 0N 135 0W
Yunnan □, *China* .... **60** 25 0N 102 30 E
Yuzhno-Sakhalinsk,
U.S.S.R. .... **49** 46 58N 142 45 E

Z

Zaandam, *Neth.* ..... **36** 52 26N   4 49 E
Zabrze, *Pol.* .... **43** 50 18N 18 50 E
Zagorsk, *U.S.S.R.* ... **46** 56 20N 38 10 E
Zagreb, *Yug.* .... **40** 45 50N 16 0 E
Zagros Mts., *Iran* ... **56** 33 45N 47 0 E
Zahlah, *Leb.* .... **57** 33 52N 35 50 E
Zaïre ■, *Africa* ...... **80** 3 0S 23 0 E
Zaïre →, *Africa* ..... **80** 6 4S 12 24 E

Zákinthos, *Greece* .... **41** 37 47N 20 57 E
Zambezi →, *Africa* .. **81** 18 55S 36 4 E
Zambia ■, *Africa* .... **81** 15 0S 28 0 E
Zamboanga, *Phil.* .... **63** 6 59N 122 3 E
Zamora, *Sp.* **37** 41 30N   5 45W
Zante = Zákinthos,
Greece .... **41** 37 47N 20 57 E
Zanzibar, *Tanz.* ..... **80** 6 12S 39 12 E
Zaporozhye, *U.S.S.R.* . **47** 47 50N 35 10 E
Zaragoza, *Sp.* **37** 41 39N   0 53W
Zaria, *Nig.* .... **78** 11 0N   7 40 E
Zeebrugge, *Belg.* .... **36** 51 19N   3 12 E
Zeist, *Neth.* .... **36** 52 5N   5 15 E
Zhangjiakou, *China* ... **61** 40 48N 114 55 E
Zhangzhou, *China* .... **61** 24 30N 117 35 E
Zhanjiang, *China* .... **61** 21 15N 110 20 E
Zhdanov, *U.S.S.R.* ... **47** 47 5N 37 31 E
Zhejiang □, *China* ... **61** 29 0N 120 0 E
Zhengzhou, *China* ... **61** 34 45N 113 34 E
Zhitomir, *U.S.S.R.* .... **47** 50 20N 28 40 E
Zibo, *China* .... **61** 36 47N 118 3 E
Zielona Góra □, *Pol.* . **42** 51 57N 15 30 E
Zigong, *China* ...... **60** 29 15N 104 48 E
Ziguinchor, *Sene.* **78** 12 35N 16 20W
Žilina, *Czech.* .... **43** 49 12N 18 42 E
Zimbabwe ■, *Africa* .. **81** 20 0S 30 0 E
Zion Nat. Park, *U.S.A.* . **90** 37 25N 112 50W
Zlatoust, *U.S.S.R.* .... **46** 55 10N 59 40 E
Zonguldak, *Turk.* .... **47** 41 28N 31 50 E
Zrenjanin, *Yug.* ..... **41** 45 22N 20 23 E
Zug, *Switz.* .... **42** 47 10N   8 31 E

MAP PROJECTIONS

MAP PROJECTIONS

A map projection is the systematic depiction on a plane surface of the imaginary lines of latitude or longitude from a globe of the earth. This network of lines is called the graticule and forms the framework upon which an accurate depiction of the earth is made. The map graticule, which is the basis of any map, is constructed sometimes by graphical means, but often by using mathematical formulae to give the intersections of the graticule plotted as x and y co-ordinates. The choice between projections is based upon which properties the cartographer wishes the map to possess, the map scale and also the extent of the area to be mapped. Since the globe is three dimensional, it is not possible to depict its surface on a two dimensional plane without distortion. Preservation of one of the basic properties listed below can only be secured at the expense of the others and the choice of projection is often a compromise solution.

Correct Area

In these projections the areas from the globe are to scale on the map. For example, if you look at the diagram at the top right, areas of 10° x 10° are shown from the equator to the poles. The proportion of this area at the extremities are approximately 11:1. An equal area projection will retain that proportion in its portrayal of those areas. This is particularly useful in the mapping of densities and distributions. Projections with this property are termed **Equal Area, Equivalent or Homolographic.**

Correct Distance

In these projections the scale is correct along the meridians, or in the case of the Azimuthal Equidistant scale is true along any line drawn from the centre of the projection. They are called **Equidistant.**

Correct Shape

This property can only be true within small areas as it is achieved only by having a uniform scale distortion along both x and y axes of the projection. The projections are called **Conformal** or **Orthomorphic.**

In order to minimise the distortions at the edges of some projections, central portions of them are often selected for atlas maps. Below are listed some of the major types of projection.

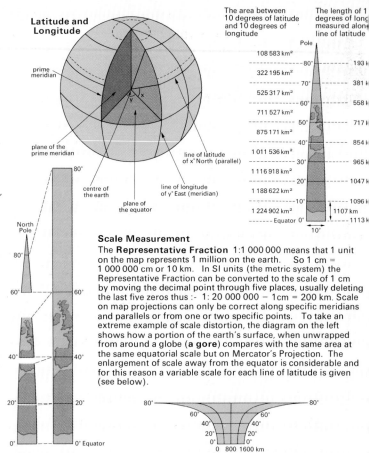

Latitude and Longitude

prime meridian
plane of the prime meridian
centre of the earth
plane of the equator
line of latitude of x° North (parallel)
line of longitude of y° East (meridian)

The area between 10 degrees of latitude and 10 degrees of longitude	The length of 1 degrees of long measured along line of latitude
Pole	
108 583 km² — 80°	193
322 195 km² — 70°	381
525 317 km² — 60°	558
711 527 km² — 50°	717
875 171 km² — 40°	854
1 011 536 km² — 30°	965
1 116 918 km² — 20°	1047
1 188 622 km² — 10°	1096
1 224 902 km² — Equator 0°	1113
	1107 km

North Pole 80° 60° 40° 20° 0° Equator

Scale Measurement

The **Representative Fraction** 1:1 000 000 means that 1 unit on the map represents 1 million on the earth. So 1 cm = 1 000 000 cm or 10 km. In SI units (the metric system) the Representative Fraction can be converted to the scale of 1 cm by moving the decimal point through five places, usually deleting the last five zeros thus :- 1: 20 000 000 – 1cm = 200 km. Scale on map projections can only be correct along specific meridians and parallels or from one or two specific points. To take an extreme example of scale distortion, the diagram on the left shows how a portion of the earth's surface, when unwrapped from around a globe (**a gore**) compares with the same area at the same equatorial scale but on Mercator's Projection. The enlargement of scale away from the equator is considerable and for this reason a variable scale for each line of latitude is given (see below).

80° 60° 40° 20° 0° 20° 40° 60° 80°

0 800 1600 km

AZIMUTHAL OR ZENITHAL PROJECTIONS

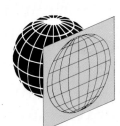

These are constructed by the projection of part of the graticule from the globe onto a plane tangential to any single point on it. This plane may be tangential to the equator (**equatorial case**), the poles (**polar case**) or any other point (**oblique case**). Any straight line drawn from the point at which the plane touches the globe is the shortest distance from that point and is known as a **great circle**. In its **Gnomonic** construction *any* straight line on the map is a great circle, but there is great exaggeration towards the edges and this reduces its general uses. There are five different ways of transferring the graticule onto the plane and these are shown on the right. The central diagram below shows how the graticules vary, using the polar case as the example.

Equidistant	Equal-Area	Orthographic	Gnomonic	Stereographic (conformal)

Oblique Case

The plane touches the globe at any point between the equator and poles. The oblique orthographic uses the distortion in azimuthal projections away from the centre to give a graphic depiction of the earth as seen from any desired point in space. It can also be used in both Polar and Equatorial cases. It is used not only for the earth but also for the moon and planets.

Polar Case

The polar case is the simplest to construct and the diagram below shows the differing effects of all five methods of construction comparing their coverage, distortion etc., using North America as the example.

Equatorial Case

The example shown here is Lambert's Equivalent Azimuthal It is the only projection which is both equal area and where bearing is true from the centre.

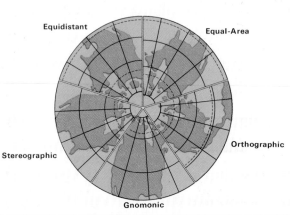

Equidistant
Equal-Area
Orthographic
Gnomonic
Stereographic

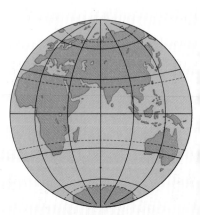